International Series in Operations Research & Management Science

Volume 190

For further volumes:
http://www.springer.com/series/6161

Gregory S. Zaric
Editor

Operations Research and Health Care Policy

Springer

Editor
Gregory S. Zaric
Ivey School of Business
University of Western Ontario
London, ON, Canada

ISSN 0884-8289
ISBN 978-1-4614-6506-5 ISBN 978-1-4614-6507-2 (eBook)
DOI 10.1007/978-1-4614-6507-2
Springer New York Heidelberg Dordrecht London

Library of Congress Control Number: 2013933991

Printed on acid-free paper

Springer is part of Springer Science+Business Media (www.springer.com)

Preface

Globally, health policy-makers face several daunting challenges. In many low-income countries, HIV, malaria, and other diseases are endemic. There are serious shortages of medicines and vaccines, along with supply-chain disruptions, all of which cause unnecessary suffering and reduced life expectancies. In many high-income countries, health-care spending already represents more than 10 % of GDP and is growing faster than the economy as a whole. Many of these countries face aging populations, which strains the sustainability of publicly funded health-care systems and creates challenges in forecasting the required capacity of health-care services in coming decades. Several middle-income countries face funding and organizational challenges as they transition to more generous publicly funded systems. Medical research is producing promising but very expensive new drugs and medical technologies. Policy-makers in all environments face difficult decisions about which new drugs and medical technologies to fund, under which conditions they should be made available, and how to pay for them.

Operations research tools are ideally suited to providing solutions and insights for many of these problems. Indeed, a growing body of literature on health policy analysis, based on operations research methods, has emerged to address the problems mentioned above and several others. The research in this field is often multidisciplinary, being conducted by teams that include not only operations researchers but also clinicians, economists, and policy analysts. The research is also often very applied, focusing on a specific question driven by a decision-maker and many times yielding a tool to assist in future decisions.

The goal of this volume was to bring together a group of papers by leading experts that could showcase the current state of the field of operations research applied to health-care policy. There are 18 chapters that illustrate the breadth of this field. The chapters use a variety of techniques, including classical operations research tools, such as optimization, queuing theory, and discrete event simulation, as well as statistics, epidemic models, and decision-analytic models. The book spans the field and includes work that ranges from highly conceptual to highly applied. An example of the former is the chapter by Kimmel and Schackman on building policy models, and an example of the latter is the chapter by Coyle and colleagues on developing a Markov model for use by an organization in Ontario that makes recommendations about the funding of new drugs. The book also includes a mix of review chapters, such as the chapter by Hutton on public health response to influenza outbreaks, and original research, such as the paper by Blake and colleagues analyzing a decision by Canadian Blood Services to consolidate services. This volume could provide an excellent introduction to the field of operations research applied to health-care policy, and it could also serve as an introduction to new areas for researchers already familiar with the topic.

The book is divided into six parts. The first part contains two chapters that describe several different applications of operations research in health policy and provide an excellent overview of the field. Parts II, III, and IV present policy models in three focused areas. Part V contains two chapters on conceptualizing and building policy models. The book concludes in Part VI with two chapters describing work that was done with policy-makers and presenting insights gained from working directly with policy-makers. A more detailed overview is provided below.

Part I Applications of Health Policy Modeling

Part I is intended to illustrate the breadth of the field and contains two chapters describing six different applications of health policy modeling. Arielle Lasry and colleagues describe three models developed by the U.S. Centers for Disease Control and Prevention. These models include an optimization model to schedule immunizations, a simulation model to estimate throughput at a vaccination clinic, and a nonlinear optimization model to allocate funds to HIV prevention programs. Margaret Brandeau discusses several more applications of health policy modeling, including economic evaluations of hepatitis vaccination programs in China and the USA, models of HIV treatment and harm reduction in Russia and Ukraine, and an evaluation of bioterrorism preparedness and control.

Part II Operations Management and Health Policy

Many health policy problems have important operational components, including capacity planning, facility location and throughput analysis, and the solutions to these problems often involve classical operations management tools. The chapters in Part II highlight the interplay between health policy and operations management. Yue Zhang and Martin Puterman present models to determine the required capacity for long-term care beds in British Columbia. Beste Kucukyazici and Vedat Verter discuss the management of chronic diseases through community-based care. Yasar Ozcan, Elena Tànfani, and Angela Testi discuss the "Clinical Pathway" concept and its application to improve the efficiency of thyroidectomy. Armann Ingolfson surveys the literature on planning and management of emergency medical services, with a focus on operational measures, such as forecasting, performance measurement, facility location, and capacity allocation. In the final chapter of this part, Marion Rauner and Michaela Schaffhauser-Linzatti discuss a number of analyses of changes in reimbursement mechanisms—and, hence, changes in incentives—on various aspects of hospital and health-system performance in Austria.

Part III HIV and Infectious Diseases

The work in this area illustrates the strong connection between operations research and public health. From a modeling perspective, the problems are difficult because models of HIV and other infectious diseases often involve nonlinear systems of differential equations for which there are no analytical solutions. From a policy perspective, the problems are equally challenging because of the costs of many of the interventions and the practical and political issues associated with targeting high-risk groups. The four chapters in this part cover a wide range of problems and methodologies. Sada Sooropanth and Stephen Chick developed a model to conduct cost-utility analyses on HIV behavioral interventions. John Stover, Carel Pretorius, and Kyeen Andersson present a model to investigate new HIV prevention technologies. Their model allows policy-makers to estimate the number of HIV infections prevented, the cost, and the cost-effectiveness of new technologies. Sabina Alistair, Margaret Brandeau, and Eduard Beck describe the Resource Allocation for Control of HIV Model, which is a formal optimization model for HIV interventions that takes account of several epidemic characteristics. They provide illustrations tailored to Uganda, Ukraine, and St. Petersburg, Russia. In the final chapter in this part, David Hutton discusses several insights obtained through mathematical modeling studies of public health responses to pandemic influenza.

Part IV Pharmaceutical Applications

Pharmaceutical policy has attracted media attention in recent years through a combination of factors, including blockbuster drugs being pulled from the market due to safety concerns and the emergence of very expensive drugs costing US$20,000–500,000 per year. The papers in this part demonstrate some of the important ways that operations research is helping to improve pharmaceutical policy. Margrét Bjarnadóttir and David Czerwinski discuss statistical tools to provide post-marketing vaccine and drug surveillance. Doug Coyle and colleagues describe the development of a Markov model that was used to help inform a funding decision for idursulfase for the treatment of Hunter disease, a rare disease affecting approximately 1 in 170,000 live births. Greg Zaric, Hui Zhang, and Reza Mahjoub review risk-sharing models and patient-access schemes, which are contracts between drug manufacturers and health-care payers in which the unit price of a drug may change, depending on either the total number of units sold or the performance of the drug, or both.

Part V Building Health Policy Models

In this part, the focus shifts to building heath policy models. The first chapter, by April Kimmel and Bruce Schackman, describes a number of high-level issues, including how to identify, conceptualize, build, and validate health policy models; it also discusses strategies for communicating results to policy-makers. The second chapter, by Malek Hannouf and Greg Zaric, describes in detail how the vast holdings of health administrative databases can be used when conducting cost-effectiveness analyses.

Part VI Working with Policy-Makers

The final part of the book is devoted to working with policy-makers. John Blake and two colleagues from Canadian Blood Services, Michelle Rogerson, and Dorothy Harris, describe an analysis that was conducted to analyze the impact of a consolidation of two facilities in Atlantic Canada. In the final chapter of the book, Jeffery Hoch describes some of the lessons that he has learned as director of the Pharmacoeconomics Research Unit at Cancer Care Ontario. The unit employs a number of modellers and health economists who provide support for managers and policy-makers at Cancer Care Ontario.

Summary

This volume covers many of the important ways in which operations research can and is contributing to improved health policy decisions. This is an exciting field that involves interdisciplinary research and the ability to have both a theoretical and a real-world impact. I believe the research and insights contained in this volume will help to enhance the value and impact of future contributions as the need for this type of work continues to grow.

Acknowledgements

I would like to thank Fred Hillier for inviting me to compile this volume and Matthew Amboy and Neil Levine from Springer for their assistance in putting it together. I would also like to acknowledge the support of the Canada Research Chairs program. Most importantly, I must thank all of the contributing authors for their commitment to bringing this volume together.

London, ON, Canada Gregory S. Zaric

Contents

Part I Applications of Health Policy Modeling

1 **Public Health Modeling at the Centers for Disease Control and Prevention** ... 3
Arielle Lasry, Michael L. Washington, Hannah K. Smalley, Faramroze Engineer, Pinar Keskinocak, and Larry Pickering

2 **OR in Public Health: A Little Help Can Go a Long Way** ... 17
Margaret L. Brandeau

Part II Health Policy and Operations

3 **Analytical Long-Term Care Capacity Planning** ... 39
Yue Zhang and Martin L. Puterman

4 **Managing Community-based Care for Chronic Diseases: The Quantitative Approach** ... 71
Beste Kucukyazici and Vedat Verter

5 **Project Management Approach to Implement Clinical Pathways: An Example for Thyroidectomy** ... 91
Yasar A. Ozcan, Elena Tànfani, and Angela Testi

6 **EMS Planning and Management** ... 105
Armann Ingolfsson

7 **Impact of Inpatient Reimbursement Systems on Hospital Performance: The Austrian Case-Based Payment Strategy** ... 129
Marion S. Rauner and Michaela M. Schaffhauser-Linzatti

Part III HIV Policy Models

8 **Assessing Prevention for Positives: Cost-Utility Assessment of Behavioral Interventions for Reducing HIV Transmission** 157
Sada Soorapanth and Stephen E. Chick

9 **Modeling the Impact of New HIV Prevention Technologies in Sub-Saharan Africa** 179
John Stover, Carel Pretorius, and Kyeen Andersson

10 **REACH: A Practical HIV Resource Allocation Tool for Decision Makers** 201
Sabina S. Alistar, Margaret L. Brandeau, and Eduard J. Beck

11 **Review of Operations Research Tools and Techniques Used for Influenza Pandemic Planning** 225
David W. Hutton

Part IV Pharmaceutical Policy

12 **Active Vaccine and Drug Surveillance: Towards a 100 Million Member System** 251
Margrét V. Bjarnadóttir and David Czerwinski

13 **Application of Operations Research to Funding Decisions for Treatments with Rare Disease** 281
Doug Coyle, Chaim M. Bell, Joe T.R. Clarke, Gerald Evans, Anita Gadhok, Janet Martin, Mona Sabharwal, and Eric Winquist

14 **Modeling Risk Sharing Agreements and Patient Access Schemes** 295
Gregory S. Zaric, Hui Zhang, and Reza Mahjoub

Part V Building Health Policy Models

15 **Considerations for Developing Applied Health Policy Models: The Example of HIV Treatment Expansion in Resource-Limited Settings** 313
April D. Kimmel and Bruce R. Schackman

16 **Cost-Effectiveness Analysis Using Registry and Administrative Data** 341
Malek B. Hannouf and Gregory S. Zaric

Part VI Working with Policy Makers

17 Evaluating Health Care Policy Decisions: Canadian Blood Services in Atlantic Canada 365
John Blake, Michelle Rogerson, and Dorothy Harris

18 Improving the Efficiency of Cost-effectiveness Analysis to Inform Policy Decisions in the Real World: Lessons from the Pharmacoeconomics Research Unit at Cancer Care Ontario 399
Jeffrey S. Hoch

Index 417

Part I
Applications of Health Policy Modeling

Chapter 1
Public Health Modeling at the Centers for Disease Control and Prevention

Arielle Lasry, Michael L. Washington, Hannah K. Smalley, Faramroze Engineer, Pinar Keskinocak, and Larry Pickering

Abstract At the Centers for Disease Control and Prevention, there is a growing interest in promoting the use of mathematical modeling to support public health policies. This chapter presents three examples of operations research models developed and employed by the Centers for Disease Control and Prevention. First, we discuss the Adult Immunization Scheduler, which uses dynamic programming methods to establish a personalized vaccination schedule for adults aged 19 and older. The second operations research project is a discrete event simulation model used to estimate the throughput and budget for mass vaccination clinics during the 2009–2010 H1N1 pandemic. Lastly, we describe a national HIV resource allocation model that uses nonlinear programming methods to optimize the allocation of funds to HIV prevention programs and populations.

A. Lasry (✉)
Division of HIV/AIDS Prevention, Centers for Disease Control and Prevention,
1600 Clifton Road, Mailstop E-48, Atlanta, GA 30333, USA
e-mail: alasry@cdc.gov

M.L. Washington
Preparedness Modeling Unit, Centers for Disease Control and Prevention,
Atlanta, GA, USA

H.K. Smalley • P. Keskinocak
H. Milton Stewart School of Industrial and Systems Engineering,
Georgia Institute of Technology, Atlanta, GA, USA

F. Engineer
School of Mathematical & Physical Sciences, University of Newcastle,
Ourimbah, NSW, Australia

L. Pickering
National Center for Immunization and Respiratory Diseases,
Centers for Disease Control and Prevention, Atlanta, GA, USA

G.S. Zaric (ed.), *Operations Research and Health Care Policy*,
International Series in Operations Research & Management Science 190,
DOI 10.1007/978-1-4614-6507-2_1,

1.1 Introduction

The application and use of modeling methods and, in particular, operations research techniques in the realm of public health have increased in the past decade. The Centers for Disease Control and Prevention (CDC), one of the national public health agencies in the USA, has demonstrated a keen interest in applying quantitative models to support policy recommendations with evidence-based, rational economic decisions. For example, in 2008, CDC created a Preparedness Modeling Unit (PMU) to serve as a focal point for the development, validation, verification, promotion, and support of policy-oriented quantitative models for use by CDC, the Department of Health and Human Services (DHHS), and state and local public health departments. The PMU provides leadership and a forum for collaborators in health-related and engineering sciences focusing on preparedness and emergency response logistics from a public health research and practice perspective. Also in 2008, the CDC established an agency-wide workgroup focused on modeling and applications to infectious disease. The workgroup meets bimonthly to share, collaborate and coordinate infectious disease modeling efforts at CDC. In December 2010, the CDC hosted the inaugural conference on "Modeling for Public Health Action: From Epidemiology to Operations," intended to foster interest in applying analytical tools for public health policy and operational decision-making. These activities show a growing interest in promoting, using and coordinating mathematical modeling in public health at the CDC.

In this chapter we present three examples of operations research models developed and employed by CDC. First, we discuss the Adult Immunization Scheduler, which uses dynamic programming methods to establish a personalized vaccination schedule for adults aged 19 and older. The second operations research project is a discrete event simulation model used to estimate the throughput and budget for mass vaccination clinics during the 2009–2010 H1N1 pandemic. Lastly, we describe a national HIV resource allocation model that uses nonlinear programming methods to optimize the allocation of funds to HIV prevention programs and populations.

1.2 The Adult Immunization Scheduler

To aid in the timely and appropriate vaccination of adults aged 19 and older, a recommended immunization schedule based on age and medical condition is published annually by the Advisory Committee on Immunization Practices (ACIP) [1]. The schedule is accompanied by a series of footnotes specifying the recommended timing between doses and identifying high risk groups for which specific vaccines are recommended. While the importance of immunizing children is widely accepted, many adults fail to receive their recommended vaccines on time, whether due to misinformation or changes in medical condition, work environment, or lifestyle. Following the 2007 National Immunization Survey of Adults [2], up-to-date coverage levels for the tetanus, diphtheria vaccine (Td) were reported at 57.2 % among persons aged 18–64 and 44.1 % among persons aged 65 and older. Only 65.6 % of persons 65 and older had received the pneumococcal vaccine, which is recommended for everyone in that age group.

Failure to receive immunizations when recommended can have serious consequences for both the unvaccinated adult and family members, including children. For example, from January through October of 2010, 211 infants in California, too young to be fully immunized against pertussis, were hospitalized due to pertussis infection, and ten pertussis-related deaths occurred in infants younger than 3 months [3]. Following a study of laboratory-confirmed infant pertussis cases, it was reported that sources of transmission to infants younger than 6 months include parents (55 % of source cases), aunts and uncles (10 %), and grandparents and part-time caregivers (8 %) [4]. Thus, on-time immunization of adults can be vital to protect infants too young to be fully immunized.

With the goal of protecting adults and those close to them against vaccine-preventable diseases, a decision support tool was developed which constructs catch-up immunization schedules for adults aged 19 and older. This tool, the Adult Immunization Scheduler, is a companion tool to the Catch-up Immunization Scheduler for children through age 6 [5]. Both have been verified and validated through physicians who normally provide immunizations to these populations.

The adult immunization scheduling problem is one of determining the best schedule of missed and required vaccine shots needed to make an individual's immunization record up to date according to ACIP recommendations. Constructing an immunization schedule for an adult requires the adult's date of birth, dates of previous immunizations, and details regarding his or her medical condition, place of work, and lifestyle. In addition, the requirements about the spacing between the doses for each individual vaccine must be available. Each vaccine dose has a feasible age window, recommended age window, and minimum and recommended gaps between previous and successive doses. Vaccines are recommended in some circumstances (e.g., the adult works in healthcare) and contraindicated in others (e.g., the adult's immune system is suppressed by disease or medical treatment). Therefore, conditions for which vaccination is recommended or not must also be available.

Similar to the Catch-up Immunization Scheduler for Children which was released in June 2008, the Adult Immunization Scheduler has three main components: (1) user-interface, (2) vaccine library, and (3) dynamic programming algorithm. User-specific information is entered into the user-interface, including date of birth, vaccination history, and the additional necessary input which is compiled based on the user's answers to a series of questions. A screenshot of the user-interface is shown in Fig. 1.1. Timing restrictions for each vaccine were compiled based on the ACIP recommendations and entered into a table which is contained in the vaccine library. These tables are simple to modify by authorized personnel when changes to the recommendations occur.

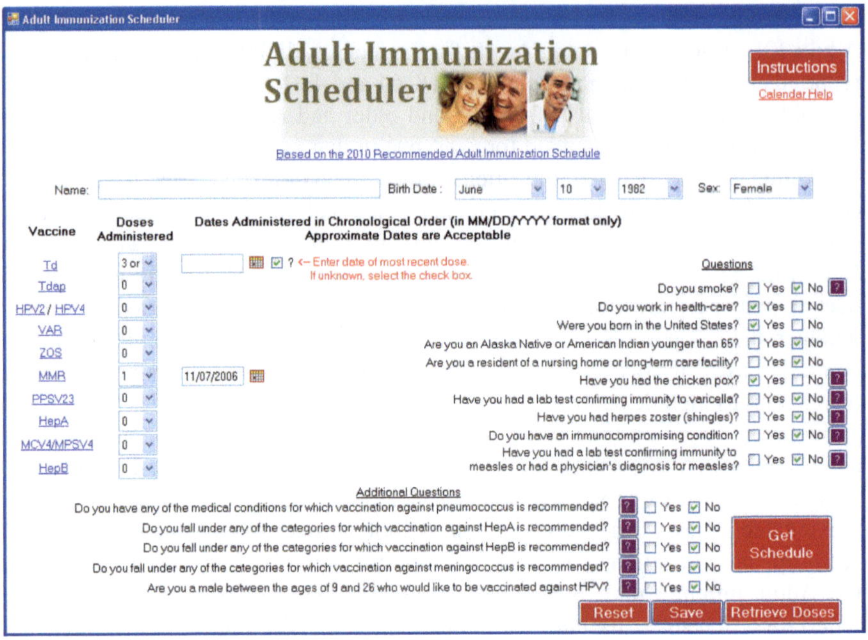

Fig. 1.1 Screenshot of the user interface for the Adult Immunization Scheduler

Given the necessary input from the user and vaccine-specific feasibility requirements provided within the vaccine library, the Adult Immunization Scheduler constructs an optimal catch-up schedule for an adult using a dynamic programming algorithm. The optimal schedule for an individual seeks to achieve the greatest level of coverage against vaccine-preventable diseases. Thus, the objectives are to (1) maximize the number of complete vaccination series' scheduled so as to fully immunize the individual against the most diseases possible, (2) minimize the total delay in administering doses and thereby maximize the individual's coverage as soon as possible, and (3) maximize the total number of doses given to ensure that individuals receive as many doses of a vaccine as possible, even if it is not possible to complete the entire vaccination series. Rather than enumerating all possible schedules to determine the best schedule for optimizing coverage, the algorithm iteratively discards schedules which are infeasible or dominated by another schedule. Details of the algorithm and criteria for determining schedule dominance are described elsewhere [6].

The Adult Immunization Scheduler is posted on the Centers for Disease Control and Prevention's (CDC) Web site at http://www.cdc.gov/vaccines/recs/Scheduler/AdultScheduler.htm and can be downloaded for free. The tool is easy to use and provides an optimal immunization schedule to users within seconds. The intended users are adults, aged 19 and above, seeking to determine the best immunization schedule that is customized to their age, medical conditions, and current

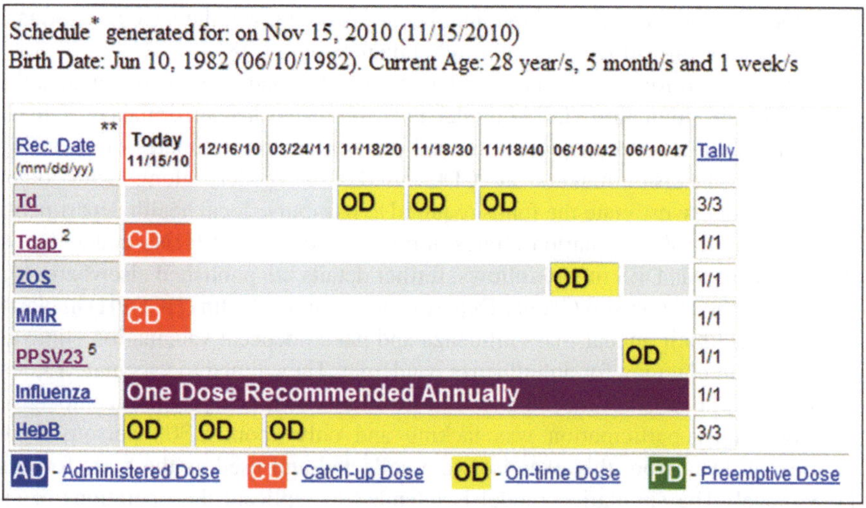

Fig. 1.2 Example of immunization schedule produced by the Adult Immunization Scheduler

vaccination status. They may share the resulting schedule with their primary care physician. An example of a schedule produced by the tool is shown in Fig. 1.2.

A rise in immunization coverage levels among adults is important for personal protection and for reducing potential for outbreaks of certain vaccine-preventable diseases among children. However, many adults are unaware that immunizations are recommended for them, thus creating a significant barrier to increased immunization rates. The Adult Immunization Scheduler provides an added means of informing the public regarding recommended immunizations, and allows those recommendations to be applied on an individual basis.

An Adolescent Immunization Scheduler targeting children and adolescents aged 7 through 18 years was released in 2011 and posted to the CDC Web site at http://www.cdc.gov/vaccines/recs/Scheduler/AdolescentScheduler.htm. Also, Spanish language versions of the childhood, adult, and adolescent vaccine scheduling tools are currently under development [7].

1.3 Mass Vaccination Model During the H1N1 Pandemic

During the 2009–2010 H1N1 pandemic, supply of the 2009 H1N1 vaccine was initially limited, and the 6-week period following the release of the vaccine was characterized by high demand and very limited availability. Most state and local health departments requested that the available vaccine be administered to the high priority target groups specified by the Advisory Committee for Immunization Practices (ACIP), yet the vaccine supply was often not sufficient to meet even those target groups. Public health officials from the state and local level sought guidance from the CDC on vaccinating large numbers of people given the vaccine shortage, and the lack of infrastructure, funds and human resources [8].

In preparation for an influenza pandemic, the CDC had previously developed a discrete-event simulation (DES) model that simulates the performance of mass vaccination clinics and provides total and per person cost estimates of operating the clinics. Decision-makers at CDC used this model, along with other considerations, to estimate the funds required to reimburse local health departments for operating mass vaccination clinics during the 2009–2010 H1N1 pandemic. A description of this DES model follows, further details are published elsewhere [9].

In 2002, the Henderson County Department of Public Health (HCDPH) in North Carolina held their annual mass influenza and pneumococcal vaccination clinic as an exercise in planning for an influenza pandemic. They aimed to vaccinate 15,000 persons in 17 hours since they had vaccinated 10,000 people in previous campaigns; but community participation was lacking and only about 8,300 persons were vaccinated. Data from this exercise were collected and used as the basis for this DES model. The simulation model is intended to replicate the operations of an actual mass vaccination clinic and estimate costs from a societal perspective. Computer simulation was deemed valuable in this case because it easily creates a representation of the clinic, can generate as many "clients" as desired, and allows for experimenting with multiple variations of the clinic staffing to identify the best arrangements.

Data on processing times, client process flows, costs, materials, and the clinic layout were provided by HCDPH. Using these data, a DES model was created to estimate the throughput (or number of clients served over a period of time) of the vaccination clinic as the number of clients entering the clinic per unit time (arrival intensity) increased and evaluate whether reassigning staff members to different stations could increase throughput at minimal cost.

Three types of clients were simulated: "Medicare" clients represented 70 % of all clients; "Medicare Special" clients representing 6 % and all others known as "Cash" clients. "Medicare" and "Medicare Special" clients' vaccinations were paid for by Medicare. "Medicare Special" designates clients needing physical assistance to move through the clinic; they are vaccinated in a separate station from the two other clients types. "Cash" clients paid out-of-pocket for the vaccination, though they could subsequently get reimbursed from a private insurer. The process flow for "Cash" type client was to register and pay at one station and receive their vaccination at another station. "Medicare" and "Medicare Special" began with an additional station where their card was copied as a means to ensure that the HCDPH would be reimbursed by the Medicare program. They then proceeded to a registration station and then to receive their vaccination.

The simulation model was verified by the HCDPH and then validated against the real data (i.e., the number of people vaccinated over the same time period and the time spent by each client in the clinic). The simulation model was developed using Arena 10 (Rockwell Software, West Allis, WI). A clinic flow diagram and a screenshot of the simulation in progress are shown in Fig. 1.3.

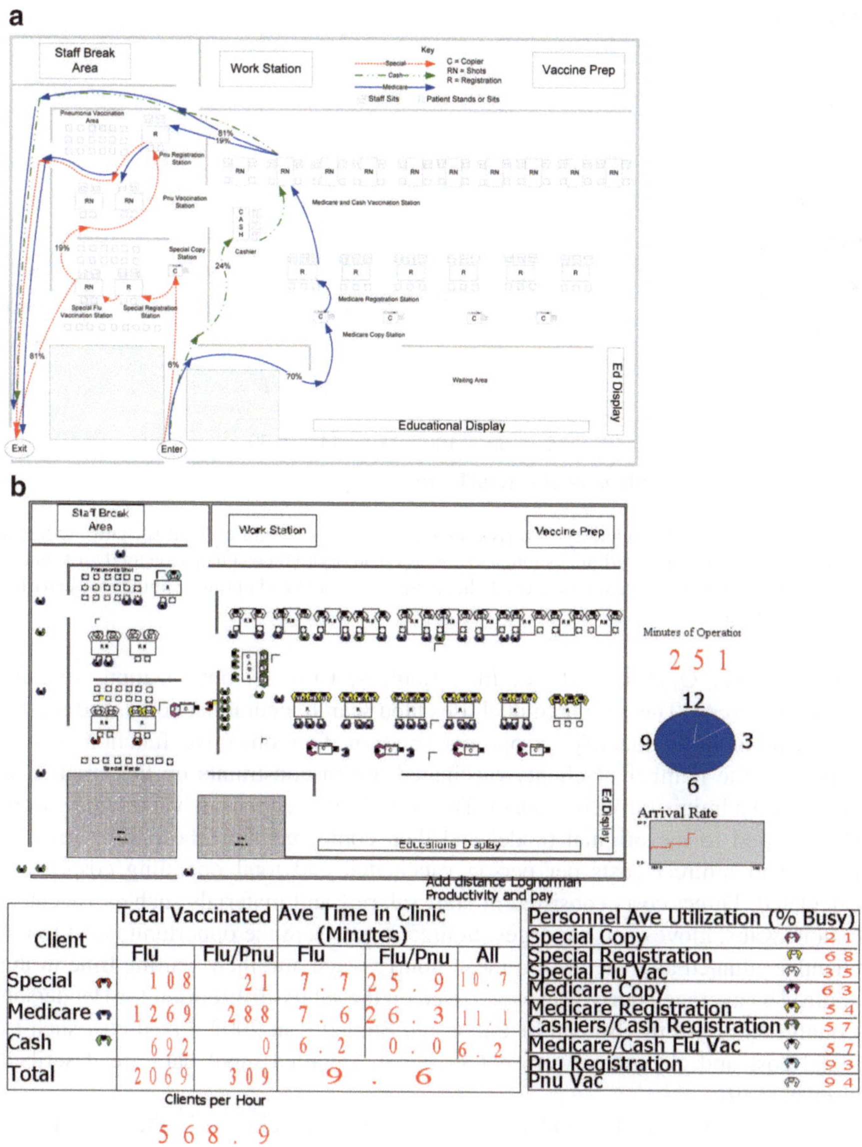

Fig. 1.3 (**a**) Facility layout and flow. (**b**) Screenshot of simulation in progress

The costs of materials, staff salaries, staff utilization, and client waiting time were considered. Two model types were created: the "original" model was designed to represent the same staff placement as that of the actual clinic and the "optimal" model was designed such that staff placement maximizes the number of client visits, or the throughput of the clinic. Arrival intensity was varied in 20 % increments; to determine the optimal model at each increment, we used OptQuest

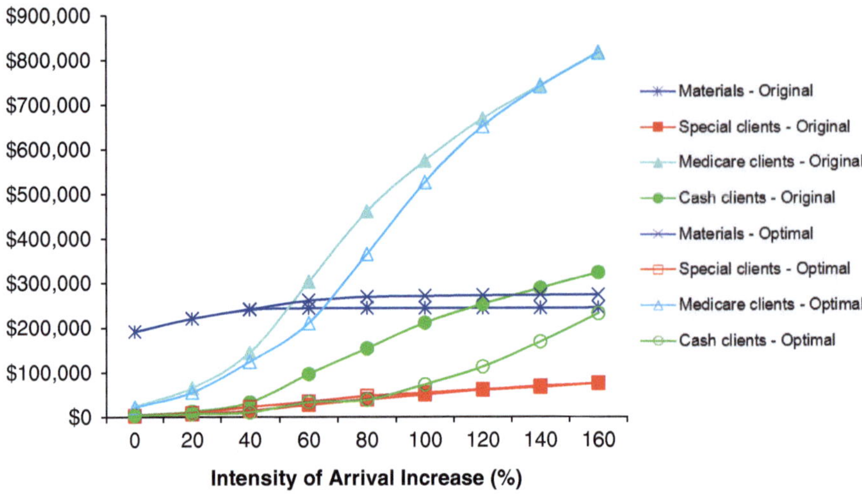

Fig. 1.4 Total costs by intensity of arrival increase for original and optimal scenario. Original designates the costs in the original simulated scenario and optimal designates the total costs under the optimal scenario. Cost data for special clients in the original and optimal simulation scenarios are overlapping

(version 10.0; OptTek Systems, Inc., Boulder, CO), an optimization software add-on to Arena. The optimal model uses tabu search, neural networks, and scatter search methods to identify an optimal solution. Our objective function was to maximize the number of clients vaccinated, given constraints on the number of nurses and administrative personnel. The 20 % increments in arrival intensity were also applied to the original model and then compared with the optimal model. Direct and indirect costs per person vaccinated and total operating costs were calculated. Direct costs consisted of staff salaries and materials such as vaccines, cotton swabs, gloves and bandages. Indirect costs were the opportunity cost to the clients evaluated as a factor of a mean hourly wage and their waiting time in the clinic. The average hourly wage was based on the salary distribution for Henderson County, NC from the Bureau of Labor and Statistics in 2002. Fixed cost such as rental cost and electricity were not included. Detailed input data are described elsewhere [9].

A maximum of 13,138 and 15,094 clients were vaccinated in the original and optimal scenarios, respectively. At the original arrival rate of 8,300 clients in 17 hours, materials were the most expensive cost component of the clinic operation in both the original and optimal models. Figure 1.4 shows the impact of the increase in arrivals on the overall costs by client type and for materials in the original and optimal scenario. The baseline case is represented by 100 % of arrival intensity on the x-axis. As the arrival intensity increases to 140 %, the costs of "Medicare" clients increase from $23,887 to $743,510 in the original model, and from $21,474 to $740,760 in the optimal model. As shown in Fig. 1.5, the direct cost per person vaccinated decreases from $22.78 to $20.19 as the arrival intensity increases in the

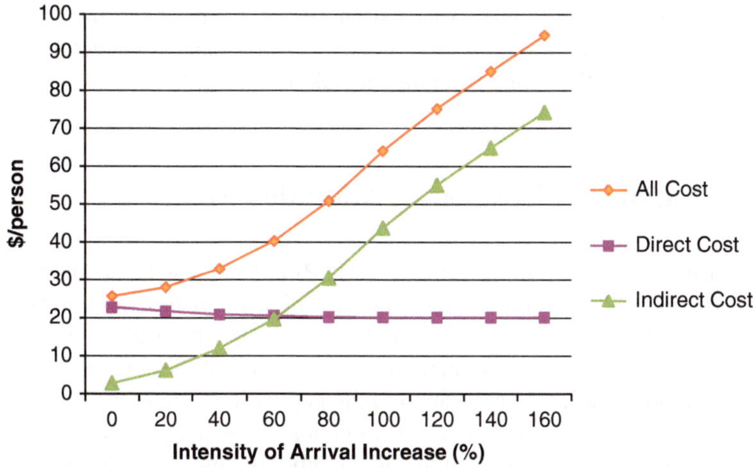

Fig. 1.5 Cost of vaccination per Medicare client in optimal scenario by intensity of arrival increase

optimal model, due to reduced idle time for nurses and administrative personnel. However, when indirect costs are included, the cost per person vaccinated increases from $25.67 to $94.54 due to the increased client waiting time.

According to the optimal model, the clinic could reach their target of 15,000 vaccinations with two fewer staff members by reallocating staff assignments from "Medicare Special" to "Medicare" and "Cash" stations. In the optimal model, "Cash" clients are targeted because they tend to get processed more quickly as they visit one fewer station, while "Medicare Special" clients spend over 250 minutes in the clinic, on average. In reality, the clinic would likely modify the staffing arrangement to ensure these clients are serviced more expeditiously.

This DES model can help decision-makers evaluate the impact of the various clinic designs without operating an actual clinic and help them determine the most efficient use of staff, supplies, and time. Though an optimal model can offer the design which maximizes throughput, decision-makers must nonetheless review the practicality of the results and their implications. Policy makers must balance the objective of serving as many people as possible with the reality that a marginal part of the population may receive inappropriate care. For example, providing a high throughput while "Medicare Special" type clients experience excessive waiting times may not be acceptable.

The model results can be generalized to similar mass vaccination clinics considering that most are staffed and designed in a similar fashion. The model can easily be modified to accommodate other staffing arrangements and results for a 30-day simulation were obtained in less than a minute.

This simulation model provides estimates of mass vaccination operating costs and costs per person vaccinated. Decision-makers at CDC used this model and other factors to estimate the funds that would be required to reimburse local health departments for operating mass vaccination clinics during the 2009–2010 H1N1 pandemic. Those results were in turn used by CDC officials as budget justification to obtain the required funding from the federal government.

1.4 A National HIV Resource Allocation Model

The Division of HIV/AIDS Prevention (DHAP) at CDC has an annual budget of approximately $325 million for funding HIV prevention programs in the USA. Prompted by the need to reduce the number of people who become infected with HIV each year, DHAP seeks to improve the allocation of these funds by targeting intervention programs to the most appropriate population subgroups. We define this HIV resource allocation problem as one of choosing the amounts to be invested in HIV prevention interventions such that the number of new infections is minimized subject to a budget constraint. We select a 5-year time horizon to match the typical strategic planning and budget cycle. To address this problem we define two models that interact. First, an epidemic model, defined as a compartmental Susceptible-Infected model, determines HIV epidemic projections given a specified allocation scenario. The epidemic model uses discrete-time approximations to the continuous system in monthly time intervals [10, 11]. Second, an optimization model, defined as a nonlinear mathematical program, generates different allocation scenarios, supplies them to the epidemic model and converges to optimality when the best outcome is reached.

The epidemic model is structured into population subgroups by gender, race/ethnicity, HIV transmission risk group and serostatus. Risk groups include high-risk heterosexuals (HRH), men who have sex with men (MSM) and injection drug users (IDU). Race is defined as blacks, Hispanics, and Other races, where Other races are primarily whites as well as Asians, Pacific Islanders, Alaskan Natives, and American Indians. Each population subgroup is then divided into three compartments, those susceptible to HIV infection, those HIV infected but undiagnosed and those HIV infected and diagnosed.

We considered two main types of HIV prevention interventions: HIV testing and HIV counseling and education programs. Those aware of their HIV seropositivity tend to engage in safer sex; therefore testing is considered a prevention intervention [12–14]. These interventions types can be targeted to the various combinations of the population subgroups (e.g., Hispanic MSM or all IDUs) and more broadly to the general US population, aged 13–64 years.

The optimization model is defined as a multi-period model with a time horizon of 5 years and the decision variables are the amount to allocate annually to each of the interventions and target groups considered. Testing interventions can be targeted to 22 combinations of the population subgroups and are aimed at identifying those infected with HIV but undiagnosed. Counseling and education programs can be targeted to 49 different combinations of the population subgroups and can be aimed specifically at those infected with HIV, those uninfected or both.

Constraints are defined to enforce a minimum and maximum penetration rate for every intervention and population subgroup, and bounds are set on the funding levels for each intervention. Details of the model's structure and methods are provided elsewhere [15].

For each population subgroup, data requirements include the following: rates of entry to and exit from each HIV-related status, the number of people living with HIV, the percentage of positives unaware of their serostatus, the current annual number of new infections, the overall size of the subgroup, and the effective contact rates for every valid pair of population subgroups. For each intervention data requirements include the following: the cost and outcome per person, the current allocation of funds, the minimum and maximum penetration rate and funding level.

The model's structure and its data inputs have undergone a rigorous validation process, including peer review by over 40 subject-matter experts internal and external to the CDC.

We compared the model's optimized allocation scenario to DHAP's current allocation scenario and key differences can be summarized into three main recommendations. First, the allocation to testing interventions should increase and further target MSM and IDUs. Second, counseling and education interventions ought to provide a greater focus on HIV-infected persons. And lastly, more funds should be allocated to those at high risk rather than the general population. We evaluated whether these main model recommendations were upheld given reasonable variations in the inputs. We conducted over 100 univariate sensitivity analysis scenarios on more than 20 model variables. Results appeared most sensitive to variations in the cost of testing, the cost and outcome of counseling and education interventions and the size of the MSM population. When the cost of testing increased, the allocation to testing MSM increased because testing MSM remains a priority in spite of the cost increase. Either reducing the cost or increasing the outcome of counseling and education programs increased the overall allocation to counseling and education programs, also, the proportion of the allocation to targeted MSM for both intervention types increases. As the size of the MSM population in the model increases, so does the allocation to testing that is targeted to MSM. These scenarios reinforce the model's recommended focus on MSM and thus demonstrate the stability of the model structure and inputs. Model results and implications are more thoroughly described elsewhere [16].

The lifetime treatment costs of an HIV-infected individual are estimated at $367,000 (US$ 2009), so even moderate reductions in new HIV infections leads to considerable savings from averted medical costs [17]. This HIV resource allocation model provides valuable guidance to the rational economic allocation of funds. Improving the use of funds by targeting the interventions and population subgroups of greatest return should lead to improved HIV outcomes.

DHAP's leadership state that the findings of this model are used, along with program and other data, to guide the Division's decision-making process for HIV resource allocation, enhance the effect of our HIV prevention efforts and progress towards the goals of the National HIV/AIDS Strategy which include reducing the number of new HIV infections and increasing the number of HIV infected persons who know their serostatus [18]. The national HIV resource allocation model provides useful guidelines that can be used to target resources to interventions and population subgroups likely to have the most impact on curtailing HIV incidence in the USA.

1.5 Conclusions and Policy Implications

In this paper, we presented three operations research models, developed at CDC, that address specific concerns or questions posed by policy makers at the agency. All the models demonstrated some impact on public health resources and priority setting. First, the Adult Immunization Scheduler was downloaded more than 17,235 times (January 2010 to April 2011) from the CDC Web site. The older Catch-up Immunization Scheduler has been downloaded 80,505 times from June 2008 until April 2011. Even if a fraction of the end users follow their optimized immunization schedule, the public health benefits in terms of herd immunity and cases of diseases averted are likely to be significant and cost-saving. Second, a discrete-event computer simulation model and other mass vaccination decision tools were recommended to local health jurisdictions by the CDC and used by the CDC to plan mass vaccination clinics during the H1N1 pandemic of 2009–2010. In addition, the discrete-event computer simulation model was one factor used by the leadership at CDC to justify and obtain the funds required to support mass vaccinations clinics in local health jurisdictions. Lastly, results of the national HIV resource allocation model were used to guide CDC's decision-making process for HIV resource allocation and support the goals of the National HIV/AIDS Strategy.

Health care modelers at, or commissioned by, the CDC benefit from proximity to policy makers, access to real data and an understanding of the problem and the context under which decision-making takes place. These advantages provide an environment that is favorable to the development of models that can have an impact on public health policy and priority setting decisions in health.

The opportunity for modeling to help guide discussions and provide clarity to health care policy debates is great. However, models have had a relatively limited impact on decision-making processes in health and public health [19–21]. Health care policy making is often influenced by qualitative factors that include social and ethical considerations, community advocacy and politics, but they are scarcely supported by quantitative models [22, 23]. To improve the contribution of models to decision-making in health and bridge the gap between insights and predictions from quantitative models and decisions about policy and practice, modeling should be considered a process to be undertaken by all parties involved, rather than a product or tool to be delivered by the modeler. Modelers should understand the requirements of their end users and the context in which they operate. Also, modelers should first find out what data are available to inform their models and then create models that make the best use of available data. An understanding of stakeholders' needs and influences is critical. Stakeholders should be engaged early in the modeling process in order to increase their willingness to cooperate in building and using the models [24]. And modelers should involve stakeholders during a model's conception phase in order to improve the quality of the model and increase the stakeholders trust in the model. The cooperation of all stakeholders is especially important in public health where societal health benefits are as important as individual health benefits and might involve tradeoffs among them [25–27].

Disclaimer: The findings and conclusions in this paper are those of the authors and do not necessarily represent the views of the Centers for Disease Control and Prevention.

References

1. Centers for Disease Control and Prevention (2010) Recommended adult immunization schedule—United States. http://www.cdc.gov/vaccines/recs/schedules/downloads/adult/2010/adult-schedule.pdf. Accessed 15 Nov 2010
2. National Center for Health Statistics—United States (2007 (Revised 2008)) Vaccination coverage among U.S. adults, National Immunization Survey—Adult. http://www.cdc.gov/vaccines/stats-surv/nis/downloads/nis-adult-summer-2007.pdf. Accessed 15 Nov 2010
3. California Department of Public Health (2010) Pertussis report. p 5
4. Wendelboe A et al. (2007) Transmission of *Bordetella pertussis* to young infants. Pediatr Infect Dis J 26(4):293–299
5. Centers for Disease Control and Prevention (2010) Catch-up Immunization Scheduler for children six years of age and younger. http://www.cdc.gov/vaccines/recs/Scheduler/catchup.htm. Accessed 15 Nov 2010
6. Engineer FG, Keskinocak P, Pickering LK (2009) OR practice—catch-up scheduling for childhood vaccination. Oper Res 57(6):1307–1319
7. Smalley HK et al. (2011) Universal tool for vaccine scheduling—applications for children and adults. Interfaces 41(5):436–454
8. Cho B-H et al. (2011) A tool for the economic analysis of mass prophylaxis operations with an application to H1N1 influenza vaccination clinics. J Public Health Manag Pract 17(1): E22–E28
9. Washington ML (2009) Evaluating the capability and cost of a mass influenza and pneumococcal vaccination clinic via computer simulation. Med Decis Making 29(4):414–423
10. Luenberger DG (1979) Introduction to dynamic systems: theory, models, and applications. Wiley, New York, p 446
11. Zaric GS et al. (1998) The effect of protease inhibitors on the spread of HIV and the development of drug resistance: a simulation study. Simulation 71:262–275
12. Marks G et al. (2005) Meta-analysis of high-risk sexual behavior in persons aware and unaware they are infected with HIV in the United States: implications for HIV prevention programs. J Acquir Immune Defic Syndr 39:446–453
13. Weinhardt LS et al. (1999) Effects of HIV counseling and testing on sexual risk behavior: a meta-analytic review of published research, 1985–1997. Am J Public Health 89(9):1397–1405
14. Marks G et al. (2009) Understanding differences in HIV sexual transmission among Latino and black men who have sex with men: the Brothers y Hermanos study. AIDS Behav 13(4):682–690
15. Lasry A et al. (2011) A model for allocating CDC's HIV prevention resources in the United States. Health Care Manag Sci 14(1):115–124

16. Lasry A et al. (2012) Allocating HIV prevention funds in the United States: recommendations from an optimization model. PLoS ONE 7(6):e37545
17. Schackman BR et al. (2006) The lifetime cost of current human immunodeficiency virus care in the United States. Med Care 44(11):990–997
18. The White House Office of National AIDS Policy (2010) National HIV/AIDS strategy for the United States. Washington, DC. p 60
19. Mooney G (1998) "Communitarian claims" as an ethical basis for allocating health care resources. Soc Sci Med 47(9):1171–1180
20. Kahn JG, Marseille E (2002) A saga in international HIV policy modeling: preventing mother-to-child HIV transmission. J Policy Anal Manag 21(3):499–505
21. McGregor M (2006) What decision-makers want and what they have been getting. Value Health 9(3):181–185
22. Lasry A, Carter MW, Zaric GS (2011) Allocating funds for HIV/AIDS: a descriptive study of KwaDukuza, South Africa. Health Policy Plan 26:33
23. Lasry A, Richter A, Lutscher F (2009) Recommendations for increasing the use of HIV/AIDS resource allocation models. BMC Public Health 9(Suppl 1):S8
24. Keeney RL (1988) Structuring objectives for problems of public interest. Oper Res 36(3):396–405
25. Pinkerton SD et al. (2002) Ethical issues in cost-effectiveness analysis. Eval Program Plann 25:71–83
26. Granata AV, Hillman AL (1998) Competing practice guidelines: using cost-effectiveness analysis to make optimal decisions. Ann Intern Med 128(1):56–63
27. Jackson T (1996) Health economics and policy: ethical dilemmas in the science of scarcity. In: Daly J (ed) Ethical intersections: health research, methods, and researcher responsibility. Westview Press, Boulder, CO, p 127–138

Chapter 2
OR in Public Health: A Little Help Can Go a Long Way

Margaret L. Brandeau

Abstract When deciding which programs to invest in, public health decision makers face a number of challenges including limited resources, competing objectives (e.g., maximize health, achieve equity), and limited information about uncertain events. Despite these difficulties, public health planners must make choices about which programs they will invest in—and the quality of these choices affects the health benefits achieved in the population. To support good decisions, information about the likely costs and health consequences of alternative interventions is needed. This is where OR-based modeling can play a role: by providing a structured framework that uses the best available evidence, imperfect as it may be, and that captures relevant uncertainties, complexities, and interactions, OR-based models can be used to evaluate the potential impact of alternative public health programs. This chapter describes modeling efforts in which OR has played and can play a role in informing public health decision making. We describe work in three areas: hepatitis B control, HIV control, and bioterrorism preparedness and response. We conclude with a discussion of lessons learned.

2.1 Introduction

The goal of public health is to improve lives through the prevention and treatment of disease. Specifically, public health focuses on population-level aspects of health, including disease prevention, infection control, prolongation of life, and promotion

M.L. Brandeau (✉)
Department of Management Science and Engineering,
Stanford University, Stanford, CA 94305, USA
e-mail: brandeau@stanford.edu

G.S. Zaric (ed.), *Operations Research and Health Care Policy*,
International Series in Operations Research & Management Science 190,
DOI 10.1007/978-1-4614-6507-2_2,

of healthy lifestyles. Early efforts in public health focused on sanitation and hygiene (e.g., clean water, sewers, garbage collection), nutrition, and mass inoculation (e.g., for smallpox). Modern public health efforts focus on these and other activities including control of the local and global spread of infectious diseases (e.g., influenza, malaria), control of chronic diseases (e.g., type 2 diabetes), and promotion of healthy behaviors (e.g., antismoking and obesity reduction campaigns).

When deciding which programs to invest in, public health decision makers face a number of challenges. They typically have limited resources to invest among many potential programs. It is never possible to achieve perfect health for everyone in the population, so they must choose where to focus their efforts. Moreover, when evaluating the worth of potential public health programs, they must consider not only the likely costs and health effects of such programs (e.g., cases of disease prevented, lives saved, or quality-adjusted life years gained as a function of resources expended) but also issues of equity and fairness. For example, it may be more expensive and less effective to target programs to certain impoverished or marginalized population groups compared to other segments of the population—but it is likely not acceptable (either politically or ethically) to ignore such groups. Additionally, public health planners frequently must make decisions with limited information about uncertain events. For example, plans for response to pandemic influenza must be made before it is even known whether such a pandemic will occur, what its magnitude may be, and what strain of influenza will predominate. Despite these difficulties, public health planners must make choices about which programs they will invest in—and the quality of these choices affects the health benefits achieved in the population.

To make good decisions, public health decision makers need information about the likely costs and health consequences of alternative interventions. The gold standard for evaluating health interventions is a randomized clinical trial. However, such trials are very often time consuming, expensive, infeasible, or unethical. This is where OR-based modeling can play a role: by providing a structured framework that uses the best available evidence, imperfect as it may be, and that captures relevant uncertainties, complexities, and interactions, OR-based models can be used to evaluate the potential impact of alternative public health programs. Of course, perfect prediction of the impact of interventions is not possible. Thus, the goal of OR-based modeling of potential health decisions must instead be to identify which alternatives are better than others—in other words, to inform good decisions.

This chapter describes modeling efforts in which OR has played and can play a role in informing public health decision making. We describe work in three areas: hepatitis B control, HIV control in Eastern Europe, and bioterrorism preparedness and response. For each area, we describe key policy questions, the types of models we used to inform decision making, and the process of dissemination of results to policy makers. We conclude with a discussion of lessons learned.

2.2 Hepatitis B Control

Hepatitis B is a blood-borne viral infection that, if untreated, can cause liver disease and cancer [1]. Individuals can acquire the infection at birth (if born to an infected mother), through sharing of blood (e.g., cuts and scrapes, sharing of toothbrushes), through unsafe blood transfusions, or through sexual contact, among other means. Some individuals who are exposed to hepatitis B can resolve the infection (their immune system generates sufficient antibodies such that they become immune to it), but some individuals go on to develop lifelong, chronic infection. Children are particularly vulnerable because the chance that an acute infection becomes chronic is higher for young children than for older children and adults. The chance of an infection becoming chronic for a newborn is approximately 90 %, whereas a 10-year-old exposed to the infection has approximately a 15 % chance of developing chronic infection and for a 20-year-old the chance is 9 % [2]. Approximately one-fourth of chronically infected individuals will die from hepatitis B-related liver disease (cirrhosis or liver cancer). Chronic hepatitis B is a silent infection: infected individuals are typically asymptomatic for decades before symptoms of the disease appear, so they can unknowingly spread the disease to others for many years.

A vaccine for hepatitis B has been available since the mid-1980s. Despite this, approximately 350 million people worldwide are infected with hepatitis B—more than ten times as many as are infected with HIV [3].

2.2.1 Hepatitis B in China

One-fourth of the world's hepatitis B cases occur in China, where an estimated 95 million people are chronically infected with hepatitis B [4, 5]. In 2002, the Chinese government included free hepatitis B vaccination for newborns in its national immunization program [4]. Although newborn vaccination rates have been relatively high in urban areas, vaccination coverage in rural areas has lagged behind [6]. It is estimated that 150 million children in China up to the age of 18 remain unprotected against hepatitis B (they have not been vaccinated, nor have they developed antibodies through exposure to the virus) [7].

A demonstration program implemented in the rural Qinghai province in China provided free hepatitis B catch-up vaccination to nearly 500,000 school children between 2006 and 2008 [8]. China's health ministry wanted to know whether such free catch-up vaccination would be economical to extend to the rest of the 150 million unprotected children in the country.

To inform this decision, we developed a model to evaluate the costs and health benefits of such catch-up vaccination [9, 10]. We considered a representative cohort of 10,000 children of a given age, and we considered different ages from 1 to 19 years old. We considered three strategies: no catch-up vaccination (which is the status quo); catch-up vaccination with no screening (children would be vaccinated

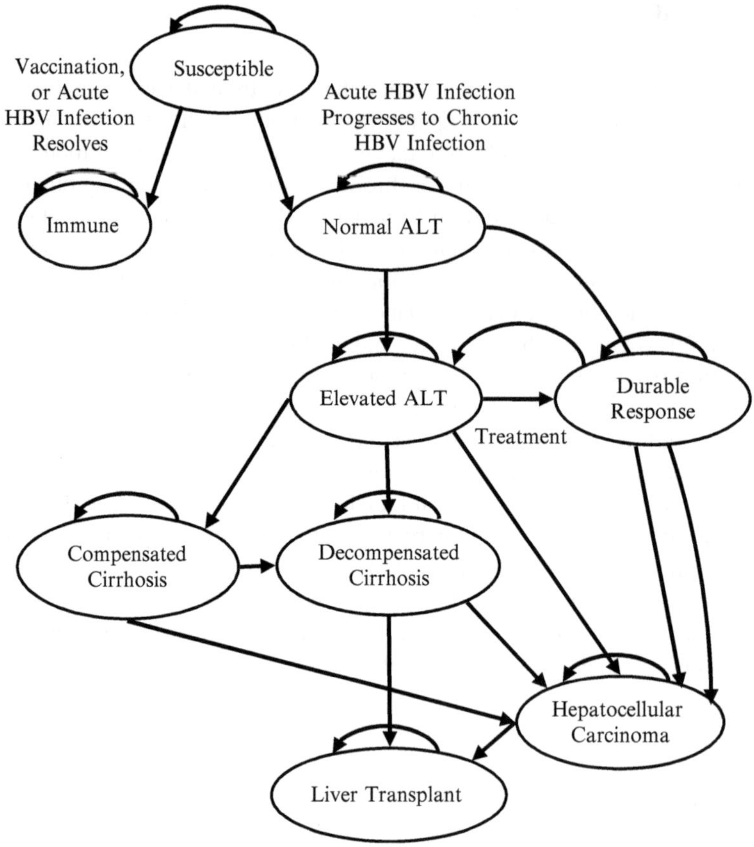

Fig. 2.1 Age-structured Markov model of hepatitis B disease states. Transitions occur annually and are associated with an age increment of 1 year. *ALT* alanine aminotransferase, a liver enzyme

unless they could provide evidence of vaccination); and catch-up vaccination with antibody screening (children with no evidence of vaccination would first be screened for hepatitis B antibodies and, if not immune to hepatitis B, would be vaccinated). For each of these strategies, we modeled costs incurred and health outcomes achieved over the lifetime of all children in the cohort. Costs included the cost of the vaccination program and all future healthcare costs for the cohort. Following standard practice in health economics [11], we measured health outcomes in terms of quality-adjusted life years (QALYs) gained, and we discounted all costs and benefits to the present.

We used an age-structured Markov model to model health states and associated costs over the lifetimes of the children in the cohort (Fig. 2.1). We developed this model in collaboration with hepatitis B experts at the US Centers for Disease Control and Prevention, at the Asian Liver Center at Stanford University, and elsewhere. Susceptible children can become immune to hepatitis B through vaccination.

Because of the large reservoir of chronically infected individuals in the population of China, we assumed that vaccination efforts would not change the chance that a child is exposed to hepatitis B; thus, we assumed a constant annual chance of a child in the cohort being exposed to hepatitis B (i.e., constant disease incidence). Children who are exposed to hepatitis B can either resolve the infection and become immune, or develop chronic infection. The first sign of liver dysfunction is an elevated level of alanine aminotransferase (ALT). If the individual is successfully treated with antiviral drugs, then a so-called durable response is achieved. Otherwise, the disease may progress further to cirrhosis and possibly liver cancer (hepatocellular carcinoma). Some individuals may receive a liver transplant. Death can occur from any state, with the rate determined by the health state and the age of the individual (for simplicity, these transitions are not shown in Fig. 2.1).

We modeled age and health state transitions in 1-year time increments. Thus, for example, a susceptible child aged 1 whose health state does not change within 1 year moves to the state for susceptible children aged 2 in the next year. Transition probabilities associated with hepatitis B disease progression were obtained from the literature and from informed judgment of hepatitis experts in China and elsewhere.

Associated with each health state is a quality multiplier reflecting the quality of life in that state. These quality multipliers, which in general can range from 0 (death) to 1 (perfect health), were drawn from the literature on hepatitis B infection. Also associated with each health state is an annual healthcare cost. These costs were obtained from demographic data and from recent studies of hepatitis B-related healthcare costs in China.

We implemented the model in an Excel spreadsheet. We simulated the cohort of 10,000 individuals in annual increments over a 100-year time horizon (reflecting the total possible lifetime of all individuals). For each year and each health state, we calculated costs incurred and QALYs experienced, and then discounted these values back to the present to calculate total costs and QALYs.

Using the model, we found that hepatitis B catch-up vaccination for children up to age 19 in China is cost-saving: the cost of the vaccination program (which is incurred now) is less than the net present savings in healthcare costs, when compared to the strategy of no catch-up vaccination. This finding was robust in sensitivity analysis: even in regions of the country where newborn vaccination coverage is already high and health care costs are low, catch-up vaccination is still cost-saving. We also found that screening before vaccination is not cost-effective: it costs more to screen a child for antibodies than to vaccinate the child, so it is cheaper to just vaccinate all children who have not been vaccinated or whose vaccination status is unknown (extra-vaccination is not harmful).

To disseminate this work, we published it in an international liver journal [9], and one member of our team (So) met multiple times with academics and health officials in China and members of the World Health Organization to share our interim results. Partly as a result of our study, in 2009 China instituted a policy of free hepatitis B catch-up vaccination to all children under the age of 15. Although a significant current expenditure of funds is required to implement the program, the future savings in healthcare costs will be quite large. We estimate that such vaccination could avert some 400,000 cases of chronic hepatitis B infection and almost 70,000 deaths due to hepatitis B, and would save China nearly $1 billion in healthcare costs [12]—a substantial impact on public health. Additionally, many individuals with chronic hepatitis B infection in China face significant discrimination in education and employment, so another benefit of the vaccination program is that it will spare hundreds of thousands of children from a lifetime of discrimination.

2.2.2 *Hepatitis B in the USA*

In the USA, which has high childhood vaccination coverage, hepatitis B infection among children is uncommon. However, the prevalence of chronic hepatitis B infection among adult Asian and Pacific Islanders (APIs) in the USA is quite high, partly because many APIs in the USA are foreign-born. Approximately 10 % of APIs in the USA are chronically infected with hepatitis B, as compared to 0.5 % of the general population [13, 14]. Because of this health disparity, a number of ad hoc hepatitis B screening, vaccination, and treatment programs have been implemented for APIs in various US cities. The US Centers for Disease Control and Prevention (CDC), which issues immunization and treatment guidelines for hepatitis B (and other diseases), wanted to decide what nationwide strategy they should recommend for hepatitis B control among APIs.

We used an age-structured Markov model similar to that in Fig. 2.1 to analyze the likely costs and health benefits of various strategies for controlling hepatitis B among APIs in the USA [15]. We obtained data for the model from the literature and from the informed judgment of our collaborator (So) and other hepatitis experts [12]. We implemented the model in an Excel spreadsheet, and instantiated and calibrated the model using an iterative process with input from hepatitis experts at the CDC and elsewhere.

We considered the following strategies: the status quo (no incremental screening, vaccination, or treatment); universal vaccination of all adult APIs; screening and treatment (screening to identify chronic infection, followed by antiviral treatment for those found to be infected); screening, treatment, and ring vaccination (screening to identify chronic infection, followed by antiviral treatment for those found to be infected and vaccination of the close contacts of infected individuals); and screening, treatment, and vaccination (screening to identify chronic infection or immunity, followed by vaccination of susceptibles and antiviral treatment for infected individuals). We considered a cohort of 10,000 adult APIs aged 40, and used the age-structured Markov model to simulate net present costs incurred and QALYs experienced over the lifetime of the cohort.

This analysis showed that the most cost-effective strategies are screening and treatment, which costs approximately $36,000 per QALY gained; and screening, treatment, and ring vaccination, which costs approximately $39,000 per QALY gained. Interventions in the USA that cost less than $50,000 per QALY gained are generally considered highly cost-effective [16–18]. In sensitivity analysis, we showed that the screen and treat and the screen, treat, and ring vaccinate strategies are cost-effective for any population in the USA for which the prevalence of chronic hepatitis B infection is 2 % or higher (e.g., individuals born in countries with endemic hepatitis B prevalence of 2 % or more). The analysis showed that the two strategies that involve vaccination of adult APIs are dominated: they cost more and yield fewer QALYs than the other strategies. This is because the probability of exposure to hepatitis B in the USA is relatively low and, for adults who do get exposed to the virus, the chance that they will develop chronic hepatitis B infection is low.

The key insight from the analysis is that there is substantial benefit to be gained from identifying adults who are chronically infected with hepatitis B, because they can then be started on antiviral treatments which can significantly reduce morbidity and mortality, but there is little benefit to be gained from vaccination of adult APIs. We published the results of this study in a widely read medical journal [15]. Additionally, we shared our results with the CDC throughout the process of developing the model and performing the analyses.

Consistent with our findings, the CDC issued updated hepatitis B recommendations in 2008 that call for hepatitis B screening of all adult APIs in the USA, as well as screening of all adults born in countries where the prevalence of chronic hepatitis B infection is 2–7 % [19, 20]. We estimate that there are approximately 600,000 APIs in the USA who are chronically infected with hepatitis B but unaware of their disease status. If all of these individuals were identified and treated, some 50,000 premature deaths from hepatitis B-related liver disease could be prevented [12]. Thus, this strategy can have a significant impact on improving public health.

2.3 HIV Control in Eastern Europe

With an estimated 33 million people worldwide infected with HIV, and 2.6 million new infections per year (an average of 7,100 new infections per day), the HIV epidemic presents a serious global challenge [21]. Prevalence of HIV is highest in sub-Saharan Africa, where two-thirds of the world's cases have occurred. However, HIV incidence (the rate of new infection) is significantly higher in other parts of the world, particularly in certain countries of Eastern Europe and Central Asia, where it has grown significantly in the past decade [21]. An estimated 1.4 million people are living with HIV in Eastern Europe and Central Asia, with approximately 90 % of them in Russia and Ukraine [21]. Since 2001, HIV prevalence in the region has doubled: an estimated 1 % of the population of Russia and 1.1 % of the population of Ukraine is now infected [21]. The rapid growth in HIV infections in this region was spurred by collapse of the Soviet Union and subsequent social and economic disruption in the mid-1990s, which led to increasing levels of injection drug use.

Originally occurring mainly in injection drug users (IDUs), the epidemic has now begun to spread heterosexually to sex partners of IDUs and to sex workers.

HIV control efforts in Eastern Europe have been somewhat limited to date. Prevention programs targeted to IDUs include "harm reduction" programs such as needle exchanges and opiate substitution therapy (with methadone or buprenorphine), as well as general education about risk reduction (e.g., safer sex, prevention of mother-to-child transmission). However, it is estimated that at most 10 % of IDUs in Eastern Europe have access to harm reduction programs [22]. In Russia, which has an estimated two million IDUs and an estimated 980,000 persons living with HIV, opiate substitution therapy is illegal, and there are only about 80 needle exchange programs in the country. Treatment coverage is also low: only 19 % of eligible individuals in Eastern Europe received lifesaving antiretroviral therapy (ART) by the end of 2009 [21]. Moreover, fewer than 14 % of treatment slots are currently allocated to IDUs, despite the fact that injection drug use accounts for 80–90 % of new HIV cases in Eastern Europe [22]. Recently, many countries in the region have focused on scaling up their prevention and treatment efforts.

2.3.1 HIV Treatment in Russia

In 2005, virtually no IDUs in Russia and only about 1 % of non-IDUs received ART [23, 24]. HIV treatment resources were targeted almost exclusively to non-IDUs, partly because of concerns that IDUs would not adhere to the medications [25]. At the time, plans had been made to significantly scale up the level of HIV treatment in the country. We performed an analysis to determine whether the country's non-IDU-focused treatment strategy would be successful in slowing the epidemic and to evaluate the impact of alternate allocations of the incremental HIV treatment resources [26].

For this analysis, we developed a dynamic compartmental model of the HIV epidemic, illustrated in Fig. 2.2. In this model, the population (of adults aged 15–49) is divided into mutually exclusive, collectively exhaustive compartments, distinguished by injection drug use status (IDUs, non-IDUs), HIV infection status (uninfected, HIV infected and asymptomatic, HIV infected and symptomatic, and AIDS), and HIV treatment status (untreated, treated). We modeled the transmission of HIV via injection drug use (between IDUs) and via sexual contact (between any members of the population).

The arrows in the diagram represent transitions. Individuals who age into the population enter as HIV-uninfected. Uninfected individuals who acquire HIV infection move to an HIV+, asymptomatic compartment. Uninfected IDUs (compartment 1) can acquire HIV through injection drug use (risky needle sharing with other IDUs) or risky sexual contacts (with IDUs or non-IDUs), while uninfected non-IDUs (compartment 7) acquire HIV only through risky sexual contacts (with IDUs or non-IDUs). Rates of infection transmission are a nonlinear function of the number of infected and uninfected individuals in the population; thus, the model is

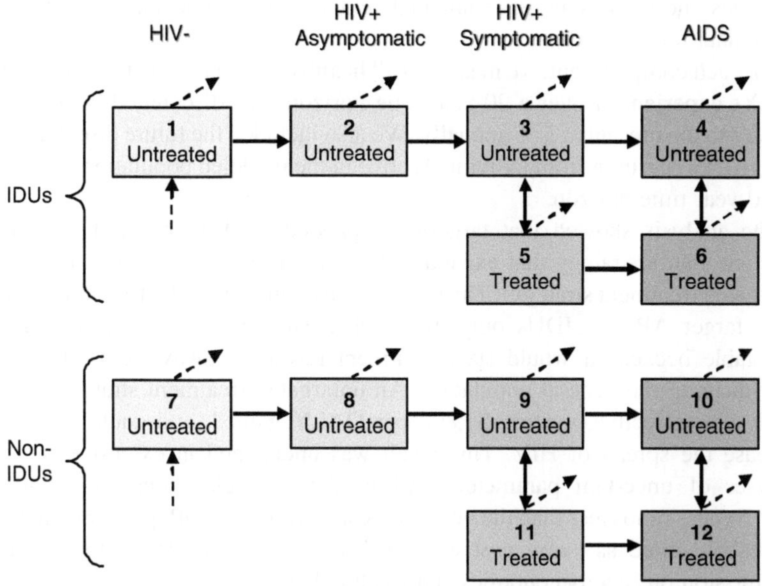

Fig. 2.2 Simplified schematic of dynamic compartmental model used to analyze HIV treatment expansion in Russia. Although not shown in the figure, individuals may transition between the IDU and non-IDU risk groups

a nonlinear dynamic system. Individuals with asymptomatic HIV infection may develop symptomatic HIV infection, and may further progress to AIDS. HIV-infected individuals with symptomatic disease or AIDS can enter treatment. Additionally, IDUs may cease injection drug use and transition to the non-IDU population, and vice versa. Deaths can occur from any compartment, as shown by the diagonal dashed arrows.

Use of a dynamic model of the HIV epidemic allowed us to capture both the individual-level and population-level effects of ART: individuals treated with ART live longer (individual benefit) and are less infectious (population benefit). The dynamic model also allowed us to capture the effects of ART on different modes of transmission (injection drug use, sexual contact) as a function of treatment levels in the IDU and non-IDU populations.

We implemented the model in an Excel spreadsheet and simulated the system over a 20-year time horizon in 1/10 year increments. In the base case, we used data for the city of Saint Petersburg, Russia, where HIV prevalence was approximately 35 % among IDUs and 0.6 % among non-IDUs. In sensitivity analysis, we used data for Barnaul, a Russian city in southwestern Siberia with an earlier-stage HIV epidemic (1.7 % HIV prevalence among IDUs and 0.06 % among non-IDUs). We obtained data for the analysis from published literature, from our expert collaborators (Galvin and Vinichenko), and directly from HIV and drug abuse experts in Russia: in 2005 our research team traveled to Russia and met with numerous individuals in governmental and non-governmental organizations to obtain data for the study.

For each compartment, we measured all health care-related costs incurred and all QALYs experienced over a 20-year time horizon. We discounted both costs and QALYs to the present at 3 % annually. We also included the future discounted costs and QALYs accruing from individuals alive in the modeled population at the end of the 20-year time horizon.

The analysis showed that targeting expanded ART to non-IDUs is far less effective than a strategy that expands ART without regard to IDU status (i.e., an untargeted treatment strategy). The most effective and cost-effective strategy would be to target ART to IDUs only, but such a strategy would not be politically acceptable because it would steer treatment resources away from HIV-infected individuals in the general population. An untargeted treatment strategy would be highly cost-effective, costing $1,800 per QALY gained, and could significantly decrease the spread of HIV. This result was unchanged in extensive sensitivity analyses of uncertain parameters. All of the strategies considered had cost-effectiveness ratios less than the gross domestic product (GDP) per capita in Russia, a threshold cited as "very cost effective" by the World Health Organization's Commission on Macroeconomics and Health [18].

For this example, the most efficient strategy—targeting ART to IDUs—is not the most equitable strategy—providing ART to all eligible individuals. By quantifying the costs and health benefits of alternative strategies, the model informs decision makers about the loss in health benefits of more equitable strategies (or indeed any strategy) compared to the most efficient strategy. Public health planners make decisions based on many considerations in addition to cost and health benefit, such as social, political, and ethical factors (e.g., see [27]). An OR-based model can quantify the likely costs and health benefits of potential decisions.

The key insight from the analysis is that providing IDUs with ART helps reduce HIV transmission not only to the IDU population but also to the non-IDU population—and neglecting IDUs when scaling up treatment is the least effective and least cost-effective strategy. We published the results of this work in an international AIDS journal as a means of informing the debate about HIV policy in the region [26] and translated the article into Russian for broader dissemination [28].

2.3.2 Harm Reduction and HIV Treatment in Ukraine

With an estimated 350,000 persons living with HIV, Ukraine has the highest HIV prevalence in Europe [21]. Originally confined to IDUs, HIV in Ukraine has recently begun to transition to other members of the population. In 2007, some 40 % of new HIV infections occurred due to risky injection practices and 40 % accrued from heterosexual transmission (often due to contact with an infected IDU) [29]. At the same time, efforts to control HIV have been limited. In 2007,

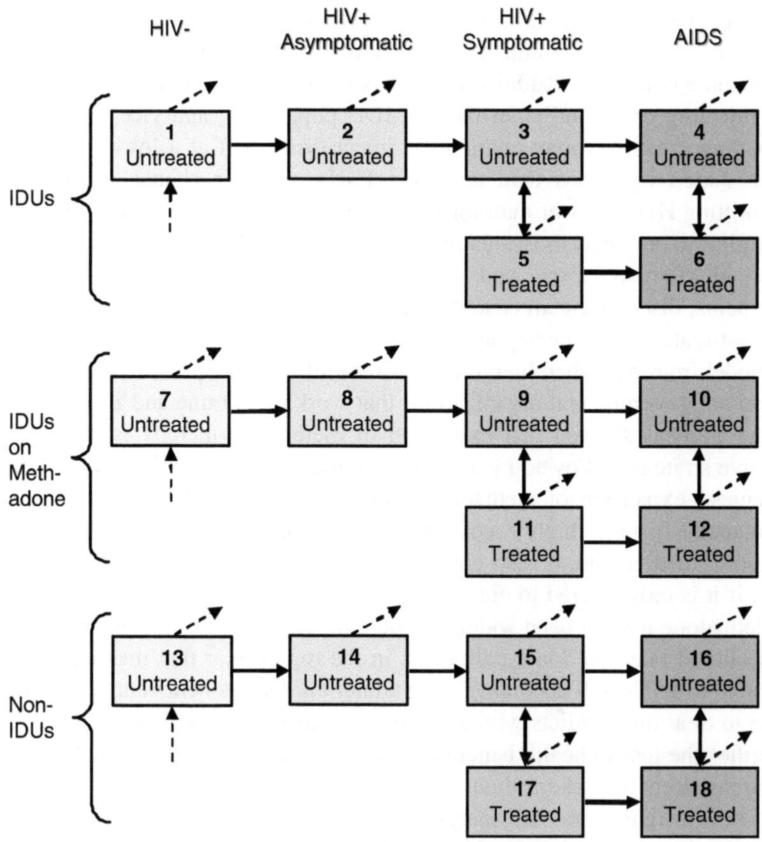

Fig. 2.3 Simplified schematic of dynamic compartmental model used to analyze methadone and HIV treatment expansion in Ukraine. Although not shown in the figure, individuals may transition between risk groups (IDUs, IDUs on methadone, Non-IDUs)

virtually none of the estimated 400,000 IDUs in Ukraine received methadone substitution therapy, and only about 10 % of eligible patients received ART [29].

At the end of 2007, Ukraine approved the use of methadone for substitution therapy and announced plans to enroll 11,000 IDUs in methadone treatment by 2011. The country also announced plans to scale up ART coverage to 90 % of eligible individuals. Because these two interventions may potentially compete for scarce resources, it is essential to determine the most cost-effective combination of these programs. We performed an analysis to determine the effectiveness and cost-effectiveness of different levels and combinations of methadone and ART scale up [30]. We analyzed strategies that focus on increasing methadone slots, ART slots, or both.

We used a dynamic compartmental model, schematically illustrated in Fig. 2.3, to evaluate costs and health outcomes of various scale-up strategies. This model is similar to that shown in Fig. 2.2 except that it also includes compartments for IDUs receiving methadone treatment. IDUs can transition into and out of methadone treatment. On leaving treatment, IDUs can return to untreated injection drug use or can become non-IDUs. Additionally, IDUs not receiving methadone treatment can stop injecting drugs and enter the non-IDU population, and vice versa. IDUs on methadone treatment may continue to inject drugs, but at a lower rate and with fewer shared injections than untreated IDUs, so their chance of acquiring or transmitting HIV is lower than for untreated IDUs, as is their mortality rate.

Similar to our analysis evaluating ART scale up in Russia, we implemented this model in Microsoft Excel and simulated the system for 20 years in 1/10 year increments, discounting all costs and health benefits back to the present, including those estimated to accrue beyond the end of the time horizon. We obtained data for the model from published literature and from information provided by governmental and nongovernmental organizations that work in Ukraine and Eastern Europe.

The analysis showed that expansion of methadone therapy is the most cost-effective strategy, followed by a strategy of methadone and ART expansion. Both strategies—expansion of methadone only or expansion of methadone and ART simultaneously—are highly cost-effective. Expansion of ART only, without expanding methadone, is also cost-effective, but less so. However, expansion of ART, if it is only offered to non-IDUs, is not cost-effective.

Methadone has not been widely adopted in Eastern Europe, primarily for social and political reasons. Some politicians in the region fear that making methadone available to IDUs will encourage drug addiction. Others believe that it is inappropriate to treat drug addicts with an addictive substance (methadone). Our analysis quantifies the loss in health benefits associated with not adopting methadone, thus informing decision makers about the cost of this political constraint.

A key insight from the analysis is that even modest levels of methadone treatment can substantially reduce the HIV epidemic in Ukraine and would be highly cost-effective. A second important insight is that methadone treatment averts the most infections, but expanded ART along with expanded methadone treatment provides the largest total increase in QALYs. This result highlights the complementary nature of these interventions. Thus, when expanding ART in Ukraine, a simultaneous expansion of methadone treatment can significantly increase the number of infections averted in a highly cost-effective manner. Because the HIV epidemic in Ukraine is representative of the HIV epidemic in Eastern Europe and Central Asia, these findings can inform HIV policy in Ukraine as well as in other countries in the region. To disseminate the results of this work, we published it in a widely read international medical journal [30]. We also translated the article into Russian for broader dissemination [31].

2.4 Bioterrorism Preparedness and Response

Although it has long been known that biological agents can be used as weapons, the 2001 anthrax attacks in the USA focused new attention on the threat of bioterrorism. Biological agents are thought to be a particularly dangerous form of terrorism because, if properly deployed, they can become weapons of mass destruction, killing large numbers of people and potentially creating mass disruption.

In 2001, the newly formed Department of Homeland Security set about developing enhanced plans to prepare for and respond to potential terrorist attacks. As part of this effort, the US Strategic National Stockpile was created. This nationally held repository of medical, pharmaceutical, and other supplies is intended for use in any type of public health emergency, including a terrorist or bioterror attack, when local supplies are insufficient [32]. The Strategic National Stockpile has two components: Push Packs and Vendor-Managed Inventories (VMI). Push Packs contain antibiotics, antidotes, and other medical supplies necessary to treat a wide range of possible biological or chemical agents and are reportedly available for local distribution within 12 h after being requested. VMI consist of additional supplies of antibiotics and medical equipment tailored to the specific needs of communities and are reported to be able to arrive at local distribution and/or dispensing sites within 36 h following the detection of an attack.

Local communities may also hold inventories of supplies for response. However, there is no consensus about the amount and type of local supplies that should be held. Some communities stock only enough supplies for first responders, whereas other communities stock enough supplies so as to be self sufficient for several days after an attack [33, 34].

In addition to the question of how much local inventory should be held, a 2003 review [35] identified the following unresolved questions regarding bioterrorism response logistics: What strategy should be used for dispensing Push Packs and VMI? How much dispensing capacity should local communities have for emergency response to a bioterror attack? What dispensing strategies should be used at local dispensing centers? To what extent will quicker detection of a bioterror attack save lives? What is the effect of large numbers of unexposed individuals requiring prophylaxis?

To address these questions, we developed a model that focuses on the case of a potential large-scale anthrax attack in an urban area [36, 37]. We focused on anthrax because it is thought to be a particularly dangerous threat: it may be possible to dispense large amounts of aerosolized anthrax without immediate detection, and the resulting pulmonary anthrax infection, if untreated, is almost uniformly fatal.

The model is designed to evaluate the costs and benefits of various strategies for pre-attack stockpiling and post-attack distribution and dispensing of medical and pharmaceutical supplies, as well as the benefits of rapid attack detection. A schematic of the model is shown in Fig. 2.4.

We assumed the following sequence of events after a large-scale anthrax attack: The attack is detected and announced to the public, and the order is given to dispense antibiotics to affected members of the public. Local dispensing centers are set up and antibiotics and other supplies are requested from the Strategic National Stockpile. Over time, exposed and potentially exposed individuals learn of the attack and go to the local dispensing centers to receive oral antibiotics. At the local dispensing centers, they are given a supply of one of two prophylactic

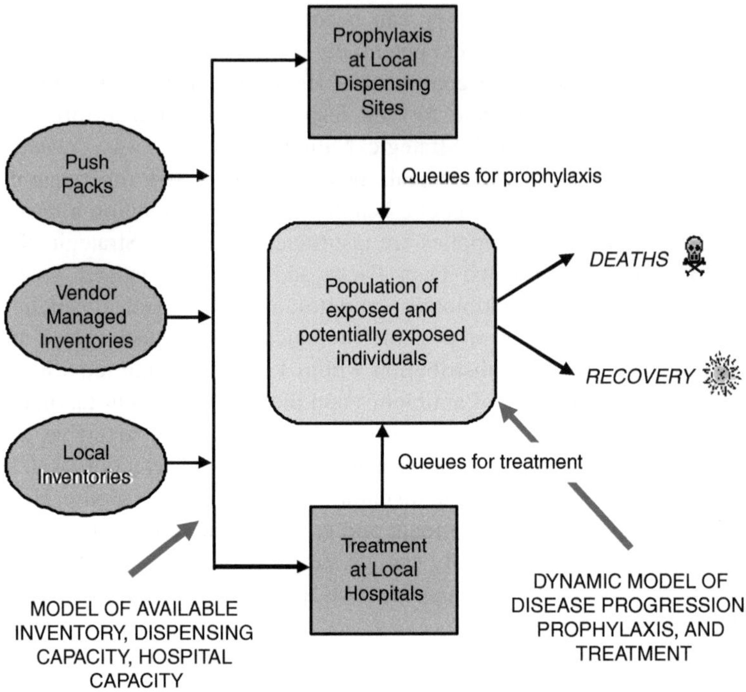

Fig. 2.4 Schematic of model used to evaluate anthrax attack scenarios and response strategies

antibiotics, ciprofloxacin or doxycycline ("prophylaxis"). Locally held inventories are dispensed until supplies from the Strategic National Stockpile arrive; these supplies may later be augmented by VMI. Symptomatic individuals are admitted to intensive care unit (ICU) beds in local hospitals ("treatment"), where they must be given intravenous antibiotics, put on a respirator, and monitored by a respiratory technician. Queues may arise for both prophylaxis and treatment.

Our model has two interconnected components: a dynamic model of disease progression, prophylaxis, and treatment in the population (disease model), and a model of local dispensing and hospital capacity and the supply chain of available inventories (logistics model). The disease model, illustrated in Fig. 2.5, is a dynamic compartmental model that incorporates five states for anthrax disease (not exposed, potentially exposed and requiring prophylaxis, infected and in the incubation period of disease, prodromal disease, and fulminant disease) and four states for individuals' awareness and care (unaware of exposure, aware of exposure or potential exposure but not receiving antibiotics, in prophylaxis, and in treatment). The incubation period of anthrax, which is asymptomatic, lasts approximately 9–13 days. This can progress to prodromal infection, which manifests with flulike symptoms and lasts 3–4 days. Prodromal infection can progress to fulminant infection, which is associated with extreme respiratory distress, lasts approximately

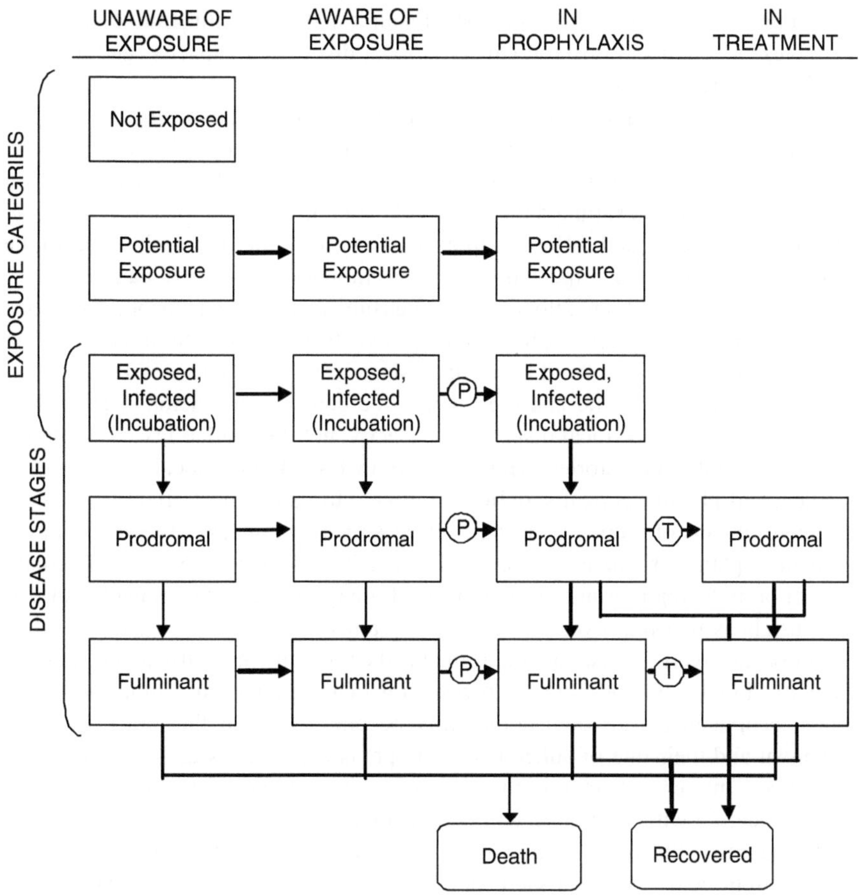

Fig. 2.5 Simplified schematic of anthrax disease model. The *circled P's* represent queues for anthrax prophylaxis and the *circled T's* represent queues for anthrax treatment. The service rates for these queues are governed by the logistics model

1 day, followed almost always by death. The probability of progression through the different disease stages depends on when (and if) the infected individual receives antibiotics to treat anthrax.

The rates at which exposed and potentially exposed individuals receive antibiotics are governed by the logistics model. Specifically, the rate at which individuals can enter prophylaxis is a function of the dispensing centers' capacity and the level of available oral antibiotics. The rate at which hospitals can accept patients for treatment is a function of the number of available ICU beds, doses of intravenous antibiotics, and respiratory technicians.

We implemented the model in an Excel spreadsheet, using data for a typical US city of five million people. Data for the disease model came from published studies, including a systematic review of inhalational anthrax cases in the USA [38]. We obtained data on costs, national antibiotic inventories, and Strategic National

Stockpile response times from published sources. We used illustrative values for variables such as local hospital capacity, local dispensing capacity, and levels of local antibiotic inventories.

We considered different scenarios for attack size (small, exposing 50,000 people, or large, exposing 250,000 people) and fraction of people in the unexposed population who are potentially exposed and thus require prophylaxis (ranging from 2 to 95 %). Then we examined the effects of different levels of local inventory and dispensing capacity, and different times to event detection. For each scenario, the model calculates total expected mortality. In addition, to evaluate the cost-effectiveness of local inventory and dispensing capacity expansion, the model calculates total local costs (the costs of inventories in the Strategic National Stockpile were not considered in the analysis, as they are a sunk cost).

A key insight from the analyses is that the constraining factor in an anthrax response is likely to be local dispensing capacity, not the availability of antibiotics and other needed inventories. This suggests that stockpiling local inventories of medical and pharmaceutical supplies is unlikely to be the most effective (or cost-effective) means of reducing mortality from an anthrax attack. Instead, the development of plans for extensive dispensing capacity will likely have a much greater impact on reducing mortality in the event of a large-scale anthrax attack. Another key insight is that improved surveillance systems that can lead to quicker attack detection can avert deaths, but only if the local community has sufficient dispensing capacity. Finally, factors related to behavior of the public, including the rate at which people in the affected community become aware of the attack and seek treatment and their rate of adherence to prophylaxis, have a significant impact on mortality. This suggests that, in the event of such an attack, effective strategies for communicating with the public will be essential.

To maximize the impact of this work, we disseminated our findings in journals in two different fields. We published some of the key findings from our analyses in a bioterror journal [36] and published a more detailed description of the model and its capabilities in a medical journal [37]. The visibility of these publications led to a subsequent invited consultation with planners at the Strategic National Stockpile regarding design of the supply chain for anthrax response. Additionally, this work led to membership of the author (Brandeau) on an Institute of Medicine Committee charged with examining the costs and benefits of prepositioned medical supplies for bioterror response in local communities [39]. Although it is not known if, when, or where an anthrax attack will occur in the USA, information about the potential costs and benefits of alternative preparedness plans can help planners now in creating effective, and cost-effective, preparedness plans.

2.5 Conclusions and Policy Implications

We have described three types of models that we have used to inform public health policy in three areas: Markov models to evaluate hepatitis B control strategies in the USA and China, dynamic compartmental models to evaluate strategies for HIV control in Eastern Europe, and a hybrid logistics/disease model to evaluate strategies for bioterrorism preparedness and response in the USA. Although the impact of all of these studies is not yet fully known, they have provided important information that can inform decision making. They have also provided useful lessons for OR modelers who wish to help improve public health decision making.

First, a successful OR-based policy analysis will *focus on a problem of importance*. In some cases, a problem may be identified as important by a public health decision maker, as was the case when the CDC asked for evidence about alternative strategies for controlling hepatitis B among adult APIs in the USA. In other cases, a problem of importance may be identified through articles in the media, through discussions with knowledgeable individuals, or through personal observations. For example, our analysis of HIV treatment strategies in Russia was inspired by discussions with members of nongovernmental organizations who were working to implement HIV prevention and treatment programs in Russia, while our analysis of methadone and ART scale up in Ukraine was inspired by articles in the media and by discussions with country-level HIV planners in Eastern Europe. No matter how the problem is identified, an OR model must examine a problem of importance in order to have impact.

Second, successful analyses of public health decisions very often require *multidisciplinary expertise*. For example, to analyze hepatitis B control strategies we collaborated with a liver surgeon (So) who is an expert on hepatitis B as well as an advocate for hepatitis B control in Asian populations. We also sought advice from and shared our ongoing work with the CDC and with other hepatitis B experts. Our analysis of anthrax preparedness strategies involved an internist (Owens), a pulmonologist (Holty), and an expert in public health disaster response (Bravata). Working with domain experts helps to ensure that models and assumptions are believable and that the most important aspects of the problem are appropriately addressed.

Third, the goal of OR modeling in public health is not to predict the impact of alternative decisions with complete precision, but instead to *identify good decisions*. A useful—and believable—model will be detailed enough so that it can appropriately evaluate the decisions at hand, but not so detailed that it relies on numerous potentially untenable assumptions and large amounts of unavailable data. One way to achieve an appropriate balance between simplicity and realism is to start with a simple model and only add detail if an essential component of the problem—one that may change the believability or the results of the analysis—has been omitted. Additionally, because uncertainty is an integral part of most public health problems, a key part of any analysis that aims to identify good decisions is sensitivity analysis. Decision makers need to know how values of uncertain parameters affect the findings of the analysis.

Fourth, although an OR model may generate many interesting findings, policy makers are most interested in the *key insights* from the analysis. For example, in our analysis of anthrax preparedness strategies, we considered many combinations of attack scenario, time to attack detection, local inventory levels, local dispensing capacity, etc., and generated a variety of detailed results. However, we focused our written reports of the work on the few most important findings. Decision makers typically want to know, "What is your main finding and how is this relevant to my decision making?" To have impact, an OR-based analysis will answer these questions concisely and clearly.

Finally, an essential component of successful OR-based modeling in public health is *dissemination of findings to decision makers*. In public health there is typically no single decision maker. Instead, public health decisions are often made by consensus among groups of individuals including public health and government officials, members of nongovernmental public health organizations, health care providers, advocacy groups, and members of the public. Thus, unlike work done for companies which can be relatively easy to report to the person (or few persons) in charge of the decision, significant effort is often required to disseminate the results of OR analyses for the public sector. An important step in this process is to publish the results in outlets where they are likely to be read by decision makers. For example, decision makers who work in the area of HIV control may read AIDS journals or general medical journals, whereas decision makers in the area of bioterror preparedness may read publications targeted to a general public health audience or a bioterror audience. For international studies, translation of the published paper into other languages may be helpful; for example, our study of hepatitis B in China was translated by the journal into Chinese, in addition to its publication in English, so as to reach a wider audience in China. Additionally, dissemination of results through conference presentations and meetings with interested individuals can increase the audience for the work. Although broad dissemination of results of OR-based public health analyses may require significant effort, such effort is essential if the work is to have impact.

Decision makers in public health face many complex problems for which OR-based analyses can provide valuable insights. Effective OR models of public health problems do not need to be highly complex, as long as they capture the salient aspects of the problem and help to identify good decisions. In this promising new area of OR application, a little help can indeed go a long way.

Acknowledgment This work was supported by grant number R01-DA15612 from the National Institute on Drug Abuse.

References

1. Centers for Disease Control and Prevention (2008) Hepatitis B fact sheet. http://www.cdc.gov/ncidod/diseases/hepatitis/b/fact.htm. Accessed 8 Apr 2008
2. Edmunds WJ et al. (1993) The influence of age on the development of the hepatitis B carrier state. Proc Biol Sci 253(1337):197–201
3. World Health Organization (2008) Hepatitis B. Fact Sheet No. 204. World Health Organization, Geneva, Switzerland
4. Centers for Disease Control and Prevention (2007) Progress in hepatitis B prevention through universal infant vaccination—China, 1997–2006. MMWR Morb Mortal Wkly Rep 56(18):441–445

5. Liu J, Fan D (2007) Hepatitis B in China. Lancet 369(9573):1582–1583
6. Chinese Ministry of Health (2008) The Ministry of Health conference on planning and hepatitis B immunization, malaria prevention and control work [Chinese]. http://www.gov.cn/xwfb/2008–04/21/content_950425.htm. Accessed 1 Aug 2008
7. United States Census Bureau (2008) China international database country summary. http://www.census.gov/ipc/www/idb/country/chportal.html#TAB. Accessed 18 Nov 2008
8. Chen JJ (2008) A model HBV catch-up immunization and education project in Qinghai, China. In: National Immunization Conference
9. Hutton DW, So SK, Brandeau ML (2010) Cost effectiveness of nationwide hepatitis B catch-up vaccination among children and adolescents in China. Hepatology 51(2):405–414
10. Hutton DW, Brandeau ML (2013) Too much of a good thing? When to stop catch-up vaccination. Working paper
11. Gold MR et al. (1996) Cost-effectiveness in health and medicine. Oxford University Press, New York
12. Hutton DW, So SK, Brandeau ML (2011) Doing good with good OR: supporting cost-effective hepatitis B interventions. Interfaces 41(3):289–300
13. Custer B et al. (2004) Global epidemiology of hepatitis B virus. J Clin Gastroenterol 38(10 Suppl):S158–S168
14. McQuillan GM, Coleman PJ, Kruszon-Moran D (1999) Prevalence of hepatitis B virus infection in the United States: the National Health and Nutrition Examination Surveys, 1976 through 1994. Am J Public Health 89(1):14–18
15. Hutton DW et al. (2007) Cost-effectiveness of screening and vaccinating Asian and Pacific Islander adults for hepatitis B. Ann Intern Med 147(7):460–469
16. Murray CJ, Lopez A (2002) World Health Report 2002: reducing risks, promoting healthy life. World Health Organization, Geneva, Switzerland, p 186
17. Owens DK (1998) Interpretation of cost-effectiveness analyses [Editorial]. J Gen Intern Med 13(10):716–717
18. World Health Organization (2003) Making choices in health: WHO guide to cost-effectiveness analysis. World Health Organization, Geneva, Switzerland
19. Weinbaum CM, Mast EE, Ward JW (2009) Recommendations for identification and public health management of persons with chronic hepatitis B virus infection. Hepatology 49(5 Suppl):S35–S44
20. Weinbaum CM et al. (2008) Recommendations for identification and public health management of persons with chronic hepatitis B virus infection. MMWR Recomm Rep 57(RR-8):1–20
21. Joint United Nations Programme on HIV/AIDS (UNAIDS) (2010) UNAIDS report on the global AIDS epidemic 2010. UNAIDS, Geneva, Switzerland
22. Open Society Institute (2008) Harm reduction developments 2008. Countries with injection-driven HIV epidemics. Open Society Institute, New York
23. Samoilov D (2004) Double discrimination: drug users living with HIV/AIDS. HIV AIDS Policy Law Rev 9(3):83–85
24. World Health Organization (2005) Summary country profile for HIV/AIDS treatment scale-up: Russian Federation, June 2005. World Health Organization, Geneva, Switzerland
25. Open Society Institute (2004) Breaking down barriers: lessons on providing HIV treatment to injection drug users. Open Society Institute, New York
26. Long EF et al. (2006) Effectiveness and cost-effectiveness of strategies to expand antiretroviral therapy in St. Petersburg, Russia. AIDS 20(17):2207–2215
27. Alistar SS, Brandeau ML (2012) Decision making for HIV prevention and treatment scale up: bridging the gap between theory and practice. Med Decis Making 32(1):105–117
28. Long EF et al. (2006) Оценка эффективности и экономической эффективности стратегии расширенной антиретровирусной терапии в Санкт-Петербурге, Россия. http://www.stanford.edu/dept/MSandE/cgi-bin/people/faculty/brandeau/brandeau.php. Accessed 31 Oct 2011

29. Joint United Nations Programme on HIV/AIDS (UNAIDS) (2008) Ukraine—National report on monitoring progress towards the UNGASS declaration of commitment on HIV/AIDS. UNAIDS, Geneva, Switzerland
30. Alistar SS, Owens DK, Brandeau ML (2011) Effectiveness and cost effectiveness of expanding harm reduction and antiretroviral therapy in a mixed HIV epidemic: a modeling analysis for Ukraine. PLoS Med 8(3):e1000423
31. Alistar SS, Owens DK, Brandeau ML (2011) Результативность и экономическая эффективность расширения программ снижения вреда и антиретровирусной терапии при «смешанной» эпидемии ВИЧ: анализ модели на примере Украины. http://www.plosmedicine.org/attachments/pmed.1000423_Russian.pdf. Accessed 31 Oct 2011
32. Koplan J (2001) CDC's strategic plan for bioterrorism preparedness and response. Public Health Rep 116(Suppl 2):9–16
33. Benson B, McKinney P (2003) Selecting and stocking antidotes to biological/chemical agents. In: Texas Society of Health-Systems Pharmacists Annual Meeting, Austin, TX
34. Case GG, West BM, McHugh CJ (2001) Hospital preparedness for biological and chemical terrorism in central New Jersey. N J Med 98(11):23–33
35. Bravata DM et al. (2003) Regionalization of bioterrorism preparedness and response (Evidence report/technology assessment). Agency for Healthcare Research and Quality, Rockville, MD
36. Bravata DM et al. (2006) Reducing mortality from anthrax bioterrorism: strategies for stockpiling and dispensing medical and pharmaceutical supplies. Biosecur Bioterror 4(3):244–262
37. Zaric GS et al. (2008) Modeling the logistics of response to anthrax bioterrorism. Med Decis Making 28(3):332–350
38. Holty JE et al. (2006) Systematic review: a century of inhalational anthrax cases from 1900 to 2005. Ann Intern Med 144(4):270–280
39. Institute of Medicine Committee on Prepositioned Medical Countermeasures (2011) Prepositioning antibiotics for anthrax. National Academies Press, Washington, DC

Part II
Health Policy and Operations

Chapter 3
Analytical Long-Term Care Capacity Planning

Yue Zhang and Martin L. Puterman

Abstract This chapter discusses the use of analytical approaches for residential long-term care (LTC) capacity planning. The recommended method integrates demographic and survival analysis, discrete event simulation, and optimization. Through a case study based in British Columbia, Canada, it illustrates results of using this approach. Further, it discusses shortcomings of a fixed-ratio approach widely used in practice and the SIPP (stationary, independent, period by period) approach and its modifications developed in the call center literature. It also proposes an easy-to-use and effective planning method, the Average Flow Model. It concludes with a discussion of policy implications and extensions.

3.1 Introduction

Long-term care (LTC) refers to a variety of medical and nonmedical services provided to people with a chronic illness or disability, especially the elderly. LTC capacity planning has become an emerging problem, because the number of people needing LTC will increase rapidly as a result of an aging population and the prolonged longevity resulting from medical advances.

This chapter focuses on determining the number of beds required to meet the needs of a frail elderly population in a geographical region. The primary focus of this article is on beds in residential facilities, but the methods apply to a wider range of health care resource planning problems. It is motivated by the Canadian

Y. Zhang
College of Business and Innovation, University of Toledo, 2801 W. Bancroft Street, Toledo, OH 43606, USA
e-mail: yue.zhang@utoledo.edu

M.L. Puterman (✉)
Sauder School of Business, University of British Columbia, 2053 Main Mall, Vancouver, BC V6T 1Z2, Canada
e-mail: martin.puterman@sauder.ubc.ca

G.S. Zaric (ed.), *Operations Research and Health Care Policy*, International Series in Operations Research & Management Science 190, DOI 10.1007/978-1-4614-6507-2_3,

experience where a considerable portion of LTC beds are provided by publicly funded provincial health systems. We find it surprising that this issue has received so little attention in the operations literature in spite of the fact that the number of people needing LTC will increase rapidly.

Worldwide, there are 600 million people aged 60 and over, and this number will double by 2025 [1]. According to Statistics Canada, the 2006 Census shows that seniors aged 65 or over accounted for 13.7% of Canada's population [2]; this proportion will increase even more rapidly when the first wave of baby boomers born in 1946 reach 65. In British Columbia (BC), Canada, the proportion of the population aged 65 and over will pass 20% in many regions over the next few years and the proportion of the population aged 85 and older is expected to double by 2031 [3].

Although this population aging is a success of public health policies and socioeconomic development, it is also posing tremendous challenges in providing timely health care for this population. According to the Canadian Medical Association, an estimated 5% of Canadians aged 65 and over live in LTC facilities [4]. These facilities provide health care and support services as well as assistance with activities of daily living.

Moreover, lack of access to LTC is often cited as the major cause of a high level of alternative level of care (ALC) patients who no longer need acute services but who are occupying expensive acute care beds while waiting to be discharged to a setting more appropriate to their needs. According to the Canadian Institute for Health Information, ALC patients accounted for 14% of hospital days in acute care hospitals; 43% of ALC patients were discharged to a LTC facility [5]. This suggests that providing sufficient LTC capacity would have a significant impact on acute care as well as the entire health system. Therefore, there is an urgent need to effectively plan to meet these needs.

The methods and observations described here were based on several applied projects we carried out in BC. The issues in each case were slightly different but in general the question raised was "How many LTC beds are needed over the next 10–20 years to ensure that care is provided in a timely fashion?" Current practice in BC, Canada, and other countries has been to use a fixed ratio of beds per population as the basis for planning [6–10]. This is problematic for several reasons and has resulted in long wait times for admission to care or excess capacity [11]. Therefore, development of rigorous mathematical tools for LTC capacity planning is critical.

This chapter describes our use of operations research techniques to improve long-term capacity planning for LTC programs and facilities. Specifically, we describe a simulation optimization approach to determine the minimal capacity level needed each year to satisfy a service level criterion based on clients' wait time. A key element is the use of demographic and survival analysis to predict arrival and length of stay (LOS) distributions for input to the simulation model. By service level, we mean the percentage of clients who must wait less than a specified number of days for admission to care.

This chapter combines and extends our two earlier papers [12, 13]. The former [12] presents technical details of our methodology that integrates simulation, optimization, and demographic and survival analysis as well as compares it to the SIPP (stationary, independent, period by period) approach and its modifications that are widely used in the call center literature (see below). The latter [13] mainly focuses on ratio policies and proposes a simple Average Flow Model (AFM) that can be easily implemented and performs relatively effectively. Through a case study of applying these methods at a regional health authority in BC, this chapter reviews the simulation optimization approach, compares it to the ratio policies, the SIPP approach and its modifications, and the AFM, and derives policy insights. In particular, the chapter presents all the relevant techniques and approaches in a more systematic manner and provides more detailed results and analysis than the two papers.

The chapter is organized as follows. The next section reviews related literature on capacity planning in health care and other areas. Section 3.3 describes the problem and the system. Our recommended methodology is described in Sect. 3.4, including the discrete event simulation model, demographic analysis, survival analysis, and two optimization techniques. Section 3.5 presents an application of this methodology, and the comparisons of using this methodology with the ratio policies and the SIPP approach and its modifications are discussed in Sects. 3.6 and 3.7. Section 3.8 describes the AFM and explores its use. In the final section, concluding remarks and policy implications are summarized, and future research directions are discussed.

3.2 Related Literature

There is little published research on capacity planning for LTC services. As far as we know, only two studies besides ours address this issue [14, 15]. Hare et al. [14] presented a deterministic system dynamics model for the entire home and community care system, which includes residential LTC as an option. Also, their model forecasts future demand for services rather than the required capacity needed to satisfy a service level criterion. Lin et al. [15] described an optimal control problem to determine the optimal capacity allocation between LTC and acute care for Medicaid so as to minimize the total expenditure over a period of time. Since both models focus on strategic level decisions at a high level of aggregation, no client is individually identifiable and no service level criterion is considered.

In contrast, several studies focus on capacity planning or utilization analysis for other specific medical services [16–18], as well as capacity allocation for various services or departments [19, 20]. These papers usually do not consider the dynamics of the systems over time. Smith-Daniels et al. [21] and Green [22] review capacity planning and management problems in health care using operations research tools.

On the other hand, the problem investigated here is similar to the operator staffing problem in call centers and other multi-server queuing systems with time-varying arrival rates, where the minimum staffing level (number of servers) in each period needs to be determined to ensure a satisfactory service level, usually based on customers' waiting time, such as 80% of customers waiting less than 5 min. Other service sectors where such a staffing problem is encountered include toll plazas, airport check-in counters, retail check-out counters, banking, telecommunications, and police patrol [23].

Prior to determining optimal staffing levels, an important issue is to evaluate system performance for specified staffing levels. In queuing theory, analytical approaches have been used to study nonstationary Markovian systems. For example, by numerically solving a system of differential equations, the steady state probability of the number of customers in the system can be calculated, and then various performance measures can be obtained [24–26]. In contrast, many papers also use simple stationary queuing models as approximations to evaluate and manage nonstationary systems, especially for non-Markovian or more general systems. These include the pointwise stationary approximation that uses the instantaneous arrival rate, the simple stationary approximation that uses the long-run average arrival rate, and the infinite-server approximation that estimates the distribution of the number of busy servers with respect to time. Jennings et al. [27] and Ingolfsson et al. [28] reviewed these approximation methods.

When required staffing levels are decision variables, they are typically determined by using available analytical results based on simple stationary queuing models [23]. Specifically, the planning horizon is divided into multiple homogeneous periods. Then, a series of stationary queuing models, usually $M/M/s$ queues, are constructed, one model for each period. Each of these models is independently solved for the minimum number of servers needed to meet the service level target in that period. They referred to this method of setting staffing requirements as the stationary, independent, period by period (SIPP) approach. The SIPP approach is closely related to the approximations mentioned above, and it usually results in the form of the "square-root rule" [29, 30]. However, the SIPP approach does not always work well. Many papers have compared the achieved performance measures derived from the solutions by the SIPP approach with the ones derived from the exact analytical approaches or simulation [23, 31–33]. For instance, Green et al. [23] and Atlason et al. [33] were mainly concerned with the linkage between staffing decisions in consecutive periods. The former showed that the SIPP approach does not produce accurate staffing levels when service times are long relative to the period length. They also suggested several modifications of the SIPP approach that perform better for long service time situations, such as the modified offered load (MOL) approach. See Gans et al. [29] and Green et al. [30] for further references regarding the square-root staffing rule and the SIPP approach and its modifications.

In addition to the SIPP approach, other analytical methods have been used in staffing problems. For example, optimal staffing levels as a function of time can be derived based on the infinite-server approximation, when the probability of delay is the service performance measure [27]. More recently, Parlar and Sharafali [34] proposed an exact analytical approach based on a stochastic dynamic programming model, to determine the optimal number of check-in counters needed for each flight to minimize an expected cost function. De Vericourt and Jennings [35] considered a nurse staffing problem by modeling medical units as closed queuing systems. Their results suggest that nurse-to-patient ratio policies cannot achieve consistently high service level. Yankovic and Green [36] investigated a more complicated nurse staffing problem taking new arrivals, departures, and transfers of patients into account. Using a two-dimensional queuing model, they evaluated system performance analytically and then chose optimal staffing levels. Again, they showed that prespecified nurse-to-patient ratio policies cannot achieve satisfactory performance across a wide range of scenarios.

Simulation is another methodology used in the literature, especially to study complex nonstationary queuing systems. However, instead of using simulation to optimize staffing, most call center papers use simulation to evaluate system performance with staffing levels identified by approximate analytical approaches, so as to verify whether the suggested staffing levels indeed produce the desired performance. A few exceptions in recent years have used simulation to study their specific staffing problems. By generating multiple simulation replications, Atlason et al. [33] transformed their staffing problem into a deterministic one, which computes the staffing level in each period to ensure that the average service level is satisfied. Feldman et al. [37] proposed a flexible simulation-based iterative-staffing algorithm for models with nonhomogeneous Poisson arrival process and customer abandonment. They divided the time horizon into many small intervals. Running multiple independent simulation replications, they estimated the distribution of the total number of customers in the system with respect to time, based on which optimal staffing levels as a function of time can be derived. By generating multiple simulation replications, they transformed their staffing problem into a deterministic one, which computes the staffing level in each period to ensure that the average service level is satisfied.

3.3 Model Description

This chapter focuses on LTC capacity planning for an individual facility or a geographic region in aggregate over a multiyear planning horizon. The system is assumed to operate as follows. Potential clients in either hospitals or the community undergo an eligibility assessment. If they meet the medically and activity based eligibility requirements, they enter a waitlist or are admitted directly to care if capacity is available. If they are not eligible, they are provided with home care and other support services if needed and capacity is available. Admitted clients remain in the LTC system until death.

A trade-off between admission requirements and capacity underlies this planning problem in two ways. When admission requirements are made more stringent there are fewer eligible clients. Further, since these clients are at higher levels of acuity, their LOSs will tend to be shorter. On the other hand, when admission requirements are relaxed, there are more eligible clients who tend to remain in care longer. Further, there may be better ways, such as home care or

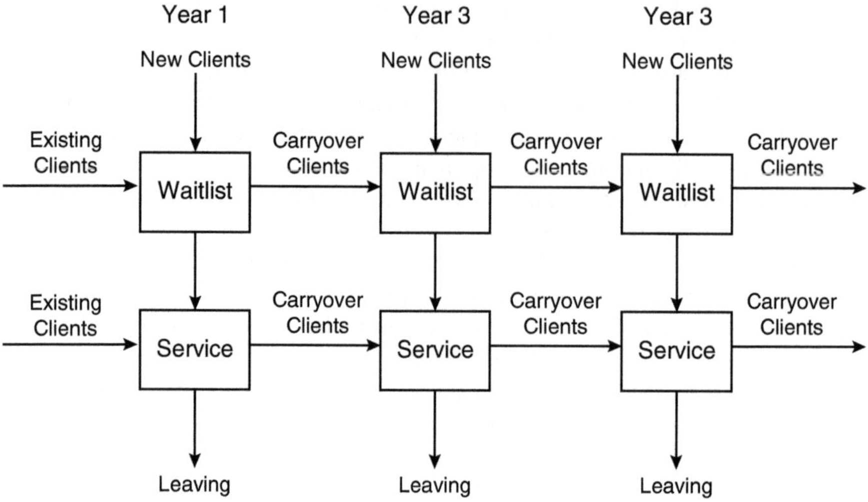

Fig. 3.1 Client flow of the system over time

assisted living, for meeting the needs of these lower acuity individuals. The issue of determining appropriate admission requirements is outside the scope of this paper and best left to health care planners and medical decision makers. However, operations research methods can quantify these trade-offs.

The system may be modeled by a multiple server queue with time varying arrival and service rates, as the arrival rate typically increases and the service rate may change due to the change of admission requirements. Since Hare et al. [14], Xie et al. [38], and our preliminary analyses for the case studied in Sect. 3.5 have shown that individuals of different ages and genders may have different arrival and LOS distributions, the model contains I classes of clients stratified on the basis of age and gender. Each stratum has its own arrival and LOS distributions. There are no constraints on the waitlist size, no departures from the waitlist, and a first-come first-served (FCFS) queue discipline. The assumption of no departures from the waitlist may be overly strong, but it would not be difficult to modify the formulation to allow reneging during waiting. In practice, if the medical condition of clients on the waitlist deteriorates, FCFS may not be appropriate.

For planning purposes assume a T year planning horizon and denote the year index as $t, t = 1, \ldots, T$. In practice T should be between 10 and 20 years depending on the specific application. For simplicity, we assume that the number of beds can only be changed at the start of each year and that at the start of the planning horizon, there are a known number of clients in care or on the waitlist in each class. Assume that the number and timing of arrivals in each class can be modeled by a Poisson process with a constant rate that can vary by year, and that the LOS distribution varies by age and gender. Since we use simulation, alternative arrival distribution can be used. Denote the number of beds provided in year t by s_t, and let s_0 denote the initial number of beds. Thus, we model the system as a series of interrelated multi-class $M_t/G/s_t$ queuing systems as shown in Fig. 3.1.

The proposed model assumes that capacity can be changed at the start of each year and by any amount. In practice, this is not feasible. Hence, the results below provide decision makers with capacity targets that can serve as inputs to optimal capacity planning decisions which take costs and constraints into account [22].

The service level optimization problem seeks to find the values for s_t, $t = 1, \ldots, T$, that achieve a prespecified service level in each year with a prespecified probability. This can be viewed as an open-loop control problem. Service levels may be based on the probability of waiting, the number of people in the system or in the queue, and average wait time. We prefer the following service level measure:

$$\Pr(W_t(s_t) \leq \gamma) \geq \tau \quad t = 1, \ldots, T, \tag{3.1}$$

where $W_t(s_t)$ denotes the wait time in year t given s_t, γ denotes a wait time threshold (in days), and τ denotes a probability threshold. This means that the probability that a typical client in year t will be placed in care within γ days is greater than or equal to τ. In other words, $\tau \times 100\%$ of arriving clients receive service within γ days each year.

In contrast, the following stronger criterion based on the simultaneous probability over the planning horizon may be preferred:

$$\Pr(W_1(s_1) \leq \gamma, \ldots, W_T(s_T) \leq \gamma) \geq \tau'. \tag{3.2}$$

Nevertheless, using the Bonferroni approach [39], expression (3.2) will hold if:

$$\Pr(W_t(s_t) \leq \gamma) \geq 1 - \frac{1 - \tau'}{T} \quad t = 1, \ldots, T. \tag{3.3}$$

Since this has exactly the same form as expression (3.1), we describe methods which seek to achieve (3.1).

Let $\tilde{s}_t$ denote the minimum number of beds that achieve the service level criterion in year t. As discussed in Atlason et al. [33], the relationship between the number of beds and the resulting steady state service level typically follows an "S-shaped" curve, i.e., a convex arc flowing into a concave arc. If an exact closed-form expression for this steady state probability is available, the number of beds required to meet the service level criterion in each year can be directly determined from:

$$\tilde{s}_t = \text{argmin}\{k \in \text{N} : \Pr(W_t(k) \leq \gamma) \geq \tau\} \quad t = 1, \ldots, T. \tag{3.4}$$

We note that this is the basis for the SIPP approach [23]. In that framework, under the assumption of exponential service times, a closed-form expression based on the stationary queue in the steady state is available to set the capacity in each year.

One significant challenge in using the SIPP approach in the LTC setting is that closed-form expressions needed to evaluate (3.4) are not available. This is because the system contains several classes of clients with different arrival and non-Markovian LOS distributions. To use the SIPP approach, we could aggregate them in a single class and further assume that the LOS follows an exponential distribution, so that the system over time is modeled by a series of $M/M/s$ queues. However, we show through examples below that the SIPP approach may fail to provide capacities that achieve the service level objective, because several of its implicit assumptions are violated:

1. *Independent Periods*. The system is not empty at the start of each year. LOSs are long relative to period length so that clients may remain in the system for several periods.
2. *Homogeneity of Clients*. Aggregating multiple classes of clients into a single class ignores widely varying client arrival rates and resource requirements.
3. *Exponentiality*. LOS distributions appear to be better modeled by a fat-tailed Weibull rather than an exponential distribution. Hence, the memoryless property will not hold.

Because of these reasons, a simulation-based optimization approach may be preferred.

3.4 Methodology

3.4.1 Discrete Event Simulation

We first describe a discrete event simulation model for evaluating service levels in the presence of a fixed prespecified capacity sequence s_t, $t = 1, \ldots, T$. The simulation has three main inputs: arrival distributions, LOS distributions, and preloaded existing clients. The simulation logic can be summarized as follows.

1. *Initialization*. At the beginning of a planning period, preload existing clients in care and on the waitlist. To each, randomly assign a remaining LOS based on the appropriate age and gender specific *conditional* LOS distribution, as discussed in Sect. 3.4.2.3.
2. *Client Generation*. In each year, generate inter-arrival times from an appropriate exponential distribution.
3. *LOS Generation*. Randomly assign a LOS to each new client based on an age and gender specific LOS distribution.
4. *Assignment to Queue and Beds*. If all beds are occupied, enter each new client into the waiting queue, otherwise assign them a bed. Upon receiving a bed, the LOS starts and the client remains in the system for that period. Length of time in the queue is recorded to measure performance.
5. *Annual Summaries and Updating*. At the end of each year, the service level is computed and arrival rates and LOS distribution parameters are updated as necessary for the subsequent year.

The discrete event simulation by itself cannot determine the appropriate capacity level each year. Hence, it must be combined with an optimization method. Then, by running multiple simulation replications, the problem becomes that of determining the minimal capacity level required each year so that on average $\tau \times 100\%$ of clients are placed in care within γ days.

3.4.2 Simulation Inputs

This section discusses the issues faced when estimating arrival and LOS distributions as well as pre-loading existing clients into the LTC planning simulation model.

3.4.2.1 Arrival Analysis

Under the assumption that the number of new arrivals of each class throughout a year follows a Poisson process with a constant rate, the time between arrivals follows an exponential distribution. This assumption appears reasonable in that most arrivals to LTC are unscheduled. Alternatively, it can be tested using data and modified if necessary.

Let $\lambda_i(t)$, $i = 1, \ldots, I$, $t = 1, \ldots, T$, denote the Poisson arrival rate parameter for clients in class i in year t. One way to estimate this quantity is to represent it as

$$\lambda_i(t) = \lambda_i N_t(t) \quad i = 1, \ldots, I. \tag{3.5}$$

where λ_i denotes the historical per capita arrival rate for class i and $N_i(t)$ denotes a population forecast for class i in year t. To estimate λ_i requires two data sources: the historical number of clients per year entering care or the waitlist, and historical population sizes. The former should be available from LTC facility data or appropriate regional records. Population data by age, gender, and year is usually available from census or administrative data. The simplest estimate of λ_i would be obtained for each class i by dividing total arrivals to the LTC facility by the population. This could be refined by using a weighted average of the past several years. The beauty of this approach is that it allows several forms of "What if?" analysis, either by varying λ_i, varying $N_i(t)$ or varying $\lambda_i(t)$ directly.

3.4.2.2 Los Analysis

In most settings, LOS distributions can be estimated using historical data for clients who have exited care. However, this ignores the effect of active clients (those who have entered care and are still in care at the end of the most recent fiscal year). If there is a considerable amount of historical data and it is believed that LOS distributions have been constant over time, ignoring those in care may still provide reliable estimates. But if LOS distributions are changing over time or there is not a lot of data, data on clients still in care must be taken into account. Unfortunately, the LOS data for those clients still in care will be *right censored*, that is only start dates are available. We observed in our studies that ignoring censored data leads to significant underestimation of LOS, since the censored clients tend to be those with longer LOSs.

The statistical field of survival analysis [40] addresses the problem of modeling time-to-event data, when a portion of data is censored. To include LOS distributions in simulations, parametric models for LOS distributions are preferable. We found that a two-parameter Weibull distribution was sufficiently flexible and robust to meet our needs. Its desirable features are that it can be tuned to have several shapes, it contains an exponential distribution as a special case, and it can represent data with long tails. Its adequacy can be investigated through *Q–Q* plots or formal goodness-of-fit tests. The cumulative distribution function (CDF) of a Weibull distribution is given by:

$$F(x) = 1 - \mathrm{e}^{-(x/\alpha)^{\beta}}, \tag{3.6}$$

where α is the scale parameter and β is the shape parameter.

The parameters α and β can be time-varying and/or class specific. These parameters can either be estimated separately for each class or through a combined Weibull regression model [40] in which the shape parameter β is constant and α is a function of age, gender, and year of admission. In the Weibull regression model if $y_1, \ldots, y_k$ denotes values for k explanatory variables; then α can then be represented by:

$$\alpha = \exp(\varphi_0 + \varphi_0 y_1 + \cdots + \varphi_k y_k), \tag{3.7}$$

where $\varphi_0, \varphi_1, \ldots, \varphi_k$ are regression coefficients to be estimated from data. Regression parameter estimates are obtained using maximum likelihood available in most statistical software packages. This analysis yields a distinct Weibull distribution for each class of clients and can also test whether the LOS varies with time.

In our applications, LOS measured the length of time in care, excluding the length of time on the waitlist because of the absence of reliable longitudinal waitlist data. If such data is available, separate models can be developed for LOS on the waitlists. Alternatively, the impact of ignoring waitlists can be explored through sensitivity analysis.

3.4.2.3 Simulation Initialization

Often, the system being modeled has been in operation for many years and contains people who were admitted to care in the past. Thus, simply allowing the system to warm-up and reach a "steady state" is not practical. To account for those clients currently in care and on the waitlist, their information must be used to initialize the simulation. For each existing client in care, the requisite information includes gender, age, and amount of time in care. The class-specific conditional LOS distribution should be used to assign a remaining LOS. The conditional Weibull distribution CDF is given by:

$$F(x|u) = 1 - e^{-(x/\alpha)^{\beta}+(u/\alpha)^{\beta}} \quad x > u, \tag{3.8}$$

where u denotes the elapsed time in care. Thus, (3.8) can be used to generate a remaining LOS for each client in care. For clients in the waitlist, the unconditional LOS distribution can be used to generate an appropriate LOS.

3.4.3 Optimization

For several decades, simulation has been used as a descriptive tool in the modeling and analysis of complex systems. With recent advances in computing technology, it now becomes feasible to integrate simulation models and optimization techniques together for decision-making. A variety of simulation optimization approaches have been proposed, and there are also several review papers and books in the literature that discuss theories and applications of these techniques [41–44].

On the other hand, optimization techniques have also been incorporated into commercial discrete event simulation tools, such as OptQuest (http://www.opttek.com/). However, these commercial tools are not well designed for this application. In our research, we developed two optimization techniques: a sequential bisection search algorithm and a simultaneous search algorithm. Since the second algorithm performs more efficiently, we describe only it in this section. Refer to Zhang et al. [13] for the sequential bisection search algorithm.

Let θ_1 and θ_2 denote two step-size parameters and K denote a maximum iteration number.

3.4.3.1 Simultaneous Search Algorithm

- Step 0: Choose appropriate values θ_1, θ_2, N, and K; for each year t, set $s_t^1 = s_0$; set $k = 0$.
- Step 1: Set $k = k + 1$; run the simulation for the entire time horizon with s_t^k, $t = 1, \ldots, T$, for N independent replications; for each replication n and each year t, record the achieved service level denoted by π_{tn} (i.e., the fraction of clients who are placed in care within the time threshold); calculate the mean service level $\bar{\pi}_t$ for each year t and the half-width of the 95% confidence interval of $\bar{\pi}_t$ denoted by ε_t.

- Step 2: If $\bar{\pi}_t - \varepsilon_t \leq \tau \leq \bar{\pi}_t + \varepsilon_t$ for each year t or $k \geq K$, set $\tilde{s}_t = s_t^k$ and stop; otherwise, for each year t, set

$$s_t^{k+1} = \begin{cases} s_t^k + \theta_1(\tau - \bar{\pi}_t) & \text{if } \tau > \bar{\pi}_t + \varepsilon_t \\ s_t^k - \theta_2(\bar{\pi}_t - \tau) & \text{if } \tau < \bar{\pi}_t - \varepsilon_t \\ s_t^k & \text{otherwise} \end{cases}$$

and go to Step 1.

In each iteration, this algorithm simulates the entire planning horizon, and adjusts the capacity level in each year based on the resulting service level in that year. Note that the adjusted capacity level may not be an integer value, and thus, it needs to be rounded to an integer. The search mechanism of this algorithm is similar to that of gradient-based methods [42], whereas the gradient information is represented by the deviation between the current service level and the target. Moreover, this algorithm would also work for more complex service level criteria or for solving capacity allocation problems.

Based on computational experiments, we chose the following parameter values to balance efficiency (finding a good solution within a reasonable amount of time) and reliability (not producing an unreasonable solution): set $\theta_1 = 0.2\ s_0$, $\theta_2 = 0.1\ s_0$, $K = 50$, and $N = 100$.

3.4.4 Implementation

To support application we developed a decision support system for LTC managers containing three main components: a discrete-event simulator, an optimizer and a front-end interface. We developed the discrete event simulation model in Arena 10.0, where we coded the simultaneous search algorithm in Visual Basic for Applications (VBA). The front-end interface developed in Excel contains all data and information to be used by the Arena simulation model, including population data and per capita arrival rates to generate arrival distributions, parameter values of LOS distributions obtained from survival analysis, information on existing clients in care and on the waitlist, a current capacity level, as well as all other relevant inputs. In addition, we used the LIFEREG procedure in SAS (http://support.sas.com/rnd/app/da/new/802ce/stat/chap6/) for survival analysis. When the simulation ends, the front-end interface stores the optimal solution and other outputs from the simulation in both graphical and tabular forms. In addition, it allows the user to set the capacity levels and determine the resulting service performance, as well as to modify the parameter values for sensitivity analysis or scenario testing.

In summary, this decision support system enables the user to:

- Estimate service levels for any sequence of prespecified capacity levels.
- Determine a sequence of optimal capacity levels required to meet the service level criterion.
- Conduct sensitivity analysis of important system input parameters, such as service levels, initial conditions, population growth rates, per capita arrival rates, and LOS distributions.

3.5 A Case Study

3.5.1 Background and Data

The following case study illustrates the use of simulation optimization and compares results to those obtained using some related methods. Vancouver Island Health Authority (VIHA) is one of six health authorities in BC, providing acute care, LTC, home care and support, and mental health care, across a widely varied geographic area covering approximately 56,000 km^2 and consisting of 15 local health areas (LHAs).

LTC is managed by the Home and Community Care program. One challenge they faced at the time we initiated this research was to plan LTC bed capacity to meet future needs. More precisely, they required a decision support system that could "forecast" long-term capacity requirement and allow ongoing scenario testing. We arrived at the objective of having a sufficient number of beds each year to ensure that 85% of clients would be placed in care within 30 days every year. In terms of expression (3.1), this corresponded to $\gamma = 30$ and $\tau = 0.85$.

We applied the above simulation-optimization approach at the LHA level for 2009–2020. Data sources for estimating the arrival and LOS distributions include: the Population Extrapolation for Organization Planning with Less Error (PEOPLE) 32 database from BC Stats and the Continuing Care Information Management System (CCIMS) database collected by VIHA. These data sources are updated on a yearly basis, are readily available to VIHA personnel, and were utilized in a manner that required the minimum of data cleaning activities.

The PEOPLE 32 database provides population forecasts and historical population sizes by geographic area, age, and gender in 1 year increments. This data was aggregated to the LHA level and stratified by gender and age (less than 55, 56–65, 66–75, 76–85, and greater than 85). The CCIMS database was used to estimate the per capita arrival rates to the system by age group, gender, and LHA, which were calculated based on the weighted moving average of the last 4 years. However, this database only contained information on admitted clients. The waitlist length in each LHA was only available for the date the database was accessed; the historical waitlist information was not available. Hence, the number of arrivals in the past was assumed to be the number of clients admitted. This implies that our analysis may

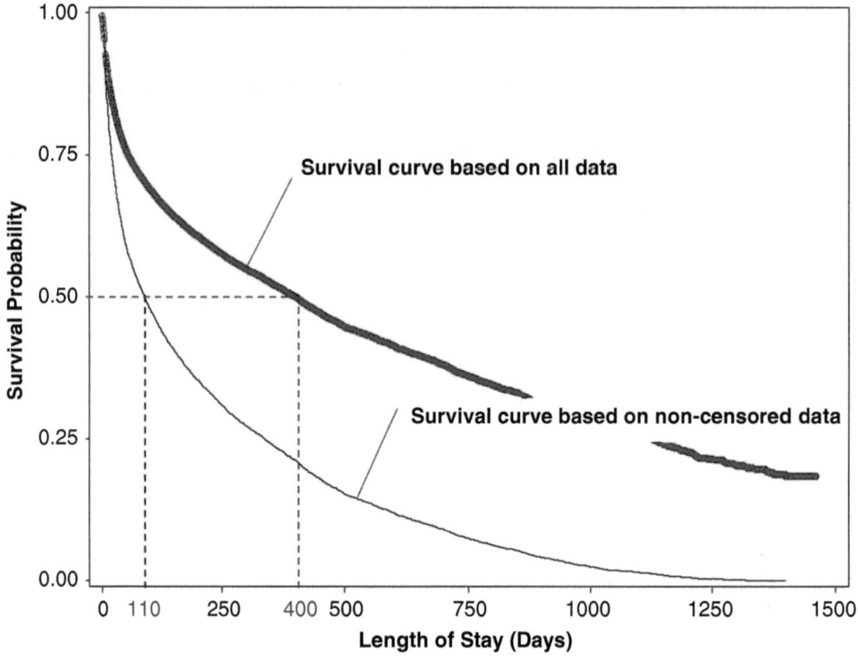

Fig. 3.2 Kaplan–Meier survival curves with and without censored data. *Dotted lines* show that the median based on using the non-censored data is significantly less than that based on all data

have underestimated the arrival rates. The impact of this assumption was investigated through sensitivity analysis.

We also used the CCIMS database to estimate the LOS distributions. It includes information on more than 40,000 clients in all the LHAs since 1990. Again, because the historical individual wait time data was unavailable, the LOS distributions may be underestimated by only using the CCIMS database. Another challenge was that new LTC admission eligibility criteria were implemented in BC in 2003 so that after that date, only clients with higher acuity levels became eligible for admission. Hence, we would expect shorter LOSs for post 2003 clients. To estimate LOS distributions, we split the clients into two groups: pre-2003 and post-2003, and estimated those for each group separately. In particular, 36% of clients in the database were admitted after 2003, and 5% of pre-2003 clients and 33% of post-2003 clients were still in care.

Figure 3.2, based on the post-2003 data, shows that not considering the information contained in the censored cases leads to significant underestimation of the LOS; median LOS changed from 400 to 110 days. Note that the survival curves were derived using the Kaplan–Meier estimation method [40]. In addition, Fig. 3.3 shows the difference in the survival curves for male and female clients, based on the post-2003 data. It is clear that the LOS of females is approximately double that of males. Moreover, analyses also showed that LOS differs significantly by age and LHA. This provided justification for separating clients into different groups by age, gender, and LHA.

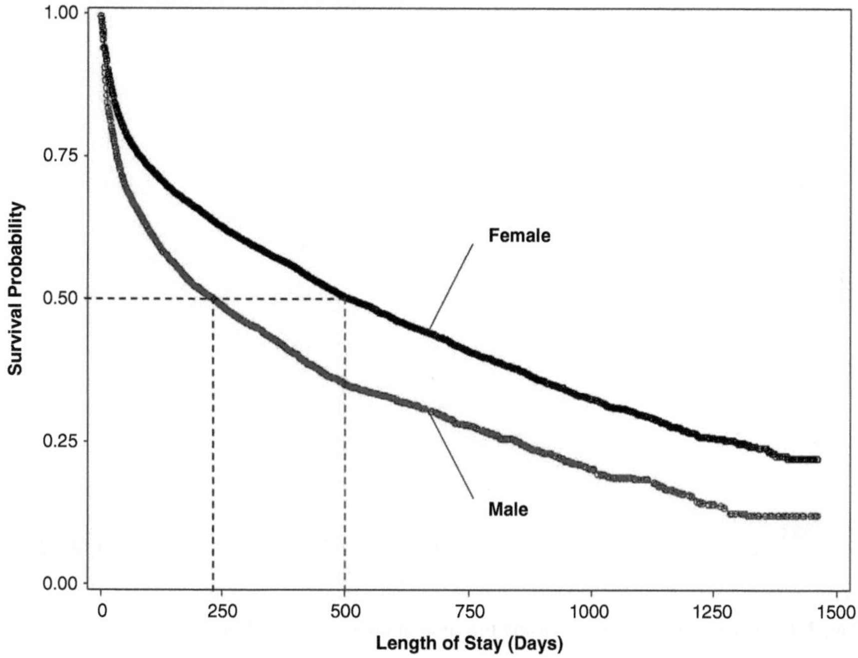

Fig. 3.3 Kaplan–Meier survival curves of male and female clients. *Dotted lines* show that the median length of stay for females is almost double that of males

In order to estimate LOS distributions as accurately as possible, we analyzed the pre- and post-2003 data (including the censored data) at the aggregate level by including age group, gender, and LHA as explanatory variables. Thus, LOS distributions for all the classes were represented by Weibull distributions with a common shape parameter value and distinct scale parameter values.

For the existing clients in care, the simulation model preloaded their information (including the age, gender, and date of entry in care) and randomly generated a remaining LOS for each of them based on the corresponding conditional Weibull distribution (3.8). Moreover, although the waitlist length in each LHA was available, there was no information about the age and gender of each client in it. We assumed that the existing clients on the waitlist can be represented by the people who entered care in the last year. Using this assumption, we split these clients in each LHA by age group and gender and then applied the same LOS distributions as for new arrivals to them.

3.5.2 Results and Analysis

We now describe results of using this method for one particular LHA (called LHA I), where all 2,392 existing beds were occupied and 240 clients were on the waitlist

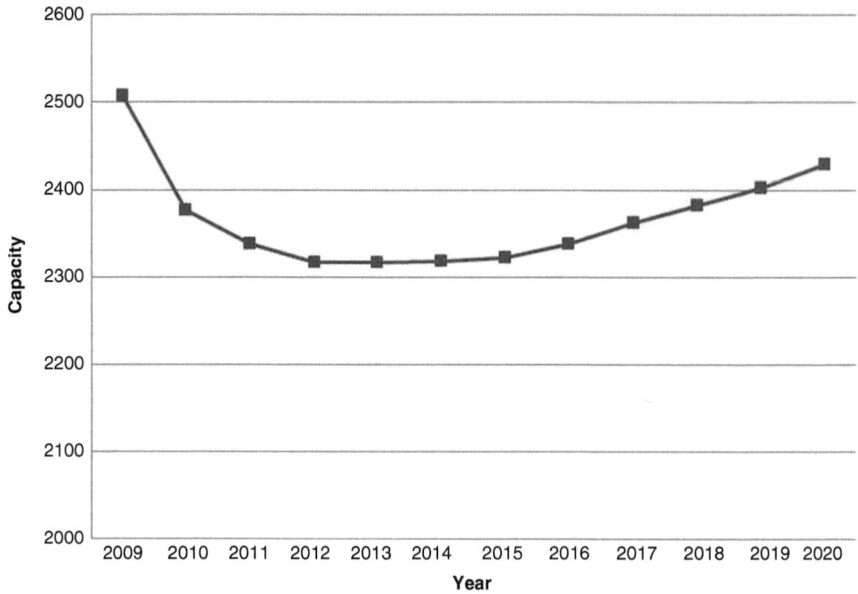

Fig. 3.4 Capacity levels obtained using the simulation approach in LHA I

when the study started. The forecasts (the number of beds required during 2009–2020) obtained using our simulation approach are displayed in Fig. 3.4. We also show the forecasted number of arrivals per year from each class in Fig. 3.5 (since the number of arrivals aged less than 65 is small and stable, we only show the classes over age 65).

The curve of the optimal capacity levels over time is "U-shaped," i.e., decreasing during 2009–2013 and then increasing during 2014–2020. Note that, when $s_t < s_{t-1}$ and all beds are occupied in year $t-1$, the simulation that we implemented does not immediately release $s_{t-1} - s_t$ beds at the beginning of year t. Instead, it makes the first $s_{t-1} - s_t$ released beds (when the current clients exit the system) unavailable for new clients. Thus, these beds are still operated for some time in year t until released. This implies that there may be more beds actually in operation during 2010–2013 than those obtained using our approach.

We believe that the required capacity increases during 2014–2020 are mainly attributable to the rapid increase of the population aged between 65 and 85. On the other hand, we identified two main reasons for the post-2009 decrease in required capacity.

- Since the service level at the time of the study was much lower than the target [45] and also there were a large number of clients on the waitlist, much extra capacity is needed to reduce the wait time and meet the service level criterion in 2009.

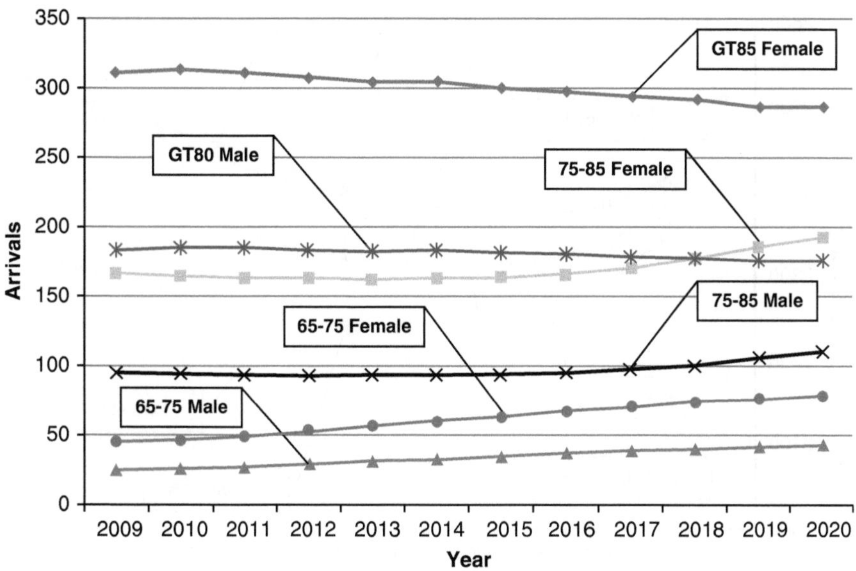

Fig. 3.5 Forecasted number of arrivals per year by client class in LHA I

- Another potential reason for this initial decrease is the change in admission criteria instituted in 2003. Clients admitted pre-2003 were of lower acuity and thus generally had longer LOS. Since many of these individuals will be leaving the system between 2009 and 2013, capacity needs will decrease.

3.5.3 Implementation and Recommendations

We delivered the decision support system based on this methodology as well as an analysis report to the Division of Operations Research of VIHA, where Arena was available and the employees there had the capability to use and revise the simulation model. We also provided training for Arena simulation, survival analysis in SAS, and other supportive documents to the employees of VIHA.

As explained earlier, in practice, it is not feasible to change capacity in each year and by any amount. Hence, our results provided the management with capacity targets that can serve as inputs to optimal capacity planning decisions which take costs and constraints into account. In this regard, the simulation model without the optimization was also useful alone, as the users could input the capacity levels and observe the resulting performance.

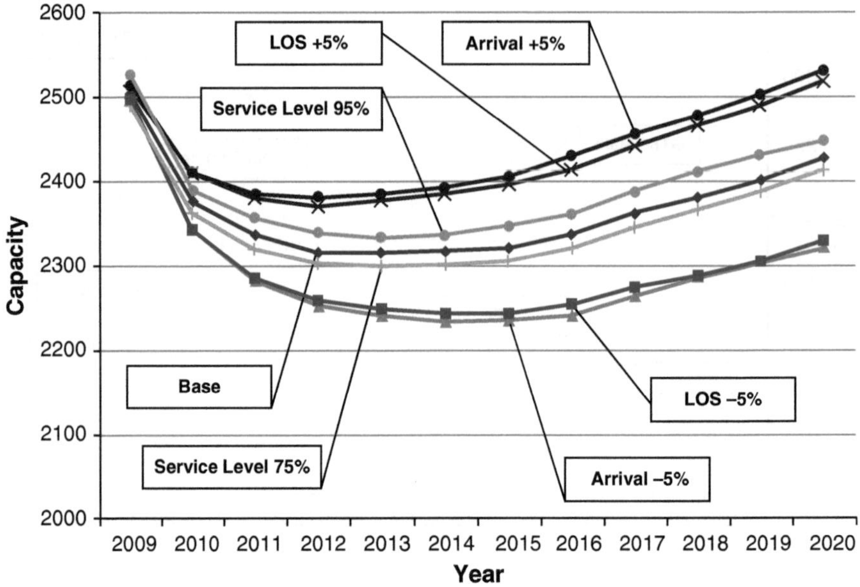

Fig. 3.6 Capacity levels for different scenarios in LHA I

In addition to the suggested methodology, we proposed several recommendations based on the results and observations.

- In most of the LHAs, capacity levels do not need to grow significantly until a few years into the future, and the current capacities in some LHAs are sufficient for the short term. Nevertheless, they should avoid reducing LTC capacity further and consider capacity expansion options for the long term.
- We recommended considering acquiring flexible capacity, perhaps through outsourcing, that would better respond to short-term demand surges.
- We also recommended not relaxing admission criteria when there is unused capacity during this period. The consequence of doing that would be that clients with lower acuity would be admitted. Since these clients would have longer LOSs, more capacity would be needed in the future when arrival rates increase.

3.5.4 Sensitivity Analysis

Several scenarios were investigated, including the base case, increasing and decreasing the LOS by 5%, increasing and decreasing the per capita arrival rates by 5%, and setting the service level criterion τ equal to 0.75 and 0.95. All scenarios were run using the methodology above to find the required capacity in each year to meet the service level criterion.

Figure 3.6 compares the base case to the other scenarios. It seems that there is no significant difference in the effect on the required capacity levels between changing the LOS and changing the per capita arrival rates. Moreover, the service level is sensitive to the capacity level. For instance, if the capacity decreases only by 20 each year, the resulting service level would drop to 75%.

3.6 Comparison to the Ratio Approach

Assuming that capacity forecasts based on our simulation model are correct, it is important to determine whether a ratio policy such as that used in practice, can obtain accurate forecasts.

We calculated the capacity levels based on the current provincial planning ratio of 75 beds per 1,000 population over 75 in BC [8]. We refer to this policy as *Current Ratio*. As also shown in Fig. 3.7, this policy significantly underestimates the capacity requirement during 2009–2018, and the resulting service levels are close to zero. Furthermore, it may significantly overestimate the capacity requirement after 2020. Nevertheless, we observed overestimation in some other LHAs by using this approach. This suggests that it does not produce accurate capacity forecasts.

The shortcomings of this ratio policy are that it ignores:

- The dynamics of the system.
- Geographic specific differences in arrival and LOS.

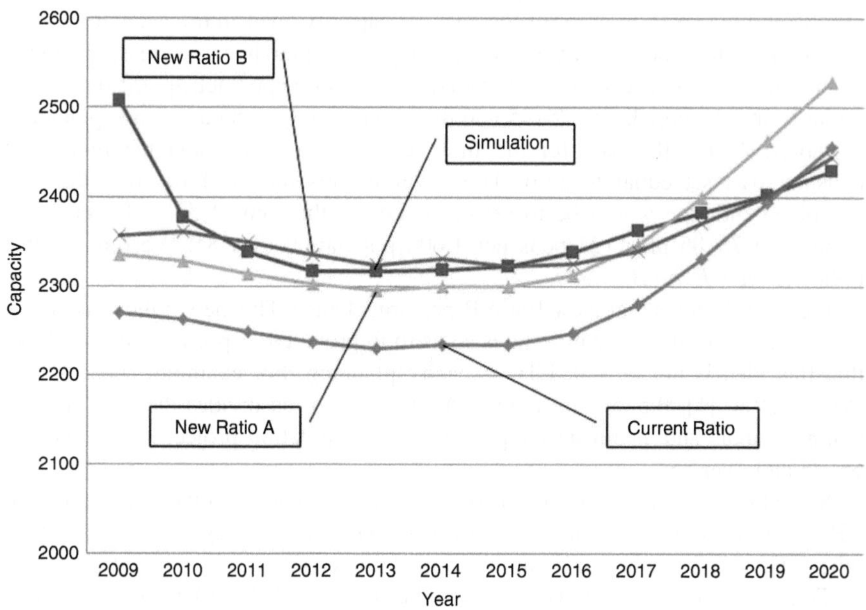

Fig. 3.7 Capacity levels obtained using the ratio-based approaches in LHA I

- Clients in care and on the waitlist at the beginning of each year.
- The population below 75, who account for 20% of total clients.
- Differences in arrival rates and LOS between the two age groups (75–85 and over 85) and between the two gender groups.

The above results suggest that the ratio for the provisional target, i.e., 75 beds per 1,000 population over 75, does not achieve service criteria or results in excess capacity. An immediate question to ask is "Is there a better ratio policy that can approximate forecasts based on the service level criterion?"

To address this issue, we first attempted to find an appropriate ratio value based only on the population over 75. A simple linear regression model was developed, using the capacity levels obtained from our simulation approach as a dependent variable and the population over 75 as an explanatory variable. In particular, we did not include the data for the first year (2009) in the regression, because it is mainly affected by the current waitlist. Also, we set the constant in the regression equal to zero. Based on this regression, the best ratio value can be estimated as 77 beds per 1,000 population over 75. We refer to this policy as *New Ratio A*.

From Fig. 3.7, it is clear that New Ratio A significantly overestimates the capacity levels after 2018. We found out that the main reason for this is that subgroups within the population over 75 are not differentiated. The population 75–85 is growing, while the population over 85 is declining. Although the size of the former population group is much larger than that of the latter one, the arrival rate per population for the former (1.5%) is also much lower than that for the latter (4.97%). In addition, the LOS distributions for these two groups are also different. Hence, this suggests that it is important to differentiate the two population groups (75–85 and over 85), in order to forecast the capacity levels more accurately.

Based on the above analysis, we developed another linear regression model, where the capacity levels obtained from our simulation approach are the dependent variable and the population 75–85 and the population over 85 are two explanatory variables. Again, the data for the first year was excluded, and the regression constant was set equal to zero. The result of this model shows that the best combined estimate would be to set capacities as the sum of 52 beds per 1,000 population 75–85 plus 127 beds per 1,000 population over 85. We refer to this policy as *New Ratio B*.

Figure 3.7 shows that New Ratio B performs better. This new policy takes into account age-specific utilization rates so as to improve the capacity forecasts. Note that this idea is not new in LTC capacity planning. For example, according to Wiener et al. [6], the nursing home program of Florida divides the state into 36 planning areas and establishes separate bed-to-population projections for people 65–75 and over 75.

Since the two ratio values of this policy were estimated based on this particular LHA, another immediate question to ask is "Does this policy also work well in other LHAs?", i.e., whether it can be applied universally.

To answer this question, we chose another LHA (called LHA II) and compared the capacity forecasts obtained from this ratio policy to those obtained from our

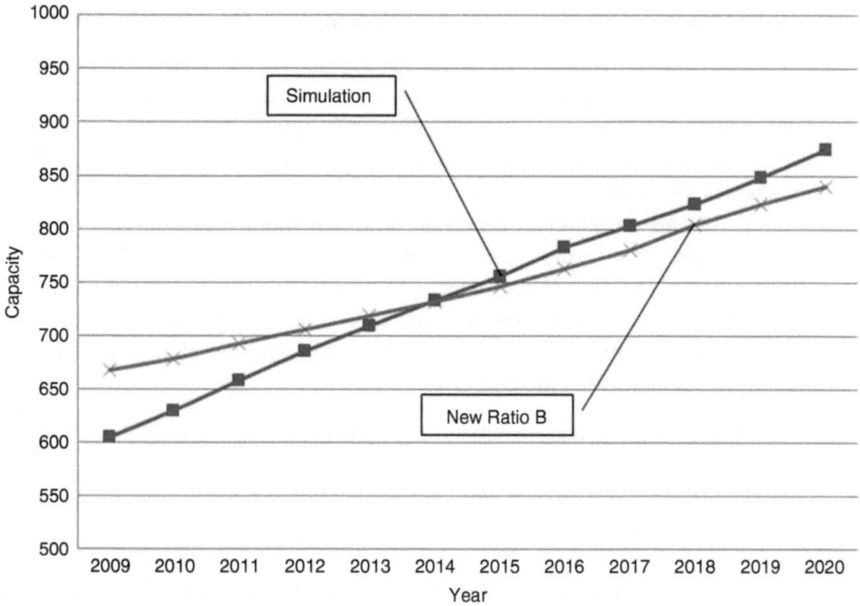

Fig. 3.8 Capacity levels obtained using the simulation and New Ratio B approaches in LHA II

simulation approach. Figure 3.8 shows that this policy does not work well in this LHA. The ratio policy overestimates the capacity levels in the first several years and then underestimates the capacity levels. Similar analyses in other LHAs also demonstrate that this policy do not perform reliably in general. This suggests that a universally valid ratio policy may not be achievable. Even if a simple ratio policy is needed, it should be customized for each region based on the results obtained from our simulation approach, which negates their value since the simulation model is required anyway.

The reasons why a universally valid policy may not be attainable are many-fold.

- LOS distributions in different regions are not identical, probably because of differences in population characteristics and possible variability in admission criteria.
- Arrival rates per population are different. For example, in rural regions, people may be less willing to live in residential care facilities, due to inconvenient access.
- Population composition is different. For instance, it would be problematic when a ratio policy only based on population over 75 is used in a region where population 55–65 have higher demands for LTC beds.

Therefore, since each region has its own characteristics, it is very hard to find a universally valid ratio policy that can address all of these differences.

3.7 Comparison to the SIPP Approach and Its Modifications

In this section, we compare the simulation-optimization approach to the SIPP approach and its modifications, including the MOL approach.

To calculate the capacity levels based on the SIPP approach, we aggregated the clients into a single class. We used the overall arrival rate and estimated the LOS distribution for this single class based on an exponential distribution. Using the closed-form expression for the *M*/*M*/*s* queueing system, we calculated the number of beds required to satisfy the service level criterion in the steady state in each year.

Figures 3.9 and 3.10 show that, for both LHA I and II, the required capacities based on the SIPP approach are significantly lower than those derived from the simulation. Reasons for this include:

- The SIPP approach ignores clients in care and on the waitlist at the beginning of each year.
- It ignores differences in arrival and LOS among the five age groups and between the two gender groups.
- Most importantly, Fig. 3.11 shows that the exponential distribution provided a much poorer fit to the Kaplan–Meier curve than the Weibull distribution did. Moreover, the mean of the estimated exponential distribution is significantly lower than that of the estimated Weibull distribution. We found that this underestimation occurs when there is a relatively large portion of censored data.

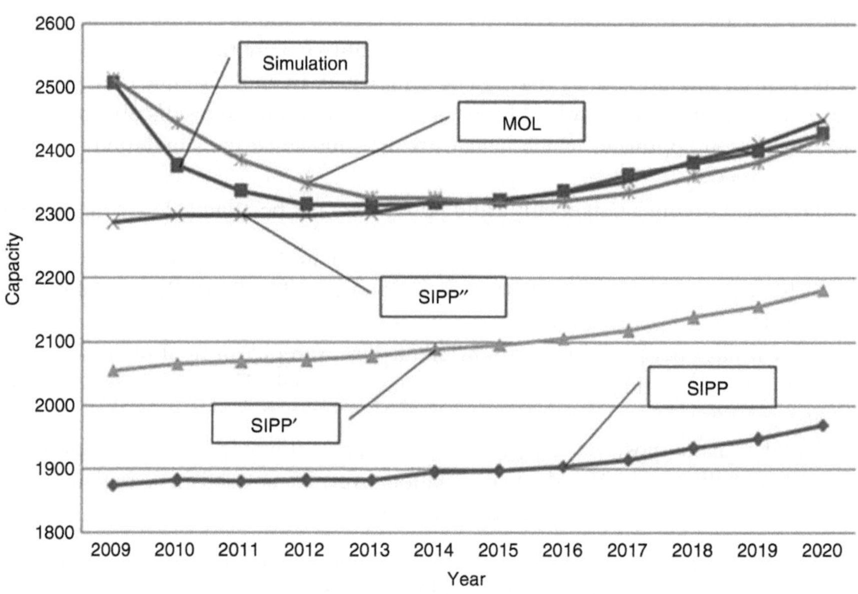

Fig. 3.9 Capacity levels obtained using the SIPP approach and its modifications in LHA I

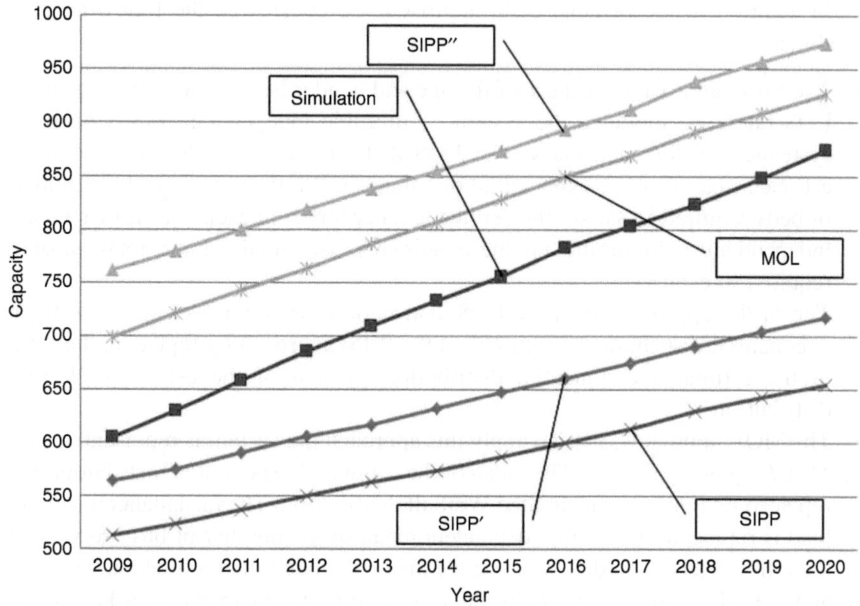

Fig. 3.10 Capacity levels obtained using the SIPP approach and its modifications in LHA II

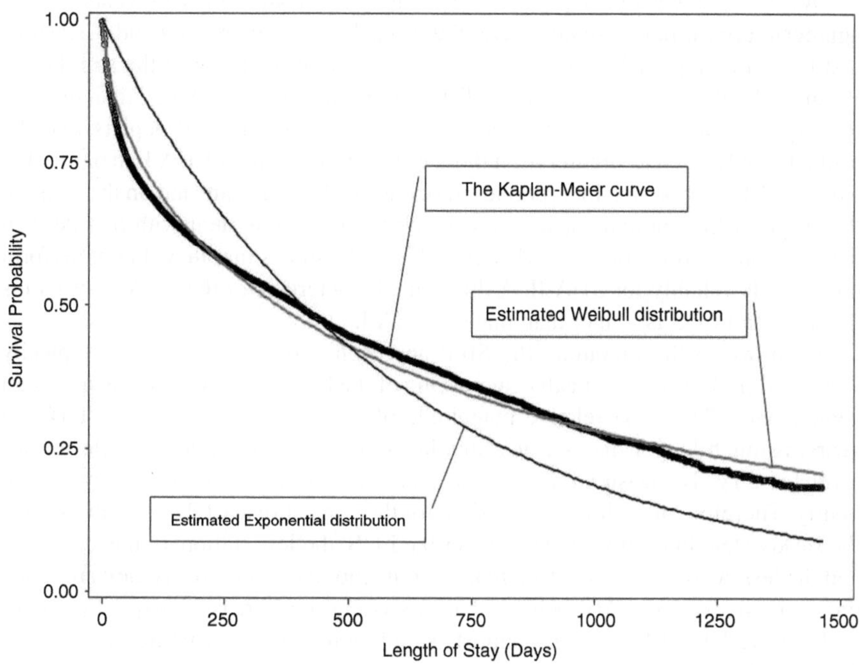

Fig. 3.11 Estimated exponential distribution versus estimated Weibull distribution compared to the Kaplan–Meier curve

In addition to the original SIPP approach, we considered the following three modifications:

- The SIPP′ approach: Because of the age and gender heterogeneity in arrival and LOS rates, we modeled the system by multiple independent $M/M/s$ queueing systems, one for each class. The LOS distribution for each class was again estimated based on an exponential distribution. We then calculated the number of beds required to satisfy the service level criterion in each year for each class independently. Summing up these numbers, we obtained the total capacity required in each year.
- The SIPP″ approach: Because LOS distributions were not well modeled by an exponential distribution; we modified the SIPP approach by replacing the mean of the estimated exponential distribution by that of the estimated Weibull distribution.
- The MOL approach [30]: To apply this approach the system is represented as an $M_t/M/s_t$ queuing system. The mean of the estimated exponential distribution was replaced by that of the estimated Weibull distribution. The instantaneous offered load is replaced by the time-dependent mean of the number of busy servers for the infinite-server model $M_t/G/\infty$; we then calculated the modified arrival rates and used the standard $M/M/s$ formula to determine the capacities. A key advantage of this approach is that existing clients in care and on the waitlist can be incorporated in the initial condition of the system.

Overall, for the above approaches, the aggregate mean LOS is 2.6 years and the aggregate arrival rate is roughly 873 clients each year. Figures 3.9 and 3.10 show that the SIPP′ approach predicts capacities still far below those of the simulation. Presumably, this is because the LOS distributions are far longer tailed than those of the exponential. For the SIPP″ and MOL approaches, Fig. 3.9 depicts that the estimates only deviate slightly from those of the simulation for LHA I; in particular, since the MOL approach incorporates the existing clients in care and on the waitlist, the shape of the optimal capacity levels over time is consistent with that derived using the simulation approach. However, Fig. 3.10 shows that they do not perform consistently reliably for LHA II. A different characteristic of the LHA II system is that its mean LOS is longer than that for LHA I.

As shown in the literature, the SIPP approach and its modifications typically work well in the context of call centers. One of the key differences between the call centers and LTC is the relative magnitude of the service time. LOS in LTC (in years) is much longer than service time in call centers (in minutes), while service level for LTC is measured yearly and that for call centers is usually measured hourly. Therefore, it is almost impossible for the nonstationary LTC system to reach the steady state in each year. The longer the LOS, the less stationary the system is, and the less accurate the SIPP approach and its modifications are, as they are based on stationary systems. We believe that this is one main reason why they do not perform well for LHA II. In contrast, simulation typically captures the system dynamics better.

This suggests that, in general, the SIPP approach may not be suitable to use when the service time is very long compared to the period length. This is consistent with the observations in Green et al. [23]. Although the modifications of the SIPP approach may perform better for this long service time situation, they are still not reliable.

3.8 The Average Flow Model

The discussions above suggest that ratio policies, the SIPP approaches and the MOL approach cannot consistently achieve desirable service levels. Although our simulation approach is a more reliable tool, it takes much effort and analytical experience to implement it, especially by practitioners. Therefore, we considered a simpler method which we refer to as the deterministic Average Flow Model (AFM). Its advantages are that can be easily implemented in a spreadsheet and appears to provide relatively good performance.

Suppose that the number of beds needed in year t to satisfy *all* demand is denoted by s_t. Denote the total number of arrivals (aggregated over age groups and gender) in year t by A_t, and the number of total departures in year t by D_t. Also, denote the aggregate mean LOS by L. The AFM is based on the following client flow relationship:

$$s_t = s_{t-1} + A_t - D_t \quad t = 1, \ldots, T. \tag{3.9}$$

The above equation means that in every year, the number of beds needed (s_t) is set equal to the number of existing clients in the system at the beginning of the year (s_{t-1}) plus the number of total arrivals in the year (A_t) minus the number of departures in the year (D_t).

According to Little's law [46], the number of total departures in a stable system is equal to the number of people in the system divided by the average time people spend in the system, i.e.,

$$D_t = \frac{s_t}{L} \quad t = 1, \ldots, T. \tag{3.10}$$

Then, s_t can be determined from the formula below:

$$s_t = \frac{(s_{t-1} + A_t)L}{1 + L} \quad t = 1, \ldots, T. \tag{3.11}$$

This simple model as well as the simulation approach, requires estimates of the aggregate LOS and the number of total arrivals in each year as inputs.

In general, we found that the AFM performs well in all the LHAs that we studied. Figures 3.12 and 3.13 show the capacity forecasts obtained from our

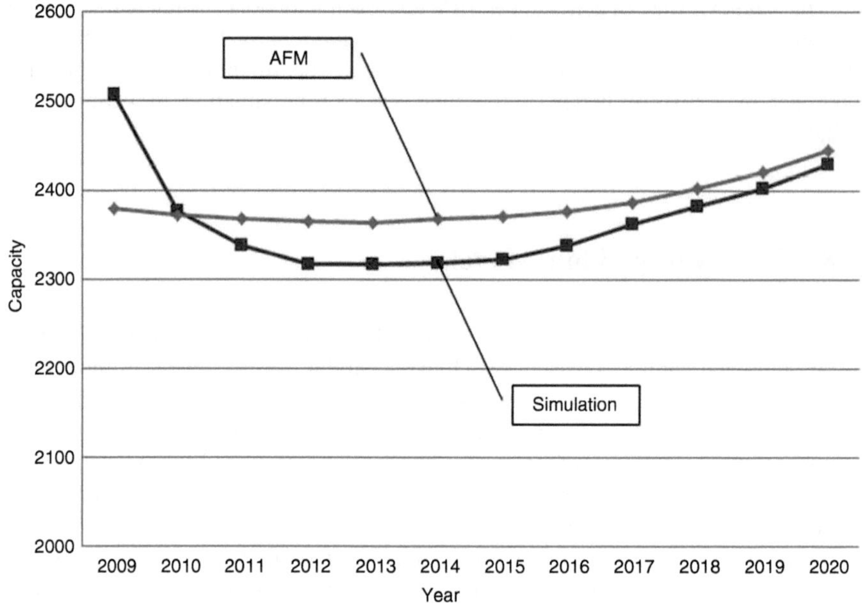

Fig. 3.12 Capacity levels obtained using the AFM in LHA I

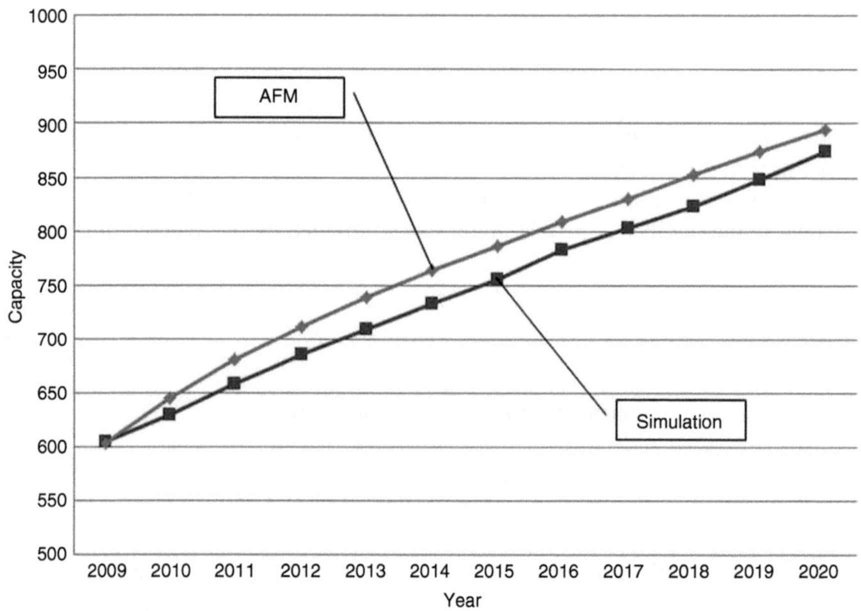

Fig. 3.13 Capacity levels obtained using the AFM in LHA II

simulation approach and the AFM in LHAs I and II. The pattern of the capacity forecasts obtained from the AFM is consistent with that obtained from our simulation approach, implying that the AFM is reliable. This is mainly because the AFM, like the simulation approach, considers the dynamics of the system.

On the other hand, in almost all the LHAs, the AFM slightly overestimates the capacity levels. The primary reason is that Little's law applies to a stable system, i.e., the system needs to remain unchanged for a long enough time; however, the system that we study is clearly not stable, since the number of arrivals and the capacities needed are typically increasing over time. Therefore, expression (3.10) is only an approximation. In particular, we found out that the number of total departures in each year is greater than that estimated from this formula.

To further study the accuracy of the AFM approach compared to the simulation approach, we conducted sensitivity analyses in the context of on a simulation of an idealized system. Also, sensitivity analyses in this setting provide an indication of when the AFM would over- or underestimate capacity needed so as to adjust it accordingly and also when it may not be appropriate to use in practice.

In this example, we set the planning horizon to 50 years. Initially, there were no existing clients in care or on the waitlist. There was only a single population of arrivals with the LOS modeled by a Weibull distribution. The number and timing of arrivals within each year was modeled by a Poisson process with a constant rate. We set the arrival rate of the first year in the planning horizon as a base, and the arrival rate of the following years increased by a 1-year growth rate (both the base and the growth rate measured in client/year). In addition, we considered the same service level criterion as before, i.e., $\tau \times 100\%$ of arriving clients must receive the service within γ days every year.

For each year t, denote the capacity forecast obtained from the simulation approach by s_t' and that from the AFM by s_t''. Since the system is initially empty, we used the first 20 years for warm-up in the simulation and focused on the relative error, defined as $(s_t'' - s_t')/s_t'$, over the rest 30 years. We expected that the four major parameters may mainly influence the accuracy, including the growth rate, Weibull scale, Weibull shape, and service level measure τ.

In the base case, we set the base of the arrival rate to 500, the growth rate to 10, the Weibull scale to 485, the Weibull shape to 0.6, and the service level measure to 85%. Note that the values of the Weibull parameters make the mean LOS equal to 2 years and make the distribution have a long fat tail. This is consistent with the real cases that we studied. In addition to the base case, we varied the values of the four parameters mentioned above to investigate their impact on the accuracy.

Table 3.1 summarizes the mean and standard deviation of the relative error with respect to the different values of the four parameters. The first column represents the error of the base case with the mean 1.06% and the standard deviation 0.68%. Any of the other eight cells in the table shows the resulting mean and standard deviation of the error when the corresponding parameter changes and the other parameters remain the same as in the base case.

In general, we observed that the absolute value of the mean of the relative error decreases in time. This suggests that the AFM is very accurate when the system is

Table 3.1 The mean and standard deviation of the error using the AFM

Growth rate	10	20	50
Relative error	(1.06%, 0.68%)	(2.56%, 0.76%)	(4.50%, 1.07%)
Weibull scale	485	970	2425
Relative error	(1.06%, 0.68%)	(5.86%, 2.11%)	(7.15%, 1.12%)
Weibull shape	0.6	0.8	1
Relative error	(1.06%, 0.68%)	(−1.04%, 0.39%)	(−1.47%, 0.37%)
Service level measure	85%	95%	99%
Relative error	(1.06%, 0.68%)	(−0.02%, 0.74%)	(−1.15%, 0.61%)

close to being stable. The first two rows of the table demonstrate that the mean of the relative error increases in both the growth rate and Weibull scale. This may suggest that the system needs more time to become relatively stable. Hence, when the expected arrivals are increasing very rapidly or the mean LOS is very large, the capacity actually needed may be less than that estimated from the AFM; in these situations, it may not be a very effective approach to use. More interestingly, the Weibull shape also has an impact on the accuracy. For instance, when it is equal to 1, the LOS distribution is an exponential distribution; the AFM in fact underestimates the capacity levels, contrary to the based case. The main reason for this is that a Weibull distribution with a small shape parameter has a longer and fatter tail than an exponential distribution, i.e., there are more people with a short LOS that would leave the system quickly; thus, less capacity is needed. This suggests that, instead of simply calculating the mean, using survival analysis to estimate the LOS distribution is critical. Finally, the service level measure clearly influences the capacity forecasts. In the AFM, there is no consideration of the service level; in contrast, in the simulation approach, the higher the service level criterion, the more the "safety" capacity is needed. It would be interesting to investigate the quality of this approximation theoretically.

3.9 Conclusions and Policy Implications

This chapter describes a methodology for setting LTC capacity levels over a multiyear planning horizon to achieve target wait time service levels. We proposed and applied an approach that integrates demographic and survival analysis, discrete event simulation, and optimization. Based on this methodology, a decision support system was developed for use in practice. We illustrated this approach through a case study. We also compared our approach to the commonly used ratio-based approaches and the SIPP approach and its modifications developed in the call center literature. Finally, we proposed the simple AFM that performs effectively.

From a methodological perspective, the innovation of this research is the combination of several operations research and statistical methods. Since our approach is driven by service levels, it is preferable to the ratio-based approaches.

Also, because LOS distributions tend not to be exponential and LOS is long relative to the period length, our approach is also preferable to the SIPP approach and its modifications.

From a practical perspective, this chapter provides rigorous tools that can be used by managers of LTC programs or facilities to evaluate system performance and to make long-term capacity planning. Although it is not realistic to expect each community or health region to develop and implement the simulation optimization approach, we believe that a provincial ministry in Canada (or a similar health department in other countries) may have the capabilities of conducting this analysis. One feasible long-term solution could be that a provincial ministry conducts this analysis once every 5 years and provides the relevant information to constituent communities or health regions so they can use it to construct "New Ratio B" type local solutions. Alternatively, when there are insufficient resources or capabilities to develop and implement the simulation optimization approach, the proposed AFM also performs effectively and can easily be implemented in a spreadsheet. We are hopeful that using the tools will result in both improved access to LTC and reduced volumes of ALC patients in acute care.

The following observations and recommendations follow from our research.

- Survival analysis reveals that LOS varies considerably by age, gender, and geographic region. This must be accounted for in estimating future capacity needs.
- An approach based on a fixed ratio of beds per population should not be used because it ignores differences in population characteristics by region and historical data.
- The SIPP approach should not be used because it ignores the large number of clients in care and on the waitlist at the beginning of each year and the observation that LOS tends to follow a Weibull distribution. The modifications of the SIPP approach, such as the MOL approach, may perform better but are not reliable due to long service times.
- System managers should avoid relaxing the admission criteria even when capacity utilization is low. Admitting lower acuity clients could result in increased LOSs and the need for more capacity in the future.
- System managers should seek flexible temporary capacity that would better respond to short-term demand surges.

Still there remain many interesting research directions in LTC capacity planning. In depth analysis of the simulation output showed great variation in the achieved service level among the replications as well as a high correlation between the achieved service levels in consecutive years. This is because the service time is very long compared to the period length. To find a more effective method to overcome the problems alluded above, one might investigate the use of an adaptive approach to LTC capacity planning where the capacity decision depends on the initial state of the system. In other words, provide policies for managers instead of a series of capacity levels. They can be represented as a look-up table that contains an upper and lower bound for the required capacity level in each year. Furthermore, there is a need for coordinated planning models that include assisted living, dementia care, and home care and as well to account for different levels of acuity within a single facility.

Acknowledgments We gratefully thank Steve Atkinson, Director of Operations Research, Vancouver Island Health Authority, Peter Kafka, Chief Executive Officer of the Louis Brier Home and Hospital for providing data and many helpful discussions. This research has been partially supported by NSERC grant RGPIN 5527.

References

1. World Health Organization (2009) http://www.who.int/ageing/primary_health_care/en/index.html
2. Statistics Canada (2009) http://www12.statcan.ca/census-recensement/2006/rt-td/as-eng.cfm
3. BC Stats (2008) British Columbia population projection—PEOPLE 32. http://www.bcstats.gov.bc.ca/
4. Canadian Medical Association (2009) http://www.cma.ca/multimedia/CMA/Content_Images/Inside_cma/WhatWePublish/LeadershipSeries/English/pg17EC.pdf
5. Canadian Institute for Health Information (2009) http://secure.cihi.ca/cihiweb/
6. Wiener JM, Stevenson DG, Goldenson SM (1998) Controlling the supply of long-term care providers at the state level. Occasional Paper Number 22, Urban Institute, Washington, DC
7. West Virginia Health Care Authority (2003) Long term care task force. http://www. hcawv.org/PolicyPlan/wr16.htm
8. Legislative Assembly of British Columbia (2006) http://www.llbc.leg.bc.ca/Public/PubDocs/bcdocs/401348/Creating Patient Flow.pdf
9. Canadian Union of Public Employees (2009) Residential long-term care in Canada: our vision for better seniors' care. http://www cupe.ca/updir/CUPE-long-term-care-seniors-care-vision.pdf
10. Gibson D, Liu Z (2008) Planning ratios and population growth: will there be a shortfall in residential aged care by 2021? Australas J Ageing 14(2):57–62
11. Cohen M, Jeremy T, Baumbusch J (2009) An uncertain future for seniors: BC's restructuring of home and community health care, 2001–2008. http://www.policyalternatives.ca/reports/2009/04/uncertain future
12. Zhang Y, Puterman ML, Nelson M, Atkins D (2012) A simulation optimization approach to long-term care capacity planning. Oper Res 60(2):1–13
13. Zhang Y, Puterman ML, Atkins D (2012) Residential long-term care capacity planning: the shortcomings of ratio-based forecasts. Healthc Policy 7(4):68–81
14. Hare WL, Alimadad A, Dodd H, Ferguson R, Rutherford A (2009) A deterministic model of home and community care client counts in British Columbia. Health Care Manag Sci 12(1):80–98
15. Lin F, Kong N, Lawley M (2012) Capacity planning for publicly funded community based long-term care services. In: Johnson MP (ed) Community-based operations research. International series in operations research & management science, vol 167. Springer, New York, pp 297–315
16. Ridge JC, Jones SK, Nielsen MS, Shahani AK (1998) Capacity planning for intensive care units. Eur J Oper Res 105:346–355
17. Green LV (2003) How many hospital beds? Inquiry 39:400–412
18. Harper PR, Shahani AK (2002) Modelling for the planning and management of bed capacities in hospitals. J Oper Res Soc 53(1):11–18

19. Kao EPC, Tung GG (1981) Bed allocation in a public health care delivery system. Manag Sci 27(5):507–520
20. Vassilacopoulos G (1985) A simulation model for bed allocation to hospital inpatient departments. Simulation 45:233–241
21. Smith-Daniels VL, Schweikhart SB, Smith-Daniels DE (1988) Capacity management in health care services: review and future research directions. Decis Sci 19:898–919
22. Green LV (2004) Capacity planning and management in hospitals. In: Brandeau ML, Sainfort F, Pierskalla WP (eds) Operations research and health care: a handbook of methods and applications. Kluwer, London
23. Green LV, Kolesar PJ, Soares J (2001) Improving the SIPP approach for staffing service systems that have cyclic demand. Oper Res 49(4):549–564
24. Green LV, Kolesar PJ (1991) The pointwise stationary approximation for queues with nonstationary arrivals. Manag Sci 37(1):84–97
25. Green LV, Kolesar PJ, Svoronos A (1991) Some effects of nonstationarity on multiserver Markovian queuing systems. Oper Res 39(3):502–511
26. Ingolfsson A, Haque MA, Umnikov A (2002) Accounting for time-varying queueing effects in workforce scheduling. Eur J Oper Res 139(3):585–597
27. Jennings OB, Mandelbaum A, Massey WA, Whitt W (1996) Server staffing to meet time-varying demand. Manag Sci 42(10):1383–1394
28. Ingolfsson A, Akhmetshina E, Budge S, Li Y, Wu X (2007) A survey and experimental comparison of service level approximation methods for non-stationary $M(t)/M/s(t)$ queueing systems. INFORMS J Comput 19(2):201–214
29. Gans N, Koole G, Mandelbaum A (2003) Telephone call centers: tutorial, review and research prospects. Manuf Serv Oper Manag 5(2):79–141
30. Green LV, Kolesar PJ, Whitt W (2007) Coping with time-varying demand when setting staffing requirements for a service system. Prod Oper Manag 16(1):13–39
31. Kwan SK, Davis MM, Greenwood AG (1988) A simulation model for determining variable worker requirements in a service operation with time-dependent customer demand. Queueing Syst 3:265–276
32. Whitt W (1991) The pointwise stationary approximation for Mt/Mt/s queues is asymptotically correct as the rates increase. Manag Sci 37(3):307–314
33. Atlason J, Epelman MA, Henderson SG (2008) Optimizing call center staffing using simulation and analytic center cutting-plane methods. ManagSci 54(2):295–309
34. Parlar M, Sharafali M (2008) Dynamic allocation of airline check-in counters: a queueing optimization approach. Manag Sci 54(8):1410–1424
35. De Vericourt F, Jennings O (2011) Nurse staffing in medical units: a queueing perspective. Oper Res 59:1320–1331
36. Yankovic N, Green LV (2011) Identifying good nursing levels: a queuing approach. Oper Res 59:942–955
37. Feldman Z, Mandelbaum A, Massey WA, Whitt W (2008) Staffing of time-varying queues to achieve time-stable performance. Manag Sci 54:324–338
38. Xie H, Chaussalet TJ, Millard PH (2006) A model-based approach to the analysis of patterns of length of stay in institutional long-term care. IEEE Trans Inf Technol Biomed 10(3):512–518
39. Miller RG (1981) Simultaneous statistical inference, 2nd edn. Springer, New York
40. Klein JP, Moeschberger ML (2003) Survival analysis, techniques for censored and truncated data, 2nd edn. Springer, New York
41. Fu MC (2002) Optimization for simulation: theory vs. practice. INFORMS J Comput 14(3):192–215
42. Tekin E, Sabuncuoglu I (2004) Simulation optimization: a comprehensive review on theory and applications. IIE Trans 36:1067–1081
43. Henderson SG, Nelson BL (2006) Handbooks in operations research and management science: simulation. Elsevier, Amsterdam

44. Hong LJ, Nelson BL (2009) A brief introduction to optimization via simulation. Winter Simulation Conference Proceedings, pp 75–85
45. Vancouver Island Health Authority (VIHA) (2009) http://www.viha.ca/NR/rdonlyres/B5AEA945-8240-47B7-8BC2-63D593924350/0/residential care admissions.pdf
46. Little JDC (1961) A proof of the queueing formula $L = \lambda W$. Oper Res 9:383–387

Chapter 4
Managing Community-based Care for Chronic Diseases: The Quantitative Approach

Beste Kucukyazici and Vedat Verter

Abstract Community-based care (C-bC) constitutes an important element of the chronic disease management programs. The design and management of C-bC systems requires the development of new resources and services, the assessment and reorganization of the existing services/facilities as well as the design of interventions. Quantitative decision models can play a major role for helping care providers and policy makers in this context. We present a systematic view of C-bC and provide selective examples of quantitative decision models developed for various chronic diseases. We outline the building blocks of C-bC systems as well as the distinguishing features of these systems that need to be incorporated in quantitative decision models. Then, we present three representative and diverse examples of prevailing quantitative approaches for managing C-bC. Finally, we discuss some avenues for future research.

4.1 Introduction

Chronic conditions cannot be cured by acute care and hence, the patient most often suffers from their symptoms during the remainder of his/her life requiring long-term care. They include non-communicable diseases (e.g., diabetes, cardiovascular disease, stroke, and asthma), long-term mental disorders and certain communicable diseases (such as HIV/AIDS). Chronic diseases are responsible for 60 % of the global disease burden [45]. They result in 1.7 million deaths each year in the U.S., which accounts for 70 % of all deaths in the country [5]. A much higher portion, 87 %, of the fatalities in Canada are due to chronic diseases, which amounts to 220,000 people annually [23]. Also, the number of persons with chronic illness is growing at an astonishing rate because of the rapid aging of the population and the

B. Kucukyazici (✉) • V. Verter
Desautels Faculty of Management, McGill University, Montreal, QC, Canada H3A 0G5
e-mail: beste.kucukyazici@mcgill.ca; vedat.verter@mcgill.ca

G.S. Zaric (ed.), *Operations Research and Health Care Policy*,
International Series in Operations Research & Management Science 190,
DOI 10.1007/978-1-4614-6507-2_4,

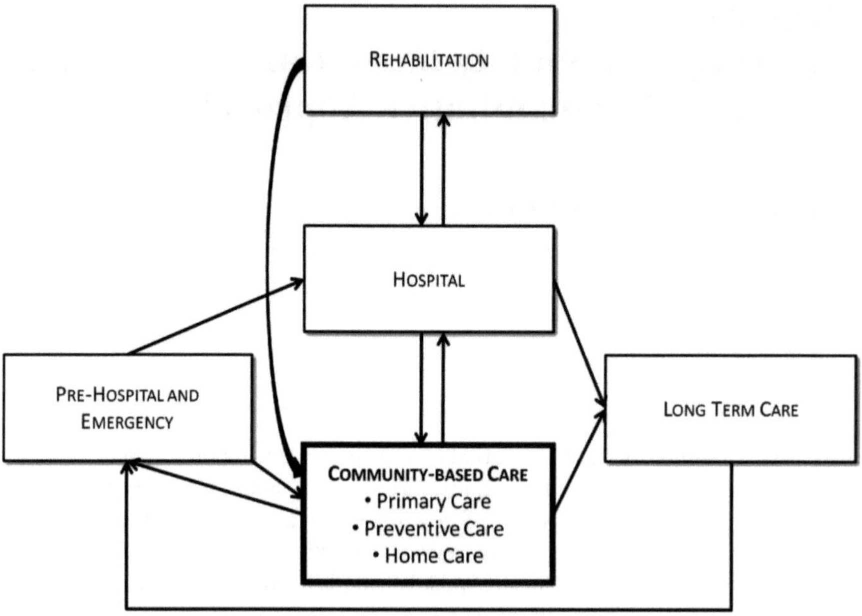

Fig. 4.1 The phases of care for chronic disease patients

greater longevity of persons with many chronic conditions [41]. In response to this growing burden, many countries around the world are developing *chronic disease management*(CDM) programs [42]. The effective management of chronic care calls for a multidisciplinary and coordinated approach spanning from prevention to community care, i.e., a coordinated chronic care programs.

In light of the fact that hospitals still account for a significant portion of healthcare spending [6], CDM programs mostly aim at shifting care out of acute care facilities. As a result, *community-based care*(C-bC), which patients receive while living at their homes, is being assigned an increased role in the healthcare continuum. C-bC encompasses a broad spectrum of services including; preventive and primary care with specialist backup as needed, community-based long term residential care, community-based rehabilitation and community health care teams.

The focus of C-bC services extends beyond the immediate medical problem to include management of one's chronic condition and environment in order to *prevent* emergency room visits, hospital admissions or transfers to long term care (LTC) facilities, all of which are less desirable for the patient and can be more costly to the health care system. In order to achieve the broader objectives of C-bC, services offered include social and educational components, and require more input and participation from the patients as well as their family and caregivers. The central nature of C-bC within the healthcare continuum is depicted in Fig. 4.1, where the nodes represent the care phases and the arcs represent the flow of patients.

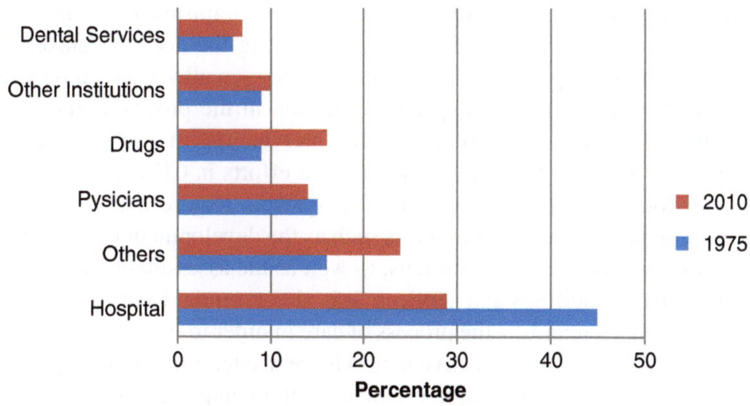

Fig. 4.2 Canadian healthcare spending 1975 and 2010 [6]

Here, we briefly focus on Canada as an example of the increasing significance of chronic diseases and C-bC. The Canadian Institute for Health Information (CIHI) identifies new drugs, medical technology, medical imaging, costly interventions and community services as the most important determinants for increased healthcare spending in Canada [6]. From a broader perspective, the "cost drivers," which are the underlying structural forces, comprise population aging, demand, inflation and increased chronic disease prevalence. In addition, the "cost escalators," which effect healthcare spending in the short and medium-term, include pharmaceuticals, new technologies, home and community services, and health human resources. As depicted in Fig. 4.2, drugs are the fastest-growing expenditure items in Canada for the past 35 years, while hospital spending has been reduced by 1/3 in terms of its share in the overall healthcare costs. The Cb-C services are included in the "others" category, whose share increased from 16 to 24 % during this period. Evidently, the prevalence of chronic care and C-bC has been increasing in the Canadian system.

It has been documented that improving chronic care delivery processes through well-designed C-bC can have a significant effect on health outcomes [15, 24, 39]. In the current practice, the main sources of inspiration for C-bC design initiatives are as follows: (1) the interventions proven by randomized controlled trials and before–after observational studies, and (2) the literature on other CDM program implementations that were successful. These previous studies, however, may not be immediately applicable since patient characteristics and care patterns vary significantly among geographic locations and chronic illnesses [39, 44]. The characteristics of the specific chronic disease and the geographic region being targeted should be taken into account while planning a community-based delivery system. Therefore, choosing elements, resource allocation, designing the required interventions and the care assignment of a C-bC system constitute crucial, but challenging, tasks for any CDM program. In the context of diabetes interventions, for example, Renders et al. [24] pointed out that these decisions have often not been based on a rigorous theoretical or empirical rationale. The lack of a road map that provides guidelines for informing the decision makers in the design/selection of the programs/interventions, resource allocation among various programs and/or interventions, capacity allocation in the program and providing insights about the effectiveness of alternative interventions in a specific health care context may be a barrier to quality improvement efforts in CDM [41].

The decisions to build and expand C-bC systems require analysis of chronic disease programs and many other factors such as the development of new resources and services, the design of interventions, as well as the assessment and reorganization of the existing facilities and services. It is also essential to introduce management practices that streamline the process of care in order to increase efficiency and generate cost savings. Thus, effective methods are needed for planning, prioritizing and decision making for the design, establishment, management and improvement of the C-bC systems. With respect to these issues, quantitative decision models can play a major role by helping care providers and policy makers to analyze tough decisions, solve critical complex problems and shape important policies [3]. However, there are very few quantitative studies focusing on decision modeling for C-bC, and particularly in the context of CDM. The aim of this chapter is to present a systematic view of this increasing important field of research and provide selective examples of quantitative decision models developed for managing C-bC for various chronic diseases. We hope that by pointing out this gap in the management science literature concerning C-bC for chronic diseases we would be able to attract the attention of our fellow researchers to this significant problem.

The remainder of this chapter is organized as follows. CDM programs and C-bC systems are described in Sect. 4.2, whereas Sect. 4.3 outlines the characteristics of the C-bC systems that need to be incorporated in quantitative decision models. In Sects. 4.4–4.6, we present examples of prevailing analytical approaches for managing C-bC for mental health, asthma and stroke, respectively. Our conclusions are summarized in Sect. 4.7 along with a discussion of future research directions.

4.2 Chronic Disease Management Programs and Community-Based Care

4.2.1 An Overview of Chronic Disease Management

A CDM program is a system redesign strategy that successfully addresses the continuing care needs of the chronically ill [11]. There are a number of strategic approaches for conceptualizing chronic care including the Chronic Care Model [42], Innovative Care for Chronic Conditions [45], Public Health Model [25] and Continuity of Care Model [22]. All these approaches acknowledge that a substantial portion of chronic care takes place outside hospitals [2] and integrate a number of elements into a plausible package designed to create informed, active patients with improved self-management skills for their chronic illnesses [4] as well as reorganize C-bC delivery systems to improve the quality of care [26].

CDM programs have received substantial interest from foundations, quality improvement organizations, physician groups, community health centers as well as national and regional health authorities [13]. For instance, most major health organizations and regions in the United States have a CDM program designed to improve care for people with chronic illnesses such as that used by the US Veteran's Affairs [5]. In Canada, British Columbia is using an Expanded Chronic Care Model, which incorporates health promotion and disease prevention [12]. Moreover, United Kingdom [29], Denmark [32], The Netherlands [33], New Zealand [43] and individual states of Australia have developed their own programs. Such a CDM program can be applied to a variety of chronic illnesses, health care settings and target populations. For example, the Indiana CDM program is developed as a result of the Medicaid legislation requiring implementation of a disease management program for patients with diabetes, asthma, congestive heart failure, hypertension, or who are at high risk of chronic disease in Indiana [14].

An efficiently designed CDM program utilizes both community services and hospital care. In this care model, the focus is on providing services in normal community settings close to the population served, while hospital stays are as brief as possible, promptly arranged and used only when necessary. That is, C-bC constitutes an important element of the CDM programs. It typically offers a wide set of services and encourages consideration of what blend of services is best suited to a particular geographical region at a particular time for a specific disease [38]. Recent studies highlight the notable impact of improvements through redesign of C-bC on the outcomes for various chronic diseases, including diabetes, asthma, stroke and congestive heart failure [17, 24, 39].

4.2.2 The Building Blocks of Community-Based Care Systems

4.2.2.1 Primary Care with Specialist Backup

The task of identifying and treating chronic diseases falls mostly to the primary care providers with specialist backup, as needed. Therefore, primary care systems constitute one of the most important components of the C-bC systems. For successful CDM, the primary care system needs to provide accessible, continued and comprehensive care. Assigning a primary care provider (e.g., family physician) to each individual, improving access to primary care, active follow-up by a *case manager* (often a primary care nurse), monitoring treatment and adjusting it if the patient does not improve, and referral to a specialist if necessary, usually lead to successful primary care [9, 28, 38, 40]. One of the common proposals considered during primary care system-design initiatives is *facilitated care* [17]. This involves transferring the care of the patient to a primary care provider or specialist, to whom the patient will have easy and fast access, when he/she needs. Facilitated care can be provided (1) with regular pro-active follow-up with planned care visits to a primary care provider or a specialist at important points during the care delivery process, such as discharge from hospital or emergency room, and (2) by defining the roles of the care providers in these visits, for ensuring that the patients receive appropriate care at the right place and at the right time with these planned interactions [17, 27]. There is now a considerable literature showing that case management and facilitated care can be effective in improving continuity of care, quality of life and patient satisfaction for chronic diseases [38, 46, 47].

4.2.2.2 Community Health Care Teams

Another building block of C-bC systems is community health care teams, which provide the full range of interventions in a certain geographical region. The increased continuity and accessibility of care constitute the main advantages of such teams. The ability of mobile teams to contact patients at home, at work and in neutral locations such as local cafes means that early relapses are identified and treated more often, and that treatment may be better adhered to [21, 38]. Recent studies have also shown that efficiently run teams can achieve reductions in hospital admissions as well as acute inpatient bed-days, while patient satisfaction is improved.

One of the successful examples of C-bC initiatives is the Integrated Diabetes Health Care Service Delivery Project in Manitoba (http://www.diabetesintegrationproject.ca). This project is based on a mobile diabetes care and treatment model that (1) addresses the needs of people already diagnosed with diabetes by providing them with direct services to help monitor their diabetes status, (2) screens and prevents further complications from developing, and (3) provides diabetes education to clients to encourage self-management. In a similar initiative run by Scrips Health, Project Dulse, community-based diabetes care and management is provided to thousands of ethnically diverse and low-income patients in San Diego County [7]. (http://www.scripps.org/services/diabetes/project-dulse)

4.2.2.3 Long-Term Community-Based Residential Care

Another important service in the context of C-bC is the long-term community-based residential care. This involves providing a wide-array of health and personal services in the home environment to people who would otherwise be cared for in nursing homes or other institutional settings. Examples include adult day care, personal care, personal emergency response system, environmental adaptations, home delivery meals, nursing care at home, transportation, and medical equipment [19, 30, 31]. They are significantly less expensive and preferable for those patients who do not need intensive nursing care [35, 36].

4.2.2.4 Community-Based Rehabilitation

One of the major objectives of CDM programs is facilitating functional independence and community reintegration [20]. Rehabilitation (including physiotherapy, occupational therapy, speech language pathology, dietitian services and social work) is the most important intervention in reducing death, disability and dependency for the chronic conditions [8]. It involves a combined and coordinated use of medical, social, educational, and vocational measures for retraining individuals to reach their maximal physical, psychological, social, and a vocational potential [27].

Community-based rehabilitation programs combine coordinated in-home care and access to in-home, and/or community ambulatory rehabilitation. The strong scientific evidence supports that for higher functioning patients; these programs reduce inpatient hospital stays and significantly improve function and quality of life [1, 20]. It also provides a cost-effective alternative to the traditional in-patient rehabilitation care [34]. Community-based rehabilitation also promotes community reintegration and provides social and emotional support for patients and their caregivers. It includes public facilities and recreation programs that assist in maintaining mobility and functional skills and provide peer support, such as clubs for the group of patients with specific chronic condition.

4.3 Characteristics of Community-Based Care

Quantitative decision models are effective tools in order to (1) understand and evaluate a C-bC system for a specific chronic illness in a specific geographic region, and (2) investigate the potential of alternative policies/interventions to improve the system. Understanding and assessment of C-bC systems, however, present a unique set of methodological challenges.

The first challenge is accounting for the *multiple care-provider patterns*. Chronic care is often delivered by multiple caregivers with different characteristics in different settings e.g., by a family physician in his/her office or by a specialist in an emergency department. Note that randomized controlled trials and observational studies usually ignore multiple care provider patterns and assume that care is given by a single provider [16]. Second, chronic care requires *repeated interaction with the patient* whose disease progression over time is a function of the time between consecutive visits and the health state and care received at the prior visit [2, 4, 7]. The third challenge is avoiding *case-mix bias*. Older patients with multiple diseases, for example, may have worse health outcomes than younger patients with a single disease, independent of the quality of care they receive. Consequently, the care-providers who see older patients may appear to provide lower quality of care than those who see younger patients with less co-morbidity. Accounting for these patient characteristics is an essential feature of fair and accurate assessment of quality of C-bC. Finally, patients with specific characteristics, such as age, sex, or

Table 4.1 Key characteristics of C-bC [37]

- *Accessibility*: patients' ability to receive care where and when it is needed
- *Autonomy*: a patient's ability to make independent decisions and choices, despite the presence of symptoms or disabilities
- *Comprehensiveness*: a service characteristic with two dimensions: (1) the extent to which a service is provided across the entire range of disease severity, and the wide range of patient characteristics; (2) the availability of the basic components of care, and their use by prioritized groups of patients
- *Continuity*: an uninterrupted series of contacts with care providers over the long term
- *Coordination*: a service characteristic resulting in coherent treatment plans for individual patients
- *Equity*: the fair distribution of resources across different patient groups

health problems, choose and remain with care-providers who have specific characteristics, such as specialty training or practice style. Patients in a care-provider's practice might therefore "cluster," that is, be more like each other and differ from patients who are drawn to another provider's practice. Accounting for *care-provider level clustering* is therefore another key feature of scientifically sound profiling of quality of care [10].

Effectively and efficiently designed C-bC services embody several key characteristics as identified by [37]. Table 4.1 depicts these principles that need to be incorporated in quantitative models.

We now turn to the distinguishing features of C-bC systems that need to be incorporated in mathematical models. It is important to recognize that the majority of C-bC services are publicly funded programs. In such non-profit and/or public care delivery models, the most natural objective is to maximize aggregate health outcomes of the target population subject to resource constraints [7]. Based on the discussion above, Table 4.2 presents taxonomy of the three papers that will be discussed in the following sections.

4.4 Community-Based Care for Mental Health

4.4.1 Background of the Problem

The first example of quantitative decision models that will be presented in the context of this chapter is one of the first papers on C-bC [18]. This paper focuses on the operational, capacity allocation and planning, decisions for community-based rehabilitation teams for the mentally ill patients. As it is the case for many other chronic diseases, a series of laws and regulations in developed countries strongly recommend on deinstitutionalization, "the process by which patients are returned to live in the least-restrictive environment." As discussed in Sect. 4.2, one way of deinstitutionalization is community-based rehabilitation (which is called

Table 4.2 Taxonomy of the representative papers on C-bC

	Leff et al. [18]	Deo et al. [7]	Kucukyazici et al. [16]
C-bC building blocks			
Primary Care with Specialist Backup			X
Community health care teams		X	
Long-term residential C-bC			
Community-based Rehabilitation	X		
C-bC principles			
Accessibility		X	X
Autonomy			X
Comprehensiveness	X	X	
Continuity	X	X	X
Coordination	X	X	
Equity			
Model components			
Dynamic/static	Dynamic (LP)	Dynamic (MDP)	Static (Markov Chain)
Stochastic/deterministic	Stochastic	Stochastic	Stochastic
Objective	Several performance measures	*Max.* total QALY for patient cohort	*Min.* # of Mortality & Admissions to LTC
Constraints	Capacity	Capacity	

Community Support System, CSS, in the paper), where the teams who provide this rehabilitation cover therapeutic and psychosocial rehabilitation services such as community residences, day treatment programs, and sheltered workshops.

While designing community-based rehabilitation services for mentally ill patients, CSS administrators are responsible for designing and managing the treatment programs for their patients by assigning a set of services that best satisfy their needs depending on resource availability. Because of limited resources, the patients compete for the limited resources. Due to the nature of the chronic disease, the patient requires repeated interactions with the CSS team. Accordingly, the patient's treatment needs to be adjusted as the patient responds to treatment over time. Ideally, CSS managers would be able to design, with no restrictions, individual programs for their patients. Therefore Leff et al. [18] present a multi-period resource planning and policy evaluation model to aid CCS administrators in making their resource allocation decisions by optimizing the decisions for allocating the resources to programs and assigning programs to patients.

4.4.2 The Methodology

In [18], Leff and his colleagues provide a framework in which to structure the resource-allocation decision faced by CSS managers. The framework has three main components: (1) patient aggregation, (2) design of programs, and (3) measurement of performance.

For patient aggregation, it is assumed that the population of chronically mentally ill persons can be clustered into relatively homogeneous categories that are meaningful for program planning; that is, patients within each category have similar needs and have similar responses to treatment. To categorize the population of chronically mentally ill persons in this way, they employ a functional level classification scheme. To be more specific, the authors define functional levels such that patients in different functional levels will have different service needs and will receive different service and treatment packages, i.e., coordination of care. Furthermore, the functional levels are defined so that the progression of patients can be viewed as improvement in functional levels. Being able to classify patients in this manner permits one to model a mental health care system as a dynamic process, in which patients move from one functional level to another depending upon the services provided. For treatment programs, it is assumed that a set of service packages can be identified, where a service package can consist of a residential assignment, and participation in specific social, psychotherapeutic, and rehabilitative programs. Service packages must meet certain minimal needs of patients. Because patients in different functional levels have different service needs, not all service packages are appropriate for all functional levels.

A patient's functional level can improve, get worse or remain the same based on the service packages assigned. It is assumed that a Markov property applies to patient transitions. Namely, the probability that a patient in functional level i makes a transition (improvement, regression, or no change) to functional level j within a certain period of time depends on the current functional level of the patient and on the service package that is assigned to the patient, which captures the effects of continuity of care (regular visits and given treatment in these visits) on health outcomes. Inherent in this assumption is an underlying time period for modeling patient transitions as well as for making resource decisions. Furthermore, for planning purposes they assume that patient transitions occur exactly at their expected value despite the probabilistic nature of individual patient movements.

The assignment of service packages to patients is restricted by a set of resource constraints. It is assumed that each service package consumes a certain amount of each resource per patient per period and that the system has limited resources in each time period. The model assigns service packages to patients in each period of the planning horizon, explicitly taking into account the end-of-period transitions and resource constraints, to optimize some multi-period measure of system performance. The methodology proposes several measures of performance, including maximizing the total of improvements in functional levels and minimizing the number of patients with minimum functional level at the end of the planning horizon.

4.4.3 *Findings and Implications*

In order to demonstrate the potential value of the planning model, the authors analyzed various scenarios using different objective functions with an illustrative data set. The mixed integer programming solution determines what service packages should be assigned to each patient group in each period. By examining the assignments of service packages over time, the authors aim to determine the dominant service package assignment for each patient type. Providing the dominant service package for each patient group is an effective way for CSS managers to allocate available resources. The dominant assignments can determine what service package mix should be available at the CSS.

An important limitation of the proposed model is that its generalizability is limited. The authors focus on a specific institution in defining the problem and developing the model. In particular the service packages are defined in an institute specific way. Furthermore, the uncertainties associated with the future outcomes of temporal decisions are not incorporated.

4.5 Capacity Allocation in Community-Based Care

4.5.1 *Background of the Problem*

As discussed in Sect. 4.2, one of the objectives of C-bC is reducing the disparities by improving the access to the healthcare. In this context, Deo and his colleagues [7] study a model of community-based health care delivery for chronic diseases in order to improve the care accessibility. To be more specific, this paper focuses on investigating how improved capacity allocation in C-bC can improve health outcomes for a population of asthmatic children.

The problem setting is on school-based mobile clinics, which provide school-based asthma care for inner city children. Such mobile clinics provide continuous patient follow-up using appointment scheduling and periodic school visits for asthmatic children. In the current implementation of the problem context, each asthma mobile clinic visits one school and serves at most certain number of scheduled patients per day. Given a list of registered active schools and a schedule of visits to these schools, the capacity allocation at each school is determined through daily patient schedules. The schedules are based on the medically recommended treatment duration of the patients and are modified based on the available capacity at each school. Scheduling is performed in two steps with disjoint operational and clinical considerations. First, physicians recommend a due date for the next visit that is primarily driven by a patient's control status. Based on the physician assignments and available mobile clinic capacity, schedulers develop a feasible allocation of capacity among the school population for that visit. In this context, the key issue to be addressed is whether a systematic framework to integrate capacity constraints directly in the recommended intervals between visits increases the effectiveness of program.

4.5.2 The Methodology

To address this problem, Deo et al. [7] formulate a discrete time finite horizon discounted Markov Decision Process (MDP) comprising patients with different health states that compete for limited appointment slots in each period. The modeling framework integrates both operational and clinical decisions. Patients periodically access care, which influences their disease progression and their health outcomes. The provider decides which class of patients to schedule at the beginning of each period. Therapy is provided to scheduled patients, which improves their health states temporarily. Patients that are not seen follow their natural disease progression. It is assumed that there is a fixed schedule of equally spaced visits to a school.

In order to capture the disease progress for patient groups with different characteristics, Deo and his colleagues [7] define a homogenous patient population of I patients, whose disease progression is governed by a Markov process over discrete health states. At the beginning of each period, patient i's health state is given by $s_{it} = (h_{it};n_{it})$, where h_{it} represents the health state at the last appointment, and n_{it} represents the time since last appointment measured by number of periods.

The natural disease progression, without any medical intervention, is characterized by per period transition matrix P. It is assumed that the treatment effect occurs immediately after the appointment, improving the patient's current health state. This is modeled by an upper triangular treatment matrix Q. After the treatment effect occurs, the patient's disease progression is again governed by P. Thus, the effective state transition of patients can be interpreted as a Markov chain with two transition rates that depend on the time since the last visit: the patient transition matrix is $Q \times P$ for the first period after the visit and P for all subsequent periods until the next appointment, where it is assumed that the natural disease progression and treatment process to be independent of each other.

At the time of making capacity allocation decisions, the beginning of period t, the health care provider does not know the current health state of the patients with certainty. Instead the provider has a belief about the patient's health state. Accordingly, random variable x_{it} is defined to denote Patient i's true health state at the beginning of Period t and the distribution of x_{it} for patient i with state $s_{it} = (h_{it};n_{it})$, is characterized. The defined distribution is referred as the information vector of patient i at the beginning of period t, which represents the health care provider's belief about patient i's true health state at the beginning of period t before a capacity allocation decision is made and the patient is seen.

The objective is maximizing the quality adjusted life years (QALY) for the entire patient cohort, where the intermediate reward for patient i is defined as the quality of life (QoL) score associated with health state k. The capacity allocation decision is a binary decision variables a_{it}, where $a_{it} = 1$ if Patient i is scheduled in period t, and $a_{it} = 0$ otherwise. Assuming that all scheduled patients attend their appointments, the total number of scheduled appointments limited to C, capacity in each period, by capacity constraint.

4.5.3 Findings and Implications

The authors characterize the optimal policy for stylized version of the problem and use this characterization to formulate a heuristic for the more general version of the problem. Following this, they calibrate operational and disease progression models using data from Mobile C.A.R.E. Foundation, a community-based provider of pediatric asthma care in Chicago. For realistic size problem instances, it is shown that the heuristic can improve the health gains of the community by up to 15 % over the current policy of Mobile C.A.R.E. Foundation. An important implication of this study is showing that significant improvement in health outcomes can be obtained by altering the scheduling policy to systematically integrate clinical and operational decisions. The proposed policy can flexibly adjust visit frequencies to accommodate limited capacity and prioritize patients in worse health states. Even with this prioritization, all patients are seen during the period of study, leading to greater access to all patients.

The authors highlight the assumption that all scheduled patients show up according to their appointment schedule as a main limitation of the model. Another assumption that constrains applicability of the model is its sole focus on returning patients. Although this makes sense from a continuity of care policy perspective, the relaxation of this assumption by incorporating the arrival of new patients in the model would be an important step at the right direction.

4.6 Improvement of Care Provider Pathways

4.6.1 Background of the Problem

Kucukyazici and her colleagues [16] develop a methodological framework in order to examine the patterns of care and the effect of these diverse patterns on health outcomes of chronic diseases. The aim is to present a systematic approach to extend the epidemiologic model to incorporate multiple care-provider patterns. The proposed analytical framework allows (1) understand and evaluating a community-based chronic care system for a specific chronic illness, and (2) investigate the potential of alternative interventions to improve the system. The methodology is built on the analytical epidemiologic model, which the authors extend so as to

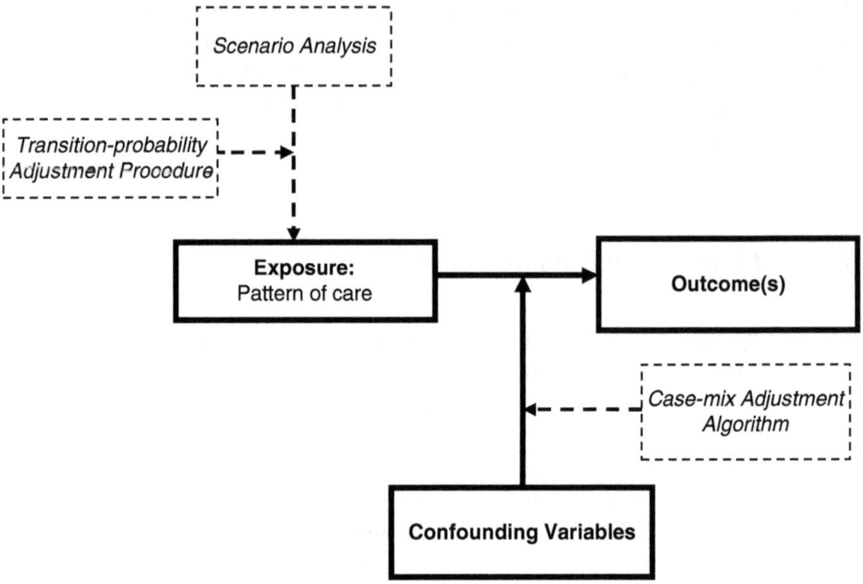

Fig. 4.3 Methodological framework of Kucukyazici et al. [16]

incorporate the distinctive features of C-bC. In particular, they model the multiple care-provider visit patterns of patients with a specific chronic illness by utilizing a patient flow approach. The patterns of care received by a group of patients are represented in a compact form by means of a Markov model that is based on a disease-specific state space. They also develop algorithms to deal with the case-mix biases and the provider level clustering of the patients. The methodology brings together epidemiological methods with operations research in modeling the patterns of C-bC. The framework enables us to investigate the system-wide impact of several plausible scenarios and to assess the effectiveness of alternative interventions.

4.6.2 The Methodology

Figure 4.3 is a schematic representation of the proposed methodology. The boldface rectangles represent the basic epidemiologic model, whereas the dashed rectangles constitute the extensions to the basic model so as to address the differentiating features of C-bC. Note that the pattern of care and the traditional health outcomes correspond to the exposure and the outcomes of the epidemiologic model, respectively. The confounding variables, also known as case-mix variables, are expected to influence the care patterns and increase the risk of poor outcomes.

The methodology comprises three phases. The first phase of the methodology focuses on describing the patterns of C-bC, i.e., the exposures in the epidemiologic model. To this end, they use a Markov model that represents the stochastic process governing the movement of a typical patient from one care-provider or health care setting to the next. In the final model the transition probabilities correspond to the likelihoods of visiting the each care-provider and transitioning to each health outcome. The Markov model can be helpful *to develop an understanding of the disease-specific chronic care process.*

The second phase is the assessment of the association between these patterns of care and selected health outcomes. The likelihood of transitioning to each health outcome, produced by a Markov model, provides inputs to examine *whether the different patterns of care are associated with differences in rates of health outcomes*. If an association is found, it is required to determine whether the association is valid i.e., the potential roles of confounders and chance need to be taken into account.

As an alternative to the homogeneity assumption of Markov models, and stratification and regression adjustments, the authors propose a *case-mix adjustment algorithm* for dealing with confounding variables, while avoiding the potential limitations of the stratification method and allowing adjustment with only stratum-specific measures rather than individual-level data. The algorithm is intended to cancel out the confounding effect of case-mix variables. To this end, the transition probabilities are adjusted to offset the differences between case-mix variables of the patient group who follows the associated sub-path and the entire patient population.

The final phase of the methodology focuses on scenario analysis in order to *evaluate the potential impact of alternative intervention strategies on health outcomes*. A typical intervention involves increasing the accessibility of a care-provider in the delivery of C-bC to a subgroup of patients. To represent this change they modify the associated transition probabilities in the model which amounts to redirecting a portion of the patient subgroup to an alternate care provider. However, the patient profiles of the original and the alternate care providers may be different and the redirected patients may not follow the patterns of care common to the patients of the alternate care provider. Therefore, the probabilities that represent transitions to/from alternate care providers may not be same as the ones in the base-line model due to the new distribution of case-mix variables of the alternate care provider. Accordingly [16], develops a transition-probability adjustment procedure in order to deal with the care-provider clustering of patients, while analyzing a scenario. Thus, the changes in the case-mix variables of the patient groups treated by both care providers are reflected in the transition probabilities via the adjustment procedure.

4.6.3 Case Study

In order to provide a basis for redesign initiatives aiming at effective community-based post-stroke care in Quebec, the authors apply their framework to the data set of about 4,000 stroke patients discharged from one of Quebec's acute care hospitals to their homes. The care-providers and settings of care for stroke survivors are classified into five major categories: known primary-care provider (PCP), new PCP, specialist, emergency room (ER), and acute-care-hospital. They define mortality and admission to long-term care as health outcomes. The data for the study were obtained from the administrative databases maintained by the provincial Ministry of Health and Social Services in Quebec, Canada. In particular, the Quebec Department of Social Insurance (RAMQ) database provides records of all fee-for-service encounters with the healthcare system. By using fee-for-service billing records, they identify the care-provider visit paths of each patient through the defined five types of care providers and two health outcomes.

The authors analyze the potential impact of various interventions that proved effective in the context of other diseases. The tested scenarios include planned care visits (1) at discharge from hospital, (2) as a follow-up to an ER visit; and (3) regular visits arranged by the case managers for rehospitalized patients. For (1) and (2), they also analyze the options of planning the visits to a PCP or a specialist in order to define the potential roles of these care providers while designing interventions.

4.6.4 Findings and Implications

The results indicate that with the information of the immediate past and current care-provider visited, the likelihood of the patterns that the patient would follow can be predicted accurately and health outcomes associated with various patterns can be projected. It is important that the rates of mortality and institutionalization were much higher following readmission to hospital (although these rates varied according to the health care contact before readmission to hospital). Therefore, their analysis points out that a window of opportunity exists for interventions designed to avoid certain critical sub-paths in providing C-bC to a stroke survivor.

Patient characteristics, including age, socioeconomic status, comorbid conditions, and health and lifestyle behaviors, have long been understood to have a direct and independent effect on health outcomes. Kucukyazici and her colleagues [16] observed that patients with specific characteristics, such as age, sex, or health problems, choose and remain with care-providers who have specific characteristics, such as specialty training or practice style. They made an explicit effort to account for "care-provider" level clustering in analyzing the potential impact of alternative interventions.

The proposed framework can be applied to a variety of chronic illnesses, health care settings and target populations in order to provide a basis for design of community-based care systems. This methodology is an effective tool that provides a road map to clinicians and system planners in developing chronic disease management strategies, and designing community-based care.

The proposed framework does not incorporate the time between consecutive visits, which amounts to the rather stringent assumption that the visits are equidistant on the timeline. A semi-Markov model would be a natural way for incorporating the actual time lags between consecutive care provider visits. Another limitation of this study is that the realized benefits could possibly remain below the anticipated levels, mainly due to the effect of some possible confounding variables that were not incorporated in the model. For example, the lifestyle choices and the behavioral characteristics of each individual can be such confounders.

4.7 Conclusions and Policy Implications

In this chapter, we present a systematic view of C-bC management and provide selective examples of quantitative decision models developed for various chronic diseases. It is evident from the schematic representation in Fig. 4.1 that effective C-bC requires a multi-disciplinary and multi-organizational effort. This involves collaboration of different health care providers in a coordinated system, i.e., a regional chain of caregivers working together in an organized way to provide adequate care at all stages of care.

A CDM system must coordinate and promote patient access to the full range of activities and services associated with all related institutions, in order to provide a comprehensive, integrated, effective and efficient approach to any chronic disease. The effectiveness of such a system is dependent on the management of the inter-component activities, as well as those within each organization. Although individual components of a CDM system may be well developed, these components often operate in isolation and the resulting lack of coordination creates bottlenecks to providing the patients with a *continuum of care* through the overall system [27].

Because of the complex dynamic structure of the chronic care, the failures in the management of one component affect the efficiency of others. It is critically important to look carefully at each component to develop an understanding on (1) how the care given in each of the distinct components can be improved, and (2) how these distinct components can be better integrated into systems of care. Quantitative decision models can play a major role in helping care providers and policy makers in designing and improving a C-bC system toward the two main goals discussed above.

The overview we provide in this chapter reveals that C-bC, particularly in the context of CDM, is an understudied area in the management science literature. Below we discuss four avenues for future research. The *allocation of resources* among hospitals (and other acute care facilities), and C-bC is a pressing challenge for many governments. Note that acute care facilities traditionally have priority over C-bC systems in terms of resource allocation. Note, however, that inadequate resources for C-bC delay inpatient discharge and may affect the efficiency of acute care. Effective delivery of C-bC improves not only the short-term health outcomes but also the long-term outcomes such as recurrence risk of the disease, complications of treatment, long-term care costs, the indirect cost of impact on caregivers and losses of economic productivity of the patient and caregiver. All these issues make the resource allocation and capacity management decisions between acute care and C-bC relatively complex. In this context, decision models are needed to support such resource allocation decisions by evaluating all these dynamic and stochastic issues, and limited availability of resources.

Another area that needs the attention of operations researchers is the *accessibility to the care*. C-bC programs have high potential to improve the outcomes by providing social and emotional support for patients and caregivers. However, the effectiveness of these programs mostly depends on the accessibility of health services. The lack of public transportation, for example, can make it difficult for some patients to go to healthcare facilities, unless their health status necessitates immediate care. The locations of C-bC programs and providing the necessary transportation system are essential in order to achieve the expected outcomes. Location and network design models can contribute significantly in this domain.

An *equitable distribution of resources* across different patient groups is one of the key characteristics of effectively and efficiently designed C-bC services. As shown in Table 4.2, however, equity is an understudied feature while modeling the design of C-bC services in the management science domain. Incorporation of this key issue in modeling efforts as well as studying the trade-offs between efficiency and equity in designing C-bC services is would be a significant contribution.

Last, but not the least, well-designed procedures are necessary for the *assignment of patients to the most suitable C-bC programs* among the alternatives. The literature recommends different alternatives for different patient groups, but the only criterion for deciding on the best option is disease severity. However, the decisions on the selection of the most appropriate C-bC program setting, timing and duration depend on many factors such as: expected prognosis of recovery, availability of caregiver support, and the match between patient's and caregiver's needs with the type and intensity of therapy [27]. Including all these factors in the decision-making process requires patient-centered procedures rather than general guidelines. Decision tools can be designed to assist these decisions taken in a quite complex environment, in order to optimize recovery, and improve quality of life.

References

1. Anderson C, Rubenach S, Mhurchu CN et al. (2000) Home or hospital for stroke rehabilitation? Results of a randomized trial. Stroke 31:1024–1031
2. Bodenheimer T, Wagner EH, Grumbach K (2002) Improving primary care for patients with chronic illness: the chronic care model, Part 2. J Am Med Assoc 288(15):1909–1914
3. Brandeau ML, Sainfort F, Pierskalla WP (2004) Operations research and health care: a handbook of methods and applications. Kluwer's International Series. Kluwer Academic, Boston

4. Casalino LP (2005) Disease management and the organization of physician practice. J Am Med Assoc 293:485–488
5. CDC (2007) Statistics on disease conditions. Center of Disease Control, Atlanta, GA
6. CIHI (2011) Health care in Canada 2010, Canadian Institute for Health Information. http://secure.cihi.ca/cihiweb/products/HCIC_2010_Web_e.pdf. Accessed 9 Aug 2011
7. Deo S, Iravani S, Jingo T, Smilowitz K, Samuelson S (2010) Improving access to community-based chronic care through improved capacity allocation. Working paper. http://ssrn.com/abstract=1700909
8. Dombovy ML, Sandok BA, Basford JR (1986) Rehabilitation of stroke: a review. Stroke 17(3):363–369
9. Gask L, Sibbald B, Creed F (1997) Evaluating models of working at the interface between mental health services and primary care. Br J Psychiatry 170:6–11
10. Greenfield S, Kaplan SH, Kahn R et al. (2002) Profiling care provided by different groups of physicians: effects of patient case-mix (bias) and physician-level clustering on quality assessment results. Ann Intern Med 36(2):111–121
11. Hindmarsh M (2008) The chronic care model. The first Canadian healthcare conference, April 2008
12. Hollander MJ, Pallan P (1995) The British Columbia continuing care system: service delivery and resource planning. Aging 7(2):94–109
13. Improving Chronic Illness Care (2007) http://www.improvingchroniccare.org/about/workwith.html. Accessed 14 Nov 2008
14. Indiana State Department of Health (2005) http://www.indianacdmprogram.com/Chronicnewsrelease.pdf. Accessed 10 July 2011
15. Jones C, Clement L, Morphew T, Kwong K, Hanley-Lopez J, Lifson F, Opas L, Guterman J (2007) Achieving and maintaining asthma control in an urban pediatric disease management program: the breathmobile program. J Allergy Clin Immunol 119(6):1445–1145
16. Kucukyazici B, Verter V, Mayo N (2011) An analytical framework for designing community-based care delivery processes for chronic diseases. Prod Oper Manag 20(3):474–488
17. Kucukyazici B, Verter V, Nadeau L, Mayo N (2009) Improving post-stroke health outcomes: can facilitated care help? Health Policy 93:180–187
18. Leff S, Dada M, Graves S (1986) An LP planning model for a mental health community support system. Manag Sci 32(2):139–155
19. Lin F, Kong N, Lawley M (2011) Capacity planning for publicly funded community based long-term care services. In: Johnson M (ed) Community-based operations research: introduction, theory and applications. Springer, New York
20. Mayo NE, Wood-Dauphinee S, Côté R (2000) There's no place like home: an evaluation of early supported discharge for stroke. Stroke 31:1016–1023
21. McDonald HP, Garg AX, Haynes RB (2002) Interventions to enhance patient adherence to medication prescriptions: scientific review. J Am Med Assoc 288:2868–2879
22. McGonigle JJ, Krouk M, Hindmarsh D, Campano-Small C (1992) Understanding partial hospitalization through a continuity-of-care model. Int J Partial Hosp 8(2):135–140
23. PHAC (2007) Canadian report on chronic diseases. Public Health Agency of Canada, Ottawa, ON
24. Renders CM, Valk GD, Griffin SJ et al. (2001) Interventions to improve the management of diabetes in primary care, outpatient, and community. Diabetes Care 24:1821–1833
25. Robles SC (2004) A public health framework for chronic disease prevention and control. Food Nutr Bull 25(2):194–199
26. Rothman AA, Wagner EH (2003) Chronic illness management: what is the role of primary care? Ann Intern Med 138:256–261
27. Schwamm LH, Pancioli A, Acker JE et al. (2005) Recommendations for the establishment of stroke systems of care. Stroke 36:690–703
28. Simon GE (2002) Evidence review: efficacy and effectiveness of anti-depressant treatment in primary care. Gen Hosp Psychiatry 24:213–224

29. Singh D, Ham C (2006) Improving care for people with long-term conditions: the review of UK and international frameworks. Report of NHS institute for innovation and improvement primary care/long term conditions program. http://www.improvingchroniccare.org/downloads/review_of_international_frameworks__chris_hamm.pdf. Accessed 7 Jan 2011
30. Smith G, O'Keefe J, Carpenter L, Doty P, Kennedy G, Burwell B, Mollica R, Williams L (2000) Understanding medicaid home and community services: a primer. U.S. Department of Health and Human Services Office of the Assistant Secretary for Planning and Evaluation, Washington DC
31. Stone R (2000) Long-term care for the elderly with disabilities: current policy, emerging trends, and implications for the twenty-first century. Milbank Memorial Fund, New York
32. Stuart M, Weinrich M (2001) Home and community based long-term care: lessons from Denmark. Gerontologist 41:474–480
33. Temmink D, Hutten JB, Francke AL et al. (2001) Rheumatology out-patient nurse clinics: a valuable addition? Arthritis Rheum 45:280–286
34. Teng J, Mayo NE, Latimer E et al. (2003) Costs and caregiver consequences of early supported discharge for stroke patients. Stroke 34:528–536
35. The Kaiser Commission on Medicaid and the Uninsured (2009) Kaiser: Medicaid: a primer. http://www.k_.org/medicaid/upload/7334-03.pdf
36. The Kaiser Family Foundation (2009) Kaiser: health care costs: a primer
37. Thornicroft G, Tansella M (1999) Translating ethical principles into outcome measures for mental health service research. Psychol Med 29:761–767
38. Thornicroft G, Tansella M (2003) What are the arguments for community-based mental health care? WHO regional office for Europe, health evidence network report, Copenhagen
39. Tsai AC, Morton SC, Mangione CM, Keeler EB (2005) A meta-analysis of interventions to improve care for chronic illnesses. Am J Manag Care 11(8):478–488
40. Von Korff M, Goldberg D (2001) Improving outcomes in depression: the whole process of care needs to be enhanced. Br Med J 323:948–949
41. Wagner EE, Austin BT, Connie D et al. (2001) Improving chronic illness care: translating evidence to action. Health Aff 20(6):64–78
42. Wagner EH (1998) Chronic disease management: what will it take to improve care for chronic illness? Eff Clin Pract 1:2–4
43. Wellingham J, Tracey J, Rea H, Gribben B (2003) The development and implementation of the Chronic Care Management Programme in Counties Manukau. J N Z Med Assoc 116:1169–1175
44. Wennberg J, Gittelsohn A (1982) Variations in medical care among small areas. Sci Am 246:120–134
45. WHO (2002) Innovative care for chronic conditions: building blocks for action. World Health Organization, Geneva
46. Ziguras SJ, Stuart GW, Jackson AC (2002) Assessing the evidence on case management. Br J Psychiatry 181:17–21
47. Ziguras SJ, Stuart GW (2000) A meta-analysis of the effectiveness of mental health case management over 20 years. Psychiatr Serv 51:1410–1421

Chapter 5
Project Management Approach to Implement Clinical Pathways: An Example for Thyroidectomy

Yasar A. Ozcan, Elena Tànfani, and Angela Testi

Abstract Clinical pathway is a concept that from a managerial point of view promotes variance reduction in the delivery of health care and, therefore, is able to reduce costs. To achieve this, health care providers must improve efficiency in the use of resources while completing delivery of care in time with expected achievements in quality. Implementation of the clinical pathways for a specific disease requires a clear identification of tasks that compose the care delivery process by a multi-professional team including physicians, nurses, various therapists and/or health technologist and so on. From this perspective, implementing clinical pathways for a disease can be, therefore, conceptualized as an integrated project with many tasks. Hence, the management of the care delivery tasks in time nicely fits into project management, an operations research tool. With this conceptualization, we test the potential use of project management to organize the integrated care delivery tasks of the thyroid disease as a project. Probabilistic and deterministic project management models have been implemented and solved for a real case study to demonstrate the estimated duration for the clinical pathway, where critical activities must be carefully monitored by the caregiving team to reduce or eliminate the variation in care delivery.

Y.A. Ozcan (✉)
Department of Health Administration, Virginia Commonwealth University, Richmond, VA 23298-0203, USA
e-mail: ozcan@vcu.edu

E. Tànfani • A. Testi
Department of Economics and Business Studies, School of Social Sciences, University of Genova, Via Vivaldi 5, Genova, Italy
e-mail: etanfani@economia.unige.it; testi@economia.unige.it

G.S. Zaric (ed.), *Operations Research and Health Care Policy*,
International Series in Operations Research & Management Science 190,
DOI 10.1007/978-1-4614-6507-2_5,

5.1 Introduction and Problem Addressed

One of the ongoing critical issues in health care is variation in clinical delivery process. Many research articles on many diseases have tried to identify this problem, but not so many have suggested systematic improvements using management science models that are readily available. "Clinical Pathway" is a concept that promotes variance reduction in delivery of health care. To achieve this, health care providers must improve efficiency in the use of resources while completing delivery of care in time with expected achievements in quality. Implementation of clinical pathways requires identification of tasks of a care delivery for a specific disease by a multi-professional team including physicians, nurses, various therapists and/or health technologist and so on [16].

Clinical pathways were first introduced in the early 1990s in UK and USA, and then their application spread throughout the Western world [17]. Clinical Pathways, also known as Integrated Care Pathways, Multidisciplinary pathways of care, Pathways of Care, Care Maps, Collaborative Care Pathways, are "health-care structured multidisciplinary plans that describe spatial and temporal sequences of activities to be performed, based on the scientific and technical knowledge and the organizational, professional and technological available resources" [2]. Clinical Pathways provide organizational and therapeutic guidelines for each phase of the healing process of a patient (therapies, surgery, etc.). They can be seen as algorithms described by flow-charts where they detail the set of decisions and treatments to be given to the patient, with a logic based on sequential phases. Hence, they can be considered an operational tool in the clinical treatment of diseases, from a patient-focused point of view [9] and can be conceptualized as flow process to the improve patients' healthcare.

More specifically, the process focuses on the patients' movement in receiving care, rather than on the care received from each specialty independently. Hence, emphasis is placed on specialty caregivers working together for the patient's given illness in coherence as a multi-professional care delivery teams. The whole process from an operations research/management science perspective can be viewed as an integrated project with many tasks. Thus, the management of the care delivery tasks in time nicely fits into a well-known operations research/management science tool, project management. In order to organize the integrated care delivery tasks as a project, all medical specialties and professions that contribute to the process must be involved in the development and implementation of this process.

A case study pertaining to thyroidectomy is presented. Thyroidectomy is a surgical intervention aimed at removing the thyroid gland when the patient has a thyroid cancer or other pathological conditions of the thyroid gland, as for example the multinodular goiter. Data have been collected through the collaboration of the Endocrine Surgery Unit of the San Martino University Hospital sited in Genova (Italy).

This chapter is organized as follows. In Sect. 5.2, the background and motivation of the study is presented, with a particular attention to clinical pathways in general and to the thyroid disease in particular. Section 5.3 includes model and project management tool, together with the data sources for the case study. In Sect. 5.4, the results of the application to thyroidectomy treatment are discussed. Finally, the conclusions and policy implications of the presented approach are presented in Sect. 5.5.

5.2 Background

According to the American Medical Association variations in health care delivery and utilization implies higher costs and less than desirable quality. Thus, to improve quality physicians and health care providers must be exposed to information on how to standardize the care [14]. Some of the variation in care can be explained through patient health status and preferences. However, the unexplained portion of the variation generally represents waste and inefficiency [15]. Hence, standardization of care delivery through operational research methods may provide the necessary information to care delivery team, including physicians. This standardization in turn could eliminate unnecessary tasks and cost and improve quality of care delivery [3, 6]. The clinical pathway is a method that enables such standardization in care delivery. This methodology has been adopted for various diseases by National Institutes of Health in various countries (including USA and UK) as well as medical associations to standardize the care.

5.2.1 Clinical Pathways

In many clinical situations pathways can describe standardized procedures to be followed by more or less than 80 % of patients while accommodating some exceptions. Whether a patient requires surgery, and whether that surgery is a day surgery or an in-patient procedure, a reliable pathway should identify just resources to meet patient demand with matched supply of services in a standardized way to reduce variation [9].

Visualizing what procedures are performed on patients during treatment processes, test results, and paperwork against key stages can highlight differences in explaining the variation. An example for the colonic pathway (Fig. 5.1), illustrated by National Health Institutes of Scotland for ten patients, helps us to understand the extent of the variation for patient treatment. In this example patients went through this pathway with specified physicians (consultants). The variation ranges between 21 and 167 days from referral to treatment. Moreover, a close examination of ten patients treated by three different consultants reveals that patients who went through the same path in their treatment spent different numbers of days in the process, and this is impacted by whom they have been seeing as consultant. For instance, patients 1, 3, 4, 5, 9, and 10 had similar treatments, but those handled

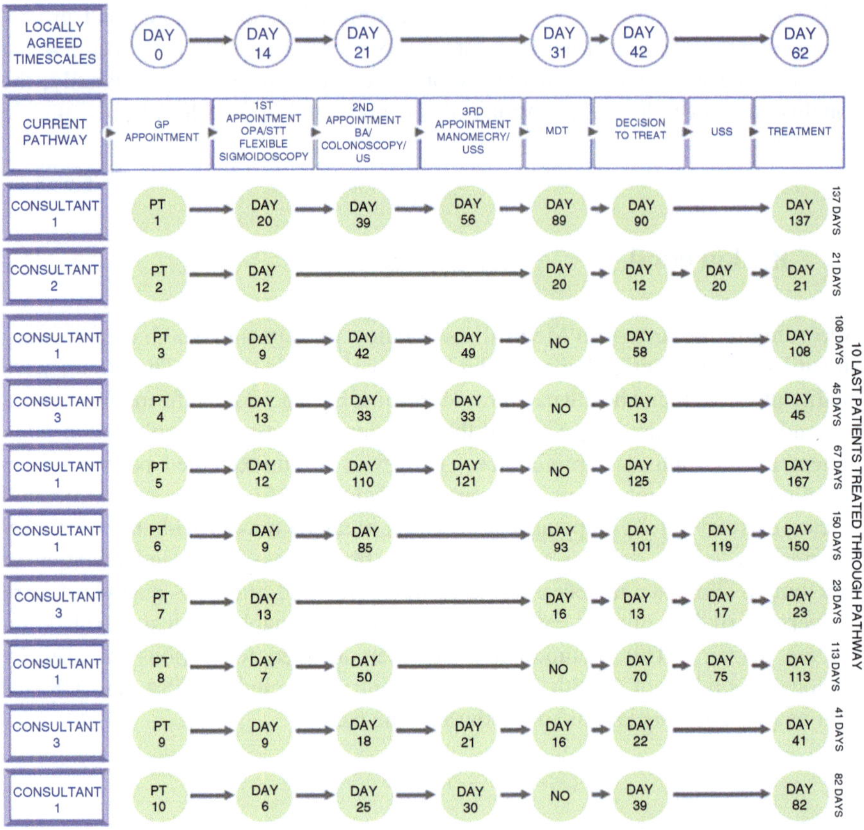

Fig. 5.1 Example of variation for colon diagnostics and therapy. (*Source*: www.nodelaysscotland.scot.nhs.uk—reprinted with permission of SHOW Team Scotland)

by consultant #1 (patients 1, 3, 5, and 10) have had significantly longer treatment period than those (patients 4 and 9) who were overseen by consultant #2. This not only demonstrates the variation, but also demonstrates where the system is constrained. A closer observation on scheduling colonoscopy by consultant #1 is much higher than consultant #3. This raises the question of whether this is due to practice style or a bottleneck in scheduling patients for consultant #1. Hence, appropriate pathway strategy and standardization of treatment may provide potential solutions to this variation.

Implementation of the clinical pathways, like those shown in the colonic pathway example, requires identification of tasks of a care delivery for a specific disease by a multi-professional team including physicians, nurses, various therapists and/or health technologist and so on. A question becomes how to select a pathology that lends itself to standardized flow management. Zander and Bower [16] suggested a list of selection criteria for selection of such pathology. The following signals may indicate that it may be useful to commit resources to establish and implement a clinical pathway for a particular condition:

- Prevalent pathology within the care setting
- Pathology with a significant risk for patients
- Pathology with a high cost for the hospital
- Predictable clinical course
- Pathology well defined and that permits a homogeneous care
- Existence of recommendations of good practices or experts opinions
- Unexplained variability of care
- Possibility of obtaining professional agreement
- Multidisciplinary implementation

Of course not all criteria may be present for a given pathology. However, using Pareto's rule, one may select the pathology when 80 % of the above conditions exist.

5.2.2 *Thyroid Disease* Conditions and Treatment

Thyroid gland surgical treatment fits the selection criteria outlined above. Endocrine surgery procedures have recently increased to constitute >20 % of the total operative volume of hospitals [5]. Even if thyroidectomy is an operation with a low incidence of morbidity and mortality is rare, the surgeon must be very capable, because some important complications may arise, as explained later [10].

It is both a high-volume and medium-cost procedure (3,000–5,000 Euros in Italy) due to the short hospitalization period and no use of costly technologies. Many private insurance companies, however, are not willing to reimburse thyroidectomy intervention due to the high risk. The major risks are the three following complications: (1) the laryngeal nerve damage (i.e., the nerve that controls the voice) in 1 out of every 250 thyroid surgeries; (2) hypoparathyroidism (surgical damage of parathyroid glands during thyroidectomy may produce hypoparathyroidism, i.e., the decreased function of the glands with under production of parathyroid hormone, leading to low levels of calcium in the blood. It can be temporary or permanent) 27.8 % of cases as temporary and 8 % as permanent; (3) hemorrhage (i.e., loss of blood from the suture area of the intervention. It is particularly dangerous because it may compress the airway, becoming life-threatening) less than 1 % of cases. Except in the case of complications, the clinical course is very predictable, recovery is immediate, and postoperative treatment is very short [4].

In thyroid treatment, patient outcomes correlate with the experience of the surgeons and surgical skills are improved with subspecialization [12]. A wide scientific and technical knowledge, recommendations of good practices, protocols, and experts opinions exist [10, 11]. Consequently the pathology is well defined and permits relatively homogeneous care (via same clinicians and nursing units and identically trained staff).

Recent studies have suggested that, appropriately implemented, clinical pathways for thyroid surgery have the potential to reduce length of stay and limit variability in care, thereby yielding cost savings, also for thyroid surgery [1, 5].

5.3 Materials and Methods

Clinical pathways can be conceptualized as flow process to improve patients' healthcare where attention is paid on the patients' movement in receiving care. In order to identify the nature of flow process, and to create a functional clinical pathway, we decided to use a simple and very familiar tool, i.e., the flowchart. Processes can be detailed on a flow chart identifying all decisions, treatments, reports related to be performed to a patient with a given pathology, with a logic based on sequential stages [2]. Of course the aim is to reduce variation in the delivery of healthcare and consequently to improve quality. We determined earlier that thyroidectomy is a pathology that fits in selection criteria, and we can, therefore, build a pathway to reduce variation in treatment of patients. The steps are presented in Fig. 5.2, where from entry to exit, patient flow is visualized and decisions and actions are identified. The particular case involves all patients that may require

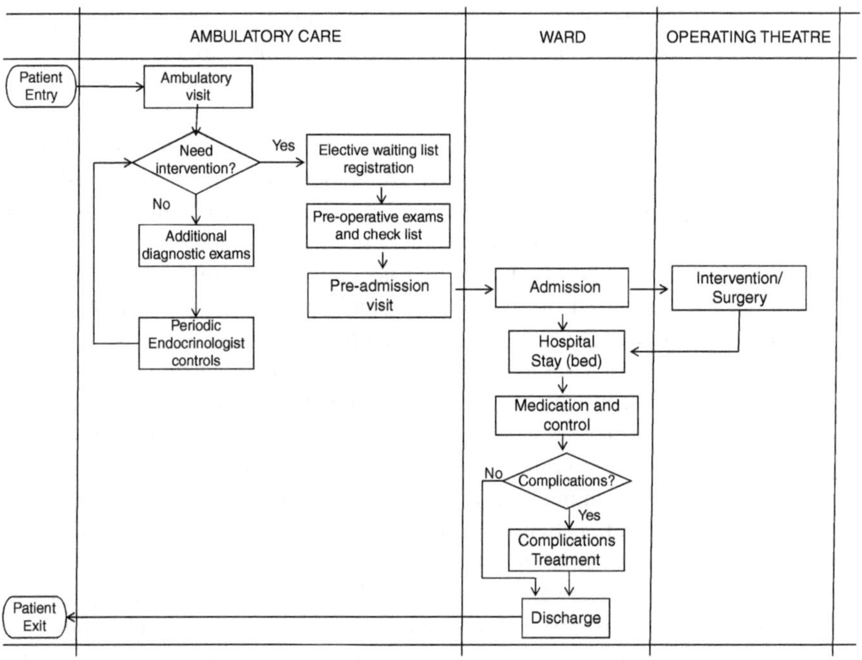

Fig. 5.2 Flowchart of the thyroidectomy pathway

surgery. This flowchart was developed by meeting all clinical and non-clinical staff in ambulatory surgery clinic, nursing units, and operating room, at the Endocrine Surgery Unit of the San Martino University Hospital in Genoa, Italy.

Note that, in Fig. 5.2 only the hospital part (ambulatory care, ward and operating theatre) of the thyroidectomy pathway is represented. In fact, some other activities before entering the ambulatory as outpatient, and also some follow up activities after discharge are excluded. For instance, another surgical visit, and medications to compensate hypoparathyroidism while remaining under the periodic control of an endocrinologist are excluded.

5.3.1 Project Management

The flowchart alone only helps to visualize the pathway, but to manage the variation one needs to quantify the time and the resources consumed throughout the process. At this stage a project management model can be used as a tool. There are four steps to construct a project management model, these are: (1) identification of activities, (2) identification of relationships among activities, (3) identification of time requirements for the activities (deterministic and probabilistic), and (4) identification of the path(s) for care delivery and its duration [8: pp. 327–329]. Once the project is identified by its paths and times, then each patient goes through the same life-cycle of this project (more/less) so that variation is minimized, and outcomes are similar with higher quality.

There are several useful methodologies available for planning and scheduling a project. The Gantt chart, the Program Evaluation and Review Technique (PERT), and the Critical Path Method (CPM) give project managers graphic displays of project activities and allow calculation of a time estimate for the project. Activities are project steps that consume resources and/or time. The crucial activities that require special attention to ensure on-time completion of the project can be identified, as well as the limits for how long others' start can be delayed. PERT and CPM are tools for planning and coordinating large projects. Once the project managers identify the project activities and times, they can estimate the project's duration, identify the activities most critical to its on-time completion, and calculate how long any activity can be delayed without delaying the project [8: p. 330].

In order to identify paths, an algorithm is used to develop the following four critical pieces of information about the project activities:

- ES: the earliest time an activity can start, if all preceding activities started as early as possible.
- LS: the latest time the activity can start and not delay the project.
- EF: the earliest time the activity can finish.
- LF: the latest time the activity can finish and not delay the project.

A macro based Excel template incorporates the four algorithms discussed above, and can be used to find the critical path[1] (see Sect. 5.4).

Any activities with zero slack time are on the critical path. Knowledge of slack times lets project managers plan with more flexibility as well as detail for how to allocate scarce resources. They can focus efforts on those critical path activities that have the greatest potential for delaying the project. It is important to recognize that activity slack times are calculated on the assumption that all the activities on the same path will start as early as possible and not exceed their expected durations. Although the activities times can be estimated in deterministic terms, the real-life projects often face situations when health care managers cannot estimate activity times with certainty. Such situations require a probabilistic approach, which uses three time estimates for each activity instead of one:

- Optimistic time (*o*): the length of time required under the best conditions.
- Pessimistic time (*p*): the length of time required under the worst conditions.
- Most likely time (*m*): the most probable length of time required.

These time estimates can be made by health care managers or by others knowledgeable about the project: contractors, subcontractors, and other professionals who have completed similar tasks or project components. They also could provide time and cost estimates for each task they are familiar with. Care should be taken to make the estimates as realistic as possible. The values can then be used to find the average or expected time for each activity t_e, and the variance of each activity time, σ^2.

That calculation uses a beta distribution, where the expected time t_e (mean) is computed as a weighted average of the three time estimates (5.1), while the variance is the square of the standard deviation among the pessimist and optimistic time (5.2), respectively, computed as follows:

$$t_e = \frac{o + 4m + p}{6} \tag{5.1}$$

$$\sigma^2 = \left(\frac{p - o}{6}\right)^2 \tag{5.2}$$

In decision making, there are methods that are useful under uncertainty, risk and near certainty platforms. The aim of decision maker is to gather data for given situation so that the decision making can be moved from uncertainty platforms to risk (outcomes are associated with probabilities), and eventually to more certainty platforms where probability of outcomes (in our case task completion times) approach to 100 %. This way reduction of the variation can be achieved. To reduce the inherent variation in the thyroid treatment, one can examine the time variations in each task and try to standardize them, CPM methodology assumes such standardization, and having standardized clinical task times, provides better planning for the health care managers.

[1] Macro-based Excel templates to solve Project Management problems are available from author Yasar A. Ozcan. Please send email to inquire: ozcan@vcu.edu.

Table 5.1 Thyroid treatment task activity relationship and probabilistic time estimates

Activity	Description	Predecessor	**Optimistic** time (*o*)	**Most likely** time (*m*)	**Pessimistic** time (*p*)
A	Pre-visit preperation		5	6	10
B	Ambulatory visit	A	25	30	45
C	Registration-elec. wait list	B	10	15	20
D	Preoperative exams	B	25	26	45
E	Checklist	D	25	25	35
F	Scheduling and planning	C, D	25	40	60
G	Preadmission visit	E	40	50	240
H	Admission	F, G	25	30	45
I	Hospital stay	H	1,400	2,790	4,004
J	Intervention/surgery	I	40	90	316
K	Post-intervention care	J	30	34	60
L	Discharge	K	35	40	45

5.3.2 Data Sources

The clinical information for thyroid treatment process identified with the flowchart presented in Fig. 5.2 was collected by interviews with the team (surgeons, nurses, and anesthesiologists) involved in thyroid treatment at the Endocrine Surgery Unit involved in our study. Starting from this flowchart, in conjunction with clinicians, nurses, and ancillary staff to ensure compliance, the execution times to perform the main activities involved in the process have been collected on 100 patients by means of a prospective study lasting about 6 months. Table 5.1 depicts the tasks and activity relationships, as well as corresponding probabilistic times for the task durations. The information contained in this table will be used to solve the project management problem, identifying the optimal length of pathway for the thyroidectomy cases under probabilistic scenario. It should be noted that all recorded times are in minutes, thus the hospital stay estimates correspond to 2–3 days. Furthermore, the time spent in post-intervention care (medications, complication treatment) activity is subtracted from hospital stay since this activity is completed during the stay.

5.4 Results

The results are presented in both probabilistic and deterministic solutions. The probabilistic solution presents the higher variability in task completions whereas the deterministic solution moves towards more standardized solution without

Length of Project =		3163.17		Project Variance =	191647.7			
Number of Critical Path(s) =		1						
Activity Name	On Critical Path	Average Time	Earliest Start	Latest Start	Earliest Finish	Latest Finish	Total Slack	Activity Variance
A	Yes	6.50	0.00	0.00	6.50	6.50	0.00	0.69
B	Yes	31.67	6.50	6.50	38.17	38.17	0.00	11.11
C	No	15.00	38.17	118.00	53.17	133.00	79.83	2.78
D	Yes	29.00	38.17	38.17	67.17	67.17	0.00	11.11
E	Yes	26.67	67.17	67.17	93.83	93.83	0.00	2.78
F	No	40.83	67.17	133.00	108.00	173.83	65.83	34.03
G	Yes	80.00	93.83	93.83	173.83	173.83	0.00	1111.11
H	Yes	31.67	173.83	173.83	205.50	205.50	0.00	11.11
I	Yes	2760.67	205.50	205.50	2966.17	2966.17	0.00	188356.00
J	Yes	119.33	2966.17	2966.17	3085.50	3085.50	0.00	2116.00
K	Yes	37.67	3085.50	3085.50	3123.17	3123.17	0.00	25.00
L	Yes	40.00	3123.17	3123.17	3163.17	3163.17	0.00	2.78

Fig. 5.3 Solution to thyroid treatment with probabilistic time (screen shot from Excel Template)

variation. Hence, this is what one would seek to standardize the care. Moving toward more deterministic solution is possible with more information about treatment process and conveying the standard treatment solutions to all caregivers.

5.4.1 *Probabilistic Solution*

A macro based Excel template solution to probabilistic thyroid treatment problem is shown in Fig. 5.3 which also depicts the ES, LS, EF, LF, and slack times which demonstrate the potential variability in the execution of each task, as approximated using the beta distribution. Such variability in time estimates introduces probability concept to project completion time.

Most of the activities are on the critical path with the exception of activity "C" (registration for elective wait list) and activity F (scheduling and planning).

The critical path dictates the thyroid treatment completion time as 3,163.2 min. Furthermore, this reflects the average completion time under probabilistic term, i.e., the probability of finishing in 52.7 h is only 50 %. Most caregivers would be interested in completion times with higher probability. By targeting the probability to certain levels, one can investigate various options and yield new completion times. As the target probability increases from 50 % to higher levels, the completion time increases too, as shown in Table 5.2. A confidence of 95 % yields approximately 64.7 h of completion time which is an additional 12 h of process time for the thyroidectomy pathway. While the aim of the research is to reduce the variability, introducing the variability into the project would make managers to understand where the variability is coming from, so that they can work on reducing the gap on optimistic and pessimistic time estimates, or altogether standardize the activities to lower pessimistic time estimates.

Table 5.2 Target probability and completion times

Target probability (%)	Desired completion time (in min)	(in h)
50	3,163.17	52.72
60	3,274.08	54.57
70	3,392.74	56.55
80	3,531.61	58.86
90	3,724.20	62.07
95	3,883.24	64.72

Note that the pathway length above computed does not include the waiting time between activities. In particular the time spent in the elective waiting list between referral and hospital admission can be particularly long and variable among patients. For example, in the Hospital under study, the elective waiting times have been recorded by a recent study to vary among 70 and 180 days [13].

5.4.2 Deterministic Solution

The clinical information for thyroid treatment process for certainty environment was also identified by interviews with the same clinical team (surgeons, nurses, and anesthesiologist). The idea behind with deterministic times is to reduce the variance in task times and achieve standardization, so that completion time of the whole procedure may be reduced. Table 5.3 shows the task times in deterministic times identified by a second round assessment by the clinical teams.

Using the deterministic times, the solution to thyroidectomy pathway is shown in Fig. 5.4. The critical path remains the same as in probabilistic solution. However, the thyroid treatment completion time decreases to 2,997.5 min (approximately 50 h) to complete treatment under standardized conditions. This solution on average decreases the completion time by 2.76 h compared to 52.7 h, with 50 % probability, or by 14.76 h, with 95 % probability, with respect to the probabilistic solutions

Note that, although reducing variability in completion time can be achieved by standardization of the task times, the further reductions of variability in the system of care may be achieved by more technical modernization of the equipment, electronic information gathering and new ways of doing the procedures and tasks.

5.4.3 Dissemination of the Results

Using project management in conjunction with clinical pathways represents a new way of thinking for disease management. More specifically, identifying the tasks, task relationships as well as task times in a clinical flow process, and

Table 5.3 Thyroid treatment task activity relationship and deterministic time estimates

Activity	Description	Predecessor	Time
A	Pre-visit preparation		7.5
B	Ambulatory visit	A	31.5
C	Registration-elec. wait list	B	12.0
D	Preoperative exams	B	31.0
E	Checklist	D	28.0
F	Scheduling and planning	C, D	37.0
G	Preadmission visit	E	52.5
H	Admission	F, G	32.0
I	Hospital stay	H	2,640
J	Intervention/surgery	I	96.0
K	Post-intervention care	J	38.0
L	Discharge	K	41.0

Length of Project =		2997.50				
Number of Critical Path(s) =		1				
Activity Name	On Critical Path	Earliest Start	Latest Start	Earliest Finish	Latest Finish	Slack (LS-ES)
A	Yes	0.00	0.00	7.50	7.50	0.00
B	Yes	7.50	7.50	39.00	39.00	0.00
C	No	39.00	101.50	51.00	113.50	62.50
D	Yes	39.00	39.00	70.00	70.00	0.00
E	Yes	70.00	70.00	98.00	98.00	0.00
F	No	70.00	113.50	107.00	150.50	43.50
G	Yes	98.00	98.00	150.50	150.50	0.00
H	Yes	150.50	150.50	182.50	182.50	0.00
I	Yes	182.50	182.50	2822.50	2822.50	0.00
J	Yes	2822.50	2822.50	2918.50	2918.50	0.00
K	Yes	2918.50	2918.50	2956.50	2956.50	0.00
L	Yes	2956.50	2956.50	2997.50	2997.50	0.00

Fig. 5.4 Solution to thyroid treatment with deterministic time (screen shot from Excel Template)

conceptualizing each patient as project are new to health care delivery. Furthermore the variability in care delivery, specific to task times, and their standardization is a challenge faced by care delivery teams in most procedures.

The results in this study showed that when the care delivery mapped and timed, reduction in the process times can be achieved due to standardization. Standardization of the task times also brings discipline to care delivery process, as well as improve the quality of care since these task will be applied to each project (i.e., patient) same way.

Thus, the caregiving teams must be retrained to learn and adhere the task times that are achievable under deterministic estimates to provide timely and quality care to patients.

5.5 Conclusions and Policy Implications

The aim of this research was to show how project management can help in designing a clinical pathway appropriately. Clinical data was collected to demonstrate a real situation, in particular a subspecialty of Endocrine Surgery Unit in a University Hospital. The particular clinical pathway was designed for thyroidectomy procedure that satisfies the main requirements suggested by literature.

The example presented here further shows how implementation of clinical pathways requires strict collaboration between clinical and operations research competences to integrate different steps including the following: (1) building a flowchart to describe process, (2) identifying activities and times to develop single tasks, (3) applying project management tools. In particular both probabilistic and deterministic methods were used to identify the critical activities requiring special attention to ensure on-time completion of the treatment. When and if standardization is achieved, its impact on reduction of completion times can be demonstrated by CPM deterministic models.

Standardization of care delivery through operational research methods described in above steps sets the expectations for the care delivery team, in turn helps to eliminate unnecessary tasks and cost. More importantly, following the same pathway for majority of patients in a given procedure naturally improves quality [6]. The implications of this approach for health care policy are obvious as the quality improves and the overall costs decrease through standardization. Many countries, including USA, encouraged such standardizations in the past for set of diseases through published protocols for practice. However, incentives to practice efficiently or in a more standard way were lacking. Now with tight budgets and curtailed payments in every economy, health care providers must take the initiative to standardize the care wherever possible through methods (such as pathways) discussed in this chapter.

Clinical practice variation which increases resource consumption as well as quality problems can be assessed using other operational research methodologies such as Data Envelopment Analysis (DEA). More specifically, one can identify practice styles for a specific disease for group of health care providers, and assess the impact when the practices use most preferred style of clinical work. This could be done in two stage DEA analysis using weight restricted/cone ratio models, where at the first stage all providers assessed in current practice, then preference equations imposed through weight restrictions (forming various cones) to assess potential resource savings if certain practices (i.e., clinical pathways) followed. Furthermore, once the clinical pathway processes are implemented and functioning, practice variation can be measured before and after the implementation using Malmquist method to demonstrate the improvements [7].

Acknowledgments The authors acknowledge support from the Italian Ministry of Education, University and Research (MIUR), under the grand FIRB n. RBFR081KSB. The authors wish to thank the staff of the Endocrine Surgery Unit of the San Martino Hospital for providing data and collaboration in this study.

References

1. D'Hubert E, Proske JM (2010) How to optimize the economic viability of thyroid surgery in French public hospital? J Visc Surg 147:259–263
2. De Blaser L, Depreitere R, De Waele K, vanhaecht K, Vlayen J, Sermeus W (2006) Defining pathways. J Nurs Manag 14:553–563
3. Jappelli T, Pistaferri L, Weber G (2007) Health care quality, economic inequality, and precautionary saving. Health Econ 16(4):327–436
4. Karamanakos SN, Markou KB, Panagopoulos K, Karavias D, Vagianos CE, Scopa CD, Fotopoulou V, Liava A, Vagenas K (2010) Complications and risk factors related to the extent of surgery in thyroidectomy. Results from 2,043 procedures. Hormones 9(4):318–325
5. Kulkarni RP, Ituarte PHG, Gunderson D, Yeh MW (2011) Clinical pathways improve hospital resource use in endocrine surgery. J Am Coll Surg 212(1):35–41
6. Mant J (2001) What causes the variation in outcome between health care providers. Int J Qual Health Care 13(6):475–480
7. Ozcan YA (2008) Health care benchmarking and performance evaluation: an assessment using data envelopment analysis (DEA). Springer, Newton, MA
8. Ozcan YA (2009) Quantitative methods in health care management: techniques and applications, 2nd edn. Jossey-Bass/Wiley, San Francisco, CA
9. Panella M, Marchisio S, Di Stanislao F (2003) Reducing clinical variations with clinical pathways: do pathways work? Int J Qual Health Care 15:509–521
10. Ramanujam LN, Cheah WK (2005) Improvements in health care for patients undergoing thyroidectomy. Asian J Surg 28(4):266–270
11. Soria-Aledo V, Flores-Pastor B, Candel-Arenas MF, Carrillo-Alcaraz A, Campillo-Soto A, Miguel-Perelló J, Carrasco Prats M, Aguayo-Albasini JL (2008) Evaluation and monitoring of the clinical pathway for thyroidectomy. Am Surg 74:29–36
12. Sosa JA, Bowman HM, Tielsch JM, Powe NR, Gordon TA, Udelsman R (1998) The importance of surgeon experience for clinical and economic outcomes from thyroidectomy. Ann Surg 228:320–330
13. Valente R, Testi A, Tanfani E, Fato M, Porro I, Santori G, Santo M, Ansaldo GL, Torre GC (2009) A model to prioritize access to elective surgery on the base of clinical urgency and waiting time. BMC Health Serv Res 9:1. doi: 10.1186/1472-6963-9-1
14. www.ama-assn.org/go/healthcarecosts/variation-delivery-utilization.pdf
15. www.dartmouthatlas.org. Accessed 2 Jan 2012
16. Zander K, Bower K (1987) Nursing case management. Blueprint for Transformation
17. Zander K (2002) Integrated care pathways: eleven international trends. J Integr Care Pathw 6:101–107

Chapter 6
EMS Planning and Management

Armann Ingolfsson

Abstract In this chapter I survey research on planning and management for emergency medical services, emphasizing four topics: forecasting demand, response times, and workload; measuring performance; choosing station locations; and allocating ambulances to stations, based on predictable and unpredictable changes in demand and travel times. I focus on empirical work and the use of analytical stochastic models.

6.1 EMS Scope and Scale

Emergency medical services (EMS) refers to the provision of out-of-hospital acute medical care and the transport of patients to hospitals for definitive care. In 1792, Dominique Jean Larrey, a surgeon in Napoleon Bonaparte's Imperial Guard, was the first to develop *ambulances* [54], in the modern sense of specially equipped vehicles for carrying sick or injured people, usually to hospital. In the 220 years since, EMS has evolved and expanded to become a significant component of modern health-care systems.

Table 6.1 provides a sense of the scale of EMS, with statistics on call volumes, resources, and operating expenses in Canada [25, 2, 9]; London, England [38]; the United States [17]; and rural Iceland, Scotland, and Sweden [23]. These statistics suggest that a person in any one of these jurisdictions calls EMS an average of once every 5 to 12 years and that the cost of providing EMS (financed through a combination of public funding and user fees) ranges from US$40 to US$90 per capita, per year.

A. Ingolfsson (✉)
School of Business, University of Alberta, Edmonton, AB T6G 2R6, Canada
e-mail: armann.ingolfsson@ualberta.ca

G.S. Zaric (ed.), *Operations Research and Health Care Policy*,
International Series in Operations Research & Management Science 190,
DOI 10.1007/978-1-4614-6507-2_6,

Table 6.1 EMS statistics

Region	Canada	London, England	United States	Rural Iceland, Scotland, Sweden
Year	(2012)	(2009)	(2011)	(2007)
Population (000)	5,104	7,754	313,625	586
Annual calls per capita	1/8.8	1/5.24	1/8.54	1/12.1
Ambulances per capita	1/8,954	1/8,615	1/3,858	1/5,581
EMS professionals per capita	Not available	1/1,551	1/380	1/750
Annual operating expenses per capita	US$92 (Alberta), US$64 (Toronto)	US$55	Not available	US$41

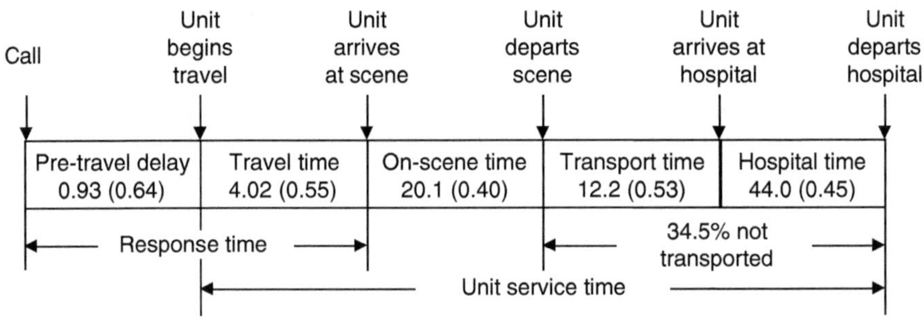

Fig. 6.1 Events and time intervals for an EMS call, with median minutes (coefficients of variation) for each interval, based on 2003 Calgary EMS data

EMS planning and management are challenging, because the volume, location, and severity of EMS calls are highly variable, making it difficult to decide where to position ambulances and their crews while they wait for their next call. Planning is facilitated, however, by the ever-increasing quantity and quality of data collected by modern EMS agencies, through computer-aided dispatch (CAD) and global positioning system (GPS) technologies. CAD systems typically collect times tamps for all the events associated with a typical EMS call that are shown in Fig. 6.1 (from [5]), for the geographical coordinates of the ambulance at the time of dispatch and for the call address. In addition to improving the real-time information available to dispatchers, these data make it possible to model and predict call volumes and response times more realistically. Partly because of the increased availability of data, perhaps, the number of publications in the operations research and management science (OR/MS) literature that includes "emergency medical services" or "ambulances" as keywords has grown rapidly during the last decade, as demonstrated in Fig. 6.2 (data obtained from the ISI Web of Science).

This chapter summarizes recent OR/MS contributions to EMS planning and management. Several related survey articles have been published during the last

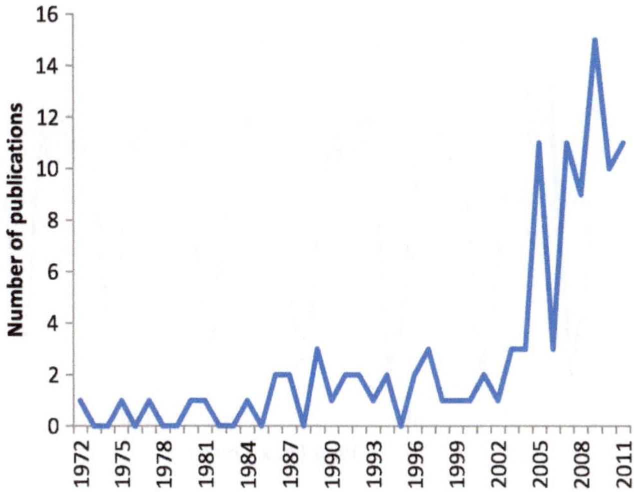

Fig. 6.2 Number of OR/MS publications with keywords "emergency medical service" or "ambulances"

four decades, including general surveys on emergency response planning for EMS, fire, and police [6, 56, 21]; a survey of OR/MS methods aimed at EMS practitioners [20]; surveys that focus on optimal facility location models [3, 37]; and surveys focusing on the use of simulation [28]. In comparison, this chapter places greater emphasis on forecasting EMS demand, response times, and workload; EMS performance measures; and the use of stochastic models to predict the performance of EMS systems.

The remainder of this chapter is organized as follows. Section 6.2 addresses the prediction of demand, response times, and workload. Section 6.3 summarizes EMS performance measures, and Sect. 6.4 outlines stochastic models to predict the performance of EMS systems. Section 6.5 discusses optimization models for station planning and allocation of ambulances to stations.

6.2 Predicting Demand, Response Times, and Workload

Mathematical models of EMS systems require three components as input information: (1) demand—how call volumes vary over time and space; (2) response times—how the response time to a call varies with the distance that the ambulance must travel and perhaps other factors; and (3) workload—how long an ambulance and its crew will be occupied with a call. Researchers have started to use the call-by-call data that modern EMS systems collect, together with road network information, in order to investigate each of these components in detail.

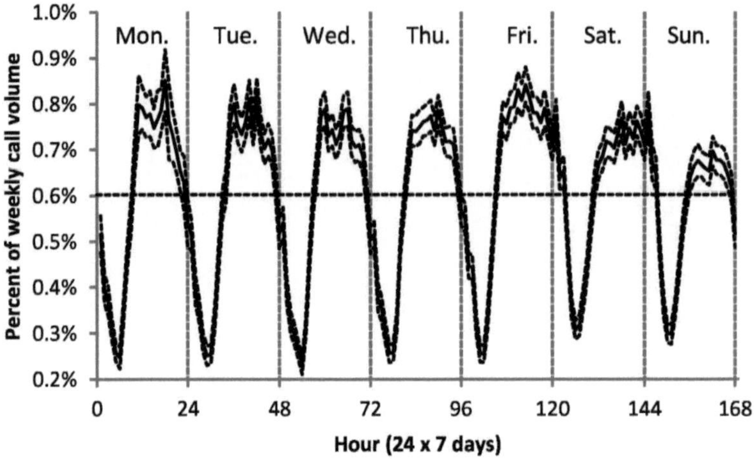

Fig. 6.3 Average hourly call volume as a percentage of weekly volume, with 95% confidence intervals (2000–2004 Calgary EMS data, adapted from [7])

6.2.1 Demand

EMS call volumes vary predictably by month, day of the week, and hour of the day. Figure 6.3 shows a typical weekly pattern for average call volumes, revealing a regular diurnal cycle each weekday, higher volumes on Friday and Saturday night (which carry on into early Saturday and Sunday morning), and lower volumes on Sundays. This weekly pattern is crucial for planning purposes, particularly for shift scheduling. Figure 6.4 displays the annual cycle for Calgary, Canada. Other predictable patterns include higher-than-average volumes on certain holidays (e.g., New Year's Day) and during certain annual festivals or other special events. See [7] for time series models that incorporate both seasonal patterns and special events. Extreme weather events and natural or human-caused disasters are other special events for which timing is more difficult to predict, but the impact on call volume can be predicted to some extent [43].

It is commonly assumed in planning models that call volumes follow a stationary or time-varying Poisson process. This assumption is supported by theoretical arguments [27] and empirical evidence [22, 61]. It is often appropriate, however, to view the Poisson arrival rate as a random variable, with a distribution that is narrower for time periods closer to the present. To be more precise, suppose that the call volume on day $t + n$ (where call volumes are known up to and including day t and n is the forecast horizon) is Y_{t+n}, that the arrival rate for day $t + n$ is $\Lambda_{t+n} = B_{t+n}\lambda_{t+n}$ (where B_{t+n} has a mean of 1 and a standard deviation $\sigma_{B_{t+n}}$), and that conditional on $\Lambda_{t+n} = \lambda$, Y_{t+n} is Poisson-distributed with mean λ. One can interpret λ_{t+n} as a long-term average call volume for day $t + n$ and B_{t+n} as a "busyness factor" that perturbs the average call volume away from its long-term value,

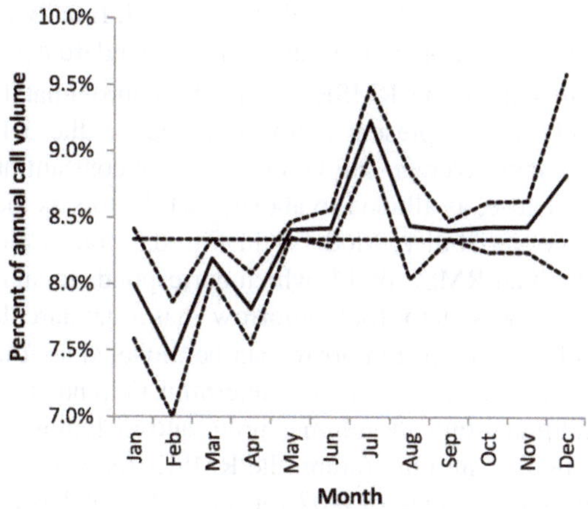

Fig. 6.4 Average monthly call volume as a percentage of annual volume, with 95% confidence intervals (2000–2004 Calgary EMS data, adapted from [7])

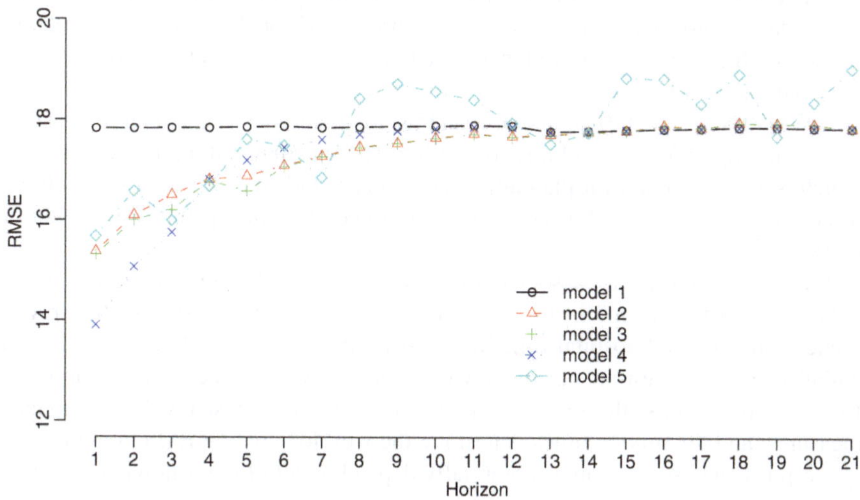

Fig. 6.5 Root-mean-square forecast error for daily call volume forecasts from 1 to 21 days into the future. (2000–2004 Calgary EMS data, from [7])

because of such factors as the weather. To the extent that these factors persist from one day to the next, one would expect that information on the actual call volume on day t should make it possible to forecast the call volume on day $t + 1$ with greater accuracy.

As an example, Fig. 6.5 shows the root-mean-square forecast error (RMSE—the square root of the average of the squared forecast errors) for daily EMS call volumes in Calgary using five time series methods described in [7]. We focus on

Models 1 and 4. The average daily call volume was 174. If daily call volumes were Poisson distributed with a mean of 174/day, then the standard deviation of the daily call volumes, estimated by the RMSE, should be approximately $\sqrt{174} = 13.2$. This estimate is likely to represent a lower bound on the achievable forecast accuracy for two reasons: average call volumes are not constant but have seasonality and trend and because, as alluded to above, such factors as the weather tend to increase call volume variability. Model 4 in Fig. 6.5 comes close to this lower bound, however, with an RMSE of 14, which corresponds to an estimate of 0.027 for $\sigma_{B_{t+1}}$; thus, the busyness factor for "tomorrow" has a standard deviation of 2.7%. Put differently, call arrivals for tomorrow can be modeled as following a Poisson process, the arrival rate of which is almost deterministic (and can be forecast using Model 4) and conditional on call volumes up to and including today. In contrast, when forecasting 14 days into the future, the RMSEs for Models 1 and 4 are both 18, corresponding to an estimate of 0.07 for $\sigma_{B_{t+14}}$. Model 1 is a linear regression model with an intercept and trend term and dummy variables for month of the year, hour of the week, New Year's Day, and a special event that occurs every year in Calgary (the Calgary Stampede). Model 4 is a time series regression model, with the same independent variables as Model 1, some interaction terms added, and error terms that are modeled as an autoregressive process. (Models 2 and 3 are similar to Model 4, differing only in which interaction terms are included. Model 5 is a seasonal ARIMA model).

See Matteson et al. [40] and Vile et al. [58] for additional research on forecasting the evolution of EMS call volumes over time. The spatial distribution of EMS calls, which is also important for planning, has not been studied as much as call volume forecasting has. See [53] for recent work on forecasting the spatial distribution of EMS calls.

Each EMS call has an associated *response time* (R, the sum of the pre-travel delay and the travel time in Fig. 6.1) and *service time* (S, the sum of the travel, scene, transport, and hospital time in Fig. 6.1—the time interval during which an ambulance and its crew are occupied with a call). These time intervals are important for different reasons: the response time is the basis for most EMS performance measures, and the service times determine the workload on the EMS system.

Response and service times potentially depend on all of the following factors:

- The time when the call arrived
- The location of the call (i) and the location of the responding ambulance (j)
- The system *load*, which I will consider to be the number of busy ambulances when the call arrived
- The urgency of the call

In the remainder of this section, I summarize some of the available evidence on whether and how response and service times depend on these factors, but there is much that we have yet to learn about this issue. To illustrate the potential benefits of further research, consider that average service times appear to increase with system load, as discussed later in this section. Future research could address three types of questions:

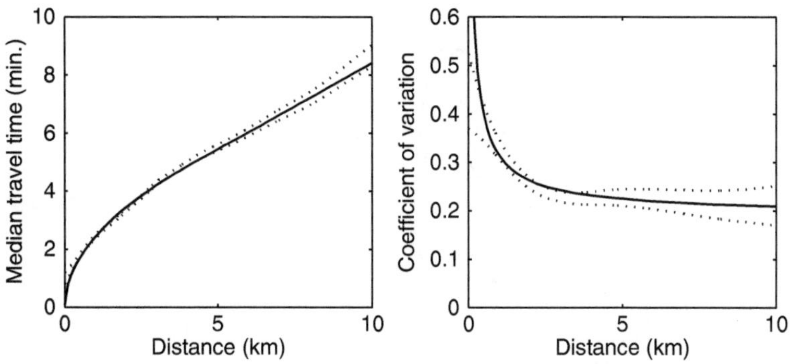

Fig. 6.6 Parametric estimates of median and coefficient of variation of travel time functions with nonparametric 95% confidence limits (2003 Calgary EMS data, from [5])

Fundamental knowledge: Does average service time vary with system load? If so, why? Does the strength and nature of the relationship vary among geographic regions or depend on the way EMS service is organized?

Modeling: How can load-dependent average service times be incorporated into mathematical models of EMS systems? How do the validity, tractability, and scalability of different modeling approaches compare?

Implications for planning: How do the recommended number of ambulances and the predicted system performance differ as a function of the incorporation of load-dependent average service times?

6.2.2 Response Times

Travel time is usually the largest component of response time. Statistical analysis of EMS travel times has focused either on predicting travel time based on the characteristics of the links in a transport network that are included in the trip (e.g., the length and the road type for each link) [59] or on predicting travel time based only on the distance between the responding ambulance and the call location [34, 5]. Both of these approaches incorporate dependence of travel time on locations of the responding ambulance and call address. The latter approach is more parsimonious, and the calculations needed to predict travel times are simpler and require fewer data (e.g., Euclidean distance can be used instead of road network distance, if desired). Focusing on the latter approach, Fig. 6.6 shows how estimated medians and coefficients of variation of travel time vary with distance, based on 2003 Calgary data [5]. The median travel time curve is concave because average speeds are typically higher for longer trips.

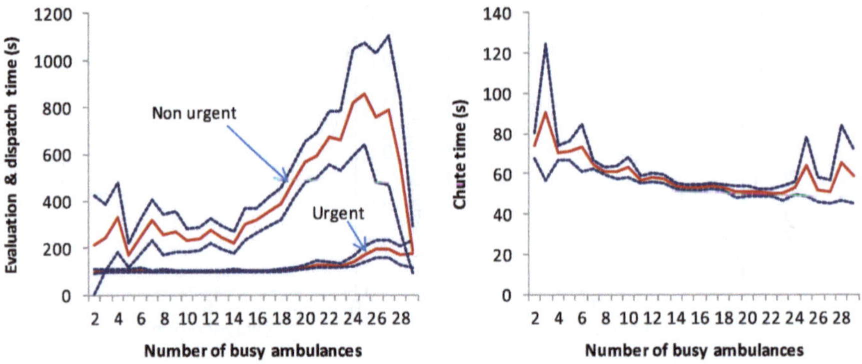

Fig. 6.7 Means and 95% confidence intervals for evaluation and dispatch time and for chute time (2008 Edmonton EMS data, from [1])

EMS travel speeds tend to be higher for urgent calls [5, 59] and lower during rush hours, but the rush-hour effect is less pronounced for urgent "lights-and-siren" calls [59].

The pretravel delay can be decomposed into evaluation and dispatch time and chute time (the time from dispatch until the dispatched ambulance starts its travel toward the call address). Evaluation and dispatch times are shorter for urgent calls [1], and there is some evidence (left panel of Fig. 6.7) that they depend on the system load for nonurgent calls, perhaps indicating that dispatching is delayed for nonurgent calls when the system is congested. Chute times tend to be shorter when the system is more highly loaded (right panel of Fig. 6.7), because the responding ambulance is more likely to be traveling rather than to waiting at a station.

If one can predict the response-time distribution for a representative set of combinations of ambulance locations and call addresses, then one can plot probability of coverage maps, as shown in Fig. 6.8. *Coverage* refers to the proportion of calls with response time below a time standard, such as 9 min (see Sect. 6.3 for further discussion). The map on the right of Fig. 6.8 is based on the assumption that all stations have an available ambulance, whereas the map on the left incorporates the probability that an ambulance is available at each station, as calculated using the Hypercube Queueing Model (a Markov chain model with a state variable for the status of every ambulance; see Sect. 6.4 for further information). A visual comparison of these two maps can help planners diagnose which regions of a city require additional stations and which regions could benefit from more ambulances. The lack of coverage in the northwest area of the city that is apparent on map (a), for example, could be attributable to an inadequate number of stations in the area or an inadequate number of ambulances allocated to those stations. Map (b), which is based on the assumption of unlimited ambulance availability, indicates that coverage in the northwest could be increased considerably by allocating more ambulances to the stations already in that area, without building any new stations. In contrast, having unlimited ambulance availability appears not to address the lack of coverage in the northeast, suggesting that it is necessary to build new stations in order to improve coverage in that area.

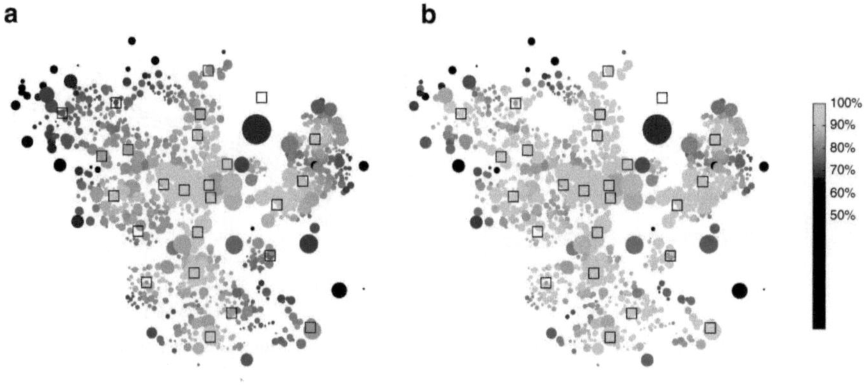

Fig. 6.8 Probability-of-coverage map. Locations of ambulance stations are depicted as black squares. The colors of the other locations (neighborhoods aggregated to a single point) indicate the probability of coverage. Unshaded regions represent areas with sparse or no population. (**a**) Closest available ambulance responds. (**b**) Closest station responds (2003 Calgary EMS data, from [5])

6.2.3 Workload

The most obvious reason for EMS service times to depend on the location of the responding ambulance and the call address is that travel time, which depends on travel distance, is part of service time. This dependence has driven generalizations of the Hypercube Queueing Model [31], for example. The dependence of travel times on travel distances should induce a dependence of travel times on the system load, because, when the system is more highly loaded, the average distance from a call address to the closest available ambulance should be higher. Considerably less attention has been devoted to the study of service time components other than travel time, but these other components also appear to depend on the system load. I have already discussed how chute time appears to decrease with load, as shown in Fig. 6.7. Hospital time is the component that appears to be most strongly influenced by system load, as the right panel of Fig. 6.9 shows, revealing average hospital times that are approximately 30 min longer when the system is most highly loaded [1], likely because emergency departments (EDs) tend to be highly loaded when an EMS system is highly loaded. In contrast, average length of stay in at least some hospital wards has been found to be *shorter* under heavier load [32]. It is not clear why average hospital times decrease at extreme loads, but the effect may be linked to protocols that operate in EDs when the number of patients is deemed to have exceeded capacity.

I believe that further study should seek to determine if EMS service times depend more on the locations of the responding ambulance (i) and the call address (j) than they do on the system load and if the dependence on (i, j) can be captured via the load (as is done in the repositioning model proposed in [1]). These issues have modeling implications, because models with a single state variable for the system load are likely to be more scalable than are models that keep track of the address and the identity of the responding ambulance for every call in progress.

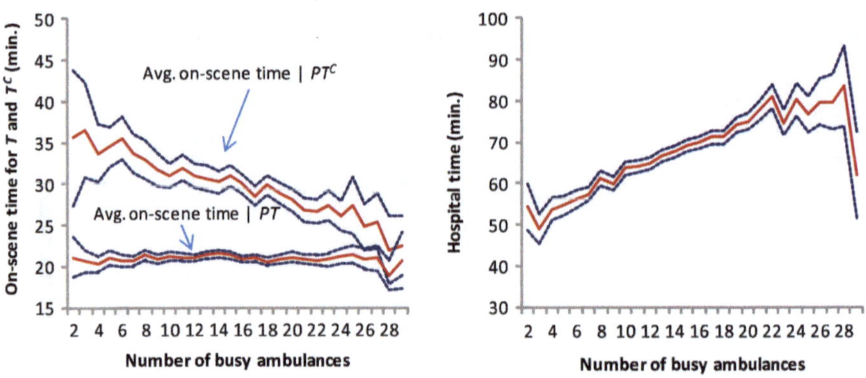

Fig. 6.9 Means and 95% confidence intervals for on-scene time and hospital time (2008 Edmonton EMS data, from [1]). On-scene times are shown separately for patients who were transported to hospital (*PT*) and those who were not (PT^C)

6.3 Performance Measures

Where EMS systems are publicly funded, their operations should presumably aim to deliver maximum benefit to the public, given their budget. But measuring the benefits that EMS systems provide is no straightforward matter. Ideally, the benefit would be measured in such concrete and easily interpreted units as lives saved—units that facilitate comparisons between competing uses of funds [15]. But this is typically not the case. Most EMS systems use such system-wide response-time statistics as the proportion of urgent calls with a response time within a certain time standard. The US National Fire Protection Association, for instance, recommends a target of 90% within 4 min for the first response to an urgent EMS call, followed by an Advanced Life Support (ALS) response within 8 min [46, Sects. 5.3.3.4.2-3]. Reaching 90% of urgent urban EMS calls in 9 min is a common target in North America [19]. The National Health Service in the UK sets targets of 75% in 8 min and 95% in 19 min for urgent urban EMS calls [12]. The advantage of response-time performance targets is the fact that response-time data are relatively easy to collect and understand. There are disadvantages, however: the link between response-times and medical outcomes is not clear, and response time standards and percentages are necessarily arbitrary.

Optimization models for EMS station location and ambulance allocation (discussed in Sect. 6.5) typically aim to maximize *coverage*, which corresponds to the EMS response time being within a time standard. For the sake of simplicity, some models assume a deterministic relationship between distance and response time, implying that all call locations within a given distance from an available ambulance are covered and that all locations that are further away are not covered. Other models use a probability of coverage, p_{ij}, of a call location i by an available ambulance at location j, where p_{ij} is estimated using such methods as the estimated travel time distributions discussed in [5].

Planners must answer a variety of questions when recommending appropriate EMS performance measures, including:

- Should one report response-time statistics or medical outcome statistics?
- When reporting response times, should one report averages, quantiles (such as medians or 90th percentiles), or fractiles (the proportion of response times within a time standard)?
- Should one use different standards for different call priorities?
- Should one use different standards for urban and rural areas?
- Should one report system-wide measures or separate measures for different geographical regions?

The last two questions concern equity. Economies of scale typically make it more difficult to achieve a response-time standard in city suburbs than in the more densely populated downtown core and more difficult still in rural areas. As Felder and Brinkmann [18] point out, the objectives of providing equal access to EMS versus minimizing system-wide response times lead to different deployment patterns. Response-time standards and actual performance typically differ for urban and rural areas in the USA, UK, and Germany [18, 19], indicating that the standard setters have decided against equal access. As Felder and Brinkmann [18] note, although a policy of equal access may appear difficult to criticize, such a policy does imply that lives are valued more highly in more sparsely populated areas.

As two examples of the political issues involved with access to medical care in remote areas, the cities of Edmonton, Canada and Reykjavik, Iceland both have two airports—an international airport that is relatively far from the city center and a smaller domestic airport close to the center. In Edmonton, the decision has been made to close the City Centre Airport, and in Reykjavik, there is a continuing debate about whether to close all or part of its domestic airport. In both cases [26, 60], advocates for rural areas have raised the issue of longer transport times to hospital for patients that are flown to the city by air ambulance, pitting urban interest in reducing sprawl against rural concerns about access to medical care.

Although the link between EMS response times and medical outcomes is not always clear, this issue has been studied extensively for patients experiencing cardiac arrest. A study by Valenzuela et al. [57] illustrates the type of knowledge generated by medical researchers. They used data from Tucson, AZ, and King County, WA, to fit logistic regression models that predict the probability of survival as a function of various factors. One of their prediction equations was:

$$s(I_{\mathrm{CPR}}, I_{\mathrm{Defib}}) = 1/(1 + \exp(-0.260 + 0.106 I_{\mathrm{CPR}} + 0.139 I_{\mathrm{Defib}})) ,$$

where $s(.)$ is the survival probability, I_{CPR} is the duration from collapse to cardiopulmonary resuscitation (CPR), and I_{Defib} is the duration from collapse to defibrillation. By combining this survival function with assumptions about such factors as the proportion of cardiac arrests witnessed, the proportion of cardiac arrest patients that receive CPR from a bystander, and estimates of the distribution of EMS response time as a function of distance, Erkut et al. [15] estimated the

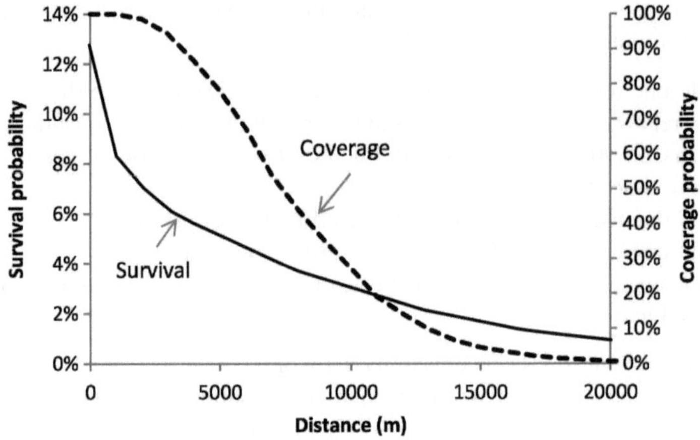

Fig. 6.10 Estimated survival probability and coverage probability as a function of distance for cardiac arrest patients (adapted from [15])

relationship between distance and survival probability shown in Fig. 6.10. They found that replacing coverage with a survival probability did not greatly complicate optimization models for EMS station location and ambulance allocation. They also found that coverage-maximizing models in which the relationship between distance and coverage is probabilistic are much better proxies for maximizing the expected number of survivors than are deterministic coverage models. Figure 6.10 compares the shape of a survival probability function and a probabilistic coverage function. Although the two functions have different shapes, they share two characteristics that may explain why one is a good proxy for the other: (1) the benefit decays *gradually* with distance from the closest ambulance, in contrast to a deterministic coverage function that drops from one to zero at the coverage distance standard, and (2) the benefit approaches and remains close to zero after a certain distance, in contrast to a linear decrease in benefit that continues indefinitely, as implied by minimization of average distance.

Work continues on the incorporation of survival probabilities in EMS planning models (see, e.g., [47, 42, 44, 33]). Although a shift of focus from coverage to medical outcomes appears to be relatively straightforward from the point of view of mathematical modeling, shifting the focus of EMS planners to outcome-based measures will likely involve challenges. One of these challenges is the collection of information about events prior to the arrival of an ambulance at the scene (for a cardiac arrest patient, e.g., was CPR administered and how long ago did the cardiac arrest occur?), about medical outcomes after EMS has transferred care of the patient to a hospital, and the linking of both types of information to the response-time data that EMS agencies typically collect.

6.4 Performance Evaluation

In this section, I focus on the use of stochastic models to predict how EMS system performance changes as the deployment of ambulances changes. To compute EMS system performance measures, it is often convenient to condition on the call location (j) and the location of the ambulance that responds to the call (i). One first requires an estimate of the performance measure of interest for calls from j that are responded to from i, which I will denote with p_{ij}. I leave the interpretation of p_{ij} open, but it could, for example, represent average response time, proportion of calls with a response time under 9 min, or the probability of survival. Second, one requires the *dispatch probability*, f_{ij}, that an ambulance from location i responds, given that the call is from location j.

I focus on stochastic models that can be solved analytically rather than simulation models. Simulation models of EMS systems have been discussed by [30, 28, 39], among others. Both simulation models and analytical models have their uses, and they can be utilized to complement each other. A primary advantage of analytical models is their short computation time, which is important when using such a model as a component in a procedure to search for optimal or near-optimal deployment plans or as a component in a decision support system that allows EMS planners to experiment with deployment policies and to (almost) immediately see the likely consequences for system performance. Such a system would be frustrating to use if one had to wait several minutes each time a change was made.

To simplify the discussion in this section, I assume that the model parameters do not vary with time or with the system state. Some of the models that I discuss, however, can incorporate time- or state-dependent parameters. For further information, please refer to the references that I cite for each model.

To illustrate the models, I use an example with two single-vehicle ambulance stations and two *demand nodes* (ambulance call locations), shown in Fig. 6.11. (The figure shows all the input parameters that I use, but the simpler models do not require all the parameters.) In this example, the demand nodes correspond to the catchment areas around the two stations. I assume throughout that the closest available ambulance responds to every incoming call. When both ambulances are busy, with probability B, incoming calls are responded to by backup systems—for example, by EMS supervisors or the fire service. The situation when all ambulances are busy is sometimes referred to as "code red."

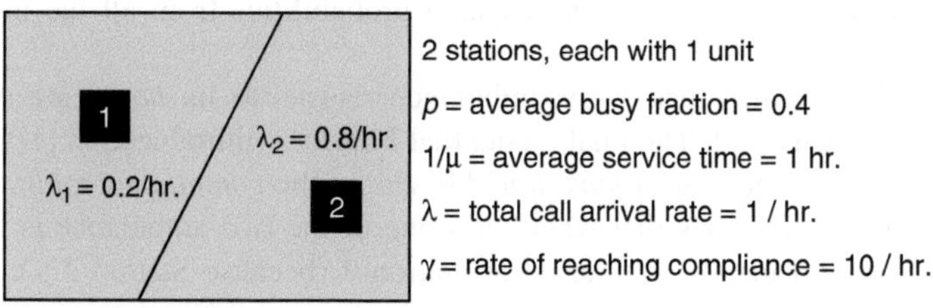

Fig. 6.11 Performance evaluation example

The simplest model assumes that both stations have an available ambulance at all times, which implies that $f_{11} = f_{22} = 1, f_{12} = f_{21} = 0$, and $B = 0$. This is the model implicitly used in such optimal facility location models as the maximal covering location problem (MCLP) [8]. The simplest model that accounts for ambulance unavailability is based on the assumption that at any given time, each ambulance is unavailable with probability p (the "average busy fraction," assumed equal to 0.4 in our example) and available with probability $1 - p$, independent of all other ambulances. This *binomial model* is implicit in the maximum expected covering location model (MEXCLP) [10] and implies that $f_{11} = f_{22} = 1 - p = 0.6$, $f_{12} = f_{21} = p(1 - p) = 0.24$, and $B = p^2 = 0.16$.

Up to this point, the only input parameter that I have used is the busy fraction p. Next, suppose that we model the system as an Erlang B (i.e., $M/M/2/2$) loss system, with arrival rate $\lambda = 1$ per hour and service rate $\mu = 1$ per hour. Standard calculations reveal that $B = 0.\ 2$, the average ambulance utilization is 0.4 (I chose λ and μ so as to obtain an average ambulance utilization equal to p), the probability of both ambulances being free is 0.4, and the probability of one ambulance being free is 0.4. We calculate the dispatch probabilities for demand node 1 as follows:

$$\begin{aligned} f_{11} &= \Pr\{\text{both ambulances free}\} \\ &\quad + \Pr\{\text{Ambulance1 free} \mid \text{one ambulance free}\} \Pr\{\text{one ambulance free}\} \\ &= 0.4 + 0.5 \times 0.4 = 0.6 \\ f_{21} &= \Pr\{\text{Ambulance 2 free} \mid \text{one ambulance free}\} \Pr\{\text{one ambulance free}\} \\ &= 0.5 \times 0.4 \end{aligned}$$

By symmetry, $f_{11} = f_{22}$ and $f_{12} = f_{21}$. Observe that the probability of the closest ambulance responding is the same $(1 - p)$ as in the binomial model, but the probability of the second-closest ambulance responding is different, because the Erlang B model incorporates dependence—essentially, given that Ambulance 1 is busy, the probability that Ambulance 2 is busy $(0.2/(0.2 + 0.2) = 0.5)$ is higher than the average busy fraction $(p = 0.\ 4)$.

Next, I use the Hypercube Queueing Model (HQM, [35]) to compute the dispatch probabilities. Unlike the models I have considered so far, the HQM views the two ambulances as distinguishable, taking into account that 80% of the arrivals are to the Station 2 catchment area and that Ambulance 2 is therefore likely to be busier than Ambulance 1. The HQM dispatch probabilities are obtained by computing the steady-state probabilities for the Markov chain shown in Fig. 6.12; they are shown, together with the dispatch probabilities from all the models, in Table 6.2.

The HQM assumes that every ambulance returns to its *home station* at the conclusion of every call. The final model that I discuss (introduced in [1]) assumes instead that ambulances are *repositioned* based on the *compliance table* shown in Fig. 6.13, which indicates that when only one of the two ambulance is free, that ambulance should ideally be located at Station 2 (because Station 2's catchment

Fig. 6.12 Transition diagram for the Hypercube Queueing Model

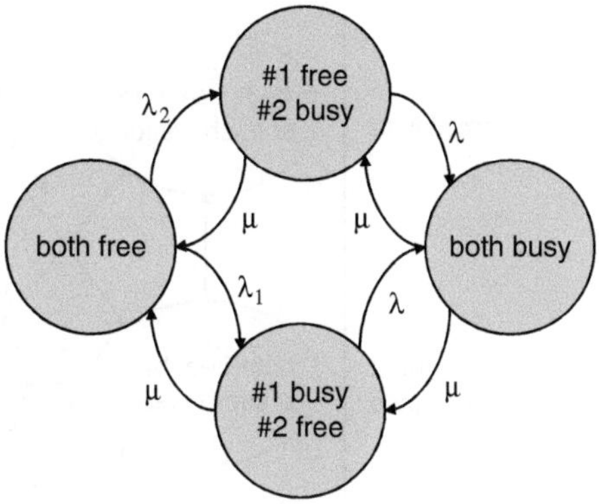

Table 6.2 Dispatch probabilities

Model	f_{11}	f_{21}	f_{12}	f_{22}	B	Performance
Always available	1	0	0	1	0	0.95
Binomial	0.600	0.240	0.240	0.600	0.16	0.69
Erlang B	0.600	0.200	0.200	0.600	0.20	0.67
HQM	0.660	0.140	0.260	0.540	0.20	0.65
Repositioning	0.448	0.352	0.085	0.715	0.20	0.70
	p_{11}	p_{21}	p_{12}	p_{22}		
	0.95	0.5	0.95	0.5		

area has a higher call rate). This Markov chain model, the transition diagram of which is shown in Fig. 6.13, has one state variable for the number of busy ambulances and another state variable indicating if the system is "in compliance." When the system is out of compliance, I assume that an ambulance is moved to another station, an action that takes 6 min on average, implying that the "rate of reaching compliance" is $\gamma = 10$ per hour.

Table 6.2 shows the dispatch probabilities and the code red probabilities B, as computed with each of the five performance evaluation models. The bottom row of the table also shows a possible performance measure, which could be thought of as the probability that the response time R is within some time standard—that is,

$$p_{ij} = \Pr\{R \leq \text{ time standard} \mid \text{station } i \text{ responds, call from location } j\}.$$

I show the conditional performance estimate for each combination of call location and ambulance location at the bottom of the table, and display the system-wide expected performance in the rightmost column. The system-wide performance is computed using

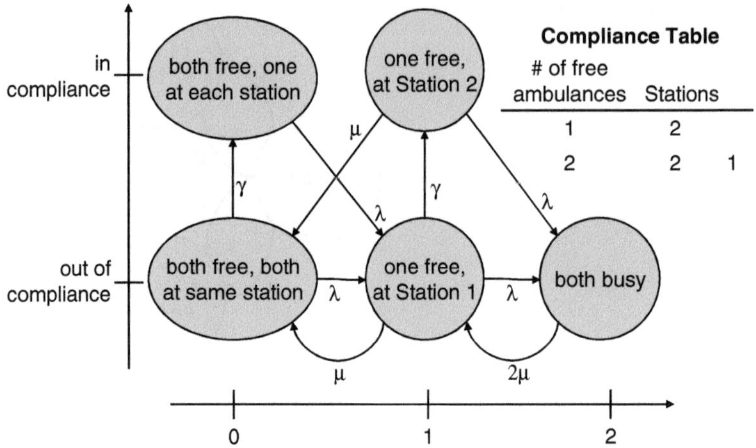

Fig. 6.13 Transition diagram for the repositioning model

$$\text{Performance} = \sum_{j=1}^{2} \frac{\lambda_j}{\lambda} \sum_{i=1}^{2} f_{ij} p_{ij} \,.$$

The optimistic "always available" model provides an upper bound on performance. The Erlang B model predicts lower performance than the binomial model does, because the dependence between the statuses of Ambulances 1 and 2 leads to a higher code red probability. The HQM predicts lower performance than the Erlang B model does because the HQM incorporates the inefficiencies that result from the demand imbalance between the catchment areas for Stations 1 and 2, which leads to better performance for the low-demand Station 1 region and worse performance for the high-demand Station 2 region. The repositioning strategy is intended to address this imbalance by favoring Station 2 when only one ambulance is available. We see that repositioning is predicted to increase the performance by 5 percentage points, compared to the "return to home station" that is implicit in the HQM.

The operation of the system is held constant in the first four rows of Table 6.2, and changes in estimated performance are therefore attributable to improved model realism as one moves down the rows in the table. In contrast, the performance estimates for the last two rows show the impact of changing the way the system operates, by repositioning ambulances based on the system state. The first four models represent different trade-offs between model tractability and accuracy. The HQM has a state space the size of which increases exponentially with the number of ambulances, rendering that model intractable for systems with more than 36 ambulances [4, online supplement], based on typical computer storage capacities available in 2009, but approximate versions of the HQM [36, 31, 4] improve its scalability. The simpler "always available" and binomial models have been used in station planning and ambulance allocation optimization models, in order to make it possible to formulate and solve the models as mathematical programs.

Incorporating the HQM into a mathematical program is difficult, but the HQM can be incorporated into optimization heuristics, such as the tabu search heuristic discussed in [13]. The "always available" model remains relevant because it facilitates decoupling station planning models from ambulance allocation models, as discussed in Sec. 6.5.1.

The repositioning model is more scalable than the HQM, with a state space that grows only linearly with the number of ambulances. As an example of the benefits of repositioning policies in a real system, a simulation study of the Edmonton, Canada EMS system [14] estimated that the use of repositioning increased the percentage of urgent calls reached in 9 min or less from 77% to 85%. Repositioning policies do increase workload for EMS staff, which may lead to back problems [45] and increased fatigue, but these potential impacts require further investigation. Studnek et al. [55] linked back pain among EMS professionals to various factors, but failed to find a statistically significant relationship with call volume.

6.5 Station Planning and Ambulance Allocation

Having discussed the prediction of EMS model inputs, EMS performance measures, and models to predict performance, I now turn to optimization models designed to help planners decide where ambulance stations should be located and how to assign ambulances and their crews to stations. The choice of locations for ambulance stations is a long-term decision, but the assignment of ambulances to stations can change over time to provide a better match for supply and demand on a timescale of days and hours.

6.5.1 Station Planning

By *ambulance station*, I mean a structure in which ambulances can be stored, cleaned, and restocked with medical supplies. Ambulance crews typically begin and end their shifts at an ambulance station and return to an ambulance station between calls. There are exceptions, however. In some systems, ambulance crews wait for their next call in locations with no dedicated infrastructure. Other systems have a single start station [30, 48], in order to increase efficiency in maintenance and inventory.

I choose to focus on the typical situation, in which planners must decide where to build ambulance stations. Perhaps the best-known model for this purpose is the MCLP [8], which selects locations for q stations so as to maximize the proportion of demand within a coverage distance standard of the closest station. This model is based on several assumptions, including:

- A coverage distance standard is an adequate proxy for a coverage time standard. This assumption is relatively easy to relax—see the MCLP with probabilistic response times (MCLP + PR) [11, 16].
- The system is to be designed from scratch. This assumption is also easy to relax, by adding constraints to the MCLP or MCLP + PR integer program to account for preexisting stations.
- Every station has an available ambulance at all times. This assumption implies that the coverage values obtained from the MCLP and the MCLP + PR are upper bounds on the coverage that can be achieved with a finite number of ambulances. Such models as the MEXCLP [10], which relax this assumption, can be seen as combining station planning and the allocation of ambulances to stations.
- All ambulance responses start from a station. In reality, however, ambulances often respond while in transit.

Using the MCLP, the MCLP + PR, or other similar optimization problem formulations to inform EMS station planning requires not only reliable data but also good judgment [24]. How does one choose the potential station locations, for example? If a municipality-operated EMS service constrains itself to locations with publicly owned land where current zoning allows the building of EMS stations, then the list of possible sites could be very short. It could be worthwhile to include more potential sites and use the model to quantify the amount by which EMS response times could be reduced by relaxing zoning regulations. Conversely, when EMS operates separately from fire services, but the fire service provides first response to EMS calls, one should perhaps include the current fire station locations and use the model to find a set of EMS station locations that complement the fire stations in a way that minimizes first response times.

Station planning and ambulance allocation are closely linked: on the one hand, station locations constrain the way in which ambulances can be deployed. On the other hand, the way in which ambulances are deployed determines the performance of a plan that indicates where stations should be located. According to one point of view, one should therefore develop models that simultaneously optimize station locations and ambulance allocation. Another point of view is that it is natural and appropriate to separate the two, given that station planning is a strategic issue, whereas ambulance allocation is a tactical and operational issue. Furthermore, integrated models may oversimplify ambulance allocation, because they do not take into consideration how the allocation should change as a function of day of the week and hour of the day in order to match demand patterns, for example.

6.5.2 Ambulance Allocation

Notwithstanding the need to consider how ambulance allocation should vary with time to match daily and weekly demand patterns, I begin by discussing optimization models for allocating ambulances to stations in a static situation. These models are

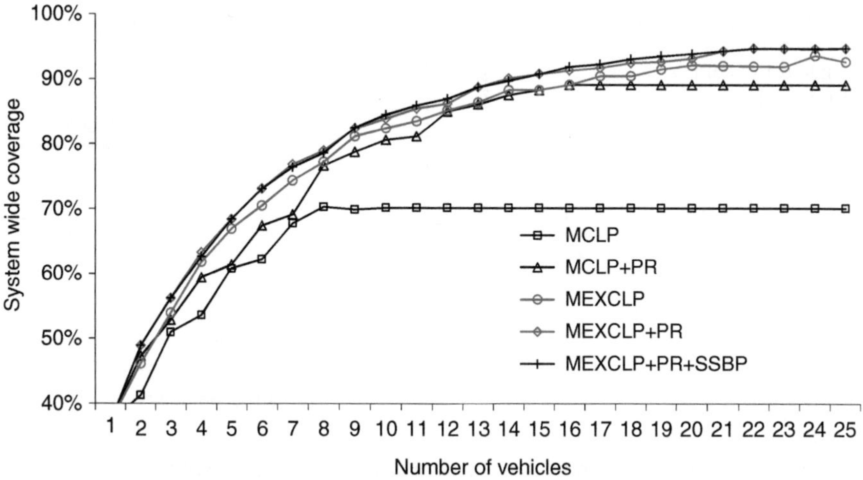

Fig. 6.14 Expected coverage for various ambulance allocation models, evaluated using the approximate hypercube model. MCLP, maximum coverage location problem; MEXCLP, maximum expected coverage location problem; PR, probabilistic response times; SSBP, station-specific busy probabilities (from [16])

based on the assumption that every ambulance will return to the station to which it has been assigned at the conclusion of every call. Several such models are compared in [16] the MCLP, the MCLP + PR, the MEXCLP, and variations of MEXLCP that incorporate probabilistic response times and busy probabilities that vary by station. Figure 6.14 shows how expected coverage, as evaluated using the approximate hypercube model and incorporating stochastic response times, varies as the number of ambulances that are allocated to a set of 16 stations increases from 1 to 25. The more realistic models result in expected coverage that is considerably higher, especially when the number of ambulances is larger than the number of stations.

All the models that [16] compare are formulated as mathematical programs, and such formulations require some simplifications. Alternatively, one can formulate the problem more directly, as follows:

$$P : \text{maximize } \operatorname{cov}(z_1, \ldots, z_n),$$
$$\text{subject to } \sum_{i=1}^{n} z_j = q;\ z_j \in \{0, \ldots, c_j\},$$

where cov(.) is the expected coverage, evaluated with the approximate hypercube model, for example; c_j and z_j are the capacity and the number of ambulances assigned to station j, respectively; n is the number of stations; and q is the number of ambulances to be allocated. Erdogan et al. [13] describe a tabu search heuristic to

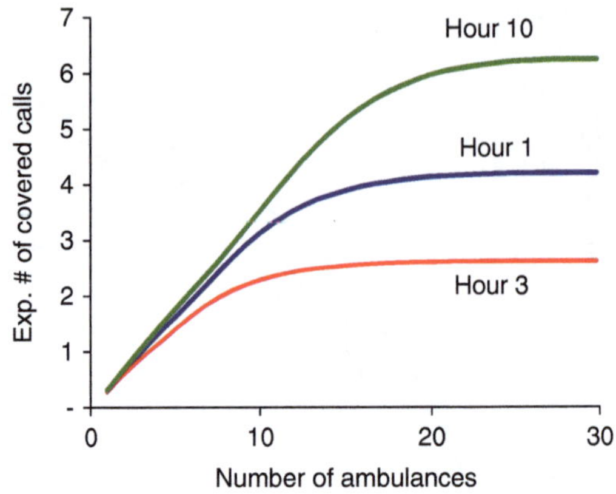

Fig. 6.15 Expected number of covered calls as a function of number of ambulances (based on [16]

solve this problem, and report that the tabu search finds better solutions in less time than does the mathematical programming-based heuristic discussed in [16].

Erdogan et al. [13] present one way of planning ambulance deployment over a weekly time horizon. First, solve problem P repeatedly, for each hour of the week and for every possible total number of ambulances, in order to generate expected coverage curves like those shown in Fig. 6.15. Note that the input data for the instances of P that are solved at this stage will reflect differences in average call volume by hour of the week, and can also reflect other predictable changes in the spatial distribution of calls or in travel speeds, for example. Second, incorporate the maximum expected coverage values from the first stage into a linear integer program that simultaneously determines how many ambulances to assign for each hour of the week and weekly shifts for the ambulance crews. The solutions to P for each hour of the week specify the way to allocate the ambulances to stations. This procedure is an example of *preplanned repositioning*. Other examples of models for preplanned repositioning include [50, 49, 52].

Finally, I mention the currently active research topic of repositioning based on the system state, or *real-time repositioning*, which involves EMS dispatchers moving ambulances in real time to fill "holes" in coverage. In Sect. 6.4, I mentioned compliance table policies for real-time repositioning and a Markov chain model to analyze the performance of these policies. Other researchers have investigated the use of approximate dynamic programming to find optimal repositioning policies—see [41, 51], for example.

Some of the issues regarding repositioning that could benefit from further study include:

- If and how to integrate preplanned and real-time repositioning: All the work done so far focuses on either preplanned or real-time repositioning (although the approximate dynamic programming approach used in [41] could, in principle, incorporate both types of repositioning).
- Trade-off between improvement in performance and increase in workload: Workload is increased by repositioning, especially when done in real time for

ambulance crews that are currently idle at a station. Empirical work could clarify whether the increased workload increases fatigue, back pain, job satisfaction, or has other undesirable consequences. Further modeling work could lead to tools to help dispatchers decide if the increase in coverage resulting from a potential ambulance move outweighs the increased workload.
- Suboptimality of compliance table policies: Compliance tables are already used in practice for real-time repositioning, and they are simple to explain and to use. Approximate dynamic programming approaches, which do not restrict the form of real-time repositioning policies, could be used to investigate the performance loss resulting from the use of a compliance table policy and to determine if compliance table policies are optimal in some situations.

6.6 Conclusions and Policy Implications

The amount and scope of OR/MS research on EMS planning and management have grown rapidly in recent years, perhaps fueled by the increased availability of detailed EMS call data and persistent pressure on EMS providers to operate more efficiently. Availability of EMS call data makes it possible to investigate the accuracy of modeling assumptions used in the past and to improve understanding of the way EMS systems operate. Although it is valuable to question modeling assumptions and although computing power continues to increase, modelers should not forget about parsimony and tractability. An ideal model is one that is no more complicated than necessary to shed light on the health-care decisions or issues that prompted the development or use of the model. A more realistic model is not always a more useful model.

Although EMS data are more readily available than ever, the data collected are not always the ideal data for informing the decisions of EMS planners. EMS call data reports the journey of a patient from the moment the EMS agency receives a call until EMS staff complete their care or until they transfer care to another part of the health-care system. Linking EMS data to information about what happened to the patient before and after the EMS call is necessary in order to develop and track performance measures that emphasize medical outcomes rather than response times. A greater focus on medical outcomes could help planners and policy makers compare the consequences of competing uses of funds, particularly in jurisdictions where EMS is part of a publicly funded health-care system. Measures of medical outcomes, such as survival probabilities, can typically be incorporated into existing EMS planning models without greatly complicating them, so the challenge lies in collecting and analyzing the appropriate data—not in model formulation and solution. Linking patient data collected by different agencies also presents challenges in safeguarding patient privacy and confidentiality. In the absence of reliable information about outcome measures, models that incorporate response-time variability appear to provide better proxies for outcome measures than do models based on deterministic distance-based coverage.

Acknowledgements I thank Ms. Fernanda Campello for research assistance, Mr. Daniel Haight and Mr. Mohammad Salama for access to preliminary results of [25], the coauthors that collaborated with me on work that was surveyed in this chapter [1, 7, 16, 13, 5, 15, 30, 29, 4, 14], an anonymous referee and the editor for valuable suggestions, Nina Colwill and Dennis Anderson for editorial assistance, and Alberta Health Services for access to data. I gratefully acknowledge research support from the Natural Sciences and Engineering Research Council of Canada.

References

1. Alanis R, Ingolfsson A, Kolfal B (2012) A Markov chain model for an EMS system with repositioning. Oper Manage (Forthcoming)
2. Alberta Health Services (2011) Annual report 2010-2011
3. Brotcorne L, Laporte G, Semet F (2003) Ambulance location and relocation models. Euro J Oper Res 147(3):451–463
4. Budge S, Ingolfsson A, Erkut E (2009) Technical note–Approximating vehicle dispatch probabilities for emergency service systems with location-specific service times and multiple units per location. Oper Res 57(1):251–255
5. Budge S, Ingolfsson A, Zerom D (2010) Empirical analysis of ambulance travel times: The case of Calgary Emergency Medical Services. Manage Sci 56(4):716–723
6. Chaiken JM, Larson RC (1972) Methods for allocating urban emergency units: A survey. Manage Sci 19(4):P110–P130
7. Channouf N, L'Ecuyer P, Ingolfsson A, Avramidis A (2007) The application of forecasting techniques to modeling emergency medical system calls in Calgary, Alberta. Health Care Manage Sci 10(1):25–45
8. Church R, ReVelle C (1974) The maximal covering location problem. Pap Reg Sci 32(1):101–118
9. City of Toronto (2011) 2011 Operating Budget Summary
10. Daskin MS (1983) A maximum expected covering location model: Formulation, properties and heuristic solution. Transport Sci 17(1):48–70
11. Daskin MS (1987) Location, dispatching, and routing model for emergency services with stochastic travel times. In: Ghosh A, Rushton G (ed) Spatial analysis and location-allocation models. Van Nostrand Reinhold, New York, pp 224–265
12. Department of Health (2012) Ambulance quality indicators. www.dh.gov.uk/en/Publicationsandstatistics/Statistics/Performancedataandstatistics/AmbulanceQualityIndicators/index.htm
13. Erdogan G, Erkut E, Ingolfsson A, Laporte G (2010) Scheduling ambulance crews for maximum coverage. J Oper Res Soc 61(4):543–550 .
14. Erkut E, Ingolfsson A, Budge S, Haight D, Litchfield J, Akyol O, Holmes G, Cheng J Final report: The impact of ambulance system status management. Unpublished report, prepared for the Emergency Response Department, City of Edmonton, March 2005
15. Erkut E, Ingolfsson A, Erdogan G (2008) Ambulance location for maximum survival. Nav Res Log 55(1):42–58
16. Erkut E, Ingolfsson A, Sim T, Erdogan G (2009) Computational comparison of five maximal covering models for locating ambulances. Geogr Anal 41(1):43–65
17. Federal Interagency Committee for Emergency Medical Services (2011) National EMS assessment
18. Felder S, Brinkmann H (2002) Spatial allocation of emergency medical services: Minimising the death rate or providing equal access? Reg Sci Urban Econ 32(1):27–45
19. Fitch J (2005) Response times: Myths, measurement & management. JEMS : A J Emerg Med Services 30(1):46–56 .

20. Goldberg JB (2004) Operations research models for the deployment of emergency service vehicles. EMS Manage J 1:20–39
21. Green LV, Kolesar PJ (2004) Improving emergency responsiveness with management science. Manage Sci 50(8):1001–1014
22. Gunes E, Szechtman R (2005) A simulation model of a helicopter ambulance service. In: Proceedings of the 2005 Winter Simulation Conference. IEEE Press, Piscataway, NJ, pp 951–957
23. Gunnarsson B, Svavarsdottir H, Duason S, Sim A, Munro A, McInnes C, MacDonald R, Angquist K, Nordstrom B (2007) Ambulance Transport and Services in the Rural Areas of Iceland, Scotland and Sweden. J Emerge Primary Health Care 5(1):1–12
24. Haight D (2010) Agency uses patient-centric approach for station location: How response time goals factor into your decision. JEMS Emerge Med Services
25. Haight D, Salama M (2012) Survey of Canadian EMS operators. Unpublished, May 2012
26. Health Quality Council of Alberta (2011) Review of the safety implications for patients requiring medevac services to and from the Edmonton International Airport
27. Henderson SG (2005) Should we model dependence and nonstationarity, and if so, how? In: Proceedings of the 2005 Winter Simulation Conference. IEEE Press, Piscataway, NJ, pp 120–129
28. Henderson SG, Mason AJ (2005) Ambulance service planning: Simulation and data visualisation. In: Brandeau ML, Sainfort F, Pierskalla WP (ed) operations research and health care: A handbook of methods and applications, chap 4. Kluwer Academic, Boston, MA, pp 77–102
29. Ingolfsson A, Budge S, Erkut E (2008) Optimal ambulance location with random delays and travel times. Health Care Manage Sci 11(3):262
30. Ingolfsson A, Erkut E, Budge S (2003) Simulation of single start station for Edmonton EMS. J Oper Res Soc 54(7):736–746
31. Jarvis JP (1985) Approximating the equilibrium behavior of multi-server loss systems. Manage Sci 31(2):235–239
32. Kc DS, Terwiesch C (2009) Impact of workload on service time and patient safety: An econometric analysis of hospital operations. Manage Sci 55(9):1486–1498
33. Knight V, Harper P, Smith L (2012) Ambulance allocation for maximal survival with heterogeneous outcome measures. Omega 40(6):918–926
34. Kolesar P, Walker W, Hausner J (1975) Determining the relation between fire engine travel times and travel distances in New York City. Oper Res 23(4):614–628
35. Larson RC (1974) A hypercube queuing model for facility location and redistricting in urban emergency services. Comput Oper Res 1(1):67–95
36. Larson RC (1975) Approximating the performance of urban emergency service systems. Oper Res 23(5):845–868
37. Li X, Zhao Z, Zhu X, Wyatt T (2011) Covering models and optimization techniques for emergency response facility location and planning: A review. Math Methods Oper Res 74(3):281–310
38. London Ambulance Service (2010) Annual report 2009/10, June 2010
39. Mason A (2012) Simulation and real-time optimised relocation for improving ambulance operations. In: Denton B (ed) Healthcare Operations Management: A Handbook of Methods and Applications
40. Matteson DS, McLean MW, Woodard DB, Henderson SG (2011) Forecasting emergency medical service call arrival rates. Ann App Stat 5(2B):1379–1406
41. Maxwell MS, Restrepo M, Henderson SG, Topaloglu H (2010) Approximate dynamic programming for ambulance redeployment. INFORMS J Comput 22(2):266–281
42. McLay L, Mayorga M (2010) Evaluating emergency medical service performance measures. Health Care Manage Sci 13(2):124–136

43. McLay, LA, Boone EL, Brooks JP (2012) Analyzing the volume and nature of emergency medical calls during severe weather events using regression methodologies. Socio-Econ Plan Sci 46(1):55–66
44. McLay LA, Mayorga ME (2011) Evaluating the impact of performance goals on dispatching decisions in emergency medical service. IIE Transactions on Healthcare Systems Engineering 1(3):185–196
45. Morneau PM, Stothart JP (1999) My aching back. The effects of system status management & ambulance design on EMS personnel. JEMS : A J Emerge Med Services 24(8):36–50, 78–81
46. NFPA (2004) NFPA 1710: Standard for the organization and deployment of fire suppression operations, emergency medical operations, and special operations to the public, by career fire departments. National Fire Protection Assocation, Quincy, MA
47. Noyan N (2010) Alternate risk measures for emergency medical service system design. Ann Oper Res 181(1):559–589
48. Ottawa Paramedic Service (2012) Service reliability. Accessed 1 June 2012
49. Rajagopalan HK, Saydam C, Xiao J (2008) A multiperiod set covering location model for dynamic redeployment of ambulances. Comput Oper Res 35(3):814–826
50. Repede JF, Bernardo JJ (1994) Developing and validating a decision support system for locating emergency medical vehicles in Louisville, Kentucky. Eur J Oper Res 75(3):567–581
51. Schmid V (2012) Solving the dynamic ambulance relocation and dispatching problem using approximate dynamic programming. Eur J Oper Res 219(3):611–621
52. Schmid V, Doerner KF (2010) Ambulance location and relocation problems with time-dependent travel times. Eur J Oper Res 207(3):1293–1303 .
53. Setzler H, Saydam C, Park S (2009) EMS call volume predictions: A comparative study. Comput Opera Res 36(6):1843–1851
54. Skandalakis P, Lainas P, Zoras O, Skandalakis J, Mirilas P (2006) "To afford the wounded speedy assistance": Dominique Jean Larrey and Napoleon. World J Surg 30(8):1392–1399 10.1007/s00268-005-0436-8.
55. Studnek JR, Crawford JM, Wilkins J, Pennell ML (2010) Back problems among emergency medical services professionals: The leads health and wellness follow-up study. Am J Ind Med 53(1):12–22
56. Swersey AJ (1994) The deployment of police, fire, and emergency medical units. In: Rothkopf MH, Pollock SM, Barnett A (ed) Operations Research and The Public Sector. Handbooks in Operations Research and Management Science, vol 6. Elsevier, pp 151–200
57. Valenzuela TD, Roe DJ, Cretin S, Spaite DW, Larsen MP (1997) Estimating effectiveness of cardiac arrest interventions : A logistic regression survival model. Circulation 96(10):3308–3313
58. Vile JL, Gillard JW, Harper PR, Knight VA (2012) Predicting ambulance demand using singular spectrum analysis. J Oper Res Soc 63(11):1556–1565 (Advance online publication).
59. Westgate BS, Woodard DB, Matteson DS, Henderson SG (2012) Travel time estimation for ambulances using Bayesian data augmentation. Working paper
60. Wikipedia. Reykjavik airport, 2012. en.wikipedia.org/wiki/Reykjavik_Airport, accessed 30 May 2012
61. Zhu Z, McKnew MA, Lee J (1992) Effects of time-varied arrival rates: An investigation in emergency ambulance service systems. In: Proceedings of the 1992 Winter Simulation Conference. IEEE Press, Piscataway, NJ, pp 1180–1186

Chapter 7
Impact of Inpatient Reimbursement Systems on Hospital Performance: The Austrian Case-Based Payment Strategy

Marion S. Rauner and Michaela M. Schaffhauser-Linzatti

Abstract Due to cost-intensive technological advances in high-end medicine and increased life expectancy accompanied by a rising number of multi-morbid elderly people, the health care sector consumes a large part of the gross national product of Austria. As the hospital sector is the main contributor to this increasingly unaffordable cost explosion, reimbursement systems for inpatients worldwide have been undergoing massive restructuring. Case-based systems such as the Austrian performance-oriented LKF-system have been introduced to curb the cost explosion. While macro-perspective studies analyze the efficiency of hospitals based on aggregated input and output data using DEA techniques, micro-perspective studies focus on the main incentives of the LKF-system on several outcome measures using empirical data on inpatients with certain major diseases. This study illustrates its impact on hospitals' performance as well as on the hospitals' management subsystem of strategic technology management. Such studies support health regulators in improving their reimbursement schemes by closing loopholes.

M.S. Rauner (✉)
Department of Innovation and Technology Management, University of Vienna,
Bruenner Str. 72, 1210 Vienna, Austria
e-mail: Marion.Rauner@univie.ac.at

M.M. Schaffhauser-Linzatti
Department of External Accounting, University of Vienna,
Bruenner Str. 72, 1210 Vienna, Austria
e-mail: Michaela.Linzatti@univie.ac.at

G.S. Zaric (ed.), *Operations Research and Health Care Policy*,
International Series in Operations Research & Management Science 190,
DOI 10.1007/978-1-4614-6507-2_7,

7.1 Introduction

Austria has over eight million inhabitants and ranks among the richest countries in the world [43]. A lot of attention is paid to health care by policymakers [62]. The Austrian health care system is financed by a solidarity-based funding principle which guarantees equal access to health services for all inhabitants, independent of their income, age, sex, and origin. In 2007, over 10 % of the Austrian gross domestic product was spent on the health care sector, which was above the average consumed by the European Union (EU)-15 members [12]. About 76 % of the total health care expenditure was raised by both public sources and social insurance. Inpatient care consumed the highest share of the total health care expenditure (33.5 %) and the total expenditure for long-term care (12.4 %) also contained some expenditure for inpatient care, while about 18.2 % of the health care budget was spent on out-patient care. Medical supplies for out-patients accounted for about 17.1 % of total health care costs.

Cost-intensive technological advances in high-end medicine and increased life expectancy accompanied by a rising number of multi-morbid elderly people lead to the consequence that the health care sector consumes a large part of gross national product [30]. The hospital sector is the main contributor to this increasingly unaffordable cost explosion. In addition, new drugs are often discussed as an important cost contributor [1, 25].

In order to contain costs in the hospital sector, reimbursement systems for inpatients worldwide have been undergoing massive restructuring [38]. In 1997, Austria introduced a performance-oriented, case-based payment system for inpatients (called Leistungsorientierte Krankenhausfinanzierung, LKF-system) to overcome problems with the old day-based payment system. This LKF-system follows the idea of a diagnosis-related (DRG)-based payment scheme in which inpatients are reimbursed based on their diagnoses, treatments, and care.

Quantitative models for analyzing the effects of alternative reimbursement systems on hospital efficiency (macro effects) and inpatient care (micro effects) represent key decision-making tools for hospital administrators and policymakers. In this review, micro-perspective policy models for the Austrian case-based LKF-system are discussed. Several of these models also compare the Austrian case-based LKF-system with other reimbursement systems. Most of the results for the LKF-system are general enough to be transferred to other case-based reimbursement systems internationally.

The next section outlines general incentives of different inpatient payment strategies for hospitals. Section 7.3 then describes the Austrian performance-oriented case-based LKF-system. Section 7.4 presents and discusses quantitative studies on main incentives of the LKF-system for hospitals with a focus on micro-perspective-based policy models. For each key quantitative approach, policy implications are drawn and future research questions are outlined. Section 7.5 illustrates the impact of the LKF-system on a hospital's management subsystem using the example of strategic technology management. Conclusions and further research are summarized in the final section.

7.2 General Incentives of Inpatient Payment Strategies for Hospitals

Reimbursement systems for inpatients can be generally divided into four general types [40]: (1) single procedure-based payment (fee-for-service payment), (2) payment for day-based grouped performances (day-based payment), (3) payment for case-based grouped performances (case-based payment), (4) and payment for overall performances per accounting period (global budget-based payment with either a flexible or a fixed budget). Side-payments for quality care can be additionally considered. These systems have different incentives for hospitals to modify factor input and production prices for single procedures as illustrated in Fig. 7.1.

If hospitals are reimbursed for all single procedures, they will have a high incentive to increase reimbursement by performing more single procedures, by means of increasing the number of nursing days, and/or by raising the number of inpatients treated [40]. On the factor level side, these hospitals will try to save money. Due to these severe drawbacks, this payment system is mainly applied for reimbursing private inpatients and has nearly vanished as reimbursement strategy for public inpatients worldwide [38].

An improved payment scheme for curbing hospital costs is the day-based payment strategy because a fixed amount per inpatient day independent of treatment and care is reimbursed instead of all single performances for inpatients. Under this payment strategy, hospitals can only increase reimbursement by expanding the

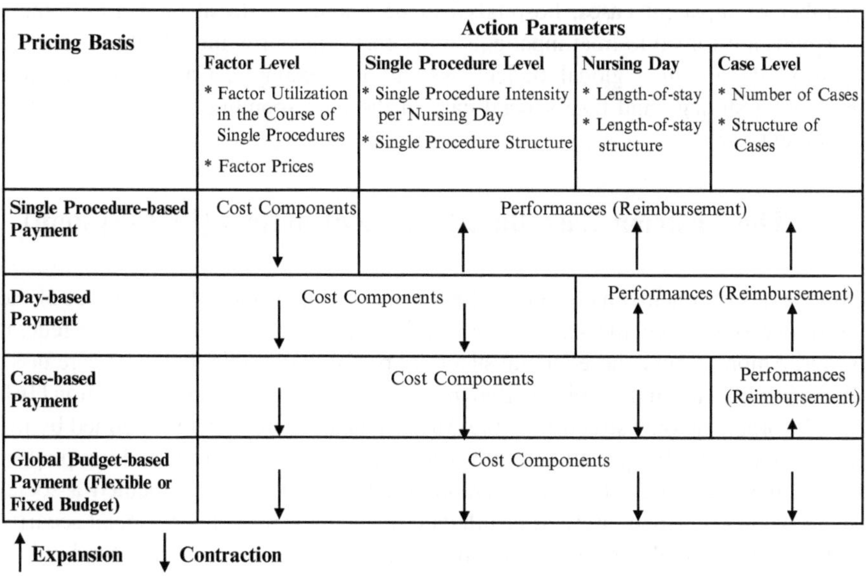

Fig. 7.1 General incentives of inpatient payment strategies for hospitals [40]

number of inpatient days or cases treated. As this payment strategy still contains many disadvantages, many countries such as Austria have abandoned day-based payment strategies [12, 38].

If policymakers want to force hospitals to discharge patients earlier, a case-based payment strategy will have to be introduced. Then, the payment depends on a differentiated case with standardized treatment and care as well as a certain range for the length-of-stay. Hospitals can only increase reimbursement by raising the number of inpatient cases. This is why many countries worldwide use this payment strategy. In the USA, a DRG-based payment system for medicare patients was introduced in the 1980s to enforce economic efficiency and cost reductions in hospitals [18]. The Australian Refined Diagnosis Related Groups (AR-DRGs) influenced the German DRG-system that was implemented in 2003 [27]. Further examples of case-based systems include the Austrian LKF-system or the French Groupes homogènes de malades (GHM) [12, 26].

For example, Rauner and Schaffhauser [49] generally analyzed the case-based Austrian payment system with its main incentives for hospitals which will be discussed in detail in Sect. 7.3.2: (1) optimized admission, (2) risk selection, (3) up-coding and DRG-creep, (4) DRG-point gathering, (5) unbundling, (6) optimized discharge, and (7) effect. Depending on the external environment (general environment groups, regulators, venders and suppliers, payers, recipients and impactees, health care providers) and internal environment of the hospital, hospitals react differently to a case-based system. This study added to the general overview by Pfeiffer [44] and a general system review by Sommersguter-Reichmann and Stepan [60] as well as Stepan and Sommersguter-Reichmann [63].

In order to overcome the incentive to increase reimbursement by raising the number of inpatient cases, hospitals can be granted a global budget. Although hospitals are forced to treat inpatients most cost-efficiently, they might reduce the quality of care in a global budget system. For example, Canada applies this budgeting strategy and take special care of the corresponding quality of medical treatment [39].

7.3 The Austrian Case-Based Payment System (LKF-System)

Austria has been a member state of the European Union since 1995 and part of the euro zone as well as of the Schengen area. It is a democratic republic with nine federal states. Among others, these federal states are partly responsible for health care tasks such as public hospitals, social welfare money, care allowances, and prevention [16].

The organizational structure of the Austrian health care system is defined by the interaction of public, private non-profit-making, and private profit-making players [31]. Like many other European Union countries, Austria implemented a social security system. About 50 % of health care financing is provided by social security contributions and about 20 % by public means that are mainly used to fund public and nonprofit private hospitals. The remaining 30 % of the health care funds are raised by public households.

In Austria, more than 80 % of the hospital beds are acute care beds [11]. About 70 % of the hospital beds are general hospital beds and 30 % are specialized hospital beds. Due to the geographic and demographic structure of the small country, about 56 % of all hospital beds are located in small and medium-sized hospitals with less than 499 beds, while about 23 and 21 % of the beds are located in big and central hospitals, respectively.

To cope with the target of cost reductions and efficiency increases the LKF-system introduced in 1997 applies a case-based reimbursement model for inpatients. Among others, it differs from other similar DRG-based systems by including day clinics, ambulances, by developing an individual catalogue to identify cost-homogeneous groups of inpatients, and by defining upper and lower boundaries for the length-of-stay (LOS) [21, 27, 39, 65]. The key distinction from other systems is the centralized cap of the overall budget and the decentralized influences of the federal states at the same time. While country-wide identical LDF-points are allocated to inpatients according to their diagnoses and treatments, federal state-specific influences weight these LDF-points individually. As the LDF-points are finally transformed into monetary values, this allocation mechanism might result in a different reimbursement for one and the same diagnoses and treatment in each federal state [45].

7.3.1 *The Development of the Austrian Case-Based Payment System*

7.3.1.1 The Day-Based Payment Strategy Before 1997

Before 1997, Austria followed a day-based payment strategy (cf. Fig. 7.1). By law, the Krankenanstaltenzusammenarbeitsfonds (KRAZAF) was established to control and to fund public and nonprofit private hospitals [19]. This fund was reimbursed by a fixed percentage of the value added tax levied by the federal government, federal states, and municipalities as well as by the association of Austrian social insurance institutions [35]. The complicated allocation mechanism of the financial means comprised two parts: (1) a federal states quota which was divided among the federal states according to a fixed percentage and was used for hospitals' reimbursement, and (2) a structural quota to cover defined investments and special medical performances such as ambulances [19].

The federal states regulated the public and nonprofit private hospitals' reimbursement which was based on a day-based payment per inpatient independent of diagnoses and treatments. Disadvantages of this day-based lump-sum payment comprised the tendency to maximize the inpatients' LOS and the hospitals' bed occupancy rate in order to increase performances. Because hospitals did not face tight budget restraints and because losses were covered, an overall efficient and effective resource allocation was neglected [51].

7.3.1.2 The Initial Case-Based LKF-System Introduced in 1997

The Austrian day-based payment strategy which was applied before 1997 proved inadequate for cost containment. In order to overcome the drawbacks of this system (cf. Sect. 7.2), Austria abandoned this undifferentiated day-based lump-sum reimbursement in 1997 and installed the performance-oriented LKF-system for effective and efficient cost management, coordinated performances among hospitals, medically optimal LOS, and—for the first time—a detailed documentation of an inpatient's diagnoses and treatments.

When introducing the LKF-system, Austria radically restructured the financial and medical performances of its hospitals [31]. In general, the universal Austrian health care system is structured on a national and a regional level in the nine federal states [12]. Since abandoning the KRAZAF in 1997, in each federal state, a Federal Health Fund with its Regional Health Platform has been responsible for the reimbursement of its fund hospitals under the LKF-system, including all public hospitals and nonprofit private hospitals [31]. In 2006, 50.4 % of the Austrian hospitals were federal fund hospitals financed by Regional Health Funds. These fund hospitals comprised 133 public and nonprofit hospitals with 48,870 beds apart from the emergency hospitals in 2006 [11]. Only 16.3 % or 43 hospitals with 4,031 beds were for-profit private hospitals funded by Private Hospital Funds (DRG-based) and about 33.3 % or 88 hospitals with 10,453 beds were for-profit private hospitals run by private owners (non-DRG-based).

The federal government, federal states, municipalities, social insurance and other institutions distributed financial means to the Federal Health Funds by a fixed formula. These funds were then responsible for financing their units and departments; ambulance care; and departmental cost centers [14, 49].

In order to create an economic basis for the new case-based LKF-system, the performances for 5,000 socially insured inpatients of 20 hospitals were calculated. These results entered into a performance catalogue and finally led to the so-called LDF-points (points allocated to a Leistungsorientierte Diagnosefallgruppe as discussed in "Core Part" section) which represent a fictitious value that is gained for a performance. These points are transformed into monetary values at the end of each financial period as will be shown in Sect. 7.3.1.3 [9, 14].

The performance catalogue and the thus defined LDF-points became obligatory for all Austrian fund hospitals included in the LKF-system [10]. In 1997, the LKF-system was applied to general inpatients who were covered by social insurance. It excluded nursing and asylum cases as well as private inpatients. Semi-stationary patients of psychiatric departments as well as inpatients of other defined departments were still reimbursed by a lump-sum per day [9].

Figure 7.2 shows the general structure of the LKF-system as introduced in 1997. Until now, this structure has not been changed fundamentally but undergoes regular revisions for improvement. Details and current status of the LKF-system will be presented in Sect. 7.3.1.3 Each Federal Health Fund provides a lump sum for inpatient care which is split into two parts: the national core part and the federal regulation part.

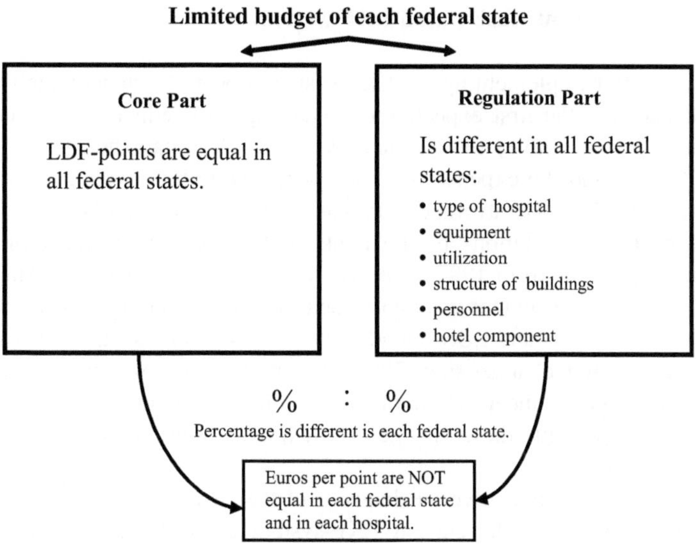

Fig. 7.2 Influence of the core and regulation parts on inpatient reimbursement in federal states

The core part is defined identically in all federal states (cf. "Core Part" section). It contains a DRG-like reimbursement system to allocate the LDF-points for diagnoses and medical performances on inpatients. For identical performances, the same amount of LDF-points is allocated to the performing hospital for its inpatient.

The regulation part is defined individually in each federal state. In 1997, it took into account the structure-specific quality criteria of hospitals, i.e., type of hospital, equipment, utilization, structure of buildings, personnel, and hotel component. Please note that these criteria have been replaced in the latest LKF-model (cf. "Regulation Part" section). Reimbursement of hospitals in and among federal states differs considerably due to the weight of the financial split between core and regulation parts for the units and departments; the inclusion and treatment of ambulance care and other departmental cost centers; and the refunding of losses [49].

The overall limited budget of each federal state is allocated to the core part and to the regulation part. The budget allocated to the core part is divided by all gathered LDF-points of the hospitals in a federal state to calculate the amount of each LDF-point in euro. These LDF-points are distributed for reported diagnoses and performances on an identical basis for each hospital. However, due to the different weights on the core and regulation parts in the federal states, the total LDF-points of each hospital may be differently weighted. Under the premises of these different weights and of a limited budget, the LDF-points of one and the same treatment may result in different payments in euro for each hospital. For example, in some federal states the LDF-points of the core part are multiplied by a special factor to account for the special characteristics of hospitals, while in other hospitals LDF-points for the regulation part are added to the LDF-points from the core part.

7.3.1.3 The Current Case-Based LKF-System

Only 1 year after implementing the LKF-system, hospitals changed their financial behavior and met the first expectations regarding cost reductions and efficiency gains [51]. For example, the financial losses of Vienna's hospitals decreased by about 24 % and the expenses by about 4 %, while the revenues increased by approximately 16 %. The average LOS was reduced by about 9 %.

Retrospective calculations of inpatients' data sets and recalculations of the economic LKF-basis from 1997 have been conducted regularly to update, among other things, the performance catalogue, identification of cost-homogenous groups, amount of LDF-points and LOS-boundaries (cf. "Core Part" section). These results have induced system changes since 2002 [45] which have proven necessary in order to counteract negative incentives to maximize reimbursement [10, 56]. The following Sect. 7.3.2 presents these changes and explains how they could reduce such system weaknesses.

To understand the incentive mechanisms of the LKF-system, its details will be presented by means of the current LKF-system 2011. Figure 7.3 displays the complex system of the performance-oriented LDF-point allocation algorithm for the core part and the regulation part of the LKF-model of 2011 [13].

Core Part

The core part is regulated identically on a national basis. Figure 7.3 shows the path how LDF-points are allocated to diagnoses and treatments of an inpatient.

Following the Federal Ministry of Health [13], the hospital first has to categorize inpatients at the admission as

1. Asylum or nursing cases, which are still not integrated in the LKF-system
2. Semi-stationary cases comprising psychiatry, acute geriatrics, psychosomatic medicine and psychotherapy, which are allocated a predefined treatment component per day as defined below and are still not integrated in the LKF-system
3. Inpatients, day clinics, and rehabilitation cases which are again divided into
   (a) Special function departments which do not accommodate general inpatients and which are defined by the Federal Ministry of Health, comprising among others
      - Remobilization/post care, which are allocated LDF-points per day
      - Palliative units which are allocated LDF-points per day and decreasing points per day after an upper boundary of length-of-stay (LOS)
      - Acute neurological post care as well as child and youth psychiatry which are allocated points per day depending on treatment patterns

   (b) Non-special function departments hosting general inpatients not especially allocated to other departments as defined by the Federal Ministry of Health

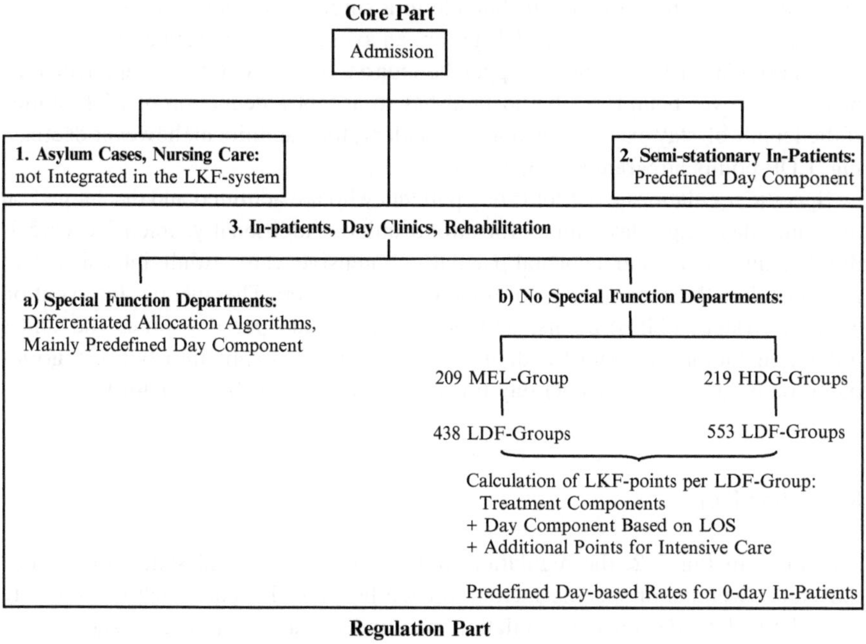

Fig. 7.3 The Austrian LKF-system of 2011

Inpatients in departments with no special function represent the main standard cases and are consequently described in the following paragraphs in more detail. Treatment for these inpatients is first divided into [13,14]:

1. Procedure-related groups (based on an Austria-specific standardized listing of procedure codes), called Medizinische Einzelleistungen (MEL)
2. Main diagnosis groups-related to the ICD-10 BMSG 2001 (International Classification of Diseases 10th edition, Modification of the Federal Ministry of Health) called Hauptdiagnose-Gruppen (HDG), also leading to LDF-groups

Both MEL-groups and HDG-groups lead to diversified performance-oriented diagnosis-related groups, called Leistungsorienterte Diagnosefallgruppen (LDF-groups) which may be again split into subgroups subject to criteria such as age or gender. These LDF-groups are similar to other DRG group-based systems [38]. Their number and characteristics are revised every year. For the year 2011, 209 MEL-groups and 438 corresponding LDF-groups as well as 219 HDG-groups and 553 corresponding LDF-groups are established [13]. The assignment of each inpatient to one specific LDF-group follows a certain path in a defined regression tree that identifies cost-homogeneous groups of inpatients.

Each LDF-group is granted LDF-points which are a compound of a treatment component and a day component. The treatment component includes single costs of treatments such as personnel costs for a surgery team. The day component includes all costs that are not directly attributable to a single treatment such as care and it depends on the LOS. For each LDF-group, an average LOS is defined for standard calculations by a lower and an upper boundary. If the LOS of an inpatient falls below the lower boundary, the hospital has to accept a deduction of LDF-points. If the length-of-stay exceeds the upper boundary, then additional, however decreasing, LDF-points are granted [13,49,51].

Specific regulations exist for 0-day patients who are admitted and discharged on the same day (e.g., day clinics for stroke units). Additionally, intensive care is divided into adult and neonatal/paediatric intensive care. Adult intensive care accounts for three categories of inpatients based on Therapeutic Intervention Scoring System (TISS)-points, and predefined points per day times the unit's utilization factor. Neonatal/paediatric intensive care is split into two categories based on predefined points per day times a so-called plausibility factor [13].

Regulation Part

As shown in Fig. 7.2, the regulation part allows each federal state to introduce individual weights of specific factors in each hospital. Because each federal state was allowed to design the regulation part individually, all federal states have different regulations which undergo slight alterations every year [5, 32, 33, 45, 49, 50, 53]. In the LFK-system of 1997, the regulation part considered aspects of type, equipment, utilization, structure of the buildings, the personnel, and the hotel component. The newly designed regulation part of the LKF-model of 2011 permits the recognition of the following region-specific supply side factors accounting for hospital size and/or specialization: (1) central supply (e.g., university clinic Graz), (2) priority supply (e.g., federal capital hospital Klagenfurt), (3) specific specialist supply (e.g., Orthopedic Hospital Speising, Vienna), and (4) specific regional supply (e.g., Klosterneuburg hospital) [14]. As a consequence of this system-immanent system encouraging individual regulations, the LDF-points identically calculated in the core part can be weighted according to the supply side factors of the regulation part. In order to demonstrate the influence of the regulation part, the Federal Health Fund of Styria uses a fixed coefficient per hospital for the regulation part. In 2006, the LDF-points of the university clinic of Graz are weighted by 1.3, while the LDF-points of two other main federal hospitals are weighted by 1.05 and the LDF-points of general hospitals are weighted by 1.0 [24].

7.3.2 Key Changes to the Case-Based LKF-System Between 1997 and 2011

In order to improve the accuracy of the LKF-model and to prevent hospital managers from exploiting such a system's weaknesses [7, 18, 21, 40, 41, 69], the

LKF's core part as well as the regulation part undergo alterations and adaptations at regular intervals [5, 32, 33, 45, 49, 53]. Among others, these changes could abolish or at least reduce counterproductive strategies such as bureaucratic and time structure optimization strategies, performance optimization strategies, and quantity optimization strategies [54].

7.3.2.1 Bureaucratic and Time Structure Optimization Strategies

Relevant parameters of the LKF-system such as LDF-points or LOS are revised annually. The recalculations in 2002, 2009, and 2010 [28] mainly suppressed DRG-creep via up-coding [34, 66], i.e., allocating inpatients to more expensive DRG-groups than the adequate cheaper case groups [45]; DRG-point gathering by conducting additionally funded performances; and exploitation of specific extra-paid regulations. For example, the LKF-model of 2009 introduced regulations for charging multiple performances and patient splitting, i.e., splitting an inpatient into several cases.

Optimizing the LOS of inpatients may not lead to better treatment quality and to an overall reduction in costs in the long run [2, 45,51, 57, 64, 65, 67]. As described in Sect. 7.3.1.2, the LKF-system regularly revises the upper and lower boundaries of the core part's day component to provide the medically optimal length-of-stay [28]. Major recalculations were performed in 2002.

Among other questionable practices, hospitals might admit inpatients more frequently on certain days (optimized admission), or might discharge inpatients on certain days more frequently or too early (optimized discharge), which could result in a rise of complications and readmissions rates, particularly with 0-day patients (cf. also the subsequent section).

7.3.2.2 Performance Optimization Strategies

In general, fund hospitals have to admit all inpatients. This is meant to prevent hospitals from repositioning their range of services towards profitable groups of inpatients [20, 37, 61] by risk selection. This hospital's strategy comprises "cream-skimming," i.e., the explicit selection of preferred patients [42]; and "patient dumping," i.e., the explicit avoidance of high-severity patients [7]. However, special units and departments have to be authorized by the federal state. For example, the LKF-systems from 1998 to 2001 developed guidelines for intensive care and psychiatric units, while the LKF-systems from 2002 to 2008 significantly expanded their catalogues of treatments, surgery, or special departments [28].

Unbundling, i.e., shifting expensive treatments to other hospitals [17], was especially revealed for stroke and 0-day patients [55]. Therefore, the LKF-system of 2000 introduced strict criteria for allocating LDF-points to stroke patients [28]. Also, the regulations for intensive care units were restructured in 1999 and 2002;

since then, they have been subject to annual supervision. As 0-day patients at intensive care units were exploited to maximize LDF-points in the past, they only get full remuneration in case of death or transfer to other hospitals now [49, 50, 53, 54].

7.3.2.3 Quantity Optimization Strategies

A further popular strategy is the revolving-door effect [8, 53, 68] by which inpatients are prematurely discharged and readmitted in order to be reimbursed again. For example, to mitigate the problem of lucrative 0-day patients, the LKF-system of 2002 introduced the day clinic model with strict regulations such as application only for selected MEL, no emergencies, and provision of a bed and post care [28]. Also, discontinued stays of inpatients were newly defined in the LKF-systems of 2010 and 2011 to fight the revolving-door effect [15].

7.4 Quantitative Studies on the Case-Based LKF-System for Hospitals

7.4.1 Macro-perspective Studies on Hospital Efficiency

Several studies used Data Envelopment Analysis (DEA) techniques to quantitatively analyze the effects of the case-based Austrian LKF-system on hospitals based on aggregated input and output data from a macro-perspective. First studies investigated the influence of the LKF-system on the efficiency of hospitals or efficiency changes due to the introduction of the LKF-system in 1997 [58, 59]. For example, Sommersguter-Reichmann [58] found a positive technology shift for a sample of 22 hospitals from a particular federal state between 1996 and 1998. Hofmarcher et al. [29] disclosed LDF-point gathering, an increase in the number of cases (could be a sign of the revolving-door effect), and a decrease in LOS (could be due to the revolving-door effect, unbundling, optimized discharge, and/or admission) in 44 low-profile acute care hospitals from 1997 to 2000.

A more recent DEA study by Czypionka et al. [4] analyzed efficiency differences between hospitals due to ownership and hospital types for Austria in the year 2006. Using multiple input data and LDF-points as output data, they disclosed higher efficiencies for order hospitals and larger nonteaching hospitals. Order hospitals were forced to operate more efficiently due to a limited loss coverage by the LKF-system compared to public hospitals. They furthermore illustrated that in several federal states, order hospitals were significantly discriminated against public hospitals regarding loss coverage. Currently, Sommersguter-Reichmann and colleagues are investigating the efficiency of nonteaching fund hospitals up to 500 beds from 2002 to 2009.

7.4.2 Micro-perspective Studies on Incentives for Hospitals

In contrast to the macro-perspective efficiency studies, micro-perspective studies evaluate the incentives of the LKF-system for hospitals on inpatient care. Table 7.1 displays their main quantitative studies and underlying methodologies to illustrate different incentives of the case-based Austrian LKF-system which are discussed in this section. Section 7.5 reviews additional empirical studies on the impact of the LKF-system on strategic technology management in hospitals representative for a certain hospital management subsystem.

Rauner [45] as well as Schaffhauser-Linzatti and Rauner [54] qualitatively summarized the LKF-system's effects on hospital management disclosed in their early empirical studies [39, 53]. This current review extends these two previous reviews by discussing the main results of the studies by Rauner et al. [48, 52], as well as Schaffhauser-Linzatti et al. [55]. In addition, the new study by Rauner et al. [47] on the impact of the LKF-system on strategic technology management is outlined as well.

As a starting point, Rauner and Schaffhauser [51] analytically identified and validated the benefits and problems of the newly introduced Austrian case-based LKF-system by a system-dynamics model. The results showed that the LKF-system has already led to a more effective and efficient reimbursement strategy for hospitals in the first year after introduction. For example, the LKF-system resulted in multiple health care improvements such as a reduction in inpatients' LOS, increased cost awareness, or improved documentation and planning. However, looking at both the ambulatory sector of hospitals and the extramural sector showed that curbing total health care costs rather than hospitals costs alone was unavoidable.

The study mentioned above together with Rauner and Schaffhauser [50] provided a basis for understanding the case-based LKF-system's impacts on its stakeholders and technology management. Furthermore, they revealed systemic and hospital management-related strategic incentives to exploit the new regulations and to maximize budgets. Several drawbacks have been mitigated by ongoing system advancements such as day care centers and the limitation of LDF-point gathering in intensive care stations [28, 56]. However, the necessity to eliminate the remaining misleading incentives still exists.

Based on Rauner and Schaffhauser [50, 51], the quantitative policy models of Leonard et al. [39], Rauner et al. [53], as well as Schaffhauser-Linzatti et al. [55] empirically proved the main incentives of the LKF-system using statistical approaches (statistical tests, generalized linear models, and regression models). A comparison of the incentives of the Austrian case-based system compared to the Canadian global budget system on admission and discharge policies of hospitals can be found in Leonard et al. [39]. Rauner et al. [52] used a nonlinear optimization model for investigating an optimized allocation of both variable budgets (case-based payment system) and fixed budgets (global budget-based payment system) as well as inpatients with different treatments among hospitals within a geographic region such as Vienna, Austria. This model optimized overall quality of treatment

Table 7.1 Micro-perspective quantitative studies that analyze the incentives of the LKF-system for policymaking in Austrian hospitals

References	Rauner and Schaff-hauser-Linzatti [51]	Leonard et al. [39]	Rauner et al. [53]	Rauner et al. [52]	Rauner et al. [48]	Schaffhauser-Linzatti et al. [55]
Method	System dynamics	Statistical tests	Generalized linear models	Nonlinear optimization	Discrete- event simulation	Regression models
Incentive						
Optimized admission	X	X	X		X	X
Risk selection	X			X	X	
Up-coding and DRG-creep	X				X	
DRG-point gathering	X	X	X	X	X	X
Unbundling	X		X		X	
Optimized discharge	X	X	X		X	X
Revolving-door effect	X		X			X

provided by the hospitals. Using discrete-event simulation, Rauner et al. [48] provided a hospital game based on empirical data to illustrate the competition of hospitals under different reimbursement systems including day-based, case-based, and global budget-based payment strategies. In the following subsections, the findings of these quantitative policy models are explained in detail.

7.4.2.1 Impact of the Austrian Case-Based System and the Canadian Global Budget-Based Payment System on Day of Week Admissions and Discharges

Due to the insights from Rauner and Schaffhauser-Linzatti [49, 51], the authors decided to empirically investigate several incentives of the case-based Austrian LKF-system. For the year 1998, they obtained a major LKF-data set from the Austrian Ministry of Health on both surgical and nonsurgical diagnosis groups for which the days of the week for admissions and discharges, types of admissions and discharges, as well as the total LOS of inpatients were recorded. As examples for such major nonsurgical diagnosis groups, acute myocardial infarct, asthma, and stroke were selected, while prostatectomy, cholecystectomy, and hip replacement were chosen for surgical diagnosis groups.

Leonard et al. [39] investigated the different incentives of the Austrian case-based and the Canadian global budget-based payment system on clinical LOS of different inpatient groups and their day of the week admissions and discharges using data from 1998 by statistical tests. Canada had comparable universal health coverage and similar hospital care expenditures but applied a global budgeting reimbursement system for inpatients. As outlined in Sect. 7.2, the Canadian system has high incentives for hospitals to discharge inpatients as early as possible because no extra payment can be obtained by increasing LOS of inpatients (optimized discharge). The inpatients' mean LOS was chosen as the main indicator as it is widely used to reflect care efficiency and can be changed by, among other factors, improved planning of general procedures, devices, and equipment, experienced staff, new or revised nonsurgical and surgical diagnoses, and better drugs.

The statistical analysis of the Austrian and Canadian data on day of admission and day of discharge for six clinical diagnoses, three of them surgical and three nonsurgical, revealed different effects of discharge and admission policies in both countries as well as Austrian LDF-point gathering by LOS variation (DRG-point gathering). Frequencies for admission and discharge of inpatients were not equally distributed over all days of the week in either Austria or Canada (optimized admission, optimized discharge). Whereas Canadian inpatients were preferably discharged Monday or Friday to avoid administrative work during weekends, Austrian hospitals reacted to the predetermined boundaries and preferred discharges after the weekend, especially for surgical inpatients. For most diagnoses, the average inpatients' LOS was shorter in Canada. For example, for inpatients with asthma the average LOS in Austria (6.82 days) was more than three times higher compared to Canada (2.11 days). As explained above, a global budget system such as in Canada has high incentives for hospitals to discharge patients as early as possible. Compared to Canada, the average LOS was significantly longer in Austria, because payment is dependent on the LOS of an inpatient and decreases once it exceeds the upper boundary of the respective LDF-group (i.e., disease or treatment category).

The paper concluded that inpatients' LOS was dependent on the reimbursement system such as the Austrian case-based payment as well as the Canadian global budgeting payment strategy. A reduction of Austria's LOS-boundaries and the inclusion of the out-patient care were recommended to increase the incentives for Austrian hospitals to discharge inpatients earlier. Several adaptations of the Austrian LKF-system such as the modification of LOS boundaries and consideration of day clinics in hospitals have taken place since 2002 (cf. Sect. 7.3.2). In Austria, we revealed a high potential for evening out admissions and discharges of elective inpatients throughout the week to lower LOS which ultimately leads to a decrease in health care expenditures and an increase in health care effectiveness. Further research with data after the 2002 system changes might reveal different admission and discharge patterns compared to the 1998 data due to learning effects of the hospitals.

7.4.2.2 Impact of the Case-Based Austrian LKF-System on the LOS of Inpatients

Leonard et al. [39] investigated the day and week of admission of inpatients and their LOS, while the influence of the month of admission and the type of admission and discharge were not analyzed in detail for the Austrian case-based payment system. Using generalized linear Quasi-Poisson models, Rauner et al. [53] modeled the LOS for major disease groups (dependent variable) for the Austrian LKF-system in 1998. They showed significant interdependencies among the dependent variable and the explanatory variables (day and month of admission, type of admission and discharge) including a constant term. They revealed problematic hospital behavior which is induced by case-based payment systems (cf. Sect. 7.2) such as unbundling and the revolving-door effect depending on disease categories and their underlying codes. Furthermore, tendencies of LDF-point gathering (DRG-point gathering) by varying the LOS were found.

This analysis highlighted four main effects and its underlying incentives that impacted on the inpatients' LOS and allowed for appropriate strategies for hospital managers as well as health care decision-makers to be derived.

First, hospitals should be encouraged to rethink their capacity planning regarding surgical teams and facilities by considering their admission and discharge strategies. The earlier inpatients were admitted during the week (optimized admission), the earlier they were discharged because chances are higher that inpatients could be discharged before the weekend. During the weekend, fewer inpatients were discharged (optimized discharge). While nonsurgical inpatients tended to be admitted more evenly during the week, this effect was not found for surgical inpatients who were preferably admitted at the beginning of the week. For example, surgical patients with Cataract Extraction or Hysterectomy who were admitted on Sundays, had a shorter average mean of LOS compared to inpatients admitted on the other days of the week. Policymakers should especially focus on an advanced planning for elective patients.

Second, the LOS significantly depended on the month in which inpatients were admitted. For example, inpatients with asthma admitted between January and March stayed longer in hospitals compared to the other months, while during summertime, inpatients with acute myocardial infarct had a shorter LOS compared to the rest of the year. The only general pattern was that LOS was shorter in December for many surgical and nonsurgical inpatients as inpatients wanted to be discharged before Christmas.

Third, this study revealed unbundling effects as the LOS depended on the type of admission and discharge and hospitals tended to shift inpatients with complex medical needs, mainly with surgical diagnoses, to other hospitals. They disclosed that effect in particular for stroke patients who should be cared in specialized departments. In the last years, stroke units were established in Vienna and ambulances took inpatients with suspicion for stroke preferable to these specialized units.

Fourth, hospitals tended to readmit 0-day patients in order to increase reimbursement due to patient splitting. They found that effect again for inpatients with stroke. Therefore, stroke units with special reimbursement were introduced to improve the LKF-system of the early years. As mentioned before, in a case-based system such the Austrian LKF-system, once an inpatient stay is split into two inpatients stays, payment for the second stay is granted (revolving-door effect). In a global budget system like the Canadian system, such a strategy does not lead to increased reimbursement.

This study disclosed potentials for the improvement of misleading incentives within the case-based LKF-system and for policy implications on how to take countermeasures. For example, the introduction of the first day clinics in hospitals in the year 2002 lowered the fourth incentive of patient splitting as described above (revolving-door effect). It left open further questions for ongoing research, mainly longitudinal studies which are now possible due to longer time series of the data and differences among the Austrian federal states. Further, it will be interesting to analyze whether the current changes in the case-based LKF-system have reduced the revealed negative incentives.

7.4.2.3 Impact of Case-Based and Global-Budget Payment Systems on Regional Inpatient Allocation

Using a nonlinear optimization model, Rauner et al. [52] investigated the optimal allocation of both variable budgets (case-based payment system) and fixed budgets (global budget-based payment system) as well as inpatients with different treatments among hospitals within a geographic region such as Vienna, Austria. This model optimized the overall quality of treatment of certain in-patient categories provided by the hospitals under consideration of various constraints such as hospital capacities, number of inpatients to be treated, and percentage of emergency cases for inpatients with certain treatments. Elective inpatients were then assigned to those hospitals with optimal cost–quality relation, while emergency inpatients had to be treated by all hospitals. Due to this optimal allocation, negative risk selection strategies and LDF-point gathering (DRG-point gathering) of hospitals could be restricted. At that time, the combination of hospital location-allocation models and economic models to solve advanced inpatient allocation in a region was unique.

In most of the policy scenarios analyzed, fixed budgets (global budget-based payment system) outperformed variable budgets (case-based payment system) as less money had to be invested for an incremental unit of quality of care provided. Similarly, Leonard et al. [39] also showed that global fixed budget-based payment systems such as the Canadian one were advantageous compared to case-based payments systems such as the Austrian one once it can be granted that quality of hospital care will not drop. These findings empirically confirm the general incentives for hospitals of these two payments strategies as discussed in Sect. 7.2. Rauner et al. [52] identified inefficient hospitals, which helped policymakers to restructure the hospital region. They proposed a merger of a specialized hospital with a bigger hospital because it was inefficient in the sense that it had a relatively high euro per quality of treatment. A small hospital should be transformed into a nursing home due to the small number of inpatients in each of the efficient allocations.

As further research, Rauner et al. [52] noted that more components of location-allocation models such as travelling distance and time of individual inpatients to different hospitals could be considered. In addition, different shapes of learning curves for optimal resource allocation could also be subject of future investigation.

7.4.2.4 Competition of Hospitals Under Different Payment Systems

Hospital management games help policymakers, practitioners, and students improve planning for scarce resources in times of growing health care demand and increasing technology costs [36]. As the hospitals compete for inpatients and reimbursement in a region, this aspect has to be considered in a realistic hospital management game. In the last few years, Internet-based games were introduced to bring together players from all over the world by overcoming the distance and time problem of time-bounded and location-bounded management games.

Rauner et al. [48] designed an Internet-based hospital simulation game based on empirical data to illustrate the competition of hospitals in a region under different reimbursement systems. This hospital management game considered four types of inpatient payment systems (cf. Sect. 7.2): (1) day-based systems, (2) case-based (DRG-based) systems with unlimited budget, (3) case-based (DRG-based) systems with limited budget (e.g., the Austrian LKF-system), and (4) global budget-based systems. Only few hospital games (e.g., [3]) accounted for financial management in combination with resource and process management [36].

This hospital management game of [48] simulated real world situations in a hospital. The players ran main departments of a hospital and had to admit and discharge inpatients. It could be used for both teaching and management training. For example, this game could also be used to illustrate the potential for teaching operations research in the classroom (e.g., queuing theory, agency/game theory, system dynamics, forecasting, stock-keeping). Currently, the final improvements to this discrete-event simulation game are implemented by the PhD student Jörg Gesslbauer.

The players of this hospital game did not only investigate main incentives of different reimbursement systems (except for the revolving-door effect) for hospitals but also their impact on resource and process management over a longer period. For example, depending on the policies of other hospitals as well as on general conditions such as the regional health policy, the labor market, and the radiology technology market, the players chose best possible decisions in different areas such as management, surgery, radiology, and nursing for running a hospital over a certain period.

For example, players of a particular hospital selected optimized admission and discharge strategies to increase reimbursement. Furthermore, those players could try to attract more lucrative inpatients from the region depending on the strategies of the other hospitals and the regional health policy which reflected the incentive of risk selection. To account for the incentive of up-coding and DRG-creep of case-based reimbursement systems, the management player of a particular hospital determined the percentage of DRG-creep in each period keeping in mind that too high misqualification rates would increase the risk of being financially punished by a regulatory agency. In the case-based LKF-system player mode, LDF-point gathering (DRG-point gathering) and unbundling were indirectly reflected by LOS variations of the inpatients. In addition to the above policy decisions, advanced resource management such as investment in radiology machines, opening/closing of surgery rooms, hiring/firing of staff, and investment in staff education positively impacted reimbursement as well. Furthermore, advanced process management such as optimized scheduling of inpatients for surgery or radiology also improved reimbursement.

By playing such a hospital management game, policymakers, practitioners, and students can study running a hospital under alternative reimbursement systems in an artificial setting with high learning effects. For example, players can experience that inpatients might have a longer LOS in day-based payment systems compared to case-based payment systems in which an additional inpatient day does not generally lead to increased reimbursement (cf. Sect. 7.2). In global budget-based payment systems a short LOS of inpatients is most beneficial for hospitals. Future research could contain experimental economics to investigate both teaching (e.g., game situation) and policy issues (e.g., impact of reimbursement systems).

7.4.2.5 Impact of the Case-Based LKF-System on Treatment Patterns in the Federal States

Schaffhauser-Linzatti et al. [55] added to the former analyses by being the first paper to investigate differences among the case-based LKF-system in the Austrian federal states and of hospital infrastructure. They analyzed effects of LDF-point gathering (DRG-point gathering), patient splitting tendencies due to the number of cases treated (revolving-door effect), and optimized admission and discharge policies (due to the length-of-stay) using semi-logarithmic linear regression models for longitudinal observations from 2002 to 2006 of inpatients with knee joint problems for both surgical and nonsurgical groups.

The findings of the study showed that the nine federal state-specific reimbursement features of the LKF-system (cf. Sect. 7.3) had some impact on the two dependent variables, LOS and reimbursements for identical diagnoses and treatments. However, the federal state-specific big-ticket technologies such as magnetic resonance imaging and the age of the inpatients were identified as more significant explanatory variables for the above two dependent variables. For example, older inpatients were mostly applied to non-surgical diagnosis and staid longer than younger patients with mainly surgical treatments. However, the influence of modern technology such as magnetic resonance imaging (MRI) was expected to be higher but could be partly explained that the number of MRIs did not increase significantly except in 2003.

The authors drew two main conclusions from this study. First, the regulation part of the LKF-system, which is individually determined by each federal state, should be harmonized. Second, further research could analyze inpatient data on an individual basis to investigate effects of up-coding and DRG-creep. Finally, diagnoses such as stroke might be valuable illustrative examples to reveal effects such as patient splitting (revolving-door effect), unbundling, end-of-the-week discharges (optimized discharge), and technology shifts.

7.5 Impact of the Case-Based LKF-System on Hospital Technology Management

As an example of the effect of the case-based Austrian LKF-system on a hospital management subsystem, Rauner and Schaffhauser-Linzatti [50] concentrated on the implications of the LKF-system's introduction for hospitals' stakeholders [6]. They illustrated the interplay between the new reimbursement system for inpatients and hospital health care technology management in correlation with the external and internal hospital environment as well as the main incentives of the LKF-system. Management of medical technologies enabled hospitals to improve their financial positions relative to other hospitals in the same federal state because of the limited budget and helped them survive within the new LKF-system. In this way, the integration of strategic management of health care technology served as an important function for Austrian hospitals, which was shown by Rauner and Heidenberger [46].

Based on these previous studies, Rauner et al. [47] surveyed the impact of the case-based LKF-system on strategic technology management regarding planning, purchasing, and evaluating of different types of technologies in hospitals in Vienna. According to Geisler and Heller [22], the authors concentrated on the following main technology types: (1) medical devices and systems, (2) drugs and pharmaceuticals, (3) information technology, (4) disposables, (5) medical/surgical procedures and services, (6) strategies and policies regarding technology, (7) administrative rules, procedures and workflows on technology, and (8) technology education training.

Due to the higher economic and efficiency pressure induced by the LKF-system, technology decision-making for many medical technologies shifted from the top level to respective departments and users to better execute strategic changes on the operational level. The executive board, central purchasing, and the purchasing department were identified as new key decision-makers. Health technology assessment has gained in importance for decision-making. However, the Austrian Health Care Structure Plan limits the investment in technology management for fund hospitals regarding several big-ticket technologies and provision of certain medical services [12, 23].

Decision-makers particularly invested in technology types that directly impacted on the reimbursement such as medical devices and systems, medical/surgical procedures and services, as well as information technology. Especially, e-health and telemedicine were regarded as fields of high potential for the future by policymakers. Furthermore, the external networks to other health care providers were planned to be expanded.

Hospitals adapted their organizational structures (e.g., opening, extending, and closing of medical specializations and beds) subject to the LKF-system and the external environment. Especially those medical specializations such as surgery, radiology, as well as medical and chemical laboratory diagnostics with a high impact on improving process management of inpatients were identified as current and future investment areas.

For further research, this study could be extended to other Austrian federal states or other countries. Such studies could support health regulators in improving their hospital reimbursement schemes by closing loopholes.

7.6 Conclusions and Policy Implications

This study illustrated the impact of inpatient reimbursement systems on hospital performance by means of the Austrian LKF-system. While macro-perspective studies analyzed the efficiency of hospitals on aggregated input and output data using DEA techniques, micro-perspective policy models focused on the main incentives of the LKF-system on several outcome measures using empirical data on inpatients with certain major diseases. Such studies could support health regulators in improving their reimbursement schemes by closing loopholes.

DEA models disclosed efficiency differences depending on ownership and hospital size in Austria from a macro-perspective. Several micro-perspective studies used different quantitative techniques such as system dynamics, discrete-event simulation, optimization, as well as statistical approaches (statistical tests, generalized linear models, and regression models) and models to investigate the incentives of the LKF-system on inpatient treatment. This literature review found evidence for all main incentives for hospitals such as optimized admission, risk selection; up-coding and DRG-creep, unbundling, optizimized discharge, and the revolving-door effect.

As the LKF-system has evolved since its introduction in the year 1997, longitudinal studies that investigate the main changes of the system together with differences among federal states are subject to further research. Schaffhauser-Linzatti et al. [55] were among the first to investigate that effect on inpatients with knee joint problems from 2002 to 2006 on a micro-perspective level, while Sommersguter-Reichmann and colleagues are studying these effects on nonteaching fund hospitals up to 500 beds from 2002 to 2009 on a macro-perspective level. Schaffhauser-Linzatti et al. [55] could only prove tendencies of behavior distances among inpatient treatment in federal states due to changes in technology as well as population differences. The effect of federal states should be analyzed on less technology-intensive treatment patters for certain inpatient groups. As the expansion of the day clinics for many inpatients groups comprised a crucial system change to fight early discharges, patient splitting, and the revolving-door effect, this area could be also investigated in the future.

Rauner et al. [47] demonstrated the impact of the LKF-system on the management subsystem of technology management. The LKF-system forced Vienna hospitals to efficiently treat inpatients by focusing on lucrative departments/units and by investing in certain technologies such as medical devices and systems, medical/surgical procedures and services, as well as information technology. In addition, decision-making shifted from the top level to the respective departments and users. Furthermore, hospitals more frequently applied health technology assessment techniques compared to the earlier years after the introduction of the LKF-system. Potential for further research could lie in expanding the insights of this study of Vienna hospitals to all Austrian hospitals or other countries. At last, the impact of the LKF-system on other management subsystems could be studied.

Acknowledgments Special thanks are due to Wolfgang Bartosik of the Federal Ministry of Health who has provided us with all essential data on the LKF-system since 1997. We are also grateful to several students who surveyed data on Austrian hospitals and the LKF-system, especially Sabrina Herndl who investigated key data on the LKF-system for the years 1997 to 2010. We are indebted to practitioners at Austrian hospitals for providing us with hospital-specific data.

References

1. Anonymous (2004) Survey: the health of nations. Economist 372(8384):3–4
2. Crane M (2001) Discharge patients sooner, or we'll discharge you. Med Econ 78(13):100–101

3. Cromwell DA, Priddis D, Hindle D (1998) Using simulation to educate hospital staff about casemix. Health Care Manag Sci 1(2):87–93
4. Czypionka T, Roehrling G, Kraus M, Schnabl A, Eichwalder S (2008) Fondsspitaeler in Oesterreich: ein Leistungs- und Finanzierungsvergleich. Project report, Institute for Advanced Studies, Vienna
5. Dienesch S, Heitzenberger G (1998) Krankenanstaltenfinanzierung 9 mal anders—Ein Streifzug durch den Finanzierungsdschungel in den oesterreichischen Bundeslaendern. Nycomed, Hallein, Austria
6. Dezsy J, Fritz R (2000) Analyse und Vorschlaege zur Finanzierung von Gesundheitsleistungen. Oesterreichische Krankenhauszeitung 41(2): 53–58
7. Ellis R (1998) Creaming, skimping and dumping: provider competition on the intensive and extensive margins. J Health Econ 17(5):537–555
8. Engelke H, Fricke H (2003) Komplizierte Wiederaufnahmen—Erste Zweifelsfragen bei der Abrechnung von DRGs. Krankenhaus Umschau 72(5):366–367
9. Federal Ministry of Labour, Health, and Social Affairs (1997) Leistungsorientierte Krankenhausfinanzierung LKF 1998. Federal Ministry of Labour, Health, and Social Affairs, Vienna
10. Federal Ministry of Health (2006) The Austrian health care system, key facts. Federal Ministry of Health, Vienna
11. Federal Ministry of Health, Family and Youth (2008) Krankenanstalten in Oesterreich, Hospitals in Austria 2008. Federal Ministry of Health, Family and Youth, Vienna
12. Federal Ministry of Health (2010) The Austrian health care system, key facts. Federal Ministry of Health, Vienna
13. Federal Ministry of Health (2010) Leistungsorientierte Krankenhausfinanzierung—LKF—Modell 2011. Federal Ministry of Health, Vienna
14. Federal Ministry of Health (2010) Leistungsorientierte Krankenhausfinanzierung—LKF—System 2011. Federal Ministry of Health, Vienna
15. Federal Ministry of Health (2010) Leistungsorientierte Krankenhausfinanzierung—LKF—Aenderungen 2011. Federal Ministry of Health, Vienna
16. Federal Ministry of Health (2012) www.gesundheit.gv.at. Accessed Mar 2012
17. Feldstein P (1993) Health care economics. Thomson Delmar Learning, New York
18. Fetter R (1991) Diagnosis related groups: understanding hospital performance. Interfaces 21(1):6–26
19. Flemmich G, Ivansits H (1994) Einfuehrung in das Gesundheitsrecht und in die Gesundheitsleistungen. Verlag des Oesterreichischen Gewerkschaftsbundes, Vienna
20. Flessa S (2007) Grundzuege der Krankenhausbetriebslehre. Muenchen, Oldenbourg
21. Fuloria P, Zenios S (2001) Outcomes-adjusted reimbursement in a health care delivery system. Manag Sci 47(6):735–751
22. Geisler E, Heller O (eds) (1996) Managing technology in health care. Kluwer, Boston
23. Gesundheit Oesterreich GmbH (2010) Austrian health care structure plan. Federal Ministry of Health, Vienna
24. Gesundheitsplattform Steiermark (2006) LKF-Abrechnungssystem—Steiermark 2006, Beilage zu Top 6c der 3. Sitzung der Gesundheitsplattform, 6 July 2006
25. Gottlieb S (2007) The war on (expensive) drugs. Wall St J, 30. August, 11–12
26. Gridchyna I, Aulois-Griot M, Maurain C, Bégaud B (2012) How innovative are pharmaceutical innovations? The case of medicines financed through add-on payments outside of the French DRG-based hospital payment system. Health Policy 104(1):69–75
27. Guentert B, Klein P, Kriegel J (2005) Fallpauschalierte Entgeltsysteme im Krankenhauswesen—Ein Vergleich von LKF und G-DRG. Wirtschaftspolitische Blaetter 53(4):515–525
28. Herndl S (2010) Die Evolution des oesterreichischen leistungsorientierten Krankenhausfinanzierungssystems. Master thesis, University of Vienna, Department of Innovation and Technology Management, Austria

29. Hofmarcher MM, Lietz C, Schnabl A (2005) Inefficiency in Austrian in-patient care: identifying ailing providers based on DEA results. CEJOR 13(4):341–363
30. Hofmarcher MM, Paterson I, Riedel M (2002) Measuring hospital efficiency in Austria—a DEA approach. Health Care Manag Sci 5(1):7–14
31. Hofmacher MM, Rack HM (2001) Gesundheitssysteme im Wandel, Kopenhagen: European Observatory on Health Care Systems. European Observatory on Health Care Systems: Gesundheitssysteme im Wandel—Oesterreich 2001, Kopenhagen 2001
32. Hofmacher MM, Rack HM (2006) Health care systems in transition. European Observatory on Health Care Systems, Kopenhagen, Austria
33. Hofmarcher MM, Riedel M (2001) Gesundheitsausgaben in der EU: Ohne Privat kein Staat, Schwerpunktthema. Das oesterreichische Krankenanstaltenwesen—eines oder neun Systeme? Health System Watch, No. 1. Institute for Advanced Studies, Vienna
34. Hsia D, Ahern C, Ritchie B, Moscoe LM, Krushat WM (1992) Medicare reimbursement accuracy: under the prospective payment system, 1985 to 1988. J Am Med Assoc 268 (7):896–899
35. Ingruber H (1994) Krankenhausbetriebslehre. Goeschl, Vienna.
36. Kraus M, Rauner MS, Schwarz S (2010) Operations research and management games with a special focus on health care games. CEJOR 18(4):567–591
37. Kuntz L, Scholtes S, Vera A (2007) Incorporating efficiency in hospital-capacity planning in Germany. Eur J Health Econ 8(3):213–223
38. Leidl R (ed) (1998) Health care and its financing in the single European market. IOS Press, Amsterdam
39. Leonard KJ, Rauner MS, Schaffhauser-Linzatti MM, Yap R (2003) The effect of funding policy on day of week admissions and discharges in hospitals: the cases of Canada and Austria. Health Policy 63(3):239–257
40. Neubauer G, Demmler G (1991) Bausteine eines rationalen Krankenverguetungssystems. In: Neubauer G, Sieben G (eds) Alternative Entgeltverfahren in der Krankenhausversorgung: Beitraege zur Gesundheitsoekonomie, 24th edn. Gerlingen, Bleicher, pp 13–42
41. Neubauer G, Sonnenholzner-Roche A, Unterhuber H (1987) Die Problematik einer Fallgruppenbildung im Krankenhaus. Krankenhaus Umschau 56(1):27–34
42. Newhouse J (1996) Reimbursing health plans and health providers: efficiency in production versus selection. J Econ Lit 34(3):1236–1263
43. OECD (2012) Country-specific statistical profiles. http://www.oecd-ilibrary.org/economics. Accessed Mar 2012
44. Pfeiffer KP (1996) The possible effects of a new hospital financing system in Austria. In: Schwartz W, Glennester H, Saltman R (eds) Fixing health budgets: experience from Europe and North America, Chichester. Wiley, Chichester, pp 203–212
45. Rauner MS (2007) Ein Rueckblick auf die Leistungsorientierte Krankenhausfinanzierung in Oesterreich von 1997–2006 unter besonderer Beruecksichtung der Anreizwirkungen auf Krankenhaeuser. In: Braeuning D, Greiling D (eds) Stand und Perspektiven der oeffentlichen Betriebswirtschaftslehre, Festschrift fuer Professor Dr. Peter Eichhorn. Berliner Wissenschaftsverlag, Berlin, pp 163–175
46. Rauner MS, Heidenberger K (2002) Scope and role of strategic technology management in hospitals: the case of Vienna, Austria. Int J Healthc Technol Manag 4(3/4):239–258
47. Rauner MS, Heidenberger K, Hermescec D, Mokic A, Zsifkovits M (2011) Scope and role of technology management in Vienna hospitals. Int J Healthc Technol Manag 12(3/4):250–279
48. Rauner MS, Schwarz S, Kraus M (2008) Competition under different reimbursement systems: the concept of an internet-based hospital management game. Eur J Oper Res 185(3):948–963
49. Rauner MS, Schaffhauser-Linzatti MM (1999) Evaluation of the new Austrian in-patient reimbursement system. In: De Angelis V, Ricciardi N, Storchi G (eds) Monitoring, evaluating, planning health services, Proceedings of the 24th meeting of the European working group on operational research applied to health services, Rome, Italy, July 19–24, 1998, World Scientific Publishing, Singapore, pp 221–233

50. Rauner MS, Schaffhauser-Linzatti MM (2001) Interplay between in-patient reimbursement systems and health care technology management: the Austrian case. Int J Healthc Technol Manag 3(1–2):1–23
51. Rauner MS, Schaffhauser-Linzatti M-M (2002) Impact of international in-patient payment strategies on health technology management: a system-dynamics-model for Austria. Socioecon Plann Sci 36(3):133–154
52. Rauner MS, Schneider G, Heidenberger K (2005) Reimbursement systems and regional in-patient allocation: a non-linear optimisation model. IMA J Manag Math 16(3):217–237
53. Rauner MS, Zeileis A, Schaffhauser-Linzatti MM, Hornik K (2003) Modelling the effects of the Austrian in-patient reimbursement system on length-of-stay distributions. OR-Spectrum 25 (2):183–206
54. Schaffhauser-Linzatti MM, Rauner MS (2008) Quo vadis Leistungsorientierte Krankenhaus-finanzierung? Oesterreichische Erfahrungen und Perspektiven. In: Schauer R, Helmig B, Purtschert R, Wirt D (eds) Steuerung und Kontrolle in Nonprofit-Organisationen, 8. Colloquium der NPO-Forscher im deutschsprachigen Raum, Johannes Kepler Universität Linz, 17.-18. April 2008. Trauner, Linz, pp 335–364
55. Schaffhauser-Linzatti MM, Zeileis A, Rauner M (2009) Effects of the Austrian performance-oriented in-patient reimbursement system on treatment patterns: illustrated on cases with knee-joint problems. CEJOR 17(3):293–314
56. Sebek W (2009) Entwicklung des LKF-Systems 1997–2009. http://www.prikraf.at/forum/lkf2009/pdf/Beitrag_Sebek.pdf. Accessed 5 Oct 2009
57. Selbmann HK (2005) Es entstehen neue Problemzonen—Bedeutung des Qualitaets-managements im DRG-Zeitalter. Krankenhaus Umschau, ku-Special Controlling 74(4):8–11
58. Sommersguter-Reichmann M (2000) The impact of the Austrian hospital financing reform on hospital productivity: empirical evidence on efficiency and technology changes using a non-parametric input-based Malmquist approach. Health Care Manag Sci 3(4):309–321
59. Sommersguter-Reichmann M (2003) Analysing hospital productivity changes using non-parametric approaches. OR Spectrum 25(2):145–160
60. Sommersguter-Reichmann M, Stepan A (2000) Evaluating the new activity-based hospital financing system in Austria. In: Dockner E, Hartl R, Luptacik M, Sorger G (eds) Optimization, dynamics, and economic analysis. Physika, Heidelberg, pp 49–63
61. Stepan A (1985) Moeglichkeiten eines leistungsgerechten Finanzierungssystems fuer oesterreichische Krankenhaeuser. Zeitschrift für oeffentliche und gemeinnuetzige Unternehmen 8(4):432–445
62. Stepan A, Sommersguter-Reichmann M (1999) Priority setting in Austria. Health Policy 50(1–2):91–104
63. Stepan A, Sommersguter-Reichmann M (2002) Analyse des neuen leistungsorientierten Krankenanstalten-Finanzierungssystems in Österreich. In: Wille E (ed) Anreizkompatible Verguetungssysteme im Gesundheitswesen, Gesundheitsoekonomische Beitraege, Vol. 38. Baden-Baden, Nomos, pp 109–141
64. Taheri PA, Butz DA, Greenfield LJ (2000) Length-of-stay has minimal impact on the cost of hospital admission. J Am Coll Surg 191(2):123–130
65. Theurl E, Winner H (2005) Die Reform der Krankenhausfinanzierung in Oesterreich und ihre Auswirkungen auf die Verweildauer. Wirtschaftspolitische Blaetter 52(4):504–514
66. Vaul JH (1998) DRG benchmarking study establishes national coding norms. Healthc Financ Manage 52(8):52–54
67. Westphal E (1996) Fallbezogene Krankenhausfinanzierung und Monistik—Kostendaempfung nach dem Beispiel von Oesterreich. Die Krankenversicherung 47:220–223
68. Wray N, Petersen NJ, Souchek J, Ashton CM, Hollingsworth JC, Geraci JM (1999) The hospital multistay rate as an indicator of quality of care. Health Serv Res 34(3):777–790
69. Zakoworotny C (1993) Strategies to optimize DRG reimbursement. Topics in Health Care Financing 20(1):53–60

Part III
HIV Policy Models

Chapter 8
Assessing Prevention for Positives: Cost-Utility Assessment of Behavioral Interventions for Reducing HIV Transmission

Sada Soorapanth and Stephen E. Chick

Abstract Typical studies of HIV behavioral interventions measure relative risk reduction for HIV transmission. Here, we also consider the health benefits of such interventions on secondary transmission. In addition, a sensitivity analysis explores the potential additional benefits that may accrue if partners of those in the intervention group also adopt the risk reducing behavior. To do this, we developed an ordinary differential equation (ODE) model to analyze the cost and utility (measured in quality-adjusted life years, or QALYs) of a published behavioral HIV intervention that aims to reduce the risk of transmission from HIV-infected persons to their sexual partners. The ODE model maps measurements of behavioral risk reduction parameters, estimated from sampling, into costs and QALYs. Monte Carlo sampling was used to perform a probabilistic sensitivity analysis to quantify uncertainty in costs and QALYs due to parameter estimation error for the behavioral HIV intervention. The results suggest that the behavioral intervention is most likely to be cost-saving or, at least, cost-effective. The analysis highlights the step of converting uncertainty about estimates of mean values of parameters that are commonly reported in the literature to uncertainty about the costs and health benefits of an intervention. It also shows the potential importance of considering secondary transmission of HIV and the partial adoption of behavior change by partners of the individuals who undergo the intervention.

S. Soorapanth (✉)
Decision Sciences Department, San Francisco State University, 1600 Holloway Avenue, San Francisco, CA 94132, USA
e-mail: sada@sfsu.edu

S.E. Chick
Technology and Operations Management Area, INSEAD, Boulevard de Constance, 77300, Fontainebleau, Paris, France

G.S. Zaric (ed.), *Operations Research and Health Care Policy*, International Series in Operations Research & Management Science 190,
DOI 10.1007/978-1-4614-6507-2_8,

8.1 Introduction

At the end of 2006, the Centers for Disease Control and Prevention (CDC) estimated that 1.1 million people were living with HIV in the USA, and that 56,300 people were newly infected each year [1]. Because of the success of HIV treatment in recent years, HIV-infected persons live longer than before. The challenge of managing the risk of transmission to the uninfected population remains important. In 2003, the CDC announced the Advancing HIV Prevention initiative to intensify HIV prevention efforts. One of the initiative's four strategies, called "prevention with positives," was to reduce risky behaviors among HIV-infected persons which could lead to the transmission of HIV to uninfected sexual partners [2].

A number of studies have demonstrated the efficacy of HIV behavioral interventions in reducing risk behaviors. The efficacy findings from these studies, however, were measured in various forms of risk behaviors, such as increase in condom use and reduction in number of HIV-negative and unknown-status partners [3, 4, 5]. Without a common measure of efficacy, the benefits of these interventions cannot be compared with each other and with other types of HIV intervention prevention programs.

Cost-utility analysis (CUA) is a standard approach for comparing and evaluating multiple health interventions. CUA is based on common measure of effectiveness, i.e., quality-adjusted live years (QALYs), and costs associated with the interventions. The results from a CUA can provide useful information for public health policy makers in determining which HIV intervention would be most cost-effective, and hence inform resource allocation decisions for HIV prevention. Only a limited number of cost-effectiveness or CUA studies for HIV behavioral interventions have appeared. These studies did not focus on interventions for HIV-positive adults in the USA and were mostly conducted before 2001.

This chapter develops a mathematical model to assess the costs and benefits (as measured in QALYs) of behavioral interventions for HIV-infected individuals. We considered behavioral studies of interventions delivered to individuals or small groups whose participants were heterosexual men and women in the USA and we present the results of analyzing one of the interventions [6]. Results from analyzing other interventions were similar and can be found elsewhere [7]. The benefits of the intervention were modeled as the reduction in primary infections from HIV-infected individuals to their sexual partners. We also modeled the indirect benefits of the intervention as the reduction in the secondary infections between these sexual partners and other sexual partners in the general population.

We also analyzed the effect of the duration over which the intervention remains effective. Some studies have indicated that relapse can occur in relatively short periods of time [8, 9, 10, 11]. Our analysis demonstrated the degree to which an intervention's cost-effectiveness varies as a function of the duration of its effectiveness.

Additionally, we analyzed the partial adoption of the behavioral intervention by the partners of the individuals who undergo the intervention. To do this, we modeled the effects of potential HIV transmission from index cases to their partners. We also modeled transmission between partners of index cases and the general population. Secondary transmission of infection from partners to the general population is a health outcome that is not always gathered in studies of HIV behavioral interventions. This chapter describes what would happen if there were benefits that result from the adoption of risk reducing behaviors by partners of those in an intervention. This is evaluated by means of a sensitivity analysis that evaluates the total number of infections (primary and secondary) averted as a function of the degree of adoption of a risk-reducing behavior by partners of index cases of a behavioral intervention.

The outcomes of the analysis below included the cost per HIV infection prevented and the cost per QALY gained, although the papers that reported on the behavioral studies had a different outcome, such as the percent reduction of certain risky behaviors. Moreover, parameter values that are typically reported in such studies include a measure of potential error in their estimation such as with standard errors. This chapter used probabilistic sensitivity analysis (PSA) to convert uncertainty about such parameters into statements of uncertainty that are associated with the potential financial costs and health benefits for a program that implements such an intervention. The model was implemented in Microsoft Excel with the design goals of being transparent, user-friendly, and usable by cross-disciplinary collaborators.

8.2 Methods

We first describe a simple compartmental model of HIV transmission from HIV-infected index cases to their partners. The model incorporates the effects of a behavioral intervention that aims to reduce the risk of HIV transmission from these index cases to uninfected partners. We then describe how we fit the parameters of the model to data from the behavioral intervention described by Kalichman et al. [6]. The parameters of our HIV transmission model were estimated by matching them to general population statistics as well as to parameter estimates of behavioral changes from the clinical control trials of the interventions studies. Next we describe how the model was extended to account for transmissions from partners of index cases to their other partners, as well as for transmission from the partners of partners to uninfected partners of index cases. This section concludes with a description of how we mapped uncertainty about the parameter estimates from the studies due to sampling error to a Monte Carlo simulation that assesses how parameter uncertainty influences uncertainty about the intervention's costs and benefits.

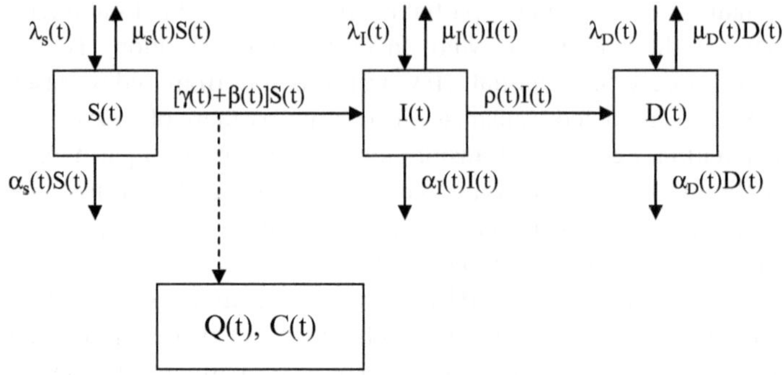

Fig. 8.1 Continuous-time system dynamic infection model of sexual partners per index case

8.2.1 HIV Infection Model

We used the compartmental model in Fig. 8.1 to describe the HIV infection transmission dynamics. The parameters of the model were varied through time in an attempt to assess how the behaviors of partners were influenced by the behavioral interventions. By running the model, we could assess the change in the number of HIV transmissions from index cases to their partners. We used that information to assess the lifetime QALYs and treatment costs associated with such HIV transmissions. In this way, we assessed the incremental costs and QALYs associated with an intervention as compared to the case of no intervention.

We refer to an HIV-positive individual participating in the behavioral intervention program as an index case. The variable $S(t)$ was used to describe the number of susceptible partners of index cases per index case in the behavioral intervention, as a function of time. For example, if there were 100 index cases at time t and 325 partners of those index cases who were not HIV positive then $S(t) = 3.25$. The dynamics of the model evolved according to the ordinary differential equations (ODEs) in (8.1) to (8.5).

$$\mathrm{d}S(t)/\mathrm{d}t = \lambda_S(t) - [\mu_S(t) + \gamma(t) + \beta(t) + \alpha_S(t)]S(t) \tag{8.1}$$

$$\mathrm{d}I(t)/\mathrm{d}t = \lambda_I(t) + [\gamma(t) + \beta(t)]S(t) - [\mu_I(t) + \rho(t) + \alpha_I(t)]I(t) \tag{8.2}$$

$$\mathrm{d}D(t)/\mathrm{d}t = \lambda_D(t) + \rho(t)I(t) - [\mu_D(t) + \alpha_D(t)]D(t) \tag{8.3}$$

$$\mathrm{d}C(t)/\mathrm{d}t = [\gamma(t) + \beta(t)]S(t)c\mathrm{e}^{-rt} \tag{8.4}$$

$$\mathrm{d}Q(t)/\mathrm{d}t = [\gamma(t) + \beta(t)]S(t)q\mathrm{e}^{-rt} \tag{8.5}$$

Equation (8.1) describes the rate of change in the number of susceptible partners per index case over time. These partners, once infected, could further transmit the infections to other sexual partners in the general population, as described further in Sect. 8.2.3 below. We focus now on primary transmission of infection.

The term $\lambda_S(t)$ determines the rate at which an index case acquires new susceptible sexual partners. The value of $\lambda_S(t)$ was set by dividing the mean number of HIV-negative sexual partners per index case by the mean duration of a partnership. The term $\mu_S(t)$ is the rate at which a susceptible partner leaves the partnership with the index case per time period. The rate at which a susceptible partner becomes infected during the partnership with an index case is $\gamma(t) + \beta(t)$, where $\gamma(t)$ is the rate of infection transmission from the index case and $\beta(t)$ is the transmission rate due to sexual contacts with other HIV-infected individuals in the general population (other than the index case). The death rate of partners who are susceptible to HIV is $\alpha_S(t)$.

Equations (8.2) and (8.3) describe the rates of change in the number of asymptomatically infected partners per index case, $I(t)$, and the rate of change in the number of partners with AIDS per index case, $D(t)$. The first terms of those equations, $\lambda_I(t)$ and $\lambda_D(t)$, represent the rates at which an index case acquires asymptomatically infected sexual partners and partners with AIDS, respectively. The terms $\lambda_I(t)$ and $\lambda_D(t)$ were estimated by dividing the mean numbers of asymptomatically infected partners and the mean numbers of partners with AIDS, respectively, by the average duration of a partnership. The rates of termination of a partnership with an index case are $\mu_I(t)$ and $\mu_D(t)$ for an asymptomatically infected partner and for a partner with AIDS, respectively. Both $\mu_I(t)$ and $\mu_D(t)$ were assumed to equal $\mu_S(t)$. An infected individual develops AIDS at the rate of $\rho(t)$. The death rate of partners with AIDS is $\alpha_D(t)$. It was assumed that all infected individuals develop AIDS before death, hence we assumed $\alpha_I(t) = 0$.

Each newly infected partner was assumed to incur a lifetime HIV treatment costs of c and a loss of q quality-adjusted life years (QALYs). The accumulation of HIV treatment costs, $C(t)$, and the QALYs lost, $Q(t)$, associated with newly infected partners changes, was described by (8.4) and (8.5). Both rates were discounted at an annual discount rate of r. We also considered the undiscounted QALYs lost per infection.

The transmission rate, $\gamma(t)$, was estimated by examining its interpretation with respect to a corresponding stochastic model. Specifically, the number of protected sexual contacts (i.e., with condom use) causing infection per time period, x_{p}, was assumed to be Poisson random variable with mean $m_{\mathrm{p}}(t)p_{\mathrm{p}}$, and the number of unprotected sexual contacts (i.e., without condom use) causing infection per time period, x_{u}, is assumed to be a Poisson random variable with mean $m_{\mathrm{u}}(t)p_{\mathrm{u}}$. The Poisson distribution is consistent with the stochastic Markov chain process approach to epidemic modeling, and is consistent with the compartmental model approach that we have taken here if a large population limit is taken [12]. The spreadsheet implementation of the model can be adapted in applications if other distributions are deemed to be more appropriate. The means $m_{\mathrm{p}}(t)$ and $m_{\mathrm{u}}(t)$ were the mean number of protected and unprotected sexual contacts, respectively, per individual. The probabilities p_{p} and p_{u} were the transmission probabilities per protected contact and per unprotected contact, respectively. These were used to define $P(t)$, the probability that at least one infection occurs during the time period t to $t + dt$, as follows:

$$\begin{aligned} P(t) &= P(X_p > 0) + P(X_u > 0) - P(X_p > 0)P(X_u > 0) \\ &= [1 - e^{-m_p(t)p_p dt}] + [1 - e^{-m_u(t)p_u dt}] - [1 - e^{-m_p(t)p_p dt}][1 - e^{-m_u(t)p_u dt}] \end{aligned} \quad (8.6)$$

Thus, the rate of infection $\gamma(t)$ at time t was modeled by $-[\ln(1 - P(t))]/dt$.

The transmission rate $\beta(t)$ between susceptible partners and other HIV-infected individuals in the general population (excluding the index case) was modeled by

$$\beta(t) = (k/y)(y - 1)P_{\mathrm{HIV}}p_u \quad (8.7)$$

where k is the number of unprotected sexual contacts per period among heterosexual women and men, y is the number of sexual partners per individual among heterosexual women and men in the USA, and P_{HIV} is the HIV prevalence in the US population. The term k/y approximates the number of unprotected sexual contacts per sexual partner per period. The number of HIV-positive sexual partners, excluding the index case, equals $(y - 1)P_{\mathrm{HIV}}$. By multiplying that with the transmission probability per unprotected sexual contact, p_u, we obtained the rate of transmission $\beta(t)$. The death rate of susceptible partners, $\alpha_S(t)$, was estimated by the annual death rate among US adults.

A closed-form solution for the ODE that determines $S(t)$ can be found for certain special cases. For example, the Appendix describes the closed-form solution for $S(t)$ when the parameters are piecewise constant on a sequence of time intervals.

We simulated the ODE model in a spreadsheet by using the Euler-forward method [13]. This method, while offering less numerical stability than some other ODE solution methods, offers ease of implementation in spreadsheets and more flexibility to adapt (8.1)–(8.5) to accommodate a less restrictive set of assumptions about how the parameters may vary through time and the distribution of the number of potentially infectious contacts in each period of time. The Euler-forward method updates states on a discrete time grid, such as by

$$x_{j+1} = x_j + f(x_j, t_j)\Delta t$$

where x_j is the state of the system at time $t_j = j\Delta t$ and $f(x_j, t_j) = dx/dt$. We followed the dynamics of the system over a period of 20 years. The initial values of the state variables were $S(0) = s_0 =$ the mean number of sexual partners per index case (which will be random in the probabilistic sensitivity analysis, because of measurement uncertainty in estimating this mean) and $I(0) = D(0) = 0$.

Table 8.1 summarizes the model's parameter values for HIV transmission, treatment cost, and QALYs in the base case. All costs were converted to 2009 US $ using the consumer price index for medical care [14].

The most appropriate values for the HIV prevalence and transmission probabilities in the model depend upon the prevalence in the potential population

Table 8.1 Parameter values for HIV transmission, treatment cost, and QALYs

Parameter	Base-case	References
HIV prevalence among heterosexual men and women	0.0100	[15, 19]
Transition rate from HIV to AIDS (events per patient-year)	0.0585	[19]
Transition rate from HIV to death (events per patient-year)	0.0000	Assumption
Transition rate from AIDS to death (events per patient-year)	0.0339	[19]
Average annual, age-adjusted death rate in USA (2003–2005)	0.0081	[20]
Percent reduction in transmission probability from condom use	90 %	[21]
Per-act transmission probability (unprotected, male-to-female vaginal sex)	0.001	[21]
Average duration of partnership (years)	1	Assumption
Number of QALYs lost per HIV infection	8.22	[22]
Lifetime cost of treating HIV/AIDS costs per infection (in 2009 US$)	$466,579	[23]
Annual discount rate for costs and QALYs	3 %	Assumption

for which it is intended. For this paper, we chose 1 % for the HIV prevalence among heterosexual men and women because it is a threshold that has been recommended by the CDC in general guidance for whether to recommend or target HIV counseling and testing [15]. For the HIV transmission probabilities, some studies indicated that the per-act transmission probability from female to male was half of that from male to female [16, 17]. Another study showed that the two transmission probabilities were more similar [18]. In the numerical example below we assumed that both transmission probabilities were equal.

The behavioral interventions described below may cause some of these parameter values to change.

8.2.2 HIV Behavioral Intervention for HIV-Positive Individuals

We searched the published literature on HIV behavioral interventions in PubMed, including meta-analytic and systematic reviews [3, 4, 5, 24, 25] and articles included in those reviews. We focused on individual and small group interventions for HIV-infected individuals that aimed at changing behaviors through counseling. We only considered studies with quantitative results; we did not consider studies with dichotomous or categorical measures (such as [26, 27]).

We selected three studies for our analysis: Kalichman et al. [6], Patterson et al. [28], and Rotheram-Borus et al. [29]. Although some interventions also targeted drug risk behaviors, we only focused on sexual risk behaviors in our analysis. Kalichman et al. [6] examined a group intervention focused on strategies for practicing safer sex. Patterson et al. [28] studied a brief counseling intervention that focused on condom use, safer-sex negotiation, and serostatus disclosure. Rotheram-Borus et al. [29] studied a two-module counseling intervention focused

Table 8.2 Parameter values for risky behaviors for with and without behavioral intervention

Study	Setting	Parameter values: without intervention; with intervention
Kalichman et al. [6]	Community-based service agency	Mean (SE) number of sex partners in the preceding 3 months: 1.6 (0.18); 1.2 (0.14) Mean number of unprotected sex acts (vaginal and anal) in the past 3 months: 2.7 (0.67); 1.2 (0.33)

Table 8.3 Summary of program cost calculations for the intervention of Kalichman et al. [6]

Intervention	Intervention's details	Total counselor time* hourly pay	Total counselor's cost per participant	Total program cost per participant
Kalichman et al. [6]	Number of sessions: 5 Length of session: 2 h Number of counselors: 2 Number of participants: 8	US$604.24	US$75.53	US$302.12

on (1) coping with one's serostatus and staying healthy, and (2) reducing substance use and unprotected sexual acts.

Although we analyzed all three interventions, we only report here the results of our analysis of the intervention studied by Kalichman et al. [6]. The results of our analyses based on the other two studies were similar to those of our analysis of Kalichman et al. [6]. We reported a subset of those results elsewhere [7]. Table 8.2 presents parameter values related to sexual behaviors we modeled.

Because the costs of the intervention (also called program costs) were not reported for that study, we estimated program costs based on provided details about intervention delivery, including the number of program staff delivering the intervention, the total number of sessions, the session duration, and the average number of clients served per session. Table 8.3 summarizes the estimated counselor times and expenses required by the intervention.

In deriving those costs, we assumed that the program's delivery facilitators had an educational background similar to that of a medical and public health social worker. We multiplied the total program delivery time by the average hourly wage of a social worker in the USA in 2009 ($23.24 [30]) plus 30 % for fringe benefits to obtain an estimated total cost for a facilitator of $604.24. We divided this quantity by the number of program participants to obtain per-client facilitator costs ($75.53 = $604.24/8).

In order to estimate more complete program costs, including those for recruitment, training, supervision, administration, supplies, equipment, facility space and participant costs, we examined two additional cost studies involving HIV-infected persons. One was an ART adherence case management program in Los Angeles

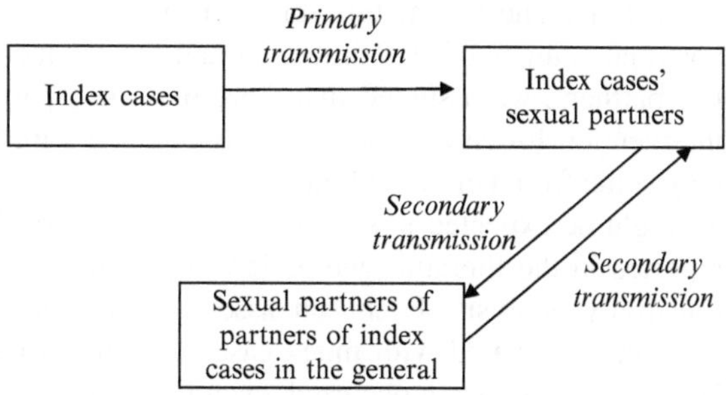

Fig. 8.2 HIV transmission chain

County in which clients met one-on-one with a case manager 14 times on average during a 6-month period to address barriers to ART adherence [31]. The other was a ten-session program for up to 15 participants per session to reduce risk behaviors among HIV-infected injection drug users in four US cities [32].

Based on the data from these two cost studies, we estimated the ratio of the cost of a case manager's time to the total societal cost to be 0.25. Therefore, we assumed that the facilitator costs estimated for the program considered in this study were 25 % of total program costs. To arrive at the total program cost per participant, we thus multiplied the facilitator costs by 4 ($302.12 = $75.53 × 4). All the costs in Table 8.3 were in 2009 US$.

8.2.3 Secondary Infection Model

The benefits of the HIV intervention are modeled as the reduction of HIV transmission among different population groups as summarized in Fig. 8.2. The potential types of transmissions we considered are the following:

- *Primary transmission.* Transmission from the index cases to their uninfected sexual partners
- *Secondary transmission.* Transmission involving sexual partners of index cases
  - Transmission from partners of index cases who become infected to their other sexual partners in the general population.
  - Transmission from HIV-infected individuals in the general population to uninfected partners of the index cases.

Almost all studies of behavioral interventions for HIV-infected individuals that we reviewed focused on primary transmission to partners. These studies did not measure endpoints that would quantify secondary transmission from the partners of index cases to their partners more broadly, or a change in infection transmission to partners of index cases from third parties.

This section describes how we adapted our model to account for secondary transmission. We did so by running a sequence of experiments. Each experiment instantiated the system dynamics model in Fig. 8.1 with somewhat different parameters. The parameters for each run were set so as to model the number of potential sources of HIV infection and the number of potential infected persons. For partners, we assumed that there may be a partial adoption of the behavioral intervention for risk reduction by association with the index case. Such a benefit may come from behavioral mimicry in response to change in behavior of a partner, as might be expected in social networks. Data for the degree of adoption was not reported in the literature we reviewed, so the degree of adoption was varied in a sensitivity analysis. Each run assessed the costs, benefits and potential transmissions associated with index cases or their partners for a period of time up to 20 years, unless death occurred, even if the duration of the effect of the behavioral intervention was shorter than that time horizon.

We now summarize the parameters we used and experiments we carried out for that analysis.

Let $\gamma_{\text{intervention}}$ and $\gamma_{\text{w/o intervention}}$ be the rate of infection transmission from the index case to his or her sexual partners when the index case receives and does not receive the intervention, respectively. These terms were computed based on the risky behaviors of the intervention and control groups ("with intervention" and "without intervention" parameter values in Table 8.2, respectively). Similarly, let $\lambda_{S,\text{intervention}}$ and $\lambda_{S,\text{w/o intervention}}$ be the rate at which an index case acquires new susceptible sexual partners, when the index case receives and does not receive the intervention, respectively. These terms were computed based on the values for "with intervention" and "without intervention" in Table 8.2, respectively.

To model the benefit of the intervention in secondary transmissions that are attributable to potential behavior changes in partners of index cases, we applied a multiplier ζ, $0 \leq \zeta \leq 1$, which represents the percentage reduction of risky behaviors of the index case's partner.

We defined t_0 be the time that the invention becomes effective at reducing risky behaviors and t_1 to be the time that the intervention becomes ineffective. In order to compute the number of new infections averted by the intervention, we ran the model in multiple scenarios, each with a different set of parameter values. We ran five scenarios with the following parameter inputs.

Scenario 1. None of the index cases receives the intervention. Parameters associated with the risky behaviors follow those of the control group reported in Kalichman et al. [6] or "without intervention" parameters in Table 8.2. The key input parameters were as follows:

$$\gamma(t) = \gamma_{\text{w/o intervention}}, \quad \lambda_S(t) = \lambda_{S,\text{w/o intervention}}, \quad \text{for all } t.$$

The simulation output for this scenario Y_1 was the total number of new infections among index cases' partners per index case, *without* intervention.

Scenario 2. The index cases receive the intervention reported in Kalichman et al. [6]. The benefit of the intervention was modeled as the reduction in risky behaviors among the index cases that lead to the primary transmission to their sexual partners. The key input parameters were as follows:

$$\gamma(t) = \gamma_{\text{intervention}},\ \lambda_S(t) = \lambda_{S,\text{intervention}},\ \text{for } t \in [t_0,\ t_1],$$

$$\gamma(t) = \gamma_{\text{w/o intervention}},\ \lambda_S(t) = \lambda_{S,\text{w/o intervention}},\ \text{for } t \notin [t_0,\ t_1].$$

The simulation output for this scenario Y_2 was the total number of new infections among index cases' partners per index case, *with* intervention.

Scenario 3. The index cases received a partial benefit of the behavioral intervention that was reported in Kalichman et al. [6]. The benefits of the intervention included a reduction in primary transmission stemming from the reduction in the risky behaviors of the index cases, and reductions in secondary transmission stemming from the partial reduction in the risky behavior of the index cases' partners. The key input parameters were as follows:

$$\gamma(t) = \gamma_{\text{intervention}},\ \lambda_S(t) = \lambda_{S,\text{intervention}},$$
$$\beta(t) = \zeta\beta\frac{\lambda_{S,\text{intervention}}}{\lambda_{S,\text{w/o intervention}}} + (1-\zeta)\beta,\ \text{for } t \in [t_0,\ t_1],$$

$$\gamma(t) = \gamma_{\text{w/o intervention}},\ \lambda_S(t) = \lambda_{S,\text{w/o intervention}},\ \beta(t) = \beta,\quad \text{for } t \notin [t_0,\ t_1].$$

Here β is the base value of the transmission rate due to sexual contacts with other HIV-infected individuals in the general population. The simulation output for this scenario Y_3 was the total number of new infections among the index cases' partners per index case, with intervention.

Scenario 4. In addition to primary transmission from index cases to their partners, we calculated the secondary transmission from the index cases' partners, who become infected, to their other partners in the general population, when there is no intervention. The simulation output for this scenario Y_4 was the total number of new infections among the partners (in the general population) of the index cases' partners per index case, when the intervention is not implemented. If the index case's partners have similar risk behaviors to the index case, then each infected partner can further infect, on average, Y_1 other partners in the general population. We therefore assumed that Y_4 equals $(Y_1)^2$. This is reasonable given the assumed HIV prevalence and that the time horizon for primary and secondary infections was the same.

Scenario 5. In addition to primary transmission from index cases to their partners, we calculated the secondary transmission from the index cases' partners to their other partners in the general population, assuming that the intervention is implemented and has a partial effect on reducing the risky behaviors of partners of index cases. The key input parameters are as follows:

$$\gamma(t) = \zeta\gamma_{\text{intervention}} + (1-\zeta)\gamma_{\text{w/o intervention}},$$
$$\lambda_S(t) = \zeta\lambda_{S,\text{intervention}} + (1-\zeta)\lambda_{S,\text{w/o intervention}},$$

$$\beta(t) = \zeta\beta_{\text{intervention}}(\lambda_{S,\text{intervention}}/\lambda_{S,\text{w/o intervention}}) + (1-\zeta)\beta_{\text{w/o intervention}}.$$

The simulation output for this scenario $Y_{5,\text{partner}}$ was the total number of new infections among the partners in the general population *per index case's partner*, when the intervention is implemented. Given that a newly infected partner of an index case may further infect $Y_{5,\text{partner}}$ partners, we modeled the total number of new infections among the partners in the general population *per index case* by $Y_5 = Y_{5,\text{partner}} \cdot Y_3$.

Scenarios 4 and 5, in which the partners of index cases became the index cases, require an assumption about the number of susceptible partners that the partners of the index cases have. Formally, that number would be best modeled as the conditional mean number of partners beyond the index case given that they have at least one partner (the index case). Such data is not available in any of the studies that we examined. In the analysis below, we assumed that this conditional mean equals the mean number of partners of the index case. This is consistent with an assumption that the number of partners is geometrically distributed (a consequence of the memoryless property of the geometric distribution). If better data were available about the mean number of partners of partners of index cases, that could be incorporated directly into our analysis for Scenarios 4 and 5.

The total number of infections averted by the intervention per index case was thus $(Y_1 - Y_2)$ when considering primary transmission only, and was $(Y_1 - Y_3) + (Y_4 - Y_5)$, when including both primary and secondary transmission. We did not consider more distant infections in the transmission chain.

8.2.4 Probabilistic Sensitivity Analysis

Probabilistic sensitivity analysis (PSA) is a tool that accounts for the uncertainty in key parameters of mathematical models. That uncertainty may be due to a lack of data—for example when expert judgment is involved—or due to parameter estimation errors from limited sample sizes. Thus, a precise assessment of the cost-effectiveness of a health intervention cannot be known with certainty. Decisions involving a cost-effectiveness analysis should therefore account for the fact that uncertainty exists. Indeed, the UK National Institute for Health and Clinical Excellence (NICE) has updated its methods guidance for technology assessment to require the use of PSA [33].

We used Monte Carlo sampling to explore the effect of parameter uncertainty on the cost and effectiveness results. Since we focused on the effect of the intervention on risky sexual behaviors and infection transmission among partners, we only sampled parameters related to sexual behaviors. Table 8.4 presents the selected model parameters and the sampling distributions. We assumed that these parameters are independent and the number of sexual partners and the number of unprotected sexual contacts follow gamma distributions. The parameters of the gamma distribution, a and b, were derived from the mean ($\mu = ab$) and standard errors ($\text{SE} = \text{sqrt}(ab^2)$), reported in Kalichman et al. [6], i.e., $a = \mu^2/\text{SE}^2$, and $b = \text{SE}^2/\mu$.

Table 8.4 Monte Carlo sampling distributions used in probabilistic sensitivity analysis

Intervention	Model parameter	Sampling distribution
Kalichman et al. [6]	Mean number of sexual partners in the past 3 months	
	Without intervention	Gamma (82.22, 0.019)
	With intervention	Gamma (73.80, 0.016)
	Mean number of unprotected sex acts (vaginal and anal) in the past 3 months	
	Without intervention	Gamma (16.29, 0.166)
	With intervention	Gamma (13.16, 0.091)

8.2.5 *Cost-Utility Analysis and the Program Cost Threshold Analysis*

For each of the five scenarios, the model was run for 100 iterations using parameters from Tables 8.2, 8.3, and 8.4. In each simulation run, the model calculated the total number of HIV infections among partners per index case for all scenarios (i.e., Y_1 to Y_5), the total number of HIV infections averted by the intervention per index case, the discounted QALYs saved per index case, and the discounted HIV lifetime treatment cost saved per index case. The method of common random numbers was used for all scenarios.

The mean discounted lifetime HIV treatment costs saved and the mean discounted QALYs saved were computed by averaging the values from all simulation runs. This determined the incremental cost-effectiveness ratio (ICER),

$$\text{ICER} = \frac{\text{Program Costs} - \text{Mean Discounted Lifetime HIV Treatment Costs Saved}}{\text{Mean Discounted QALYs Saved}}$$

A program was considered cost-saving if the savings in total lifetime HIV treatment costs exceed the program costs (a negative ICER). A program was considered cost-effective if the ICER was less than or equal to \$50,000 [34, 35], a widely used threshold in public health economic evaluation.

We also performed a threshold analyses to determine the upper bound for the program cost of the behavioral intervention such that the program is cost-effective. In the USA, the program might be considered cost-effective if the ICER is less than \$50,000 per QALYs saved. With this value, the program cost threshold is as follows:

$$\begin{aligned}\text{Progra cost threshold} &= \$50{,}000 \times \text{QALYs Saved per Index Case} \\ &\quad + \text{Mean DiscountedLifetime HIV Treatment} \\ &\quad\quad \text{Cost mathrm Saved per Index Case.}\end{aligned}$$

Another criterion, considered by the World Health Organization, is that the program is cost-effective if its cost per QALYs gained is less than a country's per capita GDP [36]. The program cost threshold could be readily adapted to those contexts by substituting the appropriate value for the cost per QALY conversion factor.

8.3 Results and Discussion

Table 8.5 shows our simulation estimates of the cost and effectiveness of an HIV behavioral intervention such as that studied by Kalichman et al. [6] when compared to the "Without Intervention" scenario. When the index case received the risk reduction intervention and modified his or her risk behaviors for 1 year, the mean (SE) number of primary infections prevented was 0.0114 (0.0005) per index case. Assuming that the intervention partially affects the index cases' partners by reducing their risky behaviors by 20 %, the mean (SE) total number of primary and secondary infections prevented was 0.0164 (0.0009) per index case. The prevention of these HIV infections resulted in the mean (SE) discounted QALYs saved per index case of 0.0908 (0.0046) for the primary infection prevention and 0.1205 (0.0066) for the primary and secondary infections prevention respectively. On average, the intervention would save discounted lifetime HIV treatment costs of \$5,155 (SE = \$258) per index case from the primary infection prevented, and \$6,840 (SE = \$376) per index case from the primary and secondary infections prevented, respectively.

The intervention was cost-saving when the model used the sample mean as a point estimate of the given parameters. When uncertainty was accounted for in the parameter estimates, we estimated that the probability that the intervention was cost-saving or at least cost-effective was 0.98.

Figure 8.3 shows the mean number of HIV infections prevented per index case as a function of the degree of adoption of the behavior intervention by an index case's partners, and when the duration of intervention effectiveness was varied from 1 to 3 years. The solid lines quantify the mean number of infections averted per index case when secondary transmission to and from partners of the index cases were included. If partners of index cases adopted more of the risk-reduction behavior of the index cases (as ζ increases), the number of infections averted increased. The broken lines, which correspond to the number of infections averted from only index cases to their partners, are horizontal since they are independent of the parameter ζ.

We observed that the topmost dashed line in Fig. 8.3 is below the middle solid line when $\zeta = 1$. This indicates that there were more infections averted by a behavioral intervention whose effects last 2 years when the risk reductions are also fully adopted by partners, as compared with an intervention which lasts 3 years but is not at all successful at changing the risk behavior of partners of index cases with their other partners. This indicates that there may be value in studies that also

Table 8.5 Mean and standard errors (SE) of costs and health outcomes when comparing the "with intervention" scenario of Kalichman et al. [6] to the "without intervention" scenario and using $\zeta = 0.2$ and a duration of intervention effectiveness of 1 year

Outcome	Include primary transmission only	Include primary and secondary transmissions
Mean (SE) number of partners' infections averted per index case	0.0114 (0.0005)	0.0164 (0.0009)
Mean (SE) discounted QALYs saved due to partners' infections per index case	0.0908 (0.0046)	0.1205 (0.0066)
Mean (SE) discounted lifetime treatment costs saved due to partners' infections per index case	$5,155 ($258)	$6,840 ($376)
Program cost per index case	$302.12	$302.12
Incremental cost per QALY saved (ICER)	Cost-saving	Cost-saving
Proportion of runs with negative ICER (cost-saving) or with ICER ≤ $50,000 (cost-effective)	0.98	0.98

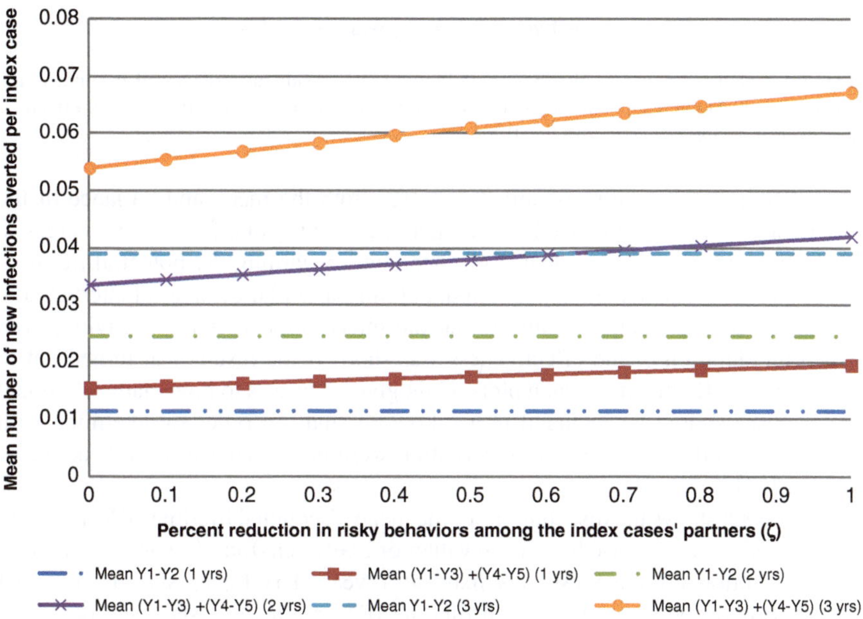

Fig. 8.3 Mean number of new HIV infections averted per index case by the intervention when considering primary transmission only (*broken lines*) and when considering both primary and secondary transmission (*solid lines*) (based on 100 Monte Carlo simulation runs)

assess the degree to which social adoption of behavioral interventions may influence HIV transmission.

Figure 8.4 shows the distributions of the mean discounted lifetime HIV treatment costs saved per index case when the duration of intervention effectiveness was

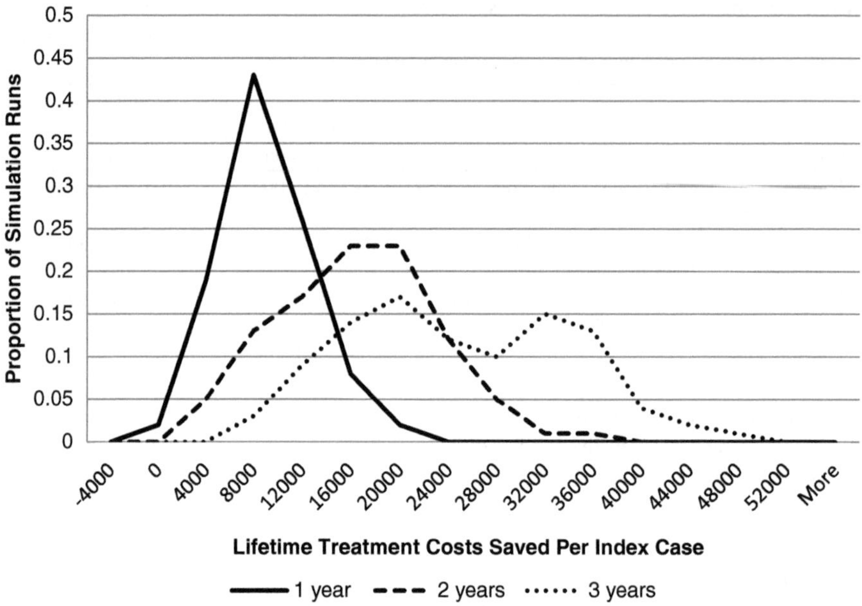

Fig. 8.4 Relative frequency distribution of lifetime HIV treatment costs saved per index case (based on 100 Monte Carlo simulation runs) when varying the duration of intervention effectiveness from 1 to 3 years, assuming $\zeta = 0.2$

varied from 1 to 3 years, assuming $\zeta = 0.2$. Both the mean and variance of the discounted lifetime costs saved increased as the duration of effectiveness increases. This PSA indicated a high degree of uncertainty regarding the potential life time treatment costs due to the risk reduction. For this particular behavioral intervention, there was only a small probability that the intervention is not cost-saving, even when the duration of the effectiveness was short. If the results had turned out to indicate less effectiveness, such plots might give a sense as to how many additional index cases should be included in a follow-up study in order to determine with higher probability whether the intervention were cost saving or cost-effective or neither [37].

Figure 8.5 shows the distributions of the mean discounted lifetime HIV treatment costs saved per index case for several values of ζ between 0 and 1, when the duration of intervention effectiveness was fixed at 1 year. The figure also displays the distribution of the mean discounted lifetime HIV treatment costs saved per index case when only primary infections were considered. There was considerable variation in the mean discounted lifetime treatment costs saved per index case even when only primary infections were considered. The variation, which was due to uncertainty about the parameters due to the statistical error in their estimates as presented in the source studies, showed that the intervention is most likely cost saving, but that there is some probability that it is not. This figure therefore shows explicitly the influence of parameter uncertainty on the uncertainty of economic outcomes.

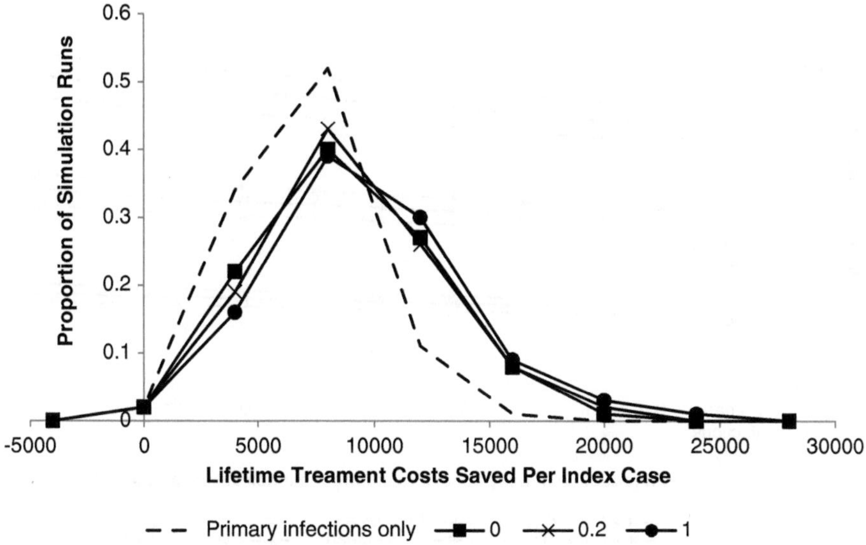

Fig. 8.5 Relative frequency distribution of the lifetime HIV treatment costs saved per index case (based on 100 Monte Carlo simulation runs) for $\zeta = 0$, 0.2, and 1, assuming a 1-year duration of intervention effectiveness

The distribution with $\zeta = 0$ differs from the curve for primary infections only in that it also included transmissions to and from partners of index cases with other individuals. As ζ was increased, the distribution shifted to the right. This corresponds to statistically larger cost savings. Qualitatively, the mean cost savings per index case is similar to the mean number of infections averted per index case shown in Fig. 8.3.

Figure 8.6 shows the averages and 95 % confidence intervals of the cost-effectiveness thresholds when the duration of effectiveness was varied from 1 to 3 years. We examined the case when primary transmission only was considered and when secondary transmission was also considered. Each threshold value is the upper bound of the program cost below which the intervention would be considered cost-effective. This threshold information determines the maximum cost-effective program cost if the intervention were to be implemented. The analysis showed that the average program cost threshold can range from $9,932 to $15,233 per index case, assuming the duration of effectiveness of the intervention was 1 year. The cost threshold doubled when the duration of effectiveness was extended from 1 to 2 years and increased by approximately 60 % when the duration was extended from 2 to 3 years. The cost threshold also increases by at least 30 % when we included the effects of the intervention on secondary transmission for various levels of ζ.

The robustness of the cost and effectiveness results depends significantly on the assumptions we made to overcome four main challenges encountered in our study of the three published behavioral interventions. One, the lack of comparable sexual behavior data from the three studies made it difficult to develop comparable projections of the number of infections averted and QALY saved. Two, not all studies

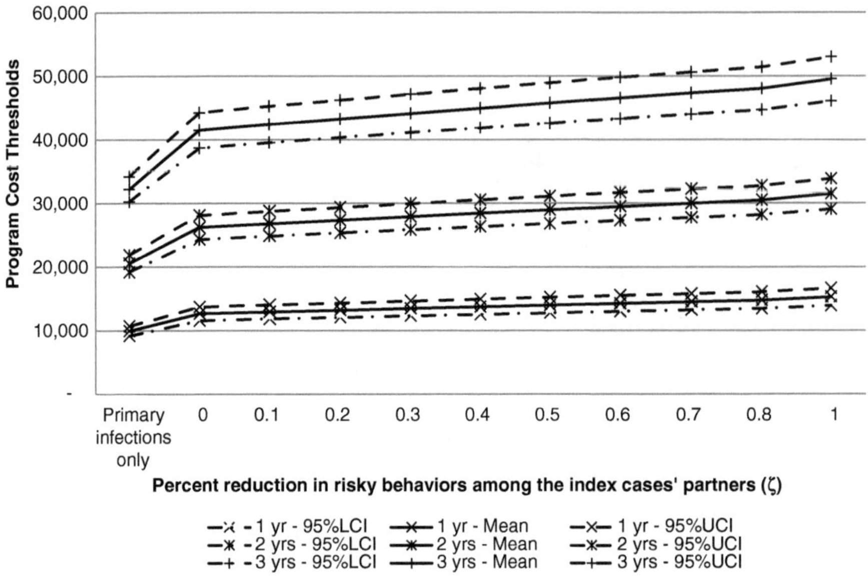

Fig. 8.6 Program cost threshold: mean and 95 % confidence intervals for upper-bound value on total program cost, below which the behavioral intervention would be considered cost-effective (based on 100 Monte Carlo simulation runs), for different values of ζ, assuming duration of intervention effectiveness of 1, 2, and 3 years

provided a measure of variation of the measured behavioral outcomes. This limited our ability to perform accurate sensitivity analyses. Three, none of these studies, except Rotheram-Borus et al. [29], reported intervention program costs. We estimated these costs based on available information and assumptions about resource use. Program costs may vary significantly for the same intervention in different settings. Four, our model did not account for the increase in viral load and consequent increase in infectivity during the acute phase of HIV infection (that is, shortly after initial infection) [38, 39]. For partners that partially adopt the risk reductions of an index case, a behavioral intervention is likely to be ongoing at the time of infection of those partners by index cases. Thus, this analysis may understate the benefits of the partial adoption of risk-reducing behaviors by partners of index cases.

8.4 Conclusions and Policy Implications

We conducted cost-effectiveness analysis of interventions that aim to reduce risk behaviors of HIV-positive individuals. We used an ODE model, coupled with cost estimates, to extend the intermediate outcomes reported by studies of behavioral interventions (e.g., reductions in number of sex partners, hours per counseling session) into cost-effectiveness values that can be used to compare interventions. We drew values for potential intervention efficacy from published studies.

We estimated intervention costs based on the details of the intervention delivery published in the studies. We used the model to perform sensitivity analysis on the duration of infection and, importantly, on the degree to which partners of index cases also reduce risky behaviors with their other partners.

Our results suggest that behavioral interventions targeted to HIV-positive individuals, such as the intervention described by Kalichman et al. [6], can reduce HIV transmission in the population, particularly if the behavioral changes are sustained over time. Information regarding the duration of intervention effects and the duration of sexual partnerships is important to better estimate HIV transmission risk and intervention effectiveness. The duration of these behavioral changes seem to strongly influence the magnitude of the cost-effectiveness of these programs, but the duration of effectiveness seems to be an open question. The cost-effectiveness analyses also showed that the intervention we studied was most likely to be cost-saving, or at least cost-effective, because the program cost estimate was much lower than the savings in lifetime HIV treatment costs.

Our results also indicate that the degree to which partners adopt risk reduction behaviors can have a significant effect on the total number of HIV infections averted (when considering primary infections from index cases to their initially uninfected partners, as well as potential secondary transmissions from partners of index cases who get infected and then infect other individuals). This data is typically not reported in the literature that we observed, and is likely not collected. Given current interest in behavioral interventions and the diffusion of behaviors through social networks, our model suggests that field studies may be warranted to better understand the degree to which behavioral interventions for infectious disease transmission risk reduction are diffused to those individuals who are initially susceptible and close to infected individuals.

Appendix

The ODE for $S(t)$ in (8.1) and the discounted cost and QALY equations in (8.4) and (8.5) drive the analysis. The term $S(t)$ is readily solvable in closed form when the time-varying parameters are assumed to be piecewise constant on a sequence of intervals in (8.1). For the behavioral interventions that we modeled, we assumed that these parameters were indeed piecewise constant on intervals. In particular, the functional form of (8.1) for the studies that we analyzed is

$$\mathrm{d}S(t)/\mathrm{d}t = a_i + b_i S(t), \quad \text{for } t \in [\tau_i, \ \tau_{i+1})$$

where $\tau_0 = 0$, τ_1 is the time of initiation of the behavioral intervention, $\tau_2 - \tau_1$ is the duration of the intervention, τ_3 is the time through which infections are counted for the purpose of the endpoint of the study, and $\tau_4 = \infty$ allows $S(t)$ to be defined for all $t \geq 0$. We assumed that $\tau_i \leq \tau_{i+1}$ for $i = 0, 1, 2, 3$, meaning that

$a_i = \lambda_S(t)$ and $b_i = -[\mu_S(t) + \gamma(t) + \beta(t) + \alpha_S(t)]$ were constant for t in $[\tau_i, \tau_{i+1})$. The constants may differ depending on the intervention for each i.

The solution is straightforward by a quick change of variables for each interval $[\tau_i, \tau_{i+1})$. If we set $T(t) = a_i + b_i S(t)$, we obtain $dT(t)/dt = b_i T(t)$, which has solution $T(t) = c_i \exp[b_i t]$ for some constant c_i. Solving for $S(t)$ we get

$$S(t) = c_i \exp[b_i t]/b_i - a_i/b_i, \text{for } t \in [\tau_i, \tau_{i+1}).$$

The value of c_i is determined by the preceding equation, which implies $c_i = b_i s_i + a_i$, and the initial condition $S(\tau_0) = s_0$. We evaluate this first for $i = 0$ to obtain

$$S(t) = s_0 \exp[b_0 t]/b_0 - a_0(\exp[b_0 t] - 1)/b_0, \text{for } t \in [\tau_0, \tau_1).$$

This determines $s_{i+1} = S(\tau_{i+1}) = s_i \exp[b_i(\tau_{i+1} - \tau_i)] - a_i/b_i(\exp[b_i (\tau_{i+1} - \tau_i)] - 1)$, which we sequentially evaluate for $i = 0, 1, 2, 3$. Thus, a closed-form expression for $S(t)$ is found by iterating over each time interval, with the parameters of the intervention set to constants in each interval. A similar analysis can be used obtain an iterated closed-form solution for the number of individuals infected up to a given time t.

This analysis was used to debug the spreadsheet code, which implements a forward Euler finite difference approximation to the ODE. The spreadsheet code additionally can be modified to have more flexibility than allowed by the piecewise linear assumption for the parameters.

References

1. CDC (2010) Projecting possible future courses of the HIV epidemic in the United States. http://www.cdc.gov/hiv/resources/factsheets/us-epi-future-courses.htm. Accessed 13 Nov 2011
2. Janssen R, Onorato I, Valdiserri R et al. (2003) Advancing HIV prevention: new strategies for a changing epidemic—United States. Morb Mortal Wkly Rep 52:329–332
3. Johnson B, Carey M, Chaudoir S et al. (2006) Sexual risk reduction for persons living with HIV: research synthesis of randomized controlled trials, 1993 to 2004. J Acquir Immune Defic Syndr 41:642–650
4. Herbst J, Sherba R, Crepaz N et al. (2005) A meta-analytic review of HIV behavioral interventions for reducing sexual risk behavior of men who have sex with men. J Acquir Immune Defic Syndr 39:228–241
5. Lyles C, Kay L, Crepaz N et al. (2007) Best-evidence interventions: findings from a systematic review of HIV behavioral interventions for US populations at high risk, 2000–2004. Am J Public Health 97:133–143
6. Kalichman S, Rompa D, Cage M et al. (2001) Effectiveness of an intervention to reduce HIV transmission risks in HIV-positive people. Am J Prev Med 21:84–92

7. Soorapanth S, Chick SE (2010) Cost-utility analysis of behavioral interventions for HIV-infected persons to reduce HIV transmission in the USA. In: Johansson B, Jain S, Montoya-Torres J, Hugan J, Yücesan E (eds) Proc Winter Sim Conf. IEEE, Piscataway, NJ, pp 2433–2443
8. Ekstrand ML, Coates TJ (1990) Maintenance of safer sexual behavior and predictors of risky sex: the San Francisco Men's Health Study. Am J Public Health 80:973–977
9. Stall R, Ekstrand ML, Pollack L et al. (1990) Relapse from safer sex: the next challenge for AIDS prevention efforts. J Acquir Immune Defic Syndr 3:1181–1187
10. Adib SM, Joseph JG, Ostrow DG et al. (1991) Relapse in sexual behavior among homosexual men: a 2-year follow-up from the Chicago MACS/CCS. AIDS 5:757–760
11. Brandeau ML, Owens K (1994) When women return to risk: costs and benefits of HIV screening in the presence of relapse. In: Kaplan EH, Brandeau ML (eds) Modeling the AIDS epidemic: planning, policy and prediction. Raven, New York
12. Diekmann O, Heesterbeek JAP (2000) Mathematical epidemiology of infectious diseases: model building, analysis and interpretation. Wiley, Chichester, England
13. Brennan A, Chick SE, Davies R (2006) A taxonomy of model structures for economic evaluation of health technologies. Health Econ 15:1295–1310
14. US Bureau of Labor Statistics (2009) Consumer price index databases. http://www.bls.gov/cpi/cpi_dr.htm. Accessed 6 Apr 2010
15. CDC (2001) Revised guidelines for HIV counseling, testing, and referral. Morb Mortal Wkly Rep 50(RR19):1–58. www.cdc.gov/mmwr/preview/mmwrhtml/rr5019a1.htm. Accessed 15 Nov 2011
16. European study group on heterosexual transmission of HIV (1992) Comparison of female to male and male to female transmission of HIV in 563 stable couples. BMJ 304(6830):809–813. doi: 10.1136/bmj.304.6830.809. PMC 1881672. PMID 1392708
17. Varghese B, Maher JE, Peterman TA et al. (2002) Reducing the risk of sexual HIV transmission: quantifying the per-act risk for HIV on the basis of choice of partner, sex act, and condom use. Sex Transm Dis 29(1):38–43. doi: 10.1097/00007435-200201000-00007. PMID 11773877
18. Boily MC, Baggaley RF, Wang L et al. (2009) Heterosexual risk of HIV-1 infection per sexual act: systematic review and meta-analysis of observational studies. Lancet Infect Dis 9(2):118–129. doi: 10.1016/S1473-3099(09)70021-0. PMID 19179227
19. Sanders G, Bayoumi A, Sundaram V et al. (2005) Cost-effectiveness of screening for HIV in the era of highly active antiretroviral therapy. N Engl J Med 352:570–585
20. National Center for Health Statistics (2009) Health, United States, 2008, With Cartbook, Hyattville, MD. http://www.cdc.gov/nchs/data/hus/hus08.pdf#026. Accessed 16 Sept 2009
21. Cohen D, Wu SY, Farley T (2004) Comparing the cost-effectiveness of HIV prevention interventions. J Acquir Immune Defic Syndr 37:1404–1414
22. Pinkerton S, Holtgrave D, DiFranceisco W et al. (2000) Cost-threshold analyses of the National AIDS demonstration research HIV prevention interventions. AIDS 14:1257–1268
23. Schackman B, Gebo K, Walensky R et al. (2006) The lifetime cost of current human immunodeficiency virus care in the United States. Med Care 44:990–997
24. Kelly J, Kalichman S (2002) Behavioral research in HIV/AIDS primary and secondary prevention: recent advances and future directions. J Consult Clin Psychol 70:626–639
25. Crepaz N, Lyles C, Wolitski R (2006) Do prevention interventions reduce HIV risk behaviours among people living with HIV? A meta-analytic review of controlled trials. AIDS 20:143–157
26. Wolitsky R, Gomez C, Parson J et al. (2005) Effects of a peer-led behavioral intervention to reduce HIV transmission and promote serostatus disclosure among HIV-seropositive gay and bisexual men. AIDS 19:S99–S109
27. Richardson J, Milam J, McCutchan A (2004) Effect of brief safer-sex counseling by medical providers to HIV-1 seropositive patients: a multi-clinic assessment. AIDS 18:1179–1186
28. Patterson T, Shaw W, Semple S (2003) Reducing the sexual risk behaviors of HIV + individuals: outcome of a randomized controlled trial. Ann Behav Med 25:137–145

29. Rotheram-Borus M, Swendeman D, Comulada W et al. (2004) Prevention for substance-using HIV-positive young people telephone and in-person delivery. J Acquir Immune Defic Syndr 37(Suppl 2):S68–S77
30. US Bureau of Labor Statistics (2009) National occupational employment and wage estimates United States. http://www.bls.gov/oes/2009/may/oes_nat.htm. Accessed 25 Oct 2011
31. Garland W, Wohl A, Valencia R et al. (2007) The acceptability of a directly-administered antiretroviral therapy (DAART) intervention among patients in public HIV clinics in Los Angeles, California. AIDS Care 19:159–167
32. Tuli K, Sansom S, Purcell D et al. (2005) Economic evaluation of an HIV prevention intervention for seropositive injection drug users. J Public Health Manag Pract 11:508–515
33. Claxton K, Sculpher M, McCabe C et al. (2005) Probabilistic sensitivity analysis for NICE technology assessment: not an optional extra. Health Econ 14(4):339–347
34. Owens DK (1998) Interpretation of cost-effectiveness analyses. J Gen Intern Med 13(10):716–717
35. Grosse SD (2008) Assessing cost-effectiveness in healthcare: history of the $50,000 per QALY threshold. Expert Rev Pharmacoecon Outcomes Res 8(2):165–178
36. Macroeconomics and health (2001) Investing in health for economic development. Report of the Commission on Macroeconomics and Health (CMH) of the World Health Organization, S.J. D, Editor, World Health Organization, Geneva
37. Ng SH, Chick SE (2006) Reducing parameter uncertainty for stochastic systems. ACM TOMACS 15(1):26–51
38. Koopman J, Jacquez J, Welch G et al. (1997) The role of early HIV infection in the spread of HIV through populations. J Acquir Immune Defic Syndr Hum Retrovirol 14:249–258
39. Vimalanand P, Farnham P, Hutchinson A et al. (2011) Cost-effectiveness of HIV screening in STD clinics, emergency departments, and inpatient units: a model-based analysis. PLoS One 6(5):e19936. doi:10.1371/journal.pone.0019936

Chapter 9
Modeling the Impact of New HIV Prevention Technologies in Sub-Saharan Africa

John Stover, Carel Pretorius, and Kyeen Andersson

Abstract Research has shown that several new technologies can be effective in reducing the transmission of HIV infection. Male circumcision was shown to reduce susceptibility to new infection by about 60 % in trials in 2005 and 2007. In 2009, a large scale trial of an HIV vaccine showed some protective benefits. Research results released in 2010 showed effectiveness of oral pre-exposure prophylaxis and topical pre-exposure prophylaxis at levels around 40 %. When new technologies become available national policy makers are faced with questions about whether to implement them, how much they will cost and how they should be implemented. Funders face similar questions. We have developed computer models to aid in policy development and planning. These models are intended to investigate questions such as "What will the impact be in terms of infections averted?", "How much would a new program cost?", and "Would the new program be cost-effective?" This chapter discusses models for male circumcision, pre-exposure prophylaxis, and HIV vaccines and their applications to inform policy makers.

9.1 Introduction

Mathematical models of HIV epidemics have a variety of uses. Applications include explaining or exploring the role of behavioral and contextual factors in the spread of HIV, projecting the future course of epidemics, estimating the need for HIV-related services such as treatment and prophylaxis, evaluating the impact of past programs, and informing policy and program decisions. Models have a special role in the planning for the introduction of new technologies or approaches

J. Stover (✉) • C. Pretorius • K. Andersson
Futures Institute, Glastonbury, CT, USA
e-mail: jstover@futuresinstitute.org

G.S. Zaric (ed.), *Operations Research and Health Care Policy*,
International Series in Operations Research & Management Science 190,
DOI 10.1007/978-1-4614-6507-2_9,

since they can be used to test alternative implementation strategies or even different technology characteristics when the new technology is not fully developed. Such models may help funders decide what research to support based on potential for future impact and which available approaches to support with implementation funding. Models can also assist national policy makers to decide whether to implement new approaches and how to implement them. In the field of HIV, organizations funding research need to decide whether they should be supporting studies of new technologies such as pre-exposure prophylaxis, microbicides, new antiretroviral drugs, and HIV vaccines. International organizations funding program implementation and national AIDS control programs need to decide how much funding to allocate to new technologies such as medical male circumcision and new approaches to preventing mother-to-child transmission of HIV as well as new approaches such as universal test and treat (where general population testing takes place annually and treatment is provided to all HIV + individuals) and combination prevention (which involves scaling-up the most cost-effective prevention intervention, usually male circumcision, ART, prevention of mother-to-child transmission and targeted programs for sex workers, men who have sex with men and injecting drug users).

Modeling can be useful in answering several questions of interest to policy makers and funders, such as the following:

- How much impact can we expect if we introduce a new technology or approach? How many infections and deaths can be averted?
- How should we target new programs? Should they be provided for all adults or targeted to particular population groups, such as young people, most-at-risk populations, or discordant couples?
- How much will new programs cost?
- Are new approaches cost-effective when compared with other available approaches for HIV prevention or compared against guidelines for health intervention?
- Will new programs be cost savings if they avert future costs of treatment, mitigation or productivity losses?
- What are the costs of delay? Will impact be greater if we start now or delay for several years?

HIV/AIDS models have been applied to a wide variety of key issues. Topics to which models have been applied recently include the characteristics of epidemics driven by men who have sex with men (MSM) and injecting drug user (IDU) transmission, estimating HIV incidence, using models to influence policy makers, uptake of biomedical interventions, the emergence of drug resistance, and the prevention impact of treatment [1].

This chapter discusses the use of mathematical modeling to examine key issues around three new HIV prevention technologies: medical male circumcision, pre-exposure prophylaxis (PrEP), and HIV vaccines.

9.2 The Impact of Medical Male Circumcision on New HIV Infections

It had long been noted that there is an association between the prevalence of male circumcision and HIV prevalence. In countries with the highest levels of prevalence in sub-Saharan Africa, primarily in Eastern and Southern Africa, males are not routinely circumcised, while male circumcision is nearly universal in most countries in West Africa where HIV prevalence levels are low [2]. A study designed to explain the difference between cities with high HIV prevalence (Kisumu, Kenya and Ndola, Zambia) and cities with low HIV prevalence (Cotonou, Benin and Younde, Cameroon) found only two factors that stood out: male circumcision (high in Contonou and Yaounde and low in Kisumu and Ndola) and the age difference between male and female partners [3, 4]. A meta-analysis of anthropological information estimated that male circumcision has a protective effect of 50–60 % [2].

Beginning in 2005 three randomized controlled trials of male circumcision in South Africa [5], Kenya [6], and Uganda [7] showed that medical male circumcision (MC) among men 15–49 could reduce men's risk of acquiring HIV by about 60 %. As a result policy makers in many countries began considering whether they should implement programs to provide medical MC. The most urgent need was in the countries in East and Southern Africa with high levels of HIV prevalence and low levels of MC. National policy makers and donor organizations that might support MC programs wanted to know several things: "What would be the national impact on new infections in my country if we started programs to provide male circumcision?", "Should we target specific population groups (neonates, 15-year-olds, high risk men) and, if so, which ones?", and "How many circumcisions will we need to perform and what are the requirements in terms of personnel and cost?"

A number of research groups developed mathematical models to address these questions. Williams developed an aggregate model of national populations and fitted it to data from 42 countries in sub-Saharan Africa to estimate the impact of scaling up male circumcision programs [8]. Nagelkerke applied both a random mixing model and a compartmental model to epidemics in Botswana and Nyanza province in western Kenya [9]. Gray applied a stochastic model to Rakai, Uganda and explored the effects of various scenarios on the epidemic reproductive rate [10]. Hallett developed a model for Zimbabwe that showed that HIV incidence could be reduced by 25–35 % after 10 years [11]. White developed an individual-based model and applied it to a typical southern African epidemic to investigate who should be targeted for MC services and the effect of risk compensation (where men who are circumcised adopt riskier behaviors because they believe they are no longer susceptible to HIV) on overall impact [12]. Alsallaq applied a deterministic compartmental model to Rakai, Uganda and Kisumu, Kenya and found that MC could reduce HIV prevalence by 14–19 % by 2020 [13].

Kahn [14] and Auvert [15] found MC to be cost-effective in the South Africa context while Bollinger found it to be cost-effective in Botswana [16]. Martin and colleagues collected detailed cost information and used it to model cost-effectiveness in Lesotho, Swaziland and Zambia [17]. Binagwaho applied a cost-effectiveness model to Rwanda and found that the most cost-effective approaches were neonatal circumcision, followed by adolescent programs, followed by programs that reach all adult men [18].

These studies showed the benefits of male circumcision in specific settings but did not address all the issues important to policy makers trying to develop national policies. To support that policy dialogue we developed a simple model that replicates the key findings of the detailed modeling studies but that could be easily set-up for any country context and used to explore the impact of various program options. The model also included a component to determine the costs of implementing a male circumcision program.

The impact model tracks males and females separately in two age groups: 15–24 and 24–49 to allow for various targeting options. Circumcision for neonates is also included and affects the adult model when children reach age 15.

New HIV infections are determined from the force of infection r and the prevalence in the partner populations, which is an average of the prevalence in each of the two age groups of the opposite sex weighted by the proportion of contacts with that age group.

$$I_{a,s,t} = r_{a,s,t}\left(P_{15-24,s',t} \times c_{a,15-24,s'} + P_{24-49,s',t} \times c_{a,25-49,s'}\right)$$

where

$I_{a,s,t}$ = New infections in age group a, sex s, at time t
$r_{a,s,t}$ = Force of infection for age group a, sex s, at time t
$P_{a,s,t}$ = HIV prevalence of age group a, sex s, at time t
$c_{a,a',s}$ = Proportion of contacts between age group a and a' for partner sex s

The force of infection during the historical period is determined by fitting the modeled prevalence to estimates of prevalence derived from surveys or surveillance data. The equation is based on a model of male circumcision described by Williams [8]. The fitting involves three parameters:

r': The force of infection at the start of the epidemic.
α: A parameter describing the rate of decline in the average risk for the susceptible population as prevalence increases. Risk is assumed to decline as those with the highest risk get infected first leaving a susceptible population with lower risk.
ε: A parameter describing the reduction in risk due to behavior change.

The force of infection during the projection period is further modified by the change in the proportion of adult men that are circumcised.

$$r_{a,s,t} = r'_{a,s} \times e^{-\alpha \times p_{a,s,t}} \times \varepsilon_{a,s,t} \times \mathrm{mc}_{a,t}$$

In this equation the basic force of infection, r', is modified by changes in the average level of risky behavior ($e^{-\alpha P}$) in the partner population, changes in behaviors (ε) of the susceptible population, and the effects of MC (mc).

Behavior change is assumed to occur as knowledge of AIDS increases due to the increasing number of people who die from AIDS. Thus the behavior change parameter ε is determined as a function of a constant ε' and the cumulative number of AIDS deaths,

$$\varepsilon_{a,s,t} = e^{-\varepsilon'_{a,s}} \times D_t$$

The effect of increasing prevalence of male circumcision, mc, is determined by the change in the proportion circumcised, χ, and the reduction in transmission for men who are circumcised compared to those who are not, π.

$$\mathrm{mc}_{a,t} = \left(\chi_{a,s,t} - \chi_{a,s,1}\right)\pi$$

The costs of male circumcision are a function of the source of the service (public, private or NGO hospital; public, private or NGO clinic; mobile vans), the time required of each personnel type (surgeon, nurse) and local costs for salaries, facilities, supplies and outreach.

The model allows planners to investigate the impact of alternative implementation scenarios on impact and cost. The model is typically used by planners developing an MC strategy to investigate three key questions:

- How much impact could be expected? In terms of deaths averted or life years gained.
- How much would the program cost?
- What is the cost per infection averted?

A full analysis usually examines alternate implementation scenarios. Among the implementation characteristics that can be investigated are the following:

- The target coverage level to be achieved at some future date. Typical values are 60–90 %.
- The pace of scale-up. How does the time required to reach the target coverage affect the ultimate impact? Programs often try scale-up periods of 5–10 years.
- The target population. This can be set to all adult males, 15–24-year-old males, adolescent males prior to sexual debut, high risk males or neonates or any combination of the above. Coverage levels may vary by population group.

A full description of the impact model and the model itself can be downloaded as an Excel file from www.FuturesInstitute.org.

The model has been applied in a number of countries to support policy and planning. For example, the national AIDS program in Botswana used the model in 2008 to support initial program development [16]. The model has also been used to test the application of a single implementation strategy in all 14 countries in

Sub-Saharan Africa likely to benefit the most from scaling up male circumcision [19]. In that case the key questions were how many circumcisions would have to be performed each year to reach 80 % coverage by 2015 and how much funding would be required.

The Sub-Saharan Africa analysis tested a scenario of achieving 80 % coverage of adult males 15–49 and neonates by 2015. The findings indicate that such a program would avert over four million new infections between 2009 and 2025, require almost 12 million circumcisions a year in the peak years of scale-up and four to five million circumcisions to maintain the target coverage level. The cost would be about US$ 2.5 billion between 2009 and 2025 resulting in a cost per infection averted of about US$662. Since the costs of treatment are considerably higher than this the program would actually save costs in the long run. While the benefits are large there are serious challenges to implementing a program that could provide so many circumcisions per year.

Most countries that have used the model have moved forward with male circumcision programs because of the trial results and funding from donors. The model has helped some programs decide on the best approach while other countries planned their programs without this model. Some are targeting high risk groups (such as military recruits and university students in Rwanda) while others are providing services to all adult males. Progress has been slower than envisioned in most countries as programs learn how to recruit new acceptors and provide services in a cost-effective manner. Nevertheless, these programs offer the promise of significant reductions in HIV incidence in some of the most severely affected countries in Africa.

As of April 2010 nine countries in Africa reported program statistics for their new MC programs. Kenya led the way with 110,000 circumcisions performed. Altogether countries in sub-Saharan Africa reported completing over 170,000 new circumcisions. Since then progress has been even more rapid. The program in Kenya provided 50,000 circumcisions in November and December 2010 alone through a campaign in Nyanza province. South Africa has rapidly scaled up its efforts, and Swaziland is mounting a major campaign in 2011. Progress reports and other information on male circumcision are available from the male circumcision clearinghouse at www.malecircumcision.org

9.3 Pre-exposure Prophylaxis for HIV Prevention

9.3.1 Description of Intervention

Antiretroviral therapy (ART) is the basis of many HIV-related treatment and prophylactic strategies [20]. Combination therapy regimens are now reaching a large number of those in need, resulting in a sharp reduction in mortality among many living with HIV/AIDS [21, 22]. The use of antiretroviral regimens has been very effective in preventing transmissions (pre- and post-partum) from mother to child [23]. Post-exposure prophylaxis (PEP) using mostly zidovudine is recommended for individuals following recognized recent exposure to HIV.

Pre-exposure prophylaxis (PrEP) is a new approach to ART-based prevention. It advocates the use of antiretroviral therapy by individuals who anticipate exposure to HIV infection. A wide range of prevention strategies can be formulated with PrEP, but it is likely that cost-effectiveness arguments will focus attention on those at highest risk of infection: commercial sex workers (CSW), men who have sex with men (MSM), injecting drug users (IDU) and serodiscordant partners of high risk individuals.

9.3.2 Effectiveness Trials

A number of trials are underway and a few have reported results. Results from a microbicide trial conducted by the Centre for the AIDS Programme of Research in South Africa (CAPRISA) for determining the efficacy of topical PrEP [24] found that a microbicide gel containing 1 % tenofovir disopoxyl fumarate (TDF) used by women at high risk of infection in KwaZulu-Natal, South Africa reduced incidence by 39 %. Results from the Preexposure Prophylaxis Initiative (abbreviated to "iPrEx") showed that PrEP in the form of oral emtricitabine (FTC) and TDF combination reduced the risk of HIV infection by 44 % in men and in transgender women who have sex with men [25]. Both studies found higher effectiveness among those who adhered to the recommended regimen but overall adherence levels were low, leading to very large confidence bounds around the efficacy estimates.

Another implementation challenge is the possibility of risk compensation. Both technologies are hailed as a timely female-based control method for women at high risk of infection, whether they are partners of high-risk men or are engaging in high-risk sex themselves (e.g., sex workers, injecting drug users (IDU) and women who have unprotected anal sex with men). These women are often not able to negotiate condom use. (Oral PrEP is unique in that it can provide protection for female IDU who often rely on their partners for their—often used—needles.) The concern is that these women will use condoms less frequently to protect themselves. A general decline in condom use may also result from the perceptions that risk of infection will be reduced at community level following the introduction of these technologies in community-wide interventions.

9.3.3 Modeling Impact

We set out to investigate the implementation challenges to a possible PrEP rollout in the generalized HIV epidemic of South Africa [26]. How will the expanding ART program in South Africa influence the impact of PrEP? Will condom substitution nullify the benefits of PrEP? What is an optimal prioritizing strategy when PrEP is used as a female-based tool? These questions relate to concerns of efficacy, risk compensation and female-based prioritizing respectively. Although studied as challenges in oral PrEP implementation, the lessons learned apply *mutatis mutandis* to questions in topical PrEP implementation.

We developed an age structured demographic HIV compartmental model to evaluate the impact and cost-effectiveness of PrEP for susceptibles alongside ART for HIV-positives and condom-use interventions in South Africa [26, 27]. The model is informed by national HIV and demographic surveys and pays close attention to the distribution of relative infection risks between age categories. It includes dynamical effects usually not explicitly modeled (most transmission models focus on risk and not age categories), such as age-dependent condom use, partner turnover rates and partner choice. The condom-use trends suggested by household surveys (in 1998, 2002, 2005 and 2008) are noteworthy: condom use has increased since the mid-1990s, predominantly among young women, and decreases with age, as shown in Fig. 5a in [27].

The transmission mechanism used in the model is designed from the point of view of women. The model views the spread of HIV as a process governed by the rate at which women meet new male partners, much like demographic models view population dynamics as the result of female fertility. The reason for these choices lies in the fact that women are more closely monitored (in antenatal clinics) than men. This choice was also guided by the requirement to describe data from South Africa's expanding PMTCT programs and to account for HIV among young children, as shown in Fig. 6b in [27].

We can put these ideas together in the following equations for force of infection for women (λ_{f}) and men (λ_{m}) receiving PrEP:

$$\lambda_{\mathrm{f}}(t,\ x) = 1 - \exp\left(-p_{\mathrm{f}}(1-\varphi)(1-c(t,\ x))r(x)\sum_{z} s(x,\ z)J_{\mathrm{m}}(t,\ z)/N_{\mathrm{m}}(t,\ z)\right)$$

$$\lambda_{\mathrm{m}}(t,\ x) = 1 - \exp\left(-p_{\mathrm{m}}\sum_{z}(1-\varphi)(1-c(t,\ z)r(z)s(z,\ x)J_{\mathrm{f}}(t,\ z)/N_{\mathrm{f}}(t,\ z)\right)$$

The force of infection depends on the probability of transmission per sex act (p_{f} and p_{m} are the per relationship transmission probabilities for women and men respectively), the effect of PrEP in reducing this probability (φ), the level of condom use ($c(t, x)$ is the probability that a condom is used during sex at year t and age x) and the rate of partner change ($r(x)$ is the rate at which women at age x meet sexual partners, $s(x, z)$ is the probability that she will form a relationship with a man of age z, $J_s(t, z)$ is the total number of HIV positive men and $N_s(t, z)$ is the total number of men (or women) of age z and sex s) [26].

The model gives a good fit to the overall population pyramid of South Africa, its crude death rate, the age-aggregated prevalence among women and disaggregated

HIV prevalence among women and men. Without direct measurements of incidence, the model's fit to incidence cannot be validated. However, it fits the UNAIDS and ASSA estimates for estimates among incidence among adults (15–49-year-old individuals) in 2008 relatively well.

9.3.4 *Programmatic Assumptions*

We made simple programmatic assumptions about ART and PrEP. The model accounts for the current baseline ART enrollment rate. We estimate a parameter of 9.6 years before initiating treatment, based on fitted data for the number of individuals receiving ART, as shown in Fig. 8b in [27]. (At the time of this analysis South Africa used a "less than 200 CD4 count" criterion for adults and recently a "less than 350 CD4 count" criterion for pregnant women.) A parameter adjusting ART enrollment rate is used to model expansion of ART, possibly to Universal Test and Treat (UTT) like coverage [28]. For PrEP the model uses a simple "uptake" parameter. We assume that the ART expansion and PrEP programs start in 2014 and will be fully scaled up by 2019 to achieve a given enrollment rate. A dropout rate of 1.5 % is assumed for both programs. These assumptions are used to test the contribution of PrEP in a context where ART scale-up is happening and expected to continue.

Our assumptions are as follows: $600 per person per year for ART and $150 per person per year for oral PrEP [27]. The cost estimate for PrEP is based on $12 for counseling and testing (VCT) (DOH 2007), $4 for serum creatinine tests (the National Health Laboratory Service of South Africa currently perform these at less than $5 per test) and $134 for the TDF-based regimen.

9.3.5 *Prioritizing Prep*

The inclusion of an age variable offers a direct way of studying age-structured prioritizing strategies. In South Africa, for example, there is particular interest to use PrEP as control strategy among young women (e.g., 15–24-year-olds). However, our model shows that the highest risk category would be 25–35-year-old women. To which age category should PrEP be prioritized?

We studied a number of PrEP prioritizing strategies: to 15–35-year-old women, to 15–25-year-old women and to 25–35-year-old women. We considered optimistic and realistic PrEP efficacy assumptions of 90 % and 70 % respectively. (Following the release of the iPEx results after the publication of modeling results, it seems that even 70 % should be considered optimistic.) However, given that the finding that ART can be 92 % effective in preventing new infections [30], and given the expectation that reducing infectiousness (ART) should have a greater impact than reducing susceptibility (PrEP), we wanted to be optimistic about the potential impact of PrEP.

9.3.6 Results

Our results show that PrEP can avert 10–25 % more infections (i.e., in addition to a continuation of the current ART scale-up trajectory) of women in the 15–35-year-old age group, and 12–27 % of additional infections in both the 15–25- and 25–35-year-old age groups. The population-level effect would be 5–12 %, 3.7–8.7 % and 3.7–9.3 % in these age groups respectively. The impact of PrEP increases if the incidence declines more gradually. Assuming, for example, that baseline incidence will be closer to 0.8 % per year in 2025 PrEP results in 13–28 % of new infections averted among 15–35-year-old women.

The model shows that prioritizing PrEP to 25–35-year-old women would have only a marginally higher impact on the HIV epidemic than prioritizing it to 15–25-year-old women. For this reason, we argue that an age-structured prioritization strategy to combat the generalized South African HIV epidemic cannot be based on incidence alone: at the national level incidence does not vary enough between these age groups to do so. Sub-national strategies, prioritizing for example young women in the KwaZulu-Natal province of South Africa (who are at very high risk of HIV infection) are more likely to be based partly on impact and cost-effectiveness arguments.

A continuation of the current ART scale-up trajectory would see twice as many individuals receiving ART in 2025 compared to 2010. When this ratio reaches levels of 3–3.5, our model shows a rapidly diminishing return in PrEP investment: the number of infections averted per unit coverage increase in PrEP drops dramatically. At this level of coverage ART will reach so many infected individuals that it will substantially control the HIV epidemics, leaving few infections for PrEP to avert. This conclusion hinges, somewhat delicately, on the assumption that ART will reduce the risk of new infections by 90 % by drastically reducing viral load and infectiousness, an impact which has recently been confirmed by the HPTN052 trial that showed a 96 % reduction in transmission in couples when the infected partner was on ART [29].

We find that a 30 % decrease in condom use will not nullify the impact of PrEP, but results in a 25 % reduction in the number of new infections averted. This impact is much smaller than expected by [31], who warned that marginal reductions in condom use can nullify the benefits of PrEP. We attribute the difference between our findings to the condom use trends suggested by DHS data: condom use declines with age. When evaluating the impact of condom substitution over long periods of time, we suggest that condom-substitution analysis should account for the extra complexity of declining condom use as a function of age.

The 10–25 % reduction in new infections that can be attributed to a female-based PrEP strategy will require a significant amount of additional financing. It would require coverage of 30–60 % and would cost $12,500–$20,000 per infection averted. If we consider different scenarios of PrEP efficacy and coverage and ART coverage by 2025 an estimate close to $20,000 seems realistic. If we assume baseline incidence that declines more gradually to 0.8 % by 2025, the lower bound for cost per infection averted by PrEP could be closer to $10,000, which is closer to the estimates of [31]. However, if ART expands to achieve, at 2025, 3–3.5 times the number of individuals receiving ART in 2010, this cost will increase rapidly beyond $35,000, even if baseline incidence at 2025 is higher than 0.5 %.

We cannot predict how policy makers will interpret our estimates that PrEP will be a relatively expensive prevention strategy. At $10,000–$20,000 per infection averted it lies in a similar cost range to ART. Prioritizing PrEP to the general population, even if the recipients are predominantly women, will raise the question of whether PrEP could be given to susceptible women before all HIV + cases eligible for treatment have been enrolled for ART. ART has the additional benefit of being a treatment tool. On the other hand, it must also be considered that a cost of $10,000–$20,000 per infection averted by PrEP is much less than the lifetime costs of ART should a person become infected and become eligible for treatment.

The debate of whether ART for treatment must be expanded before PrEP is introduced has another dimension: drug resistance. Many researchers are concerned about the possibility that high levels of ART resistance will result from the mono-therapeutic use of TDF [20], especially in countries where TDF is used in a first line treatment regimen. We did not include details of drug resistance in our analysis, but note a recent modeling result which suggests that the biggest contribution to resistance in a program with overlapping ART and PrEP regimens will come from the ART part of the program [32]. Using different regimens for PrEP and ART (if new PrEP regimens are developed) will minimize any drug resistance that might arise due to PrEP in combination with ART for treatment, and will also make the case for ART expansion before the introduction of PrEP less compelling.

Is there a window of opportunity for PrEP and how long will it last? Our analysis shows this depends on the rate at which ART coverage expands. Although based on optimistic assumptions, our analysis shows that well managed and prioritized PrEP interventions can have a non-negligible impact on incidence reduction, and the window of opportunity for its impact may turn out to be long.

9.4 HIV Vaccines

9.4.1 Description of Intervention

Current HIV prevention programs generally include a range of programs including behavioral interventions such as condom promotion and syringe exchange programs, as well as biomedical interventions such as male circumcision and the potential use of pre-exposure prophylaxis. These programs are already having an enormous impact on the HIV epidemic and the global number of new infections has recently started to decrease [33]. However, other prevention technologies—in particular a safe and effective HIV vaccine—are still urgently needed. At least 25 potential HIV vaccine candidates are in various stages of clinical testing globally

[34] and many more candidates are in preclinical development. Additionally, there have been enormous scientific challenges in developing HIV vaccines over the past several decades such as determining appropriate correlates of immunity and the ability of the virus to rapidly mutate in response to selective pressure. Because of this, vaccine candidates with only partial efficacy will certainly be considered for licensure and use [35].

There are generally two types of HIV vaccines under development: preventative and disease-modifying. A preventative vaccine would stimulate a broadly neutralizing antibody response and reduce (partially or entirely) the probability of infection from all routes, including sexual and intravenous transmission. These vaccines would prevent infection at the individual level and would provide the greatest chance of halting the HIV epidemic. However, because of scientific challenges in developing preventive vaccines, disease-modifying vaccines that stimulate cellular immunity via cytotoxic T lymphocyte-based responses are also currently under development. These vaccines would be able to decrease viral load and/or disease progression in those that are already infected, and might decrease HIV transmission at the population level through decreased infectivity in addition to lessening the impact of the disease at the individual level.

9.4.2 Effectiveness Trials

Only two vaccine candidates have made it through the pipeline of preclinical development and early clinical safety (Phase I) and immunogenicity (Phase II) trials to the large, multicenter, randomized controlled trials of effectiveness (Phase III) needed to prove that a vaccine candidate can reduce the likelihood of infection with HIV in humans. The first vaccine candidate to complete clinical trials—in North America, Europe, and Asia—failed to show evidence of protection from HIV infection [36]. The second vaccine candidate (ALVAC/AIDSVAX) to undergo Phase III effectiveness clinical trials was recently completed in Thailand (trial RV144) and demonstrated the first evidence of a protective effect from an HIV vaccine [37]. The modified intention-to-treat analysis revealed an overall efficacy of 31.2 % (95 % CI 1.1 %, 51.2 %) in preventing HIV infection for vaccinated individuals. Although this efficacy level was initially viewed by policy makers and the scientific community as too low for licensing consideration, the trial data indicated that this reduction may have been much higher during the first year following vaccination.

When clinical trials for prevention technologies are concluded and demonstrate efficacy in reducing HIV transmission, immediate decisions must be made regarding their potential use in terms of licensure and implementation. Policy makers must rely on the available empirical data from the clinical trials and modeling data for decision-making, rather than wait for long-term data on program outcomes. After the conclusion of the RV144 trial in Thailand, a group of international experts met with the Thai Ministry of Health to develop recommendations and next steps on the future use of the RV144 candidate [38]. One of these recommendations was that modeling methods be used to explore the implications of the trial results and the potential utility of this vaccine. We examined the potential impact of an HIV vaccine with rapidly waning efficacy—approximating the characteristics of the RV144 candidate—as an example of how modeling can be used to estimate the potential population impact of new prevention technologies concluding clinical trials.

9.4.3 Modeling Impact

9.4.3.1 Overview

We conducted this study at the national level for South Africa to explore the impact of vaccines with rapidly waning efficacy in a generalized, predominantly heterosexual epidemic. Because of the dynamics of the HIV epidemic in South Africa and the lower cost of vaccines compared to PrEP, we considered a vaccination campaign which reached the entire adult population (ages 15–49) rather than vaccination strategies which prioritized specific groups of individuals at higher risk of infection. Given the context of combination prevention and therefore the simultaneous implementation of multiple prevention programs, we explored the impact of various vaccination scenarios under different assumptions regarding the coverage levels of other biomedical and behavioral prevention interventions, as well as antiretroviral therapy (ART) coverage.

We used the Spectrum suite of models (Version 4.23, Beta 22, Futures Institute, Glastonbury, CT), which includes a vaccine component [39] that has been used previously to examine the impact of potential HIV vaccination scenarios in the country-specific settings of Brazil [40], Uganda [41], and Kenya [42] as well as at the global level [43]. The majority of inputs in Spectrum are from published sources including national surveys and surveillance data. Additionally, Spectrum allows for the impact of a vaccination program to be evaluated within the context of increasing or decreasing levels of other prevention programs such as condom promotion, volunteer counseling and testing, and male circumcision.

The vaccine model in Spectrum divides the population aged 15–49 by male and female and six risk groups: not sexually active, stable couples, casual sex, commercial sex, men who have sex with men, and injecting drug users. Transmission of HIV depends on a number of factors including the following:

- Base probability of transmission per act, r
- HIV prevalence in the partner population, P
- The number of acts per partner per year, a
- The number of different partners per year, p
- Vaccine efficacy, Ve, and coverage, Vc
- Male circumcision efficacy, Me, and coverage, M_C

- Condom efficacy, Ce, and coverage, Cc
- The prevalence of other STIs, Sp, and the multiplier on transmission when other STIs are present, Sm
- The multiplier on transmission for stage of infection, R

The number of new infections occurring to sex s, risk group g, at time t is a function of the number of susceptible, $N_{s,g,t}$ multiplied by the probability of becoming infected in that year, which is given by

$$(1-(P_{s',g,t}(1-r\times R_t\times \mathrm{MC}_{g,t}\times C_{g,t}\times V_{g,t}\times S_{g,t})^a+\ (1-P_{s',g,t})))^n$$

where the influence of male circumcision MC, condoms C, and vaccines V is calculated as one minus the product of the effectiveness and the coverage. For example:

$$V_{g,t}=1-\mathrm{Ve}\times\mathrm{Vc}$$

$$C_{g,t}=1-\mathrm{Ce}\times\mathrm{Cc}$$

The influence of stage of infection, R, is the weighted average of the proportion of the HIV-positive population in each stage (primary infection, asymptomatic, symptomatic, or on ART) and the relative transmission by stage.

Although the model can incorporate any combination of a reduction in susceptibility to infection, decreased infectiousness in those who are infected, and an increase in survival time for those who are HIV positive, we explored only the impact of reduced susceptibility in this analysis as the RV144 trial did not show evidence of reduction in viremia for those who were HIV positive. We assumed that vaccination provided complete protection to only a portion of those vaccinated and no protection to the rest of those vaccinated, such that the vaccine efficacy found in the RV144 trial was replicated in the overall population of vaccinated individuals in the model. We also assumed individuals were vaccinated without testing for HIV.

9.4.3.2 RV144 Trial Parameters

New analysis of the RV144 trial data has revealed substantially higher efficacy levels during the first year of vaccination than the overall efficacy found in 42 months of follow-up in the trial. Therefore we fit the trial data to an appropriate exponential decay function for vaccine efficacy, $\mathrm{Ve}=0.78\exp[-0.06\ t]$ where t is time in months since vaccination, to simulate rapidly waning levels of protection from the vaccine over time (John Glasser and Donald Stablein, personal communication). The equation specifies a vaccine efficacy which starts at 78 % and declines exponentially over time. We calculated the average duration of protection for this function as 1.43 years and used these parameters to model population-level efficacy, which approximated the RV144 clinical trial results.

9.4.3.3 Impact of Other Prevention Programs

Because the levels of other prevention program activities will determine the potential impact of a vaccination program, we explored different assumptions regarding the scale-up of 14 existing biomedical and behavioral prevention programs including condom distribution, volunteer counseling and testing, educational and outreach programs, male circumcision, and the provision of ART [44, 45]. All vaccination programs were evaluated for two different scenarios, a "baseline" prevention scenario and a "scaled up" prevention scenario. In the baseline prevention scenario we assume that coverage of other prevention programs will remain at their current levels over time, while in the scaled-up prevention scenario we assume that coverage of other prevention programs will be rapidly scaled up from their current levels to universal access country targets by 2015 and then maintained. We used Spectrum to create demographic projections for the baseline and scaled-up prevention scenarios in South Africa and then used these as the base case to simulate the additional impact of vaccination scenarios by creating separate projections for each of the vaccination scenarios examined.

9.4.3.4 Vaccination Scenarios

We explored the impact of varying levels of population vaccination coverage (20, 40, 60, and 80 %) which were maintained over time, such that new individuals were vaccinated and previously vaccinated individuals were revaccinated continuously. We assumed that individuals could not be revaccinated until their protection had waned completely and that revaccination provided the same benefits in terms of efficacy and duration of protection as initial vaccination. Although there was no data on the potential effects of booster vaccinations in the trial [37], current studies are attempting to assess whether and how booster vaccination might provide additional protection [38].

We assumed that levels of risk behavior such as condom use and number of sex partners remained constant over time in vaccinated individuals, as no evidence for increases in risky behavior were found in the trial. However, we allowed for changes in risk behavior due to the scale-up of behavioral prevention programs in the scaled-up prevention scenarios. We assumed that the vaccine would become available in 2020 so that vaccination could begin in that year and increase linearly to achieve target coverage levels by 2025. We assumed that vaccination would then continue through 2030. We also explored the impact of higher and lower levels of vaccine efficacy (30 %, 50 %, 50 %, 70 %, 90 %), while keeping the duration of protection constant.

We calculated program outcomes in terms of the number of new HIV infections, the number and percentage of expected HIV infections averted, the total number of vaccinations for a given strategy, and the number of vaccinations needed per infection averted. We used a 10-year time horizon (2020–2030) for measurement of program impact.

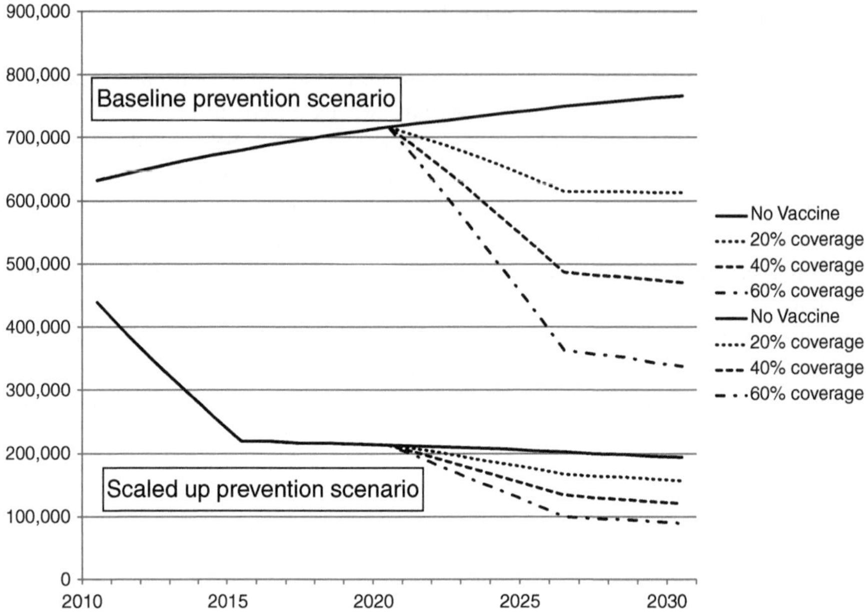

Fig. 9.1 New adult HIV Infections in South Africa. The annual number of new adult HIV infections in South Africa for various scenarios with general population vaccination beginning in 2020, reaching target coverage levels (20%, 40%, 60%, 80%) by 2025, and maintained thereafter. All scenarios considered a vaccine with efficacy and duration of protection approximated to RV144 trial conditions. All simulations were performed for two different background prevention scenarios: (1) baseline prevention scenario, in which coverage levels of all other prevention interventions remain constant over time at present levels, and (2) scaled-up prevention scenario, in which coverage levels of all other prevention interventions are scaled up from present levels by 2015 and maintained thereafter (Adapted from Andersson & Stover, *Vaccine*)

9.4.4 Results

The projections for the baseline prevention scenario and the scaled-up prevention scenario in South Africa are illustrated in Fig. 9.1. Scaling up levels of other prevention programs produces a steep decline in the number of new HIV infections over time: In the baseline prevention scenario, 8.2 million new infections will occur between 2020 and 2030 whereas in the scaled-up prevention scenario, the number of new infections over the 10-year period drops by 66 % (2.2 million).

Vaccination programs had a substantial impact on the number of new infections in the baseline prevention scenario (Fig. 9.1), even at the more modest coverage levels of 20 and 40 %. At 60 % coverage, the vaccination program would reduce the annual number of new infections by more than 50 % in the year 2030. At a very optimistic coverage level of 80 %, the 10-year vaccination program would reduce the number of new infections by the year 2030 almost as much as scaling up all other prevention programs immediately to universal access levels by 2015 and maintaining these levels until 2030 (without a vaccine). In the scaled-up prevention scenario, the vaccination programs had less effect as the other prevention programs were already impacting the number of new infections to a large degree (Fig. 9.1). However, the immediate scale-up of all other current prevention program activities is not enough to bring the annual number of new infections to zero and the vaccination programs would still provide additional needed benefits.

To quantify these benefits, we calculated total infections prevented and the percentage of cumulative infections prevented from 2020 to 2030. For the baseline prevention scenario, 20 % vaccination coverage would prevent 1,042,000 (13 %) infections, 40 % coverage would prevent 2,034,000 (25 %) infections, 60 % coverage would prevent 2,977,000 (36 %) infections, and 80 % coverage would prevent 3,845,000 (47 %) infections. For the scaled-up prevention scenario, 20 % vaccination coverage would prevent 268,000 (12 %) infections, 40 % coverage would prevent 525,000 (23 %) infections, 60 % coverage would prevent 773,000 (34 %) infections, and 80 % coverage would prevent 1,009,000 (45 %) infections. Overall, the vaccination programs in the baseline and scaled-up prevention scenarios prevented very similar proportions of expected HIV infections but the actual numbers were substantially less in the scaled-up prevention scenario due to the significant impact of the other prevention programs in reducing the number of expected infections.

We next examined the number of vaccinations that would be needed to achieve these goals. In the baseline prevention scenario, 38–154 million vaccinations would be needed between 2020 and 2030, depending on the target coverage level. The efficiency of the program would be relatively high, as only 37–40 vaccinations would be needed for each infection averted. In the scaled-up prevention scenario, a similar number of vaccinations (42–167 million) would be needed, but the efficiency of the program would be lower, as 156–166 vaccinations would be needed for each infection averted, depending on the target coverage level. Overall the number of vaccinations needed per infection averted was not sensitive to the program coverage levels but was sensitive to the levels of other prevention program activities.

Finally we explored the impact of varying levels of vaccine efficacy while keeping the short duration of protection found in the RV144 trial constant and assuming the baseline prevention scenario and 60 % target coverage levels. We found that the impact on infections prevented was generally as sensitive to vaccine efficacy as it was to program coverage levels, and that the number of vaccinations per infection averted was also sensitive to vaccine efficacy despite not being sensitive to program coverage levels. A 30 % effective vaccine would prevent 823,000 (10 %) infections but would require 141 vaccinations per infection averted; a 50 % effective vaccine would prevent 1,782,000 (22 %) infections but would require 65 vaccinations per infection averted; a 70 % effective vaccine would prevent 2,652,000 (32 %) infections and require 44 vaccinations per infection averted; and, a 90 % effective vaccine would prevent 3,439,000 (42 %) infections and only require 34 vaccinations per infection averted. Therefore higher coverage levels of a lower efficacy vaccine could result in similar outcomes to lower coverage levels of a higher efficacy vaccine in terms of infections prevented, but the efficiencies of the program would be different as the low efficacy vaccines would necessitate much higher numbers of vaccinations needed per infection averted.

Assuming a vaccine would not be available until 2020 and would have rapidly waning protection similar to that found in the RV144 trial, vaccination programs could produce very steep declines in the annual number of new infections in South Africa with relatively high efficiency. If all other prevention programs were scaled up immediately to universal access targets by 2015, the annual number of new infections in South Africa would drop substantially but vaccination programs like those described here could still make a significant additional impact, although the number of infections averted would be decreased and the vaccinations needed would be much greater. These conclusions depend on the ability of revaccination to produce efficacy levels at least as high as initial vaccination, and therefore studies to confirm the impact of booster vaccinations are needed.

9.5 Conclusions and Policy Implications

New prevention technologies such as male circumcision, pre-exposure prophylaxis, and vaccination potentially hold great promise for HIV control. Policy makers are well aware that detailed planning and accounting for nuances, such as efficacy, adherence, and prioritizing, are necessary for the successful implementation of any new prevention strategy. They also want to know how trial results may translate into impact in their countries where the epidemic may be very different from that in the trial locations. With many interventions already in place, such as prevention of mother to child transmission (PMTCT), antiretroviral therapy (ART) for treatment and condom programs, and with commitments to ensure their continuation, programmatic planning is now more challenging than ever in the HIV prevention arena.

When introducing new technologies into comprehensive prevention programs there are synergies to exploit and antagonisms to avoid. Prevention programs cannot accommodate expansion of all strategies, old and new. Cost tradeoffs must be considered and prioritizing strategies formulated. Mathematical models provide a sound platform for policy makers to compare alternative program designs, in terms of both impact and cost. The models discussed above are effective in translating the results of efficacy trials to real-world problems in specific countries. In these models, new interventions interact and compete with existing interventions in order to prevent new infections. The result is country specific planning tools which assign costs and impacts to different strategies. The models also look to the future in accounting for constraints such as the expected expansion of PMTCT and ART for treatment programs. The models are detailed enough to reflect and tentatively project the course of national epidemics. The focus of modeling on costs and efficiency does, however, necessitate that additional consideration be given to ethical issues surrounding equity, access, and the potential for stigma in program design. No model is a crystal ball, but country-specific tools based on mathematical models do help drive debate, and encourage policy makers to be explicit about the critical assumptions underlying decisions around current and future HIV intervention programs.

References

1. Garnett G, Wilson DP (2011) Epidemic modeling. Curr Opin HIV AIDS 6:1–140
2. Weiss H, Quigley MA, Hayes RJ (2000) Male circumcision and risk of HIV infection in sub-Saharan Africa: a systematic review and meta-analysis. AIDS 14:2361–2370
3. Buvé A, Carael M, Hayes RB, Auvert B et al. (2001) Multicentre study on factors determining differences in rate of spread of HIV in sub-Saharan Africa: methods and prevalence of HIV infection. AIDS 15(Suppl 4):S5–S14
4. Auvert B, Buvé A, Lagarde E et al. (2001) Male circumcision and HIV infection in four cities in sub-Saharan Africa. AIDS 15(Suppl 4):S31–S40
5. Auvert B, Taljaard D, Lagarde E et al. (2005) Randomized, controlled intervention trial of male circumcision for reduction of HIV infection risk: the ANRS 1265 trial. PLoS Med 2: e298. doi:10.1371/journal.pmed.0020298
6. Bailey RC, Moses S, Parker CB et al. (2007) Male circumcision HIV prevention young men in Kisumu, Kenya: a randomized controlled trial. Lancet 369:643–656
7. Gray RH, Kigozi G, Serwdda D et al. (2007) Male circumcision for HIV prevention in men in Rakai, Uganda: a randomized trial. Lancet 359:657–666
8. Williams BG, Lloyd-Smith JO, Gouws E, Hankins C, Getz WM et al. (2006) The potential impact of male circumcision on HIV in Sub-Saharan Africa. PLoS Med 3:e262. doi:10.1371/journal.pmed.0030262
9. Nagelkerke NJ, Moses S, de Vlas SJ, Bailey RC (2007) Modelling the public health impact of male circumcision for HIV prevention in high prevalence areas in Africa. BMC Infect Dis 7:16
10. Gray RH, Li X, Kigozi G, Serwadda D, Nalugoda F et al. (2007) The impact of male circumcision on HIV incidence and cost per infection prevented: a stochastic simulation model from Rakai, Uganda. AIDS 21:845–850
11. Hallett TB, Singh K, Smith JA, White RG, Abu-Raddad LJ et al. (2008) Understanding the impact of male circumcision interventions on the spread of HIV in southern Africa. PLoS One 3:e2212. doi:10.1371/journal.pone.0002212
12. White RG, Glynn JR, Orroth KK, Freeman EE, Bakker R et al. (2008) Male circumcision for HIV prevention in sub-Saharan Africa: who, what and when? AIDS 22:1841–1850
13. Alsallaq R, Abu-Raddad L (2008) Male circumcision is a leading actor behind the differential HIV prevalence in sub-Saharan Africa [Poster MOPE0254]. In: Proceedings of the XVII international AIDS conference, Mexico City, Mexico. http://www.aids2008-abstracts.org/. Accessed 13 Aug 2009
14. Kahn JG, Marseille E, Auvert B (2006) Cost effectiveness of male circumcision for HIV prevention in a South African setting. PLoS Med 3:e517. doi:10.1371/journal.pmed.0030517
15. Auvert B, Marseille E, Korenromp EL, Lloyd-Smith J, Sitta R et al. (2008) Estimating the resources needed and savings anticipated from rollout of adult male circumcision in sub-Saharan Africa. PLoS One 3:e2679. doi:10.1371/journal.pone.0002679
16. Bollinger L, Stover J, Musuka G et al. (2009) The cost and impact of male circumcision on HIV/AIDS in Botswana. J Int AIDS Soc 12:7. doi:10.11861/1758-2652-12-7

17. Martin G, Bollinger L, Pandit-Rajani T, Tshehlo R, Nkambula R et al. (2007) Costing male circumcision in Lesotho, Swaziland, and Zambia: implications for the cost-effectiveness of circumcision as an HIV intervention. USAID Health Policy Initiative, Washington, DC. http://www.healthpolicyinitiative.com/Publications/Documents/419_1_Joint_MC_Costing_Technical_Report_FINAL2.pdf. Accessed 13 Aug 2009
18. Binagwaho A, Pegurri E, Muita J, Bertozzi S (2010) Male circumcision at different ages in Rwanda: a cost-effectiveness study. PLoS Med 7(1):e1000211. doi:10.1371/journal.pmed.1000211
19. Njeuhmeli E, Forsythe S, Reed J, Opuni M, Bollinger L et al. (2011) Voluntary medical male circumcision: modeling the impact and cost of expanding male circumcision for HIV prevention in eastern and Southern Africa. PLoS Med 8(11):e1001132. doi:10.1371/journal.pmed.1001132
20. Grant R (2010) Antiretroviral agents used by HIV-uninfected persons for prevention: pre- and post-exposure prophylaxis. Clin Infect Dis 50:96–101
21. Braitstein P, Brinkhof M, Dabis F, Schechter M, Boulle A et al. (2006) Mortality of HIV-1-infected patients in the first year of antiretroviral therapy: comparison between low-income and high-income countries. Lancet 367:817–824
22. Jahn A, Floyd S, Crampin A, Mwaungulu F, Mvula H et al. (2008) Population level effect of HIV on adult mortality and early evidence of reversal after introduction of antiretroviral therapy in Malawi. Lancet 371:1603–1611
23. Guay L, Musoke P, Fleming T, Bagenda D, Allen M et al. (1999) Intrapartum and neonatal single-dose nevirapine compared with zidovudine for prevention of mother-to-child transmission of HIV-1 in Kampala, Uganda: HIVNET 012 randomised trial. Lancet 354:795–802
24. Abdool Karim Q, Abdool Karim SS, Frohlich JA, Grobler AC, Baxter C, Mansoor LE et al. (2010) Effectiveness and safety of tenofovir gel, an antiretroviral microbicide, for the prevention of HIV infection in women. Science 329:1168–1174
25. Grant RM, Lama JR, Anderson PL, McMahan V, Liu AY, Vargas L et al. (2010) Preexposure chemoprophylaxis for HIV prevention in men who have sex with men. N Engl J Med 363:2587–2599
26. Pretorius C, Stover J, Bollinger L, Bacaer N, Williams B (2010) Evaluating the cost-effectiveness of pre-exposure prophylaxis (PrEP) and its impact on HIV-1 transmission in South Africa. PLoS One 5(11):e13646
27. Bacaer N, Pretorius C, Auvert B (2010) An age-structured model for the potential impact of generalized access to antiretrovirals on the South African HIV epidemic. Bull Math Biol 72:2180–2198. doi:10.1007/s11538-010-9535-2
28. Granich R, Gilks C, Dye C, De Cock K, Williams B (2009) Universal voluntary HIV testing with immediate antiretroviral therapy as a strategy for elimination of HIV transmission: a mathematical model. Lancet 373:48–57
29. Donnell D, Baeten J, Kiarie J, Thomas K, Stevens W et al. (2010) Heterosexual HIV-1 transmission after initiation of antiretroviral therapy: a prospective cohort analysis. Lancet 375:2092–2098
30. Cohen MS, Chen YQ, McCauley M, Gamble T, Hosseinipour MC, Kumarasamy N et al. (2011) Prevention of HIV-1 infection with early antiretroviral therapy. N Engl J Med 365:493–505. doi:10.1056/NEJMoa1105243
31. Abbas U, Anderson R, Mellors J (2007) Potential impact of antiretroviral chemoprophylaxis on HIV-1 transmission in resource-limited settings. PLoS One 2:e875
32. Abbas U, Glaubius R, Mubayi A, Hood G, Mellors J (2011) Predicting the impact of ART and PrEP with overlapping regiments on HIV transmission and drug resistance in South Africa. Paper # 98LB, Presented at 18th conference on retroviruses and opportunistic infections, Boston
33. Global report UNAIDS (2010) UNAIDS report on the global AIDS epidemic 2010, Joint United Nations Programme on HIV/AIDS, Geneva

34. International AIDS Vaccine Initiative Database of AIDS vaccine candidates in clinical trials. International AIDS Vaccine Inititative, New York. www.iavi.org. Accessed 28 Mar 2011
35. Future access to HIV vaccines UNAIDS (2001) Report from a WHO-UNAIDS Consultation, Geneva, 2–3 Oct 2000, 15:W27–W44
36. Francis DP, Heyward WL, Popovic V, Orozco-Cronin P, Orelind K, Gee C et al. (2003) Candidate HIV/AIDS vaccines: lessons learned from the World's first phase III efficacy trials. AIDS 17:147–156
37. Rerks-Ngarm S, Pitisuttithum P, Nitayaphan S, Kaewkungwal J, Chiu J, Paris R et al. (2009) Vaccination with ALVAC and AIDSVAX to prevent HIV-1 infection in Thailand. N Engl J Med 361:2209–2220
38. Hankins C, Macklin R, Michael N, Stablein D and the participants at the March meeting in Bangkok Thailand Recommendations for the future utility of the RV144 vaccines to the Thai Ministry of Health. Report on meeting in Bangkok, Thailand 16–18 Mar 2010, Global HIV Vaccine Enterprise, WHO-UNAIDS, Thai Ministry of Public Health, and U.S. Military HIV Research Program, Bangkok. http://www.vaccineenterprise.org/sites/default/files/RV144_March16-18_Meeting_Report_FINAL.pdf. Accessed 14 Feb 2011
39. Bollinger L, Stover J, Forsythe S (2009) Estimating long-term global resource needs for AIDS through 2031. Results for Development Institute, Futures Institute, and the aids2031 Costs and Financing Working Group, Glastonbury, CT. http://www.resultsfordevelopment.org/publications/estimating-long-term-global-resource-needs-aids-through-2031. Accessed 14 Feb 2011
40. Fonseca MGP, Forsythe S, Menezes A, Vuthoori S, Possas C, Veloso V et al. (2010) Modeling HIV vaccines in Brazil: assessing the impact of a future HIV vaccine on reducing new infections, mortality and number of people receiving ARV. PLoS One 5:e11736
41. International AIDS Vaccine Initiative(a) (2009) Uganda: estimating the potential impact of an AIDS vaccine. Policy Brief 23. International AIDS Vaccine Initiative, New York. http://www.iavi.org/publications-resources/Pages/PublicationDetail.aspx?pubID=454d7f8e-f58a-4bf0%979694%9736447fa52211. Accessed 12 Feb 2011
42. International AIDS Vaccine Initiative(a) (2009) Kenya: estimating the potential impact of an AIDS vaccine. Policy Brief 24. International AIDS Vaccine Initiative, New York. http://www.iavi.org. Accessed 12 Feb 2011
43. Stover J, Bollinger L, Hecht R, Williams C, Roca E (2007) The impact of an AIDS vaccine in developing countries: a new model and initial results. Health Aff 26:1147–1158
44. Hecht R, Stover J, Bollinger L, Muhib F, Case K, de Ferranti D (2010) Financing of HIV/AIDS programme scale-up in low-income and middle-income countries, 2009–31. Lancet 376:1254–1260
45. Bollinger L, Stover J (2006) HIV vaccine: a model for examining the effects of an HIV vaccine. Futures Institute, Glastonbury, CT. http://futuresinstitute.org/Download/Spectrum/Manuals/Vaccine%20Manual.pdf. Accessed 12 Feb 2011

Chapter 10
REACH: A Practical HIV Resource Allocation Tool for Decision Makers

Sabina S. Alistar, Margaret L. Brandeau, and Eduard J. Beck

Abstract With more than 34 million people currently living with HIV and 1.8 million dying from HIV annually, there is a great need for continued HIV control efforts. However, funds for HIV prevention and treatment continue to fall short of estimated need and are further jeopardized by the current global economic downturn. Thus, efficient allocation of resources among interventions for preventing and treating HIV is crucial. Decision makers, who face budget constraints and other practical considerations, need tools to help them identify sets of interventions that will yield optimal results for their specific settings in terms of their demographic, epidemic, cultural, and economic contexts and resources available to them. Existing theoretical models are often too complex for practical use by decision makers, whereas the practical tools that have been developed are often too simple. As a result, decisions are often made based on historical patterns, political interests, and decision maker heuristics, and may not make the most effective use of limited HIV control resources. To address this gap between theory and practice, we developed a planning tool for use by regional and country-level decision makers in evaluating potential resource allocations. The Resource Allocation for Control of HIV (REACH) model, implemented in Microsoft Excel, has a user-friendly design and allows users to customize key parameters to their own setting, such as demographics, epidemic characteristics and transmission modes, and economic setting. In addition, the model incorporates epidemic dynamics; accounts for how intervention effectiveness depends on the target population and the level of scale up; captures benefit and cost differentials for combinations of interventions versus single interventions, including both treatment and prevention interventions;

S.S. Alistar (✉) • M.L. Brandeau
Department of Management Science and Engineering, Stanford University, Stanford, CA 94305, USA
e-mail: ssabina@stanford.edu

E.J. Beck
Department of the Deputy Executive Director, Programme Branch, UNAIDS, 20 Avenue Appia, Geneva 27, 1211, Switzerland

G.S. Zaric (ed.), *Operations Research and Health Care Policy*, International Series in Operations Research & Management Science 190, DOI 10.1007/978-1-4614-6507-2_10,

incorporates key constraints on potential funding allocations; identifies optimal or near-optimal solutions based on epidemic characteristics, local realities, and available level of investment; and estimates the impact of HIV interventions on the health care system and resulting resource needs. In this chapter we describe the model and then present example analyses for three different settings, Uganda, Ukraine, and Saint Petersburg, Russia. We conclude with a discussion of insights gained from application of the model thus far, and we describe our ongoing work in further developing and applying the model.

10.1 Introduction

Combating and controlling the HIV epidemic is one of eight United Nations Millennium Development Goals and a top priority for governments around the world [1]. The Joint United Nations Programme on HIV/AIDS (UNAIDS) estimates that approximately 34 million people are currently living with HIV, with 2.6 million new infections and 1.8 million HIV-related deaths occurring in 2009 [2]. This corresponds to 5 new infections and more than 3 deaths every minute.

Considerable progress has been made in increasing the level of financing for HIV programs in the past decade, but available funds still fall short of the estimated need. UNAIDS estimated that $16 billion per year was needed to combat HIV in 2011, increasing to $21.5 billion by 2020 [3]. This is the estimated cost of universal access to treatment for infected individuals as defined at the country level, plus the cost to scale up prevention programs adequately to ensure that vulnerable individuals around the world are reached. However, in 2009, only $14.5 billion, a reduction of 6.8 % from 2008, was available to combat HIV, and the gap is likely to increase due to the global economic downturn [2]. Diminished resources are expected to have a particularly significant impact on low-income countries, many of which have a high burden from HIV and rely heavily on international donations for HIV control efforts.

Efforts to control HIV include treatment, care, and support programs for infected and affected individuals, and prevention programs. Antiretroviral therapy (ART) has been refined in the past decade and has extended life and improved quality of life for millions of persons living with HIV. ART has an additional benefit: by reducing the viral load of treated individuals, ART reduces the likelihood that the virus will be transmitted to an uninfected person during an unprotected contact [4]. Because there is no cure for HIV, prevention remains an essential component of HIV control. Current key prevention interventions include programs to prevent mother-to-child transmission such as ART for infected pregnant women and those who are breastfeeding; programs to reduce risk among injection drug users such as needle and syringe exchange programs, opiate substitution therapy, and other harm reduction programs; programs to reduce sexual risk through partnership reduction and condom promotion programs; male circumcision; and general education programs.

In recent years, treatment efforts have been significantly scaled up. A six-fold increase in financing for HIV programs in low- and middle-income countries from 2001 to 2007 increased by ten-fold the number of people receiving ART [5]. In 2009, 1.2 million people started ART and, at the end of 2009, 5.2 million HIV-infected people in low- and middle-income countries were receiving ART [2]. However, it is estimated that another 10 million people in these countries still need treatment [2].

Prevention efforts have lagged behind treatment in many parts of the world, even though they are considered essential for reversing the epidemic. It is estimated that for every one patient newly enrolled in ART, two people have become infected with HIV [2].

Decision makers, who are constrained by limited budgets and other practical considerations, must determine the most effective allocation of available HIV funds. However, finding the optimal balance between treatment, prevention, and palliative interventions remains a challenge. Decision makers have few tools to help them identify sets of interventions that will yield optimal results for their specific settings in terms of their demographic, epidemic, cultural, and economic contexts and resources available to them [6]. Furthermore, many political and social considerations affect decision making [6–8]. In practice, there is often a mismatch between investment levels and need [9–11]. In some cases, funds have been spent on largely ineffective programs—such as programs promoting abstinence only [9, 12, 13]—and have not been invested in programs known to be effective in controlling HIV such as opiate substitution therapy or needle exchange programs.

10.2 Prior Research and Current Practice

Despite extensive research estimating the cost-effectiveness of various HIV interventions, decision makers still have little guidance as to which interventions or combinations of interventions will yield optimal results under their particular constraints. Current UNAIDS guidelines are limited because even though they provide a framework for decision makers to analyze their epidemic through programs such as "Know Your Epidemic, Know Your Response," they do not specify which sets of interventions are optimal for each setting [14]. Moreover, although a number of researchers have considered the problem of HIV resource allocation, the gap between these academic models and practical tools that planners can use for such decision making is significant [6].

Models used in academic studies of HIV are typically unsuitable as general decision tools for several reasons. Many times, studies compare a few interventions in one specific population in a specific setting, and it is unclear how transferable these results are between different settings, such as between low-income versus middle- or high-income countries, or settings with different transmission patterns and key populations [14–16].

Few studies look at how the effects of combined interventions differ from simply adding the effects of two or more single interventions. Depending on which concurrent interventions are chosen, the overlap can have significant effects, since it may decrease or increase total costs or total benefits, due to synergies or nonadditive results [14]. For example, a study of expanded HIV screening and treatment in the USA found that strategies that increase both screening and treatment avert more HIV infections than the sum of infections prevented from each individual intervention [17]. Conversely, a study on expanding methadone and HIV treatment programs in Ukraine found that the sum of HIV infections prevented from combined strategies that scale up both methadone programs and HIV treatment is less than the sum of infections prevented by the individual interventions [18]. Accounting for the combined effects of different interventions is important for understanding the impact of packages of interventions.

Only a limited number of studies analyze the impact of decreasing or increasing returns to scale for specific interventions, or sets of interventions, and how investment returns depend on the level of funding. Most times, a linear relationship is assumed between funds or efforts invested and outcomes, which may distort results when attempting to scale up programs [15, 16]. Empirical data suggests that program effects do not scale up linearly with expense. In some cases, programs may become proportionally more effective as they are scaled up; this has been observed for expansion of voluntary HIV counseling and testing programs [19]. Other types of programs, such as needle exchanges [20], may become proportionally less effective as they are scaled up.

Finally, academic attempts to create accurate models have yielded complex, inaccessible systems that are not user friendly and cannot be easily adopted by decision makers [6, 21]. In an effort to include a significant number of details and model reality as closely as possible, many academic models become difficult to understand, and require the use of software that may not be readily accessible to decision makers. Although a number of theoretical HIV resource allocation studies have been developed (e.g., [22–25]), they have generally not been designed for use by planners and could be difficult to implement in practice.

Existing practical resource allocation tools for decision makers also have limitations. Aside from decentralized country-level efforts, the most notable comprehensive model currently available to decision makers is the Futures Group International's Goals Model [26]. The model, designed in Microsoft Excel, provides a relatively user-friendly interface, allows users to enter a variety of parameters characterizing their local situation, and allows decision makers to compare the results of various budget allocations between prevention, care and mitigation. However, the Goals Model does not recommend appropriate sets of interventions for specific settings, nor does it optimize results given the available level of resources. Users must try various budget splits and compare results, which can be a time consuming process and may not lead to the best use of scarce resources. Moreover, decreasing or increasing returns to scale of investment are not considered in the model, nor is the impact of combinations of interventions versus single interventions explicitly modeled. Additionally, the model considers only sexual transmission of HIV, and does not account for potential transmission via injection drug use, which is increasingly becoming a key epidemic driver in many parts of the world.

A recent study identified the following features needed in a planning tool to support HIV resource allocation decisions [6]. First, the model must be *usable*: it must have a user-friendly design and structure, be easily accessible, and include calibration and validation tools that allow users to verify model outputs. Second, the model must be *flexible*: it must allow for parameter customization based on local constraints, including key demographics, epidemic characteristics and transmission modes, and economic setting, and must capture uncertainty in input parameters. Third, the model must incorporate certain *key technical features*: it must capture epidemic effects; account for how intervention effectiveness depends on the target population and the level of scale up; capture benefit and cost differentials for combinations of interventions versus single interventions, including both treatment and prevention interventions; incorporate key constraints on potential funding allocations; identify optimal or near-optimal solutions based on epidemic characteristics, local realities, and available level of investment; and estimate the impact of HIV interventions on the health care system and resulting resource needs.

10.3 Reach: An OR-Based Resource Allocation Tool

We have created the REACH model (Resource Allocation for Controlling HIV) for use by regional and country-level decision makers who must allocate resources for HIV prevention and treatment. The model incorporates the key required features identified above. The model is implemented in Microsoft Excel and has a modular structure, with an Inputs sheet, several Model Calculation sheets, and an Outputs sheet. A schematic of the model is shown in Fig. 10.1.

On the Inputs sheet, the user enters input data describing local conditions. This includes demographic, behavioral and epidemic data; data on available programs and key populations (individuals at increased risk of infection); estimated costs to scale up programs; health care costs; and specification of relevant constraints on allocations. Depending on the key populations that the user specifies, different model modules corresponding to those populations are activated. The individual modules are contained in separate sheets in the Excel model, and link back to the Inputs and Outputs sheets. From these modules, the model calculates the impact of alternate allocations of resources using a dynamic epidemic model and determines the allocation of resources that maximizes health outcomes. On the Outputs sheet, the model reports the outcomes of alternative portfolios of programs, including HIV prevalence and incidence, AIDS deaths, HIV infections averted, life years (LYs) gained, quality-adjusted life years (QALYs) gained, and cost per QALY gained, as well as the allocation of resources that maximizes health benefits given the input data. Additionally, the Outputs sheet includes estimates of the health care resources needed to support the allocations (e.g., health workers, facilities, supplies).

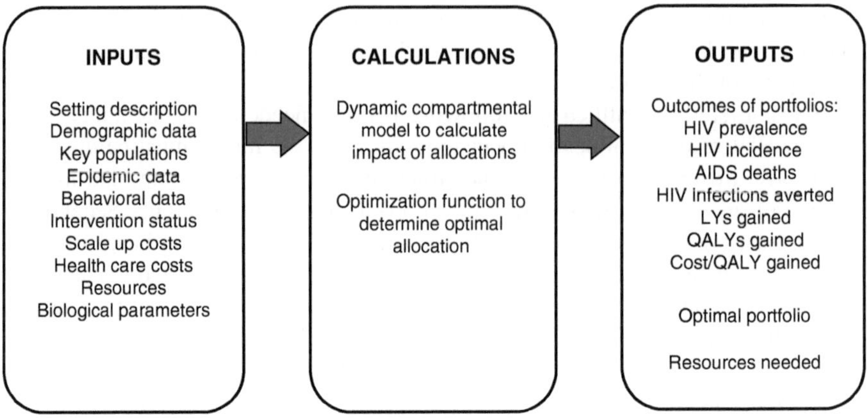

Fig. 10.1 Schematic of the REACH model

10.3.1 Model Inputs

Setting: At the top of the Inputs sheet, the user enters information that broadly describes the setting. The user specifies the country under consideration, key populations involved in HIV transmission, and the HIV prevention and treatment programs considered for scale up.

The user selects from a menu of potential key populations so as to identify the key populations involved with driving the epidemic in the setting under consideration. The model allows for three key populations—injection drug users (IDUs), men who have sex with men (MSM), and sex workers (SWs)—in addition to the general population. In any setting, the model can include any or all of these key populations, as well as the general population.

The user also selects from a menu of potential interventions to indicate which interventions could receive investment. Interventions considered can include any of the following HIV prevention and treatment interventions:

- Antiretroviral therapy (ART)
- Condom promotion targeted to the general population or to selected key populations
- Needle and syringe programs (NSP)
- Opiate substitution therapy (OST)
- Oral pre-exposure prophylaxis (PrEP) for MSM
- Topical vaginal gels with ART for SWs
- Programs for prevention of mother-to-child transmission (PMTCT)

Demographic data: The user enters data on the number of people in the population, including adults 15–49 years old, the male-to-female ratio, and birth and death rates. Such data is typically available from national country statistics. The population segment aged 15–49 years old has until recently been considered to be the main group responsible for sexual and IDU-related transmission but older people may also become infected with HIV, and many people living with HIV are now older than 49. If desired, the user can define a different age range for the population of interest by including, for instance, individuals up to age 64.

Key populations: The user enters the estimated number of individuals in each key population, as well as annual rates of entry into these populations. Estimates for these population group sizes may be available from national statistics. Choosing a zero value—where zero is defined as "below a certain threshold"—for a key population means "turning off" that module in the model.

We chose a modular approach because while there are multiple key populations potentially involved in HIV transmission, some of these groups may be less important to the spread of the epidemic in certain settings. For example, some HIV epidemics in sub-Saharan Africa are mainly driven by heterosexual and mother-to-child transmission, whereas in Asia SWs may play a more important role, and in Eastern Europe injection drug use causes more than half of new infections. However, over time, the involvement of key populations in propagating country epidemics may change. By specifying those key populations most relevant to the particular setting under consideration, the user activates the corresponding epidemic modules that are used in the model calculations. This is described further in the Model Calculations subsection below.

HIVepidemic data: For all population groups, the user must specify estimated HIV prevalence and the distribution of the population across three HIV disease stages: early HIV infection, late HIV infection, and AIDS. The latter values are a reflection of the stage of the epidemic: for example, in a setting with a rapidly growing HIV epidemic, more individuals would be in the early stages of HIV infection than in a setting with a stable epidemic.

Default values are used for other parameters needed to project the epidemic, including the average time in each disease state (i.e., rates of disease progression), infectivity per sexual contact and per needle-sharing contact, and quality-of-life multipliers for each disease state. These values, shown at the bottom of the Inputs sheet with other default values used by the model, were obtained from published literature and are assumed to be common to all settings. If there is reason to believe that some of these parameter values would not apply in a given setting, they can be changed by the user.

Behavioral parameters: Behavioral parameters must be specified for each population group. Specifically, the user inputs details about the sexual and drug use behavior of the general population and key populations. This includes average number of sexual partners, rate of condom usage, average number of customers of an SW, average number of injections per IDU and percentage of injections that are shared, as well as preferential mixing parameters that may be relevant to either sexual or needle-sharing HIV transmission.

Intervention status: For each possible intervention, the user must specify the current percentage of the population reached by the intervention, and estimated current effectiveness. The measure of effectiveness depends on the intervention: for example, a measure of NSP effectiveness is reduction in risky needle-sharing behavior, while a measure of effectiveness for a condom promotion program is level of condom use. Such data can be obtained from reports about national HIV response plans or, if generic, from published literature.

Scale up costs: The user enters information about the "production functions" for the available interventions. These functions describe output achieved as a function of expenditure. For example, for an OST program the production function describes the number of IDUs on OST as a function of total expenditure on the program, while for a condom promotion program the production function describes average rates of condom use in the target population as a function of the total amount spent on the campaign. Information about such functions is needed to account for the fact that the return on investment can change as a function of the level of investment in an intervention.

In practice, the shape of the production functions can be determined from available data on project scale up or can be determined mathematically [27, 28]. While it may not be entirely intuitive for decision makers to consider such production functions, it has been demonstrated that production functions for HIV interventions can be estimated based on a few simple data points elicited directly from the decision maker [27]. On the Inputs sheet the user enters an estimate of potential program effectiveness for one level of program investment. With this point, and with an investment-effectiveness point corresponding to the status quo, the model estimates a production function for each intervention assuming a decreasing exponential shape, which corresponds to diminishing returns to scale. Depending on the cost values input by the user, the level of diminishing returns may range from almost zero to relatively large. For ART scale up, however, the model assumes a linear production function; that is, no diseconomies of scale occur as ART is scaled up.

Most HIV resource allocation decisions are likely to be constrained, so the user must also specify relevant bounds on investment in each potential intervention. The user must indicate which interventions cannot be implemented, perhaps due to political, social or ethical concerns or HIV program capabilities in the region, as well as interventions that require a minimal level of investment due to historical reasons or strategic priorities, and interventions for which there is a maximum allowed level of investment. To specify these constraints, the user inputs any relevant budget limits for each type of intervention. A budget of zero for an intervention means that it will not be considered by the decision maker. In addition, the user must specify the total budget available for allocation.

Health care costs: In addition to the data on the cost of interventions embedded in the production functions, the user must specify the fixed costs of the interventions, the per person cost of each intervention, and the cost of HIV-related and non-HIV-related health care. The model discounts all costs and benefits to the present, based on the user-specified discount rate.

Resources: A key consideration in implementing HIV prevention and treatment programs is the healthcare infrastructure that is required to support such implementation. Thus, the model estimates the levels and types of health resources needed to support various portfolios of investment. To support such estimation, the user enters data on health resources needed to support each intervention. This includes the estimated number of health workers needed for each intervention increment, facility requirements, and supplies—such as condoms, needles, and ART doses—needed for those interventions.

Biological parameters: In addition to the parameters described above, the model calculations rely on biological parameters whose default values are obtained from published literature. For transparency, the values of these parameters are shown on the Inputs sheet. These parameters include disease progression rates, expressed in terms of the time spent in each HIV disease stage; the transmission probability per sexual partnership and per risky shared injection; the reduction in these transmission probabilities due to ART, to oral PrEP, and to topical vaginal gels; and quality-of-life multipliers for each population group and disease stage. The disease stages include: uninfected; early HIV infection with a CD4 count above 350 cells/mm^3; late HIV infection with a CD4 count between 200 and 350 cells/mm^3, and AIDS, with a CD4 count below 200 cells/mm^3. Although not recommended, it is possible for the user to change the values of the biological parameters if there is compelling evidence that a different value is appropriate in the user's particular setting.

10.3.2 Model Calculations

Dynamic compartmental model to evaluate impact of allocations: The effects of investments in prevention and treatment are modeled using dynamic compartmental models that estimate costs and health outcomes over a 20-year time horizon. Model calculations are contained in four sheets in the model, one for each of the key population modules—IDUs, MSM, and SWs—and one sheet that integrates the results from the modules with the general population.

In the dynamic compartmental models, individuals move through a series of mutually exclusive, collectively exhaustive states, each of which contains individuals with homogeneous characteristics. The model dynamics are reflected by a system of nonlinear differential equations. Similar to other work in the literature [18, 29, 30], the differential equations are discretized into time increments of 1/10 year, which is reasonable in terms of disease dynamics and length of stay in the various disease compartments. The population compartments in each module distinguish individuals by HIV disease stage and treatment status (not on ART, on ART) and by whether they are reached by relevant key interventions. For simplicity and tractability, each module includes a relatively small number of compartments.

To illustrate how the model works, we describe the IDU module in detail. The IDU module distinguishes individuals by HIV disease stage (uninfected, early HIV, late HIV, and AIDS), HIV treatment status (not on ART, on ART), and OST status

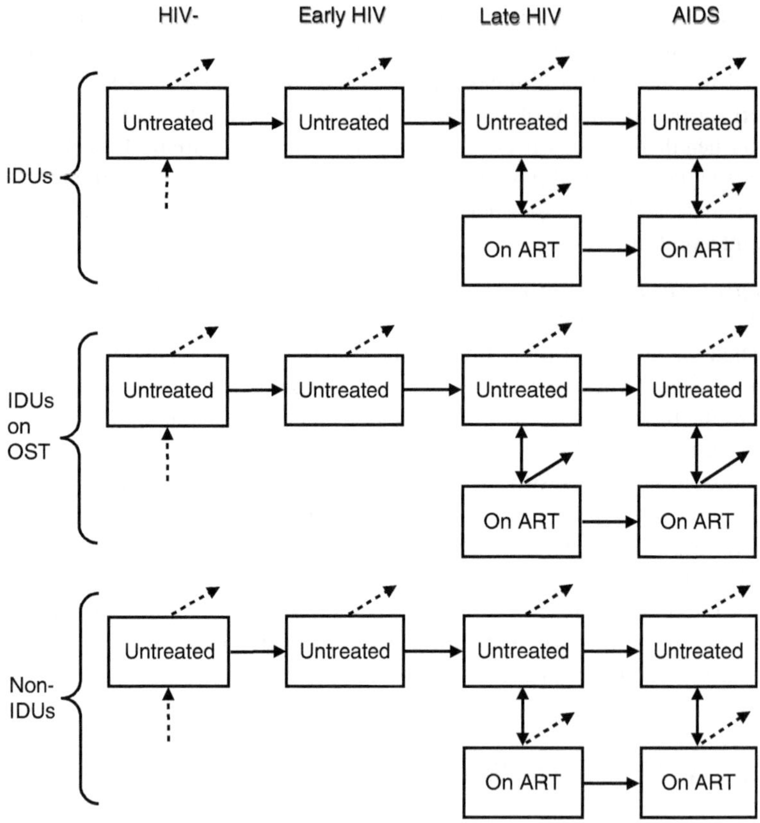

Fig. 10.2 Simplified schematic of the dynamic compartmental model used in the REACH model's IDU module. Although not shown in the figure, individuals may transition between the three population groups (IDUs, IDUs on opiate substitution therapy (OST), and non-IDUs)

(on OST, not on OST), leading to a total of 18 compartments (Fig. 10.2). The general population module, which is contained in a different calculations sheet, has six compartments which are similar to the non-IDU compartments in the bottom third of Fig. 10.2.

Individuals transition between disease stages with parameters based on models of HIV natural history available from the literature [31]. We assume that the intrinsic biology of the disease—for example, rates of disease progression in untreated individuals—does not change across settings and that treatment delays progression to the more advanced stages of the disease. Individuals become eligible for treatment according to current international guidelines when their CD4 count falls below 350 cells/mm^3.

In the IDU module, HIV transmission occurs via sexual contacts and injection equipment sharing. The risk of acquiring HIV from injections for an uninfected IDU is calculated based on annual number of injections, percentage of injections involving shared equipment, the likelihood of sharing with an HIV-infected individual, and the probability of HIV transmission per contact. Contact infectivity varies depending on the disease and ART status of the infected individual since both affect viral load. For sexual transmission, we consider the average number of annual new partnerships, which is typically higher for IDUs than non-IDUs. We assume random mixing in sexual partnerships, but that IDUs preferentially pair with other IDUs. The model estimates the annual risk of sexual HIV transmission to an uninfected individual per partnership based on disease stage of partner, condom usage rate, and condom effectiveness.

Within each compartment, homogeneous mixing is assumed for simplicity, thus neglecting the effects of geographical distancing and distribution of infected individuals. A network-based model or microsimulation model could incorporate such effects, but would be difficult for decision makers to use in practice because it would require significant amounts of data that are often unavailable or unknown, such as a detailed description of sexual mixing patterns. At a high level of aggregation such as national or regional levels, the assumption of homogeneous mixing is likely to hold. For modeling sexual transmission, individuals in the general population are assumed to mix homogeneously across disease states. The same assumption is made for IDUs for sexual and needle-sharing transmission. However, we account for preferential sexual mixing of IDUs with other IDUs, which is a behavior often observed in practice, by imposing a percentage on the number of sexual contacts shared with non-IDUs, scaled by the number of individuals in each group.

Investment in interventions affects the dynamics of the disease. For example, in the IDU module, OST, ART, NSPs, and condom promotion programs all affect the disease dynamics—and thus estimated epidemic outcomes and costs. Changes in the level of available OST and ART slots change the flow of individuals into those compartments. NSPs modify the chance of HIV transmission via injection equipment sharing, and OST programs modify the average number of injections and shared injections. Other risk reduction programs can reduce the chance of transmission via injection equipment sharing or via sexual contact, depending on the types of behaviors targeted by the intervention.

As described above, the model includes a module for each key population—IDUs, MSM, and SWs—and one for the general population. The latter module, if used alone with no key populations, reflects a generalized epidemic. If the user has activated any of the key population modules, then the outcomes from the modules are aggregated using the assumption that the key populations each interact with the general population but not with each other.

Optimization function to determine optimal allocation: In addition to evaluating the health outcomes and costs associated with specific choices of investments, the model determines the optimal allocation of resources. Here, the optimal allocation is defined as the allocation that maximizes health outcomes, subject to the investment constraints entered by the user in terms of minimum and maximum allowable level of investment in each intervention, as well as the total available budget. The optimization function can consider HIV infections averted, LYs gained, or QALYs gained as the health objective, and time horizons of 5, 10, or 20 years. We consider these different objectives because they can lead to different optimal portfolios: if the goal is to maximize HIV infections averted, then prevention interventions may be favored, whereas if the goal is to maximize LYs or QALYs gained, then treatment will become relatively more favorable.

The model determines the optimal resource allocation numerically by iterating over all allowable allocations of funds in increments of 1, 5, or 10 % of the total budget, depending on the potential scale of the program: for programs that are small compared to the total budget, the model uses a finer search grid. The model's exhaustive search algorithm executes quickly on a personal computer with average capability and identifies the optimal allocation with a reasonable degree of precision. Although calculations can take up to a day if all population modules are activated and many potential interventions are considered, most analyses can be produced within 15 minutes.

10.3.3 Model Outputs

Outcomes of portfolios: For any budget allocation, the Outputs sheet reports both HIV infections averted, to capture benefits of prevention interventions, and LYs and QALYs gained, to capture benefits of treatment, over 5-, 10-, and 20-year time horizons. Costs associated with each allocation are also reported. The Outputs sheet also reports HIV prevalence and incidence over each time horizon, AIDS deaths over each time horizon, cost per HIV infection averted, cost per LY gained, and cost per QALY gained. Additionally, the Outputs sheet reports estimated levels of health-care resources needed for each allocation, including estimates of quantities of personnel, facilities, and supplies needed to support each allocation.

These outcomes are shown for eight different budget allocations, each in a separate column in the Outputs sheet: the status quo, the allocation proposed by the user, and the optimal allocations calculated by the model that maximize infections averted and LYs gained for a 5-, 10-, and 20-year time horizon. Summary measures for each of these allocations—such as the split of funds between interventions, and HIV infections averted and LYs gained compared to the status quo—are presented at the top of the Outputs sheet, and then details of outcomes for each allocation are provided below in the sheet.

The Outputs sheet shows the allocations that maximize LYs gained over the three considered time horizons, as this is a common health measure considered by policy makers. If desired, the Outputs sheet can instead show the allocations that maximize QALYs gained.

10.4 Example Analyses

Thus far, we have implemented the model using data for four countries—Uganda, Ukraine, Brazil, and Thailand—and for one city—Saint Petersburg, Russia. We created these examples as part of the process of model development. These implementations allowed us to test the model in different settings, and to iteratively improve the model based on feedback from planners at UNAIDS and the World Health Organization (WHO). Additionally, the implementations helped generate insights into the HIV resource allocation problems faced by planners.

These examples are representative of the diverse settings to which the model can be applied, as they involve two different types of epidemics, generalized and concentrated, and two different levels of decision making, country-level and city-level. Data for the analyses were obtained from a variety of sources, including reports published by governmental and non-governmental sources (e.g., WHO and UNAIDS) and from published journal articles. The analyses are preliminary and are based on simplified estimates of costs. Nonetheless, they provide useful insights into the tradeoffs a decision maker may face in the process of allocating resources for HIV control. Here we describe results for Uganda, Ukraine, and Saint Petersburg.

10.4.1 Uganda

Uganda has a generalized heterosexual epidemic according to UNAIDS [32], with more than 1 % of the population living with HIV. In the last two decades, a national HIV prevention campaign with a strong condom promotion element has helped to slow the epidemic in Uganda. In 2001, an estimated 7.0 % of the adult population was HIV infected, whereas in 2009, prevalence had decreased to 6.5 % of the adult population [2]. Nonetheless, an estimated 1.2 million people are living with HIV in Uganda, with some 120,000 new HIV infections occurring in 2009 [2], so prevention efforts are still needed. Additional treatment efforts are also needed: in 2008, only about 50 % of the 280,000 HIV-infected people needing treatment received ART [33].

We populated the REACH model with Uganda data for 2008. We considered a single prevention program that emphasizes condom promotion, as well as ART. In 2008, Uganda spent $71.4 M on treatment and $13 M on prevention, with all the funds being used for the general population. We considered a 20 % budget increase, leading to a total new budget of $101.3 M. We chose this amount because it represents a reasonable level of scale up that might be achievable in practice. Input data used in the analysis are shown in Table 10.1.

Key model outputs are summarized in Table 10.2. As described earlier, the model produces a variety of output measures, including HIV prevalence and incidence and number of AIDS deaths over 5, 10, and 20 years; here we report HIV infections averted and LYs gained over 5 years for each allocation. Because

Table 10.1 Input data for Uganda example[a]

Parameter	Value
Demographic	
Adults 15–49	14,000,000
Birth rate	0.04
Death rate	0.01
Epidemic	
Prevalence—general population	6.8%
Disease stage—early	70%
Disease stage—late	15%
Disease stage—AIDS	15%
Behavioral	
Number of sexual partners per year	1.5
Condom usage rate per contact	15%
Initial intervention status	
ART access	50%
Sexual transmission reduction due to ART	90%
Condom effectiveness	90%
Costs	
Annual non-HIV health cost	$75
Annual HIV health cost	$300
Annual ART cost	$500
Condom cost, per condom	$0.1
Constraints	
Prevention budget above	$13.0 M
Treatment budget above	$72.0 M
Production functions	
ART	Linear
Condom promotion	Decreasing exponential

[a]Parameter values were obtained from online demographic publications and UNAIDS databases and reports

Table 10.2 Results for Uganda example

Outcome	Status quo	20% budget increase	Optimal: maximize infections averted (5 years)	Optimal: maximize LYs gained (5 years)
Resources allocated				
Treatment	$71.4 M	$85.7 M	$71.4 M	$88.3 M
Prevention	$13.0 M	$15.6 M	$29.9 M	$13.0 M
Infections averted (5 years)	–	12,200	34,500	7,600
LYs gained (5 years)	–	63,700	30,900	68,500

Uganda has a generalized epidemic, only the general population module of the model is activated for this example.

We first used the portfolio analysis capability of the model to evaluate the results of a strategy that allocates the additional $16.9 M from the 20 % budget increase according to the historical spending patterns, thus maintaining the same proportional allocation of funds between treatment, at $85.7 M representing 85 % of the total budget, and prevention at $15.6 M representing 15 % of the budget. This strategy would avert 12,200 HIV infections and gain 63,700 LYs over a 5-year time horizon compared to the status quo.

We then used the optimization capability of the model to identify the best use of the additional resources. If the goal is to maximize infections averted over 5 years, it is optimal to invest all of the incremental $16.9 M in prevention, leading to a $29.9 M total prevention budget. This resource allocation would avert 34,500 infections, but would gain fewer LYs than the proportional allocation (30,900 vs. 63,700). If instead the goal is to maximize LYs gained over 5 years, then the optimal strategy is to invest all of the incremental $16.9 M in treatment, leading to a total treatment budget of $88.3 M. This allocation would increase the number of LYs gained from 63,700 in the proportional allocation to 68,500, but would avert much fewer infections (7,600 vs. 12,200). For both of these objectives, simply scaling up the current resource allocation is not the optimal choice.

10.4.2 Ukraine

With 1.6 % of its adult population infected with HIV—approximately 350,000 people—Ukraine has the highest HIV prevalence in Europe [2], and also has one of the fastest growing HIV epidemics in the world [34]. As in many countries in Eastern Europe, the HIV epidemic in Ukraine was initially fueled by increasing levels of injection drug use after the collapse of the former Soviet Union.

Currently some 40 % of the estimated 390,000 IDUs in Ukraine are HIV infected [34, 35]. Although the HIV epidemic in Ukraine was originally confined to IDUs, now nearly 40 % of new cases are thought to accrue from heterosexual transmission—though often from contact with an infected IDU [34]—thus creating concern that the epidemic is spreading to the non-IDU population.

Ukraine has a concentrated epidemic [32]: HIV prevalence is greater than 5 % in at least one key population, but HIV is not as well established in the general population. We implemented the model with 2008 data for Ukraine, summarized in Table 10.3. For this example, the IDU module is activated in the model, reflecting the importance of this population in the HIV epidemic in Ukraine.

We considered one incremental HIV prevention program—OST for injection drug users—and we considered ART. We assumed that ART could be targeted to the general population, to IDUs, and to IDUs on OST. In the status quo, $3.4 M was spent on ART, with 77.5 % of that money used to treat eligible individuals in the general population, and $0.2 M spent on OST. We considered a 200 % budget

Table 10.3 Input data for Ukraine example[a]

Parameter	Value
Demographic	
Adults 15–49	24,200,000
Birth rate	0.03
Death rate	0.005
Key population	
Injection drug users (IDUs)	390,000
Epidemic	
Prevalence—general population	0.98%
Prevalence—IDUs	41.2%
Disease stage—early	75%
Disease stage—late	15%
Disease stage—AIDS	10%
Behavioral	
Number of sexual partners—general population	1.3
Number of sexual partners—IDUs	4.3
Condom usage rate—general population	45%
Condom usage rate—IDUs	40%
Shared injections by IDUs	25%
Preference for IDU sex partner for IDUs	40%
Initial intervention status	
ART access—general population	10%
ART access—IDUs	2%
Sexual transmission reduction due to ART	90%
Needle-sharing transmission reduction due to ART	50%
Condom effectiveness	90%
OST slots	500
Sharing reduction if in OST	85%
Costs	
Annual non-HIV health cost	$310
Annual HIV health cost	$1,200
Annual ART cost	$450
Annual OST cost	$370
Constraints	
IDU prevention budget above	$0.2 M
Treatment budget above	$3.4 M
Production functions	
ART	Linear
Opiate substitution therapy (OST)	Decreasing exponential

[a]Parameter values were obtained from a recent study of HIV in Ukraine [18]

increase, which could occur if the country received a Global Fund grant, leading to a total available budget of $10.8 M. Selected outputs from the analyses are shown in Table 10.4. For this example, we show HIV infections averted over 5 years and over 20 years for each budget allocation.

Table 10.4 Results for Ukraine example

Outcome	Status quo	200% budget increase	Optimal: maximize infections averted (5 years)	Optimal: maximize infections averted (20 years)
Resources allocated				
Treatment	$3.4 M	$10.2 M	$10.6 M	$10.6 M
% to non-IDUs	77.5%	77.5%	0%	20%
% to IDUs	22.2%	22.2%	100%	80%
% to IDUs in OST	0.3%	0.3%	0%	0%
Prevention—OST	$0.2 M	$0.6 M	$0.2 M	$0.2 M
Infections averted (5 years)	–	7,400	13,900	13,200
Infections averted (20 years)	–	26,000	36,100	37,600

Using the portfolio analysis capability of the model, we first evaluated the results obtained if the current budget allocation is maintained and the additional funds are invested according to the historical spending pattern. In this case, $10.2 M is spent on treatment and $0.6 M is spent on OST. This strategy averts 7,400 infections over 5 years, and 26,000 infections over 20 years.

We then used the optimization capability of the model to determine the allocation that maximizes the number of HIV infections averted over 5 years. In the optimal allocation $10.6 M is spent on ART, and investment in OST stays at $0.2 M. All of the $10.6 M treatment funds are used for treating IDUs. This allocation averts 13,900 infections over 5 years.

We also used the model's optimization function to determine the resource allocation that would maximize infections averted over 20 years. In this case, $0.2 M is still spent on OST and $10.6 M is spent on ART. However, now 20 % of the treatment funds are allocated to treating the general population, compared to the allocation that maximizes infections averted over 5 years, which allocates no funds to the general population. This allocation would avert 37,600 infections over 20 years, but only 13,200 infections over 5 years.

The shift in the optimal allocation as the time horizon changes occurs because while the epidemic is still concentrated in IDUs in the short run, in the long run more and more heterosexual transmission is projected to occur. To maximize the number of HIV infections averted, the interventions prioritize treating the population group that is causing most of the infections.

10.4.3 Saint Petersburg, Russia

To illustrate the flexibility of the model, we applied it to decision making on a different scale, the city-level epidemic in Saint Petersburg, Russia. The second largest city in Russia, with a population of 4.6 million, Saint Petersburg has been disproportionately affected by HIV and currently is the regional jurisdiction in the Russian Federation with the largest number of registered people living with HIV [36]. Saint Petersburg's HIV epidemic is currently concentrated in IDUs, and is in many ways similar to the epidemic in Ukraine. Russia has a rapidly growing HIV epidemic, with more than 90 % of cases identified after 2000 [37]. Saint Petersburg closely mirrored these trends. Prior to 2000, fewer than 5 % of IDUs in the city were infected with HIV; by 2003 prevalence among IDUs had reached 30 % [38]. In 2008, HIV prevalence among the 83,000 IDUs in Saint Petersburg was estimated to be 50 % [39].

We populated the model with epidemic information from Saint Petersburg for the year 2008. Input data are shown in Table 10.5. In the status quo, $0.29 M is used for ART, with 32 % going to the general population and 68 % to IDUs, and no OST programs in place. We considered ART expansion, as well as implementation of OST for IDUs, and a significantly larger total budget of $1.45 M. Given the very small scale of the original budget, this situation could occur in practice if the city decided to increase its funding of HIV interventions. Results are shown in Table 10.6, where we show infections averted over 5 years.

If allocation of the new budget follows historical spending patterns, and thus all of the incremental funds are used for treatment, then 1,550 infections would be averted. To maximize infections averted over 5 years, the optimal allocation is to invest $1.15 M in OST, and in a different split of the $0.3 M in treatment funds.

In this case, 20 % of ART funds would be allocated to eligible IDUs not in OST, 80 % to IDUs in OST, and 0 % to the general population. This allocation averts 2,170 infections, 620 more than the proportional allocation. Notably, this is a different budget split than that recommended for Ukraine, which allocates all of the ART funds to IDUs not on OST.

10.5 Model Refinement and Implementation

In the above sections we have described the initial version of the REACH model. We are currently in the process of refining the model to add more functionality. A key area where we are adding model functionality is sensitivity analysis so that users can evaluate the robustness of the chosen resource allocations. We plan to modify the model to allow the user to specify bounds on input parameters, and we will add a function to the model to perform one-way sensitivity analyses on key parameters. This will include pre-designed charts that present the sensitivity analysis results in a way that is accessible to end users. The choice of parameters on which to perform sensitivity analysis will be determined based on typical findings from the literature, as well as feedback from decision makers on the parameters they consider the most important.

Another important area of model development focuses on data collection. The current version of the model contains baseline values for some model parameters, but further work in this area is needed. For example, behavioral data are generally

Table 10.5 Input data for Saint Petersburg, Russia example[a]

Parameter	Value
Demographic	
Adults 15–49	2,500,000
Birth rate	0.03
Death rate	0.005
Key populations	
Injection drug users (IDUs)	83,000
Epidemic	
Prevalence—general population	0.34%
Prevalence—IDUs	50.0%
Disease stage—early	75%
Disease stage—late	15%
Disease stage—AIDS	10%
Behavioral	
Number of sexual partners—general population	1.3
Number of sexual partners—IDUs	4.3
Condom usage rate—general population	45%
Condom usage rate—IDUs	40%
Shared injections by IDUs	40%
Preference for IDU sex partner for IDUs	35%
Initial intervention status	
ART access—general population	10%
ART access—IDUs	1%
Sexual transmission reduction due to ART	90%
Needle-sharing transmission reduction due to ART	50%
Condom effectiveness	90%
OST slots	0
Sharing reduction if in OST	85%
Costs	
Annual non-HIV health cost	$310
Annual HIV health cost	$1,200
OST	$450
Annual OST cost	$370
Constraints	
Treatment budget above	$0.18 M
Production functions	
ART	Linear
Opiate substitution therapy (OST)	Decreasing exponential

[a]Parameter values were drawn from a previous study of HIV control in Saint Petersburg [29] and from a recent study of HIV control in Ukraine [18]

scarce, and requesting the decision maker to provide accurate numbers for parameters such as "average number of yearly injections per IDU" or "average number of customers per SW" may not be an easy task. However, many countries, following WHO guidelines, are implementing increasingly comprehensive surveys of risk behaviors, both in the general population and in key populations. We plan to

Table 10.6 Results for Saint Petersburg, Russia example

Outcome	Status quo	400% budget increase	Optimal for Saint Petersburg: maximize infections averted 5 years)	Optimal for Ukraine: maximize infections averted 5 years)
Resources allocated				
Treatment	$0.29 M	$1.45 M	$0.30 M	
% to non-IDUs	32%	32%	0%	0%
% to IDUs	68%	68%	20%	100%
% to IDUs in OST	0%	0%	80%	0%
Prevention—OST	$0 M	$0 M	$1.15 M	
Infections averted (5 years)	–	1,550	2,170	

analyze typical data collected in these surveys with the aim of generating baseline values for various parameters in the model.

Information about intervention production functions is key to estimating the effects of HIV interventions. Only a few studies have been conducted to estimate such functions [16, 20, 23, 24, 28], so further work is needed to obtain data characterizing such functions. The shapes for the production functions may vary by intervention considered and the setting where the intervention is implemented. For example, some production functions may be linear, whereas others may show increasing or decreasing returns to scale. Some information is available from the literature, and we plan to evaluate available field data on HIV investments and their effects. Transforming such data into accurate estimates of production functions is likely to require extensive research and analysis. However, it is likely that general trends will be noted, which initially can be used to create reasonably approximate production functions. The sensitivity analysis capability will allow the user to consider different values and forms of the production functions.

Finally, we plan to beta-test the REACH model with decision makers and to refine the model based on feedback received. Our ultimate goal is to make the model publicly available on the UNAIDS website so that it is readily accessible to HIV policy makers around the world.

10.6 Conclusions and Policy Implications

Implementation of the model to date has generated important insights that can inform HIV investment planning. While the model must be populated with data for a given country to determine the best allocation of resources in that setting, the insights gained from our implementation of the model thus far can help guide the planning process in other settings.

First, *simply scaling up the current portfolio of investments may not be the best choice*. Use of the model can identify mismatches between current investments and key populations that are significant drivers of the epidemic in a particular setting. Moreover, the model can help planners determine the appropriate balance of investment in prevention versus treatment for a given setting. Our implementation of the model thus far has demonstrated that reallocation of resources away from the current portfolio can often achieve significantly improved health benefits.

Second, *different objectives lead to different allocations*. Focusing on HIV infections averted as the health goal may lead to a different allocation than when the goal is to maximize LYs or QALYs gained. When the goal is to maximize HIV infections averted, relatively more investment in prevention programs may be called for, whereas when the goal is to maximize LYs or QALYs gained, more investment in treatment may be appropriate. Both objectives are important. Use of the model allows planners to understand the tradeoffs between the two objectives, thus enabling them to make an informed choice regarding which prevention and treatment programs to invest in.

Third, *the length of the planning horizon matters*. For shorter time horizons, it may be best to focus relatively more resources on key populations, whereas for longer time horizons if those key populations are helping to spread HIV to the general population then it may be best to focus relatively more resources on the general population. The model allows planners to consider different planning horizons. In some cases, the allocation may change significantly when the planning horizon changes, whereas in other cases it may not.

Fourth, *choosing between allocations involves making tradeoffs between different objectives*. Because the model makes explicit the health benefits that could be achieved by any portfolio of investments that planners may wish to consider, as well as the health benefits that could be achieved by an optimal portfolio, the tradeoffs between potential sets of investments can be readily identified. This can provide planners and stakeholders with a much-needed degree of transparency in the decision making process: for any allocation they will have an estimate of the health benefits that it will generate.

Finally, *the optimal allocation of resources is likely to change with the setting*, even for relatively similar epidemics. Thus, an allocation that is best for one setting may not be the best allocation for another setting. Decision makers can customize the model with local information to determine the allocation that is best for their setting.

In an era when HIV budgets are shrinking, but the HIV epidemic continues to grow, it essential to make the best use of limited HIV funds. A recent report from UNAIDS suggests that countries must begin to allocate funds more strategically if they are to achieve control of the HIV epidemic [40]. Rather than simply scaling up each intervention that is already in place, it is suggested that a more effective approach may be to invest in a selected set of interventions with proven effectiveness, particularly interventions that are synergistic with one another.

The REACH model is ideally suited to address this and other questions about the appropriate allocation of HIV resources. Because it can evaluate the effects of different levels and combinations of HIV prevention and treatment programs, using data specific to any particular setting, the REACH model can help planners understand the consequences of different allocations of resources. Moreover, because it determines the optimal allocation for a given setting and given objective, the REACH model can help planners understand how the maximum health benefit can be achieved in their setting. Such input can improve decision making about allocation of HIV control resources, thus saving lives and improving health for populations around the world.

Acknowledgments This work was supported by grant number R01-DA15612 from the National Institute on Drug Abuse. Sabina Alistar was also supported by a Stanford Graduate Fellowship.

References

1. United Nations (UN) (2009) The millennium development goals report 2009. United Nations, New York, NY
2. Joint United Nations Programme on HIV/AIDS (UNAIDS) (2010) UNAIDS Report on the Global AIDS Epidemic 2010. UNAIDS, Geneva, Switzerland
3. Avila C (2011) Personal communication: updated estimates for HIV resource needs. UNAIDS, Geneva, Switzerland
4. Cohen MS et al. (2011) Prevention of HIV-1 infection with early antiretroviral therapy. New Engl J Med 365(6):493–505
5. Joint United Nations Programme on HIV/AIDS (UNAIDS) (2008) Report on the global AIDS epidemic. UNAIDS, Geneva, Switzerland
6. Alistar SS, Brandeau ML (2012) Decision making for HIV prevention and treatment scale up: bridging the gap between theory and practice. Med Decis Making 32(1):105–117 Epub ahead of print
7. Lasry AC, Malvankar MW, Zaric GS (2011) Allocating funds for HIV/AIDS: the case of kwaDukuza, South Africa. Health Policy Plann 26(1):33–42
8. Ruiz M et al. (eds) (2001) No time to lose: getting more from HIV prevention. National Academy Press, Washington, DC
9. Coates TJ, Richter L, Caceres C (2008) Behavioural strategies to reduce HIV transmission: how to make them work better. Lancet 372(9639):669–684
10. Piot P et al. (2008) Coming to terms with complexity: a call to action for HIV prevention. Lancet 372(9641):845–859
11. Potts M et al. (2008) Reassessing HIV prevention. Science 320(5877):749–750
12. Collins C, Coates TJ, Curran J (2008) Moving beyond the alphabet soup of HIV prevention. AIDS 22(Suppl 2):S5–S8
13. Horton R, Das P (2008) Putting prevention at the forefront of HIV/AIDS. Lancet 372(9637):421–422
14. Bautista-Arredondo S et al. (2008) Optimizing resource allocation for HIV/AIDS prevention programmes: an analytical framework. AIDS 22(Suppl 1):S67–S74
15. Brandeau ML, Zaric GS (2009) Optimal investment in HIV prevention programs: more is not always better. Health Care Manage Sci 12(1):27–37
16. Kumaranayake L (2008) The economics of scaling up: cost estimation for HIV/AIDS interventions. AIDS 22:S23–S33
17. Long EF, Brandeau ML, Owens DK (2010) The cost effectiveness and population outcomes of expanded HIV screening in the United States. Ann Intern Med 153(12):778–789

18. Alistar SS, Owens DK, Brandeau ML (2011) Effectiveness and cost effectiveness of expanding harm reduction and antiretroviral therapy in a mixed HIV epidemic: a modeling analysis for Ukraine. PLoS Med 8(3):e1000423
19. Dandona L et al. (2008) Changing cost of HIV interventions in the context of scaling-up in India. AIDS 22(Suppl 1):S43–S49
20. Kaplan EH (1995) Economic analysis of needle exchange. AIDS 9(10):1113–1119
21. Lasry A, Richter A, Lutscher F (2009) Recommendations for increasing the use of HIV/AIDS resource allocation models. BMC Public Health 9 (Suppl 1):S8
22. Brandeau ML, Zaric GS, Richter A (2003) Resource allocation for control of infectious diseases in multiple independent populations: beyond cost-effectiveness analysis. J Health Econ 22(4):575–598
23. Richter A, Brandeau ML, Owens DK (1999) An analysis of optimal resource allocation for prevention of infection with human immunodeficiency virus (HIV) in injection drug users and non-users. Med Decis Making 19(2):167–179
24. Zaric GS, Brandeau ML (2001) Optimal investment in a portfolio of HIV prevention programs. Med Decis Making 21(5):391–408
25. Zaric GS, Brandeau ML (2001) Resource allocation for epidemic control over short time horizons. Math Biosci 171(1):33–58
26. Futures Group (2011) Goals model. http://futuresgroup.com/resources/software/goals-model/. Accessed 8 Feb 2011
27. Brandeau ML, Zaric GS, De Angelis V (2005) Improved allocation of HIV prevention resources: using information about prevention program production functions. Health Care Manage Sci 8(1):19–28
28. Marseille E et al. (2007) HIV prevention costs and program scale: data from the PANCEA project in five low and middle-income countries. BMC Health Serv Res 7(1):108
29. Long EF et al. (2006) Slowing the HIV epidemic in St. Petersburg, Russia: effectiveness and cost-effectiveness of expanded antiretroviral therapy. AIDS 20(17):2207–2215
30. Zaric GS, Brandeau ML, Barnett PG (2000) Methadone maintenance treatment and HIV prevention: a cost effectiveness analysis. Manage Sci 46(8):1013–1031
31. Sanders GD et al. (2005) Cost effectiveness of screening for HIV in the era of highly active antiretroviral therapy. New Engl J Med 352(6):32–47
32. Joint United Nations Programme on HIV/AIDS (UNAIDS) (2007) Practical guidelines for intensifying HIV prevention—towards universal access. UNAIDS, Geneva, Switzerland
33. Government of Uganda (2010) United Nations General Assembly Special Session (UNGASS) country progress report, Uganda: January 2008—December 2009. Uganda Ministry of Health, Kampala, Uganda
34. Joint United Nations Programme on HIV/AIDS (UNAIDS) (2008) Ukraine—national report on monitoring progress towards the UNGASS declaration of commitment on HIV/AIDS. UNAIDS, Geneva, Switzerland
35. Kruglov YV et al. (2008) The most severe HIV epidemic in Europe: Ukraine's national HIV prevalence estimates for 2007. Sex Transm Infect 84(Suppl 1):i37–i41
36. Heimer R, White E (2010) Estimation of the number of injection drug users in St. Petersburg, Russia. Drug Alcohol Depend 109(1–3):79–83
37. World Health Organization (WHO) (2005) Summary country profile for HIV/AIDS treatment scale-up: Russian Federation, June 2005. World Health Organization, Geneva, Switzerland
38. Niccolai LM et al. (2009) The potential for bridging of HIV transmission in the Russian Federation: sex risk behaviors and HIV prevalence among drug users (DUs) and their non-DU sex partners. J Urban Health 85(Suppl 1):131–143
39. Niccolai LM et al. (2010) High HIV prevalence, suboptimal HIV testing, and low knowledge of HIV-positive serostatus among injection drug users in St. Petersburg, Russia. AIDS Behav 14(4):932–941
40. Joint United Nations Programme on HIV/AIDS (UNAIDS) (2011) Toward an improved framework for HIV investments, draft report. UNAIDS, Geneva, Switzerland

Chapter 11
Review of Operations Research Tools and Techniques Used for Influenza Pandemic Planning

David W. Hutton

Abstract Many public health officials are concerned about a possible influenza pandemic. The three pandemics in the twentieth century killed between 50 and 100 million people and the 2009 H1N1 "Swine Flu" exposed vulnerabilities that we still have to influenza epidemics. Operations research tools and techniques can analyze public health interventions to mitigate the impact of pandemic influenza. In this chapter we review an array of examples of how operations research tools can be used to improve pandemic influenza prevention and response. From this, we derive insights into the appropriateness of certain techniques for answering specific questions and we propose preliminary policy recommendations. We then discuss opportunities for future research.

11.1 Introduction

Pandemic influenza is a major global public health concern. If future pandemics are anything like past ones they could kill hundreds of millions of people. The analytical tools of operations research are capable of helping policymakers allocate resources to combat pandemic influenza in a more efficient and effective manner.

This chapter gives a brief overview of pandemic influenza and possible public health responses. We then review current examples of how operations research techniques have been applied to the problem of pandemic influenza. Finally, we see some broad policy conclusions from this research, see how different operations research tools might be best applied to certain problems, and identify areas for future application of operations research to pandemic influenza.

D.W. Hutton (✉)
Department of Health Management and Policy, University of Michigan, Ann Arbor, MI 48109, USA
e-mail: dwhutton@umich.edu

G.S. Zaric (ed.), *Operations Research and Health Care Policy*,
International Series in Operations Research & Management Science 190,
DOI 10.1007/978-1-4614-6507-2_11,

11.2 Background

Influenza pandemics have caused major loss of life over the past several hundred years. The 1918 influenza pandemic killed between 50 and 100 million people. Although records are less reliable before that, experts have identified over 10 probable pandemics in the last 300 years (Table 11.1). The pandemics seem to occur in 10–50-year intervals [1]. The 2009 H1N1 "Swine Flu" pandemic exposed vulnerabilities that we still have to emerging influenza pandemics. The CDC estimates that about 61 million people were infected and over 12,000 died from H1N1 in the USA alone [2].

Influenza experts are also concerned about the pandemic potential of other strains of influenza. Most popular is H5N1, or "bird flu." This virus has a reported case fatality proportion of over 50 % and has similar protein changes to the 1918 virus [10, 11]. The World Bank estimates that if H5N1 were to become a pandemic, it could kill over 70 million people and cause economic losses of $2 trillion [12].

The public health community does have some weapons at its disposal to combat an influenza pandemic. Broadly, the responses can be characterized as using pharmaceutical or non-pharmaceutical interventions. Pharmaceutical interventions include using vaccines or antivirals to prevent or treat influenza infection. Non-pharmaceutical interventions include encouraging hygiene, distributing facemasks, implementing social distancing (which may include ending mass gatherings or individual quarantine), to building public health response capacity. Each intervention has different strengths and weaknesses.

Table 11.1 Historical influenza pandemics

Years	Affected geographies	Loss of life	References
1729–1730	Russia, Europe	Unknown	[1, 3–5]
1732–1733	Russia, Europe, North America, South America	Unknown	[3–5]
1761–1762	America, Europe	Unknown	[5]
1781–1782	China, North America, South America, and Europe	Unknown	[1, 3–5]
1788–1790	Worldwide	Unknown	[5]
1830–1831	Asia, Europe North America	Unknown	[1, 3–5]
1833–1834	Asia, Europe North America	Unknown	[3–5]
1847–1848	Europe, North America	Unknown	[4, 5]
1889–1890	Worldwide	250,000 in Europe One million worldwide	[3–5]
1918–1919	Worldwide	½ million in the USA 50 million worldwide	[1, 3–6]
1957–1958	Worldwide	80,000 in the USA One million worldwide	[1, 5]
1968	Worldwide	34,000 in USA	[5, 7]
1977–1978	Asia, Europe, North America	No excess mortality	[5, 8]
2009–2010	Worldwide	10–50,000 in USA	[7, 9]

The pharmaceutical interventions can be costly and we are unsure how effective they will be. Vaccines usually require 6 months to develop [13], so well-matched vaccines are unlikely to be available at the start of a global influenza pandemic. However, researchers have studied a prime-boost vaccination technique against influenza H5N1. The technique uses a vaccine designed against an older strain of the H5N1 virus, but scientists have found that the vaccine can provide antibody response to H5N1 viruses circulating years later [14]. Thus, it may be possible to vaccinate individuals with a well-designed pre-pandemic vaccine to provide some partial protection. Antiviral medications such as Tamiflu (oseltamivir) and Relenza (zanamivir) have shown to be effective in both treating and prevention of seasonal and pandemic influenza infection [15]. However, the effectiveness is limited and some influenza virus strains are resistant to these antivirals. Because global production capacities of these pharmaceuticals are limited, pre-pandemic vaccines or antivirals would have to be stockpiled in advance of a pandemic [16, 17].

Non-pharmaceutical responses to pandemic influenza may also be difficult and costly to implement. Public health social distancing controls like cancelling mass gatherings, closing schools, and quarantine may be unpopular and costly. For example, school closures may cause parents to take time off work to care for their children. Stockpiling protective facewear would involve spending money in advance of a pandemic, and experts are still uncertain how effective facewear would be [18]. Some activities like encouraging better hygenie through handwashing and cough etiquette may be inexpensive, but not very effective in actual practice [19]. To prepare for a pandemic, we could make investments in improving infrastructure like hospitals and distribution centers. In the event of a pandemic, hospitals are likely to need surge capacity [20], and if masks or pharmaceuticals are stockpiled, they would need to be distributed quickly and efficiently to the public.

Decision makers planning for pandemic influenza face much complexity and uncertainty. Populations have complex patterns of social connections and a variety of interventions can be used in different population segments. We also do not know when a pandemic will occur, how many people it will infect, how deadly it will be, and how effective each of these interventions will be against it. Powerful tools are necessary to help tame these challenges.

11.3 Applications of Operations Research

Operations research tools may be helpful to deal with the variety and complexity of interventions for pandemic influenza response. These tools can also help decision makers cope with planning for this uncertain event. To address a variety of strategies and tactics for pandemic influenza, researchers have used simulation modeling, optimization, decision analysis, game theory, and supply chain analysis to provide insights into pandemic influenza response. Here we review examples of how these tools have been used, grouped by the operations research methods used.

11.3.1 Simulation Modeling

Simulation modeling is often used in operations research as a way of representing the real world and being able to estimate the impact of interventions and to improve their performance. Sometimes, these models are grouped into categories such as system dynamics, discrete event simulation, and agent-based simulations [21–23]. System dynamics models usually contain fewer details of individuals and take a high-level approach to how a system evolves. Discrete event simulations have more details and track objects as they move through a network. This is can be useful to model the flow of items through a process and how they back up in queues or bottlenecks. Agent-based models track how individual active agents move and evolve over time and interact with their environment. The behavior of the individual agents creates the overall system behavior. Each of these models may have different strengths and weaknesses for different purposes: system dynamics models typically are less complex and can capture macro-level insights quickly, whereas discrete event and agent-based simulations are more detailed and thus more time-consuming and costly but can provide more nuanced, detailed insights.

11.3.2 Simulation Modeling: System Dynamics

A system dynamics approach can capture how the changing level of infection and immunity in the population affects the spread of future infections in the population. These nonlinear infection dynamics can make analyzing influenza policies more complex. System dynamics modeling techniques have been applied to pandemic influenza preparedness problems as varied as social distancing, vaccination, antiviral treatment, and portfolio analysis of interventions.

Some influenza models assume all members of the population are similar and that a policy response will apply to all individuals equally. But Larson [24] created a simple dynamic compartmental model of influenza to examine the impact of targeting responses. Despite its simplicity, his model did have subpopulations with different frequencies of contact with each other. Because contact could lead to influenza transmission, he felt including heterogeneity in contact rates for different subpopulations was important to include. He showed with this simple model that the people with high rates of contact drove the initial growth of the epidemic and that targeting social distancing (reducing contact rates) to the correct subpopulations with high contact rates can prevent the epidemic with limited disruption to the remaining population.

Nigmatulina and Larson [25] built off that simple dynamic compartmental model of influenza to include multiple interconnected communities. Each community has citizens that interact with each other and is connected to other communities by a few travelers each day. This might represent towns near each other. They used this model to compare the impact of vaccination and travel restrictions. They find that in small communities, vaccinating highly active people early is very important. In their small model of 300,000 people, delaying vaccine administration by 10 days is similar to not vaccinating at all. They also find that travel restrictions will not be effective: only a complete 100 % travel restriction would stop or significantly slow transmission between communities. This analysis [25] and the one by Larson alone [24] use very simple models that can be implemented in spreadsheets, but they provide very powerful policy insights.

Simple system dynamics models have also been used to evaluate antiviral use. Lee and Chen created a model to represent the dynamics of influenza infection in the general population of Singapore and the population of health care workers in Singapore [26]. They then examined a policy of using antivirals for treatment and prevention of pandemic influenza in health care workers to see how it would affect the overall dynamics of infection. This is a complex analysis since health care workers are exposed to influenza from the outside influenza epidemic, but also from mini-epidemics within the hospital setting. They found that treatment of health care workers was effective at reducing the epidemic in health care workers, but that proactively giving antivirals to healthcare workers for prevention was about four times more effective at preventing absenteeism. These results support plans to stockpile antivirals for this critical population.

Khazeni et al. [27] used a system dynamics model to examine the magnitude of the impact of speeding up vaccine delivery for the 2009 H1N1 influenza pandemic. Delivering the 2009 H1N1 vaccine quickly was a challenge because of long production times and little advanced notice of the new virus strain [28, 29]. But, due to the dynamic nature of influenza infection, preventing one infection early may prevent multiple infections later. They modeled the spread of pandemic influenza infections and associated costs in a city the size of New York City. They found that releasing an H1N1 vaccine 1 month earlier (October vs. November) could have had substantial benefits in reducing infections in addition to saving more than 100 million dollars in costs for a city the size of New York. Additionally, because this was a relatively simple model, the authors were able to analyze the emerging H1N1 situation relatively quickly and share their results with vaccine policy makers before the epidemic was over.

Khazeni et al. used a similar model to examine strategies of stockpiling antivirals and pre-pandemic vaccines to use for prevention for a future H5N1 pandemic [30]. Antivirals and pre-pandemic vaccines may not be completely effective for future pandemics and they also can be quite costly. They found that stockpiling pre-pandemic vaccines may be both effective and cost-effective (when compared to other health care interventions). They also used their model to determine that the cost-effectiveness strongly depends on the likelihood of a pandemic and the uncertain effectiveness of the pre-pandemic vaccines.

Other authors have also used dynamic models to examine the cost-effectiveness of stockpiling antivirals. Lugnér and Postma [31] created a dynamic model of pandemic influenza transmission of the population of the Netherlands. They also explicitly modeled the effect of the likelihood of a pandemic occurring in order to incorporate the risk that stockpiling antivirals may have a cost with no corresponding health benefit. They found stockpiling of antivirals for treatment to be cost-effective if the risk of an influenza pandemic was 37 % over 30 years (a value they felt was reasonable). However, they also found that if distribution of antivirals during the pandemic was ineffective (<60 % of the population took antivirals), then stockpiling might not be cost-effective. This analysis shows both health and economic impacts and explicitly models how the likelihood of a pandemic would affect pre-pandemic planning decisions.

Medlock and Galvani [32] use an age-structured system dynamics model of influenza spread combined with optimization algorithms to determine how best to allocate vaccines to different age groups in the population. Older age groups might experience more morbidity and mortality from flu infections, but young children might be more likely to acquire and spread the disease. In this research, they find that, due to transmission patterns, schoolchildren should receive the bulk of vaccines. The authors conclude that if only 40 million doses of vaccine were available, their optimal vaccine allocation would cut infections in half when compared to current US Centers for Disease Control and Prevention and Advisory Committee on Immunization Practices guidelines.

System dynamics models have also been used for higher-level policy planning. Brandeau et al. [33] used dynamic models of infectious disease transmission to examine allocating health policy resources in a portfolio of interventions. Infectious disease programs may have subpopulations that are affected differently by different populations. These programs may also have increasing or decreasing marginal costs as they are expanded across a population. They built a model with nonlinear epidemic dynamics for multiple risk groups and nonlinear cost functions. The authors do not reach specific conclusions for pandemic influenza, but they determine that static cost-effectiveness ratios used commonly in health economics may not be sufficient for determining optimal resource allocation for a portfolio of infectious disease programs. These authors determine that dynamic resource allocation models may be needed for infectious disease epidemics which have nonlinear costs for different interventions.

The previous papers have all used system dynamics models to provide insights that may be valuable when making policy decisions for pandemic influenza. The system dynamics models are relatively simple and can quickly provide broad insights into how policies might affect the overall spread of disease in a large population. Different models might be appropriate for answering more detailed questions about tactics for responding to a pandemic.

11.3.3 Simulation Modeling: Discrete Event Simulation

Discrete event simulation of queuing systems can be valuable for modeling the tactics necessary for mass vaccination or distribution of antivirals or masks. This type of analysis may uncover bottlenecks in the logistical process of mass distribution. Unfortunately, very few models like this have been developed specifically to analyze pandemic influenza response. However, models have been created for other health emergencies, and these models may also have insights applicable to pandemic influenza.

In their 2006 articles, Aaby et al. [34, 35] share how they created discrete event simulation queueing network models to assist with clinic planning for distribution of vaccines in the event of an influenza pandemic. They created easy-to-use tools using common spreadsheet software to be used for clinic planning. They validated the model using data from a planning exercise where over 150 workers provided mock vaccinations to 530 people over a two-and-a-half hour period. These types of models can help local responders make capacity plans and avoid bottlenecks in distribution.

Other researchers have used a combination of discrete event simulation and optimization to improve performance of mass dispensing sites for a bioterrorist attack. Lee et al. [36] created a system that combines simulation and optimization technology to quickly find the best facility layout and staffing. In their paper, they describe scenarios for anthrax and smallpox public health disasters. When the staff allocation assignments suggested by the optimization algorithm were used in a real-world exercise, the site using the optimized clinic design and staffing outperformed all others by processing 50 % more customers. Although the examples are related to bioterrorism, the technology is general enough to apply to other infectious disease outbreaks like pandemic influenza.

In Zaric et al. [37] and Bravata et al. [38] the authors used dynamic models of disease progression and queuing systems along with economic analysis to examine the best ways to distribute medications in the case of a public health emergency. They modeled demand for treatment and disease progression along with queues as part of the medication distribution system. Although these analyses focused on another health emergency, anthrax, their conclusions should also be important for pandemic influenza planning. They both found that the ability to dispense medications quickly was more important than the local stockpile of supplies. This highlights the value of systems analysis that can look for bottlenecks across the entire response system. And, combining the queuing system model with a model of disease progression allowed them to estimate the overall impact on morbidity and mortality, not just people served.

No matter what disease they are used to evaluate, discrete event queuing models can be useful for studying distribution systems and help planners avoid costly delays in providing mass public health responses to pandemic influenza.

11.3.4 Simulation Modeling: Agent-Based Simulation

With increased computing power, agent-based simulation models have become popular for simulation of pandemic influenza. These models track individual people (agents) as they interact with other agents, such as classmates, coworkers, family members, and others in the community. They require very detailed information about the demographics and travel patterns of people in a community. By conducting thousands of stochastic simulations, researchers can estimate distributions of possible outcomes. Because of the detail in the models, researchers can provide more detailed outcome projections and distributions on those outcomes. But, with the increased data and computational burdens, these types of simulations can be very costly and time-consuming.

A research group led by Neil Ferguson has produced several agent-based simulation models of influenza to analyze portfolios of pharmaceutical and non-pharmaceutical interventions. In one project, Ferguson et al. [39] built a model of Thailand to examine how a local novel influenza epidemic emerging from Southeast Asia (a likely place for an H5N1 outbreak to begin) could be contained before becoming a global pandemic. They gathered very detailed information on geographic population distribution, children in schools, and travel distances to work to create the model. They examined an intervention where antivirals would be quickly given in a targeted fashion to close contacts of those infected in order to prevent further infection and spread of the disease. The stochastic agent-based model could capture important uncertainty about how the virus might spread or die out due to randomness. They determined that it may be possible to eliminate the pandemic at the source with a stockpile of three million courses of antiviral drugs and sufficiently effective policies for distributing antiviral medications and quarantining those near the outbreak. The second paper [40] used a similar model, but examined a portfolio of interventions to be used in the USA in the event the influenza epidemic is not stopped at the source. They found that border control is unlikely to be effective. Using antivirals for prevention and closing schools in response could reduce clinical attack rates by 40–50 %. Stockpiled vaccines could significantly reduce attack rates even if they were not very effective. These models have shown that a range of interventions used together may be effective in preventing a pandemic at the outset or at significantly reducing the burden of disease in the event of a global pandemic.

Halloran and Longini have also been collaborating and creating agent-based stochastic simulation models to evaluate pandemic influenza policies. In 2004, they used a model of a community of 2,000 people that closely matches the US population to examine the comparative effectiveness of pharmaceutical strategies [41]. They anticipated that vaccines may not be available during a pandemic, so they also examine antiviral use for prevention targeted at those who have any contact with someone who has become infected (coworkers, classmates, etc.). They found vaccination to be very effective at containing the epidemic, but that targeted antiviral use for prevention could be almost as effective. In 2005, they produced several studies. In one project, they evaluated prevention of an influenza pandemic at the source [42]. In this study, they modeled a population of 500,000 matching the geographic distribution and demographics of rural Southeast Asia. They found that using a stockpile of one million courses of antivirals in a targeted fashion for prevention could be effective at preventing a relatively slow-spreading disease. If the disease were more infectious, combination strategies adding pre-vaccination and quarantine could be successful. In research with Patel [43], they used optimization with genetic algorithms in addition to their agent-based stochastic simulation model to determine the best groups to allocate vaccines to. If vaccine supply were limited, they found that optimal vaccination strategies focus on children and could be 84 % more effective than random vaccination.

Longini collaborated with Germann and others to use an agent-based stochastic simulation model to analyze a portfolio of interventions [44]. They created an agent-based model of the entire US population. In this analysis, they found results similar to those of Ferguson et al. [40], namely, that travel restrictions are unlikely to have much of an impact, but that targeted antiviral prophylaxis and vaccination (even if poorly matched) could be successful in reducing the number individuals infected by about 75 % or more.

In 2009, Longini and Halloran collaborated with Sander and others to use the model to evaluate the economic impact of these pandemic influenza mitigation strategies [45]. They evaluated the costs and health benefits of 17 strategies representing a combination of pharmaceutical and non-pharmaceutical interventions using their agent-based model of the USA. They found that targeted antiviral use for prevention could reduce cases by over 50 % in addition to saving $60 per capita. They found vaccination with a pre-pandemic vaccine could have similar effectiveness and cost savings. School closure could be as effective as antivirals or vaccines, but at a cost of over $2,500 per capita.

Other researchers have used agent-based stochastic simulation models of influenza spread. Researchers at the National Infrastructure Simulation and Analysis Center have created a model of a community of 10,000 with detailed social network information with families, schools, and workplaces that closely matches US contact networks. Using this model, they have examined portfolios of strategies to contain pandemic influenza in a community [46]. They found that high-compliance social distancing can be valuable. Uniform national policies are also important because, if infection control is not uniform, smaller communities can be infected again from the outside. They also conclude that pre-pandemic vaccines are important for critical infrastructures to continue to operate during the pandemic. In another study, Perlroth et al. [47]use the same agent-based stochastic simulation model to again evaluate a portfolio of interventions, but this time also evaluating the cost-effectiveness of these interventions. They find that a combination strategy of social distancing, school closure, and providing antivirals would be a cost-effective strategy to deal with an influenza pandemic with moderate infectivity and mortality similar to 1918. For pandemics with lower infectivity and mortality, the authors do not find school closure to be a cost-effective addition to social distancing and antiviral use. This additional study is valuable because it quantifies the economic costs and benefits of school closure and identifies it might be worthwhile.

All of these studies show that simulation modeling can be a valuable tool to make sense of the complexity and uncertainty of pandemic influenza response. These models can all provide different but valuable insights to policymakers and response planners.

11.3.5 Optimization

Optimization is a core operations research methodology. It has been used in combination with stochastic modeling and discrete event simulation to assist with pandemic influenza planning. But, it can also be used alone. Kornish and Keeney [48] use dynamic programming to analyze the annual vaccine strain selection decision process. Each winter, the Vaccines and Related Biologic Products Advisory Committee meets several times and examines information on all the currently circulating flu strains in order to recommend which three flu virus strains should be in the fall vaccine. At each meeting, the committee must balance their desire to make an early recommendation and allow more time to produce the vaccine with their desire to wait and gather more information about which flu virus strains will be likely to be active in the fall. Using an analytical model, the authors found insights about when to commit to selecting a strain for the vaccine and when to defer and gather more information prior to making the decision. They used an example of the seasonal influenza vaccine, but the insights could also hold true for similar decisions that need to be made quickly for pandemic influenza.

Wu et al. [49] formulate the vaccine selection problem as a stochastic dynamic program to take into account the history of vaccines from prior years that might affect efficacy of future vaccines. They find that their optimization algorithm creates modest gains versus the current policy of selecting vaccine strains which ignores the history of vaccines. So, they suggest keeping the current policy. This study reminds us that optimization algorithms do not always produce profound benefits. This study encourages keeping a simple policy, which incidentally may be easier to implement in the chaos of a pandemic situation.

11.3.6 Decision Analysis

Decision analysis tools have been important operations research methods to deal with variability and uncertainty. These methods are also popular with health economists to analyze pandemic influenza health policies because of their ease-of-use and ability to represent the uncertainty so prevalent with pandemic influenza.

Several studies have evaluated interventions to stockpile antivirals using decision analytic tools. Balicer et al. [50] used a simple decision analytic model to evaluate the impact of stockpiling of antivirals. They also used results from Longini et al.'s agent-based model [41] to determine the population effect of antiviral use. They are among the few researchers to explicitly model the likelihood of an influenza pandemic occurring. They find that stockpiling antivirals for treatment is expected to be cost-saving and using antivirals for prevention is likely to be cost-saving, but depends on assumptions about the probability of pandemic occurring (if a pandemic is unlikely to occur, stockpiling would be less valuable).

The same authors who created a system dynamics model of influenza infection in Singapore [26] worked with a larger group of collaborators in 2006 and created a decision model of influenza infection in the general population of Singapore [51]. Their model represents prevention, infection, treatment, and hospitalization for pandemic influenza. They found that treatment with antivirals was an economically valuable strategy and that using antivirals for prevention may be valuable for high-risk populations or if pandemic influenza causes high fatalities.

Siddiqui and Edmunds [52] created a decision analytic model to examine the cost-effectiveness of using antiviral drugs for treatment during an influenza pandemic. They also examined testing patients prior to treatment since other diseases can have influenza-like symptoms. They found that treatment was cost-effective, but that pretreatment testing would not have significant benefits and would add large costs. Using Monte Carlo simulation to examine uncertainty in their model inputs, they confirmed their earlier conclusions.

These decision analytic tools can be relatively simple to use, but yet can provide powerful insights even in the face of the uncertainties related to pandemic influenza.

11.3.7 Game Theory and Supply Chain Analysis

Supply chain management analysis techniques can also be effectively used for improving pandemic influenza response. Several researchers have used game theory models to analyze vaccine production and stockpiling decisions. Researchers have also used tools like facility location analysis to assist with pandemic influenza response logistics.

The influenza supply chain is quite complex: the production process has uncertain yields, the vaccine is only used for a single season, and the value of vaccination is nonlinear in the number of people vaccinated due to the effects of preventing secondary infections. Chick et al. [53] developed a dynamic system model in conjunction with a game theory model to analyze contracts between health care service systems and vaccine manufacturers. They find that wholesale and payback contracts cannot coordinate the supply chain, but that cost-sharing contracts can properly incentivize both parties and improve the supply of vaccines. Although this analysis was created to analyze seasonal influenza vaccination, the authors acknowledge that it could be applicable to pandemic influenza contracts as well.

International sharing of antiviral stockpiles also introduce complications because countries want to save antivirals for their own populations, but if they share them at the beginning of a global pandemic, they could possibly prevent a nascent epidemic from reaching their countries in the first place. Sun et al. have used a game theory model to examine how countries might share or hoard their antiviral stockpiles at the beginning of a pandemic in order to prevent a global outbreak [54]. The game theory model is used along with a stochastic dynamic model of influenza spread to determine influenza infection outcomes to different nations. The addition of a stochastic dynamic model helps capture the uncertainty about initial infections, spread of the disease, and drug efficacy. The game theoretic model accounts for the selfish desires of the countries to protect their own populations. The authors show that for small between-country transmission rates, there are incentives for countries to donate stockpiles to the initially infected country. However, they also find that a central planner could create a Pareto improvement.

Another group of researchers has looked at hospital decisions to stockpile supplies for a pandemic when they have mutual-aid agreements with other hospitals. Because hospitals know they can get supplies from other hospitals, they may have lower incentives to stockpile. Game theory may provide insights into these relationships and help predict individual hospital stockpiling decisions. In two papers [55, 56], the authors determine that a Nash equilibrium exists for hospitals to stockpile supplies and they develop an algorithm to find a numerical solution. These analyses show stable equilibriums exist, but they are not necessarily optimal for the entire hospital system. These types of analyses could be modified to find and create new mutual aid contract forms that achieve better solutions for the entire system.

Other supply chain management analysis techniques have also been used to analyze pandemic influenza response. Another group has used facility location algorithms and geographical disease models to determine how to best distribute food in the case of an influenza pandemic [57]. During an influenza pandemic, the normal food distribution infrastructure may be disabled, and certain populations may be especially at risk. If new a food distribution system is set up, the points of distribution should be closest to the most vulnerable and they also should be opened to meet the needs during the local epidemic peaks. In their analysis, the authors' objective was to meet food demand while minimizing costs of serving the population. They identified heuristics that could be used to find solutions for the facility location problem. This analysis reinforces that there are a multitude of logistical challenges to pandemic influenza response and that a variety of operations research models that can be used to tackle these varied problems.

Overall, we have seen examples of a wide variety of operations research techniques applied to pandemic influenza response. Researchers have successfully used tools as varied as agent-based models and facility location algorithms to tackle complex questions as varied as preventing the global outbreak of pandemic in the first place to delivering food to local vulnerable populations.

11.3.8 Best Practices Using Operations Research Tools for Pandemic Influenza Response

Examining this research also shows common themes about how these operations research tools can best be used to tackle specific problems. We can get a sense for which tools are best used when and for what problems.

Different types of simulation models have strengths and weaknesses. System dynamics and agent-based models are typically used to simulate an influenza pandemic and the impact of interventions on the epidemic. System dynamics models are usually simpler deterministic models. That means they can provide insights much more quickly and with less effort. They can gather broad insights on a wide variety of scenarios. And they may be used to quickly analyze a nascent pandemic in real-time while testing different scenarios when disease parameters are highly uncertain. But, because they are deterministic, they do not capture the randomness inherent in disease spread. If they are too simple, they may not contain enough details to accurately represent the epidemic.

Agent-based models can provide more realism and capture more details of a growing epidemic. Agent-based models can capture the geographic spread of disease. And, they are stochastic, so they show uncertainty about how the epidemic may progress. Randomness in the disease spread can be critical at the very beginning or end of the pandemic. Thus, agent-based models are very useful for analyzing an emerging epidemic and can effectively quantify the likelihood of the epidemic dying out with certain interventions [39, 42]. However, the downside to all this detail is increased cost and time to conduct the analyses. If analyses are conducted for planning before a pandemic, time may not be an issue. But, deterministic system dynamics models may be easier to use on-the-fly during an actual pandemic. The quote attributed to Albert Einstein applies: "Make everything as simple as possible, but not simpler." Simulation models of the pandemic should be simple enough to quickly provide the needed insights, but still contain the needed complexity to provide a sufficient level of realism for the given problem.

While system dynamics and agent-based models may be useful for broad policy analysis for a large population, discrete event simulation modeling, on the other hand, is a natural fit for designing the details of mass distribution centers and hospital system responses. Queuing models can help identify bottlenecks and staffing requirements. Easy-to-use tools that have already been built and validated could prove to be very valuable in the event of an influenza pandemic.

Optimization also can be used for both policy questions like who should receive vaccines [43] and tactical questions about how to lay out mass distribution facilities [36]. When tied to simulation models, optimization can be even more valuable. But, with that additional complexity, different techniques and new heuristics may be necessary to provide solutions quickly [36, 57]. Providing solutions quickly may enable these tools to be used real-time during a pandemic.

While examining this research, we can also see that there is still substantial uncertainty about what might happen in the event of an influenza pandemic. Researchers are not sure when an influenza pandemic will happen, how many people the disease will infect, how deadly it will be, and how effective interventions will be at reducing infections or mortality. Fortunately, operations research models allow analysts to examine what might happen under different scenarios or to explicitly model their knowledge of uncertainty surrounding possible outcomes. Most of these analyses modeled different scenarios representing different levels of infectivity and mortality [24, 26, 27, 30–32, 38–47, 50–52, 54, 57, 58]. A few explicitly modeled the risk of a pandemic actually occurring [31, 50, 52]. Many also looked at uncertainty surrounding the effectiveness of interventions [24–27, 30, 32, 38–42, 44–47, 50–52, 58]. Any operations research-based analysis of pandemic influenza should account for uncertainty inherent in the analysis. Decision analysis techniques such as decision trees and value of information calculations can also be used to quantify uncertainty and give further clarity to decisions and to the value of future research.

Other operations research techniques can be successfully applied to operational challenges like managing supply chains. Because game theoretical methods deal with interacting parties, they can be used for supply chain contracts as applied to pandemic influenza [53], but they can also be used to gain insights for large-scale national stockpiling and response decisions [54]. Other operations research methods can be helpful, like facility location algorithms, but they can be much more valuable when combined with other tools like geographical disease models.

Often, the right choice of operations research method is a combination of methods. Many of the research studies reviewed here use a combination of operations research methods together [34–36, 43, 53, 54, 57]. Optimization can be used with systems or agent-based models. But, novel combinations of methods like using dynamic models with game theory can also be highly illuminating [54].

Each type of operations research technique may be useful for analyzing particular problems at particular times. However, there is another dimension of analysis to consider: should the analysis be focused on theoretical insights or practical insights? Both theoretical and practical analyses can provide value for pandemic influenza response. Theoretical models can provide broad insights for policymakers to guide pre-pandemic planning sessions, but these lessons can also be used as heuristics for quick decision-making during a pandemic event. And, theoretical insights like those from Brandeau et al. about which models to use for analysis can have applicability to pandemic influenza even though they were created for a general infectious disease [33]. Practical models can provide specific answers to specific policy decisions, but if practical models are too specific, they may not be generalizable to other situations. However, if the practical models are flexible and can be quickly updated, they may be very valuable in the event of a pandemic. For example, the practical models created by Aaby and Lee can be quickly adjusted to reflect the characteristics of an emerging pandemic [34–36].

11.4 Opportunities for Future Research

We have seen some examples of how operations research can be applied to pandemic influenza, but there are additional opportunities to improve pandemic influenza response with more analysis and improving the quality of analysis.

Broadly, main opportunities lie in the areas of handling uncertainty, improving the tactics of response, and improving analyses with better communication and coordination with public health decision makers.

There are many unknowns about a future influenza pandemic. We do not know when it will occur, how bad it will be, and how effective possible interventions will be. Operations research tools of risk and decision analysis can be used to help quantify those uncertainties. Decision analysis tools have been used, but they also can be used to calculate the value of gathering future information. And, forecasting tools can be used to predict and make the most of what little information we have about influenza pandemics. For example, operations research-based forecasting tools could be created to help predict the likelihood of an influenza pandemic emerging based on characteristics or attributes of current circulating viruses. A variety of operations research tools should be used to help deal with the uncertainty surrounding an influenza pandemic.

There also are many opportunities to help improve the tactics of responding to an influenza pandemic. One specific important area is to optimize the process of delivering antivirals for prevention to the proper people. Both Ferguson and Longini felt that this strategy, which they call "Targeted Antiviral Prophylaxis," could be highly effective at minimizing infections or even stopping a global pandemic at the source [39–42, 44, 45]. However, these strategies rely on almost all clinical influenza cases being detected. And, even more challenging, they rely on 80–90 % of all people in contact with infected persons to be given several weeks supply of antivirals within a few days of detection of the index case. This could be a very difficult logistical endeavor especially under the chaos and pressure of an influenza pandemic environment, and even more complex in a rural international location at the start of an epidemic. Optimized detection and information systems would likely be necessary. And, mass distribution systems would have to be very efficient to deliver just-in-time medications to very specific groups of people by people with specific healthcare training (e.g., pharmacists or nurses). These are systems that may be more complex and difficult-to-implement than current state-of-the art supply chains like those of Wal-Mart, Amazon, or Netflix. Operations researchers have much to contribute in this area.

Finally, to improve the relevance of operations research-based analyses to policymakers, operations researchers should get more guidance from policymakers about what their objectives are. Current research addresses objective such as minimization of infections, maximizing quality-adjusted life years, minimizing deaths. However, policymakers may have other goals such as minimizing costs. Or, they may be risk averse when facing uncertain events that can have such drastic outcomes. In order to conduct a valuable optimization analysis, the researchers must try to maximize what the policymakers or responders are trying to achieve. Operations researchers can also help guide policymakers through the discussions of trade-offs for competing objectives, such as minimizing costs and minimizing health impacts.

11.5 Conclusions and Policy Implications

These studies have come to several common conclusions about when and where specific policies might be valuable and which operations research tools might be best used to analyze pandemic influenza policies and response. The following are some of these common policy conclusions from the literature, grouped by response category:

Pharmaceuticals:

- Stockpiling antivirals for treatment is valuable [26, 31, 47, 50–52, 54]
- Stockpiling antivirals for prevention may be valuable [26, 39–42, 44, 45, 47]
- Vaccines would be valuable if available, even with modest efficacy [25, 27, 30, 40–46]
- Vaccines should first be allocated to school-age children to minimize the impact to the overall population [32, 43]

Social distancing:

- Travel restrictions are unlikely to have a major impact [25, 40]
- Social distancing interventions in general may not be as effective or cost-effective as pharmaceutical interventions [44, 47]
- Social distancing could be a key policy tool
  - At the very beginning of a pandemic outbreak [39, 42]
  - Or in a general pandemic, if the disease is highly infectious and if used in conjunction with other interventions [40, 44–47]

Multiple interventions:

- Multiple interventions used in combination are likely to be highly effective [39, 40, 42, 44–47]
- Dynamic models should be used to determine the best portfolio of interventions [33]

Distribution systems:

- System-wide models can identify bottlenecks before a pandemic [34–38]
- Properly designed operations research models can be quickly and easily used during a pandemic to improve response [34–36, 57].

A variety of different operations research tools can be used to tackle complex issues related to preparing for and responding to many different aspects of an influenza pandemic. So far, operations research methods have enabled us to come to some important policy conclusions for pandemic influenza planning and response and they hold great promise to help tackle additional challenges related to pandemic influenza (Table 11.2).

Table 11.2 Examples of research using operations research methods to analyze pandemic influenza

Author	Method	Applications	Insights
Studies mainly using system dynamics models			
Larson [24]	• Dynamic compartmental model	• Social distancing	• Social distancing of the correct populations may be very valuable
Nigmatulina and Larson [25]	• Dynamic compartmental model (heterogeneous populations)	• Vaccination • Social distancing	• Early vaccination of is important. • Partial travel restrictions are not very effective
Lee and Chen [26]	• Dynamic compartmental model	• Stockpiling antivirals	• Treatment is effective, but prevention was even more effective
Khazeni et al. [27]	• Dynamic compartmental model • Economic analysis	• Vaccination	• Earlier vaccination for H1N1 flu (1 month) could have substantial impact on infection and cost savings
Khazeni et al. [30]	• Dynamic compartmental model • Economic analysis	• Vaccination • Antiviral prophylaxis	• Pre-pandemic stockpiling of vaccines may be cost-effective • Cost-effectiveness depends on probability of pandemic and effectiveness of vaccines
Lugnér and Postma [31]	• Dynamic compartmental model • Economic analysis	• Stockpiling antivirals	• Conclusion: stockpiling for treatment is cost-effective
Medlock and Galvani [32]	• Dynamic compartmental model • Optimization	• Vaccine allocation	• Age-specific transmission dynamics are critical to consider for optimal allocation of influenza vaccines. • Current US CDC recommendations are suboptimal
Brandeau et al. [33]	• Dynamic compartmental mode • Economic analysis	• Resource allocation (portfolio of interventions)	• With nonlinear epidemic dynamics and nonlinear cost functions, dynamic resource allocation models may be needed instead of static cost-effectiveness ratios
Studies mainly using system discrete event simulation models			
Aaby et al. [34]	• Discrete-event simulation models • Queueing-system models	• Vaccination distribution	• Easy-to-use tools can be created and validated for clinic planning
Aaby et al. [35]	• Discrete-event simulation models • Queueing-system models	• Vaccination distribution	• Easy-to-use tools can be used clinic planning
Lee et al. [36]	• Discrete event simulation model • Optimization	• Facility layout • Staffing scenarios for mass distribution	• A real-time decision support system can improve throughput by 50 %

(continued)

Table 11.2 (continued)

Author	Method	Applications	Insights
Zaric et al. [37]	• Dynamic compartmental model • Queueing model • Economic analysis	• Medication distribution	• Dispensing capacity is more important than local stockpile size
Bravata et al. [38]	• Queueing Model • Economic analysis • Dynamic compartmental model	• Stockpiling • Dispensing supplies	• Local dispensing capacity can be an important bottleneck
Studies mainly using agent-based simulation models			
Ferguson et al. [39]	• Agent-based stochastic simulation model	• Containment with targeted antiviral prophylaxis • Quarantine	• Containment of an emerging disease may be possible • Multiple approaches will be more effective • Effective, efficient public health response would be required
Ferguson et al. [40]	• Agent-based stochastic simulation model	• Portfolio of interventions	• Border control unlikely to be effective • Prophylaxis and school closure could reduce clinical attack rates by 40–50 % • Vaccine stockpiled in advance could significantly reduce attack rates even if of low efficacy
Longini et al. [41]	• Agent-based stochastic simulation model	• Targeted antiviral prophylaxis • Vaccination	• Effective targeted antiviral prophylaxis could be as effective as mass vaccination
Longini et al. [42]	• Agent-based stochastic simulation model	• Portfolio of interventions	• Targeted antiviral prophylaxis could be effective if the strain is not very infectious • Combination strategies could be more effective for more infectious diseases
Patel et al. [43]	• Optimization with genetic algorithms • Agent-based stochastic simulation model	• Vaccine allocation	• Optimal vaccination strategies focus on children and could be 84 % more effective than random vaccination

Germann et al. [44]	• Agent-based stochastic simulation model	• Portfolio of interventions	• Targeted antiviral prophylaxis is likely to delay the pandemic (and more courses needed for more infectious strains) • Vaccination would reduce severity and possibly end the pandemic • Social distancing would not be as effective as vaccination • All interventions together are most effective
Sander et al. [45]	• Agent-based stochastic simulation model	• Portfolio of interventions	• Conclusion: targeted antiviral prophylaxis is a valuable mitigation strategy
Glass et al. [46]	• Agent-based stochastic simulation model	• Portfolio of interventions	• High-compliance social distancing is valuable • Uniform national policies are valuable • Pre-pandemic vaccines are important for critical infrastructures to continue to operate
Perlroth et al. [47]	• Agent-based stochastic simulation model	• Portfolio of interventions	• Combinations of social distancing interventions with antiviral use are cost-effective for moderate-to-severe pandemics
Studies mainly using optimization			
Kornish and Keeney [48]	• Optimization (dynamic programming)	• Vaccine strain selection	• When to commit to selecting a strain and when to defer
Wu et al. [49]	• Stochastic dynamic program	• New vaccine selection	• The current policy of vaccine strain selection is pretty good
Studies mainly using decision analysis			
Balicer et al. [50]	• Decision analysis • Economic analysis	• Stockpiling antivirals	• Conclusions: stockpiling for treatment is cost-saving • Prophylaxis is likely to be cost-saving, but depends on assumptions (probability of pandemic)
Lee et al. [51]	• Decision analysis • Economic analysis	• Stockpiling antivirals	• Treatment is an economically valuable strategy • Prophylaxis may be valuable for high-risk populations or a high case-fatality disease
Siddiqui and Edmunds [52]	• Decision analysis • Economic analysis	• Stockpiling antivirals	• Increase stockpile for treatment • Do not test before treating

(continued)

Table 11.2 (continued)

Author	Method	Applications	Insights
Studies mainly using game theory and supply chain management analysis techniques			
Sun et al. [54]	• Game theory • Stochastic compartmental model	• International antiviral drug stockpiling	• For small between-country transmission, there are incentives for countries to donate stockpiles to the initially infected country • But, a central planner could create a pareto improvement
Chick et al. [53]	• Dynamic compartmental model • Game theory	• Vaccine production	• Cost-sharing contract variant can improve supply of vaccines
De Laurentis et al. [55]	• Game theory	• Stockpiling hospital supplies	• Nash equilibrium exists between two hospitals
De Laurentis et al. [56]	• Game theory	• Stockpiling hospital supplies	• Nash equilibrium exists
Ekici et al. [57]	• Supply chain management (facility location) • Geographical disease model	• Emergency food distribution	• Heuristics can be developed to find solutions for the facility location problem

Acknowledgment I would like to acknowledge my colleague Nayer Khazeni for introducing me to pandemic influenza policy.

References

1. Potter CW (2001) A history of influenza. J Appl Microbiol 91:572–579
2. Centers for Disease Control and Prevention (2010) Updated CDC estimates of 2009 H1N1 influenza cases, Hospitalizations and deaths in the United States, April 2009–April 10, 2010. Centers for Disease Control and Prevention. http://www.cdc.gov/h1n1flu/estimates_2009_h1n1.htm. Accessed 13 Jan 2011
3. Cunha BA (2004) Influenza: historical aspects of epidemics and pandemics. Infect Dis Clin North Am 18:141–155
4. Crosby AW. Influenza. In: Kiple KF, editor. The Cambridge world history of human disease. Cambridge, United Kingdom: Cambridge University Press; 1993. pp. 807–811.
5. Taubenberger JK, Morens DM (2009) Pandemic influenza—including a risk assessment of H5N1. Rev Sci Tech 28:187–202
6. Johnson NP, Mueller J (2002) Updating the accounts: global mortality of the 1918–1920 "Spanish" influenza pandemic. Bull Hist Med 76:105–115
7. US Department of Health & Human Services (2012) History of Flu pandemics. http://www.flu.gov/pandemic/history/index.html. Accessed 6 Feb 2012
8. Dowdle WR (1999) Influenza A virus recycling revisited. Bull World Health Org 77:820–828
9. Viboud C, Miller M, Olson D, Osterholm M, Simonsen L (2010) Preliminary estimates of mortality and years of life lost associated with the 2009 A/H1N1 pandemic in the US and comparison with past influenza seasons. PLoS Curr 2:RRN1153
10. Taubenberger JK, Reid AH, Lourens RM, Wang R, Jin G, Fanning TG (2005) Characterization of the 1918 influenza virus polymerase genes. Nature 437:889–893
11. World Health Organization (2011) Confirmed human cases of Avian influenza A(H5N1). World Health Organization. http://www.who.int/csr/disease/avian_influenza/country/en/. Accessed 13 Jan 2011
12. Brahmbhatt M (2006) Economic impacts of Avian influenza propagation. http://web.worldbank.org/WBSITE/EXTERNAL/NEWS/0,,contentMDK:20978927~menuPK:34473~pagePK:34370~piPK:42770~theSitePK:4607,00.html. Accessed 13 Jan 2011
13. World Health Organization (2007) Questions and answers on pandemic influenza vaccine. World Health Organization. http://www.who.int/immunization/newsroom/PI_QAs/en/. Accessed 13 Jan 2011
14. Goji NA, Nolan C, Hill H, Wolff M, Noah DL, Williams TB, Rowe T, Treanor JJ (2008) Immune responses of healthy subjects to a single dose of intramuscular inactivated influenza A/Vietnam/1203/2004 (H5N1) vaccine after priming with an antigenic variant. J Infect Dis 198:635–641
15. Khazeni N, Bravata DM, Holty JE, Uyeki TM, Stave CD, Gould MK (2009) Systematic review: safety and efficacy of extended-duration antiviral chemoprophylaxis against pandemic and seasonal influenza. Ann Intern Med 151:464–473
16. Monto AS (2005) The threat of an avian influenza pandemic. N Engl J Med 352:323–325
17. Poland GA (2006) Vaccines against avian influenza—a race against time. N Engl J Med 354:1411–1413
18. Tracht SM, Del Valle SY, Hyman JM (2010) Mathematical Modeling of the effectiveness of facemasks in reducing the spread of novel influenza A (H1N1). PLoS ONE 5(2):e9018
19. Cowling BJ, Chan KH, Fang VJ, Cheng CK, Fung RO, Wai W, Sin J, Seto WH, Yung R, Chu DW, Chiu BC, Lee PW, Chiu MC, Lee HC, Uyeki TM, Houck PM, Peiris JS, Leung GM (2009) Facemasks and hand hygiene to prevent influenza transmission in households: a cluster randomized trial. Ann Intern Med 151:437–446
20. Schull MJ, Stukel TA, Vermeulen MJ, Guttmann A, Zwarenstein M (2006) Surge capacity associated with restrictions on nonurgent hospital utilization and expected admissions during

an influenza pandemic: lessons from the Toronto severe acute respiratory syndrome outbreak. Acad Emerg Med 13:1228–1231
21. Brailsford SC, Hilton NA (2001) A comparison of discrete event simulation and system dynamics for modelling health care systems
22. Brailsford, SC, Hilton NA, (2001) A comparison of discrete event simulation and system dynamics for modelling health care systems. In, Riley J, (ed.) Planning for the Future: Health Service Quality and Emergency Accessibility. Operational Research Applied to Health Services (ORAHS), Glasgow Caledonian University.
23. Samuelson DA, Macal CM (2006) Agent-based simulation comes of age. OR/MS Today 33.
24. Larson RC (2007) Simple models of influenza progression within a heterogeneous population. Oper Res 55:399–412
25. Nigmatulina KR, Larson RC. Stopping pandemic flu: government and community interventions in a multi-community model; 2007. Massachusetts Institute of Technology Engineering Systems Division Working Paper Series, No. ESD-WP-2007-28.
26. Lee VJ, Chen MI (2007) Effectiveness of neuraminidase inhibitors for preventing staff absenteeism during pandemic influenza. Emerg Infect Dis 13:449–457
27. Khazeni N, Hutton DW, Garber AM, Hupert N, Owens DK (2009) Effectiveness and cost-effectiveness of vaccination against pandemic influenza (H1N1) 2009. Ann Intern Med 151:829–839
28. DeNoon DJ (2009) Swine flu vaccine timeline: key decisions, key milestones. http://www.webmd.com/cold-and-flu/news/20090720/swine-flu-vaccine-when?page=4&print=true. Accessed 7 Feb 2012
29. World Health Organization (2009) Pandemic influenza vaccine manufacturing process and timeline. http://www.who.int/csr/disease/swineflu/notes/h1n1_vaccine_20090806/en/index.html. Accessed 7 Feb 2012
30. Khazeni N, Hutton DW, Garber AM, Owens DK (2009) Effectiveness and cost-effectiveness of expanded antiviral prophylaxis and adjuvanted vaccination strategies for an influenza A (H5N1) pandemic. Ann Intern Med 151:840–853
31. Lugner AK, Postma MJ (2009) Investment decisions in influenza pandemic contingency planning: cost-effectiveness of stockpiling antiviral drugs. Eur J Public Health 19:516–520
32. Medlock J, Galvani AP (2009) Optimizing influenza vaccine distribution. Science 325:1705–1708
33. Brandeau ML, Zaric GS, Richter A (2003) Resource allocation for control of infectious diseases in multiple independent populations: beyond cost-effectiveness analysis. J Health Econ 22:575–598
34. Aaby K, Herrmann JW, Jordan CS, Treadwell M, Wood K (2006) Montgomery Countys Public Health Service uses operations research to plan emergency mass dispensing and vaccination clinics. Interfaces 36:569–579
35. Aaby K, Abbey RL, Herrmann JW, Treadwell M, Jordan CS, Wood K (2006) Embracing computer modeling to address pandemic influenza in the 21st century. J Public Health Manag Pract 12:365
36. Lee EK, Maheshwary S, Mason J, Glisson W (2006) Decision support system for mass dispensing of medications for infectious disease outbreaks and bioterrorist attacks. Ann Oper Res 148:25–53
37. Zaric GS, Bravata DM, Holty JEC, McDonald KM, Owens DK, Brandeau ML (2008) Modeling the logistics of response to anthrax bioterrorism. Med Decis Making 28:332–350
38. Bravata D, Zaric G, Holty J, Brandeau M, Wilhelm E, McDonald K, Owens D (2006) Reducing mortality from anthrax bioterrorism: strategies for stockpiling and dispensing medical and pharmaceutical supplies. Biosecur Bioterror 4:244–262
39. Ferguson NM, Cummings DA, Cauchemez S, Fraser C, Riley S, Meeyai A, Iamsirithaworn S, Burke DS (2005) Strategies for containing an emerging influenza pandemic in Southeast Asia. Nature 437:209–214

40. Ferguson NM, Cummings DA, Fraser C, Cajka JC, Cooley PC, Burke DS (2006) Strategies for mitigating an influenza pandemic. Nature 442:448–452
41. Longini IM, Jr, Halloran ME, Nizam A, Yang Y (2004) Containing pandemic influenza with antiviral agents. Am J Epidemiol 159:623–633
42. Longini IM, Nizam A, Xu SF, Ungchusak K, Hanshaoworakul W, Cummings DAT, Halloran ME (2005) Containing pandemic influenza at the source. Science 309:1083–1087
43. Patel R, Longini IM, Halloran ME (2005) Finding optimal vaccination strategies for pandemic influenza using genetic algorithms. J Theor Biol 234:201–212
44. Germann TC, Kadau K, Longini IM, Macken CA (2006) Mitigation strategies for pandemic influenza in the United States. Proc Natl Acad Sci U S A 103:5935–5940
45. Sander B, Nizam A, Garrison LP, Postma MJ, Halloran ME, Longini IM (2009) Economic evaluation of influenza pandemic mitigation strategies in the United States using a stochastic microsimulation transmission model. Value Health 12:226–233
46. Glass RJ, Min HJ, Beyeler WE, Glass LM, 2007, "Design of Community Containment for Pandemic Influenza with Loki-Infect," SAND Number 2007–1184P. Sandia National Laboratories: Albuquerque, NM.
47. Perlroth DJ, Glass RJ, Davey VJ, Cannon D, Garber AM, Owens DK (2010) Health outcomes and costs of community mitigation strategies for an influenza pandemic in the United States. Clin Infect Dis 50:165–174
48. Kornish LJ, Keeney RL (2008) Repeated commit-or-defer decisions with a deadline: the influenza vaccine composition. Oper Res 56:527–541
49. Wu JT, Wein LM, Perelson AS (2005) Optimization of influenza vaccine selection. Oper Res 53:456–476
50. Balicer RD, Huerta M, Davidovitch N, Grotto I (2005) Cost-benefit of stockpiling drugs for influenza pandemic. Emerg Infect Dis 11:1280–1282
51. Lee VJ, Phua KH, Chen MI, Chow A, Ma S, Goh KT, Leo YS (2006) Economics of neuraminidase inhibitor stock piling for pandemic influenza, Singapore. Emerg Infect Dis 12:95–102
52. Siddiqui MR, Edmunds WJ (2008) Cost-effectiveness of antiviral stockpiling and near-patient testing for potential influenza pandemic. Emerg Infect Dis 14:267–274
53. Chick SE, Mamani H, Simchi-Levi D (2008) Supply chain coordination and influenza vaccination. Oper Res 56:1493–1506
54. Sun P, Yang L, de Vericourt F (2009) Selfish drug allocation for containing an international influenza pandemic at the onset. Oper Res 57:1320–1332
55. DeLaurentis P-C, Adida E, Lawley M (2008) A game theoretical approach for hospital stockpile in preparation for pandemics. Proceedings of the 2008 industrial engineering research conference 1772–1777. Vancouver, BC
56. DeLaurentis PC, Adida E, Lawley M (2009) Hospital stockpiling for influenza pandemics with pre-determined response levels. IEEE/INFORMS international conference on service operations, logistics and informatics, Chicago, IL, pp 37–42
57. Ekici A, Keskinocak P, Swann JL (2008) Pandemic influenza response. Proceedings of the 2008 winter simulation conference 1592–1600, Miami, FL
58. Longini IM, Jr, Halloran ME (2005) Strategy for distribution of influenza vaccine to high-risk groups and children. Am J Epidemiol 161:303–306

Part IV
Pharmaceutical Policy

Chapter 12
Active Vaccine and Drug Surveillance

Towards a 100 Million Member System

Margrét V. Bjarnadóttir and David Czerwinski

Abstract After the withdrawal of rofecoxib (known by the trade name Vioxx) from the US pharmaceutical market in 2004, post-approval drug safety and surveillance came under serious scrutiny. In 2008 the FDA announced the Sentinel Initiative, which includes an active surveillance system based on 100 million people's health-care data. In this chapter we describe a number of challenges involved in active drug and vaccine surveillance and provide an overview of state-of-the-art surveillance methodologies. We also address the statistical tradeoffs involved in surveillance, highlight some areas for future research, and frame the policy issues that designers of surveillance systems will have to address.

12.1 Introduction

The US Food and Drug Administration (FDA) is mandated with the task of ensuring drug and vaccine safety. The FDA's medical product approval process, in its modern form, dates to 1962, when the US Congress approved the Kefauver–Harris Amendment to the FD&C Act.[1] The amendment was approved after the thalidomide tragedy. Thalidomide is a sedative drug that was prescribed to pregnant women in many countries as a treatment for morning sickness. It was later found to cause horrible birth defects. The most important change introduced by the amendment was

[1] The Food, Drug, and Cosmetic (FD&C) Act was signed into law in 1938 and mandated premarket testing of the safety of all new drugs, as well as banning false therapeutic claims.

M.V. Bjarnadóttir (✉)
Van Munching Hall, College Park, MD 20742, USA
e-mail: mbjarnad@rhsmith.umd.edu

D. Czerwinski
One Washington Square, San Jose, CA 95192-0069, USA
e-mail: david.czerwinski@sjsu.edu

G.S. Zaric (ed.), *Operations Research and Health Care Policy*, International Series in Operations Research & Management Science 190,
DOI 10.1007/978-1-4614-6507-2_12,

the requirement that all new drugs demonstrate "substantial evidence" of efficacy in addition to a safety requirement introduced by the FD&C Act of 1938.

Today, before a vaccine or drug enters the market it has gone through a series of trials to ensure efficacy and safety as well as to establish dosage recommendations. However, rare side effects are unlikely to be observed in randomized clinical trials, due to limited sample sizes as well as short follow-up time. It is only after vaccines or drugs have entered the market that observations from a large population become available. Collecting and analyzing data from this population is therefore instrumental in ensuring safety.

The FDA began post-marketing surveillance in the late 1960s. Its current monitoring systems were established in the 1990s—the Vaccine Adverse Event Reporting System (VAERS) and the Adverse Event Reporting System (AERS) for drugs. Both systems are based on voluntary reports submitted by physicians, patients, and pharmaceutical companies. Although these systems have proven to be useful in many settings (e.g., [70, 72]), they have some serious limitations such as inconsistency in reporting, underreporting, uneven quality of reports, lack of a clear denominator, lack of control group, and limited long-term capability [2, 52] as well as limited ability to provide evidence of safety.

The need for more systematic surveillance was highlighted by the withdrawal of rofecoxib, better known under the brand name Vioxx, from the US market in 2004. Rofecoxib was withdrawn after being linked to increased rates of heart attacks and strokes. From 1999 to 2004 it is estimated that rofecoxib may have been responsible for tens of thousands of fatal heart attacks [26]. Could these effects have been detected more quickly?

The FDA Amendments Act of 2007 [1] had provisions intended to enhance drug safety and *"formalized the concept of life-cycle management of the risks and benefits of vaccines, from early clinical development through many years of use in large numbers of people"* [2]. The Act gave the FDA extended authority for post-marketing surveillance and action and mandated the creation of a national electronic system for active monitoring of medical products' safety. As a result, in May 2008 the FDA announced the Sentinel Initiative [65], with the goal of establishing an active (as opposed to passive) real-time drug surveillance system.

A key benefit of active surveillance is that it is not dependent on a physician or a patient recognizing a potential link between a drug or a vaccine and an adverse event. As an example, if a patient who is over 50, diabetic, hypertensive, and suffering from joint pain has a heart attack, it is unlikely that he or his physician would link the cardiac event to an increased risk associated with a pain medication. Therefore the event would not get reported to a passive system. On the other hand, an active system that includes comprehensive medical information on a large population may be able to detect increases in risk that on an individual level may not seem significant.

Drug and vaccine surveillance differ in fundamental ways. Vaccines are generally administered to healthy populations, while drugs are administered to people of varying health conditions, making controlling for coexisting conditions an important consideration. Vaccines are administered one time, while drugs are commonly taken over longer periods of time. In addition, vaccines generally have few known side effects while new drug compounds may lead to an array of different adverse events. Vaccine surveillance therefore tends to concentrate on a small subset of possible adverse events, ranging from common side effects such as fever, to more serious and rare events such as Guillain–Barre [13, 71]. Vaccine surveillance has shorter observation windows while drug surveillance can extend for years and needs to monitor multiple, and possibly unknown, adverse events. In the USA the active surveillance system includes the Vaccine Safety Datalink (VSD). The VSD is a collaboration between the Immunization Safety Office of the Centers for Disease Control (CDC) and eight managed care organizations. The VSD was established in 1990 to monitor immunization safety and address the gaps in scientific knowledge about rare and serious events following immunization.

There are a number of aspects of vaccine and drug surveillance that make it a challenging problem. First, the signal is unknown. That is, drugs (and to a lesser extent vaccines) can lead to numerous different adverse events, and all need to be monitored simultaneously. The duration that patients take the drug for is often unknown, as is the available sample size, due to the fact that the drug's adoption profile may not be clear. On top of these issues, there is the question of what is the right benchmark for acceptable risk? The goal of this chapter is to cover the state of the art methodologies for active vaccine and drug surveillance, to highlight some of the current research directions, and to pose a few unsolved aspects of these surveillance systems. Although the problem is a global one, the focus will be on developments within the United States. The rest of the chapter is organized as follows. Section 12.2 discusses the potential data sources for drug and vaccine surveillance and Sect. 12.3 surveys the analytical methods and design considerations of surveillance systems. Section 12.4 discusses statistical trade-offs in drug surveillance systems and Sect. 12.5 highlights two special topics in active surveillance: optimization in multiple hypothesis setting (Sect. 12.5.1) and long-term monitoring (Sect. 12.5.2). Finally Sect. 12.6 discusses some of the policy implications and future research avenues.

12.2 Surveillance Data

To date, a variety of data sources have been used for both actual surveillance and academic research. The minimum needed is (a) a dispense record for drugs (or administration records for a vaccine) and (b) data on adverse events. Since not all possible side effects might be known a priori, the data used to monitor adverse events generally includes information on all of the patients' encounters with the health-care system.

Administrative data collected for insurance billing and reimbursement purposes has been a boon to active surveillance. Insurance claims data provide an electronic record of a patient's interactions with the health-care system, including outpatient visits, hospital stays, and drug prescriptions. The details of what is recorded vary slightly from insurer to insurer but generally include the date of the visit, the doctor's diagnoses (recorded as International Classification of Diseases, Ninth Revision, Clinical Modification (ICD-9-CM) codes), and any procedures performed (recorded as Current Procedural Terminology (CPT) codes). When a prescription is filled, the date, the drug (recorded as a National Drug Code (NDC)), the dosage, and the number of days of supply are recorded. Basic demographic data, such as gender and date of birth, is also available as a part of a members' eligibility record.

Claims data have their imperfections, such as lack of outcome information. The data contains information about which tests were performed, e.g., an X-ray, but not the results of the test, although sometimes the results can be inferred from the subsequent treatment. The accuracy of claims data has been studied extensively. Though overall the coding of diagnoses and procedures in claims data are accurate, they can sometimes be vague [33]. The fact that databases contain such large populations outweighs their shortcomings, and claims data have over recent decades increasingly been used for medical research, ranging from identification of in-hospital complications [39, 44] to analysis of adherence to medication [24, 32] and guidelines [50] to studies of the effects of health-care policy changes [7, 49, 60].

As of 2010, the FDA's Sentinel system for drug surveillance had a cohort of 25 million people, with data drawn from health organizations across the country, both private and public [63]. The VSD has a cohort of about 9.2 million people [71] and extracts electronic data on vaccinations and outpatient and inpatient diagnoses from the medical record.

Electronic medical records (EMRs) provide the promise of more comprehensive data, though currently they are only in limited use in the USA. They may provide such key pieces of data as lab test results, patient symptoms, and physician's notes. In addition, text-mining clinical notes in EMRs may further boost estimates of the rates of adverse events [28], as sometimes conditions may not be coded as diagnoses in the medical record, but noted in the clinical notes. For example, a fever, a common side effect of vaccination, may be mentioned in the notes but not coded as a reason for a visit.

12.2.1 Details of ICD-9-CM Codes

The ICD-9-CM [18, 19] codes for recording diagnoses are organized in a hierarchical structure by organ system. The structure can be viewed as a tree. Every level of the tree represents an additional digit of the ICD-9-CM code, and the descriptions of the conditions are correspondingly more detailed. There are 17 broad categories, 110 subcategories below them, and 913 individual three-digit ICD-9-CM codes. Some diagnosis codes occur quite frequently, such as 462 Acute pharyngitis (i.e., a sore throat), while others occur very rarely, such as 032 Diphtheria. In addition, there is a further level of specificity available by adding a fourth and fifth digit to the

Table 12.1 Level 3 ICD-9 codes grouped together in the pneumonia group, a part of diseases of the respiratory system

ICD-9 code	Description
480	Viral pneumonia
481	Pneumococcal pneumonia
482	Other bacterial pneumonia
483	Pneumonia due to other specified organism
484	Pneumonia in infectious diseases classified elsewhere
485	Bronchopneumonia organism unspecified
486	Pneumonia organism unspecified

code for some diagnoses that, for example, note the location of a particular type of cancer (e.g., 162 refers to lung cancer, while 162.5 refers specifically to cancer of the lower lobe of the lung). Counting the fourth and fifth digits, there are approximately 14,000 ICD-9-CM codes.

Neighboring codes (that have the same parent) are often very similar and can be collapsed into one for the purpose of drug surveillance. As an example, codes 480 through 486 all refer to varieties of pneumonia (Table 12.1). Collapsing similar codes can also be advantageous because the further down the tree, the less common the conditions get and the less likely it would be to observe a significant shift in risk. Section 12.5.1 discusses some optimization approaches to selecting the right coding level for analysis.

There is significant variability in ICD-9-CM coding, as some health care professionals may code only to the third digit, while others to the fourth or fifth. In addition medical claims coding may start with a clinician, but it is most often completed and submitted by a separate dedicated billing operator, which introduces additional variability. Finally, the classification of a condition is sometimes ambiguous, and different doctors may code the same condition using different codes.

Currently, a transition from ICD-9-CM to ICD-10-CM is underway, though ICD-10-CM is not yet in widespread use. In general, the ICD-10-CM coding is more detailed, with approximately 68,000 diagnosis codes compared with just over 14,000 diagnosis codes in the ICD-9-CM standard. Conversion to ICD-9-CM from ICD-10-CM is in most cases possible; however, there is not always a mapping (either one-to-one or many-to-one), especially in the detailed four- and five-digit codes. The lack of mapping arises mainly because of the introduction of new concepts into the ICD-10 standard that are not in the ICD-9, and of multiple ICD-9-CM codes for a single ICD-10-CM code. For surveillance that incorporates a mix of ICD-9-CM and ICD-10-CM data sources there will therefore be some work in combining data from the two standards during the transition period, and some approximations may be necessary. The Centers for Medicare and Medicaid Services provides a "crosswalk" between the two systems that can be utilized for the coding conversion [17].

12.3 Surveillance Methodology

In any surveillance system, whether it is monitoring plastic production, systematic risk in a banking system, or adverse drug events, the designers need to address three fundamental questions: (1) What to monitor, (2) how to monitor it, and (3) what should it be compared to. These questions may seem basic, but when dealing with highly variable health care data, a seemingly simple question like what constitutes an adverse events becomes a complicated one.

In this section we introduce some of the modeling considerations that go into the design of an active drug and vaccine surveillance system, starting with how to define adverse events in terms of data (Sect. 12.3.1). We then discuss whom to monitor. That is, what populations should be monitored (Sect. 12.3.2). Once adverse events and the monitoring population are selected, a baseline needs to be created. That is, a "normal" rate of adverse events needs to be determined (Sect. 12.3.3). Lastly, an appropriate monitoring methodology must be selected. We discuss the two major considerations of any active drug surveillance system, sequential testing (Sect. 12.3.4), and multiple hypothesis control (Sect. 12.3.5). The section concludes with some remarks on the appropriate design (Sect. 12.3.6).

In general, we will call the population taking the drug under study the *treatment group*, and when outcomes for the treatment populations are being compared to another population, we will call the second population the *control group*.

12.3.1 Event Definition

What defines an event is a simple enough question. But, the question has surprisingly many details that need to be addressed before successfully monitoring drugs and their effects.

An adverse event can be the onset of a disease such as asthma or a single event, such as stroke. Events are defined using the occurrence of specific ICD-9 codes in the members' health-care data. In general, the ICD-9 codes are grouped together into diagnosis groups, where each group corresponds to an adverse event. Table 12.1 gives an example of code grouping, where six different level-3 codes for pneumonia are grouped together to form a pneumonia group. The American Health Data Institute provides a grouping by the third digit [61], but medical researchers often differ in their grouping and coding selection for specific events. The question of what constitutes an event is not just a question of appropriate code grouping but also which occurrences of diagnosis (group) codes should be counted as events once grouping is established.

An event can be defined in a number of different ways, from each code occurrence in the data counting as an event, to each episode counting as an event, or even only counting the first appearance of a code for a member as an event, ignoring all others. Researchers have suggested a number of different approaches.

Brown et al. [14] defined events as the occurrence of the diagnosis code of interest but only when assigned in an inpatient setting and with no prior coding for 180 days before the start of treatment. Bertsimas and Bjarnadottir [5] suggest monitoring only first occurrences of each diagnosis group code. When the first occurrence of a diagnosis (group) code is counted, the surveillance corresponds to monitoring the rate of initial incidence of adverse events. This approach has the benefit of increased homogeneity of the treatment and control groups, as the risk of experiencing a particular outcome (such as kidney stones or stroke) is significantly increased after experiencing the outcome for the first time (e.g., if a member has had a prior heart attack, he is much more likely to experience another). Therefore only counting first occurrences simplifies the baseline estimates (as the estimate is only based on first incidence risk as opposed to being based on both first incidence as well as reoccurrence risk), and this definition reduces the influence that any one member (that has multiple episodes) can have on the study, reducing the variance of the test statistics.

It is important to note that for some adverse effects, such as heart attacks, the way an event is defined may have very little effect on the results of drug surveillance. On the other hand, for other diseases it can be misleading to define events in certain ways. This difference depends on the nature of the events in question. Some events are a "one-time thing," such as complications of labor; others may take a long time to resolve (resulting in multiple claims over a long period); finally, some events can be the start of a long and irreversible condition, such as the onset of Alzheimer's disease. Therefore the appropriate definition of events need not be the same for every diagnosis.

12.3.2 Population Selection and Study Periods

Constructing the treatment and control groups for surveillance also requires care. Each study defines its selection criteria differently. In general the member selections is based on two types of criteria; their history prior to starting on a drug and the extent of the exposure to the drug.

One selection criteria is the minimum exposure, that is, the minimum number of days a member takes the drug. As an example, a brief exposure to some drugs is seen as unlikely to be linked to cancer, and studies may require minimum number of days for members being included. In addition, the dose level (the quantity of the drug taken) at any one time affects both efficacy and toxicity of a drug; however, active drug surveillance studies have so far not taken advantage of this fact [5, 8, 14], perhaps due to modeling complication and low data quality.

Another type of selection criteria is based on member histories, based on what has happened to a member prior to starting a drug he/she may be excluded from the surveillance. The study criteria may, for example, include a "clear" period prior to first use of a drug where no dispensing of either the treatment or control drug is allowed, nor any coding of the adverse events being studied [14].

Members with heavy disease burden generally have a high volume of health-care data and, therefore, independent of whether they are taking a treatment drug or not, have a high risk of medical complications. These members therefore bring a high variance into any estimates of a drug's risk. As an example, the top 5% of members in terms of spending in claims data account for over 60% of the overall costs [6], which is representative of their data volume. Excluding members with high health-care costs prior to the drug exposure has therefore been shown to be beneficial in controlling for false positives [5].

There are many parameters of surveillance design that are under the system designers' control and the optimal settings are still under investigation [5, 15]. Brown et al. [15] investigate several parameter settings, including reducing the "clear" period prior to first use of a drug from six months to three months. Relaxing the constraints on which patients are allowed to be in the study has the beneficial effect of increasing the sample size but the possible negative effect of allowing more noise. Their experiments led to mixed results and their recommendation is to continue to experiment with these parameters.

A patient that fulfills the study criteria is assigned to the treatment group at the time of their first dispensing of the drug of interest. How a member is assigned to the control group depends on the type of control being used. If the background rate of the adverse event in the general population is being used, then no active control group is needed. However, if the members of the treatment group, by virtue of being candidates for the treatment, are markedly different from the general population, then this approach would not be appropriate. If a control group on a comparison drug is used, the same inclusion/exclusion criteria are generally applied to the control group.

A surveillance system analyzes outcomes from members in the treatment group and compares them to outcomes of the control group or the baseline used. For how long each member is analyzed is again study dependent. In general the members are followed during an exposure period, the time from the first prescription to their last prescription plus the number supplied in their last prescription. Depending on the drug, the member may be followed for some period after the exposure; the post-toxicity time period meant to represent the time after a member stops taking a treatment drug until its toxicity no longer affects him or her. Once the post-toxicity period has passed, outcomes from the member are no longer included. Intuitively, one expects the toxicity of a drug to go down as time passes after a member stops taking the drug. The exception to this phenomenon occurs when permanent damage has been done. Appropriate time windows depend on the drug and the adverse event under study. Six months is a typical window size for the post-toxicity period, but this can vary from drug to drug. Figure 12.1 shows typical study periods.

12.3.3 Creating a Baseline

One of the major challenges of a surveillance system is to come up with a reliable baseline. If the baseline is too low, the surveillance is prone to result in a false alarm. If the baseline is too high, risks may go undetected. Researchers have addressed

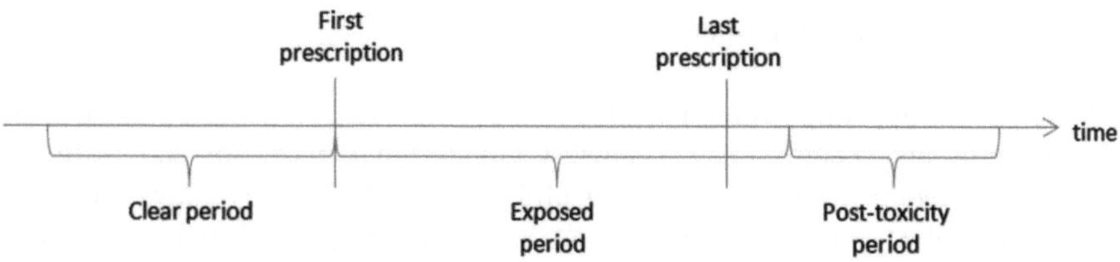

Fig. 12.1 An example of period definitions used in surveillance design. The figure shows the clear period and exposure period extending from the first prescription until the last prescription plus the days supplied by the last prescription, followed by a post-toxicity period which length depends on the drug and adverse event under study

this challenge in multiple ways: (a) using historical or concurrent controls from a separate control population, (b) using self control, or (c) using indirect control method.

With all designs, the fundamental principle is that the treatment and control groups be at equal risk of developing the outcome in the absence of drug exposure. When this comparability is achieved, increased occurrence of the outcome among the treatment group can then be linked to the use of the drug being studied.

12.3.3.1 Constructing an Active Control

An active control group can be constructed in several ways. If there are a small number of covariates to control for, then the control can be constructed by matching. In this approach, members of the treatment group are matched to someone not on the treatment who has similar covariate values to them. For example, it is common to control for age and gender in this way. Rather than one-one matching, one-many matching or stratification are commonly used.

However, if a large number of covariates need to be controlled for, then matching may be impractical because there might not be a patient who matches (exactly or even closely) on all of the covariates. This problem arises when, for instance, control is desired not only for age and gender but also for coexisting diseases, drugs that are being used concurrently, or previous treatments received.

A widely used approach is to use a control group consisting of patients who are on a drug comparable to the drug under study. As there often are biases between treatments (e.g., rofecoxib is often compared with naproxine, but the two populations are quite different in their age and gender distributions, as well as disease burden), the baseline rates are often adjusted to account for these differences.

Yet even then, if there is a reason that people are prescribed the new drug rather than the comparison drug, the comparison of risk may be biased. An alternative that has yet to be adopted for surveillance is to use propensity scores to construct the control group [43, 55]. A propensity score reflects the probability that a patient would be assigned to the treatment under investigation, *whether or not they actually are*. By balancing the treatment and control groups based on their propensity scores, bias due to covariates will be removed [54].

12.3.3.2 Indirect Adjustments

Rather than applying complicated baseline methods, Bertsimas et al. and Bjarnadottir and Zenios [5, 11] suggest monitoring the control and treatment populations independently and applying differences of differences analysis. In particular, the analysis monitors the rates of adverse events before and after the initiation of the treatment or control drugs, respectively. It then compares the change in the rates of adverse events in each population independently. If the treatment drug increases the rate of events beyond what the control drug does, an alarm is raised.

12.3.3.3 Baseline Determination for Vaccines

Vaccines are administered to the healthy population and in general to the majority of the population (in the case of infant and children's vaccination). Therefore, there is no direct comparison population, as the reasons for those who do not get vaccinated are often sickness or other characteristics that would bias a baseline. A common approach for establishing a baseline is to use historical rates, either based on the adverse event rates from comparable vaccines or based on population incidence estimates [71]. Another possible approach is self-control, for example, utilizing the self-control series method [16, 31] in which the rates for the treatment group after vaccination are compared to the rates among the same group before vaccination.

12.3.3.4 Uncertainty in Baselines

Until recently the baseline rates have been considered fixed. This is in fact the case if the comparison drug has been on the market for an extensive period of time, and therefore there is a significant amount of historical data to create baseline estimates from. However this is not always the case. Often the only suitable comparison drug is also relatively new on the market. Such was the case with the comparison of rosiglitazone[2] (trade name Avandia) and pioglitazone[3] (Actos), two diabetes drugs that have been linked to increased risk of cardiac events. This uncertainty in the baseline motivates introduction of new methods that take into account baseline uncertainty. The additional complication is that many methods with analytical

[2] Rosiglitazone is an antidiabetic drug that has been suspended from the European market and is currently being prescribed in the USA under significant restrictions. Annual sales peaked at approximately $2.5 billion in 2006, but have since declined due the potential increased risk of cardiac events and stroke.

[3] Pioglitazone is an antidiabetic drug of the same class as rosiglitazone (thiazolidinedione) and shares some of the side effects of rosiglitazone, such as increase risk of fractures in females, and it may "cause or exacerbate" congestive heart failure in some patients [64].

results become intractable, and therefore the design needs to rely on simulation to determine, for example, the rejection boundaries. We introduce one of these methods, the CmaxSPRT, below.

12.3.4 Sequential Testing and Interim Analysis

In the setting of drug surveillance, adverse events in the treatment group are observed and increased risk is tested for sequentially over time. Statistical methods for sequential surveillance mainly build on the sequential-testing framework developed by Wald [68].

12.3.4.1 SPRT

The incidence rate of adverse events in the treatment group is updated after each observation and compared to the population's baseline rate to test the null hypothesis that the incidence rate in the treatment group is the same as baseline rate. Or, in terms of relative risk (RR), $H_0 : RR = 1$.

After each observation, a decision is made whether to reject the null hypothesis, accept the null hypothesis, or continue collecting data (because the data is as of yet inconclusive). Wald showed that a sequential probability ratio test (SPRT) is optimal in this setting in the sense that it will minimize the expected number of observations required to make a decision. The probability ratio used in the test is

$$\text{PR} = \frac{P(\text{Data}|H_A)}{P(\text{Data}|H_0)}.$$

Wald also derived simple formulas for the acceptance and rejection regions for the SPRT. If the desired probability of a Type I error is α and of a Type II error is β, then the following decision boundaries can be used: $A = \frac{1-\beta}{\alpha}$ and $B = \frac{\beta}{1-\alpha}$. If $PR \geq A$, then the null hypothesis is rejected. If $PR \leq B$, then the null hypothesis is accepted. Otherwise, the experiment continues and the next data point is observed.

A limitation of Wald's approach is that it requires a sharp alternative hypothesis of the form $H_A : RR = r$, requiring a specific value r. In drug surveillance, the alternative hypothesis of interest is composite, $H_A : RR \neq 1$. (Or, if the focus is on detecting increases to the relative risk, $H_A : RR > 1$).

Kulldorf et al. [35] demonstrate the drawbacks of the need to specify r for drug surveillance. If too large a value of r is chosen, then the test will be insensitive to moderate increases to the relative risk. As a result, the time until an increased risk is detected may be prolonged or the increased risk might not be detected at all. On the other hand, using too small a value of r may lead to a delay in detecting large relative risks. This problem arises because the alternative hypothesis would be very similar to the null, and large amount of data would need to be accumulated to differentiate between them.

12.3.4.2 MaxSPRT

Kulldorf et al. [35] propose a maximized sequential probability ratio test, which they refer to as MaxSPRT. In this test, rather than using Wald's likelihood ratio, the ratio:

$$\mathrm{PR} = \max_{r>1} \frac{P(\mathrm{Data}|R = r)}{P(\mathrm{Data}|R = 1)}$$

is used with the value of r that maximizes the likelihood of the data. When the likelihood ratio is defined in this way, analytic expressions for the critical values do not exist. Rather, the critical values, can be estimated using Monte Carlo simulation. One limitation of the MaxSPRT approach is that in order to compute the appropriate critical values the intended duration of the surveillance needs to be specified in advance.

The MaxSPRT method requires a stable estimate of the baseline rate of incidence. The baseline rate is generally based on historical counts. However in some cases, such as for a rare adverse events or when the comparison population is small, the historical baseline itself will be uncertain. The SPRT does not take the variability of the estimate of the baseline rate into account and therefore can be biased, resulting in critical values that are overly tight. This bias is corrected through a refinement to MaxSPRT proposed in [71], called the conditional maxSPRT (CmaxSPRT).

12.3.4.3 Brownian Motion Approximation

As an alternative to SPRT-like methods, a recent analytical study [11] proposes using a Brownian motion approximation. The paper develops a test statistic that corresponds to the number of excess events after accounting for the number of expected events based on a comparison population. The paper proves that the test statistic is a Brownian motion, as the size of the available data becomes large. Using this approximation has the benefit of allowing tractable optimization of the surveillance boundaries, but it has yet to be tested empirically on real world data.

12.3.4.4 Sequential Monitoring of Vaccines

The statistical methods utilized in the VSD active surveillance system are SPRT-based methods, in particular maxSPRT [42], and later CmaxSPRT [41]. Other methods have been proposed for vaccine surveillance, such as case series cumulative sum charts (CUSUM) [45]. In particular it has been pointed out that when the risk periods are short compared to the overall observation window, a case series method is almost as efficient. In addition, a CUSUM-like method, that does not allow evidence in favor of the null hypothesis to accumulate, may be more suited to detecting sharp changes in risk associated with breakdowns in the supply chain (such as errors in administration, storage, and/or transportation) or risk changes associated with changes in manufacturing.

12.3.5 Multiple Hypothesis Control

When a surveillance system monitors multiple signals at a time, the probability of a false alarm goes up unless the design accounts for the multiple testing being done. Several statistical techniques are available to overcome this problem. At their core, they require a stronger level of evidence for a rejection of the null hypothesis in order to keep the probability of a false alarm at α (the family-wise error rate).[4]

A basic adjustment method is the Bonferroni correction, which tests an individual hypothesis using α / n, where n is the total number of hypotheses being tested. One of the drawbacks of this simple correction is that it greatly increases type II error rate, the probability of missing a true signal. Hence the power of the resulting surveillance design is often unsatisfactory. Another basic method is the Šidák correction, testing an individual hypothesis at $1 - (1 - \alpha)^{1/n}$. However, this approach requires that all hypotheses are independent, which may not be the case if monitoring all possible adverse events. As an example, diagnoses are not independent: a diabetic is at higher risk of foot ulcers and eye complications than other members of the population. Improvements to these methods have been suggested (e.g., [30]) but are outside the scope of this chapter.

The current practice appears to be ad hoc—the following quote describes how the VSD changed the significance level to account for larger number of hypothesis:

> The VSD, for example, reduced the alpha level in their influenza vaccine safety study to .01 to compensate for the large number of outcomes under observation.[16]

That is, rather than applying more complicated surveillance methodology, α is adjusted downwards. This approach has the benefit of being simple, but at the cost of some power loss. In addition, blindly adjusting significance level can have critical effects, as highlighted in the discussion in Sect. 12.4.

The false discovery rate (FDR) provides another way to think about false alarms in multiple testing [3, 57, 58]. The FDR measures the expected fraction of all detected signals that turn out to be false detections. When monitoring multiple number of drugs, for multiple adverse events, false signals are inevitable. It is then

[4] The family-wise error rate refers to the probability of making one or more false discoveries or type I errors among all the hypotheses being tested.

useful to control their prevalence, using the FDR, rather than controlling the less relevant probability of even a single false detection occurring, as the traditional Type I error control does.

So far there has not been much focus on multiple hypothesis error control in drug and vaccine surveillance design. Most studies focus on a handful of adverse events and ignore this aspect. A single study [5] implements a full-scale surveillance across multiple adverse events (identified as all three-digit ICD-9 codes grouped based on medical criteria), utilizing simulated boundaries and Bonferroni-like correction of the expected number of false alarm per year. From the discussion above, it is clear that there is room for improvement to maximize power of active drug surveillance design.

In addition, to overcome the complications of multiple hypothesis testing and the associated power loss, it has been proposed to monitor a single summarizing signal, as opposed to multiple adverse events. Since claims data are generated for billing purposes, each encounter with the health-care system has a cost attached to it. An individual's cost in claims data is therefore a good indicator of his/her overall health condition [6]. Therefore, instead of monitoring hundreds of adverse events, Bjarnadóttir and Guan [8] suggest monitoring cost as a summarizing signal. The paper demonstrates that by monitoring the summarizing signal, it is possible to detect faster that something is going on.

12.3.6 One Size Does Not Fit All

From the previous discussion, it is clear that there are multiple aspects of the surveillance design that need to be taken into consideration. The "right" design is dependent on both the drug/vaccine and the adverse event under study. Depending on the frequency of the adverse event, the severity of the event, and expected risk increase (if available), one statistical model may fit better than others. Sequential testing is not the answer for all. For a rare event, a one-time test may be more appropriate as it will conserve power [11]. In addition, depending on the background rate, choices about whether to use a Poisson approximation, a Binomial model, or a Brownian motion approximation may differ.

Ideally, any surveillance design should rule out any excess risk of any adverse events, at least guaranteeing that the risk is detected with some large probability $(1 - \beta)$. The challenge is that the power $(1 - \beta)$ of the design is a function of the risk increase as well as the population size. The risk increase can be specified as the minimum risk increase of interest to public health. The population size is not just a function of the database in use but also the adoption rate and market capture of the new drug as well as the member selection criteria. As the rate of different events differ, an additional consideration may be to drop from the surveillance an adverse event once the corresponding power $(1 - \beta)$ is reached, continuing with fewer hypotheses and therefore shorter time to detection for the remaining hypotheses if increased risk exists. This is especially true if controlling the family-wise error rate.

12.4 Statistical Trade-Off in Drug Surveillance

In any surveillance design, a balance needs to be struck between the rate of false positives and time until detection of real signals. Many of the early papers on drug and vaccine surveillance ignore this trade-off, but more recently it has become a topic discussed in the drug/vaccine surveillance literature [9, 41, 45].

The traditional approach to setting significance levels (α), and therefore the associated power, has been by asking what probability of a false alarm one is willing to tolerate? Once that question has been answered the associated power of the surveillance system can be calculated. A more specific question, and one that starts to address the statistical trade-off is what is the increase in the rate of false alarms that the agency is willing to accept for a certain reduction in the time to discovery of a true signals? This is a fundamental consideration for surveillance system design. What makes the calibration of the system challenging, beyond heterogeneity of different adverse events and perhaps difficulty in assigning costs to Type I and Type II errors (false alarms and undetected signals), is the uncertainty of the risk increase. In order to make any concrete statements about the trade-off, either one needs to select a *design risk increase* or assume a probability distribution over the set of possible risk increases. New drugs are often (although not always) related to other drugs already on the market with "known" safety profiles. In addition, some safety information is also available from clinical trials. Therefore, there is partial prior knowledge of what kind of adverse events a new drug may pose and the possible relative risk increases to be expected.

12.4.1 Got the Power?

In some cases, a trade-off is not feasible as the surveillance system simply is not powered sufficiently. That is, when the rate of the underlying event is small, and the risk increase not large enough, the surveillance system may not be powered to detect it. The Sentinel Initiative's aim is to have information on 100 million lives in its databases. If we assume a simple, one-signal surveillance, what would be the power of the system? The answer depends on the market penetration of the drug, the underlying rate of the adverse event, the risk increase, and the tolerance for false positives.

As an example, assume the one signal tolerance of false positive is 0.001 (which is reasonable if the surveillance system will be surveying hundreds of adverse events, for multiple drugs at a time). Figure 12.2 shows the power of the system as a function of relative risk increases of 10%, 100%, and 300% when the underlying rate of the adverse event is $p = 0.\ 1\%$ (1 in 1 thousand). Each member is assumed to experience the adverse event with probability p under the null hypothesis of no risk increase and $p \times (1 + \{\text{ risk increase}\})$ under the alternative hypothesis of a risk increase (the relative risk > 1). For example, to have a 90% chance of

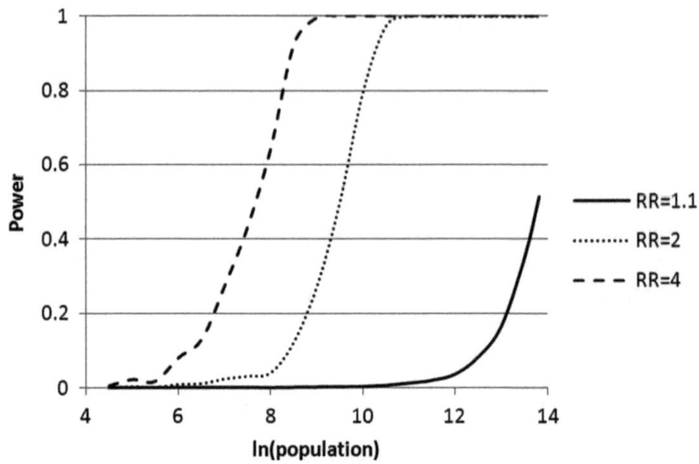

Fig. 12.2 The power of a one-time (non-sequential), one-signal surveillance system. The baseline probability of an adverse event is 0.1%. A single test for the null hypothesis of no risk increase is performed. Critical values (if the number of adverse events are above the critical value, then we raise an alarm) are calculated based on a Poisson approximation and a continuity-corrected normal approximation. RR stands for relative risk, $RR = 1.\ 1$ corresponds to a risk increase of 10%, $RR = 2$ corresponds to a 100% increase in risk, etc

detecting a 10% risk increase, a population beyond 100,000 is needed. On the other hand, if the risk is doubled, a population of approximately 36,000 is needed.

In order to put the numbers presented in Fig. 12.2 into context it is informative to review the risk increase estimates for some actual drugs. In the case of the withdrawal of robecoxib, it has been estimated that the relative risk of myocardial infarction (heart attack) was close to 1.5 (a 50% increase in risk)[14]. In the case of the recent rosiglitazone controversy the relative increase in risk of myocardial infarction was estimated by one study to be between 28% and 39% [48], and a different study estimated the risk increase to be 6% for acute myocardial infarction, 27% for stroke, and 14% for heart failure [27]. In contrast, pemoline (trade name Cylert)[5] was withdrawn after 13 deaths or liver transplants due to liver failure were linked to the drug. This rate of liver failure is estimated to be 10–25 times the rate in the general population [66]. These examples demonstrate that the risk increases vary widely. The other important factor is the background rate. The rate of liver failure is approximately 1 in 10,000 [20, 38]. While cardiac events are more common, the incidence of the first major cardiovascular event varies both with age and gender and is about 7 in 1,000 for men between 35 and 44. The average incidence of stroke is around 1.6 in 1,000 [62].

[5] Pemoline, a drug given to treat attention-deficit hyperactivity disorder, was approved by the FDA in 1975. It was withdrawn from the USA market in 2005 and can only be prescribed in the US under an "investigational new drug application."

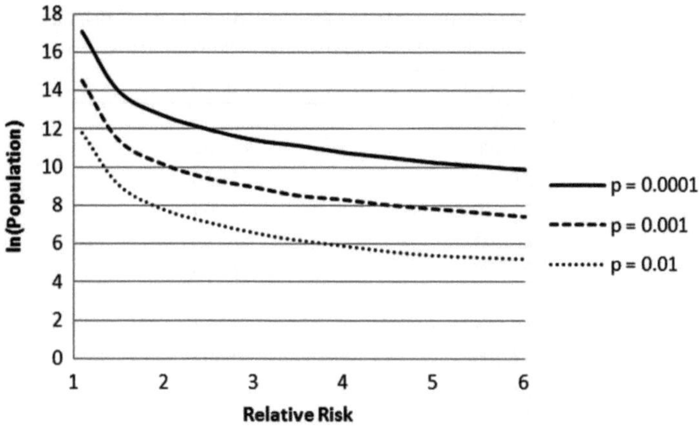

Fig. 12.3 The minimum population size needed (on a logarithmic scale) to ensure $1 - \beta \geq .9$ for different values of the underlying rate p of an adverse event. Values are found using a normal approximation with $\alpha = 0.001$

Whether a 100-million-member system will be powered to detect risk increases is in addition a function of the prevalence of the disease it treats and the market penetration of the drug. As an example, it is estimated that about 10,000 people took pemoline over the 30 years it was on the market. A system that is based on the records of 100 million people (approximately one-third of the US population) would have collected data on approximately 3,333 patients over the 30 years. With all the **major** simplifications associated with a "back of the envelope" calculation, and no sequential testing corrections, if the risk increase was 25-fold, the power would have reached 90% in year 15 if tested at a 0.05 significance level, compared to year 25 if tested at the 0.001 level. If the risk increase was in fact only tenfold, the power would not have reached 90% during the 30 years. Figure 12.3 shows the minimum population (on a logarithmic scale) needed for a simple one-signal surveillance system to have 90% power as a function of the underlying rate and risk increase. The corresponding numerical values are found in Table 12.2. As expected, if the relative risk increase is small, a large population is needed to detect the effect, and when the underlying rate of the adverse event is low, again a larger population is needed.

12.4.2 Setting the Surveillance Parameters

Assuming the system is suitably powered, the surveillance parameters need to be set, balancing the trade-off between false positive and the time to detection of true signals. For the purpose of simplicity of the discussion we will consider a single adverse event and a one-time surveillance test with a fixed population size. However the ideas presented below are extendable to sequential multiple hypothesis

Table 12.2 The population needed as a function of the underlying rate and risk increase, to ensure $1-\beta = 0.9$. Values are found using a normal approximation with $\alpha = 0.001$.

RR	$p = 0.0001$	$p = 0.001$	$p = 0.01$
0.1	25,719,653	1,977,950	135,103
0.5	1,152,300	88,504	8,844
1	321,374	25,030	2,444
1.5	156,010	12,005	1,243
2	88,705	7,720	731
2.5	66,190	4,950	493
3	46,285	4,035	371
3.5	35,885	3,054	276
4	27,500	2,505	224
4.5	22,795	2,054	203
5	18,848	1,676	186

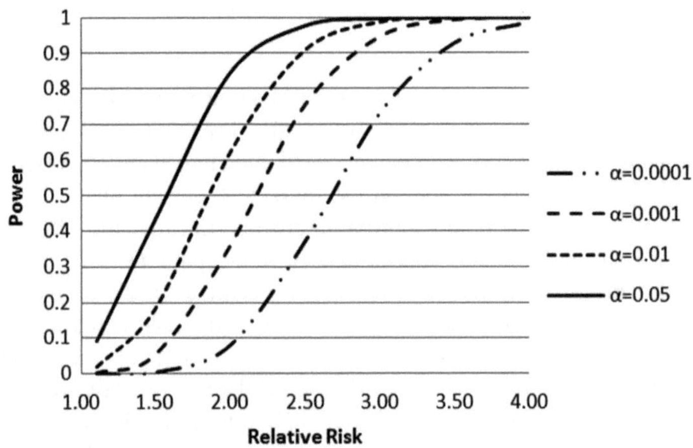

Fig. 12.4 The trade-off curves of α and β in a simple one-hypothesis setting. The population is set at 10,000 and the underlying rate of the adverse event at $p = 0.001$. Critical values are calculated based on a poisson approximation

systems. We will specify two approaches to determining the right settings: a tolerance approach and a more complex optimization approach.

The surveillance tolerance can be specified in two different ways—a maximum tolerance on the false positive probability or a minimum power required for a signal of certain size. An improvement over specifying either the tolerance for false positives α or the power $1 - \beta$ is to consider the trade-off in a more flexible manner. Analyzing trade-off curves as shown in Fig. 12.4 can help the decision maker visualize the implicit trade-off being made when α or $1 - \beta$ are specified. As expected, Fig. 12.4 shows that when the risk increase is very low, the power is low independent of the value of α. In a similar manner, when the risk increase is very high, the power is high, again independent of α. These scenarios represent very hard and very easy surveillance problems, respectively. However for intermediate risk, the selection of α can be critical for the ability to detect true signals.

Rather than specifying a certain maximum tolerance for false positive rates or minimum requirement on the power, a cost minimizing approach minimizes the overall expected cost of the surveillance, by selecting the appropriate critical value R_L. Let c^I be the cost associated with a false positive signal for the adverse event, and let $c^{II}(R)$ be the cost associated with missing a true signal of relative risk increase R, which is strictly increasing in R. These costs will be dependent on the severity of the adverse event and the market penetration of the drug. Then the objective function that minimizes the overall cost of the surveillance is

$$\min_{R_L} c^I P(R > R_L|H_0)P(H_0 \text{is true}) + \mathrm{c}^{\mathrm{II}}(\mathrm{R})\mathrm{P}(\mathrm{R} \leq \mathrm{R_L}|\mathrm{H_1}(\mathrm{R}))\mathrm{P}(\mathrm{H_1} \text{is true}).$$

In order to solve for the right risk level R_L, some assumption must be made about the probability of the null hypothesis being true as well as the distribution of R under the alternative as discussed above. If a pdf for the distribution of R is available, we can integrate the objective over all possible values of R. If such a pdf is unavailable or unattainable, a sensitivity analysis of the surveillance settings as a function of R can provide the surveillance designer some insights into good parameter settings.

In some cases there may be no acceptable parameter settings and no acceptable combination of the power and the false alarm rate. In other cases, detecting signals faster or lowering the false alarm rate can significantly improve the surveillance characteristics. One parameter is under the designer control, the population size. In order to achieve an improvement in the system characteristics, it may be possible to collect additional data, usually at a cost. The optimization problem above assumed a fixed population size but can be extended making the population size a decision variable.

What if the surveillance system gets it wrong? What does this trade-off balance boil down to? Either it withdraws a helpful vaccine/drug leaving populations exposed to a disease or members without a helpful treatment or it leaves a harmful vaccine/drug on the market, potentially leading to adverse events as severe as death. Trade-off considerations seem to have largely been overlooked. As the FDA moves to a large-scale surveillance systems, the costs and benefits need to be weighted appropriately and taken into consideration when running a multidrug multi-hypothesis drug surveillance system.

12.4.3 Adding a Dose of Reality

In traditional surveillance design it is assumed that there is just one source of false positives: an unlucky sample. In reality, an unlucky sample may be the least likely source of false positives. Others may include inaccurate background rates or inappropriate comparison groups, changes in coding behavior that have not been accounted for, coding errors in data [71], and data variability not accounted for in the statistical model, for example, due to members' short data duration [5]. At the same time, these causes may also result in "undersignaling." That is, inaccurate background rates can just as easily cause a surveillance system to miss a signal as raise a false alarm. To overcome these external sources of errors, the FDA has broken the surveillance process into three steps: hypothesis generation, signal verification, and hypothesis confirmation [2]. (Similar steps are imposed in vaccine surveillance [71].) Signal evaluation may include data verification, analysis of descriptive statistic, confounding control, and chart review.

As a result, the false-positive rate is not simply a function of statistical control but rather a function of the system design. The question of cost minimization is therefore more complicated than previously implied. A two (or three-)-step system design needs to be modeled and the tradeoff and costs associated with false alarms reaching each stage of the system and delay of signal remains to be modeled and analyzed. Refinements are needed to the methodologies, such as baseline definitions and population selection. Furthermore, to the authors knowledge, the potential issue of undersignaling resulting from the external sources of errors discussed above remains to be addressed.

12.5 Special Topics in Drug Surveillance

12.5.1 Optimizing the Hypothesis Testing

In the majority of studies it is assumed that adverse events are defined beforehand, and the surveillance monitors only a limited number of adverse events. A full-scale drug surveillance system, which would cast a wide net and monitor all possible events, increases the importance of accounting for multiple hypothesis testing.

In [22], an approach is presented to dynamically define the hypotheses to test as surveillance progresses, in order to minimize the power loss due to multiple hypothesis testing. The study considers periodic sequential surveillance. It controls the family-wise Type I error rate α across all test performed. This requires controlling across two dimensions—across the tests performed simultaneously during a single period and across the time periods of the surveillance. At each interim test the method analyzes the cumulative number of times each ICD-9-CM diagnosis has occurred in both the treatment and control groups. As with other sequential methods [14], the duration of the surveillance is specified in advance.

The approach takes advantage of the hierarchical structure of the ICD-9-CM codes and relies on two observations. First, tests for adverse events need not be conducted at the leaves (i.e., the three-digit codes). Rather, observed events can be pooled and tests conducted for effects on whole categories or subcategories. Second, the same set of tests need not be performed at each time period during surveillance nor need each test be conducted with the same probability of Type I error.

The goal is to optimize which hypotheses are tested, at which significance levels, and at each point in time. The question is, what is the right objective for the optimization? A reasonable objective could be to minimize the expected number of missed detections, alternatively, minimizing the probability of no detection or minimizing the time until detection.

Determining which tests to perform and at which significance levels in order to minimize the expected number of missed detections can be formulated as a mixed integer linear optimization problem. Estimates of the power curves for each possible hypothesis test are required, so the entire data set is partitioned, with a fraction used to estimate the power curves and the remainder used for the hypothesis tests.

Simulation results suggest that this method can be used to detect an increased risk of adverse events that are not specified in advance up to twice as quickly as controlling the Type I error rate using the Bonferroni approach and performing every test every period. Issues of initialization of the algorithm, variations of the objective, and heuristics to speed-up solution times are also discussed in [22].

The idea of taking advantage of tree structures is also explored in [36]. The authors demonstrate the use of a scan statistic [34, 46, 47] to understand the relative risks of different occupations, where similar occupations are grouped near each other in a tree structure. They propose applying the same approach to drug safety surveillance, either by grouping similar drugs together or grouping similar adverse events together. Berry and Berry [4] apply a Bayesian mixture model to detect adverse events grouped in a body-system-based hierarchy. Their study is based on clinical trials data and so does not take into account the temporal aspect of drug surveillance, but it has promise for being adapted to do so.

12.5.2 Long-Term Toxicity Effects of Drugs

For many chronic diseases, patients take drugs over years and perhaps decades. In addition, as drugs come off patents and cheaper generics become available, administering drugs as a preventive measure to large populations may not just be cost efficient, it may be cost saving, as shown with a recent cost-effectiveness study of lipid lowering strategies [51]. Given that most drug studies are short in duration (with some exceptions [25, 56, 59]), one could argue that the long-term effects of drugs are understudied. Two main challenges face the study of long-term effects of drugs: (a) data and (b) a methodology gap.

Claims data is by its nature short term. The average turnover in claims data has been observed to be about 14% per year, which is reflected by short durations of individual's data in the databases. Therefore, when the goal is to monitor large populations for extended period of time, either very large claim databases are needed (so that the subpopulation with long histories is large enough) or data from providers that provide continuous care are needed. One of such provider is Medicare, but Medicare data comes with its own challenges: an elderly population and heavy disease burden that make confounding control a difficult task. A third option is data from other countries with a single payer system, such as Canada and many European countries.

Traditionally, long-term drug studies are clinical trials that compare outcomes of a treatment group to outcome of a comparison group (a cohort taking a placebo) establishing long-term efficacy (examples include [12, 25, 53, 69]). There is an inherent ethical problem to conducting long-term safety monitoring of drugs with clinical trials. Once efficacy and baseline safety have been established, refusing half the study population the drug (those taking the placebo) for years is hard to justify. The method of virtual twins [67] has been proposed as a way to extend the duration of clinical trials. The method extends the follow-up beyond the initial trial period of the treatment arm, and compares the outcomes with estimates, based on the control arm outcomes during the initial trial period. The challenge of a large enough population still remains, as most clinical trials are not powered to detect rare events.

The literature on long-term safety of medical devices and medical interventions is related to the study of long-term effects of drugs. As an example, there is an extensive body of research on the safety of different medical devices and/or procedures for cardiac interventions (examples include [23, 37]). The analysis is closely related to that of long-term clinical trials. The studies apply methods such as Cox–Regression and Kaplan–Meier estimation and utilize statistical ideas such as hazard rates to estimate cumulative event rates. However, long-term effects of drugs differ from medical devices in that the exposure to the medical device is a one-time event while the exposure to drugs are cumulative over time, and often the toxicity is generally assumed to be increasing with increasing exposure.

The appropriate methodology for the study of long-term effects of drugs depends on how toxicity behaves. If it is assumed that exposure to a drug increases the risk of an adverse event by a fixed amount throughout a member's exposure to the drug, then traditional treatment/control design can be utilized to estimate the effects. Some of the challenges to this design are a selection of "large enough" long-term control groups and the estimation of appropriate baselines over extended periods of time.

If, on the other hand, toxicity increases with extended exposure, a self-control design may be appropriate. A self-control design compares outcomes in two succeeding periods, analyzing the treatment population only. In particular, a study of the long-term effects of statins [10] on the liver and kidneys compares the number of members that experience a particular event for the first time in the first period to the number of members that experience the same event for the first time in a follow-up period (i.e., the study compares the incidence of chronic liver and kidney conditions). A benefit from this study design is that many chronic conditions require multiple visits of a patient for an extended period of time, and therefore an "adverse event" is not a one-time interaction with the health-care system but rather consists of multiple episodes as discussed in Sect. 12.3.1. Some of the open research challenges that remain for self-control studies are extensions to all adverse events and accurately accounting for age effects, since over an extended period of time, the population gets older—and therefore the disease burden increases without any toxicity effect.

12.6 Conclusions and Policy Implications

12.6.1 Towards 100 Million Lives

Active drug and vaccine drug surveillance systems can provide public policy makers with rapid answers when questions arise, as well as automatically detect unknown excess risks of adverse events. Due to the seriousness of both false positives and false negatives, i.e., withdrawing a safe drug and leaving a harmful drug on the market, serious consideration needs to be paid to the surveillance trade-offs. This aspect of the drug surveillance becomes even more important when a system starts monitoring not only multiple events but multiple drugs. Manually decreasing the testing significance of individual hypotheses leaves potential power on the table, ignores prioritization between signals and/or drugs, and can result in an overwhelming rate of false positives.

As previously discussed, depending on the background rate and the expected increase in the rate of adverse events, different statistical methods are appropriate. With very rare events, static testing may outperform sequential designs. In addition, active drug surveillance design has focused on the discovery of unknown signals. However, there are also "common" side effects associated with drugs. The rates of these are estimated in clinical trials. The population in clinical trials is often hand selected and may therefore not reflect the experience of the average patient. In fact the general population often differs in age, comorbidities, and coprescriptions. Active drug surveillance can be further developed to monitor side effect rates of more common events in the general patient population.

Active surveillance studies have focused on diagnosis-specific adverse events. One should not forgo procedure coding, as procedures can be important indicators of toxicity and/or adverse events. A visit to the ER for a bone fracture can be a sign of dizziness or bone fragility; certain lab tests such as hepatic function panels can signal worries about deteriorating liver health—prior to an actual diagnosis being recorded. Currently, procedure codes are under utilized for drug surveillance.

Drugs and vaccines are of a global concern. As the FDA moves towards larger databases, the opportunity to detect rarer events increases as the potential statistical power of the surveillance increases. The FDA is also engaged in international collaborations, such as the World Health Organization's pilot study of the risk of Guillain–Barré Syndrome and the H1N1 influenza vaccination. With new drugs, the population taking them is initially small. With new seasonal vaccines (such as the H1N1), the time to signal is critical as vaccines are administered in a short period of time. In these cases, international collaboration may be especially valuable as it can easily double the sample size.

It is clear that in order for 100-million-member system to succeed, more methodological development and systems thinking are needed. Especially if the goal is not simply to monitor prespecified adverse events for a limited number of drugs, but rather take advantage of the range of opportunities for improving drug and vaccine safety that the system can bring. Building flexibility into the Sentinel system, to have the option of adjusting and expanding the surveillance as new questions get asked and new concern raised, has potentially enormous public benefit.

12.6.2 Unanswered Challenges

Even with 100 million lives, the challenge of monitoring subpopulations is still unanswered. That is, how do we monitor the elderly, those with preexisting heart conditions, or those with clinical depression? In many cases, these subpopulations are at greater risk for particular adverse events. As soon as the surveillance is focused on subpopulations, the sample size becomes a challenge, and the surveillance may not be adequately powered. In addition these sicker subpopulations make confounding control significantly harder and in general have greater variance in their coding.

Not all drugs are taken over an extensive period of time. In particular, a number of drugs are given in a hospital and/or treatment setting. A meta-analysis by Lazarou [40] suggests that adverse reactions to drugs killed approximately 100,000 hospital patients in 1994 in the USA and seriously harmed many more. For example, the anticoagulant warfarin is used primarily in hospitals to prevent blood clots from forming or growing larger. It carries a risk of bleeding which may be increased in patients on dialysis. How to monitor site-specific (drug given prior to dialysis vs. stroke prevention) drug use is an open research question. The use of electronic health records and innovative modeling may be the key to success.

Finally, related to the first challenge presented is the challenge of drug interactions. Drug interactions are not only hard to monitor because of smaller population size (if we assume 1% of the population are taking each drug, independently of each other, then the population on both is only 0.01%) but also because of difficult confounding control and high disease burden. Monitoring drug interactions is a unanswered challenge for modern data mining techniques.

12.6.3 Opportunities Up for Grabs

The chapter so far has focused on the surveillance for adverse events. In order to minimize the time to discovery of signals of increased risks, one-sided tests are used. But surveillance can also be used in the "opposite direction" to discover unknown *benefits* of drugs.

The fact that the Sentinel project will combine information on 100 million lives provides unprecedented opportunities for data exploration, and discovery of new medical knowledge. Medical information on 100 million lives can be mined, allowing for searches for unknown associations and identification of successful care patterns to improve quality of care and decrease health-care costs. The question is if regulatory barriers can be overcome and information security ensured.

12.6.4 Do No Harm

As a final thought, what is acceptable risk? The fact of the matter is that acceptable risk is different from one patient to the next and from one drug to the next. In particular there may be a patient population for whom the risk is warranted, given the known benefit. Although rofecoxib was associated with increased risk of heart attacks, stroke, and renal complications and therefore unacceptable as a general painkiller taken over extended periods of time, it was also popular with cancer patients (as is evident from cancer coding associated with patients taking rofecoxib in claims data). For an ill cancer patient, perhaps the long-term risk of heart attack is outweighed by the benefit. In fact, both American and Canadian health advisory boards voted shortly after the voluntary withdrawal to allow rofecoxib back on the market [21, 29].

References

1. 110th US Congress (2007) Food and drug administration amendments act. http://www.premierinc.com/safety/topics/pediatrics/downloads/FDA-Peds-Med-Device-Act-Title-3-2007.pdf. Accessed 10 June 2011
2. Ball R, Horne D, Izurieta H, Sutherland A, Walderhaug M, Hsu H (2011) Statistical, epidemiological, and risk-assessment approaches to evaluating safety of vaccines throughout the life cycle at the food and drug administration. Pediatrics 127(Suppl 1):S31–S38
3. Benjamini Y, Hochberg Y (1995) Controlling the false discovery rate: A practical and powerful approach to multiple testing. J Roy Stat Soc B Met 57(1):289–300
4. Berry SM, Berry DA (2004) Accounting for multiplicities in assessing drug safety: A three-level hierarchical mixture model. Biometrics 60(2):418–426
5. Bertsimas D, Bjarnadottir MV, Kane MA Real-time post-marketing drug surveillance. Working paper
6. Bertsimas D, Bjarnadottir MV, Kane MA, Kryder JC, Panday R, Vempala S, Wang G (2008) Algorithmic prediction of health-care costs. Oper Res 56:1382–1392
7. Bishop CE, Ryan AM, Gilden DM, Kubisiak J, Thomas CP (2009) Effect of an expenditure cap on low-income seniors drug use and spending in a state pharmacy assistance program. Health Serv Res 44:1010–1028
8. Bjarnadottir MV, Guan Y Follow the money: Real-time drug surveillance by monitoring costs in health care claims data. Workingpaper
9. Bjarnadottir MV, Guan Y (2010) Statistical tradeoff in real-time post-marketing drug surveillance. In: Proceedings of the 5th informs workshop on data mining and health informatics, 2010
10. Bjarnadottir MV, Kane MA, Ghimire S Long-term effects of drugs: A case study of statins. Working paper
11. Bjarnadottir MV, Zenios S Analytics of drug surveillance systems. Working paper

12. Black DM, Schwartz AV, Ensrud KE, Cauley JA, Levis S, Quandt SA, Satterfield S, Wallace RB, Bauer DC, Palermo L, Wehren LE, Lombardi A, Santora AC, Cummings SR, FLEX Research Group (2006) Effects of continuing or stopping alendronate after 5 years of treatment: The fracture intervention trial long-term extension (flex): A randomized trial. J Am Med Assoc 296(24):2927–2938
13. Braun MM (2008) Toward better vaccine safety data and safer vaccination. Pediatrics 121(3):625–626
14. Brown JS, Kulldorff M, Chan KA, Davis RL, Graham D, Pettus PT, Andrade SE, Raebel MA, Herrinton L, Roblin D, Boudreau D, Smith D, Gurwitz JH, Gunter MJ, Platt R (2007) Early detection of adverse drug events within population-based health networks: Application of sequential testing methods. Pharmacoepidemiol Drug Saf 16(12):1275–1284
15. Brown JS, Kulldorff M, Petronis KR, Reynolds R, Chan KA, Davis RL, Graham D, Andrade SE, Raebel MA, Herrinton L, Roblin D, Boudreau D, Smith D, Gurwitz JH, Gunter MJ, Platt R (2009) Early adverse drug event signal detection within population-based health networks using sequential methods: Key methodologic considerations. Pharmacoepidemiol Drug Saf 18(3):226–234
16. Brown JS, Velentgas P, Kulldorff M, Moore KM, Duddy A, Platt R (2008) Using electronic health data for influenza vaccine safety: New methodologies and considerations. In: Implementation of rapic cycle analysis for detection of potential excess risk of adverse events following influenza vaccination: A policy maker's guide. Web. Accessed 13 June 2011
17. Centers for Medicare and Medicaid Services (2012) Icd-10: 2012 icd-10-cm and gems. http://www.cms.gov/ICD10/11b14_2012_ICD10CM_and_GEMs.asp. Accessed 3 Jan 2012
18. Centers for Medicare and Medicaid Services (2012) Icd-10: Overview. http://www.cms.gov/ICD10/. Accessed 3 Jan 2012
19. Centers for Medicare and Medicaid Services (2012) Icd-9 provider and diagnostic codes. http://www.cms.gov/ICD9ProviderDiagnosticCodes/. Accessed 3 Jan 2012
20. Chan KA, Truman A, Gurwitz JH, Hurley JS, Martinson B, Platt R, Everhart JE, Moseley RH, Terrault N, Ackerson L, Selby JV (2003) A cohort study of the incidence of serious acute liver injury in diabetic patients treated with hypoglycemic agents. Arch Intern Med 163(6):728–734
21. CNN (2005) Celebrex, bextra, vioxx can stay: Fda panel says the painkillers should stay on the market despite risks; vioxx draws a split vote. http://money.cnn.com/2005/02/18/news/fortune500/merck_drugs/. Accessed 12 June 2011
22. Czerwinski D (2008) Quality of care and drug surveillance: A data-driven perspective. PhD thesis, Massachusetts Institute of Technology
23. Daemen J, Boersma E, Flather M, Booth J, Stables R, Rodriguez A, Rodriguez-Granillo G, Hueb WA, Lemos PA, Serruys PW (2008) Long-term safety and efficacy of percutaneous coronary intervention with stenting and coronary artery bypass surgery for multivessel coronary artery disease: A meta-analysis with 5-year patient-level data from the arts, eraci-ii, mass-ii, and sos trials. Circulation 118(11):1146–1154
24. Dragomir A, Ct R, Roy L, Blais L, Lalonde L, Brard A, Perreault S (2010) Impact of adherence to antihypertensive agents on clinical outcomes and hospitalization costs. Med Care 48:418–425
25. Glassman AH, Bigger JT, Gaffney M (2009) Psychiatric characteristics associated with long-term mortality among 361 patients having an acute coronary syndrome and major depression: seven-year follow-up of sadhart participants. Arch Gen Psychiatry 66(9):1022–1029
26. Graham DJ, Campen D, Hui R, Spence M, Cheetham C, Levy G, Shoor S, Ray WA (2005) Risk of acute myocardial infarction and sudden cardiac death in patients treated with cyclo-oxygenase 2 selective and non-selective non-steroidal anti-inflammatory drugs: Nested case-control study. The Lancet 365:475–481
27. Graham DJ, Ouellet-Hellstrom R, MaCurdy TE, Ali F, Sholley C, Worrall C, Kelman JA (2010) Risk of acute myocardial infarction, stroke, heart failure, and death in elderly medicare patients treated with rosiglitazone or pioglitazone. J Am Med Assoc 304(4):411–418

28. Hazlehurst B, Naleway A, Mullooly J (2009) Detecting possible vaccine adverse events in clinical notes of the electronic medical record. Vaccine 27(14):2077–2083
29. Health Canada (2005) Summary: Report of the expert advisory panel on the safety of cox-2 selective non-steroidal anti-inflammatory drugs (nsaids). http://www.hc-sc.gc.ca/dhp-mps/alt_formats/hpfb-dgpsa/pdf/prodpharma/sap_summary_gcs_sommaire_cox2-eng.pdf. Accessed 13 June 2011
30. Hochberg Y (1988) A sharper bonferroni procedure for multiple tests of significance. Biometrika 75:800–802
31. Hocine MN, Musonda P, Andrews NJ, Farrington CP (2009) Sequential case series analysis for pharmacovigilance. J Roy Stat Soc A (Sta) 172(1):213–236
32. Jackevicius CA, Mamdani M, Tu JV (2002) Adherence with statin therapy in elderly patients with and without acute coronary syndromes. J Am Med Assoc 288(4):462–467
33. Kashner TM (1998) Agreement between administrative files and written medical records: A case of the department of veterans affairs. Med Care 36:1324–1336
34. Kulldorff M (1997) A spatial scan statistic. Commun Stat Theor 26(6):1481–1496
35. Kulldorff M, Davis RL, Kolczak M, Lewis E, Plattl TLR (2011) A maximized sequential probability ratio test for drug and vaccine safety surveillance. Sequential Anal 30:58–78
36. Kulldorff M, Fang Z, Walsh SJ (2003) A tree-based scan statistic for database disease surveillance. Biometrics 59(2):323–331
37. Lagerqvist B, James SK, Stenestrand U, Lindbck J, Nilsson T, Wallentin L, SCAAR Study Group (2007) Long-term outcomes with drug-eluting stents versus bare-metal stents in sweden. New Engl J Med 356(10):1009–1019
38. Lanza LL, Walker AM, Bortnichak EA, Gause DO, Dreyer NA (1995) Incidence of symptomatic liver function abnormalities in a cohort of nsaid users. Pharmacoepidemiol Drug Saf 4:231–237
39. Lawthers AG, McCarthy EP, Davis RB, Peterson LE, Palmer RH, Iezzoni LI (2000) Identification of in-hospital complications from claims data. is it valid? Med Care 38(8):785–795
40. Lazarou J, Pomeranz BH, Corey PN (1998) Incidence of adverse drug reactions in hospitalized patients: A meta-analysis of prospective studies. J Am Med Assoc 279(15):1200–1205
41. Li L, Kulldorff M (2010) A conditional maximized sequential probability ratio test for pharmacovigilance. Stat Med 29(2):284–295
42. Lieu TA, Kulldorff M, Davis RL, Lewis EM, Weintraub E, Yih K, Yin R, Brown JS, Platt R, for the Vaccine Safety Datalink Rapid Cycle Analysis Team (2007) Real-time vaccine safety surveillance for the early detection of adverse events. Med Care 45(10 Suppl 2):S89–S95
43. Little RJ, Rubin DB (2000) Causal effects in clinical and epidemiological studies via potential outcomes: Concepts and analytical approaches. Annu Rev Publ Health 21:121–145
44. Mitchell JB, Ballard DJ, Whisnant JP, Ammering CJ, Matchar DB, Samsa GP (1996) Using physician claims to identify postoperative complications of carotid endarterectomy. Health Serv Res 31:141–152
45. Musonda P, Hocine MN, Andrews NJ, Tubert-Bitter P, Farrington CP (2008) Monitoring vaccine safety using case series cumulative sum charts. Vaccine 26(42):5358–5367
46. Naus JI (1965) Clustering of random points in two dimensions. Biometrika 52(1/2):263–267
47. Naus JI (1965) The distribution of the size of the maximum cluster of points on a line. J Am Med Assoc 60(310): 532–538
48. Nissen SE, Wolski K (2010) Rosiglitazone revisited: An updated meta-analysis of risk for myocardial infarction and cardiovascular mortality. Arch Intern Med 170(14):1191–1201
49. Okunseri C, Szabo A, Jackson S, Pajewski NM, Garcia RI (2009) Increased childrens access to fluoride varnish treatment by involving medical care providers: Effect of a medicaid policy change. Health Serv Res 44:1144–1156
50. Piecoro LT, Potoski M, Talbert JC, Doherty DE (2002) Asthma prevalence, cost, and adherence with expert guidelines on the utilization of health care services and costs in a state medicaid population. Health Serv Res 36:357–371

51. Pletcher MJ, Lazar L, Bibbins-Domingo K, Moran A, Rodondi N, Coxson P, Lightwood J, Williams L, Goldman L (2011) Comparing impact and cost-effectiveness of primary prevention strategies for lipid-lowering. Ann Intern Med 150:243–254
52. Postila V, Kilpi T (2004) Use of vaccine surveillance data in the evaluation of safety of vaccines. Vaccine 22(15–16):2076–2079
53. Reginster J-Y, Felsenberg D, Boonen S, Diez-Perez A, Rizzoli R, Brandi M-L, Spector TD, Brixen K, Goemaere S, Cormier C, Balogh A, Delmas PD, Meunier PJ (2008) Effects of long-term strontium ranelate treatment on the risk of nonvertebral and vertebral fractures in postmenopausal osteoporosis: Results of a five-year, randomized, placebo-controlled trial. Arthritis Rheum 58(6):1687–1695
54. Rosenbaum PR, Rubin DB (1983) The central role of the propensity score in observational studies for causal effects. Biometrika 70(1):41–55
55. Rosenbaum PR, Rubin DB (1985) Constructing a control group using multivariate matched sampling methods that incorporate the propensity score. The Am Stat 39:33–38
56. Scandinavian Simvastatin Survival Study Group (1994) Randomised trial of cholesterol lowering in 4444 patients with coronary heart disease: The scandinavian simvastatin survival study (4s). The Lancet 344:1383–1389
57. Storey JD (2002) A direct approach to false discovery rates. J Roy Stat Soc B (Stat Met) 64(3):479–498
58. Storey JD (2003) The positive false discovery rate: A bayesian interpretation and the q-value. The Ann Stat 31(6):2013–2035
59. Strandberg TE, Pyrl K, Cook TJ, Wilhelmsen L, Faergeman O, Thorgeirsson G, Pedersen TR, Kjekshus J, S Group (2004) Mortality and incidence of cancer during 10-year follow-up of the scandinavian simvastatin survival study (4s). Lancet 364(9436):771–777
60. R. Tamblyn, R. Laprise, J. A. Hanley, M. Abrahamowicz, S. Scott, N. Mayo, J. Hurley, R. Grad, E. Latimer, R. Perreault, P. McLeod, A. Huang, P. Larochelle, and L. Mallet (2001) Adverse events associated with prescription drug cost-sharing among poor and elderly persons. J Am Med Assoc 285(4):421–429
61. The American Health Data Institute (2011) Icd-9 outline. http://www.ahdi.com/ICD9.pdf. Accessed 27 July 2011
62. Thom T, Haase N, Rosamond W, Howard VJ, Rumsfeld J, Manolio T, Zheng Z-J, Flegal K, O'Donnell C, Kittner S, Lloyd-Jones D, Goff DC, Hong Y, Adams R, Friday G, Furie K, Gorelick P, Kissela B, Marler J, Meigs J, Roger V, Sidney S, Sorlie P, Steinberger J, Wasserthiel-Smoller S, Wilson M, Wolf P, American Heart Association Statistics Committee, Stroke Statistics Subcommittee (2006) Heart disease and stroke statistics–2006 update: A report from the american heart association statistics committee and stroke statistics subcommittee. Circulation 113(6):e85–151
63. US Department of health and Human Services, the U.S. Food and Drug Administration (2010) The sentinel initiative. an update on fda's progress in building a national electronic system for monitoring the postmarket safety of fda-approved drugs and other medical products. http://www.fda.gov/downloads/Safety/FDAsSentinelInitiative/UCM233360.pdf. Accessed 12 June 2011
64. US Food and Drug Administration (2011) Actos-prescribing information. http://www.accessdata.fda.gov/drugsatfda_docs/label/2007/021073s031lbl.pdf. Accessed 15 June 2011
65. US Food and Drug Administration (2010) The sentinel initiative: National strategy for monitoring medical product safety. http://www.fda.gov/Safety/FDAsSentinelInitiative/default.htm. Accessed 27 May 2011
66. US Food and Drug Administration (2005) Alert for healthcare professionals pemoline tablets and chewable tablets (marketed as cylert). http://www.fda.gov/downloads/Drugs/DrugSafety/PostmarketDrugSafetyInformationforPatientsandProviders/ucm126462.pdf. Accessed 14 June 2011

67. Vittinghoff E, McCulloch CE, Woo C, Cummings SR (2010) Estimating long-term effects of treatment from placebo-controlled trials with an extension period, using virtual twins. Stat Med 29:1127–1136
68. Wald A (1945) Sequential tests of statistical hypotheses. The Ann Math Stat 16:117–186
69. Weinstein RS, Roberson PK, Manolagas SC (2009) Giant osteoclast formation and long-term oral bisphosphonate therapy. N Engl J Med 360(1):53–62
70. Wysowski DK, Swartz L (2005) Adverse drug event surveillance and drug withdrawals in the united states, 1969–2002: The importance of reporting suspected reactions. Arch Intern Med 165(12):1363–1369
71. Yih WK, Kulldorff M, Fireman BH, Shui IM, Lewis EM, Klein NP, Baggs J, Weintraub ES, Belongia EA, Naleway A, Gee J, Platt R, Lieu TA (2011) Active surveillance for adverse events: The experience of the vaccine safety datalink project. Pediatrics 127:S54–S64
72. Zhou W, Pool V, Iskander JK, English-Bullard R, Ball R, Wise RP, Haber P, Pless RP, Mootrey G, Ellenberg SS, Braun MM, Chen RT (2003) Surveillance for safety after immunization: Vaccine adverse event reporting system (vaers)–united states, 1991–2001. MMWR Surveill Summ 52(1):1–24

Chapter 13
Application of Operations Research to Funding Decisions for Treatments with Rare Disease

Doug Coyle, Chaim M. Bell, Joe T.R. Clarke, Gerald Evans, Anita Gadhok, Janet Martin, Mona Sabharwal, and Eric Winquist

Abstract In this chapter, the focus is on the application of decision analytic tools to assist in reimbursement decisions related to drugs for rare diseases. Focus is on the evaluative framework developed by the Ontario Ministry of Health's Drugs for Rare Diseases Working Group. The chapter describes the framework and illustrates the role of decision analytic methods through the application of the framework to idursulfase treatment of Hunter disease, an enzyme deficiency syndrome. The chapter highlights the development of a Markov model designed to mirror

D. Coyle (✉)
Department of Epidemiology and Community Medicine, University of Ottawa, Ottawa, ON, Canada
e-mail: dcoyle@uottawa.ca

C.M. Bell
Keenan Research Centre, Li Ka Shing Knowledge Institute, St. Michael's Hospital, Toronto, ON, Canada

Departments of Medicine and Health Policy Management and Evaluation, University of Toronto, Toronto, ON, Canada

J.T.R. Clarke
Hospital for Sick Children, Toronto, ON, Canada

Centre Hospitalier Universitaire, Sherbrooke, QC, Canada

G. Evans
Kingston General Hospital and School of Medicine, Queen's University, Kingston, ON, Canada

A. Gadhok • M. Sabharwal
Ontario Public Drug Programs, Ontario Ministry of Health and Long-term Care, Toronto, ON, Canada

J. Martin • E. Winquist
London Health Sciences Centre and Schulich School of Medicine & Dentistry, University of Western Ontario, London, ON, Canada

G.S. Zaric (ed.), *Operations Research and Health Care Policy*, International Series in Operations Research & Management Science 190,
DOI 10.1007/978-1-4614-6507-2_13,

the natural disease history and to simulate the possible benefits of treatment. This process led to the Ministry of Health developing funding recommendations for the treatment of Hunter disease.

13.1 Introduction

Economic evaluation using decision analytic modeling plays a key role in funding decisions for new technologies in many countries. Such analyses often require development of disease models, combining data on the natural history or epidemiology of disease with data on the predicted effect treatment will have on the course of the disease. Models often take the form of Markov models which represent the progression of a cohort of individuals by estimating the proportion of the cohort in each of a set of mutually exclusive health [1, 2] The health states reflect the natural history of the disease and the effect of interventions. The cohort moves between health states over time based on a series of transition probabilities obtained from the available clinical literature. Markov models are by necessity a simplification of the real world, capturing the essential relationships between interventions and disease progression.

When models incorporate both cost and utility weights, which are applied to the health states within the model, the cost effectiveness of alternate interventions can be assessed [2]. This information is frequently used to facilitate policy decisions relating to the funding of interventions [3]. However, there are difficulties in applying this framework to rare diseases [4].

Long term large sample observational studies are recognized as the best source of data for modeling the course of disease [5]. Typically, rare diseases by their nature have a paucity of information about the natural history of the disease. Combined with greater heterogeneity of disease, this leads to practical problems in developing natural history models.

A further problem with applying this framework to rare diseases is the difficulty in conducting adequate studies of the effectiveness of new treatments. Often randomized controlled trials (RCTs), which are the gold standard methodology for assessing treatment efficacy, are not feasible for rare diseases given the inability to recruit a sufficiently large study sample. Although RCTs are primarily a means of assessing treatment efficacy, they are relevant inputs into economic models designed to assess treatment effectiveness and the absence of such data limits the feasibility of developing reasonable estimates of cost effectiveness. When an RCT is feasible there are two further limitations; the lack of validated measures of treatment response and the lack of a defined standard of care to which the new treatment is compared.

Finally, the nature of rare diseases has meant that the per-patient costs of new treatments have been much higher than standard therapies for other diseases; for example the costs of Soliris for paroxysmal nocturnal hemoglobinuria are estimated to be greater than CAN $500,000 per patient per year. Thus, the high acquisition costs of new treatments once on the market, given the low ratio of benefit to cost, usually precludes them from meeting conventional criteria for cost-effectiveness required by funders who are making decisions within limited set of resources.

It has been suggested that, given a limited budget available for health care, rare diseases should not be considered differently than other diseases, and therefore, the same framework can be applied with the result that treatments for rare diseases will be infrequently funded [4, 6, 7]. These arguments are based within the concept of utility maximization: that the purpose of health care funding is to maximize the benefit from health care regardless of the distribution of benefits.

Several authors have critiqued this view of "maximization," primarily focusing on the inter-related issues of equity concerns and pointing to studies demonstrating societal preferences for funding of rare disease treatments rather than "maximization" alone (social value) [8, 9]. Some organizations have promoted the argument that due to the rarity of disease; treatments for rare diseases should be funded regardless of their cost, effectiveness or cost effectiveness [10]. Alternatively, a more reasoned approach has been to call for alternative funding frameworks for treatments for rare diseases; although, no explicit framework has been suggested [4, 9, 11]

The chapter focuses on the use of decision analytic modeling within a framework adopted by the Ontario Ministry of Health and Long Term Care. The chapter starts with a brief discussion on the development of the framework and its structure. This is followed by a description of a disease which was considered under this framework—Hunter disease. This is then followed by the development of a decision analytic model of Hunter disease which was used to determine the potential impact of a newly available treatment which in turn facilitated a policy decision around the funding of this treatment. The chapter concludes with policy recommendations relating to the funding of new treatments for rare diseases.

13.2 Ontario Framework for Evaluating Drugs for Rare Diseases

In Ontario, the Committee to Evaluate Drugs (CED) makes recommendations for drug funding to the Executive Officer of Ontario Public Drug Programs considering recommendations from the Canadian Drug Expert Committee (CDEC formerly CEDAC) and through further review of the available clinical, safety, and cost-effectiveness data of relevance to the jurisdiction [12, 13]. The Executive Officer makes a funding decision as they are accountable for spending under the publicly funded drug programs in the province. Both the CED and CEDAC have consistently recommended against funding drugs for rare diseases as they failed to meet conventional criteria for evidence of effectiveness and cost-effectiveness applied to other drugs [4]. Given the consistency of such decisions, Ontario Public Drug Programs (OPDP) convened the Drugs for Rare Diseases (DRD) Working Group with the aim to develop a funding framework specifically for drugs for rare diseases.

A systematic framework was then drafted which consists of seven necessary steps that should be undertaken before decisions regarding funding can be made. The framework was presented to stakeholder groups representing patients, clinicians, and the pharmaceutical industry for comments.

Briefly, the seven steps of the DRD evaluation framework consist of the following:

1. Confirm the condition for treatment with the candidate drug is truly "rare": the DRD defines a rare disease as having an incidence of less than 1 in 100,000 live births—note that other definitions are used in other jurisdictions but often for reasons other than developing reimbursement mechanisms—for example in the USA, a citeria of 1 in 1,500 is used with respect to encouragement for research in rare diseases—not with respect to funding of treatments.
2. Understand the basic pathophysiology, natural history, and health effects of the condition under consideration.
3. Understand the potential value of the drug under consideration, given the available evidence.
4. Model the potential clinical effectiveness of the drug under consideration.
5. Evaluate the budget impact of funding the new drug and make a funding recommendation.
6. Review the application of the framework with disease experts and stakeholders.
7. Reassessment of the funding decision as further data comes available.

The framework was tested by the case study of idursulfase for Hunter disease. The following chapter provides details of this application with particular focus on step 4 which required the development of a decision analytic model to model the natural history of Hunter disease and the potential impact of treatment.

13.3 Application of Framework to Hunter Disease

13.3.1 Hunter Disease

Hunter disease (or mucopolysaccharidosis Type II) is an inherited disease. It is named after Charles Hunter—a Canadian/Scottish physician who first described patients with the inherent characteristics of the disease [14].

Hunter disease belongs to the family of lysosomal storage disorders. It is caused by deficiency of the activity of a specific lysosomal enzyme, iduronate 2-sulfatase (I2S), which leads to accumulation of glycosaminoglycans (GAG) which contribute to the signs and symptoms of the disorder [15].

Hunter disease primarily affects males—although rare cases do occur in females. The birth incidence of Hunter disease is estimated to be 1 in 170,000 live births [16]. Accumulation of GAG in the skin, bones, ligaments, joints, heart valves and brain with secondary fibrosis of periarticular tissues and heart valves lead to the signs and symptoms of disease [16–19]. Hunter disease is a degenerative disorder leading to complications related most importantly to the musculoskeletal, respiratory and cardiovascular systems. Hunter disease is typically differentiated as either Type A or Type B disease. Type A is characterized by an early-onset neurodegenerative course with death in the early to mid teens [19]. Type B is characterized by the absence of neurodegeneration, more variable clinical course, and survival, in some cases into mid adulthood [18].

Idursulfase is a synthetic version of I2S which has been approved as an enzyme replacement therapy (ERT) for Hunter disease. ERTs replace the deficient enzyme in patients but do not reverse preexisting irreversible complications arising from disease nor does it correct the underlying disorder. However, in theory if ERT works further progression of disease can be halted. A RCT of idursulfase has been conducted which has demonstrated biological evidence of activity through use of a composite outcome of both a 6 min walk test and forced vital capacity [20]. Idursulfase had previously not been recommended for funding by both CEDAC and CED [21, 22].

The DRD Working group was asked to consider idursulfase under the newly developed framework for evaluating drugs for rare diseases. Given the level of information available for Hunter disease and the evidence of potential effect of treatment, idursulfase passed the first three steps of the evaluative framework. The next section relates to step 4: modeling the potential effectiveness of treatment.

13.3.2 Modeling the Potential Effectiveness of Idursulfase

13.3.2.1 Development of the Markov Model

A Markov model representing the course of disease was developed with input from DRD working group and validation with external clinical experts. The epidemiology of the disease was formulated relying on available case series data, and informed expert opinion when necessary to fill in the gap in the limited evidence base which consists of a small number of case reports and case series and one recent small randomized controlled trial (i.e., 16–20). The model had 6-month cycle lengths and adopted a lifetime horizon with a maximum age at death for patients of 80 years. Once the original model was developed, it was subject to assessment of both face and content validity through consultation with two disease experts who were not involved in developing the original model.

The Markov model incorporates the two types of disease: Type A—progression of symptoms with neurodegeneration—and Type B—progression of symptoms without neurodegeneration. Thus, the progression can be classified as disease progression (modeling of disease progression without neurodegeneration) and neurodegeneration.

Disease progression was assumed to incorporate the following progression of symptoms: diagnosis to musculoskeletal (MSK) symptoms to respiratory symptoms

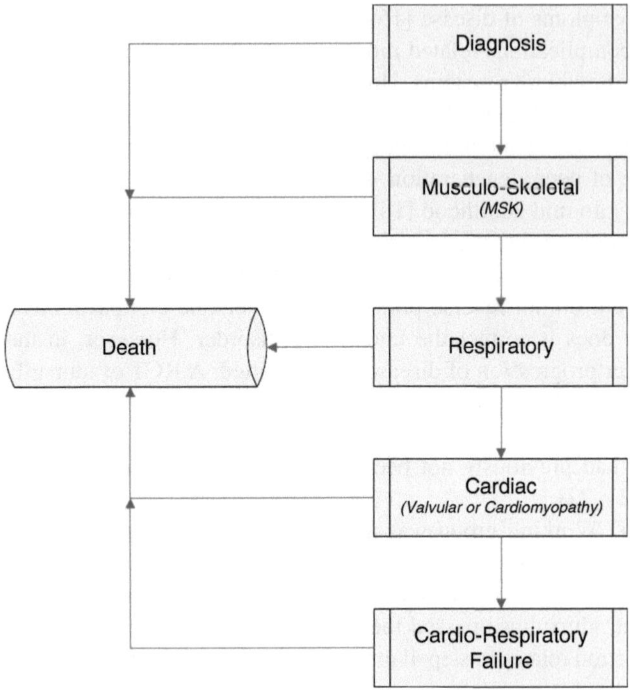

Fig. 13.1 Schematic representation of Markov model for Type B Hunter disease

to cardiovascular symptoms to cardiorespiratory failure. Figure 13.1 is a graphic representation of the disease progression for Hunter disease within the disease model. The health states are cumulative in the sense that it is assumed that patients would first develop MSK syndromes, then respiratory symptoms, and so on down the remaining possible health states based on transition probabilities.

The following summarizes the assumptions made with respect to disease progression:

- By age 3–4, 50 % of patients will develop MSK symptoms
- By age 10, 99 % of patients will develop MSK symptoms
- By age 6, 50 % of patients will develop respiratory symptoms
- By age 12, 80 % of patients will develop respiratory symptoms
- By age 20, 50 % of patients will develop cardiac symptoms
- By age 30, 90 % of patients will develop cardiac symptoms
- Within 5 years of developing cardiac problems, 50 % of patients will develop cardiorespiratory failure
- Within 10 years of developing cardiac problems, 99 % of patients will develop cardiorespiratory failure
- Patients with MSK symptoms will have the same probability of death as the male general population

- For those developing respiratory symptoms, 25 % will be dead by age 20
- For those developing cardiac problems, 25 % will be dead by age 25; for those developing cardiorespiratory failure the median survival will be 1 year.

Constant hazard rates were developed which allowed replication of the assumptions relating to incidence and prevalence listed above Neurodegeneration was derived from the same sources as physical symptoms and were depicted through three health states representing decline in neurocognitive functioning. Patients with Type A disease will therefore have a combination of both a neurodegenerative state and a disease progression state (Fig. 13.2). The first sign of neurodegeneration will be evidence of mild neurological complications (delayed progress). Within Type A patients, 50 % will develop mild complications by 2 years with 10 % of patients developing mild complications by age 6. Moderate neurological complications (Arrest) will develop in 50 % of Type A patients by age 3–5 and in 100 % before age 10. Severe neurological complications (Regression) will develop in 50 % of patients by age 6–8. Patients with mild neurological complications will have no additional mortality effect in addition to the mortality associated with their disease progression. For patients with moderate neurological complications, mortality will be 10 % by age 9 years. For patients with severe neurological complications, mortality will be 50 % by age 12 years.

With Hunter disease 2/3 of patients will have Type A disease. The nature of Type A disease means that although Hunter disease can be diagnosed early in life due to the physical symptoms of disease, the ability to discriminate between Type A and Type B is limited until age 6 when the existence of neurodegeneration becomes clear. Thus, Type B disease can not be confirmed until a patient is at least 6 years of age. This leads to a third category of patients: those for whom it is "too young to tell" whether they have Type B disease but no evidence currently suggests Type A disease. For this group the proportion which will eventually be diagnosed with Type A will decline with age.

A set of transition probabilities was determined which reproduces the data detailed above (Table 13.1). From this the average life expectancy of cohorts of Hunter disease patients based on their age and current health status can be estimated.

13.3.2.2 Projected Life Expectancy of Patients with Hunter Disease

Life expectancy will vary by a patient's age, current level of disease progression/ neurodegeneration and type of disease.

Figure 13.3 provides survival curves for two cohorts both aged 7 with respiratory symptoms—one cohort having Type A disease with moderate neurodegeneration and the other having Type B. The figure illustrates the substantive difference in prognosis between the two types with a median age at death for the Type A patient cohort of 7.5 and for the cohort of Type B patients of 22.5.

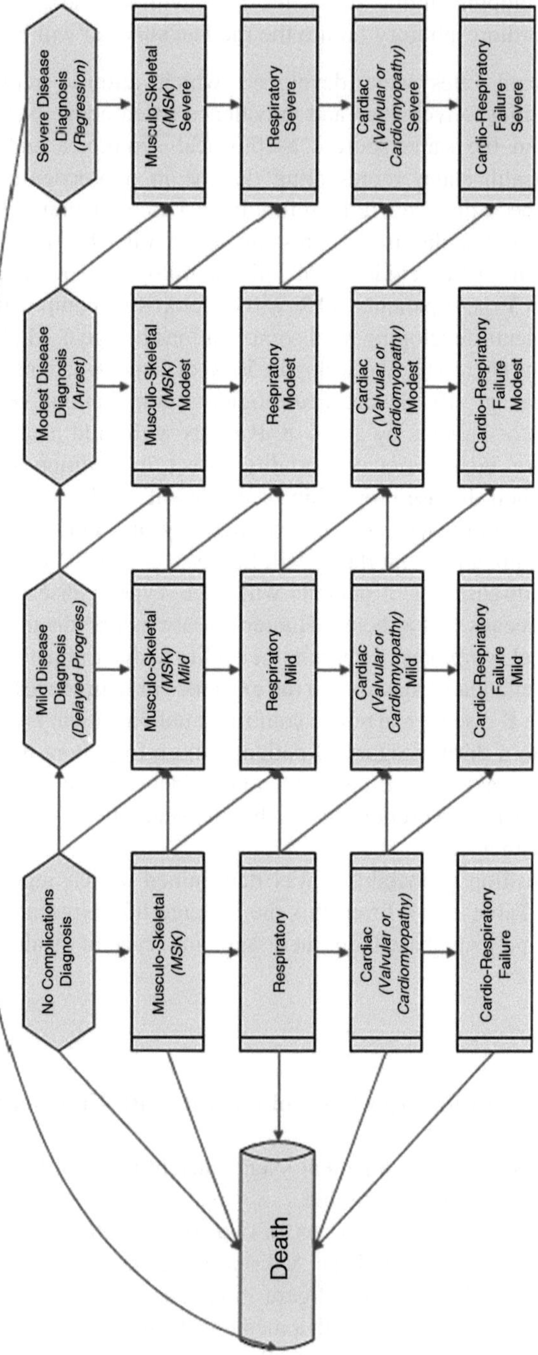

Fig. 13.2 Schematic representation of Markov model for Type A Hunter disease

Table 13.1 Natural history parameters for Hunter disease Markov model

Parameter	Derived estimate
Probability of disease progression within 6-month cycle	
Probability of developing MSK symptoms	
0–4 years	0.095
4 years +	0.257
Probability of developing respiratory symptoms	
0–6 years	0.175
6 years+	0.083
Probability of developing cardiac symptoms	
0–20 years	0.033
20 years+	0.091
Probability of developing cardiorespiratory failure	
20–25 years	0.126
25 years +	0.242
Probability of neurodegeneration within 6-month cycle	
Probability of developing mild neurological complications	
0–6 years	0.16
6 years+	0.42
Probability of developing moderate neurological complications	
0–10 years	0.19
10 years+	0.52
Probability of developing severe neurological complications	0.13
Probability of dying within 6-month cycle	
Diagnosis/MSK symptoms	Male general population
Respiratory symptoms	0.007
Cardiac symptoms	0.017
Cardiorespiratory failure	0.5
Relative risks	
Relative risk of mortality with mild neurological complications	1
Relative risk of mortality with moderate neurological complications	1.5
Relative risk of mortality with severe neurological complications	9.6

Table 13.2 provides estimates of life expectancy without treatment for a larger selection of patient profiles. The table illustrates the heterogeneity of the course of Type B disease. The mean life expectancy for a Hunter disease patient if diagnosed at age 1 with MSK symptoms will be about 15 years. If the patient survives until age 5 without development of further symptoms life expectancy will be 22 years. If the patient survives until age 12 without development of further symptoms life expectancy will be 29 years and if the patient survives until age 30 without progression, life expectancy will be 45 years.

Table 13.2 also illustrates the reduction in life expectancy which occurs with the progression of disease: a type B patient with MSK symptoms has a life expectancy of 29 years whilst a type B patient with respiratory symptoms has a life expectancy of only 25 years; whilst a type B patient with cardiac symptoms at age 12 has

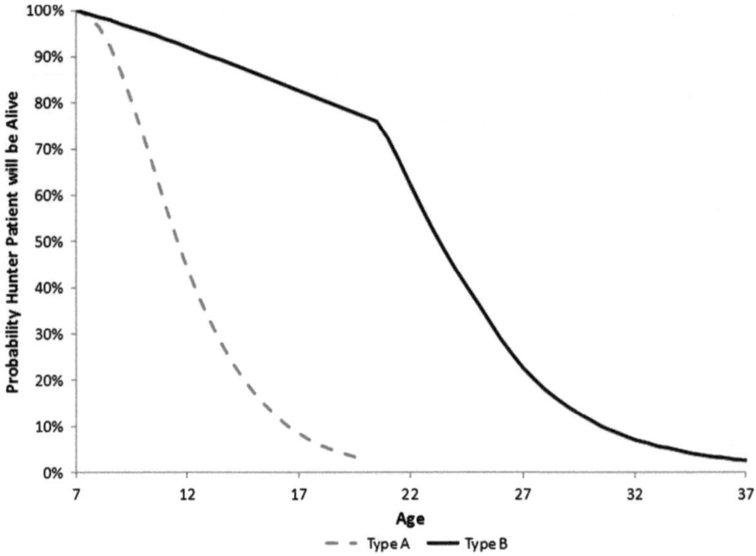

Fig. 13.3 Survival curve for Hunter disease patients based on natural history of disease. Type A patient cohort with mild neurodegeneration and respiratory symptom. Type B patient cohort with respiratory symptoms

Table 13.2 Mean age at death of hunter disease patients with and without treatment

Patient cohort	No treatment	With treatment RR = 0.9	With treatment RR = 0.8	With treatment RR = 0.5
Type A aged 1 mild neurodegeneration with MSK symptoms	9.39	9.59	9.81	10.65
Type A aged 7 severe neurodegeneration with cardiac symptoms	8.78	8.78	8.78	8.78
Too young to tell aged 1 with MSK symptoms	15.25	15.63	16.10	18.61
Too young to tell aged 5 with MSK symptoms	21.90	22.53	23.34	27.83
Type B aged 12 with cardiac symptoms	22.11	22.11	22.11	22.11
Type B aged 12 with respiratory symptoms	25.37	25.80	26.33	29.07
Type B aged 12 with MSK symptoms	28.69	29.68	30.92	37.52
Type B aged 30 with MSK symptoms	44.73	45.83	47.17	53.42

RR relative risk

a life expectancy of 22 years. In addition, the table demonstrates the reduction in life expectancy once neurodegeneration has been confirmed: a reduction from 15 to 9 years for patients aged 1 with MSK symptoms. The table also illustrates the relative homogeneity of Type A versus Type B in that patients following the established course of progression of Type A have similar life expectancies.

13.3.2.3 Potential Effectiveness of Idursulfase

In the RCT for idursulfase, patients treated weekly with idursulfase had a greater improvement in mean distance walked during the 6-Minute Walk Test (6MWT) compared to placebo [20]. Idursulfase patients also had greater improvement in forced vital capacity (FVC) compared to placebo although this was not statistically significant.

Based on this evidence, the DRD working group concluded that there *may* be evidence to suggest that idursulfase reduces the likelihood of development of MSK and respiratory symptoms and that it may reduce the progression from these symptoms to cardiac symptoms—albeit with great uncertainty in the evidence base, given the small samples and short follow-up. The group concluded that there was no evidence nor biologic plausibility to suggest there is impact of idursulfase on neurodegeneration or on the progression of cardiac disease and cardiorespiratory failure.

Based on these conclusions, the modeling exercise estimated the impact on life expectancy of varying the probabilities relating to the transitions from diagnosis to MSK symptoms, MSK symptoms to respiratory symptoms, and respiratory symptoms to cardiac symptoms. Analysis in Table 13.2 assumed three possible rates of reductions—equivalent to a relevant risk of transition of 0.9, 0.8, and 0.5—although for illustration the text provides results only for a relative risk of 0.8. It was assumed that treatment does not impact mortality within the current health state of a patient but will reduce transitions to states with higher risks of death.

Type A patients have limited benefit from treatment—i.e., for a 1-year-old patient with mild neurodegeneration, life expectancy would only be increased by 0.42 years from treatment. Patients with cardiac involvement would not benefit from treatment as there is no evidence that treatment impacts progression from this state. For patients who are "too young to tell", the benefit from treatment will increase as the patient ages without neurodegeneration—as the likelihood of neurodegeneration falls by age. For patients with Type B disease the benefits of treatment do not seem to vary by age—for a patient with MSK symptoms aged 30 the increase in life expectancy is 2.44 years whilst for a 12-year-old patient with similar characteristics it is 2.23 years. For patients with Type B disease, treatment of those with more advanced disease progression yields a lower increase of life expectancy: for a 12-year-old with respiratory symptoms the increase is 0.96 years.

13.3.3 Funding Policy with Respect to Idursulfase for Hunter Disease

Hypothetical analysis in the preceding section suggests that there is potential for a noticeable increase in life expectancy for Type B patients with MSK or respiratory symptoms when treated with idursulfase. Analysis suggests that the increase in life expectancy with Type A patients will be minimal due to the lack of impact on neurodegeneration. Life expectancy gains for patients who are too young to tell (regarding neurologic involvement) are greater the closer the patient is to age 6—the age by which neurodegeneration would have been recognized.

Thus, if idursulfase is to be funded, then limiting funding to patients with Type B disease rather than providing it to all patients with a confirmed diagnosis of Hunter syndrome would maximize the likely return for investment. In addition, as stated earlier, in theory, enzyme replacement therapy could completely halt disease progression. If patients who are provided the drug still progress with treatment it is likely evidence that the treatment is not working. Thus, this model suggests that it would be optimal to restrict continued funding of the drug only to patients for whom there is no subsequent disease progression while on treatment.

Based on the above findings, the Executive Officer decided in 2009 that the province will publicly fund idursulfase for patients with confirmed diagnosis of Hunter disease who are aged 6 years or older and who have no or minimal nonprogressive neurocognitive impairment.

13.4 Conclusions and Policy Implications

The framework developed by the DRD working group in Ontario was based on policy principles of fairness, transparency, consistency and the ethical principles of "accountability for reasonableness" developed by Daniels and Sabin [23]. The framework was presented to groups of stakeholders; physicians, patients and industry: to provide input and guidance. Furthermore, a subsequent report by the Ontario Citizen's Council concluded that the evaluation framework was in harmony with the values identified by the Council [24].

Based on the application of the framework to Hunter disease and idursulfase, the Executive Officer of the Ontario Public Drug Programs decided to approve funding for idursulfase for specific sub-groups of patients [25]. This was contrary to the previous recommendations from the Ontario CED to reject funding to all patients with Hunter disease [22]. Thus, the case study included in this chapter provides an example of the difficulty in reviewing treatments for rare diseases using established mechanisms for reimbursement decisions. The case study also illustrates how a framework for reviewing treatments for rare diseases can be established and applied which considered concerns regarding incomplete evidence, equity and cost containment.

The proposed framework does have a number of limitations. If there is insufficient information to derive even a basic natural history model of the disease then the framework cannot be applied. However, this may be sufficient evidence alone to conclude that the potential effectiveness of a candidate drug cannot be determined and funding should not be considered.

The framework adopts more of a Bayesian approach to evidence synthesis than standard evidence based medicine. Estimates from the disease models are speculative but represent the "best achievable evidence" relevant to the disease and the framework includes a commitment to adapt the model as further data become available.

A further limitation relating to the evidence basis in this field is the lack of outlets for such analyses as contained in this chapter. The rarity of such diseases necessarily limits the potential audiences for such studies which have by their nature an even more limited audience than clinical studies in this area.

The adoption of the evaluative framework provides a model for policy making with respect to the funding of rare diseases. Opinion on the funding for treatments for rare disease tends to be polarized either supporting funding for all treatments of rare diseases [10] or supporting funding treatments for rare diseases under the same conditions that are applied to treatment options for other more common diseases [6]. The framework represents a consensus building exercise providing a middle ground which allows consideration of societal concerns for fairness balanced with concerns for efficient management of government expenditures [24]. Therefore, policy makers have an alternative to two established but extremely divergent positions.

Acknowledgments Dr. Bell is supported by a Canadian Institutes of Health Research and Canadian Patient Safety Institute Chair in Patient Safety and Continuity of Care.

References

1. Sonnenberg FA, Beck JR (1993) Markov models in medical decision making: a practical guide. Med Decis Making 13(4):322–338
2. Briggs A, Sculpher M (1998) An introduction to Markov modelling for economic evaluation. Pharmacoeconomics 13(4):397–409
3. Laupacis A (2005) Incorporating economic evaluations into decision-making: the Ontario experience. Med Care 43(7 Suppl):15–19
4. Clarke JT (2006) Is the current approach to reviewing new drugs condemning the victims of rare diseases to death? A call for a national orphan drug review policy. CMAJ 174(2):189–190
5. Cooper N, Coyle D, Abrams K, Mugford M, Sutton A (2005) Use of evidence in decision models: an appraisal of health technology assessments in the UK since 1997. J Health Serv Res Policy 10(4):245–250
6. McCabe C, Claxton K, Tsuchiya A (2005) Orphan drugs and the NHS: should we value rarity? Br Med J 331:1016–1019
7. McCabe C, Tsuchiya A, Claxton K, Raftery J (2006) Orphan drugs revisited. QJM 99(5):341–345; discussion 350–351
8. Drummond MF, Wilson DA, Kanavos P, Ubel P, Rovira J (2007) Assessing the economic challenges posed by orphan drugs. Int J Technol Assess Health Care 23(1):36–42
9. Hughes DA, Tunnage B, Yeo ST (2005) Drugs for exceptionally rare diseases: do they deserve special status for funding? QJM 98(11):829–836
10. Canadian Organization for Rare Disorders (2005). Canada's Orphan Drug Policy: Learning from the Best. http://www.raredisorders.ca/documents/CanadaOrphanDPFinal.pdf. Accessed 19 Dec 2011
11. Panju AH, Bell CM (2010) Policy alternatives for treatments for rare diseases. CMAJ 182(17):E787–E792.

12. CADTH (2011) Procedures for common drug review. http://www.cadth.ca/media/cdr/process/CDR_Procedure_e.pdf. Accessed 19 Dec 2011
13. Ontario Ministry of Health (2010) The committee to evaluate drugs: terms of reference and administrative guidelines. http://www.health.gov.on.ca/english/providers/program/drugs/how_drugs_approv/documents/ced_terms.pdf. Accessed 17 Mar 2011
14. Hunter C (1917) A rare disease in two brothers. Proc R Soc Med 10:104–116
15. Bach G, Eisenberg F Jr, Cantz M, Neufeld EF (1973) The defect in the Hunter syndrome: deficiency of sulfoiduronate sulfatase. Proc Natl Acad Sci U S A 70(7):2134–2138
16. Martin R, Beck M, Eng C, Giugliani R, Harmatz P, Muñoz V, Muenzer J (2008) Recognition and diagnosis of mucopolysaccharidosis II (Hunter syndrome). Pediatrics 121(2):e377–e386
17. Morini SR, Steiner CE, Gerson LB (2010) Mucopolysaccharidosis type II: skeletal-muscle system involvement. J Pediatr Orthop B 19(4):313–317
18. Young ID, Harper PS (1982) Mild form of Hunter's syndrome: clinical delineation based on 31 cases. Arch Dis Child 57(11):828–836
19. Young ID, Harper PS (1983) The natural history of the severe form of Hunter's syndrome: a study based on 52 cases. Dev Med Child Neurol 25(4):481–489
20. Muenzer J, Wraith JE, Beck M et al. (2006) A phase II/III clinical study of enzyme replacement therapy with idursulfase in mucopolysaccharidosis II (Hunter syndrome). Genet Med 8(8):465–473
21. CADTH (2007) CEDAC recommendation and reasons for recommendation: idursulfase. http://www.cadth.ca/media/cdr/complete/cdr_complete_Elaprase_Dec-19-2007.pdf. Accessed 19 Dec 2011
22. Ontario Ministry of Health (2009) Committee to evaluate drugs (CED) recommendations and reasons: idursulfase—September, 2009. http://www.health.gov.on.ca/english/providers/program/drugs/ced/pdf/idursulfase.pdf. Accessed 19 Dec 2011
23. Daniels N, Sabin J (2002) Setting limits fairly: can we learn to share medical resources. Oxford University Press , Oxford, UK,
24. Ontario Citizen's Council (2010) Considerations for funding drugs for rare diseases: a report of the Ontario citizens' council. http://www.health.gov.on.ca/en/public/programs/drugs/councils/report/report_201003.pdf. Accessed 19 Dec 2011
25. Ontario public drug programs exceptional access program elaprase (idursulfase)—reimbursement guidelines version 2—October, 2009. http://www.health.gov.on.ca/english/providers/program/drugs/pdf/elaprase_reimburse.pdf. Accessed 19 Dec 2011

Chapter 14
Modeling Risk Sharing Agreements and Patient Access Schemes

Gregory S. Zaric, Hui Zhang, and Reza Mahjoub

Abstract Risk sharing agreements are becoming an increasingly common type of contract between drug manufacturers and third party payers such as private insurance companies and public sector health plans. In a risk sharing agreement a payer will agree to include a drug on its formulary in the presence of a contract that reduces some of the payer's risk. Payer risk may be caused by high uncertainty in sales volume, cost, effectiveness, or cost-effectiveness of a new drug. In this chapter we review the literature on risk sharing agreements, identify some opportunities for future research in the area, and highlight some policy implications associated with their use.

14.1 Introduction

A formulary is a list of drugs that will be reimbursed by an insurance provider, such as a private insurance company or a national health plan (often referred to as a "third party payer" or "payer"). A drug is said to be "listed" if it is on the formulary and available for reimbursement. In addition to listing drugs, formularies may also contain information about allowable uses. In many countries the formulary is separate from the regulatory agencies that grant approval for the drug to be available in the marketplace, which is usually granted on the basis of safety and efficacy. Thus, the conditions for use imposed by a formulary may be more restrictive than the uses that receive regulatory approval and many drugs that are approved by regulatory agencies are not approved by formularies. For example, the Bayer dug Ciprofloxacin is an anti-infective with many potential uses. However,

G.S. Zaric (✉) • R. Mahjoub
Ivey School of Business, Western University, London, Canada N6A 3K7
e-mail: gzaric@ivey.uwo.ca

H. Zhang
Faculty of Business Administration, Lakehead University, Thunder Bay, Canada P7B 5E1

G.S. Zaric (ed.), *Operations Research and Health Care Policy*,
International Series in Operations Research & Management Science 190,
DOI 10.1007/978-1-4614-6507-2_14,

the Ontario Drug Benefits Plan will only reimburse ciprofloxacin for certain conditions [1].

Payers increasingly demand value for money when making formulary listing decisions. Many formularies have formal requirements for submission of a cost-effectiveness analysis as part of the process of requesting formulary listing [2]. Demonstrating cost-effectiveness has become such a common requirement that it is sometimes referred to as "the fourth hurdle" for reimbursement [3] (the other three hurdles being safety, efficacy and quality). The motivation for value for money concerns is apparent: in many high-income countries, expenditures on drugs are growing faster than expenditures on healthcare as a whole [4], and are also growing faster than the economy as a whole [4, 5]; there are now several drugs that cost more than $50,000 per year [6]; and clinical trials for some new drugs suggest that they might only be effective or cost-effective in a subset of the population [6].

Formulary access is a critical health policy issue for patients, payers, and drug companies. For patients, the formulary can determine which drugs are available for treatment. Some expensive drugs will be unaffordable and hence inaccessible when there are high copayments or when a drug is not listed and the entire cost must be paid "out-of-pocket." For example, many formularies use tiered copayments [7]. A formulary using a tiered copayment system might include all drugs, but use very high copayments for some expensive drugs (e.g., patients required to pay 40 %—or more—of the cost out of pocket).

For payers, the formulary will have a role in determining the portion of total health care expenditures attributable to drugs, and may also have an impact on total healthcare costs. For manufacturers, formulary access can determine whether there will be any revenue generated from their products. For example, the Director of Health Economics for the Canadian subsidiary of a major pharmaceutical company indicated that his company assumes that there will be no sales of their more expensive products if they are not listed on the formulary. This is because patients will face a strong incentive to substitute for other similar products that are listed.

Despite the use of formularies and considerations of cost-effectiveness, payers still face considerable risk when adding new products to a formulary. Important sources of uncertainty include the following: the effectiveness of a drug in real-world use may be less than what was observed in the clinical trials that led to regulatory approval; the drug may have a less favorable cost-effectiveness ratio than was predicted at the time of formulary listing; and demand may be much greater than anticipated.

The pressures faced by payers (cost control and ensuring value for money) and manufacturers (ensuring formulary access) have led to the development of contracts between payers and pharmaceutical manufacturers that go by several names including "risk sharing agreements," "patient access schemes," "outcomes guarantees," and "performance based agreements." The wording may suggest different motivations. For example, risk sharing agreements are typically viewed by payers as a tool to reduce some of the risks associated with adopting a new product, and patient access schemes are seen as a tool to facilitate formulary listing and thus ensure patient access to new drugs. However, the terms are often used interchangeably and lead to similar results: a new drug is added to a formulary in the presence of a contract which may, under specific conditions, reduce the net financial cost to the payer. For the remainder of the chapter we shall only use the term risk sharing agreement (RSA).

Types of risk sharing contracts are varied and each contract type is associated with many questions about its potential impact on the health system. Concerns include the impact on drug prices, total payer costs, patient access and population health. Manufacturers may wish to develop optimal strategies in anticipation of facing risk sharing schemes, and payers may wish to design risk sharing contracts in such a way that they lead to optimal results. The purpose of this chapter is threefold. First, in Sect. 14.2, we discuss a number of risk sharing agreements and patient access schemes that have been implemented around the world. Second, in Sect. 14.3 we review the modeling literature on risk sharing agreements. We conclude and discuss policy implications in Sect. 14.4.

14.2 Risk Sharing Agreements in Practice

In this section we briefly describe some examples of different types of risk sharing and patient access schemes to give an indication of the breadth of these types of contracts. The focus in the section is on providing a high-level overview of each RSA rather than a detailed mechanics of implementing the agreements, which may involve complex measurement and verification issues, as well as multiple transfers of funds. Towse and Garrison [8] and Carlson et al. [9] provide taxonomies of RSAs, and a paper by Adamski et al. reviews several RSAs that have been implemented around the world [10].

The simplest form of RSA is a reduction in price. In August 2009, the UK National Institute for Health and Clinical Excellence (NICE) recommended cetuximab (Erbitux) for certain patients with metastatic colorectal cancer following a 16 % price reduction from Merck [11].

A second simple type of RSA is one in which one or more courses of treatment are paid for by the manufacturer rather than the payer. These contracts generally take two forms depending on whether the free treatment is provided at the beginning of treatment or for treatment beyond a certain point in time. For example, sunitinib (Sutent) for kidney cancer was recommended by NICE after an agreement with the manufacturer, Pfizer, in which the manufacturer agreed to pay for the first 6-week cycle of treatment [12]. This benefits the payer by reducing the average treatment cost and by reducing the risk that payment will be directed to cases where the drug is not successful or cannot be tolerated since patients who do not experience success will likely not continue on treatment beyond the first cycle. This first type of "free treatment" contract might be appealing to a payer if a high proportion of patients enrolled in the clinical trials had to switch to a different regimen after a short period of time. In the second type of "free treatment" contract, treatment is paid for by the manufacturer for patients who remain on treatment beyond a specified period of time (e.g., more than 2 years). This form of agreement, sometimes called a "dose cap," was implemented in the UK in July 2009 for lenalidomide (Revlimid) for multiple myeloma [13]. This type of RSA benefits the payer by reducing the financial risk associated with unanticipated long term usage. This type of contract might be appealing to a payer if clinical trials were conducted over a relatively short time frame and there is uncertainty about how long patients may remain on the drug in real world settings, or if the drug treats a chronic condition and some patients may receive the drug for a very long time.

Price–volume agreements are another type of RSA. A typical price–volume agreement operates as follows. The payer and manufacturer agree to a volume threshold. If the total units sold (or total value of units sold, depending on the details of the implementation) exceeds the threshold, then the manufacturer must return a proportion of revenues for sales in excess of the threshold to the payer. In some jurisdictions the amount returned may exceed 100 % to account for administrative or pharmacy dispensing costs. From a payer's perspective this reduces risk associated with uncertainty in sales volume, which may be caused by uncertainty about market share in the target indication, uncertainty about the potential for either unapproved or unlisted indications, or other factors. Price–volume agreements are relatively easy for a payer to implement since the payer only needs to track claims. However, they may be challenging for manufacturers to manage when there are several payers, each having different volume thresholds, as it may not be obvious in real time how much volume is accounted for by each payer. Also, if these agreements are negotiated strictly on the basis of total volume then there might not be any control over appropriate usage. However, it is often assumed that the negotiated volume threshold would be the size of the target indication, and thus, the price–volume agreement would reduce or eliminate the incentive for promotion and sales outside of the target indication.

RSAs can also be implemented based on clinical indicators, such as the agreement recommended in October 2007 for bortezomib (Velcade) in the treatment of multiple myeloma [14]. Under this agreement the UK National Health Service (NHS) agreed to pay for 4 cycles of treatment for all patients. At the end of 4 cycles, treatment success would be determined by change in serum monoclonal protein level. If a patient's treatment was considered a failure, then the drug manufacturer would reimburse the NHS for treatment until either the time of failure or the end of four treatment cycles. If treatment was a success, then the patient could continue to receive the drug, funded by the NHS. This particular RSA structure may seem appealing because of the use of clinical indicators and the presence of clearly defined criteria for success and failure. However, it has been suggested that there are several implementation challenges associated with monitoring and verification, and these may lead to the NHS losing rebate revenue [15]. RSAs based on performance have also been negotiated in other jurisdictions. For example, in one agreement Merck agreed to rebate a portion of drug costs for two of its diabetes drugs if they did not help patients to control their blood sugar levels [16].

RSAs can also be based on the impact that a new drug or health technology has on other health system costs. For example, in the USA an agreement between

Genomic Health and United Health Care involving the 21-gene assay (Oncotype Dx) linked the price of the test to the rate of chemotherapy use among breast cancer patients insured by United Health Care [17]. In another case, the seller of risedronic acid (Actonel), an osteoporosis drug, agreed to reimburse an insurer for a portion of costs of fractures among patients taking the drug [16].

An RSA based on cost-effectiveness was implemented in the UK for beta interferon and glatirmamir acetate for the treatment of multiple sclerosis [18]. Under this agreement all patients could have access to these drugs. All patients receiving these drugs would be enrolled in a registry to track their status over 10 years. At the end of 10 years, a formula specified by the RSA contract would be used to determine the cost-effectiveness of the drugs. If the calculated incremental cost-effectiveness ratio (ICER) was above a negotiated threshold (£36,000/quality adjusted life year gained in this case) then the manufacturers would be required to rebate the NHS an amount that would have made the use of the drugs cost-effective. This form of agreement is appealing because it should ensure that real world usage of the drug is cost-effective. However, it has been criticized as being overly complex [19–21]. Although this was the first major risk sharing agreement negotiated by the NHS, the NHS has not used this format again.

In addition to the RSAs described above there are several other related pharmaceutical policies, such as the use of trial periods, delisting and coverage with evidence development, all of which may help to mitigate risk on the part of payers and increase patient access.

14.3 Modeling Risk Sharing Agreements

The previous section demonstrates a wide variety of possible risk sharing contracts. In this section we review some of the modeling literature that addresses management and design issues related to RSAs. We divide the literature into three groups based on the perspective of the study and the modeling approach.

14.3.1 Optimal Manufacturer Decision Making in Response to Risk Sharing Agreements

The first group of RSA papers investigates optimal decision making by drug manufacturers who are faced with an RSA. Zaric and O'Brien [22] analyzed a manufacturer's response to a price–volume agreement. In their model the manufacturer states a total budget impact x to the payer. The manufacturer assumes that the probability of getting listed on the formulary is a decreasing function of x. If the drug is listed on the formulary then x is treated as the threshold level in a price–volume agreement. The manufacturer pays a rebate proportion α, $0 \leq \alpha \leq 1$, to the payer on all sales in excess of the threshold. The manufacturer chooses the level x to maximize expected profit.

They showed that the optimal value of x, x^*, is increasing in the rebate rate and the manufacturing cost per unit, and decreasing in sales price per unit. They found that the "forecast error," defined as the difference between x and the expected number of units sold, was also increasing in the rebate rate and the cost per unit and decreasing in the sales price per unit. That is, when the rebate is high or when the manufacturing cost is high, the manufacturer cannot afford to give a rebate. Thus, it is optimal for the manufacturer to state a high threshold at the risk of not being listed. They provided estimates of the probability of the manufacturer losing money and showed this to be relatively small. They also discussed the integration of cost-effectiveness and price–volume agreements. They demonstrated how a price–volume agreement could be used to ensure that the expected ICER for a product would fall below a given willingness to pay threshold.

Zaric and Xie [23] compared delisting after a trial period versus rebates on the basis of net monetary benefit. The authors developed a two-period model for each type of RSA. In both models the manufacturer determines the price, p, at the beginning of the first period, as well as the marketing effort, m_i, $i = 1, 2$, in each period, to maximize total expected profit over two periods. They assumed that the true effectiveness of the drug in each period is a random variable whose value is unknown at the beginning of each period and becomes known before the end of the period. Total demand is assumed to follow a Cobb–Douglas function. In the delisting model, the manufacturer is only allowed to sell in the second period if the drug was cost-effective (i.e., had positive net monetary benefit) in the first period. In the rebates model, which was inspired by the RSA for MS drugs in the UK, the manufacturer is allowed to sell in both periods, but must pay a rebate at the end of each period if the drug was not cost-effective (i.e., had negative net monetary benefit). When a rebate is paid, the value of the rebate is the minimum amount required so that use of the drug would have been cost-effective. In each model the manufacturer chooses p and m_i to maximize total expected profit over two periods.

Analytical solutions were provided for the optimal p, m_1, and m_2 for the case of a uniform distribution of effectiveness. Comparisons between the contracts for other quantities of interest, such as total market size, expected health benefits, or manufacturer profits, were not possible analytically so they were estimated numerically. Numerical analyses identified two important parameters for all comparisons: the nondrug portion of the incremental cost, and the potential variability in effectiveness.

In all comparisons presented the authors showed that total market size in the first period was greater under delisting than rebates. Thus, the threat of delisting and losing sales in the second period created an incentive to make pricing and marketing decisions that result in larger sales in the first period. They also examined the ratio of total expected profits of the manufacturer to total expected benefits purchased by the payer under both arrangements. They showed that all four combinations of the two RSAs being preferred or not preferred by each party are possible. This highlights the need for careful planning and analysis when negotiating an RSA:

under some combinations of parameters, both parties prefer delisting, while under others both parties prefer rebates, and under others the two parties have opposite preferences.

Zhang and Zaric [24] investigated whether a price–volume agreement could be used to control "leakage," which they defined as use of a drug either for an unapproved "off label" indication or for an approved but unlisted indication. To represent this, their model included three markets indexed by i: $i = 0$, corresponding to approved and listed indications; $i = 1$, corresponding to indications that have regulatory approval but are not listed; and $i = 2$ corresponding to indications that do not have regulatory approval and are thus not listed. The manufacturer determines marketing effort m_i in each market to maximize profit. Total sales are determined by marketing effort in each market as well as "spillover" effects, whereby promotional effort in one market can increase sales for another indication. A volume threshold for a price–volume agreement was assumed to be previously determined by the payer. They assumed that the payer could observe total sales but would not be able to determine the market in which the sales occurred. Thus, the price–volume agreement was based on total sales over all markets.

They found that, in general, a price–volume agreement with an exogenously determined volume threshold cannot be used to control leakage. They evaluated and compared two cases: a general model in which off-label promotion is allowed (i.e., $m_2 > 0$ is allowed), and a restricted case in which off-label promotion is prohibited (i.e., a constraint $m_2 = 0$ was added to the model) corresponding to the regulatory environment in many countries. They found that, when off-label promotion is prohibited, promotion in markets 0 and 1 rise to compensate. In a numerical example they found that the impact of this constraint on total marketing, net monetary benefit and manufacturer's profit was relatively modest.

Several of the RSAs described in Sect. 14.2 make use of information about clinical success, either explicitly (through measurement of biomarkers) or implicitly (by considering whether individuals are still receiving treatment after a specified period of time). This suggests that there may be some utility to incorporating models of disease progression into RSA models. Practical models could include health states defined according to symptoms, levels or presence of biomarkers, overall health, drug response, type of therapy, or some combination. A benefit of this approach is that it could directly incorporate knowledge from clinical trials and allow consideration of multiple definitions of success as part of the model.

To our knowledge there is only one RSA model to date that incorporates a disease progression model [25]. The authors model a "pay-for-performance" RSA similar to the bortezomib agreement in the UK [18]. They modeled disease progression using a continuous time Markov chain with three states representing stable (no response), responding, and progression. The RSA has two contract parameters: a rebate rate, α, and T_e representing "time of evaluation of response." All patients begin receiving the drug at time 0; at time T_e they are evaluated, and the manufacturer pays a rebate to the payer for all patients who are not in the responding state at time T_e. They use this model to show how the manufacturer's profit level varies with the contract parameters T_e and rebate rate, as well as other model parameters. They find conditions under which an optimal evaluation time exists and find a threshold level for the rebate rate, above which the manufacturer would not be able to achieve positive profit.

The authors discussed extending their model to incorporate both first order uncertainty and second order uncertainty. First order uncertainty would model the experiences of individuals and produce a distribution of outcomes. This approach might be appropriate if a very small number of patients will receive the drug—for example, in the case of an "orphan disease" (a very rare disease, sometimes defined as prevalence of less than 1/1,000). Second order uncertainty would reflect uncertainty on the true values of model parameters. Incorporating second order uncertainty would be appropriate if payers were concerned that the clinical trials conditions would not be reflective of real world usage.

14.3.2 Social Welfare Impact of Risk Sharing Agreements

The second group of papers investigates the social impact of RSAs, which has implications for whether payers should consider entering into such agreements. The three papers in this category all make the general comparison of "risk sharing" versus "no risk sharing."

Lilico [26] developed a model in which risk averse patients choose whether or not to initiate treatment and treatment success is a Bernoulli random variable. Risk aversion is modeled by assuming that patients have a utility function that is concave in wealth. There is a disutility associated with receiving treatment and a disutility associated with remaining sick, both of which can be expressed in monetary terms. The disutility associated with being sick can occur either by not being treated or by treatment being unsuccessful. In the "no risk sharing" model all patients who choose treatment pay drug cost p^*, whereas in the "risk sharing" model patients whose treatment is successful pay $p^{**} > p^*$ and patients whose treatment is unsuccessful pay nothing. In both models he assumed that drug prices would be set so that manufacturers earn zero profits.

There are a number of general implications of this model: (1) The expected wealth for patients is the same under both scenarios; (2) Risk sharing is always found to be welfare increasing relative to no risk sharing, which is a consequence of patients having concave utility functions; (3) The gains associated with risk sharing are greater for more risk averse patients; (4) The gains of risk sharing are greater as the disutility of remaining sick increases.

Lilico [26] also considered the possibility that risk sharing might attract new patients into treatment, and that these new patients would have a different probability of being successfully treated than those treated in the absence of risk sharing. This would happen after formulary negotiations had taken place and the price had been set. He found that this would not benefit the manufacturer if the new patients had a lower probability of being successfully treated than those in the trials. In other words, the manufacturer would be worse off with risk sharing than without risk sharing if risk sharing resulted in sicker or harder to treat patients being drawn into treatment.

Two additional papers in this group used a similar framework to investigate RSAs [27, 28]. In both models the authors assumed that a new drug provides a benefit b per patient if treatment is successful. The drug is successful with probability π in [0,1] and the population is hetrogenous with respect to π, with known distribution. The manufacturer sells the drug at price p and faces a marginal production cost of w. In both models, under risk sharing, there is a cost per patient receiving the drug to verify whether or not treatment has been successful. The two models differ in how the price is determined: in one this is resolved through backwards induction [27] and in the other a Nash bargaining process is used [28].

The first of these analyses [27] considers interactions involving the manufacturer, the NHS, physicians, and patients. The authors assume that physicians make prescribing decisions for their patients and act as perfect agents on behalf of the NHS, meaning that physicians make decisions that would be optimal from the perspective of the NHS. This simplifies the model to one with two agents, physicians and the manufacturer. Given a drug price, physicians choose a cut off value of π, π^*, such that only patients with $\pi > \pi^*$ will receive treatment. Physicians observe the probability that a patient will be successfully treated (π) and then make a prescription decision. With physicians acting as agents for the NHS the threshold is chosen so that treatment is cost-effective in the treated group. The manufacturer acts as a monopolist seller and chooses the price p to maximize profits, in anticipation of the optimal choice of π^* by physicians.

The optimal price (and corresponding optimal threshold) is found via backwards induction. They find expressions for π^* as a function of p under risk sharing and no risk sharing but are not able to find closed form expressions for p. If the verification cost is zero, then under risk sharing all patients are treated, the manufacturer sets a price equal to the average benefit of treatment, and the payer derives no net benefit from treatment. In general, they find that risk sharing may increase or decrease total social welfare depending on when the RSA is negotiated (either before or after a price has been set) and several model parameters. They introduced the concept of a modified verification cost that could be used to ensure that the solutions obtained would be optimal from the perspective of a social planner.

As an extension the author discusses incorporating "detailing" (a form of promotional effort by drug manufacturers) into the model. They assume that detailing would increase a physician's valuation of the drug, thus making her more likely to prescribe for a given probability of cure. They find that marketing activities may increase or decrease under a RSA.

In the second analysis [28] the authors assumed that under no risk sharing all patients receive the drug and the manufacturer is reimbursed for all sales. Under risk sharing, the health authority determines a cure threshold π^* such that only patients with $\pi > \pi^*$ are treated and the manufacturer is only reimbursed if treatment is successful (similar to [27]). As in [27], under risk sharing there is a verification cost to verify that treatment was successful. In this model, in both cases (with and without risk sharing) there is an also administration cost per patient receiving treatment (this cost was not present in [27]).

The optimal prices with and without risk sharing are determined by solving a Nash bargaining game between the health authority and the manufacturer. In the case of risk sharing the optimal price is a function of the threshold chosen by the payer. The objective function is the product of each party's objective raised to an exponent representing the relative bargaining power of that party. In the case of risk sharing, the optimal threshold is solved by maximizing the payer's utility given the optimal pricing policy. They find that the health authority may prefer either risk sharing or no risk sharing, depending on the distribution of patients with respect to the probability of being cured and other model parameters. They also find that, if the health authority could set the clinical threshold in the no risk sharing case, then the no risk sharing option would always be preferred. Note that this is in contrast to Lilico who found that risk sharing would always be welfare improving [26].

14.3.3 Design of Risk Sharing Agreements

The third group of papers investigates the design of an RSA from a payer's perspective. All four papers in this group model uncertainty, either in the effectiveness of the drug [26, 29] or in the total sales volume [30, 31]. In one paper the terms of the agreement are determined passively through pricing rules based on achieving cost-effectiveness [29]. The other three use principal-agent models [26, 30, 31], and two of these explicitly investigate optimal design from the payer's perspective [30, 31].

A principal-agent model is often a natural choice when considering the design of an RSA. A typical model setup would involve a principal (a government payer) offering an RSA contract to an agent (a drug manufacturer). The contract terms offered to the agent depend on the specific RSA being modeled, and the principal's objective is to choose optimal contract terms. The agent then responds by potentially revealing some private information and accepting or rejecting the contract. In some instances, after the agent has accepted the contract he may make further decisions.

Principal agent formulations allow for modeling uncertainty and participation constraints. The participation constraints ensure that both parties will be willing to enter into the RSA. Uncertainty is typically represented in three ways:

1. Asymmetric information. One or both parties know something that the other does not. For example, the manufacturer may have superior knowledge of the effectiveness of the drug or of off-label potential. The manufacturer's superior information may be the result of experience in the drug development process, experience with the drug in other jurisdictions or knowledge of future marketing plans. The payer may also have private information about its

total budget, willingness to pay, other drugs available or being considered for similar conditions.

2. Hidden action. The outcome for the principal depends on the actions of the agent, but the principal cannot directly observe the actions of the agent. This may be useful for modeling promotional effort by manufacturers since the total cost incurred by the principal will depend on the number of units sold but the principal cannot directly observe the manufacturer's promotional effort.
3. General uncertainty. Some values may be uncertain to both parties. This can be modeled by including a stochastic error term.

In an extension of the base model described earlier, Lilico [26] provided part of a principal agent formulation. The model included individual rationality constraints to ensure participation of both parties but it did not include an objective function for the principal (the payer) and thus did not address the issue of optimal design. He developed a "2-type" model in which the drug's effectiveness could either be "high" or "low" and assumed asymmetric information about the drug's effectiveness. In particular, the manufacturer knows the true effectiveness whereas the payer has a distribution of beliefs about effectiveness. He derived a necessary condition under which the payer would purchase the drug and discussed conditions under which a firm would offer a risk sharing contract.

Zhang et al. [31] investigated the optimal design of a price–volume agreement in the presence of asymmetric information about market size. They assumed that a government payer is negotiating an RSA with a drug manufacturer, and that the manufacturer has superior information about total expected market size. In the model the payer offers the manufacturer a menu of contracts consisting of a unit sales price and a rebate rate on sales in excess of the threshold. The manufacturer then states the expected mean sales which is used as the threshold in the price–volume agreement. The payer's objective is to minimize the expected cost of the contract and the manufacturer's objective is to maximize expected profit. Individual rationality constraints ensure that the manufacturer earns a minimum profit and that the overall contract has positive net monetary benefit from the payer's perspective.

An important parameter in their model is the social cost of capital, which represents administrative cost or overhead associated with managing a public health care system. In the first best case they found that, when the social cost is positive, the optimal contract never includes rebates. However, when the social cost is negative the optimal contract may include a rebate rate of 100 %. In the second best case the optimal contract depends on several parameters. In some instances the payer can achieve first best results, but this is not generally true. In many cases they found that the optimal solution for the payer can be any value within a range. They suggested that in these cases the payer may also wish to consider the manufacturer's profit as a secondary objective and choose, among all possible optimal solutions, the one that will maximize manufacturer profits.

In a numerical example they found that the optimal price was decreasing in market size and the optimal rebate rate could be increasing or decreasing in market size, depending on other parameters. The impact of asymmetric information on the payer's total cost was non-monotonic, being smallest for either small or large market sizes.

Zhang et al. [30] developed a model to investigate the optimal design of a price–volume agreement in the presence of unobservable promotional effort by the manufacturer. There is little debate that promotional effort increases sales, and a number of explanations of the mechanism by which this happens have been suggested. There is, however, debate about the effects of pharmaceutical promotion on patient health. Some argue that marketing is *informative* and can let patients know their options, improve adherence, and possibly lead to earlier diagnosis and treatment. Others argue that it is *persuasive*, leading to higher volumes of sales but not necessarily better decisions.

They model the impact of promotional effort on health benefits, $b(m)$, using a concave quadratic function. This allows for consideration of both informative marketing (when $b'(m) > 0$) and persuasive marketing (when $b'(m) < 0$). In this model the rebate rate is exogenous. The payer chooses a base price and the manufacturer chooses promotional effort (m), which takes place after a contract between the parties is agreed upon. They consider three scenarios depending on when the threshold is chosen and which party chooses the threshold level. In all scenarios the payer aims to maximize the expected total health benefits achieved subject to a constraint on the overall net monetary benefit of the contract, and the manufacturer aims to maximize expected profits. For all scenarios they compare the second best situation, where marketing effort is not observable, with the first best, where marketing is observable and contractible.

They found that first best results are, in general, not achievable. They also found that the payer sometimes chooses a contract in which strictly persuasive marketing occurs. The most significant result relates to which party chooses the threshold level in the second best case. The payer always does best if it is allowed to choose the threshold. However, in some instances the payer can do just as well when allowing the manufacturer to choose the threshold. Thus, in some instances payers could simplify their negotiation process with manufacturers by allowing them to choose the threshold. This would require a reliable method of identifying these situations.

A fourth paper looked at design of an RSA but did not use game theory [29]. Instead, the author suggests that if the payer is risk neutral in cost but risk averse in health benefits then there may be an incentive to enter into risk sharing agreements. They define a risk-adjusted ICER which accounts for the payer's risk aversion with respect to health benefits and assume that the price of the new drug is set so that the risk adjusted ICER is equal to the payer's willingness-to-pay threshold. They then show how a risk sharing scheme could be constructed by reducing the price if the observed drug effectiveness was less than a threshold value.

14.4 Conclusions and Policy Implications

In this chapter we discussed RSAs and provided a review of the modeling literature on the topic. Although RSAs are becoming increasingly common [10], there is debate about their role in the future. According to Cook, "risk sharing plans. . .may become a staple feature of the market" [32]. In contrast, de Pouverville stated that "it is not clear that risk sharing will be accepted" and suggested a much more limited role for RSAs for "innovative drugs with low competition, for very specific target populations" [33]. Neumann et al. suggest that risk sharing is appealing because of "tightening budgets, uncertain evidence, and frustration with existing 'crude' pricing models" [34]. However, they note that there are many implementation challenges.

In some instances, such as agreements involving the Ontario Drug Benefits Plan or agreements involving private insurers, the details may be kept confidential. However, in others, such as agreements with the UK NHS, details of the plans are made public and often described by the media (e.g., [11, 13, 14]). A study in Australia found 73 drugs listed with "special pricing arrangements" but details on these arrangements were not publicly available [35]. Agreements in which details are made public will provide many opportunities to identify directions for future research. Taxonomies of existing RSAs (e.g., [9]) can also provide valuable ideas for future research. Modellers can seek explanations for how or why such agreements should work. As more agreements are struck, empirical researchers can look for evidence of the effectiveness of RSAs and of the factors that caused one contract design to be more or less effective than another. Gathering empirical evidence on the effectiveness of various forms of RSAs would be a very useful direction for future research.

Several of the models that we reviewed included monitoring or administration costs [26–28] which may be quite large in practice [34]. Many of these models assumed a single payer. Monitoring and verification may become much more complicated in a system where there were several payers, each having different contract terms, and drugs are sold through a supply chain that involves at least one intermediate wholesaler. A recent report suggested that, even in the single payer system of the UK, the NHS might be missing out on collecting full rebate amounts due to complexity of paperwork [15, 36]. To implement RSAs effectively, accurate monitoring of sales and/or clinical results are necessary. One commentary suggested that "the most challenging operational barrier to widespread implementation of [outcomes-based risk-sharing agreements] in the USA is having the clinical and information technology infrastructure to support successful implementation of the programs" [16]. We note that similar issues were identified several years ago regarding models of revenue sharing in the video rental industry [37, 38].

There is a large body of research on the impact of pricing or other regulation on incentives for pharmaceutical R&D (e.g., [39–43]). More recently, some authors have specifically started to consider the specific impact of RSAs on manufacturer incentives [44, 45]. According to one study, under a pay-for-performance

Table 14.1 Summary of types of risk sharing agreements

Type of Agreement	Description	Example	Strengths	Weaknesses
Price reduction	Reduction in price of all units	Cetuximab for colorectal cancer in the UK	Relatively easy to implement	May not address all payer concerns
Free doses—At the beginning of treatment	First dose or first course of treatment for free	Sunitinib for kidney cancer in the UK	Easy to implement, may address concerns about uncertainty in effectiveness	May not address concerns about value for money or unlimited liability
Free doses—At the end of treatment	Doses provided free for patients still on treatment beyond specified time	Lenalidomide for multiple myeloma in the UK	Easy to understand, partially addresses concerns about total expenditure	May not address concerns about effectiveness or value for money
Price–volume agreement	Rebate equal to a portion of sales in excess of a threshold	Commonly used in Ontario	Easy to understand, addresses concerns about total expenditure	May not address concerns about effectiveness or value for money
Clinical indicators	Rebate for those patients who do not achieve a clinical success	Bortezomib in the treatment of multiple myeloma in the UK	Addresses concerns about uncertainty in effectiveness	Complicated to design and implement
Resource utilization	Manufacturer of one technology pays a rebate if use of other health services does not decrease	Private sector agreement regarding the use of the OncotypeDx test	Ties reimbursement to value created by system-wide cost impact	Complicated to implement, in some cases cost changes may not be due to the new technology
Cost-effectiveness	Rebate to the payer if real-world experience suggests that a new drug was not cost-effective	Beta interferon and glatiramir acetate for the treatment of multiple sclerosis in the UK	Theoretically appealing due to relationship between cost-effectiveness and resource allocation	Complicated to design and implement., may involve significant transaction costs

guarantee, "the manufacturer has a stronger incentive to maximize the number of patients with a response, not merely the number of patients treated or doses sold" [44]. Two of the models reviewed in this chapter considered R&D incentives by suggesting that, in situations where multiple optima exist, the payer consider the manufacturer's profit as a secondary objective [30, 31]. The long term impact of RSAs on R&D incentives remains an open question (Table 14.1).

References

1. Ontario Ministry of Health (2008) Ontario Drug Benefit Formulary/Comparative Drug Index No. 41. Queen's Printer for Ontario, Toronto
2. Tilson L, Barry M (2005) European pharmaceutical pricing and reimbursement strategies. National Centre for Pharmacoeocnomics, Dublin, Ireland, p 166
3. Taylor RS et al. (2004) Inclusion of cost effectiveness in licensing requirements of new drugs: the fourth hurdle. BMJ 329:972–975
4. OECD (2005) Drug spending in OECD countries up by nearly a third since 1998, according to new OECD data. http://www.oecd.org/document/25/0,2340,en_2649_201185_34967193_1_1_1_1,00.html. Accessed 15 Nov 2011
5. OECD (2011) Quarterly National Accounts MetaData: Quarterly Growth Rates of real GDP, change over previous quarter. http://www.oecd.org/document/25/0,2340,en_2649_201185_34967193_1_1_1_1,00.html. Accessed 23 Nov 2011
6. Sullivan R et al. (2011) Delivering affordable cancer care in high-income countries. Lancet Oncol 12(10):933–980
7. Lowry F (2010) Erlotinib for advanced NSCLC is "marginally" cost effective. Medscape Medical News. http://www.medscape.com/viewarticle/717585. Accessed 15 Nov 2011
8. Towse A, Garrison LP Jr (2010) Can't get no satisfaction? Will pay for performance help? Toward an economic framework for understanding performance-based risk-sharing agreements for innovative medical products. Pharmacoeconomics 28(2):93–102
9. Carlson JJ et al. (2010) Linking payment to health outcomes: a taxonomy and examination of performance-based reimbursement schemes between healthcare payers and manufacturers. Health Policy 96(3):179–190
10. Adamski J et al. (2010) Risk sharing arrangements for pharmaceuticals: potential considerations and recommendations for European payers. BMC Health Serv Res 10:153
11. BBC News (2009) Green light for bowel cancer drug. http://news.bbc.co.uk/2/hi/health/8077515.stm. Accessed 15 Nov 2011
12. Devlin K (2009) Kidney cancer patients should get Sutent on the NHS, says NICE. In: The Telegraph. London. http://www.telegraph.co.uk/health/healthnews/4449605/Kidney-cancer-patients-should-get-Student-on-the-NHS-says-NICE.html. Accessed 7 Feb 2013
13. BBC News (2009) Deal reached on NHS myeloma drug. http://news.bbc.co.uk/2/hi/health/7859053.stm. Accessed 15 Nov 2011
14. BBC News (2007) Cancer-drug refund scheme backed. http://news.bbc.co.uk/2/hi/6713503.stm
15. Wilkinson E (2010) NHS missing out on cancer drug payments. BBC News, London
16. Schuler C, Faulker LP (2009) Pay for play. PharmaExec.com
17. Pollack A (2007) Pricing pills by the results. New York Times, New York
18. National Institute for Clinical Excellence (2002) Technology appraisal No. 32. Guidance on the use of beta interferon and glatiramer acetate for the treatment of multiple sclerosis. National Institute for Clinical Excellence, London, UK, p 25
19. Rafferty J (2010) Multiple sclerosis risk sharing scheme: a costly failure. BMJ 340:c1672

20. McCabe C et al. (2010) Continuing the multiple sclerosis risk sharing scheme is unjustified. BMJ 340:c1786
21. Ebers GC (2010) Commentary: Outcome measures were flawed. BMJ 340:c2693
22. Zaric GS, O'Brien BJ (2005) Analysis of a pharmaceutical risk sharing agreement based on the purchaser's total budget. Health Econ **14**(8):793–803
23. Zaric GS, Xie B (2009) A comparison of two risk sharing agreements. Value in Health 12(5):838–845
24. Zhang H, Zaric GS (2011) Promotion and leakage under a pharmaceutical price-volume agreement. INFOR 49(4):247–253
25. Mahjoub R, Odegaard FK, Zaric GS (2011) Modeling the dynamics of a risk sharing agreement. INFORMS Healthcare, Montreal
26. Lilico A (2003) Risk-sharing pricing models in the distribution of pharmaceuticals. Staff Working Paper. Europe Economics, London
27. Barros PP (2011) The simple economics of risk-sharing agreements between the nhs and the pharmaceutical industry. Health Econ 20(4):461–470
28. Antonanzas F, Juarez-Castello C, Rodriguez-Ibeas R (2011) Should health authorities offer risk-sharing contracts to pharmaceutical firms? A theoretical approach. Health Econ Policy Law 6(3):391–403
29. Gandjour A (2009) Pharmaceutical risk sharing agreements. Pharmacoeconomics 27(5):431–432
30. Zhang H, Huang T, Zaric GS (2011) Optimal design of a price volume agreement in the presence of unobservable marketing effort. Working paper
31. Zhang H, Zaric GS, Huang T (2011) Optimal design of a pharmaceutical price-volume agreement under asymmetric information about expected market size. Prod Oper Manage 20(3):334–346
32. Cook JP, Vernon JA, Manning R (2008) Pharmaceutical risk-sharing agreements. Pharmacoeconomics 26(7):551–556
33. de Pouvourville G (2006) Risk-sharing agreements for innovative drugs: a new solution to old problems? Eur J Health Econ 7(3):155–157
34. Neumann PJ et al. (2011) Risk-sharing arrangements that link payment for drugs to health outcomes are proving hard to implement. Health Aff (Millwood) 30(12):2329–2337
35. Robertson J, Walkom EJ, Henry DA (2009) Transparency in pricing arrangements for medicines listed on the Australian Pharmaceutical Benefits Scheme. Aust Health Rev 33(2):192–199
36. Williamson S (2010) Patient access schemes for high-cost cancer medicines. Lancet Oncol 11 (2):111–112
37. Dana JD, Spier KE (2001) Revenue sharing and vertical control in the video rental industry. J Ind Econ 49(3):223–245
38. Cachon GP, Lariviere MA (2001) Contracting to assure supply: how to share demand forecasts in a supply chain. Manage Sci 47(5):629–646
39. Jena AB, Philipson TJ (2008) Cost-effectiveness analysis and innovation. J Health Econ 27(5):1224–1236
40. Pearson SD (2007) Getting the innovation we want. Health Aff (Millwood) 26(5):1506–1507
41. Ingram J (2011) Eliminating innovation: how price controls limit access. J Leg Med 32(1):115–128
42. Scherer FM (2009) Price controls and global pharmaceutical progress. Health Aff (Millwood) 28(1):161–164
43. Lakdawalla DN et al. (2009) US pharmaceutical policy in a global marketplace. Health Aff (Millwood) 28(1):138–150
44. Garber AM, McClellan MB (2007) Satisfaction guaranteed—"Payment by Results" for biologic agents. N Engl J Med 357:1575–1577
45. Garrison LP et al. (2008) Paying for pills by result: Performance-based rewards for innovation. ISPOR Annual Meeting, Toronto

Part V
Building Health Policy Models

Chapter 15
Considerations for Developing Applied Health Policy Models: The Example of HIV Treatment Expansion in Resource-Limited Settings

April D. Kimmel and Bruce R. Schackman

Abstract This chapter describes steps for developing health policy models. The discussion begins with considerations for identifying a research question and developing a model conceptual framework. It next provides guidance on how to build and implement the model, as well as how to populate or parameterize a model. We end by examining the techniques for verifying model performance. Special emphasis is placed on developing applied health policy models, particularly those used to inform policy decisions in resource-limited settings.

15.1 Introduction

Health policy models are analytic tools that researchers, policy makers, and other consumers can rely on to help inform the decision making process. Health-related mathematical models are used to make predictions about health or economic consequences, allocation of resources, or trade-offs of different interventions related to a specific disease or target population. These forecasting models typically synthesize data from primary and/or secondary sources, reflect events that occur over time and across populations, and can account for uncertainty in the data used to populate a model [1]. They can be used to assist policy or other decision makers in making real-world choices about which intervention(s) may have the best expected health outcomes, how much the interventions may cost, and which are the best value for money.

A.D. Kimmel (✉)
Department of Healthcare Policy and Research, Virginia Commonwealth University School of Medicine, Richmond, VA, USA
e-mail: adkimmel@vcu.edu

B.R. Schackman
Department of Public Health, Weill Cornell Medical College, New York, NY, USA

G.S. Zaric (ed.), *Operations Research and Health Care Policy*, International Series in Operations Research & Management Science 190, DOI 10.1007/978-1-4614-6507-2_15,

Development of applied health policy models is a lengthy but systematic process. In the text that follows, we describe some steps for developing, implementing, populating, and utilizing these types of models. While these steps are applicable in any setting, special considerations may be required for applying these models in resource-limited settings. For example, in order to forecast policy relevant outcomes useful for decision makers, particular attention may be required to identify contextually appropriate, country-specific information. Further, emphasizing development of conceptually simple model structures, implementing models with widely available software, and using reproducible data analysis techniques can promote transparency and acceptability of results to policy makers in these settings.

Our aim is to illustrate and deepen the reader's understanding of each of these steps. We also want to demonstrate some unique considerations for applying health policy models in resource-limited settings in a way that can be used for real-world policy making. Therefore, after outlining each step, we present a practical example of a health policy model applied to HIV treatment expansion in resource-limited settings.

15.2 Defining the Research Question and Conceptualizing the Model

Identifying, defining, and bounding the research question may be the most difficult aspects of performing research. Doing so allows the researcher to focus the research and provides a detailed roadmap for moving forward in the study. In the text below, we examine some processes we have undertaken when using applied health policy models. We begin by discussing the importance of identifying policy relevant, timely research questions. Next, we consider the model conceptualization process. We end by illustrating with a concrete example on forecasting the health consequences of HIV treatment expansion in resource-limited settings.

15.2.1 Identifying, Defining, and Bounding the Research Question

We define the process of identifying, defining, and bounding a research question as consisting of two main steps: identifying the research area and honing the area into a manageable research question. For the researcher either just embarking on a research agenda or continuing a more well-established one, a number of mechanisms exist by which to identify an initial policy relevant area in a defined health domain. These include reviewing disease-specific treatment guidelines for the evidence base regarding a particular recommendation, examining grant-related requests for application (RFAs), and considering foundation and institute areas of focus.

Other mechanisms are to evaluate the literature for expert opinion on emerging research priorities, engage in discussion with clinical and policy experts on-the-ground, attend national and international meetings, and monitor the popular press for problems and important policy topics. All can be used to assist in identifying a policy question about which consensus does not exist or for which inadequate evidence is available.

The next step in the process involves defining and articulating a clear, concise research question. The process may begin with a review of the literature to identify previous work, existing knowledge gaps, and how the proposed research can add to the evidence base. The process necessarily becomes iterative as the research moves from a broader inquiry to a narrower proposal with well-defined boundaries and an a priori hypothesis. Additional considerations when defining the research question include manageability of the question given time, geographic, funding, and/or other logistical constraints.

15.2.2 Conceptualizing a Model and Developing a Model Framework

Once the research question is defined, the researcher and his or her team are charged with developing the "conceptual framework" of the study. That is, given the research question, what mathematical modeling approach will be used to address the research question and how can this approach be articulated graphically? This approach often can be outlined using a model schematic, one type of conceptual framework. In a model schematic, the model's structure is diagramed as a series of linkages among elements (e.g., health states) of a particular public health problem [2, 3]. Conceptual frameworks used in applied health policy models mainly provide a means to illustrate pathways, or transitions, among different stages of disease or systems of care. The different elements of the problem are linked together by arrows. The arrows can be interpreted mathematically as probabilities ranging from 0 to 1 (e.g., state-transition models, simulation models) or rates ranging from zero to infinity (e.g., dynamic compartmental model).

The uses of a conceptual framework can go beyond providing a map for the development of the applied health policy model. Depending on the complexity of the schematic, they also can serve as a useful tool with which to communicate to policy makers or other interested readers who may not be familiar with mathematical models. For example, presentation of a basic model structure (e.g., a simple model with Well, Sick, or Dead health states) can show decision makers how the analyst thinks about different elements of disease and its treatment. By showing different health states and transitions among those health states, conceptual frameworks can also articulate how researchers hypothesize different pathways in the disease or system impact outcomes. Conceptual frameworks can be used to illustrate gaps in knowledge where data may not exist. For example, the analyst can modify the way arrows are depicted (e.g., via the color or size of an arrow) to indicate broadly the transitions between health states where data are available or unavailable, or where the evidence is strong or relatively uncertain. Finally, conceptual frameworks can be modified (e.g., by circling arrows) to show how transitions between health states reflect the different interventions under consideration.

Development of the conceptual framework is also influenced by other factors. For example, in settings where data may be limited or of poor quality, the conceptual framework may be informed by the availability of data to populate the health policy model. Conceptual frameworks often require targeted modification of the model to available local data, and model development thus necessarily becomes iterative. That is, the analyst develops a conceptual framework, identifies data sources that will inform relationships between different elements of the schematic, and modifies the framework in part based on data availability. In other cases, the conceptual framework is informed by trade-offs between model complexity and model tractability. That is, given underlying goals of using models to inform policy, analysts may choose a simpler, more transparent structure in order to improve accessibility of the model and its results to policymakers.

15.2.3 Example: Context and Framework to Develop an Applied HIV Policy Model for Resource-Limited Settings

15.2.3.1 Policy Context: Funding Uncertainty for HIV Treatment Expansion

Antiretroviral therapy (ART) has been shown to be highly effective for the treatment of HIV [4–6]. Major advances in biomedical research along with unprecedented donor initiatives and increasing in-country commitments have transformed HIV from a terminal disease into a chronic one. This progress has facilitated rapid increases in the numbers tested and receiving treatment in low- and middle-income countries, with an over 13-fold increase in the number of HIV-infected individuals receiving ART in these settings over a 6-year time horizon [7].

These developments and a recently reinvigorated US campaign suggest reason for optimism [8]. However, the global economic crisis, and diminishing political commitment to HIV prevention and treatment have resulted in declines in donor disbursements for ART provision and decreasing country-level budgets [9–11]. This occurs at a time when need for ART is increasing. Rising demand has been fueled by improved case identification and linkage to and retention of HIV-infected individuals in care [12, 13]; an independent effect of HIV treatment on reducing mortality in HIV-infected individuals [4–6]; revised international guidelines that recommend treatment initiation earlier in the course of disease [14, 15]; and evidence suggesting ART can decrease the risk of HIV transmission [16, 17].

Against a backdrop of decreasing donor funding and increasing need, resource availability for expanded HIV treatment provision in some countries remains uncertain.

In this context, it is possible to partner with clinicians and policymakers to pinpoint the question(s) of immediate policy relevance on a national scale: How many deaths could be averted due to further expansion of HIV treatment in a particular setting? How many lives could be lost should further expansion be limited? How many new HIV infections could be averted? What is the value for money of further treatment expansion and is it affordable? By addressing these questions, it is possible to shed light on how HIV treatment-related resources can be efficiently and effectively targeted in order to improve health outcomes.

15.2.3.2 Model Conceptual Structure

An iterative process—including creating a conceptual framework, implementing the model, deriving parameter inputs, and verifying the model's performance—was required to develop an applied model for HIV treatment expansion in resource-limited settings. In this process, patient- and population-level data, as well as current HIV clinical practice in the setting of interest and internationally [14], were used to develop a state-transition, multi-cohort model of treated and untreated HIV disease.

In the first stage of conceptualizing the model, we began by identifying those aspects of HIV disease progression relevant to the policy question. Because we were interested in expanding HIV treatment through treatment initiation earlier in disease progression [14, 15], distinct stages of disease were modeled that correspond with different treatment initiation policies and available country-specific data. For consistency and clinical relevance, the natural history of HIV disease (i.e., untreated HIV disease) was modeled similarly. When conceptualizing untreated and treated HIV disease progression for this model, we did so in the context of available country-specific, patient-level data. These data allowed customization of the model structure to local data.

We also identified main model outcomes relevant to our policy question. These outcomes included the number of HIV-related deaths annually as well as the number of HIV-infected individuals receiving treatment each year. In general, the main outcomes of interest required less clinical detail than used in other HIV forecasting models [18–22]. This allowed for a relatively simple model structure that would improve transparency to policy makers and other consumers of model results. We also considered secondary annual outcome measures, such as the number of HIV-infected individuals in care, the number lost from care, and treatment capacity, since variation in these parameters could impact the main outcome measure. While inclusion of cost-related outcomes was considered, it was ultimately determined that it was beyond the scope of the initial model development effort. However, the model was structured in order to accommodate this outcome in future efforts.

By the end of the iterative process, in order to characterize disease progression for each individual cohort in the model, we defined three mutually exclusive and collectively exhaustive stages of untreated HIV disease: Asymptomatic disease

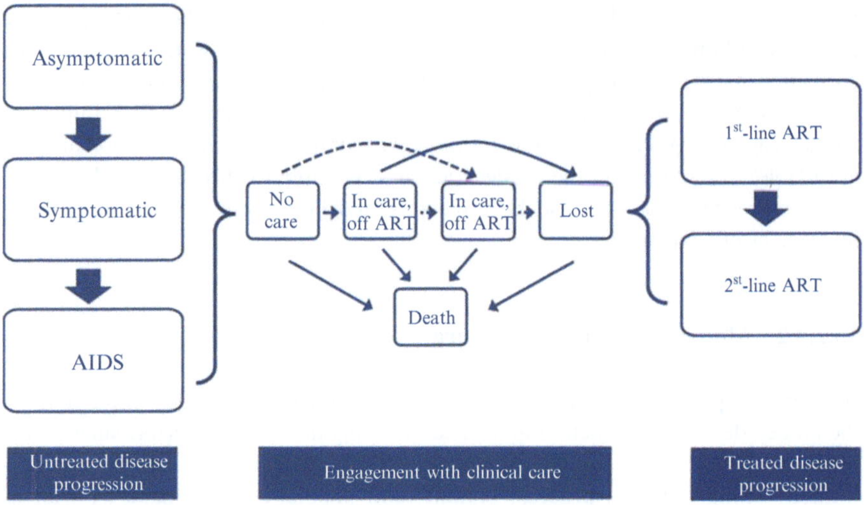

Fig. 15.1 Conceptual framework for the applied HIV policy model. The model is conceptualized such that each cohort of HIV-infected individuals in the model may experience untreated (*left-hand side*) or treated (*right-hand side*) disease progression. Untreated disease progression occurs in one of three mutually exclusive stages of HIV disease, with disease stage severity increasing as HIV-infected individuals progress from asymptomatic disease to symptomatic disease to AIDS. Within each disease stage, a fraction of the cohort may engage with clinical care (*middle*). This occurs through HIV case detection and linkage to care, ART initiation, or loss from treatment or care. Disease progression and movement through different clinical care-related events is governed by transition probabilities, which are denoted by *arrows*. The *dashed arrows* imply that transitions to or from a particular event can only arise among those individuals eligible for ART. HIV treatment expansion, as recommended in current international HIV treatment guidelines, implies HIV-infected individuals who are either Symptomatic or have AIDS are eligible to initiate ART [14]. Death can occur from any stage and may be due to AIDS-or non-AIDS-related causes. Abbreviations: *ART* antiretroviral therapy, *Lost* loss from treatment or care

(i.e., CD4 count >350 cells/μL), Symptomatic disease (CD4 count 200–350 cells/μL), and AIDS (CD4 count <200 cells/μL) (Fig. 15.1) [14, 15]. These health states reflected clinically meaningfully stages of disease progression as well as implementation of the revised international treatment guidelines. That is, current guidelines recommend treatment expansion to include treatment provision for HIV-infected individuals with Symptomatic disease as well as with AIDS [14]. Within each disease stage, events could occur that were defined according to engagement with HIV clinical care. A fraction of each cohort could be detected as HIV-infected but not in care; detected and in care, but not receiving ART; in care and receiving ART; lost from treatment or care; or dead from AIDS- or non-AIDS-related causes. Those individuals who were in clinical care and receiving ART could receive either a first- or second-line sequential ART regimen. Disease progression and engagement with clinical care would occur according to transition probabilities (see Sect. 15.4).

In conceptualizing the model, a state-transition, multi-cohort framework was selected. The model begins with a prevalent HIV-infected cohort, with fractions of the prevalent cohort distributed across the different defined health stages. In subsequent time periods, incident, or newly HIV-infected, individuals enter the model in the untreated, asymptomatic disease stage. At specified time intervals, the fraction of the total population in each stage of disease can remain in or transition to another stage of disease.

A multi-cohort approach, versus an individual cohort approach, was chosen for several reasons. First, it can provide population-level summary results for health (and economic) consequences both cross-sectionally and over time [23]. Second, this type of model structure can leverage availability of public health data for model calibration (See Sect. 15.5) [23]. Third, it can accommodate the unique characteristics of a starting (i.e., prevalent) cohort by allowing the entire eligible HIV-infected population—versus a single incident cohort—to experience the impact of changes in treatment expansion policies [24].

Several additional decisions were made in the model conceptualization process. For example, in order to simplify the model structure, population-level disease dynamics are not incorporated in the model, which includes only HIV-infected individuals and excludes disease transmission. While recent evidence suggests ART may decrease HIV transmission [16, 17], a relatively small impact on population-level results of treatment expansion was hypothesized given the short analytic time horizon chosen (See Sects. 15.3.1.1 and 15.3.2.1). However, the model was structured to accommodate user-defined variation in the number of newly HIV-infected individuals annually, including decreasing new infections over time.

In sum, the model framework reflects policy-relevant health outcomes, relies on availability of country-specific data, and captures important aspects of disease progression and clinical care. The relatively simple model structure promotes both transparency and accessibility. Finally, while designed to address a specific research question, it can be adapted to assess other HIV-related policy questions in resource-limited settings.

15.3 Building and Implementing the Model

Once the model has been conceptualized, the analyst must attend to other practical matters. These include, for example, determining an analytic time horizon [25–27], choosing a cycle length [25, 26, 28, 29], and identifying a software platform with which to build and implement the model [30]. In the sections that follow, we discuss each of these areas and follow with an example using the applied HIV policy model for resource-limited settings.

15.3.1 Some Practical Matters

15.3.1.1 Determining an Analytic Time Horizon

The time horizon in health-related mathematical models is the overall duration of time over which relevant health and/or economic consequences are forecast. If the model requires a "burn-in" period to achieve a steady-state or is calibrated to historical data, the overall model time horizon may be distinct from the analytic time horizon. The analytic time horizon refers to the period of time over which alternative strategies or scenarios are evaluated against each other. The analytic time horizon should be of sufficient duration to be policy relevant, as well as demonstrate relevant differences in health and/or economic consequences across strategies. Longer analytic time horizons (e.g., lifetime) may be more appropriate when treatment strategies have individual survival rates that vary differently over time, while shorter term analytic time horizons (e.g., 5 or 10 years) may be justified if longer term conditions or disease progression do not vary across strategies [31]. Mathematical models that rely on shorter term analytic time horizons can also be useful to decision makers who require short-term health- and cost-related information in order to assist them in making policy decisions while still allowing consideration of long term effects if the model includes terminal rewards. Shorter time horizons also avoid uncertainties about long-term population trends, but they may not adequately capture epidemic effects important for decision making.

15.3.1.2 Choosing a Cycle Length

The cycle length represents a discrete time interval during which a single transition to a clinical or other event related to the disease or system process may occur. More precisely, it is defined as a unit of time within the analytic time horizon, where units of time are divided in equal increments across the time horizon. Determining the unit of time (e.g., 1 month, 1 year) is based primarily on clinical relevance, such that the cycle length reflects a suitable time frame during which related clinical events can occur. One transition from one health state or event to another occurs within a single cycle.

A cycle length that does not adequately reflect clinical or system follow-up may introduce bias into model results. This can occur when too few events occur in a single cycle (i.e., if a cycle length is too long) or when events do not last their full clinical duration (i.e., if a cycle length is too short) [29]. At times, the cycle length may be determined by data availability [32]. Decisions about cycle length can also be influenced by computational efficiency [33]. For example, if a disease is modeled that has a relatively long analytic time horizon, a shorter cycle time could increase computing time. Computing time would further increase as more complexity is introduced into the model (e.g., increased number of health states or adoption of a stochastic model structure).

15.3.1.3 Implementing the Model

A number of different software platforms exist to assist the analyst in building and implementing the conceptual model. These include specialized software for health-related decision analytic, Markov models, and Monte Carlo simulations (e.g., TreeAge Pro, winDM); discrete event simulation (e.g., Arena/SIMAN, Simul8, TreeAge Pro); dynamic epidemiologic models (e.g., Berkeley Madonna); and agent-based modeling (e.g., Swarm). Other general programming and statistical languages (e.g., Matlab, R) can be used to implement almost all of these types of models. While commercially available software packages can facilitate implementing the model, they may require excessive computing time, advanced operational skills, or other resources that may diminish the feasibility of their use in some settings. When model complexity surpasses the capabilities of commercially available software, health policy models can be built using a general-purpose computer programming languages (e.g., C++), although intensive computing time and high-level programming skills are often required. Simpler health policy models may rely on spreadsheet software (e.g., Microsoft Excel). Given the wide availability of spreadsheet software, spreadsheet models may facilitate more transparent understanding of health policy models, improve their accessibility, and promote sharing of the model and results across settings [34, 35].

15.3.2 Example: An Applied HIV Policy Model for Resource-Limited Settings

15.3.2.1 Nuts and Bolts: Time Horizon and Cycle Length

In developing the applied HIV policy model for resource-limited settings, the model was partitioned into distinct time horizons to assess two policy-relevant eras of HIV/AIDS treatment: (1) a 5-year antiretroviral scale-up period that could be compared to country-level empirical data, and (2) a 10-year policy projection period that reflected a period of uncertainty regarding further HIV treatment expansion.

The duration of the first time horizon—the antiretroviral scale-up period—was chosen based on availability of publically available data. Historical, population-level data on HIV treatment scale-up coupled with patient-level data on treated and untreated disease progression allowed for formal model performance assessment, as well as for derivation of model inputs for those parameters that were highly uncertain (see Sect. 15.5) [36]. The subsequent era of HIV/AIDS treatment represents an analytic time horizon that would be relevant for policy makers in a resource-limited setting and from which they would need information to make policy decisions. Results from a longer analytic time horizon (e.g., 20 years, lifetime) may be subject to uncertainty, since disease-specific hazard functions may not be constant over time and disease transmission dynamics are not adequately captured [25, 27, 37]. A shorter analytic time horizon (e.g., 1 year) may not reveal significant differences in results across the alternative HIV treatment expansion strategies or communicate policy-relevant outcomes to decision makers.

After defining the time horizon, a cycle length was chosen. We considered a number of matters regarding cycle length, including the timing of clinical events relevant to the research question and availability of data. We began by examining the main health outcomes of interest: mortality, the number of HIV-infected individuals receiving HIV treatment, and treatment coverage, or the fraction of those HIV-infected individuals eligible to receive treatment who actually received it. Because a 1-year interval between events reflected a clinically relevant interval during which transitions to different events could realistically occur, it was decided that reporting of these outcomes would occur annually. In addition, an annual cycle length reflected how population-level data, which also could be used to calibrate the model (see Sect. 15.5), were reported [38]. While a 1-year cycle length was chosen for these reasons, concerns existed that this relatively long cycle would allow too few events to occur in a single cycle and therefore underestimate model outcomes over the analytic time horizon. For example, in the original model conceptual framework, HIV-infected individuals transitioned sequentially from No Care to In Care, Off ART and then to In Care, on ART (see Fig. 15.1). With an annual cycle length, this implies that it would take a minimum of two cycles (i.e., 2 years) for a newly identified HIV-infected individual to initiate ART. While this 2-year duration may be realistic for cases identified early in the course of disease (e.g., Asymptomatic), it may overestimate time in the clinical care pathway and thus underestimate deaths among cases identified, linked to care, and enrolled on ART in later stages of disease (e.g., Symptomatic or AIDS) when ART initiation among newly identified cases may occur more rapidly. To accommodate this limitation, additional transitions among health states (e.g., No Care to In Care, on ART) were included in the model structure. After making these model refinements, we were able to evaluate choice of cycle length by formally assessing model performance, which involved comparing model predictions to empiric patient-level data (see Sects. 15.5.1.2 and 15.5.2).

15.3.2.2 Model Software and Usability: How Much the "Black Box"?

A major consideration in building an applied model involves understanding how the consumers of the model—e.g., policy makers—will use, digest, and relay results. Policy makers may have little access to or training in the more sophisticated methods and software typically used to build policy models. Therefore, in implementing the model, it was important that it be conceptually simple, transparent in design, efficient to use, and easy to understand. In the initial plans to conceptualize and build the model, it was intended that the model not only rigorously address the policy question of interest but that it could be used, with guidance, by policy makers in resource-limited settings. It was decided, therefore, to build the model in spreadsheet format using Microsoft Excel, a widely available spreadsheet tool (Fig. 15.2). This straightforward and intuitive user interface allows

a

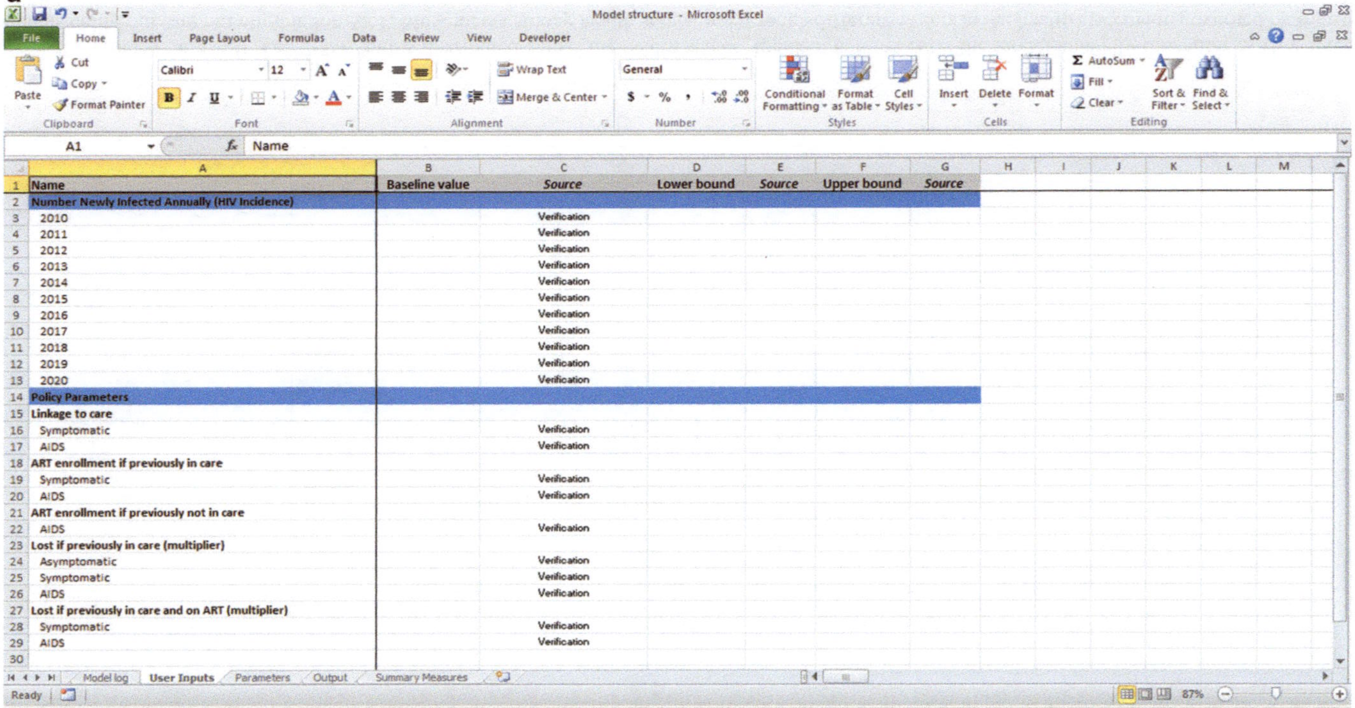

Fig. 15.2 The applied HIV policy model. Shown is an abbreviated model in spreadsheet format (Microsoft Excel). Panel (**a**) shows selected parameter values entered by the model user. The first column shows the different user-defined parameters. The columns that follow allow for entry of the baseline value, lower and upper bounds, and related sources. Panel (**b**) shows the structure for model output. The first column lists different health stages and events that a cohort can experience. Time, by year, is displayed horizontally in the upper rows. Each cell in the subsequent columns shows, once model inputs are derived and the model implemented, the number of HIV-infected individuals experiencing a particular event annually. The starting, or prevalent, cohort enters the model

b

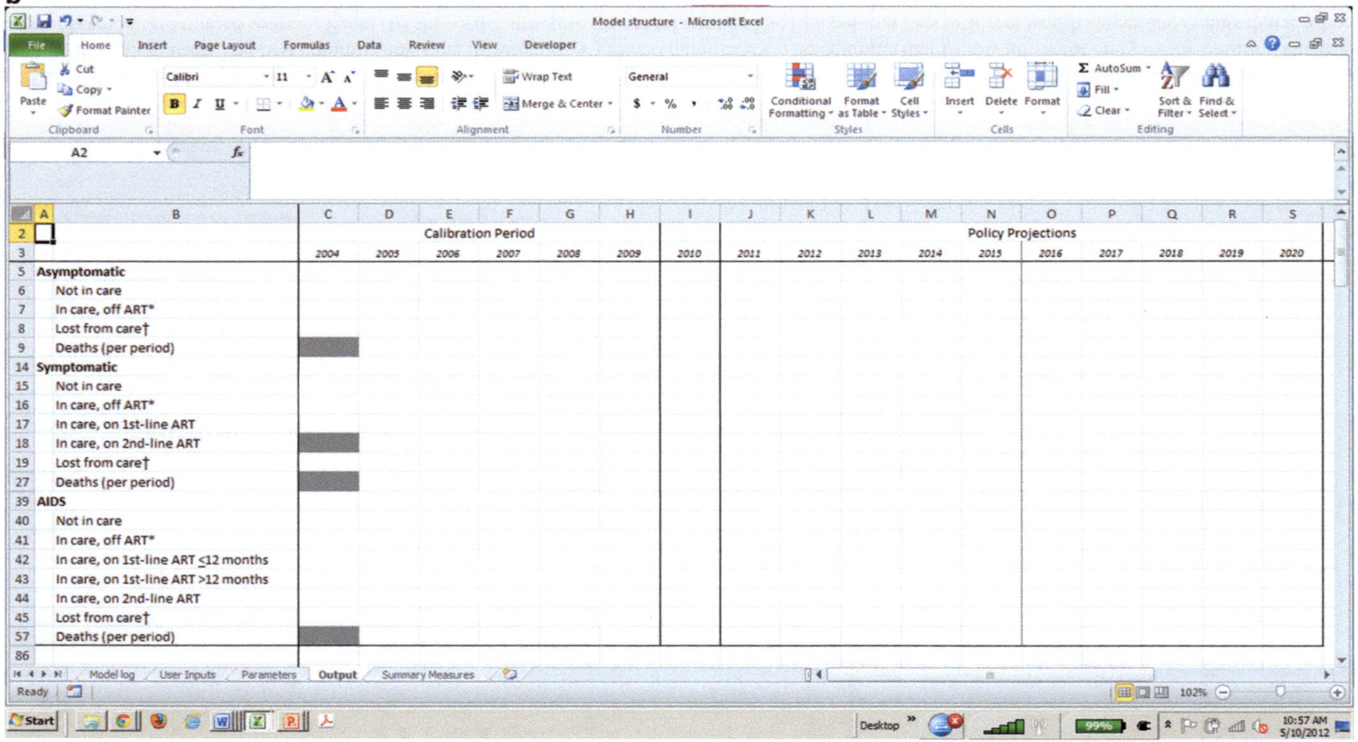

Fig. 15.2 (continued) at $t = 0$ (i.e., 2004) and is distributed across the health stages. Incident cohorts enter the model annually thereafter as HIV-infected individuals neither in care nor eligible for ART. Movements among health stages and through different events in the health system are governed by transition probabilities. The model consists of two eras of HIV treatment, including historical ART scale-up (i.e., the model calibration period) between 2004 and 2009 and 10-year policy projections in subsequent years. The three main health states are shown: Asymptomatic disease (i.e., CD4 count >350 cells/μL), Symptomatic disease (CD4 count 200–350 cells/μL), and AIDS (CD4 count <200 cells/μL). Abbreviations: *ART* antiretroviral therapy

the user to control variation in relevant model inputs, can accommodate built-in logic checks to promote correct input of model parameter estimates, display model formula or macros clearly to interested users, and be designed to succinctly summarize results [39].

15.4 Model Inputs

After the model has been conceptualized and the framework implemented, model parameters (i.e., model inputs) are derived and/or estimated. Sources for model parameters are varied and can include primary patient-level data, the existing literature, population-level reports, or, at times, other modeling studies or model calibration exercises. We discuss some of these sources and associated methods for deriving model inputs below and invite the interested reader to consult other relevant references on the topic [23, 31, 40].

15.4.1 Methods and Sources for Obtaining Parameter Estimates

15.4.1.1 Estimating Parameter Inputs from Patient-Level Data

For applied models generated from multidisciplinary partnerships among policy analysts, clinicians, and decision makers, it may be possible to capitalize on access to country-specific, patient-level data. These data may come from observational studies, clinical trials, national monitoring systems, or other databases (e.g., clinic-based electronic records), with relatively basic statistical analysis required to estimate model inputs. In cases where disease progression and access to treatment and care may vary significantly by setting, patient-level data not only improves the contextual and policy relevance of the model, but can also provide key scientific insights that inform the model structure and research question(s).

To reflect treated and/or untreated disease progression of individual cohorts, patient-level primary data can be used to derive inputs—in the form of transition rates or probabilities—for use in a model. Incidence density analysis can be performed to estimate the rate at which different events occur (i.e., progression from one health state to another) [41]:

$$\text{Incidence density} = \frac{\text{Number of events observed during interval}}{\text{Person time at risk for event during interval}}$$

Ideally suited for situations in which long-term event failure rates do not vary across the strategies under evaluation, incidence density analysis assumes events occur in a Poisson process (i.e., continuously, independently, and at a constant rate). The time between the events has an exponential distribution, which allows conversion of a constant event rate (r) over a period of time (t) to a probability (p) [42]:

$$p = 1 - \exp(-rt)$$

It is critical for the analyst to use the appropriate data input—either a rate or a probability, depending on the model structure—since there are important differences between the two [23, 43]. Rates represent the number of events for a given number of individuals per unit time [43]; a probability, on the other hand, is defined as the chance an event will occur over a defined period of time [23]. Similarly, the two have different mathematical properties: Rates can be added, subtracted, multiplied, and divided. Probabilities, however, cannot since they are conditional on having been event free at the beginning of the time interval; therefore, a 1-year probability of death is not the same as 3-year probability of death divided by 3. We direct the reader to Briggs, Claxton, and Sculpher as well as Kuntz and Weinstein for further information [23, 43].

One important feature of incidence density analysis is that the estimated rates, and derived probabilities, are constant. It is possible to estimate model inputs that vary over time [43], and in some instances this is the most appropriate approach for deriving model inputs (e.g., age-adjusted mortality risk for models with a lifetime analytic time horizon). However, there are advantages to using incidence density analysis for applied health policy models in resource-limited settings, particularly when the analytic time horizon is relatively short. First, the methodological concept is simple and transparent, such that policy makers can understand how model inputs are derived. Second, this data analysis requires relatively basic statistical skills and software programming competency. Therefore, incidence density analysis is both teachable and reproducible, allowing for technology transfer and research capacity building in settings that could benefit from it.

15.4.1.2 Estimating Parameter Inputs from the Literature

When primary patient-level data are unavailable, other sources are available to the analyst, including disease registries, publically available reports and, as an alternative but less recommended option, expert opinion. An additional common source from which to derive model inputs is secondary data from the medical and health-related literature.

The first step in estimating model inputs from secondary data is to amass all relevant evidence specific to a particular model parameter. Published estimates from randomized, controlled clinical trials or meta-analyses of randomized trials are useful for determining the effect (i.e., efficacy) of an intervention relative to another intervention under ideal circumstances. Published estimates from cohort studies and related meta-analyses may be useful in determining the effect (here, effectiveness) under more real-world, representative conditions [44]. At times, health policy models may have less complex structures that do not account for the many factors that may alter trial-based estimates. Other times, models may be applied to settings in which effectiveness estimates may differ substantially from efficacy estimates, a common situation in resource-limited settings. In these cases, cohort studies may provide a more realistic source from which to derive model inputs.

An important consideration when using applied policy models in resource-limited settings is the use of country- or setting-specific estimates and knowing how to appropriately bound the gathered information. While data synthesis is critical to understanding the evidence base and an important component of the model parameter estimation process, the analyst should use discretion about the appropriateness of using all available data when deriving model inputs. For example, estimates of HIV-related retention in treatment may differ according to setting or target population. The inclusion of some secondary data, therefore, may vary depending on the research question under consideration.

Secondary data rarely are presented in a way that the analyst can immediately enter the data into the model. For example, the literature may report the cumulative probability of an event, when an annual probability is required as a model input parameter. After identifying and, if necessary, synthesizing the data, they should be transformed appropriately for use in the model. It is beyond the scope of this chapter to present different mathematical tricks of the trade regarding data manipulation. However, the interested reader is referred to Kuntz and Weinstein for further information on this topic [23].

15.4.1.3 Estimating Parameter Inputs Through Model Calibration

At times, neither primary nor secondary data may be available to populate model parameters, and expert opinion may not provide a sufficiently reliable data source. Other times, model structure simplifications may result in model predictions that poorly approximate observed data. In these cases, model calibration may be used as a means to estimate or revise model inputs within a range informed by the available data. The calibration process also serves as one component of a broader model verification process. Later sections describe this process in further detail (see Sect. 15.5).

15.4.2 Example: Model Inputs for an Applied HIV Policy Model

The applied HIV health policy model capitalizes on availability of primary patient-level data on treated and untreated HIV disease progression. Incidence density analysis is performed to estimate the total number of events (e.g., the number of untreated symptomatic individuals progressing to AIDS), relative to the total person-time at risk for the event. Reflecting the state-transition model structure (see Sect. 15.2.3.2), the constant event rates estimated from the primary data are converted to probabilities for use as input parameters in the model [42]. For each estimated event, the 95 % confidence intervals, which represent the uncertainty of the point estimate, are used as upper and lower bounds in sensitivity analysis.

Due to a paucity of data, the number of newly HIV-infected individuals annually and their engagement with clinical care—including linkage to care, pre-ART retention in care, and ART enrollment—come from modeled estimates obtained during model verification (see Sect. 15.5). For the interested reader, Table 15.1 shows a sample shell table of model inputs in which selected input values from both the primary data estimation process and model verification are presented.

15.5 Model Verification

Model verification is a formal, systematic process that involves assessing the degree to which models are able to represent the real-world. This process is a time consuming aspect of model building. It is also an essential component of the model building and implementation process, since it can encourage confidence in the analyst, policy makers, and other consumers that the model will provide useful predictions [45].

A number of iterative steps can be taken in order to verify model performance, with the duration of this process continuing as long as new data continue to emerge and new or reanalysis is sought. In the text that follows, we outline some steps that can be taken during model verification, discuss methods to complete these steps, and end with an example using the applied HIV policy model for resource-limited settings. We also direct the interested reader to external literature that addresses this topic [1, 36, 46–52], as well as to several applied examples of model verification [46, 52–57].

15.5.1 Methods for Verifying Model Performance

15.5.1.1 Internal Consistency

The first stage in assessing model performance begins directly after the model has been constructed. Internal consistency consists mainly of debugging, where model inputs are at the extreme (e.g., 0 or 1, if using probabilities) and the outputs then evaluated for reasonableness. That is, the analyst evaluates specific outcomes and trends in those outcomes to ensure the model is doing what the analyst expects that it would. For example, if the probability of mortality from a treatment intervention were set equal to 1, then the analyst would expect that death would not only occur in

Table 15.1 Presenting model inputs: sample parameters for the HIV policy model

Panel A

Parameter	Value	Range	Source(s)
Prevalent cohort			
Number HIV-infected			
Number receiving ART			
Incident cohorts			
Number newly infected annually			Verification[a]

Panel B

Parameter	Events/100 PYs	Annual Probability	Range	Source(s)
Untreated disease progression				
Sympt if Asympt				Verification[a]
AIDS if Sympt				Verification[a]
Death if Asympt				
Death if Sympt				
Death if AIDS				
Treated disease progression				
ART2 if Early ART1				
ART2 if Late ART1				
Death if Early ART				
Death if Late ART				
Linkage to care and treatment				
Care if Sympt				Verification[a]
Care if AIDS				Verification[a]
ART if Sympt				Verification[a]
ART if AIDS				Verification[a]
Loss from ART				
Loss if Early ART				Verification[a]
Loss if Late ART				Verification[a]

Abbreviations: Verification model verification process, *PYs* person-years, *Sympt* symptomatic HIV disease, *Asympt* asymptomatic HIV disease, *ART* antiretroviral therapy, *ART2* second-line antiretroviral therapy, *ART1* first-line antiretroviral therapy, *Early* eligibility for antiretroviral therapy initiation during symptomatic HIV disease, *Late* eligibility for antiretroviral therapy initiation if AIDS

[a]The model verification process was used to confirm that model projections correspond with historical, population-level data. In this process, multiple, uncertain model input parameters were systematically varied. The input values that resulted in model outcomes best approximating empirical data were then identified [38]

all who received treatment, but that the fraction of the cohort dying would occur faster than in a scenario in which the probability were set equal to 0. While it is possible to evaluate computer code for typographical or logic errors, it is far more efficient for the analyst to test the model structure in this manner [1]. In addition, if the model structure involves lengthy or complicated calculations, internal consistency can be checked more easily by structuring model formulae into smaller component parts rather than a single long or complex formula. Verification of internal consistency continues throughout the model-building and development process. Each time a structural or coding-related change is made to the model, basic logic checks and other quality control measures should be conducted.

15.5.1.2 Internal Validation and Calibration

The second stage in the model verification process involves internal validation and, if necessary, internal calibration. In internal validation, the analyst confirms the quality of the model by comparing model predictions to the empiric data used to parameterize the model. If the model predictions do not adequately approximate the empiric data used to derive model inputs, and there is no model structure or coding error, internal calibration can then be performed. Here, specific model inputs are systematically varied in order to achieve a better fit of model predictions to the observed data used to parameterize the model.

The accuracy with which this approximation should occur as well as the methods used to assess internal validity and perform internal calibration are still emerging in the health-related modeling literature. Taylor and colleagues outline 4 iterative main steps in the calibration process: (1) identifying endpoints, (2) establishing measures of goodness-of-fit, (3) adjusting, if necessary, model input parameters, and (4) evaluating the model outcomes resulting from the revised model input parameters [46]. Karnon and Vanni further clarify the process by suggesting the analyst identify the specific parameters to be varied, characterize the parameter search strategy, and outlining acceptable goodness of fit and termination rules [50, 51]. Endpoints used in this process will vary and will reflect the data available to the analyst. They could include, for example, mortality, rates of comorbid illnesses, or probability of event-free "survival" (e.g., remaining on first-line HIV treatment). Goodness-of-fit measures also vary and include (in the order of least to most complex) visual fit, target window approaches, relative or absolute distances from the observed point estimate, likelihood-based approaches, and parameter search algorithms such as grid or random searches. Choice of goodness-of-fit is dependent on a multitude of factors, including availability of analyst and computer time and programming know-how.

An important consideration in the calibration process is to appreciate the degree of sophistication and complexity necessary to adequately calibrate a model. The analyst should always account for available resources—computing, technical, personnel, time—and balance the feasibility of different calibration techniques with additional precision gained by using a more complex method. Concerns about data availability and quality may also impact endpoint target or choice of calibration method; these concerns may be particularly salient in resource-limited settings.

15.5.1.3 External Calibration and Validation

At times, the analyst may have access to empiric data that is not used to derive model inputs. It is then possible to leverage availability of these data and externally calibrate the model. In this stage of model verification and performance assessment, the calibration process followed is similar to that described above (Sect. 15.5.1.2). In brief, empiric data not used to parameterize the model (i.e., "external" data) are identified. Uncertain model parameters are then varied such that model outcomes approximate the external empiric data. The external empiric data, which serve as the calibration endpoints, can represent a wide variety of different outcomes, including incidence or prevalence of disease. This stage of the process is particularly valuable when the analyst has uncertain or unknown information about the natural history and treatment of disease, and it can be used to shed light on unknown disease processes [53, 58].

For applied health policy models, it is particularly important to appreciate the quality of the data to which the model is externally calibrated. In resource-limited settings, for example, it is possible that available data may be based on limited surveillance or are subject to under-reporting (e.g., mortality) or over-reporting (e.g., number receiving treatment). While that should not prohibit use of the data, this limitation should be acknowledged in the external calibration process and appropriate calibration methods chosen, such that over-fitting of model predictions to empiric data is avoided.

A final step in the model verification process involves external validation, or comparison of model predictions to observed data using alternative data sources. This can be done in several ways. One method is to use an alternative, but representative data source to derive parameter inputs with which the model is initialized. Transition rates or probabilities as derived from the original sources remain the same. Model outcomes are then compared with empirical data from the alternative source. This method would evaluate the generalizability of model results to other target populations or settings. An alternative method, sometimes termed corroboration, is to compare model predictions with predictions generated by another mathematical model. This alternative method allows the analyst to compare the model structure to model frameworks developed by other researchers. These formal comparisons can highlight differences and similarities across models. At times, model results may not be comparable with predictions from other models, due to differences in model structure. However, other times, similarities in results across different models can provide model consumers with further confidence that the model is a reasonable representation of reality.

15.5.2 Validation and Calibration of an Applied HIV Policy Model for Resource-Limited Settings

We verified performance of the HIV policy model for resource-limited settings in a multistage, iterative process. We began by assessing internal consistency, or logic, of the model through a systematic debugging process. For each entering cohort in the model, all parameter inputs were varied individually in order to confirm that a given model input produced an expected model outcome. For example, when we assumed the probability of death was zero among individuals receiving HIV treatment, the expected model outcome was that the fraction of each cohort dying while on HIV treatment annually was zero. Unexpected outcomes were evaluated and the model revised accordingly.

The next stage of the model verification process involved internal validation and calibration in order to evaluate model outcome correspondence with the empiric patient-level data used to parameterize the model. The process began by identifying events or health state transitions corresponding with the empiric data (e.g., Symptomatic disease to AIDS). We then generated Kaplan-Meier, event-free survival estimates for each transition or series of transitions. Goodness-of-fit of the model predictions to the empiric data was determined through visual assessment of trend and by calculating the fraction of observations for a given transition(s) that fell within the 95% confidence intervals of the empiric data.

In some cases, the model outcomes did not adequately approximate the empiric patient-level data used to parameterize the model, due mainly to simplifications in the model structure. For example, the model did not initially account for increased mortality in the first year among individuals initiating ART in the AIDS health state. Therefore, a new health state was added to improve model fit to the empiric patient-level data (Fig. 15.3). If model structure changes were not considered appropriate, however, internal calibration was performed. For example, to simplify the model's structure, the decision was made for untreated disease to progress from Asymptomatic disease to Symptomatic disease to AIDS; the model structure did not allow for a transition from Asymptomatic disease to AIDS. Therefore, transitions between Asymptomatic and Symptomatic disease, as well as Symptomatic disease and AIDS were systematically varied over a plausible range. Model inputs were selected based on minimizing the mean percentage deviation between model predictions and the empiric data over 5- and 10-year time horizons. Model fit among calibrated parameters was then confirmed visually.

The final stage of the model verification process involved external calibration. Here, uncertain model inputs were systematically varied so that model outcomes approximated HIV treatment data that were not used to parameterize the model [38]. A wide range of HIV-related, population-level data—including the number on ART, estimated HIV prevalence, estimated HIV incidence, and estimated ART coverage—is available for resource-limited settings and can be drawn upon to externally calibrate applied policy models. In this case, it was decided to limit the main external calibration data source to the number of individuals on ART, since other available population-level data, while informative, were estimates from other mathematical models. Models from which these data were estimated have their own assumptions and it was determined that these estimates would be better suited for corroborating model results than for performing external calibration.

The external calibration process involved several steps. First, we identified uncertain parameters and made assumptions about the relationships among these

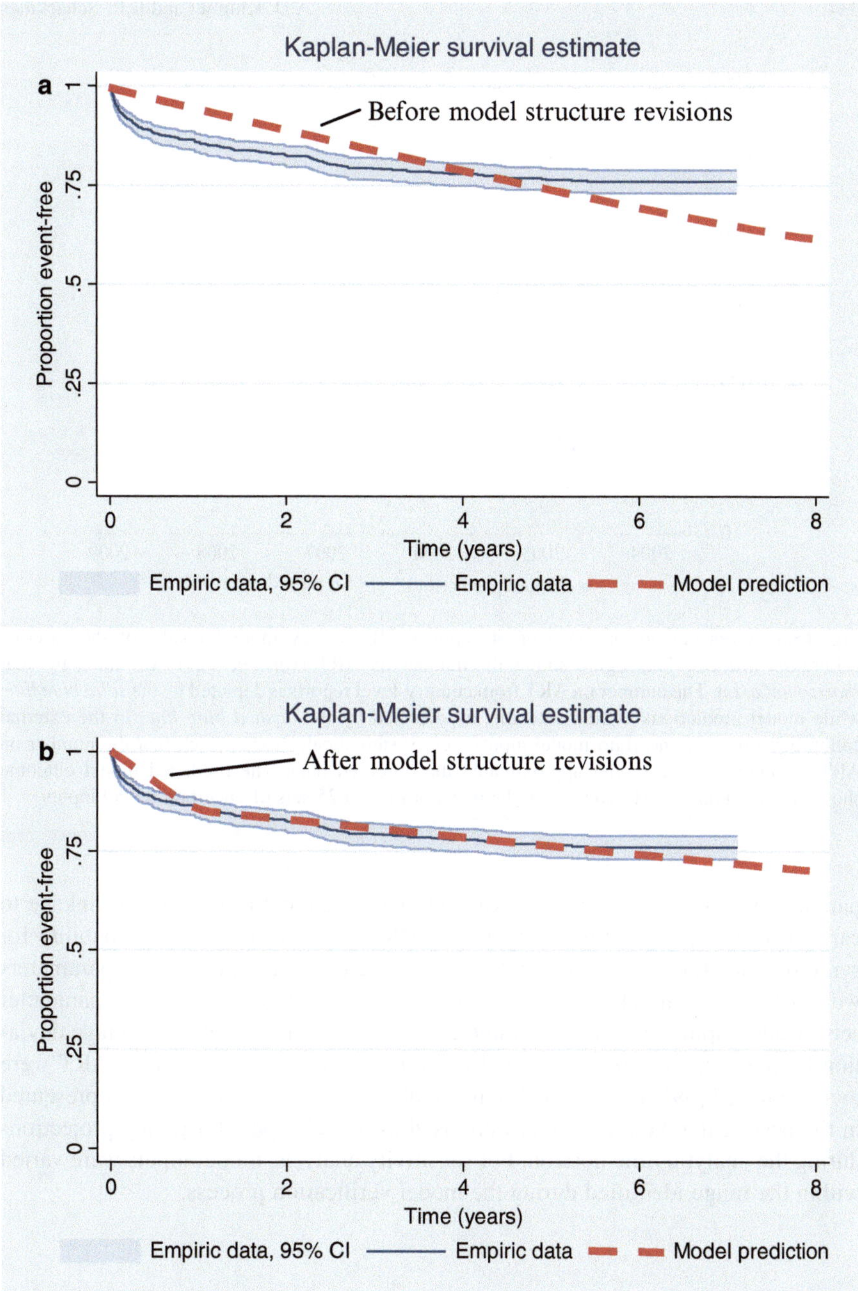

Fig. 15.3 Assessing performance of the applied HIV policy model: results of the internal validation process. This figure shows survival of an HIV-infected cohort with AIDS initiating first line ART, comparing estimates from the patient-level data with predictions form the model. The proportion of the cohort surviving (*vertical axis*) is shown over time (*horizontal axis*). Survival estimates from the empiric patient-level data are depicted by the *solid black line*, with 95 % confidence intervals shown *shaded in grey*. Survival as predicted by the model is shown by the *dashed red line*. In panel (**a**), the model did not account for increased mortality in the first year among individuals initiating ART in the AIDS health state. In panel (**b**), the model structure was revised by adding a new health state and model fit improves

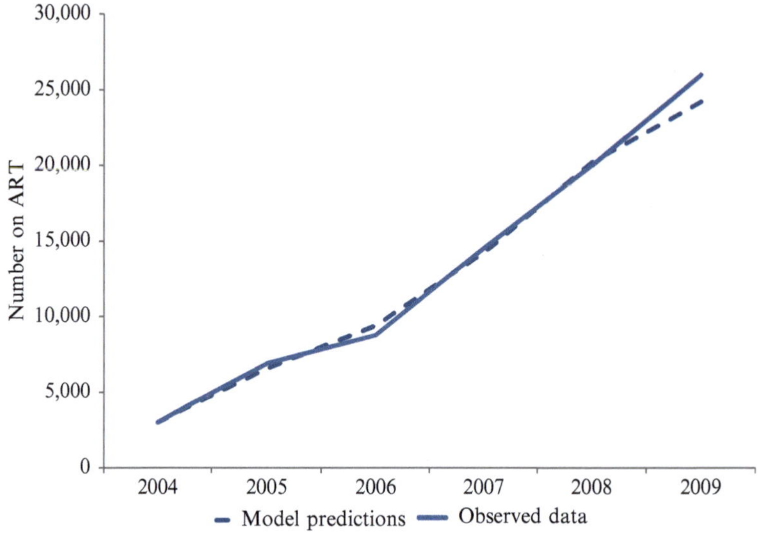

Fig. 15.4 Assessing performance of the applied HIV policy model: results of the external calibration process. This figure shows the number on ART (*vertical axis*) over time, by year (*horizontal axis*). The number on ART from country-level reports is depicted by the *solid blue line*, while model predictions of this outcome are depicted by the *dashed blue line*. In the external calibration process, uncertain model inputs were systematically varied such that the number on ART predicted by the model approximated the observed data. The predicted model outcome shown in this figure is estimated from the mean of the top 25 sets of uncertain model inputs

parameters. For example, it was assumed that the annual probability of linkage to care for HIV-infected individuals with AIDS exceeded the annual probability for symptomatic HIV-infected individuals. Multiple uncertain model input parameters were then systematically and simultaneously varied to generate unique parameter sets. Model input values from parameter sets that minimized the percentage deviation between model predictions and historical data for the number on ART were then identified [59] (Fig. 15.4). The mean of the uncertain input values represented in the best-fitting parameter sets were used as model inputs for policy projections during the analytic time horizon. For sensitivity analysis, model inputs were varied within the range identified during the model verification process.

15.6 Communicating Model Results to Policymakers

An important consideration in developing applied health policy models is understanding how to effectively communicate model results to policymakers, applied researchers, and other public health professionals. Integrating mathematical modeling methods and public health practice can pose unique communication challenges.

To combat these challenges, it is necessary to understand to whom the research is ultimately targeted. For applied health policy models, the primary target group includes policy makers, public health practitioners, public health researchers, and other decision makers. Therefore, deliberate steps should be taken from the time of model conception in order to effectively communicate research-related outcomes to the target audience. These include developing the most simple model structure possible and including increased complexity only if a policy concern warrants this complexity. Another involves; appropriately verifying model performance for historical comparison, such that model results are "believable". Identifying and projecting results for alternative, policy-relevant strategies for patient care represents an additional way to improve how information is consumed by the target audience. Finally, the methods and results of the research should be communicated in a way that is useful, useable, and digestible for policy makers, decision makers, and other public health researchers.

Practically, these steps can involve the following: (1) Formal partnerships between methodologists, public health professionals, policymakers, and clinical specialists to ensure that the model framework is understandable and that proposed strategies or interventions under evaluation are policy relevant, (2) Leveraging available empiric data to perform model performance verification in order to instill confidence in decision makers about the accuracy of model predictions, and (3) Presenting the research throughout the entire duration of the model development period to a variety of local, regional, and national audiences; publicizing the research and inviting critique at a wide range of public health, policy, and clinical conferences; and developing manuscripts that are targeted to the appropriate policy audience. Alistar and Brandeau make additional recommendations regarding input flexibility (e.g., customization to local conditions, incorporating uncertainty in the parameters); technical capability (e.g., dynamic effects, nonlinear treatment scale-up effects, intervention packages); and usability (e.g., public accessibility of the model) [35].

15.7 Conclusions and Policy Implications

In this chapter, we outlined a series of steps to be undertaken and considerations for building applied health policy models. We described some important stages in the process, from defining the research question and conceptualizing the model to verifying the performance of the applied model. For each, we provided a real-world example of a health policy model applied to HIV treatment expansion in a resource-limited setting. In so doing, we demonstrate the rigor with which these types of models can be implemented despite data or other resource limitations that the analyst will encounter. We do so while using a model that is understandable to individuals outside the research setting.

Operations research and decision analytic techniques are playing an increasing role in the development of applied health policy models. At a time when demand is growing globally for evidence of efficiency in delivery of health care and value for money of prevention and treatment interventions, researchers have the opportunity to draw on these methods in order to add to the evidence base for policy makers, health care consumers, and researchers alike. Applied health policy models play a unique role in this process. The degree to which results are understandable and communicated beyond the specialist user hinges on creating models that are simple, transparent, and useable by audiences well beyond the analyst. Developing applied health policy models that strike a reasonable balance between necessary model complexity, tractability, and usability remains one of the great challenges of the field.

References

1. Weinstein MC, Toy EL, Sandberg EA, Neumann PJ, Evans JS et al. (2001) Modeling for health care and other policy decisions: uses, roles, and validity. Value Health 4:348–361
2. Earp JA, Ennett ST (1991) Conceptual models for health education research and practice. Health Educ Res 6:163–171
3. Paradies Y, Stevens M (2005) Conceptual diagrams in public health research. J Epidemiol Community Health 59:1012–1013
4. (2008) Life expectancy of individuals on combination antiretroviral therapy in high-income countries: a collaborative analysis of 14 cohort studies. Lancet 372:293–299
5. Lima VD, Hogg RS, Harrigan PR, Moore D, Yip B et al. (2007) Continued improvement in survival among HIV-infected individuals with newer forms of highly active antiretroviral therapy. AIDS 21:685–692
6. Mills EJ, Bakanda C, Birungi J, Chan K, Ford N et al. (2011) Life expectancy of persons receiving combination antiretroviral therapy in low-income countries: a cohort analysis from Uganda. Ann Intern Med 155:209–216
7. World Health Organization, UNAIDS, UNICEF (2010) Towards universal access: scaling up priority HIV/AIDS interventions in the health sector. Progress Report 2010. World Health Organization, Geneva. http://www.who.int/hiv/pub/2010progressreport/summary_en.pdf
8. Clinton HR (2011) Remarks on "creating an AIDS-free generation". Bethesda. http://www.state.gov/secretary/rm/2011/11/176810.htm
9. Bonnel R, de Beyer J, Bennett D (2009) The global economic crisis and HIV prevention and treatment programmes: vulnerabilities and impact. The World Bank and UNAIDS. http://data.unaids.org/pub/Report/2009/jc1734_econ_crisis_hiv_response_en.pdf
10. Kates J, Wexler A, Lief E, Avila C, Gobet B (2011) Financing the response to AIDS in low- and middle-income countries: international assistance from the G8, European Commission and other donor governments in 2010. http://www.kff.org/hivaids/upload/7347–07.pdf
11. Moszynski P (2011) Global fund suspends new projects until 2014 because of lack of funding. BMJ 343:d7755
12. Rosen S, Fox MP, Gill CJ (2007) Patient retention in antiretroviral therapy programs in sub-Saharan Africa: a systematic review. PLoS Med 4:e298
13. World Health Organization (2011) Global health sector strategy on HIV/AIDS 2011–2015. World Health Organization. http://whqlibdoc.who.int/publications/2011/9789241501651_eng.pdf
14. World Health Organization (2010) Antiretroviral therapy for HIV infection in adults and adolescents: recommendations for a public health approach. 2010 revision. http://whqlibdoc.who.int/publications/2010/9789241599764_eng.pdf

15. World Health Organization (2006) Antiretroviral therapy for HIV infection in adults and adolescents in resource-limited settings: towards universal access. Recommendations for a public health approach. 2006 revision. World Health Organization,Geneva. http://www.who.int/hiv/pub/guidelines/artadultguidelines.pdf
16. Cohen MS, Chen YQ, McCauley M, Gamble T, Hosseinipour MC et al. (2011) Prevention of HIV-1 infection with early antiretroviral therapy. N Engl J Med 365:493–505
17. Donnell D, Baeten JM, Kiarie J, Thomas KK, Stevens W et al. (2010) Heterosexual HIV-1 transmission after initiation of antiretroviral therapy: a prospective cohort analysis. Lancet 375:2092–2098
18. Walensky RP, Wood R, Fofana MO, Martinson NA, Losina E et al. (2011) The clinical impact and cost-effectiveness of routine, voluntary HIV screening in South Africa. J Acquir Immune Defic Syndr 56:26–35
19. Kimmel AD, Weinstein MC, Anglaret X, Goldie SJ, Losina E et al. (2010) Laboratory monitoring to guide switching antiretroviral therapy in resource-limited settings: clinical benefits and cost-effectiveness. J Acquir Immune Defic Syndr 54:258–268
20. Bishai D, Colchero A, Durack DT (2007) The cost effectiveness of antiretroviral treatment strategies in resource-limited settings. AIDS 21:1333–1340
21. Bendavid E, Grant P, Talbot A, Owens DK, Zolopa A (2011) Cost-effectiveness of antiretroviral regimens in the World Health Organization's treatment guidelines: a South African analysis. AIDS 25:211–220
22. Braithwaite RS, Nucifora KA, Yiannoutsos CT, Musick B, Kimaiyo S et al. (2011) Alternative antiretroviral monitoring strategies for HIV-infected patients in east Africa: opportunities to save more lives? J Int AIDS Soc 14:38
23. Kuntz KM, Weinstein MC (2001) Modelling in economic evaluation. In: Drummond M, McGuire A (eds) Economic evaluation in health care: merging theory with practice. Oxford University Press, New York
24. Dewilde S, Anderson R (2004) The cost-effectiveness of screening programs using single and multiple birth cohort simulations: a comparison using a model of cervical cancer. Med Decis Making 24:486–492
25. Beck JR, Pauker SG (1983) The Markov process in medical prognosis. Med Decis Making 3:419–458
26. Sonnenberg FA, Beck JR (1993) Markov models in medical decision making: a practical guide. Med Decis Making 13:322–338
27. Benbassat J, Baumal R (2007) The time horizons of formal decision analyses. QJM 100:383–388
28. Naimark D, Krahn MD, Naglie G, Redelmeier DA, Detsky AS (1997) Primer on medical decision analysis: part 5—working with Markov processes. Med Decis Making 17:152–159
29. Price MJ, Briggs AH (2002) Development of an economic model to assess the cost effectiveness of asthma management strategies. Pharmacoeconomics 20:183–194
30. Stahl JE (2008) Modelling methods for pharmacoeconomics and health technology assessment: an overview and guide. Pharmacoeconomics 26:131–148
31. Weinstein MC, O'Brien B, Hornberger J, Jackson J, Johannesson M et al. (2003) Principles of good practice for decision analytic modeling in health-care evaluation: report of the ISPOR task force on good research practices—modeling studies. Value Health 6:9–17
32. Goldie SJ, Corso PS (2003) Decision analysis. In: Haddix AC, Teutsch SM, Corso PS (eds) Prevention effectiveness, 2nd edn. Oxford University Press, New York
33. Siebert U, Alagoz O, Bayoumi AM, Jahn B, Owens DK et al. (In press) State-transition modeling: a report of the ISPOR-SMDM modeling good research practices task force working group—part 5. Value Health
34. Kimmel AD, Fitzgerald DW, Charles M, Edwards AM, Marcelin A et al. (2012) Internal validation and calibration of a model to forecast HIV treatment demand and capacity in Haiti. Med Decis Making 32:E123

35. Alistar SS, Brandeau ML (2012) Decision making for HIV prevention and treatment scale up: bridging the gap between theory and practice. Med Decis Making 32:105–117
36. Weinstein MC (2006) Recent developments in decision-analytic modelling for economic evaluation. Pharmacoeconomics 24:1043–1053
37. Kuntz KM, Weinstein MC (1995) Life expectancy biases in clinical decision modeling. Med Decis Making 15:158–169
38. UNAIDS (2011) AIDSinfo database. http://www.aidsinfoonline.org/
39. Greasley A (1998) An example of a discrete-event simulation on a spreadsheet. Simulation 70:148–166
40. Briggs AH, Fenwick E, Karnon J, Paltiel AD, Schulpher M et al. (2012) DRAFT model parameter estimation and uncertainty: a report of the ISPOR-SMDM modeling good research practices task force working group-6. http://www.ispor.org/workpaper/modeling_methods/DRAFT-Modeling-Task-Force_Model-Parameter-Estimation-and-Uncertainty-Report.pdf
41. Porta MS (ed) (2008) A dictionary of epidemiology. Oxford University Press, Oxford
42. Lindgren BW (1993) Statistical theory. Chapman & Hall, New York, NY
43. Briggs AH, Claxton K, Sculpher M (2006) Decision modelling for health economic evaluation. Oxford University Press, New York
44. Concato J, Peduzzi P, Huang GD, O'Leary TJ, Kupersmith J (2010) Comparative effectiveness research: what kind of studies do we need? J Investig Med 58:764–769
45. Gold MR, Siegel JE, Russell LB, Weinstein MC (eds) (1996) Cost-effectiveness in health and medicine. Oxford University Press, New York
46. Taylor DC, Pawar V, Kruzikas D, Gilmore KE, Pandya A et al. (2010) Methods of model calibration: observations from a mathematical model of cervical cancer. Pharmacoeconomics 28:995–1000
47. Eddy DM, Hollingworth W, Caro JJ, Tsevat J, McDonald KM et al. (2012) DRAFT—model transparency and validation: a report of the ISPOR-SMDM modeling good research practices task force working group—part 4. http://www.ispor.org/workpaper/modeling_methods/DRAFT-Modeling-Task-Froce_Validation-and-Transparency-Report.pdf
48. Stout NK, Knudsen AB, Kong CY, McMahon PM, Gazelle GS (2009) Calibration methods used in cancer simulation models and suggested reporting guidelines. Pharmacoeconomics 27:533–545
49. McCabe C, Dixon S (2000) Testing the validity of cost-effectiveness models. Pharmacoeconomics 17:501–513
50. Karnon J, Vanni T (2011) Calibrating models in economic evaluation: a comparison of alternative measures of goodness of fit, parameter search strategies and convergence criteria. Pharmacoeconomics 29:51–62
51. Vanni T, Karnon J, Madan J, White RG, Edmunds WJ et al. (2011) Calibrating models in economic evaluation: a seven-step approach. Pharmacoeconomics 29:35–49
52. Hammerschmidt T, Goertz A, Wagenpfeil S, Neiss A, Wutzler P et al. (2003) Validation of health economic models: the example of EVITA. Value Health 6:551–559
53. Kim JJ, Kuntz KM, Stout NK, Mahmud S, Villa LL et al. (2007) Multiparameter calibration of a natural history model of cervical cancer. Am J Epidemiol 166:137–150
54. Salomon JA, Weinstein MC, Hammitt JK, Goldie SJ (2002) Empirically calibrated model of hepatitis C virus infection in the United States. Am J Epidemiol 156:761–773
55. Yeh JM, Kuntz KM, Ezzati M, Hur C, Kong CY et al. (2008) Development of an empirically calibrated model of gastric cancer in two high-risk countries. Cancer Epidemiol Biomarkers Prev 17:1179–1187
56. Rydzak CE, Cotich KL, Sax PE, Hsu HE, Wang B et al. (2010) Assessing the performance of a computer-based policy model of HIV and AIDS. PLoS One 5(9):e12647
57. Vanni T, Legood R, White RG (2010) Calibration of disease simulation model using an engineering approach. Value Health 13:157

58. Fryback DG, Stout NK, Rosenberg MA, Trentham-Dietz A, Kuruchittham V et al. (2006) The wisconsin breast cancer epidemiology simulation model. J Natl Cancer Inst Monogr (36):37–47
59. UNAIDS (2011) Country fact sheet: Haiti. http://www.unaids.org/en/dataanalysis/tools/aidsinfo/countryfactsheets/

Chapter 16
Cost-Effectiveness Analysis Using Registry and Administrative Data

Malek B. Hannouf and Gregory S. Zaric

Abstract Health administrative databases and disease registries can serve as valuable data sources for decision modeling and cost-effectiveness analyses. In this chapter, we give an overview of administrative databases in Canada and discuss how data from multiple registries and administrative databases can be linked, analyzed, and combined with experimental data to fit a decision analytic model. We illustrate with two examples of cost-effectiveness analyses of genetic tests used in cancer diagnosis and treatment decisions.

16.1 Introduction

Cost effectiveness analysis (CEA) is commonly used to assess the "value-for-money" of new medical technologies such as drugs, devices, policies, and procedures. Decision-making bodies in many jurisdictions have formally incorporated CEA into their processes for reviewing new medical technologies [1]. For example, the National Institutes for Health and Clinical Excellence (NICE) in the UK [2], the Pharmaceutical Benefits Advisory Committee (PBAC) in Australia [3], and the Common Drug Review (CDR) in Canada [4] all make use of CEA when considering reimbursement of new drugs.

CEA involves a formal comparison of the incremental costs and incremental benefits associated with switching from an existing technology or standard of care

M.B. Hannouf
Department of Epidemiology and Biostatistics, Schulich School of Medicine and Dentistry
Western University, London, ON, Canada

G.S. Zaric (✉)
Department of Epidemiology and Biostatistics, Schulich School of Medicine and Dentistry
Western University, London, ON, Canada

Richard Ivey School of Business, Western University, London, ON, Canada N6C 1A4
e-mail: gzaric@ivey.uwo.ca

G.S. Zaric (ed.), *Operations Research and Health Care Policy*,
International Series in Operations Research & Management Science 190,
DOI 10.1007/978-1-4614-6507-2_16,

to a new one. The results of a CEA are typically presented in the form of a ratio called the incremental cost-effectiveness ratio (ICER). The ICER associated with switching from an "Old" technology to a "New" one is given as ICER $= (\text{Cost}_{\text{New}} - \text{Cost}_{\text{Old}})/(\text{Health}_{\text{New}} - \text{Health}_{\text{Old}})$. Costs are expressed in currency units, and benefits are often expressed in common units, including life years gained or quality-adjusted life years (QALYs) gained. (QALYs are life years that have been adjusted by a value between 0 and 1 to reflect a difference in quality of life for different health conditions.)

CEAs often involve synthesis of data from multiple sources. When CEAs are used to inform health technology adoption decisions, policy-makers typically want evidence that is relevant to their jurisdiction or population. This information includes the use of local costs, consideration of local clinical practice and clinical guidelines, and appropriate comparators (i.e., an appropriate definition for "Old" in the ICER equation). These requirements are reflected in the formal CEA guidelines set out by several national agencies that produce and evaluate CEAs. In this regard, CEAs that are based entirely on secondary literature or on a single clinical trial might not be seen as appropriate or convincing to policy-makers; however, the use of local health databases, such as registries and administrative health databases, represents one way of incorporating local data into CEA.

The purpose of this chapter is to illustrate how disease registries and administrative databases can be used as sources of relevant local data in CEAs. We include a discussion of some of the decision analytic models that are often used in CEA and in the statistical analysis necessary to estimate parameter values in such models. In the remainder of this chapter, we discuss general approaches to CEA and provide an overview of some of the disease registries and administrative health databases available in Canada. We illustrate in detail with an example of a CEA of a prognostic test for guiding breast cancer treatment decisions. We also briefly illustrate with a discussion of a CEA of a diagnostic test that aids in the diagnosis of cancer of an unknown primary origin.

16.2 Models and Parameterization in CEA

There are two common approaches for conducting CEA. In the first, data for the CEA are estimated directly from a single clinical trial. Ideally, data on resource utilization are collected concurrently with the clinical trial. In this case, the economic data can be viewed as experimental and are typically analyzed in the same way as the clinical data [5]. Some authors have argued that CEAs that use experimental data are the most internally valid and that, as a result of this degree of validity, the differences between the medical interventions being compared are unlikely to be biased [6]. However, several factors may still limit the usefulness of such analyses in some health-technology adoption decisions.

Clinical trials usually include only a small fraction of the targeted general population, possibly as a result of strict inclusion criteria. Thus, the experience of participants in these trials may not reflect the experience of the targeted general population [7, 8]. Because trials take place under controlled conditions, the efficacy observed in clinical trials may not necessary reflect the real-world effectiveness of the treatments or technologies under investigation [9, 10]. Clinical trials are usually of limited duration relative to the possible duration of the impact of the alternatives, whereas many CEA guidelines call for use of a "lifetime" horizon. Moreover, under certain circumstances, this approach to CEAs is not even possible. For example, randomization might not be possible in studies aiming to investigate the impact of adherence to drug treatment on clinical outcomes in real-world settings. Further, clinical trials might not include all relevant comparators when multiple clinical options exist; even when a correct comparator is chosen, the definition of an appropriate comparator may change over the time horizon of the trial.

The second common approach to CEA involves the use of decision analytic models, such as decision trees, Markov models, and simulation models. In this approach, several different data sources are commonly used [11], including experimental data, observational data, routine statistics, local surveys, and publicly available pricing data, as well as expert opinion. This approach overcomes some of the limitations of conducting CEAs based exclusively on clinical trials data and allows generalizations beyond clinical trial settings. However, the reliance on published, secondary data may involve alternatives, populations, or settings that are not relevant for the policy question under consideration [12]. Hall et al. suggest that data used in CEAs should be extracted from settings that represent socioeconomic variability and are likely to reflect the regular clinical and economic experience of the relevant patient population under investigation in the studied geographic region within long follow-up periods [13].

Disease registries and administrative health databases, which contain records of events that have occurred under real-world conditions as opposed to clinical trials, can provide a valuable alternate source of clinical and economic data for CEAs [14]. These databases are often population-based, which minimizes selection bias; they have high rates of disease ascertainment; and they include a large population and a long follow-up period, which allows for extensive subgroup analysis [15, 16]. Thus, CEAs produced with this type of data may prove valuable to policy-makers who seek insights regarding local, real-world conditions [13].

16.3 Administrative Health Data and Disease Registries in Canada

16.3.1 National Administrative Health Databases

The Canadian Institute for Health Information (CIHI) facilitates the development and maintenance of an integrated health information system at a national level. In particular, CIHI, in co-operation with the provincial governments, develops data standards for some databases, such as inpatient care, ambulatory care, and pharmaceuticals. The provinces maintain their own data systems, which may be more complete than the requirements specified by CIHI, and they submit their patient or client data on hospital care and physician care to CIHI on a quarterly or annual basis, using the CIHI standards. The CIHI databases are very useful to researchers who seek to obtain data on overall counts of services and on overall costs. However, unique identification—and, hence, linking across databases and registries—is not always available to researchers outside CIHI, thus limiting the usefulness of CIHI data for some applications.

16.3.2 Provincial Administrative Health Databases

In Canada, provincial governments are responsible for funding necessary health services as per the Canada Health Act [17]. The definition of "necessary" varies by province but generally includes most inpatient and outpatient hospital and physician services. In addition, some provincial governments fund other non-physician professional services, such as chiropractic or optometry; prescription drugs, typically with eligibility criteria; vaccines; home care; and long-term care. Each provincial government maintains records of utilization for most of these services, and the resulting records form the provincial administrative health databases (Table 16.1).

Each province also maintains a population registry wherein each resident is assigned a unique identifier, often in the form of a health-plan number. For example, in Ontario, the unique identifier is the Ontario Health Insurance Plan (OHIP) number, which is used to record each service in the provincial databases. Via the unique identifier, an analyst can link available records for drugs, physician visits, hospital discharges, and certain outpatient visits in order to form a complete patient record. This record could include *all* information related to health services utilization at an individual (as opposed to aggregate) level.

Linkage of databases is useful for a number of reasons. One such application is to allow analysts to use one database to identify patients with specific characteristics and to then gather additional information about those patients using other databases. For example, a researcher may wish to investigate the use of family physician services in Ontario before and after emergency-department visits. This examination could be performed by identifying patients who received hospital-based emergency care using the National Ambulatory Care Reporting System (NACRS). After this group of patients has been identified, their physician billing in the months before and after their emergency department visit can be determined through linkage with the physician billing database. The specific fee codes included in the physician billing database could provide insight into the type and intensity of services consumed.

Table 16.1 Provincial data availability by Canadian provinces

Population registries	British Colombia	Alberta	Saskatchewan	Manitoba	Ontario	Quebec	New Brunswick	Nova Scotia	Prince Edward Island	Newfoundland and labrador
Hospital inpatient data	Yes	Yes	Yes	Yes	Yes	Yes	Yes	Yes	Yes	Yes
Hospital outpatient data	No	Yes	No	No	Yes	Yes	No	No	No	No
Physician services data	Yes	Yes	Yes	Yes	Yes	Yes	Yes	Yes	Yes	Yes
Continuing care	Yes	Yes	No	Yes	Yes	No	No	No	No	No
Outpatient prescription drugs data	Yes	Yes	Yes	Yes	Yes	Yes	Yes	Yes	No	No
Home care data	No	Yes	No	Yes	Yes	No	No	No	No	No
Case costing data	Yes	Yes	No	No	Yes	No	No	No	No	No

16.3.3 Disease Registries

Disease registries are surveillance systems that maintain records of patterns of medical history, diagnostics, or treatment in patients with a specific disease, and that follow outcomes or survival patterns among the patients over time. In Canada, patients are often identified using the same unique identifiers as those used in the population registry, a practice that allows researchers to link disease registries with administrative databases to build detailed longitudinal records of their treatments and health-care utilization. As discussed later in this chapter, for the purposes of this study, we used this approach to identify health-care costs for groups of patients with certain types of cancer.

Canada possesses several disease registries, and the most well-established ones are the cancer registries, which cover the entire population. The overall coverage for cancer incidence data is estimated to be at least 95 % [18]. All provincial and territorial registries report to the Canadian Cancer Registry (CCR), and comparable surveillance data from each province are reported up to the CCR level. The registries differ somewhat in their methods, however, and each registry can make independent decisions to record data that is not required by CCR. Thus, variations exist in the types of data recorded in the registries.

Various other disease registries in Canada have also instituted surveillance operations and built databases pertaining to patients with specific diseases. Some examples include the following:

- The Canadian Organ Replacement Registry, managed by CIHI, organizes organ replacement and end-stage renal failure records for all 84 organ replacement centres across the country.
- Starting in May 2001, the Canadian Joint Replacement Registry (CJRR), managed by CIHI and orthopedic surgeons, has collected information on hip and knee joint replacements performed in Canada. The CJRR follows joint replacement patients over time to monitor their revision rates and outcomes.
- The National Trauma Registry maintains data on injuries that lead to hospitalizations.
- The Institute for Clinical Evaluative Sciences (ICES) has recently received funding to develop a Canadian stroke registry.

16.4 Cost and Cost-Effectiveness Studies Using Registries and Administrative Databases

In Canada, the utility of administrative data has been demonstrated in a number of costing studies. For example, Krahn et al. [19] used the Ontario Cancer Registry, Discharge Abstract Database, Claims History Database of the OHIP, National Ambulatory Care Reporting System, and other administrative databases in Ontario to estimate the total health-care costs and costs attributable to prostate cancer across all stages of disease. In another analysis, Carriere et al. [20] used the CIHI's Inpatient Discharge Abstract Database for the province of Alberta and Alberta Health Insurance Plan Registry to determine the cost per day for the treatment of community-acquired pneumonia.

The use of this type of data to conduct CEAs in Canada remains relatively new. In one of the first economic evaluations using Canadian administrative data, Brown et al. [21] studied the cost-effectiveness of New Brunswick's Extra-Mural Hospital home health-care program using population-based administrative data on physician services utilization. Brown et al. used these data to examine whether home-care services act indirectly as substitutes for physician services. Najafzadeh et al. [22] studied the cost-effectiveness of herpes zoster vaccine versus status quo (no herpes zoster vaccine) from the perspective of the Canadian health-care payer. In this study, Najafzadeh et al. used administrative data retrieved from British Colombia to study health resource utilization. In addition, Sander et al. [23] used Ontario health administrative data to compile an economic evaluation of Ontario's universal influenza immunization program compared to a targeted influenza immunization program.

16.5 Example: CEA of a Prognostic Test in Patients with Early-Stage Breast Cancer Using Administrative Health Data in Canada

In this section, we discuss a CEA of a 21-gene assay for breast cancer (Oncotype DX™) in which many parameters were estimated with data from the Manitoba Cancer Registry and from administrative databases held by Manitoba Health. The 21-gene assay analyzes the expression of 21 genes in a tumor to determine a recurrence score (RS) that corresponds to a specific likelihood of breast cancer recurrence (i.e., return of breast cancer after a period of time in which no cancer could be detected) within 10 years of initial diagnosis; this analysis also determines the benefit from adjuvant treatment (i.e., treatment that is given in addition to the primary, main, or initial treatment) [24–26]. The RS ranges from 1 to 100. Women with a score below 18 have a low risk of recurrence and respond well from endocrine therapy alone, whereas those with a score of 31 or more have a high risk of recurrence and gain the largest benefit from the addition of chemotherapy to endocrine therapy. Women with a score of 18–30 have an intermediate risk, and it is not yet known whether or not these women benefit from chemotherapy [27,28].

The purpose of this study was to conduct a CEA of the 21-gene assay versus current Canadian clinical practice (CCP) to guide adjuvant chemotherapy decision-making in women with early-stage, estrogen- or progesterone-receptor-positive (ER+/PR+), axillary lymph-node negative or one to three axillary lymph-node positive (LN−/1–3LN+) breast cancer (ESBC) from the perspective of the Canadian health-care system. Some aspects of this study have been described elsewhere [29].

16.5.1 Model Description

We developed a decision analytic model (Fig. 16.1) to project the lifetime clinical and economic consequences of early-stage breast cancer under two different treatment strategies. In the LN− disease setting, the model begins with a decision to use the 21-gene assay or to continue with CCP (Fig. 16.1a). We assumed that each strategy (RS or CCP) classified patients into risk levels (low, intermediate, and high) and corresponding treatment regimens (endocrine therapy plus chemotherapy versus endocrine therapy alone). In the LN+ disease setting, no risk classification criteria have been defined in current CCP [30]. Thus, for LN+ women, we assumed that the CCP-based strategy would classify patients to different treatment regimens only. In both settings, patients receiving endocrine therapy alone enter model "E" (Fig. 16.1b), and those receiving chemotherapy plus endocrine therapy enter model "C" (Fig. 16.1c). Model "C" differs from model "E" in that it has additional states to account for possible chemotherapy-related serious adverse effects (CSAE).

Model "E" simulates monthly transitions among the following four distinct health states: (1) remission, (2) loco-regional recurrence (LR), (3) distant recurrence (DR), and (4) death. Model "C" simulates monthly transitions among the following five distinct health states: (1) remission with no CSAE, (2) remission with CSAE, (3) LR, (4) DR, and (5) death. We used a lifetime horizon in both models. Future costs and benefits were discounted at 5 % annually, according to Canadian guidelines [31].

16.5.2 Use of Manitoba Administrative Databases and Linking Strategy

We used the Manitoba Cancer Registry (MCR) and Manitoba administrative databases held by Manitoba Health as the main data source for this analysis. The Manitoba administrative databases included the Hospital Discharge Database, Physician Claims Database and the Drug Program Information Network (DPIN). The linking strategy is depicted in Fig. 16.2.

The MCR is a provincial database that contains the records for more than 99.5 % of all cases of cancer in Manitoba [32]. The MCR is comprehensive and collects information on primary tumor location, tumor size, grade differentiation, lymph-node status, ER and PR status, age, local recurrence, regional recurrence, distant recurrence, second primary cancer, death, and treatments including surgery, radiation therapy, endocrine therapy, and chemotherapy for primary breast cancer or for any recurrence. The MCR has also collected staging information based on the American Joint Commission on Cancer (Version 5) for breast cancers diagnosed since January 1995 [33].

The Hospital Discharge Database contains records of demographic and clinical information related to inpatient services and day-procedure (e.g., outpatient surgery) services.

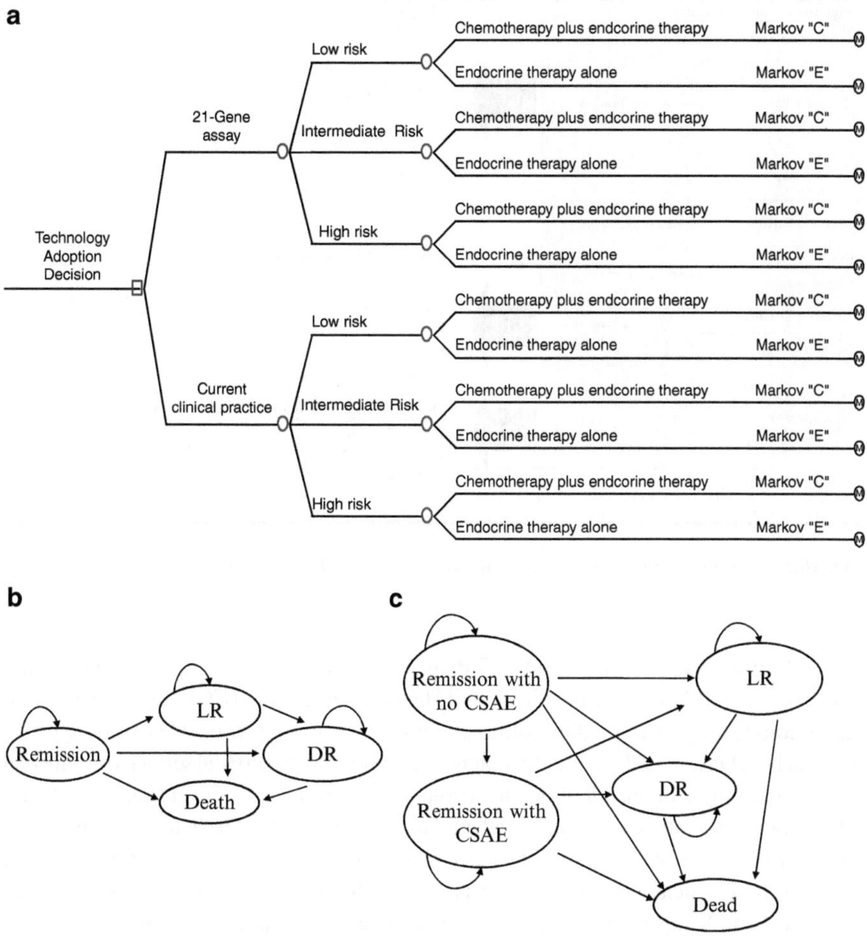

Fig. 16.1 Decision model for early-stage breast cancer. (**a**) 21-gene assay versus Canadian clinical practice for LN− women. (**b**) Schematic representation of the Markov model structure "E"*‡. (**c**) Schematic representation of the Markov model structure "C"†‡. *Patients entering Markov model "E" start the model and remain in the remission state unless they relapse (LR, DR, or Dead). †Patients entering Markov model "C" start the model in the remission state with no CSAE. Within the first cycle patients may develop CSAE. These patients will make a transition to the remission state with CSAE. During the first cycle, patients also may transition to DR, LR, and Dead states. After the first cycle, patients may remain in the two remission states unless they relapse in to LR, DR, or Dead. ‡In both Markov models, patients who developed LR remain in the LR state or make a transition to DR or Dead states. Patients who developed DR remain in the DR state or make a transition to the Dead state. The cycle length was 1 month. *LR* loco-regional recurrence, *DR* distant recurrence, *CSAE* chemotherapy-related serious adverse effects

Manitoba Cancer Registry	
Key Data	**Uses in Study**
Diagnosis	Cohort identification
Loco-regional recurrence	Transition probabilities between health states
Distant recurrence	
Death	
Surgery	Identification of surgery treated patients
Radiation therapy	Identification of radiation therapy treated patients
Hormone therapy	Identification of hormone therapy treated patients
Chemotherapy	Identification of chemotherapy treated patients
Cohort description	
Women were diagnosed with ER+/ PR+ ESBC during the period from January 1, 2000, to December 31, 2002.	

Hospital Discharge Database	
Key Data	**Uses in Study**
Breast cancer surgery-related hospital abstracts	Type and cost of breast cancer surgery
Radiation therapy-related hospital abstracts	Cost of radiation therapy
Chemotherapy-related hospital abstracts	Cost of chemotherapy therapy
Comorbidity related hospital abstracts	Charlson comorbidity index
Serious adverse effects-related hospital abstracts	Cost and rate of Chemotherapy-related serious adverse effects
Physician Claims Database	
Key Data	**Uses in Study**
Surveillance and monitoring-related physician claims	Cost of surveillance
Chemotherapy-related physician claims	Type and cost of chemotherapy
Radiation therapy-related physician claims	Radiation therapy Cost of radiation therapy
Drug Program Information Network (DPIN)	
Key Data	**Uses in Study**
Hormone therapy-related drug claims	Type, usage, and cost of hormone therapy
Follow-up	
Seven years of follow-up data from date of diagnosis.	

Fig. 16.2 Linking strategy and key data and uses in the evaluation of the 21-gene assay

Clinical information includes up to 25 diagnosis codes and 20 procedure codes using ICD-10-CA and Canadian Classification of Health Interventions (CCI). Inpatient refers to admissions to hospital (including both acute and chronic) and stays of at least one night in a hospital bed. Day procedure refers to diagnostic, treatment, or surgical services provided in a hospital setting without admission to hospital. The Physician Claims Database includes billing for visits in offices, hospitals, and outpatient departments. The database contains the date; numeric tariff index (a service-specific code used for physician compensation and provided by physicians when filing for payment); fee-for-service components for tests, such as lab and X-ray procedures performed in offices and hospitals (including emergency room and outpatient departments); and payments for on-call agreements (e.g., anesthetists) that are not attributed to individual patients. The DPIN contains prescription information, including the drug identification number (DIN), dosage, prescription date, drug cost claimed and paid, and professional fee claimed and paid (e.g., pharmacist's fee). Non-prescription drugs or over-the-counter drug products possessing a DIN allowed by the drug plan may also be present.

We used the MCR to identify a study cohort consisting of all premenopausal (defined as age <50 years) and postmenopausal (age ≥ 50 years) women living in Manitoba and diagnosed with ER+/PR+ LN−/1–3LN+ ESBC (stage I/II/III) during the period from January 1, 2000, to December 31, 2002. We used data from women diagnosed during this period so that a long follow-up period (i.e., 7 years from the date of diagnosis) would be available for each patient. Information available during the follow-up period included survival, breast cancer recurrence (LR and DR), and all treatments (surgery, radiation therapy, endocrine therapy, and chemotherapy).

We linked patients in our study cohort with their administrative data found in the Hospital Discharge Database, the Physician Claims Database, and the DPIN (Fig. 16.2). To protect confidentiality, the linkage in this study was performed using the Scrambled Personal Health Identification Number and anonymized versions of these databases. The main reason for linkage was to estimate the costs associated with breast cancer treatments and adverse effects during the follow-up period; however, linkage also allowed for cross-validation, as described in the next section.

16.5.3 Cross-Validation

Wherever possible, we cross-validated our results using multiple databases. For instance, the surgery data recorded by MCR were validated by linking the study population with the Hospital Discharge Database. This process allowed us to identify those patients who had received breast cancer surgeries (either breast-conserving surgery or mastectomy) using the ICD-9-CM procedure codes for these surgeries, and thus gave us data on the occurrence of surgery from two separate databases. Using the numeric tariff index specific to each service, radiation therapy and chemotherapy data recorded in the MCR were validated by linking the study population with the Physician Claims Database to identify those patients who had received any of these treatments. Using the drug identification numbers of the specific treatments (tamoxifen or aromatase inhibitors), endocrine therapy data recorded in the MCR were validated by linking with the DPIN to identify those patients who had received endocrine therapy.

Due to a lack of specificity of codes, some difficulties arose in determining the types of endocrine therapy and chemotherapy agents from MCR. However, by linking with the Physician Claims Database, we were able to identify the type of endocrine therapy (tamoxifen or aromatase inhibitors) and chemotherapy (non-anthracycline, anthracycline, or taxane-containing regimens) by using the specific tariff index of these agents' services.

16.5.4 Estimating Transition Probabilities

We estimated monthly transition probabilities in the Markov models using data from MCR, validation trials involving the 21-gene assay, and Canadian life tables.

16.5.4.1 Estimating Transition Probabilities from MCR

Our first step was to assign members of the study cohort to risk levels. According to the CCP guidelines for women with LN− disease, risk can be specified on the basis

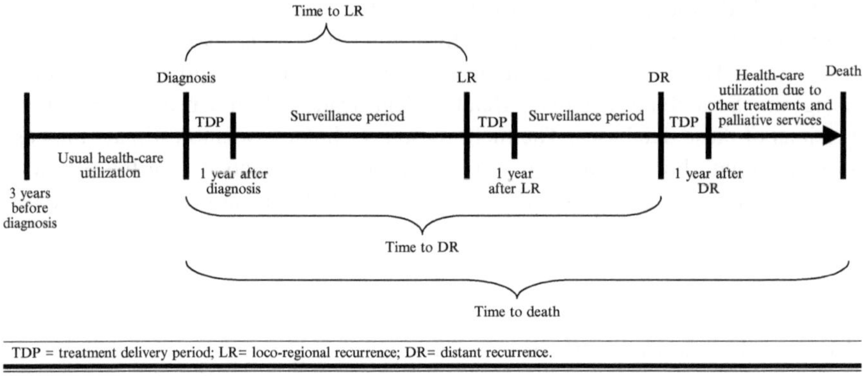

Fig. 16.3 Events time line considered in survival and cost analyses. *TDP* treatment delivery period, *LR* loco-regional recurrence, *DR* distant recurrence

of tumor size, histologic or nuclear grade, and lymphatic and vascular invasion [34]. MCR collects this information, with the exception of lymphatic and vascular invasion. Given the significant correlation between tumor size and lymphatic and vascular invasion [35], we classified premenopausal and postmenopausal women with LN− disease for this analysis as belonging to three risk levels (low-, intermediate-, and high-risk), based on tumor size and histologic or nuclear grade only. In particular, we defined low-risk premenopausal women by tumor diameter of 1 cm or less with grade 1 and low-risk postmenopausal women by tumor less than 2 cm in size with grade 1. We defined high-risk premenopausal or postmenopausal women by tumor more than 3 cm irrespective of any other factors or tumor more than 1 cm associated with grade 3. We defined intermediate-risk women as those who do not meet the low- or high-risk criteria.

We defined current clinical practice according to the observed administration of adjuvant therapy in the PR + LN−/1–3LN+ ESBC cohort during the study period. We conducted survival analyses using Kaplan-Meier estimates for premenopausal and postmenopausal women separately, stratified by LN status, use of adjuvant chemotherapy, and risk level (only in LN− disease) using 7 years of follow-up data from the MCR. We used the resulting Kaplan-Meier curves to estimate monthly transition probabilities to LR, DR, and Death (Fig. 16.3) in the CCP Markov models. We used a similar approach to estimate the monthly transition probabilities to DR and Death after LR, and to Death after DR (Fig. 16.3).

16.5.4.2 Transition Probabilities from Secondary Sources

Canada-specific data about the assay were not available for several reasons. First, validation analyses of the 21-gene assay have not yet been performed in Canada. In addition, the 21-gene assay is not widely used or publicly funded across Canada [36]. The assay is funded and available only in a limited fashion in a few provinces and has not yet been fully adopted into clinical practice [36,37]. Thus, there is no Canada-specific data about the assay.

For the LN− setting, we derived the risk distribution and monthly transition probabilities from remission to LR, DR, and Death over 10 years within each risk level from retrospective analyses of the NSABP chemotherapy-tamoxifen trials (B-14 and B-20) where the assay was validated in this disease setting [25,27]. For the LN+ setting, the risk distribution and monthly transition probabilities to LR, DR, and Death over 10 years within each risk level were derived from retrospective analysis of the phase III Southwest Oncology Group (SWOG)-8814, INT-0100 trial where the assay was validated in the this disease setting [38]. Detailed data from these validation studies were provided by the study authors.

There is no data suggesting that outcomes after first relapse are affected by the primary adjuvant therapy received [39]. Thus, we assumed that transition probabilities following first relapse in the 21-gene assay model would be the same as those in the CCP model.

16.5.4.3 Extrapolation of Transition Probabilities Beyond the Follow-Up Period

To extrapolate beyond the follow-up periods of the study cohort and the clinical trials used for this study, we assumed that the observed average monthly transition probabilities from remission to LR, DR, and Death during the last observed year of follow-up would be constant over the extrapolated life time period. We used the age-adjusted female-specific life tables for Manitoba to adjust the probabilities from remission to death in order to account for the incremental mortality risk over the extrapolated time [40].

16.5.4.4 Comorbidity Index

For each woman, we estimated a comorbidity score to represent comorbid diseases presented at the time of diagnosis that may have had an impact on decisions about adjuvant chemotherapy and the development of adverse effects. We used these comorbidity indices to adjust the estimated probability of adverse effects and to identify independent associations between chemotherapy administration and the occurrence of these adverse events, as highlighted in the next section.

We determined comorbidity from the Hospital Discharge Database through diagnoses or procedures that were recorded for each patient in the study population during all patient hospital stays from 1 year before until 6 months after a breast cancer diagnosis. We found at least one hospitalization for each patient in our study population. Among those who were defined as having received chemotherapy for their primary tumor, all first hospitalizations occurred before they started their chemotherapy regimen. Thus, the estimated comorbidity score represents comorbid diseases present at the time of diagnosis that would be likely to affect the choice of chemotherapy. We used co-morbid diagnoses coded using the method developed by Charlson et al. [41], excluding cancer diagnoses.

16.5.4.5 Adjuvant Chemotherapy-Related Serious Adverse Events

We defined chemotherapy-related serious adverse events (CSAE) as hospitalization for any of the following eight diagnoses (identified by their ICD-9-CM diagnosis and procedure codes) occurring within 1 year of diagnosis with ESBC: (1) abnormal electrolytes or dehydration; (2) constitutional symptoms and nonspecific symptoms associated with therapy; (3) nausea, emesis, and diarrhea; (4) infection and fever; (5) malnutrition; (6) anemia and red cell transfusion; (7) neutropenia or thrombocytopenia; (8) deep venous thrombosis or pulmonary embolus [42,43]. These diagnoses were selected based on their association with chemotherapy in previous clinical trials [44].

We used the study cohort to compare the frequency of occurrence of CSAEs in hospital abstracts of adjuvant chemotherapy recipients versus non-recipients, stratified by menopausal and lymph node status. We used multivariate logistic regression models to estimate the odds of occurrence of CSAEs within each patient group, adjusted for comorbidity indices. We used these models to identify independent associations between chemotherapy administration and occurrence of CSAEs.

16.5.5 Costs

All relevant treatment costs for ESBC, including surgery, radiation therapy, chemotherapy, endocrine therapy, surveillance, and CSAE, are publicly funded in Manitoba and are thus recorded in the administrative databases (Fig. 16.2). For each patient in the study cohort, we gathered all treatment costs for the first 7 years following diagnosis with primary breast cancer (Fig. 16.3). We stratified the analysis by menopausal and lymph node status. We used this data to estimate the cost per unit time in each Markov state. The cost of hospitalization included inpatient costs, hospital day-procedure costs, and physician costs. Inpatient costs included all direct-care costs for nursing, diagnostics and therapeutics, supplies, and drugs, as well as allocated overhead and administration costs. Patient-specific inpatient costs and hospital day-procedure costs are not available in hospital abstracts, so we used inpatient hospital cost estimates per day and hospital-day procedure cost estimates reported in the cost list for Manitoba health services.

The cost list for Manitoba health services classifies hospital costs into Refined Diagnostic Related Groups (RDRGs). According to RDRGs, patients are classified into clinically meaningful groups and use similar amounts of hospital resources. The RDRGs further divide patients in most diagnostic categories according to levels of severity, as defined by complications or co-morbidities that would be likely have an impact on the amount of hospital resources used. We calculated the cost of inpatient hospitalization for a specific treatment by estimating the mean duration of hospitalization (in days) for this treatment among the study cohort and multiplying this figure by the inpatient hospital cost per day for that particular treatment from the cost list for Manitoba health services. Full details for specific cost elements are found in Table 16.2.

16.5.6 Results

16.5.6.1 Base Case

There were 109 premenopausal and 389 postmenopausal women diagnosed with ER+/PR + LN− ESBC, and 161 postmenopausal women diagnosed with ER+ or PR+ 1–3 LN+ ESBC in Manitoba from January 1, 2000, to December 31, 2002. The median age was 44 years (range 29–49 years) in premenopausal women, 62 years (range 50–88) in postmenopausal women with LN− disease, and 61 years (range 50–89 years) in postmenopausal women with LN+ disease. The vast majority of women ($\geq$97 %) received surgery (mastectomy or breast-conserving surgery) for their primary breast cancer. Radiation therapy, endocrine therapy (tamoxifen or aromatase inhibitors), and adjuvant chemotherapy were administered in 63, 70, and 68 % of premenopausal LN− women, in 52, 71, and 19 % of postmenopausal LN− women, and in 60, 89, and 64 % of postmenopausal LN+ (respectively) for their primary breast cancer.

In premenopausal LN− women, the 21-gene assay led to an increase of 0.05 QALY per person and to a decrease in cost of $50 per person, resulting in a cost saving compared to CCP. In postmenopausal LN− women, the 21-gene assay led to an increase of 0.062 QALY per person and to an increase in cost of $3,900 per person, resulting in an incremental cost effectiveness ratio (ICER) of $ 63,600 per QALY gained compared to CCP.

16.5.6.2 Sensitivity Analysis

We performed extensive deterministic sensitivity analysis on all 21-gene assay-related risk classification and survival outcome parameters, and on short-term adjuvant chemotherapy-related utility, cost, and adverse effects. Many of these results are reported elsewhere [29]. Here we report results of sensitivity analysis on the long-term side effects of adjuvant chemotherapy. In premenopausal LN− women, when the utility of chemotherapy-treated patients after completion of adjuvant chemotherapy was reduced by 2 % to account for long-term side effects of adjuvant chemotherapy, the 21-gene assay led to an increase of 0.20 QALY per person, resulting in a more robust cost saving. In postmenopausal LN− women, the utility of chemotherapy-treated patients after completion of adjuvant chemotherapy did not influence our base-case analyses. In postmenopausal LN+ women, when the utility of chemotherapy-treated patients after completion of adjuvant chemotherapy

Table 16.2 Details for some specific cost elements

Type of cost	Data sources	Description
Breast cancer surgery	The Hospital Discharge Database The Physician Claims Database	We used the Hospital Discharge Database and Physician Claims Database to estimate the mean cost of hospitalization due to any breast cancer surgery (including 1-day hospitalizations) within 1 year after diagnosis with ESBC or LR
Radiation therapy	The Physician Claims Database The Cost List for Manitoba Health Services	The cost of radiation therapy included cost of radiation therapy–related physician claims in addition to hospital day-procedure costs. We used the Physician Claims Database to estimate the mean cost of radiation therapy–related physician claims (using the tariff code for a medical claim) within 1 year of diagnosis with ESBC and LR. Hospital day-procedure costs were derived from the Cost List for Manitoba Health Services
Endocrine therapy	DPIN	We used the DPIN to estimate the mean cost of tamoxifen and aromatase inhibitors (using the drug identification number for a drug claim) within the time periods: between diagnosis with ESBC and before any relapse; and between diagnosis with LR and before any relapse
Chemotherapy	The Cost List for Manitoba Health Services The Physician Claims Database	Hospital day-procedure costs were derived from the Cost List for Manitoba Health Services. We used the Physician Claims Database to estimate the mean cost of chemotherapy-related physician claims costs (using the tariff code for a medical claim) within 1 year after diagnosis with ESBC and LR. We estimated the costs of chemotherapy regimens using market prices as of May 2010
CSAE	The Hospital Discharge Database The Physician Claims Database	We used the Hospital Discharge Database and Physician Claims Database to estimate the mean cost associated with hospitalizations due to any of the eight diagnoses that were considered CSAE among women who develop CSAE
Surveillance	The Physician Claims Database	We defined the cost of breast cancer surveillance as the incremental cost of health-care utilization (medical claims) after diagnosis with ESBC versus the time before diagnosis. We used the Physician Claims Database to collect medical claims for all women, within 3 years before and 7 years after diagnosis with ESBC. We estimated the mean cost of medical claims within 3 years before diagnosis in order to reflect the usual cost of health-care utilization. We calculated the incremental mean cost of health care utilization during the period from diagnosis with ESBC and before any relapse (excluding cost of claims related to surgery, radiation therapy, chemotherapy and CSAE) stratified by the time following diagnoses (first year versus later). Similarly, we calculated the incremental mean cost of health-care utilization after LR

LR loco-regional recurrence, *ESBC* early-stage breast cancer, *CSAE* chemotherapy-related serious adverse effects, *DPIN* Drug Program Information Network was reduced by 2 %, the 21-gene assay led to an increase of 0.18 QALY per person, resulting in a smaller ICER value of $200 per QALY gained per person.

We also performed a probabilistic sensitivity analysis and a value-of-information analysis [45]. Results of the probabilistic sensitivity analysis comparing the 21-gene assay versus CCP are reported elsewhere [29]. Here we report results of value-of-information analysis in which we estimated the expected value of removing all statistical uncertainty of the 21-gene assay-related parameters [45]. Using a willingness-to-pay threshold of $100,000 per QALY gained, the opportunity cost associated with the choice of the 21-gene assay as the optimal strategy for guiding adjuvant therapy resulted in a total expected value of perfect information (EVPI) of $61,300 per premenopausal LN− woman, $24,600 per postmenopausal LN− woman, and $4,200 per postmenopausal LN+ woman.

Based on these results, we estimated the expected value for the population that could potentially benefit from more research on the predictive value of the 21-gene assay. Out of approximately 22,000 patients diagnosed with breast cancer each year in Canada, it has been estimated that at least 10,000 women would be eligible for the 21-gene assay [36,37]. Among eligible women, approximately 15 % are premenopausal LN− women, 60 % are postmenopausal LN− women, and 25 % are postmenopausal LN+ women. The resulting population EVPI was more than $258 million per year. Thus, our value of information analysis indicated that future research that can characterize the role of this technology in real-world Canadian practice may have a large societal impact when willingness-to-pay levels of recently accepted cancer treatments are considered.

16.6 Example: CEA of a Diagnostic Test in Patients with Cancer of Unknown Primary Using Administrative Health Data in Canada

In this section, we briefly describe another application in which registry and administrative data have been used to inform a CEA model. The Canadian Cancer Society estimates that approximately 4 % of all cancer cases are of tumor types not readily classified in the course of the initial diagnostic workup [46]. Further diagnostic work-up using current Canadian guidelines does not provide the certainty that physicians need and identifies the tumor origins in only about 20–25 % of instances [47]. Consequently, over 3 % of all incident cancer cases are metastatic CUP recorded annually in tumor registries across Canada, accounting for approximately 5,000–7,000 cases of CUP annually.

A new genomic test called the "Tissue of Origin" test measures the gene-expression pattern in a challenging tumor and compares it to expression patterns of a panel of 15 known tissue types in order to identify the primary type [47,48]. Recently, this test has been validated as a diagnostic test that can reliably identify the tumor of origin in patients with metastatic tumors [47,48].

If introduced into general practice, however, the clinical impact of the test has not been determined. Furthermore, there are trade-offs associated with introducing the test. The test is expensive (the current market price is approximately US$4,400) and imperfect (70–90 % accuracy). For some patients, the test will lead to an accurate diagnosis, which may result in improved health outcomes. In other cases, however, a correct diagnosis will not lead to improved outcomes due to limited treatment options for certain cancer types. Finally, for 10–30 % of patients, the test may lead to an incorrect diagnosis. Policy-makers need to carefully evaluate these complex trade-offs to determine whether the introduction of this test in Canada represents good "value for money" in a publicly funded health-care system.

We built a decision-analytic model to investigate the use of this test in Canada. The model begins with a decision to use the test or to use the current standard of care for a cohort of patients with CUP. For patients who received the test, the process is followed by a sequence of branches for the test result and a chance node indicating whether the test result was correct. The model contains 16 separate terminal Markov models, representing the 15 underlying primary tumor types that can be identified by the test, as well as an "indeterminate" test result. Patients enter one of these Markov models, depending on whether they received the test and how they were treated.

The model was parameterized using data from cancer registries and administrative population databases in Ontario and Manitoba. The provincial cancer registries were used to identify cohorts of patients diagnosed with CUP and certain metastatic cancers where the primary is known. Data on survival, adverse events, health-care utilization, and costs are obtained by linking cancer registry data with administrative databases. Secondary data, including data from the test validation experiments, was used in instances where primary data is not available.

16.7 Conclusions and Policy Implications

The primary purpose of this chapter was to highlight the usefulness of the Canadian provincial administrative health databases and disease registries as a source of information to inform health-care decision-making and policy development in Canada. Some emerging medical technologies will not have been incorporated into general practice at the time of evaluation, thus limiting the amount of direct evidence available in the registries and administrative databases at the time when funding decisions are made. Using two examples, we have shown how researchers can parameterize decision analytic models using these databases, along with other sources, to estimate the impact of emerging medical technologies in a manner that reflects Canadian clinical practice and is based on a population that is similar to the one that will ultimately use the new technology.

Many of the databases discussed in this chapter were designed for specific and limited purposes, such as surveillance or billing. However, minor enhancements could increase their usefulness for research and policy applications. For example, in some administrative databases, billing codes are vague or very broad (e.g., a single code for "combination therapy" that does not specify which agents were used). Sometimes there is a long time-lag between the adoption of a new technology and the development of a billing code that would allow researchers to identify the use of that technology. Beyond the information required by the CCR, variability exists in the information recorded by each provincial registry. For example, the MCR does not collect information on lymphatic and vascular invasion, which is considered clinically relevant for risk classification when studying early-stage cancer patients. The Ontario Cancer Registry does not routinely collect information on staging, cancer progression, and cancer biomarkers, such as hormone receptor and human epidermal growth factor receptor (HER2) status. All of this information is useful for developing detailed clinical models. Information on genetic markers (e.g., HER2, KRAS) will be particularly important as more targeted treatments come into use.

In Canada, new drug submissions are evaluated by one or more national or provincial agencies (e.g., the Canadian Agency for Drugs and Technologies in Health, the Pan-Canadian Oncology Drug Review, the Ontario Committee to Evaluate Drugs). These committees often want—and, in some cases, formally require—Canada-specific data on costs and effectiveness. The dossiers that support new drug submissions, which includes a CEA, are typically prepared by the pharmaceutical companies. However, the databases discussed in this chapter are maintained by various government agencies, and there are often rules in place that prevent any usage by the private sector. Outside of these databases, there may be little or no published data to use in CEAs. Given the organization of new drug submissions in Canada and the value of Canadian data, there may be some benefit to allowing pharmaceutical companies to have access to these databases as part of the submission and review process.

References

1. Clement FM et al. (2009) Using effectiveness and cost-effectiveness to make drug coverage decisions: a comparison of Britain, Australia, and Canada. JAMA 302(13):1437–1443
2. Miners AH et al. (2005) Comparing estimates of cost effectiveness submitted to the National Institute for Clinical Excellence (NICE) by different organisations: retrospective study. BMJ 330(7482):65
3. Henry DA, Hill SR, Harris A (2005) Drug prices and value for money: the Australian pharmaceutical benefits scheme. JAMA 294(20):2630–2632
4. Tierney M, Manns B (2008) Optimizing the use of prescription drugs in Canada through the common drug review. CMAJ 178(4): 432–435
5. Ramsey S et al. (2005) Good research practices for cost-effectiveness analysis alongside clinical trials: the ISPOR RCT-CEA Task Force report. Value Health 8(5):521–533
6. Drummond MF (1998) Experimental versus observational data in the economic evaluation of pharmaceuticals. Med Decis Making 18(2 Suppl):S12–S18
7. Antman K et al. (1985) Selection bias in clinical trials. J Clin Oncol 3(8):1142–1147
8. Rahman ZU et al. (1997) Impact of selection process on response rate and long-term survival of potential high-dose chemotherapy candidates treated with standard-dose

doxorubicin-containing chemotherapy in patients with metastatic breast cancer. J Clin Oncol 15(10):3171–3177
9. Stiller CA (1994) Centralised treatment, entry to trials and survival. Br J Cancer 70(2):352–362
10. Braunholtz DA, Edwards SJ, Lilford RJ (2001) Are randomized clinical trials good for us (in the short term)? Evidence for a "trial effect." J Clin Epidemiol 54(3):217–224
11. Zaric GS Cost effectiveness analysis, healthcare policy, and operations research models, wiley encyclopedia of operations research and management science, edited by James J. Cochran Copyright © 2010 John Wiley & Sons, Inc.
12. Hillner BE (1987) Basic principles of cost-effectiveness analysis. Med Sect Proc 45–53
13. Hall PS et al. (2010) Health economics in drug development: efficient research to inform healthcare funding decisions. Eur J Cancer 46(15):2674–2680
14. Jacobs P, Yim R (2009) Using Canadian administrative databases to derive economic data for health technology assessments. Canadian Agency for Drugs and Technologies in Health, Ottawa, ON
15. Iron K et al. (2011) Using linked health administrative data to assess the clinical and healthcare system impact of chronic diseases in Ontario. Healthc Q 14(3):23–27
16. Ayanian JZ (1999) Using administrative data to assess health care outcomes. Eur Heart J 20(23):1689–1691
17. Health Canada (2012) Canada Health Act frequently asked questions. Health Canada 2012. http://www.hc-sc.gc.ca/hcs-sss/medi-assur/res/faq-eng.php#3. Accessed 15 July 2012
18. Canadian Cancer Society's Steering Committee on Cancer Statistics (2011) Canadian cancer statistics.Canadian Cancer Society, Toronto, ON
19. Krahn MD et al. (2010) Healthcare costs associated with prostate cancer: estimates from a population-based study. BJU Int 105(3):338–346
20. Carriere KC et al. (2004) Outcomes and costs among seniors requiring hospitalization for community-acquired pneumonia in Alberta. J Am Geriatr Soc 52(1):31–38
21. Brown MG (1995) Cost-effectiveness: the case of home health care physician services in New Brunswick, Canada. J Ambul Care Manage 18(1):13–28
22. Najafzadeh M et al. (2009) Cost effectiveness of herpes zoster vaccine in Canada. Pharmacoeconomics 27(12):991–1004
23. Sander B et al. (2010) Economic appraisal of Ontario's Universal Influenza Immunization Program: a cost-utility analysis. PLoS Med 7(4):e1000256
24. Paik S et al. (2004) A multigene assay to predict recurrence of tamoxifen-treated, node-negative breast cancer. N Engl J Med 351(27):2817–2826
25. Mamounas EP et al. (2010) Association between the 21-gene recurrence score assay and risk of locoregional recurrence in node-negative, estrogen receptor-positive breast cancer: results from NSABP B-14 and NSABP B-20. J Clin Oncol 28(10):1677–1683
26. Albain K, Barlow W, O'Malley F et al. (2004) Concurrent (CAFT) versus sequential (CAF-T) chemohormonal therapy (cyclophosphamide, doxorubicin, 5-fluorouracil, tamoxifen) versus T alone for postmenopausal, node-positive, estrogen (ER) and/or progesterone (PgR) receptor-positive breast cancer: mature outcomes and new biologic correlates on phase III intergroup trial 0100 (SWOG-8814). [Abstract] Breast Cancer Res Treat 88 (Suppl 1):A-37
27. Paik S et al. (2006) Gene expression and benefit of chemotherapy in women with node-negative, estrogen receptor-positive breast cancer. J Clin Oncol 24(23):3726–3734
28. Zujewski JA, Kamin L (2008) Trial assessing individualized options for treatment for breast cancer: the TAILORx trial. Future Oncol 4(5):603–610
29. Hannouf MB et al. (2012) Cost-effectiveness of a 21-gene recurrence score assay versus Canadian clinical practice in women with early-stage estrogen- or progesterone-receptor-positive, axillary lymph-node negative breast cancer. BMC Cancer 12(1):447
30. Levine M (2001) Clinical practice guidelines for the care and treatment of breast cancer: adjuvant systemic therapy for node-positive breast cancer (summary of the 2001 update). The

Steering Committee on Clinical Practice Guidelines for the Care and Treatment of Breast Cancer. CMAJ 164(5):644–646
31. Horlings HM et al. (2008) Gene expression profiling to identify the histogenetic origin of metastatic adenocarcinomas of unknown primary. J Clin Oncol 26(27):4435–4441
32. Latosinsky S et al. (2007) Canadian breast cancer guidelines: have they made a difference? CMAJ 176(6):771–776
33. Breast (1997) In: Fleming ID, Cooper JS, Henson D (eds) American Joint Committee on Cancer Staging Manual. 5th edn. Lippincott-Raven Publishers, Philadelphia, PA
34. The Steering Committee on Clinical Practice Guidelines for the Care and Treatment of Breast Cancer (1998) Adjuvant systemic therapy for women with node-negative breast cancer. CMAJ 158(Suppl 3):S43–S51
35. Gajdos C, Tartter PI, Bleiweiss IJ (1999) Lymphatic invasion, tumor size, and age are independent predictors of axillary lymph node metastases in women with T1 breast cancers. Ann Surg 230(5):692–696
36. Ragaz J (2010–2011) The 21-gene assay, part 2, Canada's uneven response. Report card on cancer in Canada 13:41–43
37. Ragaz J (2009–2010) The 21-gene assay: impact on breast cancer in Canada. Report card on cancer in Canada (Emerson D, Major P, Co-Chairs). Cancer Advocacy Coalition of Canada, vol 12:Winter
38. Albain KS et al. (2010) Prognostic and predictive value of the 21-gene recurrence score assay in postmenopausal women with node-positive, oestrogen-receptor-positive breast cancer on chemotherapy: a retrospective analysis of a randomised trial. Lancet Oncol 11(1) 55–65
39. Wolowacz SE et al. (2008) Docetaxel in combination with doxorubicin and cyclophosphamide as adjuvant treatment for early node-positive breast cancer: a cost-effectiveness and cost-utility analysis. J Clin Oncol 26(6):925–933
40. Statistics Canada/Health Statistics Division (2006) Life tables, Canada and the Provinces, 2000–2002. Minister of Industry, publication 84–537-XIE, Ottawa, ON, ,
41. Charlson ME et al. (1987) A new method of classifying prognostic comorbidity in longitudinal studies: development and validation. J Chronic Dis 40(5):373–383
42. Hassett MJ et al. (2006) Frequency and cost of chemotherapy-related serious adverse effects in a population sample of women with breast cancer. J Natl Cancer Inst 98(16):1108–1117
43. Du XL, Osborne C, Goodwin JS (2002) Population-based assessment of hospitalizations for toxicity from chemotherapy in older women with breast cancer. J Clin Oncol 20(24):4636–4642
44. Shapiro CL, Recht A (2001) Side effects of adjuvant treatment of breast cancer. N Engl J Med 344(26):1997–2008
45. McKenna C, Claxton K (2011) Addressing adoption and research design decisions simultaneously: the role of value of sample information analysis. Med Decis Making 31(6):853–865
46. Canadian Cancer Society (2010) General cancer statistics for 2010. http://www.cancer.ca/Ontario/About%20cancer/Cancer%20statistics/Stats%20at %20a%20glance/General%20cancer%20stats.aspx?sc_lang = en&r = 1. Accessed 13 Aug 2010
47. Dumur CI et al. (2008) Interlaboratory performance of a microarray-based gene expression test to determine tissue of origin in poorly differentiated and undifferentiated cancers. J Mol Diagn 10(1):67–77
48. Monzon FA et al. Identification of tissue of origin in carcinoma of unknown primary with a microarray-based gene expression test. Diagn Pathol 5:3

Part VI
Working with Policy Makers

Chapter 17
Evaluating Health Care Policy Decisions: Canadian Blood Services in Atlantic Canada

John Blake, Michelle Rogerson, and Dorothy Harris

Abstract In 2009, Canadian Blood Services, one of two nonprofit agencies that manage the supply of blood and blood products in Canada, announced plans to consolidate a number of its production facilities in an effort to standardize processes and workflows. One of the elements of the plan involved moving existing production facilities in Saint John, New Brunswick and Halifax, Nova Scotia, into a single facility to be located in Dartmouth, Nova Scotia. The plan drew criticism from some stakeholder groups. In this chapter, we describe how operations research techniques were used to analyze this difficult policy issue. We provide a discussion of the motivation for the study, an overview of the methodology, and the results of the studies conducted to evaluate the proposed change. The analysis involved a statistical comparison of transport modes as well as a series of simulation models to evaluate the impact of consolidation on product availability. The results of this analysis suggested that, on the balance of metrics considered, customer service would not be adversely affected by the consolidation of facilities.

17.1 Introduction

Canadian Blood Services is one of two nonprofit agencies that manage blood and blood products in Canada; Héma-Québec manages the blood supply chain in the Province of Québec, while Canadian Blood Services manages it in the remainder of Canada. Canadian Blood Services provided approximately 850,000 U (abbreviated as

J. Blake (✉)
Dalhousie University, Halifax, NS, Canada

Canadian Blood Services, Ottawa, ON, Canada
e-mail: John.Blake@dal.ca

M. Rogerson • D. Harris
Canadian Blood Services, Ottawa, ON, Canada

G.S. Zaric (ed.), *Operations Research and Health Care Policy*,
International Series in Operations Research & Management Science 190,
DOI 10.1007/978-1-4614-6507-2_17,

U henceforth) of red blood cells and 110,000 platelet doses to Canadian hospitals in fiscal year 2009/2010 [1]. The budget for its operations totalled $1B ($CAN) in 2009/2010, of which approximately 50 % was related to collection, production, testing, and distribution of transfusable products (red blood cells, plasma, and platelets). Canadian Blood Services was formed in 1998 as a successor to the Canadian Red Cross and was a key recommendation of the Krever Commission. The commission, which was initiated after contaminated blood entered the supply chain in the early 1980s, noted that the safety of the blood supply system had to be held paramount and recommended the creation of a national blood system operator. The commission furthermore stressed the need for accountability and the requirement that the system operator function independently at arm's length from governments, using the most up-to-date scientific/medical information for decision making [2].

Prior to the emergence of Canadian Blood Services, the blood supply chain in Canada was highly decentralized: every province, with the exception of Prince Edward Island, had at least one blood centre and thus transfusable products were largely collected, produced, and distributed within the same province. While inventory could be shared between provinces in the event of an emergency, the Krever Commission noted that "regular transfers ... were resisted because every province paid for the operation of the blood transfusion service within its own border" [3]; managing blood as a "national resource, [where] provincial boundaries...are not barriers to the rational distribution of blood components" [3] was a key recommendation of the Commission.

Since the inception of Canadian Blood Services the blood supply chain has become more interconnected; inventory is managed through a national supply chain forum [4] and products flow regularly between provinces from areas of higher supply to areas of higher demand. Nevertheless, until recently, the network continued to consist of vertically integrated nodes; each centre collected, tested, produced, and distributed blood and blood products largely within its own catchment area. This structure began to change in the early 2000s with the consolidation of donor testing at regional sites. In 2009 Canadian Blood Services further announced a plan to consolidate production, distribution, and some support activities in southern Ontario and in the Maritime provinces of Atlantic Canada. Facilities in Hamilton, London, and downtown Toronto, Ontario were to be consolidated into one site in Brampton, Ontario (just north-west of the city of Toronto), while two facilities in the Maritimes, one in Saint John, New Brunswick, and one in Halifax, Nova Scotia, were to be replaced by a single facility to be located in Dartmouth, Nova Scotia (just east of Halifax). In addition, all donor testing for sites in Ontario and Atlantic Canada was to be consolidated at a central facility in downtown Toronto.

The announcement of the consolidation plan was not entirely well received by all stakeholder groups in New Brunswick. Both the province's physicians' association and the provincial government itself raised objections to the plan, chiefly over issues of weather and its impact on the security of supply. The consolidation plan received considerable attention in the popular press [5] and the provincial government mooted several possible policy options in response [6], including paying for redevelopment of existing facilities in Saint John (September 2009), leaving the Canadian Blood Services network and joining Héma-Québec (October 2009), or forming its own independent blood agency (August 2010). Ultimately, stakeholders in New Brunswick opted to maintain a relationship with Canadian Blood Services (January 2012) [6], but not before an extensive analysis had been completed to compare the performance of the existing network with that of the future network. In this chapter, we provide an overview of the methods and the results of this analysis. Since the analysis took almost 2 years and was completed in phases, various aspects have been reported in other sources [4, 7]. In this chapter we provide a synopsis of the problem, the approach taken to answer questions about customer service in the future network, and the overall results of the studies. Our objective in this paper is to discuss how operational research techniques were employed in an analysis to respond to heartfelt stakeholder concerns.

17.2 Background

New Brunswick is a province in the Maritime region of Atlantic Canada. It has a population of approximately 750,000, of which 61 % live in one of seven larger census divisions [8]. The population is predominantly distributed along the St. John River valley in the west of the province and the Northumberland shore in the east of the province (Table 17.1).

New Brunswick occupies 72,000 km^2 or roughly the same area as the Benelux nations of Europe and is Canada's only constitutionally bilingual province. See Appendix A for a chart of distances between select locations in New Brunswick and Nova Scotia.

17.2.1 Current Process Description

In 2009/2010 approximately 24,000 U of red blood cells (RBC) including approximately 4,500 U of irradiated red blood cells (IRR), and 4,500 U of platelets (PLT) were shipped from the production and distribution hub in Saint John to facilities in New Brunswick. Red blood cells have a nominal shelf-life of 42 days if not irradiated;

Table 17.1 Top seven largest census areas in New Brunswick

Census area	Population
Moncton	138,644
Saint John	127,761
Fredericton	94,268
Bathurst	33,484
Miramichi	28,115
Edmundston	21,902
Campbellton	17,842

irradiated red blood cells have a maximum shelf-life of 28 days; platelets have a nominal shelf-life of 5 days. However, testing of donated units for transmissible diseases typically requires between 1 and 2 days to complete, and thus products are quarantined and not available for release to hospitals until the second day following the date on which they were collected. Once tested, products are released from quarantine, end-labelled and made available for distribution. End-labelling at the Saint John site occurs throughout the day, according to a day of week specific distribution of completion times unique to product type. Variations in the times product can be released are typically a function of staffing, which differs somewhat on weekends, when compared to weekdays. RBC labelling typically peaks between 09:00 and 12:00 each day, except Sundays, during which end-labelling peaks between 20:00 and 22:00; PLT end-labelling typically peaks between 07:00 and 11:00 daily, except on Sundays, when it peaks between 09:00 and 11:00.

A total of 20 facilities ordered blood or blood products from the Saint John distribution hub in 2009/2010. The volume of demand requested by facilities ranged in size from 8,000 to 80 U. Average demand, as measured by units shipped from the distribution hubs, is 66.3 U of RBC per day and 12.5 U of platelets per day. Demand for RBCs peaks on Fridays (71.5 U/day) typically as a result of facilities ordering ahead of weekends when regular shipments are unavailable; platelet demand conversely peaks on Mondays (16.4 U/day) typically to make up for stock which may have been depleted over the weekend. (Since platelets have a much shorter shelf life than red blood cells, defensive ordering strategies such as ordering ahead on weekends would result in an unacceptable level of outdates). The ABO/Rh status of units collected in New Brunswick differs somewhat from that of the general Canadian population in that a surfeit of type O^- blood (i.e. "universal donor") is collected. Collections, obtained on a 5 or 6-day per week cycle depending on the product type, average 95 U per day, with a low of 9.7 U on Saturdays (primarily apheresis platelets) to a high of 131.5 U on Tuesdays. RBC inventory held at the Saint John hub during 2009/2010 was typically 8–9 days of available stock (roughly 525–600 U); target inventories were set at 16–32 U for platelets and 24 U for irradiated RBCs during this time.

Demand for blood products from hospitals in New Brunswick arrives throughout the day. The distribution of demand requests is specific to the day of the week and type of product and is greater on weekdays than on weekends. See Table 17.2 for average daily demand. Demand for product is received throughout the day, but peak order arrivals occur between 09:00 and 12:00 all days, except Sundays, on which demand for RBC peaks between 18:00 and 20:00.

The current distribution network for blood and blood products to New Brunswick hospitals utilizes ground services from the Saint John facility for deliveries to hospitals. Routine (i.e. scheduled) deliveries typically employ an overnight courier service. Non-scheduled orders that cannot wait until the next routine delivery, called "as soon as possible" (ASAP) orders, are dispatched by bus parcel express. Non-scheduled deliveries necessary to meet the need of a bleeding patient are considered to be "STAT" deliveries and are dispatched using the fastest available mode of transport, including taxis and, in rare instances, police relay.

Table 17.2 Aggregate daily demand at Saint John 2009/2010

	Red blood cells		Platelets	
Day of week	Annual volume	Average daily volume	Annual volume	Average daily volume
Sunday	1,190	3.26	463	1.27
Monday	4,296	11.77	790	2.16
Tuesday	4,521	12.39	702	1.92
Wednesday	4,378	11.99	716	1.96
Thursday	4,630	12.68	810	2.22
Friday	3,617	9.91	713	1.95
Saturday	1,126	3.08	282	0.77
Holidays	276	0.76	96	0.26
Total	24,034	65.85	4,572	12.53

17.2.2 Future Process Description

The planned consolidation of production activities for the Maritime region of Atlantic Canada will bring a number of changes to the distribution and logistics network in New Brunswick. Production operations will cease in Saint John and will be replaced by a smaller site, called a stock-holding unit (SHU) that will serve as a forward store of finished goods. The SHU will continue to serve as a regional hub for collating incoming collections and will continue to collect apheresis platelets on site. Transport of raw and finished products between Dartmouth and the Saint John SHU is to be provided by a dedicated ground transport relay. The relay will transport raw materials from Saint John to Dartmouth and finished goods and collection supplies from Dartmouth to Saint John. Two vehicles will be involved and the drivers will swap trucks at a point halfway between the two centres (Aulac, New Brunswick). On the return trip to the SHU, the Saint John bound driver will stop at some hospitals in the south of the province *en route* to supply finished goods before re-stocking the SHU. The SHU will also supply a number of hospitals in the south of New Brunswick with apheresis platelets and will serve as a transhipment site for facilities in the south of the province that cannot be reached by the ground relay. In addition, the SHU will provide blood products to all hospitals in New Brunswick in the event of a cessation of ground or air services, either because of scheduled or unscheduled interruptions in service. All materials dispatched from Saint John to hospitals in New Brunswick will continue to use existing ground transport services. Facilities in the north of the province, however, will be serviced directly from Dartmouth, using overnight courier services for routine deliveries and a commercial air charter service for ASAP deliveries. STAT deliveries to hospitals in the north of the province (as well as in the south of the province) will be dispatched from Saint John using ground transport services as is presently the case. No changes to the distribution network in Nova Scotia are anticipated as a result of consolidation, since the new facility in Dartmouth (a sister city to Halifax) is less than 10 km from the existing Halifax facility. The distribution network in Nova Scotia was therefore excluded from this study.

17.3 Literature

There is an extensive operations research literature in the area of blood and blood management. While operations researchers have evaluated a wide range of issues in blood supply and management, the majority of work in the area has been devoted to inventory policies and practices [9]. See references [10, 11] for reviews of early works. Recently, a classification of the OR literature on blood products according to network topology - individual hospital, regional blood centre, or supply-chain – has been suggested [9]. The literature is identified as having historically focused on individual hospitals or regional blood centres, though in recent years there has been a growing interest in modelling operations related to "interregional blood program management" through an increased use of simulation methods [9].

The blood supply chain is a complex, multilevel problem, involving collections planning production, testing, inventory control, logistics, and distribution typically over a wide geographic region, and often involving a plenitude of organizations and/or stakeholders. OR applications in the area of blood supply chain management include demand forecasting, inventory planning, network design, and vehicle routing [12] amongst others.

There are a number of models specifically related to facility location within a blood supply chain. For instance, Pierskalla [12] describes network planning for blood systems within the context of determining the number and size of facilities (production centres, distribution sites, and demand points) within a given geographic region in the Chicago area. In Sahin et al. [13] a similar problem faced by the Turkish Red Crescent is described and a suite of models to site regional blood centres and locate distribution points is developed. As evidenced by [12, 13], most facility location models related to blood systems described in the OR literature have a strategic focus and are thus designed to operate under assumptions of aggregate, deterministic demand; day-to-day operational issues are generally not included.

There is, of course, a vast literature on vehicle routing within the operations research literature in a wide variety of settings, though the application of such models to perishable inventory problems appears to be less well developed [14]. Applications of vehicle routing models specifically in blood supply include routing of fleet vehicles [12], multi-location allocation models for products with limited availability [15], and joint vehicle routing-inventory allocation [16]. Within the broader category of perishable inventory, there are a number of instances where vehicle routing methods have been applied. For instance in [17] a model for allocating limited food supplies and distributing via truck in the event of an emergency is solved via a three-phase heuristic, while in [18] a model for allocating fleet resources to supply supermarkets in Athens is solved using a tabu-search heuristic. The focus of these models is typically on minimizing the cost of fleet operations subject to constraints on capacity and/or time windows for delivery.

The available literature addressing operational issues within blood supply chains is remarkably sparse, given the sheer size of the problem in practice. However, a simulation approach to model the flow of products within a hospital transfusion service in Finland is described in [19]. This model is used to test a set of inventory and product management policies with the intent of minimizing outdating and backorder costs, while retaining high levels of product availability. Good policies are identified through scenario analysis; transport of products is not considered. A prototype decision support system for coordinating the collection of platelets across a network of potential supply points is described in [20]. This study uses an integer programming model, under the assumption of known collection volumes, to minimize transportation costs for shuttling platelets (which must be produced within 6 h of collection) from disparate collection sites to a production facility. Model results suggest consolidation of collection nodes. In [21] a simulation approach is used to model an end-to-end blood supply chain, consisting of multiple products. The model in [21] considers a single hospital, single supplier system, but can be extended to represent a larger network; however, a distributed computing environment is required to solve network models. An operational decision support system to support inventory monitoring, analysis and rebalancing for a military blood service is described in [22]. The system consists of a multi-site inventory database to monitor inventory and usage. The system features an end-to-end inventory that is enhanced by a geographic information system (GIS). Data-mining is used to evaluate trends and agent based models issue alerts when unusual trends are detected. Inventory rebalancing decisions are made on an ad hoc basis, but transportation planning is supported by logistics features of the embedded GIS.

We conclude from the available literature that while there is an extensive operational research literature on blood and blood products, much of it is of limited applicability to the problem of evaluating changes in the production and distribution network in Maritime Canada. Given that network nodes were pre-specified, facilities location models are not applicable in this case. Furthermore, while there are issues regarding inventory levels necessary to buffer variations in logistic network reliability, the problem extends beyond inventory cost minimization. In addition, the operational research literature related to blood logistics, with its focus on fleet operations and minimizing cost through applications of vehicle routing, is not particularly germane to the problem at hand. We therefore conclude that the issue of comparing the current and proposed operations of the production and distribution network in New Brunswick has novel applications. Like many recent authors, we adopt a simulation methodology because of its flexibility and ability to model detailed operational issues [9]. We could not find any results in the literature describing either a physical test or simulated comparison of a current and proposed blood distribution network. We believe therefore that this work, while employing established methods, is novel in its scope and area of application.

17.4 Methodology

Stakeholder concerns regarding product availability and security of supply centred on the reliability of the transportation network linking the Dartmouth production facility to hospitals and to the Saint John SHU. The weather in Atlantic Canada can be variable and portions of New Brunswick are subject to heavy snowfalls in the winter. Stakeholder issues, not surprisingly, included concerns about the ability of the air charter service to reach hospitals in the north of the province as well as the reliability of the ground service between Dartmouth and Saint John. (Dartmouth and Saint John are linked by a single motorway that is subject to occasional closure [23].) The key to addressing stakeholder concerns was to evaluate the impact on customer service of changes to the distribution network with a particular emphasis on evaluating the impact of network reliability on product availability and security of supply.

To compare the existing transport system with the future system, two distinct analyses were conducted. A statistical experiment was carried out to assess the proposed air delivery service to facilities in the north of New Brunswick and to compare the new service to the existing ground based service. For facilities in the south of the province, a series of simulation models were built to evaluate network reliability and to identify inventory levels necessary at the regional stockholding unit in Saint John to ensure product availability under a range of different operational scenarios.

17.4.1 Evaluating Air Versus Ground Deliveries

Since no data existed to evaluate fully the function of an air delivery service for hospitals in northern New Brunswick, a physical test trialling the proposed network was structured. The test compared the current distribution network to that of the future distribution network under actual operational conditions and consisted of a basic feasibility test, followed by a 2-week pilot to gather data to complete power calculations, and a 1-year test period to collect operational data for comparison purposes.

A dual data collection process was implemented. A Canadian Blood Services/ customer data collection process gathered information on ground shipments from Saint John and platelet shipments delivered by air from Halifax. This consisted of logging outgoing shipments (date, time, origin, destination, mode of transport) at the distribution hubs and merging this information with manually obtained arrival times at the customer site. Customer responses were logged and, in the instances where not immediately provided, were followed up by staff at the distribution centre. Response rates accordingly were very good; of more than 1,600 records, only 16 (<1 %) were not returned, or were returned with missing data.

In the production phase of data collection there were 1,600 unique deliveries recorded by the joint Canadian Blood Services/hospital customer data collection process to all customers in northern New Brunswick; there were 1,101 unique deliveries recorded to the four regional facilities in the north-east and north-west of the province that were part of the air delivery trial since they regularly receive scheduled platelet orders. Of the total deliveries to regional facilities, eight records

Table 17.3 Number of records in the data set collected at regional hospitals

Delivery mode	Completed records	Missing records	Total records
Overnight courier	201	4	205
Bus parcel express	512	1	513
Air	372	3	375
Taxi (STAT orders)	8	0	8
Total	1,093	8	1,101

were excluded from the analysis because time and date of receipt were not recorded (Table 17.3).

Metrics for comparing the air service to existing ground services included transit time, timeliness of delivery, delivery tardiness, transit time variability, and transit mode reliability.

17.4.1.1 Transit Time

Table 17.4 indicates that the air charter has shorter average transit times, when compared to bus parcel express (BPX) and overnight courier services. Transit times are, for the purposes of this analysis, measured as the time between the scheduled departure of the delivery service and the actual time of receipt in the laboratory of the destination hospital's transfusion service. It should be noted, however, that the time products are delivered to a customer site and the time the product is received in the laboratory may differ substantially. For instance, products may arrive at the destination hospital but not be logged into the lab for some period of time due to staff availability or workload issues. Since waypoint or proof of delivery data was not available for all modes of transport, it was necessary to implement the manual data collection process and to standardize on time of receipt at the transfusion service laboratory as the end point of the delivery process.

The measured differences in transit time obtained from the manual data collection process were found to be statistically significant at a 95 % significance level when compared using either a Mann–Whitney rank test or a Robust Rank Order test. In this analysis, traditional *t*-tests could not be used since the data elements were drawn from populations with non-normal distributions. Accordingly, non-parametric methods of comparison, such as the Mann–Whitney test [24] and the Robust Rank Order test were employed. Since the Mann–Whitney rank test is predicated on an assumption of equality of variance between the comparison populations, each sample was first tested for equality of variance using Levene's test [25]. If equality of variance could not be rejected, a Mann–Whitney test was employed to compare population medians; in cases where equality of variance was rejected, the Robust Rank Order test, which relaxes the assumption of equality of variance, was employed [26].

Table 17.4 Average ($(\bar{x})$), median ($x_{0.50}$), standard deviation (s) and count (n) of transit times (in hours) by mode of transport and destination for facilities in the test plan

	Bathurst				Campbellton				Edmundston				Miramichi			
Mode	$\bar{x}$	$x_{0.50}$	s	n	$\bar{x}$	$x_{0.50}$	s	n	$\bar{x}$	$x_{0.50}$	s	n	$\bar{x}$	$x_{0.50}$	s	n
Overnight	17.1	17.0	0.6	60	19.0	18.8	0.9	57	Insufficient sample				18.9	18.8	1.0	83
BPX	**8.4**	**9.2**	**1.5**	**83**	9.8	10.8	1.3	106	**7.4**	**9.2**	**1.7**	**239**	**6.9**	**7.6**	**1.6**	**84**
Air	3.5	3.0	1.2	82	6.8	6.6	1.4	87	4.4	4.0	1.3	118	4.3	4.1	1.1	85

Comparisons against air requiring a robust rank-order test are bolded. Air transit time was found to be significantly less than that of overnight courier services or BPX in all instances

17.4.1.2 Delivery Timeliness

While transit time measures the speed of the mode used to deliver blood products to customers, all modes of delivery are scheduled commercial services and thus the time the product is delivered is a function of both the number and timing of departures for the transport mode in addition to the speed of the mode. Accordingly, a test was also formulated to compare the time of delivery to customers of air versus overnight courier and BPX. Time of delivery was measured in hours from the start of the day in which products are issued from Canadian Blood Services and the receipt of products at the blood transfusion laboratory at the destination hospital. If more than one departure per day from the origin to the destination site was scheduled, as was the case for deliveries made by BPX, only data related to the earliest possible delivery time was used for comparison purposes.

In these tests, the null hypothesis of equal medians was compared against the alternative hypothesis that the median delivery time via air was less than that of the overnight courier or BPX. All samples were tested for equality of variance between the air and overnight courier or BPX service, as applicable, using Levene's test before population medians were compared. In all instances the comparison air based deliveries arrived were significantly earlier than ground transport (95 % significance level); air delivery times, it should be noted, include all deliveries scheduled by air, including those flights that were cancelled at origin or en route and completed by other methods (Table 17.5).

17.4.1.3 Transit Time Variance

A key issue for stakeholders was the reliability of the modes of transport used to deliver products. For facilities in the north-east and north-west of New Brunswick reliability was measured according to both the variability of transit time and delivery tardiness, the non-negative difference between the actual delivery time and the scheduled delivery time. While there was little doubt from the outset of the study that air deliveries could be provided faster and at an earlier time in the day, whether air deliveries would be significantly delayed when compared to ground based transport because of weather or other issues, was an important question to be resolved by the analysis. Air based services are, of course, subject to a wider range of potential interruptions than ground based services: inclement weather (including fog), crew scheduling issues, and mechanical failures. In the case of the commercial service employed to deliver blood, a number of cancellations were noted early in the operational phase of the test and a contingency plan was developed with the commercial service provider to ensure that deliveries could be completed by ground. For the purpose of analysis, all deliveries scheduled by air, whether completed by air or by specially tasked ground runs, are considered to be air deliveries.

Table 17.5 Average $((\bar{x}))$, median ($x_{0.50}$), standard deviation (s) and count (n) of delivery times (in hours from 00:00 of day of order) by mode of transport and destination for facilities in the test plan

	Bathurst				Campbellton				Edmundston				Miramichi			
Mode	$\bar{x}$	$x_{0.50}$	s	n	$\bar{x}$	$x_{0.50}$	s	n	$\bar{x}$	$x_{0.50}$	s	n	$\bar{x}$	$x_{0.50}$	s	n
Overnight	33.1	33.0	0.6	60	34.0	34.8	0.9	57	Insufficient sample				34.8	34.8	1.0	83
Bus	16.3	16.2	0.9	83	**17.5**	**17.5**	**0.5**	**106**	**19.3**	**19.0**	**1.1**	**65**	**15.0**	**15.0**	**0.6**	**84**
Air	9.5	9.0	1.2	82	12.8	12.6	1.4	87	10.4	10.0	1.4	118	10.3	10.1	1.1	85

Comparisons against air requiring a robust rank order test are bolded. All comparisons show that air deliveries arrive significantly earlier than overnight or BPX deliveries

Transit times were, as indicated above, tested for equality of variance prior to comparisons of population medians, using Levene's test. When compared to overnight courier services, the variability of transit time for air deliveries was not statistically different at the 95 % significance level for the three facilities for which a test of variance could be completed. When compared against BPX deliveries air deliveries exhibited equivocal results. Tests of transit time variance were conducted on a facility by facility basis for each scheduled BPX departure time (each origin–destination pair had two scheduled departures). In all instances, the variance of transit time for deliveries made by air was observed to be greater than those made by ground. However, the differences were not always statistically significant.

As an additional measure of reliability, the tardiness of deliveries (Max(0, Actual Time—Scheduled Time)) of air deliveries was compared against that of overnight courier and BPX deliveries. Results of this comparison were mixed. Air deliveries were observed to be consistently more tardy than overnight courier deliveries, but when compared to BPX deliveries, air delivery was observed to be more tardy, less tardy or no different than bus based deliveries, depending on the destination and the scheduled departure time. Robust rank order tests were employed to compare the tardiness of deliveries by air against the tardiness of overnight courier and BPX services to all locations. Summary data appears in Table 17.6.

The results suggest that the median tardiness for air deliveries is greater than that of overnight courier deliveries in all instances for which a test was feasible. In comparison to bus based deliveries, the median tardiness of air based deliveries was observed to be greater than bus based deliveries to Campbellton, less tardy than bus based deliveries to Miramichi, and not statistically different than bus based deliveries to either Bathurst or Edmundston.

17.4.1.4 Air Delivery Cancellations

From the outset of discussions, stakeholder concerns specifically cited the reliability of air charter services for delivering blood and blood products to facilities in the north-east and north-west of New Brunswick. Accordingly, an analysis was also completed to quantify the magnitude of this concern.

The Canadian Blood Services/hospital customer data collection exercise listed a total of 375 air based deliveries to facilities in the north-east and north-west of New Brunswick over the production phase of the test. Of the 375 records in the joint Canadian Blood Service/customer data set, three records were excluded from the analysis because of missing or incomplete delivery data. There were, in addition, nine flights to regional facilities that were cancelled outright and thus for which no record exists in the joint Canadian Blood Service/customer data set (Table 17.7).

In total 9.9 % (38/384) of all flights involved in air deliveries were either completely or partially cancelled because of weather, crew, or mechanical issues with the plane. Only 2.9 % of all scheduled air deliveries (11/384 including the nine

Table 17.6 Average $(((\bar{x}))$, median $(x_{0.50})$, standard deviation (s) and count (n) of delivery tardiness (in minutes from scheduled time of arrival) by mode of transport and destination for facilities in the test plan

	Bathurst				Campbellton				Edmundston				Miramichi			
Mode	$\bar{x}$	$x_{0.50}$	s	n	$\bar{x}$	$x_{0.50}$	s	n	$\bar{x}$	$x_{0.50}$	s	n	$\bar{x}$	$x_{0.50}$	s	n
Overnight	No tardy deliveries				12.2	0.0*	51.0	58	Insufficient sample				6.3	0.0*	24.7	83
Bus	59.7	50.0	31.2	83	22.4	20.0*	26.0	106	49.9	35.0	53.8	239	66.3	65.0	33.5	84
Air	72.6	45.0	70.0	82	79.4	65.0	82.2	81	72.3	45.0	79.8	118	51.2	34.0	59.5	85

Median tardiness values that are statistically significant when compared to air delivery are marked with an asterisk

Table 17.7 Attempted flights by destination

Destination	Complete records in joint CBS/ customer data set	Cancelled and no record in joint CBS/ customer data set	Missing or incomplete records	Attempted flights
Bathurst	82	2	1	85
Campbellton	87	0	0	87
Edmundston	118	7	1	126
Miramichi	85	0	1	86
Total	372	9	3	384

Table 17.8 Flight completions by destination

Destination	Total deliveries cancelled	Deliveries completed by direct drive	Deliveries not completed	Total deliveries attempted	Deliveries cancelled (%)	Deliveries completed by direct drive (%)
Bathurst	5	3	2	85	5.9	3.5
Campbellton	7	6	1	87	8.0	6.9
Edmundston	22	14	8	126	17.5	11.1
Miramichi	4	4	0	86	4.7	4.7
Total	38	27	11	384	9.9	7.0

missing from the joint data set plus two listed in the data set with partial records) were not completed. More frequently, the materials were driven directly to the destination hospital in the event of a problem with a scheduled flight. During the production phase of the test 7.0 % (27/384) of air deliveries were completed by direct drive after a flight interruption en route. By comparison, 0.8 % of bus shipments (4/513) were cancelled during the same period; there were no recorded cancellations of shipments made by overnight courier during this time. A summary of flight completions by destination appears in Table 17.8.

While it might be presumed that winter weather is responsible for air cancellations, a secondary analysis (not shown) in which cancellations were compared by winter versus non-winter months showed that cancellation rates in the winter were either lower than, or statistically indistinguishable from, non-winter rates. Moreover, the results of Table 17.8 show that flight cancellation rates for deliveries to Bathurst, Campbellton, and Miramichi are statistically indistinguishable from one another, and are all significantly lower than the cancellation rate for deliveries to Edmundston. The reason for the difference in performance is likely due to higher operational ceilings required at the uncontrolled airfield used to make deliveries to this particular site. It is noteworthy that the majority of the deliveries to Edmundston that were cancelled and not completed (6 of 8) occurred in the first 4 months of the test before contingency plans in the event of a cancelled flight were fully operationalized. The proportion of flights to this destination cancelled in the first 4 months of operations (15.0 %), it should be noted, is statistically greater than the proportion of flights cancelled in the later portion of the test plan (2.3 %) for this data set.

Table 17.9 Summary of physical test results

Air versus	Transit time	Timeliness of delivery	Tardiness	Transit time variance	Cancellations
Overnight Courier	Air faster than overnight courier	Air arrives earlier in day	Air deliveries on average are more tardy	No difference	Air has more cancellations
Bus	Air faster than BPX	Air arrives earlier in day	Mixed results, depending on destination	Air has greater variance	Air has more cancellations

17.4.1.5 Air Versus Ground Summary

The results of the analysis provide evidence to support the hypothesis that, on the balance of metrics considered, customer service will not be diminished if air deliveries are used to augment ground based deliveries to facilities in northern New Brunswick. The results are not unequivocal. Air based deliveries have faster transit times than do overnight courier and BPX deliveries in all instances. In addition, air based deliveries arrive at customer sites earlier in the day than do overnight courier and BPX deliveries in all instances. While air deliveries are influenced by weather and mechanical issues and are thus more likely to be cancelled, completion rates in excess of 97 % for all sites can likely be assumed if an appropriate backup method is in place to cover in the event of a problem with the air delivery. Test results further indicate that air based deliveries have greater variability, when measured by variance of transit time, than do BPX deliveries. There is no evidence to support a conclusion that the variability of air transit times is greater than that of overnight courier deliveries. In addition, there is evidence to suggest that air deliveries are more tardy (i.e. arrive after scheduled delivery) than overnight courier services in all instances; when compared to BPX deliveries, tardiness results are inconsistent; air based deliveries may exhibit greater, lesser, or the same levels of tardiness, depending on hospital destination and the scheduled bus used to reach the facility. These results are summarized in Table 17.9.

17.4.2 Evaluating Ground Services to Saint John

In parallel to the statistical comparison of the air and ground services, a series of logistics simulations were developed to evaluate the impact of network reliability and corresponding inventory levels necessary at the SHU in Saint John to ensure high levels of product availability. Three distinct models were built: a baseline model to establish the validity of a simulation approach to represent network operations; a logistics model to establish the preliminary design of the delivery system in the south of the province; and a confirmatory simulation to verify the final design of the network under operational conditions.

Table 17.10 Comparison of remaining shelf of products shipped for actual system versus baseline simulation model, showing the mean value and the corresponding confidence interval half width

	2009/2010 data		Simulation results	
Product	Mean	CI half width	Mean	CI half width
Irradiated red blood cells (IRR)	25.65	0.28	25.43	0.25
Red blood cells (RBC)	30.86	1.77	31.79	1.04
Platelets (PLT)	1.44	0.08	1.55	0.07

17.4.2.1 Baseline Model

A baseline model of the existing production and distribution network was first built and validated against historical data from the distribution network in southern New Brunswick. See Table 17.10 for a comparison of simulated output against historical records. Once validated, the baseline model served as a platform for exploring the impact of moving production activities from Saint John to Dartmouth with respect to resupply times, inventory levels, and road closures. Experiments were conducted to represent potential closures of the road linking Nova Scotia to New Brunswick and to evaluate the impact of holding different levels of inventory at the Saint John SHU. The results of this experiment suggested that customer service levels for facilities serviced from the SHU are not necessarily affected by the location where units are produced. This result was found to be robust with respect to up to three closures per year of the road linking Nova Scotia to New Brunswick and an overall reduction in the level of red blood cells (RBCs) held at the SHU [7].

17.4.2.2 Preliminary Network Design

Once the applicability of a simulation approach to analyze the location of production had been proven, a second model was built to establish the preliminary design for the distribution network in the south of New Brunswick. A three stage approach was adopted. The first stage involved identifying feasible allocations of hospitals in the south of the province to be supported either directly from Dartmouth or via the SHU in Saint John. In the next stage of the analysis, the distributions of demand anticipated at the SHU under regular conditions, STAT orders, and in the event of a logistics network failure were calculated. This data was then incorporated into a modified version of the baseline simulation model to analyze stock requirements at the SHU [4]. Experiments were then run on the revised model, assuming different levels of platelet and RBC inventory and the impact, in terms of shortages and product outdates, was measured. The revised simulation showed that the preliminary design for the distribution network was feasible and that sufficient product could be available at the Saint John SHU in the event of emergencies. Experiments with inventory levels at the SHU suggested that red cells can be managed easily in the redeveloped distribution network; high levels of product availability could be assured for RBCs without incurring a substantial penalty in terms of outdating or transhipped units. Platelets, however, were found to be more complex to manage because of their shorter shelf-life and smaller demand profile. However, performance metrics for platelets in the proposed system were not observed to be statistically different from those of the current system [4].

17.4.2.3 Confirmatory Modelling

Having established the conceptual design of the logistics network in the south of New Brunswick, a confirmatory analysis was undertaken to evaluate the proposed logistics network under operational conditions. The simulation model was modified to incorporate the final design of the logistics network and a set of experiments was conducted to evaluate product availability and outdate rates under varying levels of inventory at the SHU.

After facilities are consolidated, hospitals in New Brunswick, as noted earlier, will receive products either directly from Dartmouth or via the stock-holding unit (SHU) in Saint John. All hospitals in New Brunswick will receive routine deliveries via an overnight courier service; products will, however, be dispatched from Dartmouth. ASAP deliveries will be primarily dispatched from Dartmouth using either a dedicated ground service for facilities in the south or the commercial air courier for facilities in the north. Routine deliveries of platelets will be dispatched by air from Dartmouth to facilities in the north. Facilities in the south will continue to receive routine platelets by ground originating in either Dartmouth or Saint John. However, STAT deliveries to all facilities in New Brunswick will be dispatched, as is presently the case, using the fastest method of transport available (typically ground) from Saint John.

The dedicated ground based delivery service in the south will function as a relay between Dartmouth and Saint John, delivering raw materials to the Dartmouth site and returning finished products to Saint John. The distance between the two cities is approximately 409 km. The ground service will also supply a number of hospitals with finished product while en route to Saint John. Six days per week, a vehicle will depart Saint John with raw materials and meet a vehicle coming from Dartmouth with finished product and collection sets at a point midway between the two cities (Aulac, NB). The drivers will switch vehicles and the Saint John driver will return with finished products and collection sets. Some of the finished goods will be distributed to facilities en route; the remainder of the finished product on board will be used to restock the SHU. While enroute, collection sets will be distributed to a permanent collection site in Moncton or the SHU in Saint John. The New Brunswick portion of the route taken by the ground service essentially follows a single path. However, the time at which the ground run departs Saint John depends on the day of week (weekdays have a different departure time than weekends) as well as the particular location of the mobile collection clinic being operated in New Brunswick. Forty-one times per year, the particular location of the mobile collection clinic is such that the outbound driver is required to make an intermediate stop somewhere to meet a vehicle coming from the clinic with freshly collected materials that necessitate minor changes to routing or the departure schedule.

17.4.2.4 Transit Times for Ground Deliveries in New Brunswick

Mean transit times for ground deliveries in New Brunswick were calculated from the scheduled routes in Table 17.11. To model variability in transit times, information on ground transport between Halifax and Saint John was adapted from historical records of test samples collected in New Brunswick and sent to Halifax for transmissible disease testing. The data set contains 386 observations collected during the period of January 2009 through August 2010. To model variability, the data was separated into two periods: winter (November-March) and non-winter (April–October) and divided through by average transit time per period. An empirical distribution was then built for transit time variability as a percentage of the expected transit time and applied to the times in Table 17.11.

17.4.2.5 Road Closures

A key aspect of product availability and security of supply is the reliability of the ground transport network. In particular, stakeholders noted that the sole road linking Nova Scotia to New Brunswick is subject to closure from time to time. Accordingly, road closures were modelled explicitly. Closure data in the simulation is based on information obtained from the highway management authorities in both Nova Scotia and New Brunswick. This data suggests that the road linking Nova Scotia to New Brunswick is closed approximately 1.6 times per year, with all closures assumed to occur between the beginning of November and the end of March. The duration of the road closure can be either short (between 1 and 8 h) with a probability of 40 % or long (between 14 and 23 h) with a probability of 60 %. The duration of short closures are modelled as a triangular distribution with parameters (1.0, 3.7, 8.0) hours; long closures are modelled as a triangular distribution with parameters (14, 20, 23) hours to match the range and mean value of the available data. It is assumed that all closures start at 00:00 and always delay the start of the Saint John bound portion of the ground relay. During a road closure demand in New Brunswick that would have been serviced from Dartmouth either by ground or air transport, is assumed to be serviced from the Saint John SHU.

17.4.2.6 Weekends and Statutory Holidays

Weekends and statutory holidays are assumed to impact both demand for blood and their distribution to hospitals. There are a total of nine statutory holidays included in the simulation. Scheduled product deliveries are halted on statutory hospitals in the

Table 17.11 New Brunswick ground relay schedule

		Transport or pick up raw materials en Route to Aulac					Drivers switch vehicles		Transport or drop off finished goods en Route to Saint John/SHU							
Clinic code	# in 2011/2012	Depart Saint John	Pick up point for mobile clinic collections	Pick up time	Arrive Moncton permanent collection site o pick up raw material	Depart Moncton permanent collection site	Arrive Aulac	Depart Aulac	Arrive Sackville hospital	Arrive Moncton permanent collection site to drop off collection materials	Depart Moncton permanent collection site	Arrive Moncton hospitals	Arrive Sussex hospital	Arrive Oromocto hospital	Arrive Fredericton hospital	Arrive Saint John site/SHU
Clinic A	153	0:00	N/A	N/A	2:00	2:15	3:00	4:00	4:30	5:15	5:30	6:00	7:15	8:45	9:30	12:00
Clinic B	10	22:00	Fredericton	0:00	2:00	2:15	3:00	4:00	4:30	5:15	5:30	6:00	N/A	8:00	8:45	11:15
Clinic C	27	0:00	Sussex	1:00	2:00	2:15	3:00	4:00	4:30	5:15	5:30	6:00	7:15	8:45	9:30	12:00
Clinic D	8	2:45	N/A	N/A	4:45	5:00	5:45	6:45	7:15	8:00	8:15	8:45	10:00	11:30	12:15	14:45
Clinic E	4	2:45	Hampton	3:15	4:45	5:00	5:45	6:45	7:15	8:00	8:15	8:45	10:00	11:30	12:15	14:45
Clinic F	4	2:45	N/A	N/A	4:45	5:00	5:45	6:45	7:15	8:00	8:15	8:45	10:00	11:30	12:15	14:45
Fri & Sat (Fixed site)	36	14:00	N/A	N/A	16:00	16:15	17:00	17:45	18:15	19:00	19:15	19:45	21:00	22:30	23:15	1:45
Fri (Mobile clinic)	12	20:00	N/A	N/A	22:00	22:15	23:00	23:45	0:15	1:00	1:15	1:45	3:00	4:30	5:15	7:45

simulation model as are regularly scheduled collections. Coincidentally, demand for products is lower on statutory holidays.

On weekends, the scheduled air delivery service is halted and thus on Saturdays and Sunday demand for products originating from facilities in northern New Brunswick are supplied from the Saint John SHU. The dedicated ground service similarly operates 6 days per week with departures scheduled for late evening Monday through Saturday, corresponding to deliveries to the SHU and facilities in the south of the province early morning Tuesdays through Sundays. Since the dedicated ground service from Dartmouth is not available on Mondays, demand that arises from facilities in the south of the province on Mondays are supplied from the SHU using commercial ground services.

17.4.2.7 Product Arrival

Products shipped from Dartmouth are assumed to be available for distribution from the SHU 1.0 h $\pm$ 15 min after the arrival of the ground service. All products arriving from Dartmouth are assumed to have been collected 2 days before their date of arrival at Saint John. Products collected in Saint John (i.e. apheresis platelets) are assumed to become available 2 days after their date of collection to account for product testing. Units collected at Saint John are assumed to be end-labelled throughout the day according to the same day-of-week specific empirical distribution used to validate the baseline simulation.

17.4.2.8 Demand Modelling at the Saint John SHU

Demand for products at the Saint John SHU is assumed to consist of four distinct streams: routine demand originating from hospitals normally supported from the Saint John SHU; STAT demand originating from all hospitals in New Brunswick; routine and ASAP demand originating from all hospitals in the south of New Brunswick as a result of a suspension of ground services between Dartmouth and Saint John and; routine and ASAP demand originating from all hospitals in the north of New Brunswick as a result of a suspension of the air delivery service.

Facilities Normally Supported from the Saint John SHU

Based on the results of earlier models, it is assumed that, as part of regular operations, RBC will be regularly provided by the SHU to two facilities in the south of the province, while platelets will be regularly supplied to five hospitals in the Saint John area, including the region's sole tertiary hospital [4]. A summary of product demand, by day of week is given in Table 17.12.

Table 17.12 Summary demand by day of week for facilities supported by the SHU

	Red blood cells		Platelets	
Day of week	Annual volume	Average daily volume	Annual volume	Average daily volume
Sunday	31	0.60	254	4.88
Monday	316	6.08	419	8.06
Tuesday	360	6.92	377	7.25
Wednesday	308	5.92	361	6.94
Thursday	289	5.56	466	8.96
Friday	223	4.29	337	6.48
Saturday	73	1.40	157	3.02
Holidays	2	0.04	51	0.98
Total	1,602	4.38	2,422	6.64

Table 17.13 Summary of volume and types of STAT demand

	RBC	Platelets
Total urgent items recorded in data	421	129
Days with urgent request	63	63
Items/request day	6.68	2.05
Maximum items requested	49	7
Estimated items/year	481.2	147.4

STAT Demand from All Facilities in New Brunswick

It is assumed that all STAT requests for blood products in New Brunswick are serviced from the Saint John SHU. Data for STAT orders was derived from data collected at the Saint John site between January 2010 and December 2010. A total of 63 days were identified in the data during which a STAT order for product was received at Saint John. On average, 5.10 days elapsed between STAT orders, from which we estimate a total of 72 days per annum with a STAT order. The number of items (RBCs and/or PLTs) ordered during a day having at least one urgent request was modelled using discrete empirical distributions (Table 17.13).

Routine and ASAP Demand Originating from All Hospitals in the South of New Brunswick During a Delivery Interruption

In the event of an interruption to the ground delivery service it is assumed that facilities in the south will be serviced from the Saint John SHU. Interruptions to the ground service linking Dartmouth to facilities in the south of New Brunswick can be scheduled (i.e. the ground service does not function on Mondays or statutory holidays) or unscheduled due to weather-related road closures. The summary data for the additional routine and ASAP demand created by facilities in the south is listed in Table 17.14.

Table 17.14 Summary demand by day of week for facilities not supported by the SHU

	Red blood cells		Platelets	
Day of week	Annual volume	Average daily volume	Annual volume	Average daily volume
Sunday	815	15.67	144	2.77
Monday	2,555	49.13	227	4.37
Tuesday	3,085	59.33	217	4.17
Wednesday	3,060	58.85	244	4.69
Thursday	2,934	56.42	211	4.06
Friday	2,865	55.10	287	5.52
Saturday	633	12.17	71	1.37
Holidays	203	16.92	31	2.58
Total	16,150	44.24	1,432	3.92

Table 17.15 Summary demand by day of week for facilities in the north of New Brunswick regularly serviced by air delivery

	Red blood cells		Platelets	
Day of week	Annual volume	Average daily volume	Annual volume	Average daily volume
Sunday	326	6.27	65	1.25
Monday	1,277	24.56	144	2.77
Tuesday	862	16.58	108	2.08
Wednesday	869	16.71	111	2.13
Thursday	1,288	24.77	133	2.56
Friday	502	9.65	89	1.71
Saturday	415	7.98	54	1.04
Holidays	65	5.42	14	1.04
Total	5,604	15.35	718	1.97

Routine and ASAP Demand Originating from All Hospitals in the North of New Brunswick

In the event of an interruption in air delivery service it is assumed that facilities in the north will be serviced from the Saint John SHU. As with the ground service, interruptions can be due to weather or a scheduled halt to service (i.e. no air deliveries on Saturdays, Sundays, or statutory holidays). In the event that the air service is not available, it is assumed that demand arising from routine and ASAP orders will be serviced by the SHU. The summary data for the additional routine and ASAP demand created by facilities in the north is listed in Table 17.15. It should be noted that in the simulation model, interruptions to air deliveries are coincident with interruptions in ground services, under the assumption that if the weather is sufficiently poor to halt ground transport, air services are not likely to function as well.

Table 17.16 Probability density function for demand for RBC arriving before or during a particular hour of day

Hour	Sunday (%)	Monday (%)	Tuesday (%)	Wednesday (%)	Thursday (%)	Friday (%)	Saturday (%)
0			1.92		1.18	0.94	
1			0.15		1.02	0.06	
2					0.07		
3				0.11			
4							4.05
5							0.02
6							
7			2.07				0.08
8		2.07	13.17	0.47	1.85	0.96	6.59
9		20.02	10.21	22.99	25.50	18.26	33.18
10		14.42	21.89	32.92	24.55	29.30	34.74
11	2.33	13.73	7.10	20.47	23.89	21.14	16.45
12	6.98	15.34	13.17	11.17	9.59	11.16	1.14
13	1.16	4.83	8.88	4.73	4.76	5.05	2.74
14	3.49	3.22	12.43	2.29	3.98	5.97	0.71
15	2.33	0.54	0.30	1.43	2.40	2.18	0.18
16	11.63	1.61	3.55	1.07	0.65	3.29	
17	1.16	8.74	4.44	0.86	0.35	0.02	0.02
18	19.77	2.91	0.15	0.04	0.04	0.04	
19	18.60	4.37		1.18	0.01	0.18	0.06
20	32.56	7.44		0.04	0.01	0.18	0.04
21		0.69	0.30	0.24	0.03	1.26	
22		0.08	0.30		0.11		
23						0.02	

17.4.2.9 Demand Arrival

Demand for product is assumed to arrive throughout the day in the simulation. The distribution of demand requests is specific to day of the week and is also specific to product type, with the peaks timed corresponding to scheduled order cut-off times. See Tables 17.16 and 17.17 for the empirical distributions describing the probability of a demand arrival occurring before or during a specific hour of the day. The distributions in these two tables are based on a total of 4,572 platelets and 24,034 RBCs shipped from Saint John during 2009/2010.

17.4.2.10 Verification and Validation

The confirmatory simulation model is an extension of the baseline model which was proven to represent accurately the logistics network in place in New Brunswick prior to consolidation and thus the overall validity of the approach is assumed to follow from that earlier work [7]. Furthermore, since the model represents a future

Table 17.17 Probability density function for demand for platelets arriving before or during a particular hour of day

Hour	Sunday (%)	Monday (%)	Tuesday (%)	Wednesday (%)	Thursday (%)	Friday (%)	Saturday (%)
0	13.79				0.78		3.79
1	13.79	0.35		2.04	0.13	2.77	0.25
2	11.21		4.88	0.72	7.62		1.39
3	1.29					0.15	0.25
4				0.92	1.42	1.31	1.26
5					0.52	2.04	0.51
6	3.88		2.85	0.82	0.78		
7	3.88	0.47	0.41	26.69	38.50	25.40	1.64
8	2.16	1.75	19.51	6.65	4.01	4.23	32.20
9	12.50	20.21	19.11	33.13	7.11	30.95	14.14
10	14.22	7.83	17.89	16.36	9.82	10.51	14.14
11	8.19	10.98	8.54	8.08	14.60	14.74	11.99
12	0.43	3.15	4.07	0.41	7.11	3.65	0.76
13		3.86	7.72	0.51	3.49	2.19	0.38
14		3.86	7.32	1.84	3.49	0.73	
15		1.87		1.64	0.52	0.44	
16		13.55	0.41	0.20	0.13		
17	2.16	19.63	0.81			0.15	
18	0.86	6.07					
19		3.39					0.25
20	6.47	1.05	1.22				0.88
21	3.45	0.93					3.41
22			5.28				5.30
23	1.72	1.05				0.73	7.45

state, there exists no definitive data against which to compare the simulation. Nevertheless, it was possible to test structural aspects unique to the current model to verify the accuracy of its representation.

A basic test of the veracity of the simulation model is its ability to reproduce expected demand at the SHU. Accordingly, the model output was tested against expected demand, which includes regular and ASAP demand originating from facilities regularly supported by the SHU; STAT demand originating from all hospitals in New Brunswick; routine and ASAP demand from facilities in the south of the province. Expected values for each demand stream were calculated deterministically. The simulation model was run for a total of 10 replications of 1 year, with an initial warm-up period of 70 days to clear transient effects. The results of the simulation model were compared to the expected values and their corresponding 95 % confidence intervals. In all instances, the confidence intervals bracket the expected values, providing evidence to support the supposition that demand data has been accurately incorporated into this version of the simulation model (Tables 17.18 and 17.19).

To confirm the timings and routings of the ground delivery relay, the arrival time at Saint John were recorded in the simulation and compared to expected values

Table 17.18 Comparison of expected demand for RBCs compared to simulated results

Demand	Expected value	Simulation mean	Difference	95 % CI half width
Regular demand SHU	1,602.0	1,581.9	20.1	28
STAT demand	481.2	479.5	1.7	46
Non-SHU demand South	2,970.8	2,975.6	4.8	90
North demand	813.4	845.6	−32.2	38

Table 17.19 Comparison of expected demand for platelets compared to simulated results

Demand	Expected value	Simulation mean	Difference	95 % CI half width
Regular demand SHU	2,422.0	2,433.0	−11	24
STAT demand	147.4	150.2	−2.8	8
Non-SHU demand South	261.5	260.0	1.5	5
North demand	134.1	131.1	3.0	6

Table 17.20 Comparison of expected and simulated arrival time at Saint John Monday–Friday (in decimal hours)

	Clinic type							
	A	B	C	D	E			
Instances per year	153	10	27	8	4	Expected value	Simulation mean	95 % CI half width
Probability	74.3 %	4.9 %	13.1 %	3.9 %	1.9 %			
Monday	0	0	0	0	0	0.0	0.00	0.00
Tuesday	12	11.3	12	14.8	14.9	12.2	12.2	0.1
Wednesday	12	11.3	12	14.8	14.9	12.2	12.3	0.5
Thursday	12	11.3	12	14.8	14.9	12.2	12.2	0.4
Friday	12	11.3	12	14.8	14.9	12.2	12.3	0.6

Table 17.21 Comparison of expected and simulated arrival time at Saint John Saturday–Sunday (in decimal hours)

	Clinic type				
	Fixed	Mobile			
Instances per year	36	12	Expected value	Simulation mean	95 % CI half width
Probability	75 %	25 %			
Saturday	1.75	7.75	3.25	3.25	0.21
Sunday	1.75	1.75	1.75	1.75	0.20

derived from the routing charts in Table 17.11. These tests also showed that the 95 % confidence intervals on the ground service departure time and arrival time bracket the expected values, again providing evidence to suggest that the model provides a representation of the proposed transport system that is not inconsistent with expected values (Tables 17.20 and 17.21).

17.4.2.11 Simulation Experiments and Results

Once the confirmatory simulation model was verified, a set of experiments was conducted using differing levels of inventory for red blood cells and platelets. Inventory levels of 120, 130, and 140 U of RBC were tested, as were platelet inventory levels of 16, 18, and 20 U. These levels were selected as representative of good, if not provably optimal, inventory levels based on results from the preliminary model of the logistics network [4]. Customer service levels were evaluated under the assumption of both a 6-day and a 7-day per week ground run to restock the SHU.

In the simulation the SHU is assumed to utilize an order-up-to policy. At the beginning of each simulated day, inventory is evaluated and compared to a target level. If the inventory is below the target level, an order is issued to bring product from Dartmouth to Saint John to restore the level. In the case of platelets, if newly available units collected locally cause inventory to exceed target levels, surplus units are shipped to Dartmouth for redistribution, except on Mondays when no service is available to return product from Saint John. Demand for product is assumed to arrive throughout the day at the SHU according to the distribution in Tables 17.16 and 17.17. As demand arrives, it is filled from units available in inventory. If an exact match cannot be found for a particular demand, a search for a compatible unit is made on the basis of ABO/Rh for RBC and ABO/CMV (cytomegalovirus) for platelets. If a compatible unit is found, the demand is filled; otherwise, the order is backlogged. If additional product becomes available over the course of the day, backlogged demand is searched and, if a match is found, the demand is satisfied at that time. The day then ends. A count of all unmatched demand is made. A final search is made to match any outstanding demand items. In the case of platelets, the restriction on compatibility matching is relaxed and all platelet orders that can be filled as a mismatch are filled. All remaining, backordered demand units that are unfilled are counted as lost demand. All units in inventory are then aged by 1 day. Any units that are eligible may be transhipped to another CBS facility and any units that have expired are removed from inventory, counted, and discarded. The daily cycle then repeats.

The simulation model was run for a total of 10 replications of 1 year using a 70-day warm-up period under the method of batch means. (All runtime parameters were established using methods suggested by Law [27].) Inventory levels for both RBC and platelets were varied as was the assumption of a 6- or 7-day per week delivery cycle. Under a 6-day per week delivery cycle, it is assumed that all materials sent from Dartmouth to the Saint John SHU are delivered by the dedicated Canadian Blood Services ground run that operates (i.e. delivers) Tuesdays through Sundays. Under a 7-day per week delivery it is assumed that on Mondays (excluding statutory holidays) that materials can be moved from Dartmouth to Saint John via the air transport service already in use to supply facilities in north-west New Brunswick.

Table 17.22 RBC unmatched demand per annum (shortage); unmatched demand for RBC in 2009/2010 is estimated to be 0.80 ± 1.80 U

	6-day per week delivery cycle		7-day per week delivery cycle	
Target inventory	Mean value	95 % CI half width	Mean value	95 % CI half width
140	2.30	2.00	1.30	0.92
130	8.40	7.20	1.20	1.57
120	12.70	8.36	9.10	5.06

Table 17.23 RBC units transhipped per annum (surplus); the actual number of surplus RBC in 2009/2010 was approximately 400 U

	6-day per week delivery cycle		7-day per week delivery cycle	
Target inventory	Mean value	95 % CI half width	Mean value	95 % CI half width
140	0.30	0.35	0.40	0.90
130	0.20	0.30	0.10	0.23
120	0.30	0.48	0.00	–

Scenarios were structured to include each RBC inventory level under the assumption of both a 6-day or 7-day per week SHU replenishment cycle. In each scenario the number shortages, as determined by the number of lost demand units, and the number of surplus units, as determined by the number of transhipped or expired units, was recorded. The results of the simulation runs appear in Tables 17.22 and 17.23:

The results of the simulation model show that managing the inventory for red blood cells at the SHU is straightforward. Policies providing both low shortages and low surpluses can be easily identified through the simulation. In all instances tested, the number of surplus RBC units was small and, in fact, statistically indistinguishable from zero at a 95 % significance level, under both a 6 and 7-day per week delivery cycle. Nevertheless, product availability can clearly be seen to be influenced by the amount of inventory on hand. In the results shown in Table 17.22 it can be seen that RBC shortages were lower at all inventory levels if a 7-day delivery cycle is available to resupply the SHU. However, the differences in shortages are not statistically significant between a 6 and 7-day delivery cycle for any of the tested levels of inventory. It can also be noted that shortages observed at an RBC inventory of 140 U under a 6-day delivery cycle is significantly lower (95 % significance level) than that observed at an inventory level of 120 U, but not statistically different from the shortage rates at an inventory level of 130 U. Similarly, the shortages observed when 140 U of RBC are held and a 7-day per week delivery cycle is assumed is significantly less (95 % significance level) than that observed at an inventory level of 120 U, but not statistically different from an inventory level of 130 U. It may therefore be concluded that an RBC inventory level of 140 U provides greater availability than does an inventory level of 120 U,

Table 17.24 Platelets unmatched units per annum (shortage); the estimated number of unmatched platelets in 2009/2010 was 12 ± 3.9 U

	6-day per week delivery cycle		7-day per week delivery cycle	
Target inventory	Mean value	95 % CI half width	Mean value	95 % CI half width
20	10.50	5.54	10.60	7.68
18	12.70	8.36	9.10	5.06
16	46.70	7.89	17.90	5.94

Table 17.25 Platelet units outdated per annum (surplus); the actual number of outdated platelets in 2009/2010 was approximately 570 U

	6-day per week delivery cycle		7-day per week delivery cycle	
Target inventory	Mean value	95 % CI half width	Mean value	95 % CI half width
20	332.90	18.92	376.20	18.92
18	220.80	14.03	254.60	19.61
16	141.40	11.31	156.90	15.73

without any significant increase in outdates or transhipped units. Moreover, it may be concluded, that red cell shortages and surplus are not affected by the selection of either a 6-day or 7-day delivery cycle.

The simulation was also run with platelet inventory levels of 16, 18, and 20 U under the assumption of both a 6 or 7-day per week delivery cycle. In each scenario the number shortages, as determined by the number of lost demand units, and the number of surplus units, as determined by the number of outdated units, was recorded. The results of the simulation runs appear in Tables 17.24 and 17.25.

The results suggest that platelets are more difficult to manage than red blood cells because of their shorter shelf-life and smaller demand profile. Little statistical difference (95 % significance level) in terms of shortages was observed between a 6 and 7-day delivery cycle; only when a platelet inventory of 16 U is assumed did a 7-day per week cycle result in statistically fewer shortages than a 6-day per week cycle. Additionally, there are statistically more shortages (95 % significance level) when an inventory of 16 U is held when compared to either an 18 or 20 U inventory regardless of whether a 6 or 7-day per week delivery cycle is assumed. Differences in platelet outdates were, however, statistically significant (95 % level) between the 6-day per week delivery cycle and the 7-day delivery cycle, with 6-day per week cycle producing a lower level of wastage. This counter-intuitive result arises because of the assumption in the model that platelet units collected in Saint John coming available on Mondays (i.e. Saturday collections) surplus to requirements cannot be shipped for redistribution to Dartmouth since no air or ground service is available to return product. Thus, the model assumes all surplus units are held at the SHU while additional units may be ordered if inventory within a particular blood group is below target. The net result is an increase in inventory and outdates without an appreciable increase in product availability. Finally, it should be noted that the differences in platelet outdates between a 6-day delivery cycle and a 7-day delivery cycle are statistically significant (95 % level) for each inventory level (16, 18, or 20).

Based on the analysis of platelet results it may be concluded that the selection of a 7-day per week delivery cycle does not appreciably increase platelet availability if 18 or more units of platelets are held at the SHU. In the simulation runs, outdates were seen to increase with inventory, but availability of product was not markedly improved when more than 18 U were held at the SHU.

It should be noted that managing platelets is, in general, a difficult problem and that shortages and surpluses observed in the simulation may not be strictly due to the proposed network configuration. To provide a comparison scenario, the simulation was modified to represent a network in which it is assumed that all platelets distributed to any New Brunswick facility are collected at Saint John and distributed through the SHU using existing ground transportation and assuming, as much as possible, that all other structural assumptions are held constant common with the scenarios reported in this analysis. The comparison scenario was executed for a total of 10 replications of 1 year, using a warm-up period of 70 days. The number of units of lost demand, representing demand for platelets not satisfied as of 23:59 each day, was recorded and found to be 12.04 ± 3.90 U. This value is not statistically different (95 % level) from the number of lost demand units recorded at inventory levels of 18 or 20 U assuming either a 6-day per week or 7-day per week delivery cycle. (Though, of course, we note that these conclusions are based upon a specific number of simulation replications, which could be altered by changing the number of observations derived from either or both of the production or the comparison models.) The number of outdating units in the comparison scenario (567.8 ± 28.82) was statistically greater than those seen in the production runs at a 95 % significance level, for all inventory levels. This result suggests that shortages experienced at the SHU are not significantly increased under the proposed production and distribution policy. It may thus be concluded that customers served out of the Saint John SHU will not be adversely affected so long as 18–20 U of platelets are ordered daily. To test the robustness of this result, the simulation was executed with double the number of expected road closures per annum. These tests showed that the number of outdates and shortages to be better, or at least not statistically different from the baseline results for both RBC and platelets.

17.4.2.12 Simulation Model Summary

After consolidation plans for production facilities in Maritime Canada were announced, stakeholders voiced concerns regarding product availability and the reliability of the transport network to resupply in the event of poor weather. Simulation modelling efforts were undertaken to address this issue and thus a series of models focusing on in-bound transportation and inventory levels necessary to buffer out variations in supply and demand was created. The models were developed in an evolutionary manner as understanding of the logistics network evolved and as questions around aspects of system reliability changed.

The baseline model was primarily intended as a proof-of-concept to indicate to decision makers both internal and external to Canadian Blood Services, that the complexity of a production and/or distribution hub could be accurately represented by a simulation. Key insights from the initial modelling efforts were related to ground transportation and weather; specifically the relative rarity of a complete road closure and a lack of clear correlation between weather and transit times for commercial ground services operating between Nova Scotia and New Brunswick. The model also indicated that the location where raw materials are processed did not necessarily impact product availability; where materials are stored and the level of stock held was clearly demonstrated to be more important than the location of production.

Once the applicability of a simulation approach had been established and the basic feasibility of the consolidation plan had been proven, modelling efforts focused on the parameters of the dedicated ground service operating between the production centre in Dartmouth, NS and the distribution hub in Saint John, NB; at first to roughly establish the layout of the ground run and to identify the products/hospital pairs to be serviced by the ground vehicle en route and later to confirm the final design of the network. Both models showed that the management of red blood cells is relatively straightforward; inventory polices resulting in low outdate and low shortage rates were easily identified with the simulation. Platelets, not unexpectedly, were more difficult to manage – some level of outdate or shortage is inevitable, given the very short shelf life of this product. The simulation model allowed exploration of differing levels of inventory and suggested to decision makers a range for outdates and shortages. While no policy was found that simultaneously resulted in low platelet outdates and shortages, acceptable policies that compare favourably to current system performance were identified.

17.5 Conclusions and Policy Implications

Canadian Blood Services succeeded the Canadian Red Cross as the operator of the blood supply chain in Canada outside of Québec as a result of recommendations in the Krever Commission. In his report, Justice Krever also cited the need for blood system operators to operate at arm's length from governments and to manage Canada's blood supply as a single, national resource. Canadian Blood Services' plan to consolidate production facilities in the Maritime Provinces to standardize processes and workflows fits within the framework of the system envisioned by Krever. Nevertheless, good stewardship dictates that the security of the blood supply in the Maritimes after consolidation be assured, as stakeholders in New Brunswick requested. The analysis described in this chapter was designed to answer the concerns of these stakeholder groups.

The analysis was extensive. The physical trial of a proposed air based distribution service was conducted over a 12 month period and involved more than 1,600 shipments to hospitals in northern New Brunswick. Three simulation models were created to evaluate various aspects of the ground based service for southern facilities and to determine the amount of inventory necessary to buffer out variations in ground service availability. The results of both sets of analysis suggest that, on the balance of measures considered, customer service will not be adversely affected by the consolidation of production facilities in Dartmouth.

It should be noted that in January of 2012, stakeholder groups in New Brunswick opted to remain with Canadian Blood Services after consolidation of production facilities in Dartmouth, subject to a monitoring process to address any issues that may arise. The new production and distribution network will be operational in 2013 and will function largely as described in this analysis. Furthermore, in June 2012, Canadian Blood Services announced that a national service call centre will be opened in New Brunswick, utilizing the space to be vacated by the existing Saint John production centre.

Appendix: Travel Distances Between Select Points

See Table 17.26.

Table 17.26 Distances (in km) for select points in New Brunswick and Nova Scotia

	Saint John	Dartmouth	Fredericton	Sussex	Hampton	Moncton	Sackville	Aulac
Saint John		409	110	77	43	160	205	213
Dartmouth			429	333	371	254	206	200
Fredericton				116	148	170	219	227
Sussex					38	84	132	140
Hampton						118	165	174
Moncton							48	56
Sackville								9
Aulac								

References

1. Canadian Blood Services (2011) Annual report 2010–2011. www.blood.ca. Accessed 27 July 2012
2. Canadian Blood Services (1998–2012) Canadian blood services: FAQs. http://www.bloodservices.ca/CentreApps/Internet/UW_V502_MainEngine.nsf/page/FAQKrever?OpenDocument. Accessed 27 July 2012
3. Krever H (1997) Commission of inquiry on the blood system in Canada. Canadian Government Pub., 1997
4. Blake JT, Hardy M (2013) Using simulation to evaluate a blood supply network in the Canadian maritime provinces. J Enterprise Inform Manage 26(1/2):119–134
5. CanadaEast.com (2011) NB to ensure top quality of blood supply. http://timestranscript.canadaeast.com/newstoday/article/1411744. Accessed 10 June 2011
6. Canadian Broadcasting Corporation (2012) Timeline: Canadian blood services controversy in New Brunswick. http://www.cbc.ca/news/canada/new-brunswick/story/2012/01/13/nb-canadian-blood-services-timeline.html. Accessed 30 Jan 2012
7. Blake JT (2012) A case study on the use of operations research to evaluate changes in a blood supply chain. In: D'Amours S (ed) Proceedings of the 4th international conference on information systems, logistics, and supply chain. Quebec City, QC
8. Statistics Canada (2012) Province of New Brunswick. http://www12.statcan.gc.ca/census-recensement/2011/as-sa/fogs-spg/Facts-pr-eng.cfm?Lang=Eng&GK=PR&GC=13. Accessed 30 May 2012
9. Beliën J, Forcé H (2012) Supply chain management of blood products: a literature review. Eur J Oper Res 217:1–16
10. Nahmias S (1982) Perishable inventory theory: a review. Oper Res 30:680–670
11. Prastacos GP (1984) Blood inventory management—an overview of theory and practice. Manage Sci 30:770–800
12. Pierskalla WP (2005) Supply chain management of blood banks. In: Brandeau ML, Sainfort F, Pierskalla WP (eds) Operations research and health care. Springer, New York
13. Sural G, Sahin H, Meral S (2007) Locational analysis for regionalization of Turkish Red Crescent blood services. Comput Oper Res 34:692–704
14. Chen HK, Hsueh CF, Chang ME (2009) Production scheduling and vehicle routing with time windows for perishable food products. Comput Oper Res 36:2311–2319
15. Brodheim E, Prastacos GP (1979) The Long Island blood distribution system as a prototype for regional blood management. Interfaces 9:3–20
16. Federgruen A, Zipkin P (1984) A combined vehicle routing and inventory allocation problem. Oper Res 32:1019–1037
17. Hwang HS (1999) A food distribution model for famine relief. Comput Ind Eng 37:335–338
18. Prindezis N, Kiranoudis CT, Marinos-Kouris D (2003) A business-to-business fleet management service provider for central food market enterprises. J Food Eng 60:203–210
19. Rytilä JS, Spens KN (2006) Using simulation to increase efficiency in blood supply chains. Manage Res N 29:801–819
20. Ghandforoush P, Sen TK (2010) A DSS to manage platelet production supply chain for regional blood centers. Decis Support Syst 50:32–42
21. Katsaliaki K, Brailsford SC (2007) Using simulation to improve the blood supply chain. J Oper Res Soc 58:219–227
22. Delen D, Erranguntla M, Mayer RJ, Wu CN (2011) Better management of blood supply-chain with GIS-based analytics. Ann Oper Res 185:181–193
23. Canadian Broadcasting Corporation (2012) Snow, wind prompt school closures. http://www.cbc.ca/news/canada/nova-scotia/story/2012/03/27/ns-snow-wind-schools-closed.html. Accessed 30 Mar 2012
24. Walpole R, Myers R, Ye S, Myers K (2012) Probability and statistics for engineers and scientists, 9th edn. Prentice-Hall, Boston

25. Levene H (1960) Robust tests for equality of variances. In: Olkin I, Ghurye SG et al. (eds) Contributions to probability and statistics: essays in honor of Harold Hotelling. Stanford University Press, Stanford, CA
26. Feltovich N (2003) Nonparametric tests of differences in medians: comparison of the Wilcoxon-Mann–Whitney and robust rank order tests. Exp Econ 6:273–279
27. Law AM (2007) Simulation modeling and analysis, 4th edn. McGraw-Hill, New York

Chapter 18
Improving the Efficiency of Cost-effectiveness Analysis to Inform Policy Decisions in the Real World: Lessons from the Pharmacoeconomics Research Unit at Cancer Care Ontario

Jeffrey S. Hoch

Abstract There are important challenges in the application of using operations research (OR) and cost-effectiveness analysis (CEA) in the real world that highlight the great divide between academic research and practical application. The difficulty is magnified in cancer. Nevertheless, the potential for CEA to inform policy decisions is also great. The best estimate of a new drug's cost-effectiveness is not knowledge for knowledge's sake; this type of information is the foundation of accountability for the hundreds of millions of dollars being spent. In 2007, Cancer Care Ontario (CCO) established Canada's first in-house Pharmacoeconomics Research Unit comprised of independent researchers. This chapter reviews the initial years of the Unit at CCO after briefly describing Canada's cancer drug funding landscape. The chapter concludes by sharing lessons from the Pharmacoeconomics Research Unit's experience and pointing out directions for future research aimed at reaching decision makers in the real world.

J.S. Hoch (✉)
Centre for Research on Inner City Health, The Keenan Research Centre, Li Ka Shing Knowledge Institute, St. Michael's Hospital, 30 Bond Street, Toronto, ON, Canada M5B 1W8

Pharmacoeconomics Research Unit, Cancer Care Ontario, Toronto, ON, Canada

Institute of Health Policy, Management and Evaluation, University of Toronto, Toronto, ON, Canada

Canadian Centre for Applied Research in Cancer Control (ARCC), Toronto, ON, Canada
e-mail: jeffrey.hoch@utoronto.ca

G.S. Zaric (ed.), *Operations Research and Health Care Policy*,
International Series in Operations Research & Management Science 190,
DOI 10.1007/978-1-4614-6507-2_18,

18.1 Introduction

18.1.1 Healthcare Costs and the Need for Operations Research Techniques

There is agreement throughout medicine and especially in oncology that the current rate of growth in healthcare expenditures is unsustainable [1, 2]. Recently published warnings have appeared in both general and specialty medical journals [3, 4]. Experts note that the direct medical costs of cancer in the USA have increased from nearly $27 billion in 1990 [5] to more than $90 billion in 2008 [6], a more than two-fold increase even after adjusting for inflation [13]. Smith and Hillner [2] report that annual direct costs in the USA for cancer care are projected to increase by over 66 % from $104 billion in 2006 [7] to over $173 billion in 2020 [8].

In cancer, there has been a pronounced focus on the cost of drugs in relation to their clinical benefits. Bach [9] observed that spending from 1997 to 2004 on Medicare's Part B drugs, "a category dominated by drugs used to treat cancer" increased by 267 % compared with overall Medicare spending which increased by 47 % during the same period. The problem of skyrocketing drug costs is compounded by evidence suggesting that increased expenditures are producing only minimal gains in terms of decreases in mortality and increases in quality of life [9]. In other words, healthcare payers are paying more and getting less. An example of this involves treatment for non-small-cell lung cancer (NSCLC). Research indicates there is a 1.2 month survival advantage from adding cetuximab to cisplatin and vinorelbine to treat patients with NSCLC, and in the USA, 18 weeks of cetuximab treatment for NSCLC costs an average of $80,000 [4]. This translates into an expenditure of $800,000 to prolong the life of one patient by 1 year [4]. This observation prompted the following call to action in the *Journal of the National Cancer Institute* [4]:

> We must deal with the escalating price of cancer therapy now. If we allow a survival advantage of 1.2 months to be worth $80,000, and by extrapolation survival of 1 year to be valued at $800,000, we would need $440 billion annually—an amount nearly 100 times the budget of the National Cancer Institute—to extend by 1 year the life of the 550,000 Americans who die of cancer annually. And no one would be cured. The current situation cannot continue. We cannot ignore the cumulative costs of the tests and treatments we recommend and prescribe.

Although the USA has taken steps to prevent the simultaneous examination of both costs and benefits of pharmaceuticals [9, 10], other countries have embraced methods from operations research to address the challenge of introducing controls in an attempt to curb healthcare spending [11].

18.1.2 Cost-Effectiveness Analysis in Theory and Practice

Of all the techniques from operations research, healthcare policy advisors and decision makers appear to be provided most frequently with partial results from a constrained optimization problem. Constrained optimization, in its simplest form, has two parts: a constraint and an objective. Typically, the fixed budget is viewed as the constraint (i.e., the amount of money that can be spent is limited). The objective in healthcare is less clear but often assumed to be to maximize the population's health, and in oncology, perhaps maximizing "quality adjusted" years of life (i.e., the QALY). Thus, when considering which healthcare treatments to reimburse, a healthcare payer in theory faces the following problem:

> Choose the optimal levels of funding (i.e., δ going from 0 to 100 %) of M Treatments (i.e., x_i for $i = 1$ to M), assuming the x_i's have health outcomes of x_i^o and costs of x_i^c with an objective of maximizing $\Sigma\delta_i x_i^o$ within a fixed budget of B (i.e., $\Sigma\delta_i x_i^c \leq B$).

Weinstein and Zeckhauser [12] considered such a problem and showed the optimal decision rule is equivalent to funding treatments or interventions when the ratio of the extra cost (ΔC) to the extra health effect (ΔE) is less than a willingness to pay threshold (λ). In other words, decision makers should fund a new treatment if $\Delta C/\Delta E < \lambda$. Zaric provides more details about the link between operations research and the calculation of the incremental cost-effectiveness ratio $\Delta C/\Delta E$ [13].

Practical applications of operations research to inform policy advisors and decision makers often involve comparing a new treatment to standard care by conducting a cost-effectiveness analysis (CEA) and providing an estimate of $\Delta C/\Delta E$. Some are critical of reporting an estimate of $\Delta C/\Delta E$, the incremental cost-effectiveness ratio (ICER), as a partial result; they view a policy recommendation stemming from one ICER as limited by assuming an all or nothing funding decision (i.e., $\delta = 0$ or 1) for one treatment (i.e., $M = 1$) based on an arbitrary willingness to pay threshold (i.e., the optimal λ is only known after all potential treatments have been considered). Others see the imperfect process using a single ICER as a compromise in the right direction. For pragmatic decision makers trying to use CEA results, tentative guidelines are available [14]. Debate about their use and misuse began upon publication in 1992 and continues to this day [15, 16].

There are important challenges in the application of operations research using CEA in the real world that highlight the great divide between academic research and practical application. The difficulty is magnified in cancer because of the intense emotions it raises and their influence on decision making, impacting treatment funding decisions. Nevertheless, the potential for CEA to inform policy decisions is also great. In 2007, Cancer Care Ontario (CCO), Ontario's provincial agency responsible for continually improving cancer services and the government's cancer advisor, established Canada's first in-house Pharmacoeconomics Research Unit comprised of independent researchers [17]. This chapter reviews the initial 5 years of the Pharmacoeconomics Research Unit at CCO. The purpose is to share lessons and point out directions for future research in operations research aimed at reaching decision makers in the real world.

18.2 Background

18.2.1 The Funding and Use of Cancer Drugs in Canada

The Canadian healthcare system is a composite of multiple healthcare systems. Each province controls its own healthcare reimbursement decisions and has a responsibility to ensure its healthcare spending is in line with the preferences of its population. There are federal laws that require necessary care be covered universally; however, the definition of "necessary" can vary by province, and drugs prescribed outside of the inpatient setting are not included in the "universal healthcare" legislation. Intravenous (IV) cancer drugs are subject to provincial funding decisions, creating the possibility for inequitable access to particular drugs across provincial formularies. In addition, many provinces may limit coverage for oral drugs to people over 65 or enrolled in social assistance. The heterogeneity of drug coverage is especially important in cancer because the high price of cancer drugs means most patients are able to receive pharmaceutical treatment only if it is paid for by someone else (e.g., through a publicly funded drug program or a compassionate access program) [18].

Chafe et al. [18] observed that even once a province's Ministry of Health (MOH) decides to fund a drug, access issues persist. Based on their findings, Fig. 18.1 shows the per capita spending rankings for fiscal year 2006/2007 of two of Canada's most populous provinces British Columbia (BC) and Ontario (ON). Figure 18.1a shows six single bars indicating extreme "mismatches" in per capita expenditures for oral drugs. For example, while BC and ON both spend the most per capita on imatinib, spending on goserelin is second highest in BC but not even in the top 10 in ON. The third greatest per capita expenditure in ON is on bicalutamide which is not in the top 10 in BC. There are four single bar mismatches between BC and ON in the top 7 IV drugs (see Fig. 18.1b). For example, while BC and ON both spend the most per capita and the second most per capita on trastuzumab and rituximab respectively, spending on oxaliplatin is third highest in BC but not even in the top 10 in ON. The mismatches show clearly that cancer patients are not obtaining the same publicly funded drugs at the same rate.

There are many reasons these mismatches can occur. Differences in quantity prescribed can occur because of physician preference or because of a difference in negotiated drug price (affecting the drug's reimbursement status in the provincial formulary). Based on Chafe et al. [18], Fig. 18.2 shows the utilization rate per 100,000 population for each drug for which BC and ON reported patient utilization data. For the IV drug docetaxel, BC covers 21.3 patients per 100,000 population,

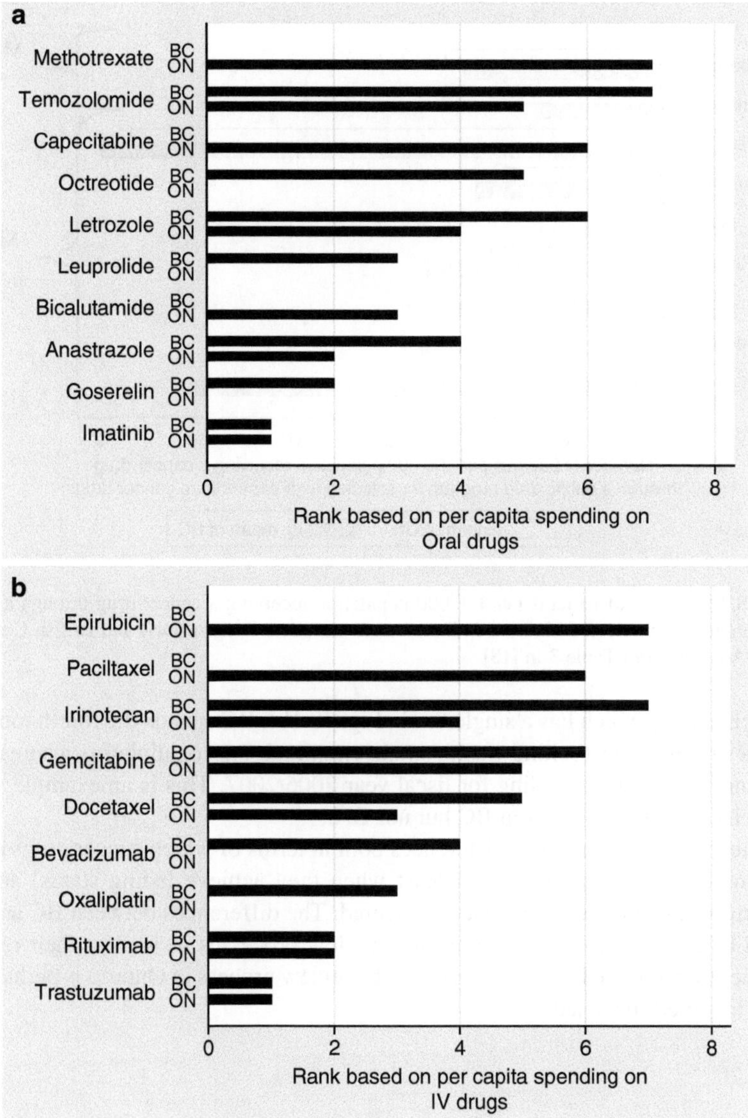

Fig. 18.1 (**a**) Top 7 oral cancer drugs for British Columbia (BC) and Ontario (ON) for 2006–2007. Adapted from Table 2 in [18]. (**b**) Top 7 IV cancer drugs for British Columbia (BC) and Ontario (ON) for 2006–2007. Adapted from Table 1 in [18]

slightly lower than the 23.7 patients per 100,000 population covered in ON. In contrast, for the oral drug letrozole, BC covers 50.5 patients per 100,000 compared to 32.5 patients per 100,000 in ON. All drugs shown in Fig. 18.2 are reimbursed by both BC and ON; thus, the per capita differences in use are due to differences in drug indication or physician preference. However, for a drug like

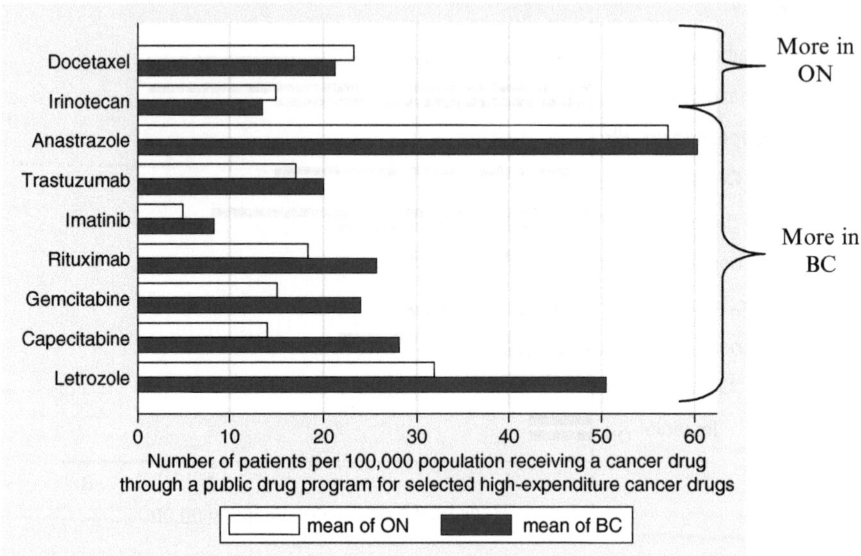

Fig. 18.2 Number of patients per 100,000 population receiving a cancer drug through a public drug program for selected high-expenditure cancer drugs in Ontario (ON) and British Columbia (BC). Adapted from Table 3 in [18]

bevacizumab, (which has a single bar in Fig. 18.1b), BC spends the fourth most per capita on this drug (behind trastuzumab, rituximab and oxaliplatin) whereas ON does not report any spending for fiscal year 2006/2007. This is an example where bevacizumab was covered in BC but not ON.

Thus, there appears to be differences both in terms of which cancer drugs are on the provincial formularies (or at least when they achieve listing status) and the patterns of use for the drugs that are covered. The differences between BC and ON could be due to the differences in their review processes as well as their relative abilities to negotiate lower drug prices. The review process in Ontario is perhaps the most involved in Canada.

18.2.2 The Funding of Cancer Drugs in Ontario

Before the recent establishment of the pan-Canadian Oncology Drug Review, Ontario's Committee to Evaluate Drugs (CED) had a subcommittee (CED–CCO) supporting oncology drug review. The CED–CCO subcommittee was established in 2005 to respond to a number of issues, including the desire to control rapidly increasing drug expenditures. The CED–CCO subcommittee was charged with evaluating the clinical and economic evidence to make a funding recommendation to the CED. The CED considers oncology agents in the context of other disease

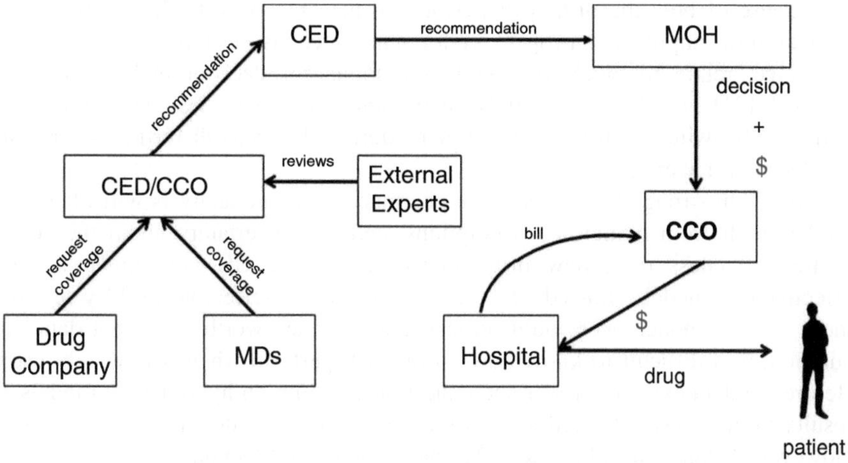

Fig. 18.3 Ontario's cancer drug reimbursement landscape (public funding) before the pan-Canadian Oncology Drug Review (pCODR). *Note*: *MDs* physicians, *CED/CCO* Committee to Evaluate Drugs, Cancer Care Ontario subcommittee, *CED* Committee to Evaluate Drugs, *CCO* Cancer Care Ontario, *MOH* Ministry of Health

areas (e.g., does this drug provide good value for money overall, not just compared to other cancer investments) and makes a final recommendation to government (the public payer). Thus, recommendations made by the CED are submitted to the Executive Officer of the Ontario Public Drugs Programs Division of the MOH (the OPDP administers Ontario's public drug programs). The process concludes with the Executive Officer's review and decision (see Fig. 18.3).

After the Executive Officer decides to fund an IV cancer drug, targeted funding then flows to CCO to reimburse hospitals for the newly approved IV cancer drugs (for oral cancer drugs funding is managed by the MOH through the Ontario Drug Benefit). The New Drug Funding Program (NDFP), administered by CCO on behalf of the MOH, was established in 1995 to administer funding to cover the cost of new, expensive IV cancer drugs [19]. The NDFP grew from a $7 million program funding six drugs for 2,354 patients in 1997–1998 to a $64 million program funding 16 drugs for over 14,000 patients in 2003/2004 [20]. Currently, more than 20 drugs are reimbursed through the NDFP.

A number of challenges exist when attempting to evaluate cancer drugs before they have been widely used. Regardless of the analytical method employed, data required to make decisions about a drug's true value are typically not available. Ideally, evidence should come from randomized controlled trials (RCTs). However, frequently the only data available are non-comparative data from phase II trials with small sample sizes [21]; without comparison groups, use of these data requires that indirect comparisons be made [21]. Moreover, the regimented clinical trial may not reflect current practice patterns in Ontario, providing a false sense of how the drug will perform in the "real world." In addition, it is unclear how unproven surrogate end points, such as response rate or tumor shrinkage, relate to more important end points for decision-makers, such as survival [21]. Lastly, some trials incorporate crossover designs (with study participants switching treatment regimens during the trial) distorting the results for decision makers [21].

Even with strong clinical data, the pharmacoeconomic analysis will likely use models built from numerous assumptions, creating uncertainty about the actual cost-effectiveness of a new drug. For example, the UK government's cost-effectiveness models showed MS drugs might be cost-effective in 20 years, but these 20-year models were built on less than 10 years worth of patient data.[1] In addition, it is difficult to know how a drug will perform when it is widely used. Before the data exist to answer such questions, relying on hypothetical models or results from industry funded studies may be preferable alternatives to guessing. However, Baker and colleagues [22] have found that "among industry studies, modelling studies are more favourable to the sponsor than administrative studies," congruent with the claim that "studies sponsored by industry are significantly more favourable to industry" [23]. Moreover, studies funded by industry are more likely to report economically attractive results [24]. Therefore, objective information about the true healthcare costs and patient outcomes is needed to determine the true value of new therapies. This type of information—describing a drug's cost, effectiveness and cost-effectiveness once it is covered by the MOH—is only available once the drug is covered by the MOH. However, the MOH's decision about whether to fund the drug must be made *a priori*. In this setting, the best estimate of a new drug's cost-effectiveness is not knowledge for knowledge's sake; this type of information is the foundation of accountability for the hundreds of millions of dollars being spent.

18.2.3 Pan-Canadian Oncology Drug Review (pCODR)

Using Ontario's established infrastructure for review of clinical and economic evidence, Canadian provinces initiated a two-step collaborative process to establish a permanent, timely, effective and efficient review and evaluation of cancer drugs throughout Canada. The first step involved setting up an interim national process for the review of cancer drugs called iJODR (the interim Joint Oncology Drug Review). For the economic evidence, pharmaceutical manufacturers were required to provide an "unlocked" version of the economic model used to support their product's submission (for external reviewers to explore). Using lessons from iJODR, the second step of the process established a permanent successor called

[1] It is interesting to note that the deal struck between the payer and the drug manufacturer in the UK was based on the assumption that the drug would be cost-effective in 10 years.

the pan-Canadian Oncology Drug Review (pCODR). iJODR began in March 2007 with provincial decision makers observing Ontario's drug review processes first-hand. At the time of this writing, pCODR is celebrating its 1 year anniversary. Because of pCODR's commitment to transparency, all of the materials used to reach a recommendation are posted online at www.pcodr.ca (the Web site also includes dates for key milestones in the process).[2]

18.3 The Pharmacoeconomics Research Unit at Cancer Care Ontario

18.3.1 Background

Shortly after the creation of the CED–CCO subcommittee, CCO hosted an invited workshop "Better Pharmacoeconomic Decisions in Oncology" where experts from around the world presented their advice to guide CCO's thinking about the creation of a Pharmacoeconomics Research Unit. Difficult questions were raised: How exactly would CEA help CCO? Would CCO place "value for money" as a guiding principle in the face of pressures that might be mounted in the popular press? These were important questions given CCO's position as the government's cancer advisor and the media's preference to feature stories devoted to the funding (and especially the non-funding) of cancer drugs.

A recent example from the Canadian Press was an article entitled "Ontario won't cover all costs of new cancer drugs" [25]. The article juxtaposed views expressed by cancer patients and views expressed by the Health Minister of Ontario. One anecdote was about a woman who was diagnosed with late-stage cancer and wanted to know "why the government felt her life was not worth the $18,000 she was billed [for her cancer drug]." [25]

> It became clear to me that early on the drugs I needed to fight my cancer were not being provided by a universal healthcare system that I, as a Canadian, have been taught to be so proud of... I'm a Canadian first and foremost—I happen to live in Ontario. Who would have thought that this would affect the type of treatment that would be available to me? ... How does the government of Ontario have the audacity to make the choices that deny their citizens the recommended standard of care that is offered in other G8 countries? [25]

[2] For example, at http://www.pcodr.ca/portal/server.pt/community/find_a_review/547/pcodr_-_find_a_review_detail_-_votrient one can see that pCODR's first submission was deemed complete on July 21, 2011 and pCODR's final recommendation was issued about 6 months later on January 5, 2012.

These concerns—"what is a life worth?", "what are needed cancer drugs?" and "why all healthcare payers do not cover the same cancer drugs?"—are all questions that an applied pharmacoeconomics research unit could help decision makers address.

The response from Ontario's health minister was also reported in the article [25]:

> There's no public or private health insurance plan in the country that could afford to pay for all of the latest cancer drugs... Ontario has more than doubled spending on new cancer drugs, but it would be impossible to cover every new medication that's developed... I can't imagine an environment, and I can't imagine leadership under any political party... that could... offer a solution that said 'every time there's a new cancer drug available on the market that a public system could pay for it.'

While, the justification for a pharmacoeconomics research unit to address the sky rocketing costs of cancer drugs is clear it is important that such a research unit should not lose sight of the fact that cancer is a devastating disease. Cancer is the leading cause of death in most developed countries, causing more than 25 % of all deaths in Canada [26]. Cancer care accounts for 2.9 % of all healthcare direct costs and 8.9 % of indirect costs in Canada [27]. Recently, the Lancet Oncology Commissioned has reasoned that "many patients with cancer would otherwise experience years to decades of good health" so "devoting appropriate resources to the prevention and treatment of cancer, and to research aimed at eradicating cancer... is essential" [28]. Thus, the Pharmacoeconomics Research Unit at CCO was established to help decision makers optimize their decisions by providing objective estimates of the extra cost and the extra benefit of various cancer investments.

18.3.2 Examples of the Pharmacoeconomics Research Unit's Work

How the Pharmacoeconomics Research Unit provides technical support related to oncology drugs depends on the route a cancer drug funding submission takes (see the lower left corner of Fig. 18.3). Submissions made by pharmaceutical manufacturers are sometimes greeted with concerns over whether "industry" reports lower ICERs than an alternative source would (e.g., one without a large financial interest at stake). For some, the fact that studies supported by pharmaceutical companies report lower ICERs in general suggests bias [24]. However, others have claimed that industry sponsored studies are focused on drugs with greater potential than those studied by others [29]. Recent studies have examined pharmacoeconomic analyses of the same drug conducted by different analysts, finding that ICER estimates by drug manufacturers were lower than those submitted by academic assessment groups *for the same product* [30, 31]. In fact, 84 % of manufacturers' estimates (21 of 25) were less than the academic assessment groups' estimates ($p < 0.001$). When Chauhan and colleagues [32] studied economic models in the UK made by both pharmaceutical manufacturers and academic groups, they found academic groups tended to estimate larger differences in cost (ΔC) and smaller differences in effectiveness (ΔE) compared with manufacturers. With $\Delta C_{\text{academics}} < \Delta C_{\text{manufacturers}}$ and $\Delta E_{\text{academics}} > \Delta E_{\text{manufacturers}}$, clearly $\Delta C/\Delta E$ estimated by academic groups will be larger than $\Delta C/\Delta E$ estimated by pharmaceutical manufacturers.

The Pharmacoeconomics Research Unit works to address the concern that Chauhan et al.'s [32] findings might hold for Canadian submissions. The Unit serves as an external reviewer for the economic evidence accompanying drug funding submissions to the cancer subcommittee of the CED. This has involved detailed "model busting" or error checking the results through various logic tests including comprehensive sensitivity analysis. In addition to producing reports reviewing pharmaceutical manufacturers' models, the Unit has been asked to present other external reviewers' reports at subcommittee meetings. It is odd that the clinical evidence is presented by the lead clinical reviewer; however, the economic evidence is not presented by the lead economic reviewer. This asymmetry may be from an earlier era where clinicians doing the reviews presented evidence to the other clinicians making the recommendations. The effectiveness of the Unit's role hinges on successfully building trust with both decision makers and policy advisors. In addition, the ability to communicate the main results of analyses and why they matter is at a premium among these audiences, not traditionally trained in operations research. We return to this theme in Sect. 18.4.

The Pharmacoeconomics Research Unit also contributes when submissions are made by physician groups (e.g., when oncologists want the MOH to pay for a treatment regimen, but the pharmaceutical manufacturer has no plans to make a formal submission to the MOH). In the past, this situation led to much consternation, as drug funding submissions must include both high quality clinical and economic evidence. Because of the extreme need for capacity building in the area of cancer pharmacoeconomics, the economic models needed for successful submissions are beyond the capacity of most oncologist groups making submissions. The Pharmacoeconomics Research Unit created several models to serve as the "economic evidence" for oncologists' submissions. Again the issue of trust looms large in this enterprise. The physicians the Unit works with must trust that the economic model will successfully capture the critical aspects of the clinical problem and the nature of the solution offered by the drug. A major concern is that if it were perceived generally that it was easier to get a drug approved if an oncologist group made the submission, pharmaceutical manufacturers might delegate this task completely. If such were the case, a much greater level of investment would be needed to support the infrastructure necessary to produce separate models for each drug submission. However, some countries (e.g., England through the National Institute for Health and Clinical Excellence) perceive sufficient value in this investment.

18.4 Lessons from the Pharmacoeconomics Research Unit

18.4.1 Limited Training ≠ Limited Capacity to Understand

As soon as the Pharmacoeconomics Research Unit was created in Fall 2007, we were affected by Canada's underinvestment in the capacity to do and understand economic evaluation. Internally, it was obvious that an entire infrastructure needed to be created de novo to meet our objectives of timely, understandable economic analysis. Externally, a pronounced knowledge transfer and exchange effort had to be launched so that the results of economic evaluation could be understood and used more effectively. To be clear, while most people involved in cancer drug funding have limited training in CEA, the majority understand the similarities between shopping, ICERs and λ. To amplify the message of how the results of CEA could help with "smart shopping," we have given over 100 invited talks to cancer researchers, clinicians, decision makers and policy advisors introducing our Unit and highlighting what audiences can do with CEA results. Our publicity push coincided with CCO's decision to list "value for money" as one of its guiding principles in the most recent version of the Ontario Cancer Plan. A natural consequence of our aggressive marketing was the interest from other areas within cancer control for "value for money" analysis, leading to additional cost-effectiveness studies in areas like cancer screening and radiation therapy. As a result, we were able to produce more opportunities for cancer system leaders to be educated about the benefits of CEA. The first years of the Pharmacoeconomics Research Unit had the feel of participatory action research where both the researchers and the knowledge users were involved in posing research questions and answering them together.

18.4.2 Type III Error + Unintelligible Language ≠ Success

It was this exposure to "real world" decision makers and their policy advisors that illustrated the chasm between academic CEA and people making recommendations or decisions. To gain more exposure to the real world, we chose to locate the Pharmacoeconomics Research Unit inside of CCO, and to their credit, CCO allowed independent researchers to set up "in-house." We were able to observe challenges firsthand; in addition, our close proximity to CCO personnel afforded unique opportunities to be invited to help with solutions in real time. An unsettling observation from our exposure to the real world was analysts' high risk of type III error (getting the right answer to the wrong question). The results from CEAs or reviews of CEAs were often accompanied by high doses of economic jargon. Simplifying the language made it clear that once people could understand what the analysis was doing, they realized they were not interested in all of the results.

Nevertheless, the requirement of "economic evidence" is firmly ensconced in both Ontario's and Canada's drug review processes.

Traditional CEA as described in Sect. 18.1.2 is based on a problem Canadian decision makers do not have. The ICER and λ from Weinstein and Zeckhauser [12] differ conceptually from most decision makers' ICER and λ. In the standard setup for constrained optimization, all decisions are made at the same time, are reversible and based on a known objective function. In Ontario, drugs decisions are not made simultaneously. In addition, they are often not reversible (e.g., delisting or removing a drug from the formulary is often politically infeasible) and the MOH's objective function is not known (and likely not fixed). Furthermore, groups like the CED, the CED–CCO, iJODR and its successor pCODR make non-binding recommendations, not decisions. Even if λ in the sense of Weinstein and Zeckhauser [12] were known to decision makers, it would be unknown to recommendation making bodies. The laws in Canada currently prevent confidentially negotiated drug prices from being disclosed. As such, the ICER and λ that recommendation making bodies consider may be quite different from the ICER and λ that decision makers entertain subsequently.

This leaves analysts with two choices: trying to nudge the real world into the theoretical world or vice versa. An initial mystery for us was this: if the ICER were the solution to a question no one in the real world was asking, why require this type of information and ask for it to be reviewed for recommendations by clinicians and patient representatives before the MOH would use it to make decisions? It seemed to us that perhaps CEA and the ICER were serving an important purpose for the MOH, but perhaps not the one exactly intended by academics. This thinking helped us begin to match more closely analytical techniques and decision/recommendation maker needs. The debate about how to use CEA results [14, 15, 16] is really a debate about what the MOH needs in order to make a decision. Working closely with decision/recommendation makers, we were able to ask them what they need. After seeking to understand, we then focused on being understood.

18.4.3 Making Things Better $\neq$ Making Things More Complicated

We frequently introduced new ways of presenting information to decision/recommendation makers. In some cases, the tools were "standard" in health economics (e.g., the cost-effectiveness acceptability curve) and in other cases we developed new tools to test. We found that presenting information could erode our credibility if that information seemed wrong. For example, we presented the results of a probabilistic sensitivity analysis (PSA) in a cost-effectiveness acceptability curve (CEAC). The model was nonlinear so the distribution of the ICER was not symmetrical. At a particular λ, the ICER $< \lambda$, but the probability that the ICER $< \lambda$ was less than 50 %. In other words, the CEA estimate meant that the new treatment was cost-effective even though there was a greater than 50 % chance that the new treatment was *not* cost-effective. Some have argued that the results from a PSA are useful for considering how to invest in future research to reduce decision making uncertainty [33]. However, none of the recommendation committees we were helping actually make research funding decisions. While we believe uncertainty is important, other options like a cost-effectiveness acceptability frontier (CEAF) or an incremental net benefit (INB) by λ curve should be considered. The advantage of the INB by λ plot is that x-intercept occurs at the ICER, the y-intercept at $-\Delta C$ and the slope of the line is ΔE. Not only are all of the key parts there to shift between ICER and INB thinking, but also adding a 95 % confidence interval for the INB to the graph allows one to illustrate the 95 % confidence interval for the ICER, indicated by the x-intercepts [34]. Another popular graph we offered to decision makers was the ICER by drug price graph. The fact that the graph was not complicated to understand or use allowed for the possibility that decision makers might use it during their confidential negotiations with drug manufacturers. The Pharmacoeconomics Research Unit looked to make things better by making things simpler and more understandable.

18.5 Future Research

Future research must identify and attack the reasons for delay in cancer drug funding recommendations. Avoidable mistakes often lead to avoidable delays. To ameliorate this, we examined the problems with CEAs submitted by drug companies to iJODR in its first year 2007, from the perspectives of reviewers, and the CED–CCO (i.e., those who used the evidence to make formulary listing recommendations). We presented the findings to analysts and researchers conducting this type of analysis, drug manufacturers who commission CEA, and a working group that was writing oncology-specific economic evaluation guidelines for Canada; we also submitted this work for publication [35]. Some of the key challenges were related to incorrect comparators and insufficient sensitivity analysis. Future research should explore whether the same problems are still a major stumbling block. The novel processes pCODR have introduced address many of the old challenges. Nevertheless, new challenges are likely to arise, and researchers must both identify them and as well as offer potential solutions.

Additionally, future research should estimate ΔC and ΔE in the real world to help decision makers calibrate funding policies. Even in countries where economic assessments are currently included in new technology coverage recommendations, such as Canada, most of the cost-effectiveness studies are based on predictive models of future events. These models often rely on efficacy findings from randomized controlled trials (RCTs) and assumptions on resource use. There is the issue of relevance to more general practice due to the selection of healthier and/or younger patients for participation in RCTs. Performing real-world cost-effectiveness analyses post-approval, allows the assessment of the true value of medicines in a real world setting. The Pharmacoeconomics Research Unit conducted a real-world CEA using retrospective registry data from Ontario, Canada; the results of this type of study reflect the real-world value of a drug in actual practice. Our cost and life-year estimates, which were based solely on observational data, differed from those reported in clinical trials and simulated models (e.g., our estimates of ΔE were smaller and our estimates of ΔC were larger than those reported in the literature), and our ICERs were in general higher than those reported in the literature, especially for the elderly [36]. Future research in this area would emphasize the message that value for money questions are still valid even after decision makers are paying.

The ability to conduct successful "value for money" studies after funding would allow payers to benefit from the differential timing of funding. For example, if one jurisdiction funded a new drug before another, studying the actual ΔC and ΔE would benefit both the funding and non-funding jurisdictions. If $\Delta E \leq 0$, this would provide impetus for future renegotiations on more favorable terms. If ΔE were substantial and robust, other payers might be persuaded to start funding the product. For this scenario to be realized, researchers in different jurisdictions would need to work together with decision makers. Currently, the Canadian Centre for Applied Research in Cancer Control [37] is working to foster such collaboration in Canada; however, there is no reason that collaboration in this area could not be multinational and multidisciplinary making use of the multitude of funding policies throughout the world and the variety of analytical challenges attending such studies (e.g., the methodological issues of analyzing censored, skewed, observational cost data combined with the public engagement work of valuing benefits that are not easily observed in administrative data could attract a variety of researchers).

18.6 Conclusions and Policy Implications

While the consequence of the application of operations research and health economics to cancer healthcare might be the denial of public funding for cancer treatment, this is not the purpose. CEA offers a framework for an organized consideration of treatment options to balance the imperatives of treating a very bad disease and not paying more than we can (or should) to do it. Researchers interested in having an applied impact must consider how to make information more understandable and useful. In addition, those seeking to be helpful must take every opportunity to earn the trust of the people they seek to help. Developing and maintaining relationships is essential. This was a top priority for us at the Pharmacoeconomics Research Unit. We leveraged our unique position of having an independent lab of investigators operating in a provincial cancer organization by talking with policy makers and advisors about the types of problems they were trying to solve and the types of information they felt they needed. While no one mentioned the ICER by name, CCO had committed to "value for money" as a guiding principle and the MOH had committed to sustainability and accountability.

It was then incumbent upon us to show clearly and exactly how what we produced could be used to meet these objectives.

When we reviewed complaints about previous CEAs meant to support decision making, we learned that complaints were mostly about simple things that were easy to fix. The people involved in recommendations and decisions do not usually have a primary focus on methods or operations research. For this reason, technical stuff for technical reasons makes no sense. This observation seems especially germane given the fact that most important drug reimbursement interactions happen behind closed doors without analysts present. Also, because decisions are made behind closed doors and recommendations are not, the advice one hears about what is useful may be from an academic or recommendation point of view, but it is usually not from a decision making point of view. For example, if there is a threshold that is used for λ, it may never be known since the real price payers receive is not reported (e.g., because there is a law against reporting it). Without the real price (that changed the ICER from $>$ to $< \lambda$), there is no way to know the real λ. Lastly, decisions made behind closed doors do not involve the capacity that was there to review the clinical and economic evidence; the audiences are different. Fancy tools may not be useful and subtle distinctions may not be appreciated.

As a field, we must continue to develop and applied new methods of analyzing data and displaying information. We must also face the reality that the purpose of our role may be to promote goals related to process rather than outcome, suggesting that getting the question of interest right may be more important for researchers than correctly solving the wrong problem. Creating the best estimate of a new drug's cost-effectiveness is not knowledge for knowledge's sake; this type of information is the foundation of accountability for the hundreds of millions of dollars being spent. There is great potential for methods from operations research and health economics to provide useful information; it is possible for the results of our analysis to be understood and used by policy makers and other decision makers in the real world. Experiences at the Pharmacoeconomics Research Unit have illustrated this potential.

Acknowledgments This chapter has benefited from comments from Greg Zaric and an anonymous reviewer. I am grateful to Cancer Care Ontario (CCO) for funding me to develop and direct an in-house Pharmacoeconomics Research Unit comprised of independent researchers. Funding in support of this publication was provided by Cancer Care Ontario. However, the analyses, conclusions, opinions and statements expressed herein are those of the author, and not necessarily those of Cancer Care Ontario.

References

1. Aaron HJ, Ginsburg PB (2009) Is health spending excessive? If so, what can we do about it? Health Aff 28:1260–1275
2. Smith TJ, Hillner BE (2011) Bending the cost curve in cancer care. N Engl J Med 364(21):2060–2065

3. Elkin EB, Bach PB (2010) Cancer's next frontier: addressing high and increasing costs. JAMA 303(11):1086–1087
4. Fojo T, Grady C (2009) How much is life worth: cetuximab, non-small cell lung cancer, and the $440 billion question. J Natl Cancer Inst 101(15):1044–1048
5. Brown ML, Lipscomb J, Snyder C (2001) The burden of illness of cancer: economic cost and quality of life. Annu Rev Public Health 22:91–113
6. National Heart, Lung, and Blood Institute. NHLBI Fact Book, Fiscal Year 2008 Bethesda, MD National Institutes of Health. http://www.nhlbi.nih.gov/about/factbook/FactBookFinal.pdf. Accessed 8 June 2010
7. National Cancer Institute. Cancer trends progress report—2009/2010 update. http://progressreport.cancer.gov/doc_detail.asp?pid=1&did=2009&chid=95&coid=926&mid=
8. Mariotto AB, Yabroff KR, Shao Y et al. (2011) Projections of the cost of cancer care in the United States: 2010–2020. J Natl Cancer Inst 103:117–128
9. Bach PB (2009) Limits on Medicare's ability to control rising spending on cancer drugs. N Engl J Med 360(6):626–633
10. Neumann PJ, Weinstein MC et al. (2010) Legislating against use of cost-effectiveness information. N Engl J Med 363(16):1495–7
11. O'Donnell JC, Pham SV, Pashos CL et al. (2009) Health technology assessment: lessons learned from around the world—an overview. Value Health Suppl 2:S1–S5
12. Weinstein M, Zeckhauser R (1973) Critical ratios and efficient allocation. J Public Econ 2:147–158
13. Zaric GS (2012) Cost effectiveness analysis, healthcare policy, and operations research models. In: Cochran JJ (ed) Wiley encyclopedia of operations research and management science
14. Laupacis A, Feeny D, Detsky AS et al. (1992) How attractive does a new technology have to be to warrant adoption and utilization? Tentative guidelines for using clinical and economic evaluations. CMAJ 146(4):473–481
15. Naylor CD, Williams JI, Basinski A et al. (1993) Technology assessment and cost-effectiveness analysis: misguided guidelines? CMAJ 148(6):921–924
16. Khor S, Djalalova D, Hoch J (2010) The Paradox of the Laupacis Parallax. Oral presentation at the CADTH symposium. http://healtheconomics.utoronto.ca/publications-presentations Accessed 8 June 2012
17. Hoch JS, Hodgson DC, Earle CC. Role of comparative effectiveness research in cancer funding decisions in Ontario, Canada. J Clin Oncol. 2012 Dec 1;30(34):4262–6.
18. Chafe R, Culyer A, Dobrow M et al. (2011) Access to cancer drugs in Canada: looking beyond coverage decisions. Healthcare Policy 6(3):27–35
19. Berry SR, Hubay S, Soibelman H et al. (2007) The effect of priority setting decisions for new cancer drugs on medical oncologists' practice in Ontario: a qualitative study. BMC Health Serv Res 7:193
20. Evidence presented to the Standing Committee on Health on Monday (2007) April 30
21. Tappenden P, Chilcott J, Ward S et al. (2006) Methodological issues in the economic analysis of cancer treatments. Eur J Cancer 42(17):2867–2875
22. Baker CB, Johnsrud MT, Crismon ML, Rosenheck RA, Woods SW (2003) Quantitative analysis of sponsorship bias in economic studies of antidepressants. Br J Psychiatry 183:498–506
23. Martin DK, Pater JL, Singer PA (2001) Priority-setting decisions for new cancer drugs: a qualitative case study. Lancet 358:1676–1681
24. Bell CM, Urbach DR, Ray JG, Bayoumi A et al. (2006) Bias in published cost effectiveness studies: systematic review. BMJ 332(7543):699–703
25. Leslie K (2007) Ontario won't cover all costs of new cancer drugs. Canadian Press. Accessed 8 June 2007 http://www.colorectal-cancer.ca/en/news-and-resources/ont-cancer-drugs/
26. Statistics Canada. www.40.statcan.ca/l01/cst01/health36.htm Accessed 8 June 2008
27. Public Health Agency of Canada (1998) The economic burden of illness. 102

28. Sullivan R, Peppercorn J, Sikora K et al. (2011) Delivering affordable cancer care in high-income countries. Lancet Oncol 12(10):933–980
29. Barbieri M, Drummond MF (2001) Conflict of interest in industry-sponsored economic evaluations: real or imagined? Curr Oncol Rep 3(5):410–413
30. Chilcott J, McCabe C, Tappenden P et al. (2003) Modelling the cost effectiveness of interferon beta and glatiramer acetate in the management of multiple sclerosis. Commentary: evaluating disease modifying treatments in multiple sclerosis. BMJ 326(7388):522
31. Miners AH, Garau M, Fidan D et al. (2005) Comparing estimates of cost effectiveness submitted to the National Institute for Clinical Excellence (NICE) by different organisations: retrospective study. BMJ 330(7482):65
32. Chauhan D, Miners AH, Fischer AJ (2007) Exploration of the difference in results of economic submissions to the National Institute of Clinical Excellence by manufacturers and assessment groups. Int J Technol Assess Health Care 23(1):96–100
33. Claxton K, Sculpher M, McCabe C et al. (2005) Probabilistic sensitivity analysis for NICE technology assessment: not an optional extra. Health Econ 14(4):339–347
34. Hoch J (2009) Improving efficiency and value in palliative care with net benefit regression: an introduction to a simple method for cost-effectiveness analysis with person-level data. J Pain and Sympt Manage 38(1):54–61
35. Yong JH, Beca J, Hoch JS.The Evaluation and Use of Economic Evidence to Inform Cancer Drug Reimbursement Decisions in Canada. Pharmacoeconomics. 2013 Jan 16.[Epub ahead of print]
36. Khor S, Beca J, Krahn M, Hodgson D et al. (2012) Real world costs and cost-effectiveness of rituximab for diffuse large b cell lymphoma patients using registry data. Pharmacoeconomics Working Paper
37. ARCC (2012) The Canadian Centre for Applied Research in Cancer Control. http://www.cc-arcc.ca Accessed 8 June 2012

Index

A
Active vaccine and drug surveillance
baseline creation
active control group, 259
indirect adjustments, 260
uncertainty in, 260–261
vaccines, 260
benefits, 252
challenges, 274
drug *vs.* vaccine surveillance, 252–253
event definition, 256–257
hypothesis testing, 270–271
ICD-9-CM codes, 254–255
insurance claims data, 253–254
long-term toxicity effects, 271–272
multiple hypothesis control, 263–264
parameters, 267–269
population selection and study periods, 257–258
sequential testing and interim analysis
Brownian motion approximation, 262
CUSUM, 262–263
MaxSPRT, 262
SPRT, 261–262
statistical trade-off, 265–267
undersignaling, 270
Adverse Event Reporting System (AERS), 252
Advisory Committee on Immunization Practices (ACIP), 4, 7
Agent-based simulation, 231–233
Age-structured system dynamics model, 230
Alanine aminotransferase (ALT), 21
Alternative level of care (ALC), 40
Applied health policy models
analytic time horizons, 320
communication result to policymakers, 334–335
conceptual framework, 315–316
cycle length, 320
HIV policy model
conceptual framework, 317–319
cycle length, 322
funding uncertainty, 316–317
model inputs, 327–328
model software and usability, 322–325
time horizons, 321–322
verification, 331–334
identification and definition, research question, 314–315
implementation, 321
model verification
description, 328
external validation and calibration, 331
internal consistency, 328–330
internal validation and calibration, 330
parameter estimation from
literature, 326–327
model calibration, 327
patient-level data, 325–326
uses, 313
Asian and Pacific Islanders (APIs), 22–23
Australian Refined Diagnosis Related Groups (AR-DRGs), 132
Austria, case-based LKF-system
bureaucratic and time structure optimization strategies, 139
current case-based LKF-system
core part, 136–138
regulation part, 138
day-based payment strategy, 133
federal states, 132
hospital technology management, 148–149
initial case-based LKF-system, 134–135
inpatient payment strategies, 131–132

G.S. Zaric (ed.), *Operations Research and Health Care Policy*, International Series in Operations Research & Management Science 190, DOI 10.1007/978-1-4614-6507-2,

Austria, case-based LKF-system (*cont.*)
LDF-points, 133
macro-perspective studies, 140
micro-perspective studies
and Canadian global budget-based payment system, 143–144
federal states, treatment patterns, 148
hospitals, competition of, 146–147
LOS, inpatients, 144–145
regional inpatient allocation, 145–146
performance optimization strategies, 139–140
quantity optimization strategies, 140
social security system, 132
Average Flow Model (AFM), 63–66

B
Bioterrorism
anthrax attacks, 28
disease model, 30
local inventory and dispensing capacity expansion, 32
oral antibiotics, 31
prodromal infection, 30
prophylaxis, 31
Push Packs, 29
US Strategic National Stockpile, 29
VMI, 29
Bird flu, 226
Bonferroni correction, 263
Bortezomib, 298
Brownian motion approximation, 262

C
Canadian blood services
air *vs.* ground deliveries
air delivery cancellations, 377–379
budget, 366
delivery timeliness, 375, 376
transit time, 373–374
transit time variance, 375, 377
blood supply chain, 370
consolidation plan, 366
ground services, Saint John
baseline model, 381
confirmatory simulation model, 382–383, 391–394
demand arrival, 388, 389
demand modelling, 385–387
preliminary network design, 381–382
product arrival, 385
road closures, 383
transit times, 383
verification and validation, 388–390
weekends and statutory holidays, 383–384
integer programming model, 371
New Brunswick (*see also* New Brunswick, blood services)
census areas in, 367
current distribution network for, 368
stock-holding unit, 369
as soon as possible (ASAP) orders, 368
Canadian Institute for Health Information (CIHI), 73, 343–344
Cancer Care Ontario (CCO)
NDFP, 405
pharmacoeconomics research unit
cancer drug funding submission, 408–409
description, 407
language, 410–411
limited training, 410
model busting, 409
PSA, 411–412
type III error, 410
Cardiopulmonary resuscitation (CPR), 115
Case series cumulative sum charts (CUSUM), 262–263
Centers for Disease Control and Prevention (CDC)
adult immunization scheduler
ACIP, 4
Catch-up Immunization Scheduler for Children, 5
dynamic programming algorithm, 6
example of, 7
pertussis infection, 5
user interface, 6
vaccine library, 5
Mass Vaccination Model, H1N1 pandemic
arrival intensity, 10
cash clients, 8
decision-makers, 11
DES model, 8
flow diagram, 9
HCDPH, 8
Medicare Special clients, 8
optimal and original model, 10
staff placement, 9
vaccination cost, 11

National HIV Resource Allocation Model, 12–14
PMU, 4
Chemotherapy-related serious adverse events (CSAE), 354
Chronic disease management (CDM), 72–74
Clinical pathways
care delivery tasks, 92
colon diagnostics and therapy, 94
deterministic solution, 101
disease management, 101
implementation of, 94
materials and methods
data sources, 99
project management model, 97–99
thyroidectomy pathway, flowchart of, 96
operational research methods, 93
organizational and therapeutic guidelines, 92
Pareto's rule, 95
probabilistic solution, 100–101
standardized procedures, 93
task times, 102
thyroid disease conditions and treatment, 95–96
Commercial sex workers (CSW), 185
Community-based care (C-bC)
capacity allocation
asthmatic children, 81
MDP, 82
Mobile C.A.R.E. Foundation, 83
natural disease progression, 82
QALY, 82
scheduled patients, 82
school-based mobile clinics, 81
care provider pathways
analytical epidemiologic model, 83
case-mix variables, 84
clinicians and system planners, 86
fee-for-service billing records, 86
Markov model, 85
methodological framework, 84
patient flow approach, 84
transition probabilities, 85
CDM program, 74–75
characteristics of, 77–78
chronic disease patients, 72
CIHI, 73
community-based rehabilitation, 77
community health care teams, 76
design initiatives, 73
long-term community-based residential care, 76
mental health
CSS administrators, 79
deinstitutionalization, 78
mixed integer programming solution, 81
patient aggregation, 80
representative papers, taxonomy of, 79
service packages, 80
primary care, specialist backup, 75–76
quantitative decision models, 74
social and educational components, 72
Community Support System (CSS), 79
Computer-aided dispatch (CAD), 106
Continuing Care Information Management System (CCIMS), 51
Cost-effectiveness analysis (CEA)
cancer drugs, in Canada, 402–406
constrained optimization, 401
disease registries, 346
healthcare costs, 400
incremental cost-effectiveness ratio, 342
models and parameterization, 342–343
operations research techniques, 400
optimal decision rule, 401
pCODR, 406–407
prognostic test, early-stage breast cancer
base case, 355
costs, 354–356
cross-validation, 351
Manitoba administrative databases and linking strategy, 348, 350–351
model description, 348, 349
recurrence score, 347
sensitivity analysis, 355, 357
transition probabilities, 351–354
provincial administrative health databases, 344–345
tissue of origin test, 357–358
Cost-utility analysis (CUA), HIV behavioral interventions
closed-form solution, 176
costs and health outcomes, 171
HIV infection model
consumer price index, 162
Euler-forward method, 162
heterosexual men and women, 163
index case, 160
lifetime HIV treatment costs, 161
ODEs, 160
parameter values, 163
transmission rate, 161

Cost-utility analysis (CUA) (*cont.*)
HIV-positive individuals
counseling, 163
HIV transmission chain, 165
individual and small group interventions, 163
injection drug users, 165
program cost calculations, 164
risky behaviors, 164
lifetime HIV treatment costs, 172
new HIV infections, 171
policy implications, 174–175
program cost threshold analysis, 169–170
PSA, 168–169
risk behaviors, 158
risk-reduction behavior, 170
secondary infection model
degree of adoption, 166
new infections, 166
primary transmission, 165
scenarios, 166–167
secondary transmission, 165
susceptible partners, 168
sensitivity analyses, 174
sexual behavior data, 173
uncertainty, 172
Critical Path Method (CPM), 97

D
Data Envelopment Analysis (DEA), 140
Decision analytic model
early-stage breast cancer, 348, 349
Ontario framework
drugs for rare diseases, 283–284
Hunter disease (*see* Hunter disease)
Discrete event simulation (DES) model, 8, 46–47, 230–231
Disease registries, in canada, 346
Division of HIV/AIDS Prevention (DHAP), 12
Dose cap, 297–298
Drug Program Information Network (DPIN), 350
Drugs for rare diseases (DRD) evaluation, 284

E
Electronic medical records (EMRs), 254
Emergency medical services (EMS)
ambulance allocation, 122–125
demand
call volumes, 108
planning purposes, 108
response and service times, 110
root-mean-square forecast error, 109
time intervals, 110
events and time intervals, 106
OR/MS publications, 107
performance evaluation
code red, 117
dispatch probabilities, 119
Erlang B model, 120
HQM, 118
MCLP, 118
optimization heuristics, 121
repositioning strategy, 120
simulation models and analytical models, 117
stochastic models, 117
transition diagram, 119
performance measures
coverage, 114
CPR, 115
medical outcomes, 116
survival and coverage probability, 116
system-wide response-time statistics, 114
policy implications, 125
response times
Calgary data, 111
chute time, 112
coverage map, probability of, 112
dispatch time, 112
travel time, 111
station planning, 121–122
statistics, 106
workload, 113–114
Enzyme replacement therapy (ERT), 285
Euler-forward method, 162
Expanded Chronic Care Model, 75

F
False discovery rate (FDR), 263–264
Forecast error, 300
Formulary access, 296
Free treatment contract, 297–298

G
Game theory, 235–236
Gantt chart, 97
Global positioning system (GPS), 106
Guillain–Barré syndrome, 273

H

Harm reduction programs, 26–28
Hauptdiagnose-Gruppen (HDG) groups, 137
Henderson County Department of Public Health (HCDPH), 8
Hepatitis B
  China
    age and health state transitions, 21
    age-structured Markov model, 20
    alanine aminotransferase, 21
    chronic infection, 21
    free catch-up vaccination, 19
    healthcare costs, 20
    newborn vaccination, 19
  USA, 22–23
High-risk heterosexuals (HRH), 12
HIV
  IDUs, 24
  infection model
    consumer price index, 162
    Euler-forward method, 162
    heterosexual men and women, 163
    index case, 160
    lifetime HIV treatment costs, 161
    ODEs, 160
    parameter values, 163
    transmission rate, 161
  policy model, resource-limited settings
    conceptual framework, 317–319
    cycle length, 322
    external calibration, 332, 334
    funding uncertainty, 316–317
    internal consistency, 331–332
    internal validation and calibration, 332
    model inputs, 327–328
    model software and usability, 322–325
    time horizons, 321–322
  positive individuals
    counseling, 163
    HIV transmission chain, 165
    individual and small group interventions, 163
    injection drug users, 165
    program cost calculations, 164
    risky behaviors, 164
  prevention technologies, in Sub-Saharan Africa (*see* Sub-Saharan Africa, HIV prevention technologies)
  Russia
    ART, 25
    dynamic compartmental model, 24
    infection transmission, 24
    public health planners, 26
    untargeted treatment strategy, 26
  Ukraine
    ART expansion, 28
    dynamic compartmental model, 27
    heterosexual transmission, 26
    methadone substitution therapy, 27
Hospital Discharge Database, 348, 350
Hunter disease
  causes, 284
  incidence, 284
  life expectancy, patients
    death age, 289, 290
    survival curve, 287, 290
  Markov model
    disease progression, 285–286
    generative state and disease progression state, 287, 288
    transition probabilities, 287, 289
  types, 285
Hypercube Queueing Model, 112
Hypothetical analysis, Hunter disease, 291–292

I

ICD-9-CM codes, 254–255
Idursulfase, Hunter disease
  description, 285
  funding policy, 291–292
  potential effectiveness of, 291
Incidence density analysis, 325–326
Incremental cost-effectiveness ratio (ICER), 169, 342, 410–413
Influenza pandemics
  historical, 226
  non-pharmaceutical responses, 227
  operations research tools
    agent-based simulation, 231–233
    decision analysis, 234–235
    discrete event simulation, 230–231
    game theory, 235–236
    optimization, 234
    practices using, 236–238
    supply chain analysis, 235–236
    system dynamics approach, 228–230
  pharmaceutical interventions, 226–227
  policy implications, 240–244
  targeted antiviral prophylaxis, 239
Injection drug users (IDUs)
  in Eastern Europe, 24
  module, 209–211

Injection drug users (IDUs) (*cont.*)
in Russia, 24–26
in Ukraine, 26–28
Inpatient reimbursement systems
Austrian case-based payment system
bureaucratic and time structure optimization strategies, 139
current case-based LKF-system, 136–138
day-based payment strategy, 133
federal states, 132
initial case-based LKF-system, 134–135
LDF-points, 133
performance optimization strategies, 139–140
quantity optimization strategies, 140
social security system, 132
general incentives of, 131–132
hospital technology management, 148–149
quantitative studies, case-based LKF-system
hospital efficiency, 140
incentives, hospitals, 141–148
Integer programming model, 371
Interim Joint Oncology Drug Review (iJODR), 406–407
Internal consistency, 328–330
Iterative process, HIV treatment, 317

K

Kaplan–Meier estimates
HIV policy model, 332, 333
long-term care capacity planning, 52, 53
premenopausal and postmenopausal women, 352
Kefauver–Harris amendment, 251
Krever Commission, 366

L

Leistungsorienterte Diagnosefallgruppen (LDF), 137
Leistungsorientierte Krankenhausfinanzierung (LKF-system), 130
Lenalidomide, 298
Levene's test, 377
LIFEREG procedure, 50
Long-term care (LTC) capacity planning
admission requirements, 43
AFM
capacity levels, 64
Little's law, 63
mean and standard deviation, 66
planning horizon, 65
sensitivity analyses, 65
simulation approach, 63
ALC patients, 40
Bonferroni approach, 45
case study
CCIMS database, 51
implementation and recommendations, 55–56
Kaplan–Meier survival curves, 52, 53
LHA, 51
LOS distributions, 52
results and analysis, 53–55
sensitivity analysis, 56–57
VIHA, 51
Weibull distributions, 53
discrete event simulation, 46–47
implementation, 50–51
LOS, 46
optimal capacity allocation, 41
optimization, 49–50
Poisson process, 44
policy implications, 66–67
population aging, 40
queuing theory, 42
ratio approach
age-specific utilization rates, 58
Current Ratio, 57
linear regression model, 58
shortcomings of, 57–58
simulation approach, 59
valid ratio policy, 59
service level criterion, 45
simulation inputs
arrival analysis, 47
LOS analysis, 47–48
simulation initialization, 48–49
SIPP approach and modifications
capacity levels, 61
Kaplan–Meier curve, 61
M/M/s queueing system, 60
MOL approach, 62
service time, 63
simulation-optimization approach, 60
stationary systems, 62
square-root rule, 42
staffing levels, 43
waitlist, 44

M

Male circumcision (MC)
behavior change, 183
force of infection, 182

implementation characteristics, 183
mathematical models, 181
neonatal circumcision, 182
policy makers, 181
randomized controlled trials, 181
Manitoba cancer registry (MCR), 348, 350
Mann–Whitney test, 373
Markov Decision Process (MDP), 82
Markov model
age-structured, in hepatitis B, 20
community-based care, 85
early-stage breast cancer, 349
Hunter disease
disease progression, 285–286
generative state and disease progression state, 287, 288
transition probabilities, 287, 289
Maximal covering location problem (MCLP), 118, 121–122
Maximum expected covering location model (MEXCLP), 118
MaxSPRT, 262
MCR. *See* Manitoba cancer registry (MCR)
Medizinische Einzelleistungen (MEL), 137
Men who have sex with men (MSM), 12, 13
Methadone, 27
Model busting, 409
Model verification process
description, 328
external validation and calibration, 331
internal consistency, 328–330
internal validation and calibration, 330
Modified offered load (MOL), 42, 62
Mucopolysaccharidosis type II disease. *See* Hunter disease
Multi-cohort approach, 319
Musculoskeletal (MSK) syndrome, 285–286

N
National Administrative Health Databases, 343–344
National Health Institutes of Scotland, 93
National Institute for Health and Clinical Excellence (NICE), 168
Needle and syringe programs (NSP), 206
New Brunswick, blood services
ABO/Rh status, 368
baseline model, 381
census areas in, 367
current distribution network for, 368
ground relay schedule, 384
road closure, 383
routine and ASAP demand, 386–387
STAT orders, 386
stock-holding unit, 369
transit times for ground deliveries, 383
travel distances for select points, 396
New Drug Funding Program (NDFP), 405

O
Ontario Health Insurance Plan (OHIP), 344
Operations research (OR), public health
bioterrorism (*see* Bioterrorism)
hepatitis B control
China, 19–22
USA, 22–23
HIV control
Russia, 24–26
Ukraine, 26–28
public health planners, 18
randomized clinical trial, 18
Opiate substitution therapy (OST), 208–210

P
Pan-Canadian Oncology Drug Review (pCODR), 406–407
Pandemic influenza. *See* Influenza pandemics
Pareto's rule, 95
Patient access schemes, 296. *See also* Risk sharing agreements (RSA)
pCODR. *See* Pan-Canadian Oncology Drug Review (pCODR)
Pfizer, 297
Physician Claims Database, 350, 351
Poisson process, 44
Population Extrapolation for Organization Planning with Less Error (PEOPLE), 51
Post-exposure prophylaxis (PEP), 185
Pre-exposure prophylaxis (PrEP), 180
ART, 188
condom-substitution analysis, 188
drug resistance, 189
effectiveness trials, 185
intervention, 184–185
modeling impact, 185–187
policy makers, 189
prioritizing strategies, 187
programmatic assumptions, 187
Preparedness Modeling Unit (PMU), 4
Price-volume agreements, 298–301
Primary-care provider (PCP), 86
Principal-agent model, 304

Probabilistic sensitivity analysis (PSA), 168–169, 357
Program Evaluation and Review Technique (PERT), 97
Propensity score, 259
Provincial administrative health databases, in canada
  description, 344–345
  prognostic test, early-stage breast cancer
    base case, 355
    costs, 354–356
    cross-validation, 351
    Manitoba administrative databases and linking strategy, 348, 350–351
    model description, 348, 349
    recurrence score, 347
    sensitivity analysis, 355, 357
    transition probabilities, 351–354
Push Packs, 29

Q
Quality-adjusted life years (QALYs), 20–23, 161–163
Quebec Department of Social Insurance (RAMQ) database, 86

R
Refined Diagnostic Related Groups (RDRGs), 354
Resource Allocation for Control of HIV (REACH)
  example analyses
    Saint Petersburg, Russia, 217–218
    Uganda, 213–215
    Ukraine, 215–217
  Futures Group International's Goals Model, 204
  interventions, 203
  methadone and HIV treatment programs, 204
  OR-based resource allocation tool
    behavioral parameters, 207
    biological parameters, 209
    demographic data, 206–207
    dynamic compartmental model, 209–211
    health care costs, 208
    HIV epidemic data, 207
    intervention status, 207–208
    key populations, 207
    model outputs, 212
    optimal allocation, 211–212
    QALY, 205
    resources, 209
    scale up costs, 208
    schematic of, 206
    setting, 206
  policy implications, 220–222
  refinement and implementation, 218–220
  UNAIDS guidelines, 203
Risk sharing agreements (RSA)
  clinical indicators, 298
  cost-effectiveness, 298
  design, 304–306
  free treatment contract, 297–298
  optimal manufacturer decision making, 299–302
  price reduction, 297
  price-volume agreements, 298
  social welfare impact, 302–304
  types of, 308
Robust Rank Order test, 373
Rofecoxib, 252

S
Saint John, blood management
  aggregate daily demand, 369
  end-labelling, 368
  ground services
    baseline model, 381
    confirmatory simulation model, 382–383, 391–394
    demand arrival, 388, 389
    demand modelling, 385–387
    preliminary network design, 381–382
    product arrival, 385
    road closures, 383
    transit times, 383
    verification and validation, 388–390
    weekends and statutory holidays, 383–384
  SHU, 369
Saint Petersburg, Russia, 217–218
Sequential probability ratio test (SPRT), 261
Sequential testing and interim analysis, drug surveillance
  Brownian motion approximation, 262
  MaxSPRT, 262
  SPRT, 261–262
Šidák correction, 263
Social welfare impact, RSA, 302–304
Stationary, independent, period by period (SIPP), 41

Stock-holding unit (SHU)
  description, 369
  Saint John, 385–387
Sub-Saharan Africa, HIV prevention technologies
  male circumcision
    behavior change, 183
    force of infection, 182
    implementation characteristics, 183
    mathematical models, 181
    neonatal circumcision, 182
    policy makers, 181
    randomized controlled trials, 181
  pre-exposure prophylaxis
    ART, 188
    condom-substitution analysis, 188
    drug resistance, 189
    effectiveness trials, 185
    intervention, 184–185
    modeling impact, 185–187
    policy makers, 189
    prioritizing strategies, 187
    programmatic assumptions, 187
  vaccines
    baseline prevention scenario, 195
    effectiveness trials, 190–191
    efficacy levels, 196
    intervention, 189–190
    overview, 191–192
    population vaccination coverage, 193
    prevention programs, 193
    RV144 trial data, 192
    scaled-up prevention scenario, 195
    South Africa, 194
Sunitinib, 297
Supply chain analysis, 235–236
System dynamics, influenza
  age-structured system, 230
  compartmental model, 228–229
  higher-level policy planning, 230
  simple system dynamics model, 229

T

Targeted antiviral prophylaxis, 239
Tenofovir disopoxyl fumarate (TDF), 185
Thyroidectomy
  CPM methodology, 98
  deterministic time, 102
  flowchart of, 96
  hemorrhage, 95
  hypoparathyroidism, 95
  laryngeal nerve damage, 95
  probabilistic time, 100
  tasks and activity relationships, 99
Tissue of origin test, 357–358
Tolerance approach, 268–269
Transition probabilities
  Canadian life tables, 353
  21-gene assay, 352–353
  MCR, 351–352
2-Type model, 305

U

Uganda, 213–215
Ukraine, 215–217
Universal Test and Treat (UTT), 187
US National Fire Protection Association, 114

V

Vaccine Adverse Event Reporting System (VAERS), 252
Vaccines
  baseline prevention scenario, 195
  effectiveness trials, 190–191
  efficacy levels, 196
  intervention, 189–190
  overview, 191–192
  population vaccination coverage, 193
  prevention programs, 193
  RV144 trial data, 192
  scaled-up prevention scenario, 195
  South Africa, 194
  surveillance system (*see* Active vaccine and drug surveillance)
Vaccine Safety Datalink (VSD), 253
Value-of-information analysis, 357
Vancouver Island Health Authority (VIHA), 51
Vehicle routing models, 370
Vendor-Managed Inventories (VMI), 29

W

Weibull regression model, 48
World Health Organization (WHO), 21, 213, 219

MIX
Papier aus verantwortungsvollen Quellen
Paper from responsible sources
FSC® C105338

If you have any concerns about our products,
you can contact us on
ProductSafety@springernature.com

In case Publisher is established outside the EU,
the EU authorized representative is:
Springer Nature Customer Service Center GmbH
Europaplatz 3, 69115 Heidelberg, Germany

Printed by Libri Plureos GmbH
in Hamburg, Germany